FLORIDA STATE
UNIVERSITY LIBRARIES

NOV 2 1999

TALLAHASSEE, FLORIDA

OXFORD HISTORICAL MONOGRAPHS

EDITORS

R. R. DAVIES   R. J. W. EVANS
P. LANGFORD   H. C. G. MATTHEW
H. M. MAYR-HARTING   A. J. NICHOLLS
            SIR KEITH THOMAS

URBAN LIBERALISM IN IMPERIAL GERMANY
Frankfurt am Main, 1866–1914

JAN PALMOWSKI

OXFORD
UNIVERSITY PRESS

Great Clarendon Street, Oxford OX2 6DP

Oxford University Press is a department of the University of Oxford.
It furthers the University's objective of excellence in research, scholarship,
and education by publishing worldwide in

Oxford New York

Athens Auckland Bangkok Bogotá Buenos Aires Calcutta
Cape Town Chennai Dar es Salaam Delhi Florence Hong Kong Istanbul
Karachi Kuala Lumpur Madrid Melbourne Mexico City Mumbai
Nairobi Paris São Paulo Singapore Taipei Tokyo Toronto Warsaw

with associated companies in Berlin Ibadan

Oxford is a registered trade mark of Oxford University Press
in the UK and in certain other countries

Published in the United States
by Oxford University Press Inc., New York

© Jan Palmowski 1999

The moral rights of the author have been asserted

First published 1999

All rights reserved. No part of this publication may be reproduced,
stored in a retrieval system, or transmitted, in any form or by any means,
without the prior permission in writing of Oxford University Press.
or as expressly permitted by law, or terms agreed with the appropriate
reprographics rights organisation, Enquiries concerning reproduction
outside the scope of the above should be sent to the Rights Department,
Oxford University Press, at the address above

You must not circulate this book in any other binding or cover
and you must impose this same condition on any acquiror

Library of Congress Cataloging in Publication Data

Palmowski, Jan.
Urban liberalism in imperial Germany: Frankfurt am Main,
1866–1914 / Jan Palmowski.
p. cm.
Includes bibliographical reference and index.
1. Liberalism—Germany—Frankfurt am Main—History—19th century.
2. Frankfurt am Main (Germany)—Politics and government. 3. Middle
class—Germany—Frankfurt am Main—History—19th century. 4. Political
parties—Germany—Frankfurt am Main—History—19th century. I. Title
DD901.F78P35 1998   320.51'0943'416409434—dc21   98–42428

ISBN 0–19–820750.6

1 3 5 7 9 10 8 6 4 2

Typeset in Ehrhardt
by Jayvee, Trivandrum, India
Printed in Great Britain
on acid-free paper by
Bookcraft Ltd., Midsomer Norton
Nr. Bath, Somerset

To
Inge, Werner, and Anja

Acknowledgements

I have been extraordinarily fortunate in the supervision I received as a graduate student; and, if anything, this appreciation has increased with the time that has passed since I finished my dissertation. With profound gratitude I acknowledge my debt to Michael John and H. C. G. Matthew, for their humanity, sympathy, and generosity. They offered invaluable support, criticism, and suggestions, far beyond the call of duty. Even after submitting my thesis I have continued to benefit enormously from their advice and experience. I shall always be indebted to them. As sub-editor Michael John also gave extremely helpful advice for the preparation of the monograph.

I am very grateful to Dieter Langewiesche, who, despite his other commitments, found time to read my dissertation and to offer detailed comments and advice. I should also like to take this opportunity to thank Ursula Bartelsheim, Christina Klausman, Dieter Langewiesche, Karl Heinrich Pohl, and especially Ralf Roth, for letting me have copies of some of their work before publication.

Thanks are due to the Friedrich-Naumann-Foundation for its generous sponsorship of my research, and to the support, since my undergraduate days, of the German National Scholarship Foundation. By electing me to a Senior Scholarship the Fellows of Lincoln College gave me a congenial environment for finishing my dissertation. Perhaps my greatest debt is due to the Students of Christ Church, who, through electing me to a Junior Research Fellowship, gave me an ideal opportunity in unique surroundings to continue my work. In Germany, Lothar Gall has provided kind support for my research. I am obliged to Dieter Rebentisch and his staff at the Institut für Stadtgeschichte for their encouragement and help. My thanks are also due to Lothar Bücheler and the extraordinarily courteous and obliging staff of the Hessian state archives in Wiesbaden. I am extremely grateful to the Institute for European History in Mainz, now under the directorship of Heinz Durchhardt, for providing an ideal working environment while I carried out my research on Frankfurt. For their help I should like to take this opportunity to thank its fellows, Ralph Melville, Claus Scharf, and especially Martin Vogt who first alerted me to the distinctiveness and the 'peculiarity' of the Frankfurt milieu. Most importantly, I owe a particular debt to Matthieu Arnold, Barbara Pitkin, and Brent Sockness, whose friendship and professional example provided an indispensable encouragement for my work both during my stay at the Institute and afterwards.

For their unfailing support I should like to thank Helen and John Adamson, who have provided a British home for me since 1988. Here in Oxford I have been sustained by the friendship of Adriano Barenco, Joe Coohill, Robin Griffith Jones, Tara Connelly, Franco De Angelis, and Norunn Bru Rem. I am particularly indebted to Tore Rem for his humour, example, and understanding. He has also been the source of much sound advice over the years. Last but not least, it is impossible to pay sufficient tribute to the help of Cressida Annesley. She has stoically and ungrudgingly proof-read everything I have written, from my undergraduate dissertation onwards. This book is no exception. Above all, I thank her for her loyalty and friendship over the years.

Words cannot convey the sense of gratitude I feel towards my parents and my sister. They have been my greatest intellectual and personal inspiration, and without their unfailing understanding, wisdom, care, encouragement, and advice, this book could never have been written. This monograph is but a tribute to their support, and it is to them that I dedicate this work.

Christ Church, Oxford J.P.
November 1997

Contents

List of Figures	xi
List of Tables	xii
List of Abbreviations	xiii

1. Introduction   1

2. The Advent of Politics   38
   - 2.1. Introduction   38
   - 2.2. Political Life before 1866   42
   - 2.3. The Birth of a Liberal City   49
   - 2.4. State and National Elections   66
   - 2.5. The Politicization of Local Government   75
   - 2.6. Liberal Politics and Municipal Administration   82
   - 2.7. Conclusion   96

3. The Diversification of Local Politics   100
   - 3.1. Introduction   100
   - 3.2. The Fragmentation of Middle-Strata Politics   105
   - 3.3. The Rise of the SPD   126
   - 3.4. Conclusion   141

4. Liberals and Education   147
   - 4.1. Introduction   147
   - 4.2. Liberalism and Religion   151
   - 4.3. Education and Self-Government   180
   - 4.4. The Quality of Primary Education   184
   - 4.5. Secondary Education   189
   - 4.6. Conclusion: The Establishment of the Civic University of Frankfurt   199

5. Liberal Social Policies   206
   - 5.1. Introduction   206

5.2.	Liberal Policies after the Annexation	210
5.3.	Frankfurt under Miquel: The Origins of 'kommunale Daseinsfürsorge'	215
5.4.	Social Policies in Wilhelmine Frankfurt	226
5.5.	Politics and Social Reform	238
5.6.	Conclusion	249

6. Liberalism and Municipal Finance — 255
   6.1. Introduction — 255
   6.2. Local Government Finance in Prussia — 258
   6.3. Municipal Expenditure — 279
   6.4. Municipal Debt — 292
   6.5. Municipal Taxation — 298
   6.6. Conclusion — 306

7. Conclusion — 311

Appendix I — 333
   Table A. General public expenditure in Frankfurt am Main, 1874–1912 (in Marks) — 333
   Table B. Actual public expenditure in Frankfurt am Main, 1895–1912 (in Marks) — 334
   Table C. Municipal debts and assets in Frankfurt am Main, 1873–1914 (in Marks) — 335
   Table D. Local taxation in Frankfurt am Main, 1868–1913 (in Marks) — 336

Appendix II — 338
   Distribution of seats in the Frankfurt City Council, 1877–1913 — 339
   The Prussian State Elections in Frankfurt am Main — 340
   National General Elections in Germany, 1871–1914 — 342
   National General Elections in Frankfurt a.M., 1871–1914 — 343

Bibliography — 345
Index — 385

List of Figures

6.1.	General budget expenditure in Frankfurt am Main, 1874–1912 (in million Marks)	280
6.2.	Actual public expenditure in Frankfurt am Main, 1874–1912 (in million Marks)	285
6.3.	Municipal debt in Frankfurt, 1873-1913 (in million Marks)	292
6.4.	Municipal wealth in Frankfurt am Main, 1890–1913 (in million Marks)	293
6.5.	Local taxation in Frankfurt am Main, 1870–1913 (in million Marks)	303
6.6.	Local taxation in Frankfurt am Main, 1868–1913 (in Marks per head)	308

List of Tables

6.1. Relative public expenditure of local, state, and national government in Prussia/Germany, 1881–1913 — 256

6.2. Local taxation in Prussia, 1869 and 1883/1884 (in Marks) — 259

6.3. State and local direct taxation in 1883/1884 (in 1,000 Marks) — 260

6.4. Proportion of property and of personal (income) taxation in % of total local direct taxation, 1869–1900 — 268

6.5. Local taxation in Prussian cities of over 10,000 inhabitants (in Marks per head) — 269

6.6. Expenditure of Prussian cities, 1869–1913 (absolute and per head) — 270

6.7. Municipal expenditure in cities with a population of over 100,000, by item of expenditure in Prussia, 1869–1911 (in Marks per head) — 271

6.8. Municipal expenditure in Frankfurt, 1879–1905, by item of expenditure (in Marks) — 281

6.9. Public expenditure in Frankfurt am Main, 1899–1912 (in Marks) — 284

Abbreviations

AFGK	*Archiv für Frankfurter Geschichte und Kunst*
AfR	*Archiv für öffentliches Recht*
AfS	*Archiv für Sozialgeschichte*
AS	Akten der Stadtverordnetenversammlung
AS P	Protokolle der Stadtverordnetenversammlung
ASA	Akten des Statistischen Amts der Stadt Frankfurt am Main
BAK	Bundesarchiv Koblenz
BAP	Bundesarchiv Potsdam
CEH	*Central European History*
CJH	*Canadian Journal of History*
CSSH	*Comparative Studies in Society and History*
EHR	*English Historical Review*
FA	*Finanzarchiv*
GG	*Geschichte und Gesellschaft*
GH	*German History*
GSR	*German Studies Review*
GWU	*Geschichte in Wissenschaft und Unterricht*
HJ	*Historical Journal*
HMRG	*Historische Mitteilungen der Ranke Gesellschaft*
hpZ	*historisch-politische Zeitschrift*
HStAW	Hessisches Hauptstaatsarchiv, Wiesbaden
HZ	*Historische Zeitschrift*
IfSG	Institut für Stadtgeschichte, Frankfurt am Main
IRSH	*International Review of Social History*
JCH	*Journal of Contemporary History*
JGVV	*Jahrbuch für Gesetzgebung, Verwaltung und Volkswirtschaft im Deutschen Reich*
JHL	*Jahrbuch für Hessische Landesgeschichte*
JLF	*Jahrbuch zur Liberalismus-Forschung*
JöR	*Jahrbuch des öffentlichen Rechts*

JSH	*Journal of Social History*
JSS	*Jahrbuch für Sozialwissenschaft und Sozialpolitik*
MA	Akten des Magistrats
MAB	*Berichte des Magistrats an die Stadtverordnetenversammlung die Verwaltung und den Stand der Gemeinde-Angelegenheiten am Schlusse des Etatsjahres ... betreffend*
MPS	*Mitteilungen aus den Protokollen der Stadtverordnetenversammlung der Stadt Frankfurt am Main*
NPL	*Neue Politische Literatur*
PJbb	*Preußische Jahrbücher*
PP	*Past and Present*
SH	*Social History*
SPAH	*Stenographische Berichte des Preußische Abgeordneten Hauses*
SPD	Sozialdemokratische Partei Deutschlands
TAJG	*Tel Aviver Jahrbuch für deutsche Geschichte*
YLBI	*Year Book of the Leo Baeck Institute*
ZfR	*Zeitschrift für Rechtsgeschichte*

1

Introduction

If I am liberal, it is in the sense of liberal-mindedness, not of Liberalism. For I am unpolitical, for the nation; but not politically minded, as a German of *bürgerlich* culture and of the Romantic era, which knew no other demand than for . . . Kaiser and Reich.[1]

Thomas Mann's description of his own bourgeois heritage, written during the twilight of the German Empire, was shared by the majority of intellectuals at the time as well as of successive generations of historians. Central to this image is the notion of the 'unpolitical German', who, influenced by a peculiarly German adherence to authority, eschewed party politics as divisive and was happy to pursue a life of culture and enterprise, leaving the business of government to the ruling élites. Accordingly, this is why the *Bürgertum*'s political alter ego, liberalism, remained peculiarly weak in comparison with other Western European liberal movements. After all, by 1914, German liberals still had not achieved a parliamentary democracy, and thus remained without direct access to power. This unique failure to gain control over government has often been attributed to the liberals' unwillingness to achieve power in the first place, and to political immaturity and other-worldliness. According to this view, German liberals are seen as entertaining the luxury of a doctrinaire rigidity suitable only for those who could never be in power, while at the same time pandering to the

---

[1] The full quotation is 'Bin ich liberal, so bin ich es im Sinne der Liberalität und nicht des Liberalismus. Denn ich bin unpolitisch, national, aber unpolitisch gesinnt, wie der Deutsche der bürgerlichen Kultur und wie der der Romantik, die keine andere politische Forderung kannte, als die hoch-nationale nach Kaiser und Reich, und die so gründlich undemokratisch war, daß nur *ihre* seelischen Nachwirkungen die Politiker, Burschenschaftler, Revolutionäre der Paulskirche das Erbkaisertum wollen ließen und sie, wie Vogt an Herwegh schrieb, "zu vollkommenen Aristokraten" machten . . .'. T. Mann, *Betrachtungen eines Unpolitischen* (Frankfurt, 1956), 108.

authorities in the hope of benevolent legislation. This view has rightly been challenged from various angles in the *Sonderweg* debate of the last two decades. And yet, this debate has largely been confined to liberal success or failure at the national level. Strangely, it has excluded the level of government where liberals had direct access to power throughout the period of the Empire, that of local government.

This book is about liberals in power in imperial Germany. It is about what liberals did to get into power, and what they did once they were in control of government. Through an analysis of urban liberal politics, the level at which liberals could actually achieve many of their ideals of a civic, cultural, and enterprising society, it is possible to determine the extent to which German liberals really were 'peculiar' and 'unpolitical' in comparison with their Western European neighbours. By focusing on one of the most progressive and important urban liberal centres in Germany, Frankfurt am Main, this study examines the liberals' astuteness in responding to the political challenges of the growth of Social Democracy, and the fragmentation of the middle classes with the corresponding growth of the *Mittelstand* protest parties. Apart from these important areas of political organization, tactics, and personalities, a second central area of investigation is that of liberal government as such. What were the main areas of liberal concern in local government, and to what extent did liberals manage to achieve their ideals? In response to this question, this work looks in greater detail at liberal policies in areas which mattered most to them, i.e. social welfare, education, religion, and taxation.

Of course, the observation that local government was an important stronghold of liberalism in imperial Germany is not new. It was first highlighted by James Sheehan's pioneering article on the subject in 1971.[2] He showed that in most cities liberals managed to hang on to the control of municipal governments until 1918, despite mounting challenges first from the Centre Party and then from the SPD. Curiously, despite this reminder of the importance of the city as a liberal power base and the place in which liberal self-government was possible, more detailed studies of liberal politics in local government have remained few and far between.

One major reason for the reluctance to investigate the party political dimensions of local government has been that such a view stands in direct contrast to the traditional explanation offered by urban historians. In their accounts, urban local government has been elevated as a showcase for the

---

[2] J. J. Sheehan, 'Liberalism and the City in Nineteenth-Century Germany', *PP*, no. 51 (1971), 116–37.

'unpolitical German'. According to the seminal studies of Helmut Croon, Wolfgang Hofmann, and Wolfgang Köllmann, in the nineteenth century, cities and municipal councils were not run by parties, but by the local notable élites, the *Honoratioren*.[3] Membership of particular clubs as well as friendship and family ties were more important than allegiance to a political party or its ideology. Until the turn of the century, there was a clear appreciation that politics had no place inside the town hall.[4] It was only as a result of a growing electorate and increasing SPD efforts to obtain a share in municipal power that municipal government became politicized from around 1900.[5] At the same time, growing politicization was counterbalanced by the fact that as municipal government grew in complexity, the city became administered by 'experts'. Whereas before the turn of the century cities were governed by the local notables, after 1900 a degree in jurisprudence and specialization in particular branches of municipal government became prerequisites for holding office in the all-powerful *Magistrat*.[6] As a result, despite growing politicization in the municipal council the executive branch of local government actually became more independent of the control of the laymen in the city council. In practice, local government remained outside the purview of party politics throughout the period. At a local level political allegiance had no role as decisions were made behind closed doors.[7]

This verdict of a local government unaffected by party political squabbles has been largely accepted by scholars of urban history, who have proceeded

---

[3] H. Croon, 'Die Stadtvertretungen in Krefeld und Bochum im 19. Jahrhundert. Ein Beitrag zur Geschichte der Selbstverwaltung der rheinischen und westfälischen Städte', in R. Dietrich and G. Oestreich (eds.), *Forschungen zu Staat und Verfassung. Festgabe für Fritz Hartung* (Berlin, 1958), 289–306. W. Hofmann, *Die Bielefelder Stadtverordneten. Ein Beitrag zur bürgerlichen Selbstverwaltung und sozialem Wandel* (Berlin, 1964). W. Köllmann, *Sozialgeschichte der Stadt Barmen* (Tübingen, 1960).

[4] Sheehan, 'Liberalism', 131.

[5] M. Niehuss, 'Party Configurations in State and Municipal Elections in Southern Germany, 1871–1914', in K. Rohe (ed.), *Elections, Parties and Political Traditions. Social Foundations of German Parties and Party Systems, 1867–1987* (Oxford, 1990), 103. J. J. Sheehan, *German Liberalism in the Nineteenth Century* (Chicago, 1978), 235–8. W. Hardtwig, 'Großstadt und Bürgerlichkeit in der politischen Ordnung des Kaiserreichs', in L. Gall (ed.), *Stadt und Bürgertum im 19. Jahrhundert* (Munich, 1990), 40–6.

[6] S. Fisch, *Stadtplanung im 19. Jahrhundert. Das Beispiel München bis zur Ära Theodor Fischer* (Munich, 1988), 43.

[7] It is striking that one of the few studies to challenge this interpretation has been based on Bochum, the same city Croon had used for his own conclusion about the importance of social élites in local government. In contrast, David Crew has emphasized the modernity of political and social conflict in Bochum during the Empire, and the fact that local élites actually failed in their attempts to manipulate social groups. D. F. Crew, *A Town in the Ruhr. A Social History of Bochum, 1860–1914* (New York, 1979).

instead to concentrate on urbanization, town planning, sanitation, architecture, and other areas such as the growth of speculation in the housing sector.[8] In these studies, the only 'political' debate has been about the locus of authority, i.e. the extent to which impulses and decisions about town planning, sanitation, and housing came from private organizations, municipal government, and the state authorities. Given the impression of an unpolitical local government, urban historians have remained faithful to the late H. J. Dyos, who failed to include the study of municipal politics in his call for the study of the city in its full complexity.[9] In this way, party politics as such have never featured prominently in urban history, even in such central and divisive areas as town planning and incorporations, provisions for the poor and social policy, and municipal finance.[10] Even though the growth of local party politics during the German Empire has been acknowledged, this process is seen as playing only a part in the growing complexity and evolution of local government, alongside bureaucratization and professionalization.[11]

Seen in this light, it appears that the city has remained a bastion of the 'unpolitical German'. In some ways, this is almost coincidental, since local government has never been part of the German *Sonderweg* debate about Germany's special path in history. Thomas Mann defined the *Bürgertum* in mainly cultural terms, with political orientations extending only as far as the support for emperor and nation. Political orientation in its immediate environment, the city, was never part of the equation. Indeed, the virtue of the monarchy was precisely that it was above party politics, at whatever level. To Mann, politics were juxtaposed to objectivity, order, and decency.

Mann's analysis was reflected in the views of contemporary historians such as Friedrich Meinecke,[12] while younger generations of scholars have

[8] For an overview of much of this literature, see C. Zimmermann, 'Urbanisierung—Stadtgeschichte—Stadtentwicklung', in *NPL* xxxviii (1993), 7–28. See also J. Reulecke, 'Federal Republic of Germany', in C. Engeli and H. Matzerath (eds.), *Modern Urban History Research in Europe, USA and Japan. A Handbook* (Oxford, 1989), 53–71.

[9] Dyos's work is best summed up in D. Cannadine and David Reeder (eds.), *Exploring the Urban Past. Essays in Urban History by H. J. Dyos* (Cambridge, 1982). See esp. Cannadine, 'Conclusion: Urban History in the United Kingdom: The "Dyos Phenomenon" and after', in Cannadine and Reeder (eds.), op. cit., 203–20.

[10] See e.g. the still central summary history of urbanization, J. Reulecke, *Geschichte der Urbanisierung in Deutschland* (Frankfurt, 1985).

[11] Ibid. 131–9. W. R. Krabbe, *Die deutsche Stadt im 19. und 20. Jahrhundert* (Göttingen, 1989), 147–8. It is characteristic that even when Krabbe discusses the growth of municipal politics before 1918, he does not analyse its implications either for municipal government and administration, or for the various parties themselves.

[12] Note esp. that a central theme of both authors is the necessity for the state to preserve a balance between its powerful ('Macht') and spiritual ('Geist') aspects, except that towards the

also largely accepted the view of the 'unpolitical German'.[13] As is well known, central to this idea of a special German path in history, the *Sonderweg*, is the perceived failure of the *Bürger*, and his political alter ego of the 1860s, German liberalism,[14] to lead German society to a 'fundamental democratisation', of the kind which developed in other European countries and most notably in England at the time.[15] Impressed by a specifically German conception of the state going back to the days of Hegel,[16] pluralist party politics were perceived as particularism, and were contrasted with the positive, integrative nature of the authoritarian state.[17] Regardless of their political ideals, liberals became passive bystanders on the political stage, their true powerlessness and other-worldliness being revealed in their 'cringing conformity towards the existing structures of power'.[18] Lack of political participation bred a distinctive lack of political responsibility and political maturity.[19] In consequence, the historiography of German

end of his life, in 1946, Meinecke could judge with hindsight this balance to have become increasingly skewed. F. Meinecke, *Die deutsche Katastrophe* (Wiesbaden, 1965), 21–4, 35–6, and *passim*.

[13] For the continuity of this type of approach in the Weimar Republic, see B. Faulenbach, *Ideologie des deutschen Weges. Die deutsche Geschichte in der Historiographie zwischen Kaiserreich und Nationalsozialismus* (Munich, 1980). Since the Second World War, the idea of the 'unpolitical German' has been advocated most effectively by Ralf Dahrendorf. See esp. ch. 21 entitled 'The Unpolitical German', in R. Dahrendorf, *Society and Democracy in Germany* (2nd edn., New York, 1979), 314–27. See also F. Stern, 'Die politischen Folgen des unpolitischen Deutschen', in M. Stürmer (ed.), *Das Kaiserliche Deutschland. Politik und Gesellschaft 1870–1918* (Düsseldorf, 1970), 168–86.

[14] Throughout the Empire, the majority of liberal support came undoubtedly from the bourgeoisie. D. Langewiesche, *Liberalismus in Deutschland* (Frankfurt, 1988), 115, 140–64. This is not to say that most *Bürger* were necessarily liberal, or that the precise nature of the relationship between liberalism and bourgeoisie has been established. In Saxony, the conservatives derived their strength from their own rootedness in the bourgeoisie. J. Retallack, 'Die "liberalen" Konservativen? Konservatismus und Antisemitismus im industrialisierten Sachsen', in S. Lässig and K. H. Pohl (eds.), *Sachsen im Kaiserreich. Politik, Wirtschaft und Gesellschaft im Umbruch* (Weimar/Cologne/Vienna, 1997), esp. 134–42. On the relationship between liberalism and the bourgeoisie, see also K. H. Pohl, 'Die Nationalliberalen—eine unbekannte Partei?', in *JLF* iii (1991), 87. More recently, see K. H. Pohl, 'Liberalismus und Bürgertum 1880–1918', in L. Gall (ed.), *Bürgertum und bürgerlich-liberale Bewegung in Mitteleuropa seit dem 18. Jahrhundert* (Munich, 1997), 242–4.

[15] H.-U. Wehler, *The German Empire 1871–1918* (Leamington Spa, 1985), 71 ff.

[16] The centrality of the 'unpolitical German' in the German intellectual tradition has been challenged for the literary field by G. A. Craig, *The Politics of the Unpolitical. German Writers and the Problem of Power 1770–1871* (New York/Oxford, 1995).

[17] T. Nipperdey, 'Grundprobleme der deutschen Parteigeschichte im 19. Jahrhundert', in G. A. Ritter, (ed.), *Die deutschen Parteien vor 1918* (Cologne, 1973), 32–55.

[18] Wehler, *German Empire*, 72.

[19] G. A. Ritter, 'The Social Bases of the German Political Parties', in Karl Rohe (ed.), *Elections, Parties and Political Traditions. Social Foundations of German Parties and Party Systems, 1867–1987* (Oxford, 1990), 30.

liberalism has tended to focus on the liberals' repeated failures to gain access to power first under Bismarck, and then in response to repeated government crises under Wilhelm II.

By contrast, critics of the *Sonderweg* have called attention to the positive aspects of German liberal political activity,[20] such as the achievement of the rule of law in German society (*Rechtsstaat*).[21] Also, they have been fiercely opposed to the principle of teleology implied in the notion that the 'unpolitical German' should have been responsible not just for the outbreak of the First World War, but also for the advent of Nazism.[22] Regarding the liberals' supposed 'other-worldliness', these scholars have highlighted the liberals' own perception of strength during the 1870s,[23] their organizational advances from the 1890s,[24] and the overall increase in the number of liberal votes cast against a background of political fragmentation and polarization.[25] Also, the traditional emphasis of the *Sonderweg* on Prussia, which left out of consideration around three-fifths of the empire's population, came under criticism.[26]

This is not the place to discuss the *Sonderweg* debate in all its nuances.[27] Towards the late 1980s, most German scholars had become extremely

---

[20] On the re-evaluation of the *Sonderweg* with regard to the liberals, see in general E. Fehrenbach, *Verfassungsstaat und Nationsbildung 1815–1871* (Munich, 1992), 104–19.

[21] M. F. John, *Politics and the Law in Late Nineteenth-Century Germany. The Origins of the Civil Code* (Oxford, 1989).

[22] D. Blackbourn and G. Eley, *The Peculiarities of German History. Bourgeois Society and Politics in Nineteenth-Century Germany* (Oxford, 1984), esp. 32–3. A rather more sophisticated analysis of the 'apolitical' German, which accepts that this was a form of wider 'political' behaviour in itself, has been undertaken in R. Koshar, *Social Life, Local Politics, and Nazism. Marburg, 1880–1935* (Chapel Hill, NC, 1986).

[23] G. Schmidt, 'Die Nationalliberalen—eine regierungsfähige Partei? Zur Problematik der inneren Reichsgründung', in G. A. Ritter (ed.), *Die deutschen Parteien vor 1918* (Cologne, 1973), 208–23.

[24] G. Eley, 'Notable Politics, the Crisis of German Liberalism, and the Electoral Transition of the 1890s', in K. H. Jarausch and L. E. Jones (eds.), *In Search of a Liberal Germany. Studies in the History of German Liberalism from 1789 to the Present* (Oxford, 1990), 187–216.

[25] Langewiesche, *Liberalismus in Deutschland*, 133.

[26] D. Blackbourn, *Class, Religion and Local Politics in Wilhelmine Germany. The Centre Party in Württemberg before 1914* (New Haven, 1980).

[27] For one of the first essays critical of the idea of the *Sonderweg*, see T. Nipperdey, 'Wehler's "Kaiserreich". Eine kritische Auseinandersetzung', *GG* i (1975), 539–60. Among the best surveys of this debate are R. G. Moeller, 'The Kaiserreich recast? Continuity and Change in Modern German Historiography', *JSH* xvii (1984), 655–83, and D. Blackbourn, 'The German Bourgeoisie: An Introduction', in D. Blackbourn and R. J. Evans (eds.), *The German Bourgeoisie* (London, 1991), 1–46. J. Retallack, 'Social History with a Vengeance? Some Reactions to H.-U. Wehler's "Das Deutsche Kaiserreich" ', *GSR* vii (1984), 423–50. J. Retallack, 'Wilhelmine Germany', in G. Martel (ed.), *Modern Germany Reconsidered, 1870–1945* (London, 1992), 33–53.

careful in using the idea of a *Sonderweg*. For instance, Jürgen Kocka accepted that it was no longer sensible to speak of the German bourgeoisie as peculiarly distinct from any other middle class, that Germany had peculiarities in the same way that other countries had their own distinctivenesses.[28] Needless to say, such a definition deprived the *Sonderweg* of much of its original meaning. Indeed, Wehler himself accepted that there was as much a British or American *Sonderweg* as there was a German one.[29] The emphasis of investigation has clearly shifted, for example on to the ways in which the coincidence of a universal male franchise and a constitutional monarchy provided a unique liability for the constitutional framework within which German liberals operated.[30]

At the same time, the *Sonderweg* is far from dead, even though it has ceased to monopolize much of the attention on German history.[31] Scholars have increasingly taken up the notion of Germany's 'peculiar' path to 'modernity'.[32] Modern political and economic elements such as a universal male suffrage and a rapidly growing industrial economy co-existed with 'traditional' authoritarian government structures and the continuing social

---

[28] J. Kocka (ed.), *Bürgertum im 19. Jahrhundert. Deutschland im europäischen Vergleich* (Munich, 1988), i. 58. J. Kocka, 'German History before Hitler: The Debate about the German *Sonderweg*', *JCH* xxiii (1988), 3–16.

[29] H.-U. Wehler, 'Deutsches Bildungsbürgertum in vergleichender Perspektive— Elemente eines "Sonderwegs"?', in J. Kocka (ed.), *Bildungsbürgertum im 19. Jahrhundert. Politischer Einfluß und gesellschaftliche Formation* (Stuttgart, 1989), iv. 215–37.

[30] D. Langewiesche, 'Deutscher Liberalismus im europäischen Vergleich: Konzeption und Ergebnisse', in D. Langewiesche (ed.), *Liberalismus im 19. Jahrhundert. Deutschland im europäischen Vergleich* (Göttingen, 1988), 14.

[31] Perhaps the best evidence for this is the recent mutually contradictory claim by two of the most prominent opponents in this debate to have won the argument. R. J. Evans, *Rereading German History 1800–1996. From Unification to Reunification* (London, 1997), ix, 12–22. H.-U. Wehler, 'A Guide to Future Research on the Kaiserreich?', *CEH* xxix (1996), 552–3 and *passim*. See also G. Eley, 'Society and Politics in Bismarckian Germany', *GH* xv (1997), 115–18, 131–2.

[32] For a brief description of the evolution of the concept of modernity, see O. Brunner, W. Conze, R. Koselleck (eds.), *Geschichtliche Grundbegriffe. Historisches Lexikon zur politisch-sozialen Sprache in Deutschland* (Stuttgart, 1978), iv. 93–131. For an illustration of the ambiguities which the term 'modernity' connoted among contemporaries, see L. Gall, *Europa auf dem Weg in die Moderne, 1850–1890* (Munich, 1989). For a defence of the usefulness of 'modernity' as a framework of analysis, see Wehler, 'Future Research on the Kaiserreich?', 549–56.

It should be emphasized that throughout this study, the term 'modernization' is not used with reference to the debates about abstract modernization theories, but rather as a summary of the transformation of economic, social, and political life in Germany up to 1914, regardless of whether and to what extent these changes were truly 'modern' or not. Such a definition can be found in D. C. Tipps, 'Modernization Theory and the Comparative Study of Societies: A Critical Perspective', *CSSH* xv (1973), 199. See also I. Roxborough, 'Modernization Theory Revisited. A Review Article', *CSSH* xxx (1988), 753–61.

predominance of agrarian élites.[33] To avid readers of Friedrich Meinecke's *Die Deutsche Katastrophe*, such an analysis of the peculiar interaction of political and economic 'modernity', and its concurrence with deeply antimodern, 'irrational', and traditional features is hardly new. Still, this notion has remained at the heart of Wehler's 'new' German *Sonderweg*, notwithstanding the warnings of scholars like Thomas Nipperdey.[34] What is new is Wehler's argument about the precise form this concurrence of 'modern' and 'anti-modern' elements took, which is discussed most eloquently in Wehler's comprehensive social history.[35] It was precisely the economic 'modernity' with which Prussian Junkers modernized their estates, for instance, that enabled them to exert such a regressive influence on German politics and society. It was the very success of capitalism and of the bourgeois culture that made the bourgeoisie defensive in the face of a growing SPD, while the state was at the same time increasing its authoritarian powers as a regulator in a fast-changing economy and society. No longer does Wehler ignore the cities, or the significance of liberals in the cities. He attributes to liberals perhaps their most impressive performance in the management of the cities. And yet, that does not appear to have had any political consequences; if anything, the persistence of notable politics in the cities owing to a restricted franchise prevented liberals from organizing themselves sufficiently to meet the challenges of a universal male franchise at the national level.[36] In many ways, Wehler simply reiterates a view found in most recent studies on local government, that until around 1900 notables in charge of local government were usually liberal in their conviction, but that their actions in the public sphere had little to do with liberal politics.[37] Like Thomas Mann, they were liberal without being Liberals, true to vague notions of liberalism and perhaps even active politically on a national level, but engaged at the local level not out of political concerns, but simply for the common weal. In much prominent writing on

[33] T. Nipperdey, 'Probleme der Modernisierung in Deutschland', in T. Nipperdey, *Nachdenken über die deutsche Geschichte* (2nd edn., Munich, 1990), 52–70. W. Hardtwig and H.-H. Brand (eds.), *Deutschlands Weg in die Moderne. Politik, Gesellschaft und Kultur im 19. Jahrhundert* (Munich, 1993). The quest for a balance between modernity and tradition characterized nationalist movements from Wilhelmine to the Nazi era. M. S. Coetzee, *The German Army League. Popular Nationalism in Wilhelmine Germany* (New York/Oxford, 1990), esp. 123–5.
[34] Nipperdey, 'Probleme der Modernisierung', 65–6.
[35] H.-U. Wehler, *Deutsche Gesellschaftsgeschichte 1849–1914*. iii. *Von der 'Deutschen Doppelrevolution' bis zum Beginn des Ersten Weltkrieges 1849–1914* (Munich, 1995). See also Wehler, 'Future Research on the Kaiserreich?', 552–6.
[36] Wehler, *Deutsche Gesellschaftsgeschichte 1849–1914*, 1053–4.
[37] Ibid. 510–43. Around 1900, the liberal notables became party politicians. Ibid. 539.

imperial Germany, therefore, the notion of the 'unpolitical German' in the cities is still intact.[38]

Doubts about the persistence of the 'unpolitical German' in the urban context have surfaced only recently, as a product of different strands of research, none of which was primarily or even immediately concerned with municipal politics as such. Important in this respect was the growing acceptance of some of the main tenets of electoral history, as introduced to Germany by M. Rainer Lepsius. He argued that the concept of the 'milieu' was central to an understanding of voting behaviour. Voters did not cast their ballots for one particular reason, but supported a party for a complex pattern of cultural as well as social reasons such as religion, regional traditions, and so on.[39]

To proponents of the *Sonderweg*, of course, such ideas are rather hard to digest by their very nature. After all, they suggest that all efforts at explaining the demise of liberalism by exposing the supposed failure of liberal élites are pointless in that the actions of the liberal élites did not significantly affect voting patterns. Yet, to be fair, there were serious flaws in Lepsius's approach which even those who were inspired by his work had to admit.[40] His model could be criticized for being artificial and thus nonhistorical.[41] More objectionable particularly to English and American scholars was the fact that Lepsius constructed his model on the a priori assumption of the 'new orthodoxy', that the German party system during the Empire impeded Germany's democratic development.[42] Finally, there was simply not enough empirical evidence available at the time to validate his assumptions. The rather more comprehensive and sophisticated models of electoral history as advocated by Karl Rohe, Peter Steinbach, and others have brought issues of regional identities and popular political cultures to more general attention.[43]

[38] See the summary of current research in H. Seier, 'Liberalismus und Bürgertum in Mitteleuropa 1850–1880. Forschung und Literatur seit 1970', in L. Gall (ed.), *Bürgertum und bürgerlich-liberale Bewegung in Mitteleuropa seit dem 18. Jahrhundert* (Munich, 1997), 215–19.

[39] M. R. Lepsius, 'Parteiensystem und Sozialstruktur. Zum Problem der Demokratisierung der deutschen Gesellschaft', in G. A. Ritter (ed.), *Die deutschen Parteien vor 1918* (Cologne, 1973), 56–80.

[40] Rohe (ed.), *Elections, Parties and Political Traditions*, 1.

[41] J. J. Sheehan, 'Klasse und Partei im Kaiserreich: Einige Gedanken zur Sozialgeschichte der deutschen Politik', in O. Pflanze (ed.), *Innenpolitische Probleme des Bismarck-Reiches* (Munich/Vienna, 1983), 21.

[42] D. Blackbourn, 'Die Zentrumspartei und die deutschen Katholiken während des Kulturkampfes und danach', in O. Pflanze (ed.), *Innenpolitische Probleme des Bismarck-Reiches* (Munich/Vienna, 1983), 75.

[43] Note particularly Rohe's studies on the Ruhr district, for example K. Rohe, *Vom Revier zum Ruhrgebiet* (Essen, 1986). For work on electoral history at the national level, see in

Against the view that the German political system was characterized by a high degree of manipulation from the top,[44] these scholars insisted that politics are better understood as a function of social, religious, and cultural identities. Instead of straightforward popular capitulation to Bismarck's whims, what was remarkable at regional level was the sheer complexity of factors which influenced the politicization and the political mobilization of voters. Politics were subject more to nationalist, social, religious, economic, and constitutional conflict at the local level, than to any straightforward manipulation from above.[45] According to Karl Rohe, these conflicts on the ground can be summarized into three basic 'camps' (*Lager*), each containing several 'socio-moral' milieux, which lasted from the period of the Empire's foundation to the late 1920s: the Roman Catholic, the Social Democrat, and the 'national camp' comprising all bourgeois parties, from conservatives to left liberals.[46] Rohe has consciously avoided the most crucial shortcoming of Lepsius's model, the assumption that social milieux were static, emphasizing instead that each milieu developed over time and had to adapt to social, political, and cultural change. While not taking the stability of these milieux for granted, he was nevertheless able to show that, measured in terms of percentage of the voting population, these camps remained remarkably stable throughout the Empire. Interestingly, other things being equal, cultural factors were seen as more important in determining social milieux than religious ones.[47] These cultural factors formed the nature of the public sphere (*Öffentlichkeit*), mentality (*Mentalität*), and codes of behaviour (*Lebensweise*),[48] which were to a large extent shaped by the traditions and peculiarities of individual regions. As a result, like any

---

particular S. Suval, *Electoral Politics in Wilhelmine Germany* (Chapel Hill, NC, 1985). See also Steinbach, 'Reichstag Elections in the Kaiserreich: The Prospects for Electoral Research in the Interdisciplinary Context', in L. E. Jones and J. Retallack (eds.), *Elections, Mass Politics and Social Change in Modern Germany. New Perspectives* (Cambridge, 1992), 119–46.

[44] Apart from Wehler's work, this view is most famously expressed in M. Stürmer, *Regierung und Reichstag im Bismarckstaat 1871–1880* (Düsseldorf, 1974).

[45] P. Steinbach, *Die Zähmung des politischen Massenmarktes. Wahlen und Wahlkämpfe im Bismarckreich im Spiegel der Hauptstadt- und Gesinnungspresse* (Passau, 1990), esp. 724–6. Steinbach, *Die Politisierung der Region. Reichs- und Landtagswahlen im Fürstentum Lippe 1866–1881* (Passau, 1989), esp. 972–3.

[46] See the introductory essay in Rohe (ed.), *Elections, Parties and Political Traditions*, 1–25. For a more detailed and developed treatment, see K. Rohe, *Wahlen und Wählertraditionen* (Frankfurt, 1992), 57–121. Despite recent criticism, this view has been reaffirmed in K. Rohe, 'Politische Kultur—politische Milieus: Zur Anwendung neuerer theoretischer Konzepte in einer modernen Landesgeschichte', in S. Lässig and K. Pohl (eds.), *Sachsen im Kaiserreich. Politik, Wirtschaft und Gesellschaft im Umbruch* (Weimar/Cologne/Vienna, 1997), 177–90.

[47] Rohe (ed.), *Elections, Parties and Political Traditions*, 3.   [48] Rohe, *Wahlen*, 18.

other party the liberals were seen as comprising many regional party systems, which to be successful had to adapt to and in some degree shape the pre-existing culture of that area.[49]

Electoral history therefore explains why people went to the polls at record numbers at a time when the parties they voted for could not have any direct influence on government decisions.[50] People voted as an affirmation of their own milieu, rather than in response to particular measures introduced by a machiavellian governing élite. In this way, electoral history can explain how individuals were drawn into the political process, i.e. how they were politicized. Moreover, this model is able to explain better than any other the divergent regional patterns in voting behaviour. It can show why, for example, the SPD had a difficult time breaking into working-class areas with a dynamic and prevalent Roman Catholic social milieu (notably the Ruhrgebiet). This approach has led to a new appreciation of Germany's local and regional political diversity, even though in its focus on national and regional elections it uncovered little new ground concerning the development of urban politics as such.

Rohe's assumption of different milieux grouped together in three distinct voting camps (*Lager*), a Social Democratic, a Roman Catholic, and a 'National' camp, has attracted its own critics, most recently by Jonathan Sperber in his groundbreaking analysis of *The Kaiser's Voters*.[51] Announcing the 'farewell to the milieu thesis',[52] Sperber showed the large extent of voter movements between opposing camps, notably from the liberals to the SPD in the 1890s, and back from the SPD to the liberals just before the First World War.[53] Sperber also highlighted the difficulty in assuming conservatives and liberals in one single, 'national' camp, noting, for example, that the greatest interchange among voters of these parties occurred not when the two parties cooperated, but when they faced each other in a competitive situation. The assumption of three separate camps also leaves unresolved the problem of frequent voter swings from liberals to Social Democrats and vice versa, in the absence of similar swings from liberals to the Roman Catholic camp.[54] To Sperber, it is the absence of such a national camp during the Empire, and its emergence, for the first time, under the National Socialist banner in 1930 and 1932, that has so much explanatory

---

[49] Rohe (ed.), *Elections, Parties and Political Traditions*, 9–11.
[50] Suval, *Electoral Politics*, 4–9.
[51] J. Sperber, *The Kaiser's Voters. Electors and Elections in Imperial Germany* (Cambridge, 1997).
[52] Ibid. 284.   [53] Ibid. 128. See also table 3.3a on 124.
[54] Ibid. 121–2, 127, 284–7. See also 270.

value for the course of German history in the twentieth century.⁵⁵ Where Rohe and Sperber clearly are in agreement, however, is over the critical importance of confession, underlined by different and distinct regional identities, for individual voting behaviour. As Sperber has shown, confessional and regional identities have much more explanatory value for the development of political parties in the Empire than class.⁵⁶

Whereas much of the work of electoral history tends to emphasize the importance of regions in the context of national politics, there have been a number of studies of politics at the state level, even though they remain relatively few in number. For the most part, these have tended to focus on the southern and western states of Baden and Württemberg, where liberal politics were relatively advanced. For instance, for Württemberg Manfred Hettling has demonstrated the importance of local government in liberal opinion there before and during 1848/9, since it was the towns that provided a crucial focus for liberal organizational life.⁵⁷ In his masterful study on Württemberg politics after 1848, Dieter Langewiesche has provided a detailed account of the political and associational life in the cities and communitites there, placing particular emphasis on the differences between liberals and democrats.⁵⁸ More recently, Paul Nolte's investigation into communal politics in Baden has provided some startling conclusions, especially to those maintaining the 'unpolitical' nature of public affairs at the grass-roots level. Even for the 1830s and 1840s, Nolte argues that 'élite and notable politics . . . were replaced by mass politics—this transition occurred half a century earlier than is generally assumed by research into social history.'⁵⁹ The particular form of liberal 'community-politics' which Nolte describes was defeated during the 1848 Revolution as the assumptions of the political movement had become obsolete in a fast-changing world.⁶⁰ Yet even though the liberalism which emerged during the 1860s was of an entirely new nature, many of the carriers of this new liberalism were those that had been involved in local liberal politics in the pre-1848

---

⁵⁵ Sperber, *Kaiser's Voters*, 318–20.   ⁵⁶ Ibid. esp. 62–3, 272–6, 281–3, 291.
⁵⁷ M. Hettling, *Reform ohne Revolution. Bürgertum, Bürokratie und kommunale Selbstverwaltung in Württemberg von 1800 bis 1850* (Göttingen, 1990).
⁵⁸ D. Langewiesche, *Liberalismus und Demokratie in Württemberg zwischen Revolution und Reichsgründung* (Düsseldorf, 1974). More generally, see D. Langewiesche, 'Frühliberalismus und Bürgertum 1815–1849', in L. Gall (ed.), *Bürgertum und bürgerlich-liberale Bewegung in Mitteleuropa seit dem 18. Jahrhundert* (Munich, 1997), 104–9.
⁵⁹ P. Nolte, *Gemeindebürgertum und Liberalismus in Baden 1800–1850* (Göttingen, 1994). The quotation is on p. 241. See also P. Nolte, 'Gemeindeliberalismus. Zur Entstehung und sozialen Verankerung der liberalen Partei in Baden 1831–1855', *HZ* cclii (1991), 57–93.
⁶⁰ See also P. Nolte, 'Bürgerideal, Gemeinde und Republik. "Klassischer Republikanismus" im frühen deutschen Liberalismus', *HZ* ccliv (1992), 609–56.

Introduction 13

era.⁶¹ Despite his different approach, Nolte neatly complemented Gall's pioneering study about Badenese liberalism 1848–71, which had described in detail the liberal bourgeois abandonment of many previously cherished social and political principles in the years before unification.⁶²

Research on other states has been less plentiful. As a state notoriously conservative in politics, Saxony has attracted the interest of a number of scholars who have, on the whole, replaced the image of a liberalism which was politically servile to the dominant conservatives with that of a pragmatic movement which managed to revive itself remarkably after 1890.⁶³ While most studies of politics at this level have looked at grass-roots political activity mainly with respect to state or national politics, a few studies have appreciated the intrinsic role of local political activity. In his much-needed study on Prussia, Thomas Kühne has noted that state elections were more often than not articulations of particular local concerns in each electoral district. His analysis is very much based on different regional social milieux, while he also notes the critical importance of local political patronage and corruption for the outcome of state elections.⁶⁴ Kühne's work was unique in scale, but his approach was not new. In his work on Hanover, Michael John had highlighted the fact that National Liberal success in the province cannot be understood without an examination of National Liberal strength in each locality. National Liberal success was thus a factor of cultural and 'national' identities in the different localities, often reinforced by religious conflict, and economic conditions.⁶⁵ In his

---

⁶¹ Nolte, *Gemeindebürgertum*, 415–31.

⁶² L. Gall, *Der Liberalismus als regierende Partei. Das Grossherzogtum Baden zwischen Restauration und Reichsgründung* (Wiesbaden, 1968).

⁶³ S. Lässig, *Wahlrechtskampf und Wahlreform in Sachsen (1895–1909)* (Weimar/Cologne/Vienna, 1996). Pohl, 'Liberalismus und Bürgertum', 287–9. A superb summary of existing research is S. Lässig and K. H. Pohl (eds.), *Sachsen im Kaiserreich. Politik, Wirtschaft und Gesellschaft im Umbruch* (Weimar/Cologne/Vienna, 1997). The most illuminative articles on the subjects are K. H. Pohl, 'Die Nationalliberalen in Sachsen vor 1914. Eine Partei der konservativen Honoratioren auf dem Wege zur Partei der Industrie', in L. Gall and D. Langewiesche, *Liberalismus und Region. Zur Geschichte des deutschen Liberalismus im 19. Jahrhundert* (Munich, 1995), 195–216. J. Retallack, 'Antisocialism and Electoral Politics in Regional Perspective: The Kingdom of Saxony', in L. E. Jones and J. Retallack (eds.), *Elections, Mass Politics, and Social Change in Modern Germany* (Cambridge, 1992), 49–91. J. Retallack, ' "What is to be done?" The Red Specter, Franchise Questions, and the Crisis of Conservative Hegemony in Saxony, 1896–1909', *CEH* xxiii (1990), 271–312.

⁶⁴ T. Kühne, *Dreiklassenwahlrecht und Wahlkultur in Preußen 1867–1914. Landtagswahlen zwischen korporativer Tradition und politischem Massenmarkt* (Düsseldorf, 1994).

⁶⁵ M. John, 'Kultur, Klasse und regionaler Liberalismus in Hannover 1848–1914', in L. Gall and D. Langewiesche (eds.), *Liberalismus und Region. Zur Geschichte des deutschen Liberalismus im 19. Jahrhundert* (Munich, 1995), 161–93. M. John, 'Associational Life and the Development of Liberalism in Hanover, 1848–66', in K. H. Jarausch and L. E. Jones (eds.), *In*

work on left liberalism in Schleswig-Holstein, Alastair Thompson has demonstrated with admirable clarity the interconnectedness of local, national, and state politics with regard to party organization, individual involvement, and political programme.[66]

A greater appreciation of the importance of politics at the local level has also been a fortunate by-product of recent research on the *Bürgertum* itself, most notably as part of Lothar Gall's research project on *Stadt und Bürgertum*.[67] In fact, the first studies that have been published suggest that the late 1860s are very much a watershed in local affairs. They mark the transition from a local community of citizens where public life was dominated by personal, informal networks of citizens through clubs and associations to a society in which local affairs became increasingly politicized, as a result of economic change, confessional conflict, and a changing national environment.[68] Hans-Werner Hahn's study on Wetzlar shows how even before 1866 a liberal city council came to oppose a conservative *Magistrat*.[69] This is despite the fact that Wetzlar could be considered a relatively static place in which traditional structures were unusually persistent.[70] Similarly, Karin Schambach has suggested that in Dortmund, too, the city council became politicized from the 1860s.[71] While the first fruits of the *Stadt und Bürgertum* project thus strongly indicate the importance of politics in local affairs by the 1870s, their focus on the bourgeoisie precludes a more detailed analysis of the nature and the extent of politicization at the local level.

Despite these studies of local urban bourgeois élites, the central problem about local politics remains, namely the extent to which public service was the result of social tradition rather than political conviction. Only too often, historians have argued that local political activity was dependent upon

Search of a Liberal Germany. Studies in the History of German Liberalism from 1789 to the Present (Oxford, 1990), 161–85. M. John, 'Liberalism and Society in Germany, 1850–1880. The Case of Hanover', in *EHR* cii (1987), 579–98.

[66] A. P. Thompson, 'Left Liberals in German State and Society 1907–1918', Ph.D. thesis (London, 1989).

[67] For a general introduction to the project's concerns, see L. Gall, 'Stadt und Bürgertum im 19. Jahrhundert. Ein Problemaufriss', in Gall (ed.), *Stadt und Bürgertum im 19. Jahrhundert*, 1–18.

[68] R. Zerback, *München und sein Stadtbürgertum. Eine Residenzstadt als Bürgergemeinde 1770–1870* (Munich, 1997), 293–4, 299.

[69] H.-W. Hahn, *Altständisches Bürgertum zwischen Beharrung und Wandel. Wetzlar 1689–1870* (Munich, 1991), 447–72, esp. 459–60.

[70] In many ways, Wetzlar fits Walker's descriptions of the German 'home towns'. M. Walker, *German Home Towns: Community, State, General Estate 1648–1871* (Ithaca, NY, 1971).

[71] K. Schambach, *Stadtbürgertum und industrieller Umbruch. Dortmund 1789–1870* (Munich, 1996), 338–41.

Introduction 15

factors such as the social prestige and the civic self-understanding of entire social groups without even taking into account the possibility that political involvement might have been most crucially a factor of political motivation.[72] In the middling Hanoverian town of Harburg, local elections were never really openly contested by political parties, and yet a highly restricted franchise allowed the council and the adminstration to be in secure National Liberal hands from the start of the Empire.[73]

It is increasingly clear that politics played a considerable part in local government throughout the Empire, even if this is often only mentioned en passant.[74] For example, in a rare study of politics at city level, Norbert Schlossmacher looks exclusively at the development of Düsseldorf party politics for state and national elections, even though he notes at one point that the first permanent election bureau was set up by the liberals in the mid-1870s for the local elections.[75] In her extremely valuable study of politics in Münster, Ute Olliges-Wieczorek does not analyse the politics of local affairs in its diversity and complexity, since her focus is equally on state and national politics. Even so, she is able to show the politicizing effects of the *Kulturkampf* on local affairs, while her general focus on the city's diverse associational life demonstrates, in this instance for the Centre Party, the value of testing general assumptions in a local study.[76]

The approaches mentioned above already give a clear indication that the view of the 'unpolitical German' in the cities is closer to myth than reality. This impression is conveyed most effectively by a growing number of investigations into the history of various cities. As a result of Rohe's work on the Ruhr area, most scholars would admit that the *Kulturkampf* provided a strong impetus for politicization,[77] and that this affected local

---

[72] H.-W. Schmuhl, 'Bürgerliche Eliten in städtischen Repräsentativorganen. Nürnberg und Braunschweig im 19. Jahrhundert', in H.-J. Puhle (ed.), *Bürger in der Gesellschaft der Neuzeit* (Göttingen, 1991), 178–98, here 178. For criticism of this type of approach, see B.-C. Padtberg, *Rheinischer Liberalismus in Köln während der politischen Reaktion in Preußen nach 1848/9* (Cologne, 1985), 12–14.

[73] P.-C. Witt, 'Kommunalpolitik in Harburg zwischen Interessen lokaler Eliten und Entstehung einer modernen Leistungsverwaltung (1867–1914)', in J. Ellermeyer et al. (eds.), *Harburg. Von der Burg zur Industriestadt* (Harburg, 1988), 219–49.

[74] Schmuhl devotes only one paragraph to the formation of liberal politics in local government in Braunschweig from the middle of the 19th century, and unfortunately he does not follow up its implications. Schmuhl, 'Bürgerliche Eliten', 191.

[75] N. Schlossmacher, *Düsseldorf im Bismarckreich. Politik und Wahlen, Parteien und Vereine* (Düsseldorf, 1985), 90.

[76] U. Olliges-Wieczorek, *Politisches Leben in Münster—Parteien und Vereine im Kaiserreich (1871–1914)* (Münster, 1995).

[77] While the occurrence of politicization as such is more or less accepted, the precise nature of this process is still unclear. At issue is whether Roman Catholicism became distinctively and

politics as well, as evidenced by the growing electoral challenge of the Centre Party in the local elections there.[78] Since the economic and demographic environment of the Ruhr area was quite unique in Germany, evidence of early politicization could easily be dismissed as an 'exception' to the rule.[79] However, it seems increasingly clear that the *Kulturkampf* provided a crucial catalyst for the politicization of local politics in a host of other cities with a strong Roman Catholic population, from Münster in the north to Freiburg in the south.[80] Moreover, the case of the Rhenish cities indicates the limits of the usefulness of deciding which towns were 'exceptional' in their political development and which were not. For example, it could also be argued that the cities of Elberfeld and Barmen, which have been heralded as models for unpolitical city government, were themselves highly 'exceptional' as the only cities in the governmental district (*Regierungsbezirk*) of Düsseldorf most of whose population was Protestant.[81]

More importantly, the small number of studies on urban politics that do exist suggest that denominational conflict provided a crucial agent of politicization even in areas unaffected by the *Kulturkampf*. In Augsburg, for instance, the latent tensions between Protestants and Roman Catholics became politicized in the 1840s, and political conflict re-emerged during the late 1850s and the 1860s. This conflict between 'conservative' Catholics and Protestant liberals extended into the city council, despite its social

---

decisively politicized during the *Kulturkampf*, or whether the development of political Catholicism occurred during the decades before, starting in 1848/9. For the former view, see, for instance, M. L. Anderson, 'The Kulturkampf and the Course of German History', *CEH* xix (1986), 82–115. For an example of the latter view, see J. Sperber, *Popular Catholicism in 19th Century Germany* (Princeton, 1984), esp. 207–76. In addition, the nature of political Catholicism, if it did exist before 1870, is unclear. For opposing views on this issue, see J. Sperber, 'Competing Counterrevolutions: Prussian State and Catholic Church in Westphalia during the 1850s', *CEH* xix (1986), 45–62, and S. Hyde, 'Roman Catholicism and the Prussian State in the Early 1850s', *CEH* xxiv (1991), 95–121.

[78] In the cities of Aachen, Cologne, and Trier, the Centre Party gained majorities in the municipal council. Krabbe, *Die deutsche Stadt*, 149. At the same time, liberals did prove surprisingly resilient, and by 1911, of 39 larger cities in the Rhineland, 30 remained in liberal-control. H. Matzerath, *Urbanisierung in Preußen 1815–1914* (Stuttgart/Berlin/Cologne/Mainz, 1985), 359.

[79] H. Pogge von Strandmann, 'The Liberal Monopolies of Power in the Cities of Imperial Germany', in L. E. Jones and J. Retallack (eds.), *Elections, Mass Politics and Social Change in Modern Germany. New Perspectives* (Cambridge, 1992), 103.

[80] H. Gründer, ' "Krieg bis auf's Messer"—Kirche, Kirchenvolk und Kulturkampf (1872–1887)', in F.-J. Jakobi (ed.), *Geschichte der Stadt Münster*. ii. *Das 19. und 20. Jahrhundert* (Münster, 1993), 131–67, esp. 131.

[81] E. G. Spencer, 'State Power and Local Interests in Prussian Cities: Police in the Düsseldorf District, 1848–1914', *CEH* xix (1986), 294–5. On the Protestant character of Barmen, see also Köllmann, *Sozialgeschichte*, 200 ff.

Introduction 17

composition of members of the bourgeois élite.[82] Another variant of this process whereby religious conflict at the local level fuelled politicization was in cases where there were glaring inequalities in privilege between a Protestant local or bureaucratic élite and a Roman Catholic popular majority. This was the case in cities such as Munich and Regensburg, although here the process of politicization in local government does not appear to have set in before the late 1860s.[83] More dramatic was the case of Osnabrück, where party friction during the early 1860s was such that local government was threatened with coming to a standstill. Here, too, confessional divisions were crucial, though Michael John has highlighted that the faultlines could also be intra-denominational, with orthodox Lutherans often finding themselves in the same camp as the Roman Catholics, against liberal Lutherans and Calvinists.[84]

The example of Osnabrück points to a second trigger of politicization, that of local identity. The religious divide was further defined by attitudes towards the Hanoverian monarchy, which had ruled the city since 1815. Protestant liberals conscious of their Westphalian identity felt no allegiance towards the Hanoverian Crown, especially after its repeated violations of the constitution. By contrast, Roman Catholics supported the Guelph dynasty following its restoration of the city's see in 1857. After 1866, political strife in local government continued, even though it changed in nature owing to the new political environment in which the city found itself after the Prussian annexation.[85] The difficulties and tensions emerging from the territorial changes in the post-Napoleonic era were not restricted to Osnabrück, but were to be found in much of Hanover.[86] Moreover,

[82] I. Fischer, *Industrialisierung, sozialer Konflikt und politische Willensbildung in der Stadtgemeinde. Ein Beitrag zur Sozialgeschichte Augsburgs* (Augsburg, 1977), 231–3. Fischer's superb study has been confirmed by the relevant articles in G. Gottlieb et al. (eds.), *Geschichte der Stadt Augsburg von der Römerzeit bis zur Gegenwart* (Stuttgart, 1984).

[83] In Regensburg and other cities, the lack of Roman Catholic representation in the local councils led to much political tension and agitation during the 1830s, though it seems that, at least in Regensburg, permanent political organizations and clubs were only established from the late 1860s. W. Chrobak, 'Politische Parteien, Verbände und Vereine in Regensburg 1869–1914. Teil II', *Verhandlungen des Historischen Vereins für Oberpfalz und Regensburg* cxx (1980), 214–40. Zerback, *München*, 278–95. R. Zerback, 'Unter der Kuratel des Staates—Die Stadt zwischen dem Gemeindeedikt von 1818 und der Gemeindeordnung von 1869', in R. Bauer (ed.), *Geschichte der Stadt München* (Munich, 1992), 274–306. E. Angermair, 'München als süddeutsche Metropole—Die Organisation des Großstadtausbaus 1870–1914', in Bauer, op. cit., esp. 327–8.

[84] John, 'Kultur, Klasse und regionaler Liberalismus', 178–83.

[85] R. Lembke, *Johannes Miquel und die Stadt Osnabrück unter besonderer Berücksichtigung der Jahre 1865–1869* (Osnabrück, 1962), 8–10.

[86] M. John, 'National and Regional Identities and the Dilemmas of Reform in Britain's "Other Province": Hanover, c.1800–c.850', in L. Brockliss and D. Eastwood (eds.), *A Union*

examples of the political effects of territorial changes are by no means limited to those territories annexed by Prussia in 1866. In many cities that had come under Prussian authority in 1814, such as Münster, Düsseldorf, and Koblenz, local friction was not simply denominational. It was caused by perceptions about a Roman Catholic majority who were the traditional (and, by implication, rightful) inhabitants, but who were deprived of their rights and their way of life by a small exogenous Prussian élite which came to dominate the bureaucracy and local politics.[87] It is only in the wake of the *Kulturkampf* in the 1870s, and owing to the growing popular acceptance of the territorial status quo under the Empire, that denominational issues came to dominate local politics while territorial identity receded into the background; but by then, politics had long become a fact of life in local affairs.

Of course, territorial or regional loyalties could politicize local affairs in the absence of added denominational hostilities. In the city of Hanover, it appears that the city council was drawn into politics, albeit reluctantly, owing to the King's persistent attempts to limit its powers. After 1866, the kingdom's annexation as a Prussian province gave the local notables such a political jolt that political dialogue within the council between supporters and opponents of the annexation stopped almost completely. Against the national trend, for most of the following two decades, the liberals were in a minority in the city council, against the dominant Guelphs.[88]

of Multiple Identities: The British Isles c.1750–c.1850 (Manchester, 1997), 179–92. H.-G. Aschoff, *Welfische Bewegung und politischer Katholizismus 1866–1918. Die Deutschhannoversche Partei und das Zentrum in der Provinz Hannover während des Kaiserreiches* (Düsseldorf, 1987), 45–9, 52–64.

[87] P. Hüttenberger, 'Die Entwicklung zur Großstadt bis zur Jahrhundertwende (1856–1900)', in *Düsseldorf. Geschichte von den Ursprüngen bis ins 20. Jahrhundert*. ii. *Von der Residenzstadt zur Beamtenstadt (1614–1900)* (Düsseldorf, 1988), esp. 589–608. P. Hüttenberger, 'Vom ausgehenden 19. Jahrhundert bis zum Ende des Ersten Weltkriegs', in *Düsseldorf. Geschichte von den Anfängen bis ins 20. Jahrhundert*. iii. *Die Industrie und Verwaltungsstadt (20. Jahrhundert)* (Düsseldorf, 1989), 82–8. H.-J. Behr, 'Zwischen Vormärz und Reichsgründung', in *Geschichte der Stadt Münster*, ii. 79–130, esp. 82. Gründer, 'Kirche, Kirchenvolk und Kulturkampf (1872–1887)', esp. 133, 147–51. J. Herres, 'Das Preussische Koblenz', in *Geschichte der Stadt Koblenz*. ii. *Von der französischen Stadt bis zur Gegenwart* (Stuttgart, 1993), 49–102. It is clear that this 'Protestant Prussian' milieu contrasted sharply with the 'indigenous traditional Roman Catholic' milieu in all three towns. However, its implications for local politics as such are only clear in the articles on Münster. It is also discussed, albeit in a more summary manner, in the study on Düsseldorf. Local politics as such are not investigated in the Koblenz history, but given the similar social and denominational circumstances, it seems reasonable to assume that national controversies such as the Cologne Church dispute of 1837 had similar politicizing effects for local politics there as they did in Münster. See also T. Mergel, *Zwischen Klasse und Konfession. Katholisches Bürgertum im Rheinland 1794–1914* (Göttingen, 1994), 132–3.

[88] D. Brosius, 'Die Industriestadt. Vom Beginn des 19. Jahrhunderts bis zum Ende des 1. Weltkriegs', in K. Mlynek and W. R. Röhrbein (eds.), *Geschichte der Stadt Hannover*.

Introduction 19

While confessional division and territorial change affected at least a substantial minority of German towns from 1814 to 1866, all were to a greater or lesser extent affected by the Revolutions of 1848/9. Even though they were fundamentally an urban phenomenon,[89] it is extremely difficult to ascertain the extent to which the politicization which they undoubtedly entailed affected attitudes towards local, as well as state, politics. Manfred Hettling has indicated for the city of Breslau that the development of liberalism there from the 1860s also affected the level of local politics. The precise extent to which this happened will only be known with the publication of his comprehensive survey of liberalism in that city.[90] Left liberals and democrats were also thriving in the university town of Königsberg from the mid-1840s, and this led to constant friction between prominent left liberals, many of whom were active in local government, and the state. This indicates a considerable degree of politicization before 1866, though in the absence of a detailed study of local politics it is impossible to say to what extent this was reflected in the conduct of local affairs.[91] Local politics in the Prussian capital of Berlin were clearly more 'peculiar' than elsewhere in the Kingdom. Yet even here, where before 1848 it had been virtually impossible to pursue liberal politics in the city council,[92] after the Revolution the city council became a major left-liberal stronghold and an example to liberals in local government elsewhere. In the late 1850s, the city council formed an important stronghold from whence leading left liberals such as Virchow and Mommsen created the German Progressive Party in 1861.[93] Berlin retained this model function throughout the duration of the Empire, not least because early SPD advances in the third class of the franchise forced Berlin liberals to articulate and realize their policies with model

---

ii. *Vom Beginn des 19. Jahrhunderts bis in die Gegenwart* (Hanover, 1994), 273–404, esp. 305–13, 340–6.

[89] Langewiesche, 'Frühliberalismus und Bürgertum', 90–3, 116–20. Seier, 'Liberalismus und Bürgertum in Mitteleuropa', 184–5.

[90] For an overview, see M. Hettling, 'Von der Hochburg zur Wagenburg. Liberalismus in Breslau von den 1860er Jahren bis 1918', in L. Gall and D. Langewiesche (eds.), *Liberalismus und Region. Zur Geschichte des deutschen Liberalismus im 19. Jahrhundert* (Munich, 1995), 253–76.

[91] F. Gause, *Die Geschichte der Stadt Königsberg in Preussen.* ii. *Von der Königskrönung bis zum Ausbruch des Ersten Weltkrieges* (Cologne/Graz, 1968), 507–55, 562–9.

[92] J. Knudsen, 'The Limits of Liberal Politics in Berlin, 1815–48', in K. H. Jarausch and L. E. Jones (eds.), *In Search of a Liberal Germany. Studies in the History of German Liberalism from 1789 to the Present* (Oxford, 1990), 111–31.

[93] G. Richter, 'Zwischen Revolution und Reichsgründung (1848–1870)', in W. Ribbe (ed.), *Geschichte Berlins.* ii. *Von der Märzrevolution bis zur Gegenwart* (Munich, 1988), 678–9. M. Erbe, 'Berlin im Kaiserreich (1871–1918)', in Ribbe (ed.), op. cit., 759–63.

sophistication and aggressiveness. Owing to the proximity between the capital's city council and the state authorities, Berlin also became a laboratory for a liberal evaluation of the role of local self-government vis-à-vis the state. Rudolf Gneist's experience first as a city councillor and then as a member of the Prussian House of Deputies inspired him to become the liberals' leading expert on local government; towards the turn of the century that distinction probably went to Hugo Preuß, who entered the council in 1896, upon finishing his first major work on local self-government.[94] Between 1850 and 1900, therefore, any notion of the Berlin city council as being unpolitical would have elicited great surprise among contemporaries, and would have to rest on an extremely narrow definition of politics.[95]

If after 1848 liberal politics became a factor in urban affairs in East-Elbian Prussia (of all places), its emergence in southern Germany should be much less surprising. Even though Petrus Müller's study of liberalism in Nuremberg does not consider local politics as such, it is reasonable to assume that the widespread extent of popular liberal support affected local affairs as well.[96] At the very least, it would appear likely that politics had some role in local government in Württemberg and Baden, the two states in which liberal politics were unusually prevalent. John Wilson has also shown the politicization and radicalization of local affairs in Ettlingen in the 1840s.[97] For the 1860s and 1870s, a pioneering and detailed study of liberal politics in the Konstanz area has emphasized the strength of political liberalism in its specific regional context.[98] Closer to the heart of Badenese politics, Lothar Gall's study of Mannheim has also indicated the importance of politics in local government from the 1860s.[99] In the case of Freiburg with its eminent see and its ancient university, it seems clear that

---

[94] H. Preuß, *Gemeinde, Staat, Reich als Gebietskörperschaften. Versuch einer deutschen Staatskonstruktion auf Grundlage der Genossenschaftstheorie* (Berlin, 1889; reprinted Aalen, 1964). S. Grassmann, *Hugo Preuß und die deutsche Selbstverwaltung* (Lübeck/Hamburg, 1965), 6–12.

[95] Especially during the 1870s, Frankfurt left-liberals looked towards local government in Berlin as a model for the conduct of left-liberal politics in the city. See, for instance, *Frankfurter Zeitung*, 22 Nov. 1872 (1. Blatt).

[96] P. Müller, *Liberalismus in Nürnberg 1860 bis 1871. Eine Fallstudie zur Ideen- und Sozialgeschichte des Liberalismus in Deutschland im 19. Jahrhundert* (Nuremberg, 1990), esp. 358–87.

[97] J. A. Wilson, *Seedbed of Protest. Social Structure and Radical Politics in Ettlingen, Grand Duchy of Baden, 1815–1850* (New York, 1992), esp. 173–4.

[98] G. Zang (ed.), *Provinzialisierung einer Region. Regionale Unterentwicklung und liberale Politik in der Stadt und im Kreis Konstanz im 19. Jahrhundert* (Frankfurt, 1978).

[99] L. Gall, *Bürgertum in Deutschland* (Berlin, 1989), 365–73.

its role as an epicentre of the Badenese *Kulturkampf* had immediate repercussions for local politics. The Freiburg liberals' efforts from 1864 to realize the state supervision of schools (*Schulaufsichtsgesetz*) locally caused the deep hostility of the Roman Catholic Church and its loyal flock, and led to a rapid process of politicization and polarization in the local public sphere.[100] Looking at Baden as a whole, Paul Nolte confirmed Gall's view that a new liberalism in small and larger towns developed during the 1850s, as a prerequisite to, and a consequence of, the liberals' ascent to power in the state government in 1860 and the consequent *Kulturkampf*.[101] Even in the absence of open religious conflict in Württemberg, politicization had advanced so much that in Stuttgart, liberal politics were a growing factor in local elections from the 1830s. A political system emerged in local affairs which was dominated by a liberal camp against one which was traditionalist and pro-governmental.[102] Politics were similarly advanced in Ulm, where the candidates' political convictions continued to be a decisive factor even during the reaction of the early 1850s. From 1860, the conflict between liberals and democrats at the state level ensured that political divisions flared up in local matters once again.[103]

Clearly, there are still too few studies of local government to make it possible to arrive at more definite conclusions about the role and the development of politics at this level. What those studies touching directly or indirectly upon politics in the locality have in common is that they all challenge the predominance of the 'unpolitical' up until 1900. Moreover, while the investigations into the government of individual cities are all case studies that may be exceptions to the rule, collectively they challenge the very concept of 'exceptionality'. It could be argued perhaps even more convincingly that those places were exceptional that did not experience either denominational conflict, recent territorial changes, or the

---

[100] G. Blod et al., 'Unruhe im "Pfaffenstädtchen". Reaktion, "Neue Ära" und Kulturkampf (1850–1870)' in H. Haumann and H. Schadek (eds.), *Geschichte der Stadt Freiburg im Breisgau*. iii. *Von der badischen Herrschaft bis zur Gegenwart* (Stuttgart, 1992), 130–64. H. Haumann et al., 'Industriestadt oder "Pensionopolis"? Im Kaiserreich (1871–1914)', in Haumann and Schadek, op. cit., 165–254, esp. 228–31. In general, see Gall, *Liberalismus als regierende Partei*, 286–311.
[101] Nolte, *Gemeindebürgertum*, 22. L. Gall, 'Die partei- und sozialgeschichtliche Problematik des badischen Kulturkampfes', reprinted in A. Schäfer (ed.), *Neue Forschungen zu Grundproblemen der badischen Geschichte im 19. und 20. Jahrhundert* (Karlsruhe, 1973), 93–132. Gall, *Liberalismus als regierende Partei*, 65–80.
[102] R. Waibel, *Frühliberalismus und Gemeindewahlen in Württemberg (1817–1855). Das Beispiel Stuttgart* (Stuttgart, 1992), e.g. 14–15.
[103] H. E. Specker (ed.), *Ulm im 19. Jahrhundert. Aspekte aus dem Leben der Stadt* (Stuttgart, 1990), 296–301.

revolutionary upheavals of 1848/9. What is most striking is that none of the studies mentioned above examine directly liberalism in local government during the German Empire. Those few studies that focus on politics in the locality concentrate on some other aspect, such as the outcomes of state and national elections, or the development of the labour movement. Despite James Sheehan's observation in 1971 that, to the extent that local government was political, it was overwhelmingly liberal, nobody seems to have heeded his call for more research in this area. Only recently have a number of scholars attempted to summarize current research on local government, and to draw some—albeit speculative—conclusions about its implications for German liberalism. While Lothar Gall has noted the intrinsic importance of local government for liberal ideals before 1848,[104] Karl Heinrich Pohl has argued for the practical importance of liberalism in local government. At the local level, liberals were flexible and power-conscious, and their insistence on the 'unpolitical' could quite possibly have been a political act in itself. Pohl also challenged scholars to take more seriously the political implications of progressive liberal policies, e.g. at the social or educational level.[105] These first attempts to bring together the wealth of disparate discussions that touch directly or indirectly upon liberalism and local government clearly show the dire need for a more detailed analysis in this area. Put crudely, current levels of knowledge about liberalism at the local level are inversely proportional to its importance.[106]

This book, therefore, aims to fill an important gap in historical scholarship. It is one of the first to consider in detail the dynamics of liberal politics in local government. In particular, it addresses the question of how liberals in local government got into power. It looks at their ideals, their rhetoric, and their policies, to assess what they did once they were in power. It then discusses what impact this had, e.g. on the behaviour of other political or social groups, or on the development of the locality. Finally, it assesses the impact of the liberals' rhetoric, ideals, and policies on electoral behaviour, to assess which policies were the most beneficial, and which the most detrimental, for their political performance.

[104] L. Gall, 'Das liberale Milieu. Die Bedeutung der Gemeinde für den deutschen Liberalismus', in *Liberalismus und Gemeinde. 3. Rastatter Tagung zur Geschichte des Liberalismus am 10./11. November 1990* (Sankt Augustin, 1991), 11–34, esp. 20–4.

[105] K. H. Pohl, '"Einig", "kraftvoll", "machtbewußt". Überlegungen zu einer Geschichte des deutschen Liberalismus aus regionaler Perspektive', *HMRG* vii (1994), 61–80.

[106] D. Langewiesche, 'Liberalismus und Region', in L. Gall and D. Langewiesche (eds.), *Liberalismus und Region. Zur Geschichte des deutschen Liberalismus im 19. Jahrhundert* (Munich, 1995), 15.

Bearing in mind the extent to which some of the findings in this case study of Frankfurt are peculiar to that city alone, an examination of liberal politics there can address a number of key issues outlined so far. Firstly, it will show what 'politics' and 'liberalism' can mean in local government. In this as in other studies, these terms have been used consistently, but it is not at all clear that 'politics' had the same connotations throughout local, state, and national government. As this study will show, at the local level the definition of what was in the purview of politics evolved over time. Throughout the period, education and the defence of local self-government against the state were central to urban liberalism, while these issues were, for obvious reasons, never really part of the national political discourse.

Secondly, this monograph will show what issues were most important for liberal politics in the locality. While a plethora of studies exist which look at various dimensions of city government, such as urban planning or municipal socialism, this study will discuss the issues that were actually important to the liberals themselves. This book's conclusion that attitudes and policies in the realms of education, social welfare, and taxation were crucial liberal concerns in Frankfurt is very likely to apply to liberals in local government elsewhere.

Thirdly, this book directly challenges allegations that Germans were inherently 'unpolitical' and 'illiberal', since they were unworldly and inept at the level of practical politics. This statement can only be true if it can be shown to apply throughout Germany, even in a city often noted for its progressivism in the German context, Frankfurt am Main. By contrast, this monograph illustrates how German liberals, once they actually were in government, could be politically astute and successful second to none.

Finally, the study will consider some of the wider implications of its findings with regard to the opportunities and challenges facing German liberalism in general. Liberalism in local government is an important enough subject in itself, but it does have critical implications for the nature of German liberalism as a whole. To what extent were politics at the local, state, and national level interdependent? Put differently, if it is the case that at the local level liberal politics were much more vital than had hitherto been presumed, how did this filter through to liberal organization and policies at the state and national levels? More specifically, this study will consider why the policies of Frankfurt liberals, despite their unique influence beyond the city, did not find their way into state or national liberal policies.

At first sight, the choice of conducting a case study of liberal politics in Frankfurt am Main may seem surprising, given that Frankfurt must be one of the best-researched cities in Germany. In fact, Siegbert Wolf has written one of the only monographs on urban liberalism by looking at Frankfurt.[107] Unfortunately, he assesses Frankfurt liberalism mostly in its local context, and most of the book is narrative, rather than argumentative. In his main section of the book, for instance, he undertakes an exhaustive description of each municipal election, essentially by rewriting contemporary newspaper reports, accepting without criticism their biased judgements. The book is a useful introduction to the liberal parties in Frankfurt, but does not engage much in critical analysis about politicization and the development of politics in the local context. More recently, Andrea Fischer has written on the evolution of municipal government, 1868–1880, but again she adds little analysis or insight into the politics or motivations of local government at that time.[108]

Wolf's analysis of the social composition of the various liberal parties has been superseded by Ralf Roth's important study of the Frankfurt bourgeoisie, written as part of Gall's project on the German *Bürgertum*.[109] Inevitably, Roth's analysis includes important conclusions about Frankfurt liberalism, and this book will enter a critical dialogue with some of Roth's major conclusions. Some of Roth's findings are extremely opportune. His analysis of liberalism's social background, in particular his attention to the dense network of clubs and societies, means that this monograph can concentrate on the organization, presentation, and content of politics itself. Meanwhile, Roth's primary objective, a portrayal of the Frankfurt bourgeoisie, means that he cannot chart the development of a liberal programme, or the ideological and tactical differences between the various liberal movements in greater detail. Roth's work illustrates well the pitfalls of looking at party politics through the prism of social history. For instance, common notable membership of the same clubs and societies leads him to speak persistently of a 'liberal' milieu which was self-sustaining. This begs the question why there were three liberal parties in operation for most of the period, and why at times there was such political acrimony between the various liberal movements.[110]

[107] S. Wolf, *Liberalismus in Frankfurt am Main. Vom Ende der Freien Stadt bis zum Ersten Weltkrieg (1866–1914)* (Frankfurt, 1987).

[108] For instance, the Democrats are characterized with the simplification that they favoured 'all municipal projects, which contributed to an increase in Frankfurt's prosperity'. A. Fischer, *Kommunale Leistungsverwaltung im 19. Jahrhundert. Frankfurt am Main unter Mumm von Schwarzenstein 1868–1880* (Berlin, 1995), here p. 98.

[109] R. Roth, *Stadt und Bürgertum in Frankfurt am Main. Ein besonderer Weg von der ständischen zur modernen Bürgergesellschaft 1760–1914* (Munich, 1996). For Roth's contradiction of Wolf's analysis, see 506–9.

[110] Roth's conclusions on liberalism in Frankfurt are summarized in R. Roth, 'Liberalismus in Frankfurt am Main 1814–1914. Probleme seiner Strukturgeschichte', in L. Gall and

Perhaps the best study on Frankfurt politics is John Rolling's unpublished thesis on the growth of social democracy in local government from 1900 until 1918.[111] His analysis of the relationship between liberals and Social Democrats remains valid in important respects, even if it represents only one aspect of liberal politics during the period. Still, his conclusion about the liberals' acceptance of tacit cooperation with the Social Democrats after 1900 raises more questions than it answers. For his image of municipal government dominated by 'unpolitical' notables until 1900 seems difficult to reconcile with his analysis of hardened, pragmatic liberal politicians thereafter.

Ursula Bartelsheim's work on the nature and the growth of municipal administration in Frankfurt is also concerned with the evolution of municipal politics.[112] Once again, her work is a good complement to, but not a replacement of, a study of liberal politics. Bartelsheim looks at local politics from the top down, from the perspective of the local administration. While some of her conclusions, chiefly about the political nature of the *Magistrat*, have given encouragement to this study's own findings, this book addresses completely different issues. It is concerned about the relationship between liberal politics and its grass roots, and the issues which were of primary concern to liberals rather than to municipal government as such.

There are a number of studies apart from these, which are of direct relevance to an investigation into the development of liberalism in Frankfurt. Like Wolf's study, however, these have been written not so much in a general historiographical context, but for an audience interested principally in Frankfurt local history.[113] Most important of these in the context of this study are Karl Maly's books on the city's municipal council. Once again, they are admirably full of narrative detail, but lack analytical depth for those having an interest beyond the confines of Frankfurt itself.[114]

D. Langewiesche (eds.), *Liberalismus und Region. Zur Geschichte des deutschen Liberalismus im 19. Jahrundert* (Munich, 1995), esp. 41–85.

[111] J. D. Rolling, 'Liberals, Socialists, and City Government in Imperial Germany: The Case of Frankfurt am Main, 1900–1918', Ph.D. thesis (Madison, 1979). Rolling's thesis stands in commendable contrast to R. Stübling's refreshingly different, but ultimately questionable, Marxist account in R. Stübling, *Die Sozialdemokratie in Frankfurt am Main von 1891 bis 1910* (Frankfurt, 1981).

[112] U. Bartelsheim, 'Die Politisierung und Demokratisierung der kommunalen Selbstverwaltung. Kommunalpolitik in Frankfurt am Main 1850–1900', D.Phil. thesis (Frankfurt, 1995).

[113] This is true for most of the publications of the Frankfurter Historische Kommission, including its periodical on Frankfurt history, the *Archiv für Frankfurter Geschichte und Kunst*.

[114] K. Maly, *Die Macht der Honoratioren. Geschichte der Stadtverordnetenversammlung 1867–1900* (Frankfurt, 1992). K. Maly, *Das Regiment der Parteien. Geschichte der Frankfurter Stadtverordnetenversammlung 1900–1933* (Frankfurt, 1995).

Given the amount of work published on Frankfurt's local administration, this monograph can afford to neglect the more detailed questions about Frankfurt's political environment. There is no need to chart in detail, for example, who comprised the *Magistrat*, or which citizens were particularly prominent in which liberal parties. For this book is not about Frankfurt per se. It is concerned with the history and the development of Frankfurt liberalism only inasmuch as it illustrates particularly well some of the underlying problems and possibilities of liberals in local government. The fundamental questions which this work seeks to address, about the ideological, organizational, electoral, and programmatic evolution of liberalism in local government, have neither been asked nor answered before. Because of this, Frankfurt offers unique advantages for a case study of urban liberalism in imperial Germany.

First and foremost, Frankfurt lends itself to an investigation into how liberals got into power, and what they did once they were in power, simply because it was one of the most prominent liberal centres in imperial Germany. Frankfurt liberals controlled the local council throughout the period, despite strong challenges first from *Mittelstand* groups and then from the SPD. Here, the Democrats, the local branch of the German People's Party, were overwhelmingly dominant. Democrats represented the city in the Reichstag until 1884, and again from 1907 to 1912. Finally, liberals continued to represent the city in the Prussian state assembly, with the balance shifting from National Liberal and Progressive Liberal representation to Democratic and Progressive Liberal representation in the late 1890s.[115]

Another important reason for choosing Frankfurt as a case study for the activities and the motivations of liberals at the local level is that local government was notoriously progressive and innovative there. After Hamburg, Frankfurt was the second city in Germany to build a drainage system from the 1860s, after intense lobbying of one of the leading German physicians at the time, Georg Varrentrapp. During the 1870s, under the First Mayor, Mumm, there was a host of municipal improvements and grandiose civic projects, such as the building of a new opera house. In the early 1880s, Mumm's successor, Johannes von Miquel, was one of the first liberal politicians to become involved with the *Verein für Sozialpolitik*'s pioneering investigations into the urban housing problem.[116] His successor, Franz

---

[115] See the relevant tables in Appendix II.
[116] B. Ladd, *Urban Planning and Civic Order in Germany, 1860–1924* (Cambridge, Mass., 1990), 141, 145–6. N. Bullock and J. Read, *The Movement for Housing Reform in Germany and France, 1840–1914* (Cambridge, 1985), 64–5.

Adickes, was regarded until the early 1900s as perhaps the leading expert on the housing question in Germany.[117] From the mid-1880s onwards, Frankfurt was at the forefront of municipal efforts to ease the tensions in the labour market brought about by rapid industrialization and early politicization of the labour force. Under Karl Flesch, the *Stadtrat* responsible for municipal social policy from 1884 to 1915, the city established a labour tribunal in 1887, and it pioneered the idea of a municipal labour exchange, established in 1895.[118] All this caused a foreign observer to note that:

> Its achievements place the city very high in the ranks of well administered municipalities. This is widely recognized, so widely that Frankfort stands upon a hill, as it were, among the municipalities of Europe. Its clean, well paved streets, swift, well-regulated and 'blessedly noiseless' street car lines, excellent lighting, water and sewerage facilities and beautiful parks are all far-famed as the earmarks of good city government.[119]

Frankfurt was undoubtedly progressive, but it was not 'peculiarly' so. If Frankfurt was more advanced in some areas of 'municipal socialism', it was behind in others; for instance, its gasworks were never municipalized, on technical schools (*Gewerbeschulen*) it followed the lead of other cities (notably Munich), and the city waited for some time to introduce unemployment insurance in 1914, well behind other pioneering cities in Germany. In the debates at the various municipal congresses held from 1900, at no point does one get the impression that Frankfurt was considered by other cities with particular reverence or esteem. For at that time, municipal socialism was in vogue, and every city tried its best to outdo the others in innovative schemes. Seen in this light, the fact that Frankfurt was more progressive than many other cities was more likely the result of its unique wealth, and thus the fact that local government could afford to experiment with a variety of new schemes, than of its unique eagerness for municipal socialism. Not by accident, in its innovations Frankfurt was regarded as a city just like any other.

---

[117] Perhaps Adickes's reputation peaked in 1903, when he outlined his views in a speech which is often seen as a portrayal of moderate liberals' principles of municipal social reform. F. Adickes and G. Beutler, *Die sozialen Aufgaben der deutschen Städte. Zwei Vorträge, gehalten auf dem ersten deutschen Städtetage zu Dresden am 2. September 1903* (Leipzig, 1903). In his speech, Beutler described Adickes as the greatest expert on social policy around ('der beste Kenner der ganzen Materie in geschichtlicher und praktischer Beziehung'), p. 93.

[118] See in particular H. K. Weitensteiner, 'Karl Flesch—Kommunale Sozialpolitik in Frankfurt am Main', D.Phil. thesis (Frankfurt, 1976).

[119] M. H. Dodge, *The Government of the City of Frankfort-on-the-Main* (New York, 1920), 103.

At the same time, the progressiveness of the Frankfurt local government, and the fact that it was uniquely unconstrained by financial limits, makes the city particularly suitable for a closer investigation into the liberals' motives and assumptions in urban government. A refusal to engage in particular policies owing to lack of funds was much less credible here than elsewhere. The example of Frankfurt raises the question of the extent to which those responsible for the innovative social policies acted out of a sense of civic duty, and the extent to which they were guided by political conviction and instinct. A study of Frankfurt liberalism can show how far some of the most progressive liberals in German cities were prepared or able to go in order to meet the social challenges of urbanization (housing, sanitation, etc.), unemployment and poverty, as well as the parallel political challenges of the rise of interest groups, a labour movement, and the advent of 'mass politics'. It will examine whether German liberals in government reacted to the changing world around them with political alertness and cunning, or whether they really were politically inept. Moreover, by uncovering the limitations of the liberals' responses, this study will contribute to the continuing debate as to whether liberalism was, by the beginning of the twentieth century, a spent force, or whether it had at least the potential of reforming itself to address the needs of a rapidly modernizing Germany.

By virtue of its traditional autonomy, Frankfurt offers the invaluable advantage of being both a city in which one can look at urban liberalism, and of being a distinct region in which it is possible to examine political culture. If the definition of a region is often ambiguous,[120] this is not the case with Frankfurt. More than many other cities, Frankfurt had developed political and cultural traditions quite distinct from those of its surrounding area.[121]

More importantly, much of the advantage of looking at Frankfurt derives from the city's position as a geographical, political, and economic link between northern and southern Germany. The former imperial city, which for centuries had been the place where the emperors of the Holy Roman Empire were crowned, became the diplomatic centre of the German Confederation after 1815. The choice of Frankfurt was not coincidental, as it was an independent city state on the edge of the Prussian sphere of influence roughly north of the Main, and of the Austrian sphere of influence to the south. Frankfurt's role as a political centre of Germany was confirmed by the national assembly, the *Nationalversammlung*, which met in the city in

[120] Rohe (ed.), *Elections, Parties and Political Traditions*, 2–4.
[121] Between 1815–1866, Frankfurt was surrounded by the Duchy of Nassau, by the *Landgrafschaft* Hesse-Homburg, the Grand Duchy of Hesse, and the Electorate of Hessen.

1848–9.[122] Frankfurt's political position between northern and southern Germany found its equivalent in the economic sphere. Although particularly since the Bavarian war of succession (1778–9) a financial centre with strong links with the south,[123] Frankfurt's entry into the *Zollverein* on 2 January 1836 signalled a recognition that at least its economic future was intertwined with that of Prussia and the more liberal trading principles it represented.[124] As a result of its income from the *Bundesversammlung*, as well as its economic and financial links with northern and southern Germany, the maintenance of the status quo was in Frankfurt's long-term interest.

On the surface, there appears to be no evidence to suggest that until the 1850s Frankfurt's political development differed significantly from that of any other city. The last years of the Free City were marked by rapid and dramatic political modernization.[125] After the moderate liberals took over the citizens' representative council, the *Bürgerrepräsentation*, in 1853, and particularly after the more radical democrats were in a majority from 1857 onwards, a number of reforms were enacted in response to the social and economic developments of the previous decades. Following the social integration of the Jews in Frankfurt's bourgeois clubs and societies, and thus their admittance to the city's social élite, they were at last fully emancipated in 1864.[126] Restrictions on trade were lifted in 1864, and in June 1866 a new, largely democratic franchise was introduced. Therefore, whereas the period before the mid-1840s was more notable for the political lethargy of the citizens of Frankfurt, in the years after the Revolution the Free City became characterized by lively political debate.[127]

Added to the discussion about the internal political and economic modernization of the city state was the debate on the German Question from 1859 onwards. Not surprisingly, Frankfurt, the former imperial city in which the emperors of the Holy Roman Empire were crowned, seat of the

---

[122] In general, see V. Valentin, *Frankfurt am Main und die Revolution von 1848/49* (Stuttgart/Berlin, 1908).

[123] R. Roth, ' "... der blühende Handel macht uns alle glücklich". Frankfurt am Main in der Umbuchszeit 1780–1825', in L. Gall (ed.), *Vom alten zum neuen Bürgertum. Die mitteleuropäische Stadt im Umbruch, 1780–1820* (Munich, 1991), 363.

[124] D. Stage, *Frankfurt am Main im Zollverein. Die Handelspolitik und die öffentliche Meinung der Freien Stadt Frankfurt am Main in den Jahren 1836–1866* (Frankfurt, 1971).

[125] For an opposing point of view, see Wolf, *Liberalismus*, 16, which is based on the assessment of H. Böhme, *Frankfurt und Hamburg. Des deutschen Reiches Silber- und Goldloch und Allerenglischste Stadt des Kontinents* (Frankfurt, 1968), 236.

[126] Roth, 'Liberalismus', 73–4.

[127] Stage, *Zollverein*, 46ff. F. Lerner, *Bürgersinn und Bürgertat. Geschichte der Polytechnischen Gesellschaft 1816–1966* (Frankfurt, 1966), 226.

National Assembly, and link between northern and southern Germany, became the focus of the supporters of the *großdeutsch* solution based on the reform of the current status quo.[128] This was manifested not only by the foundation of the German *Reformverein* there, but also by the national festivals held in Frankfurt to promote the *großdeutsch* cause, such as the German *Schützenfest* in 1862.[129] Therefore, during the last years of its existence the Free City of Frankfurt witnessed a lively political debate, both on domestic reform and on the German Question. Still, whereas it is important to acknowledge the intensity of the political debate before 1866, it must be remembered that this was a recent phenomenon. In practical terms, like the southern German states, Frankfurt was obviously more 'liberal' than Prussia with regard to political freedom. Yet it was also remarkably similar to the southern German states in that it lagged behind in an economic and 'social' sense.[130] In Frankfurt, freedom of trade (*Gewerbefreiheit*) and the full emancipation of Jews were not introduced any earlier than in the rest of southern Germany. Moreover, if one compares the various studies made in Gall's *Bürgertum* project, Frankfurt represents a distinctive mix of modernity and tradition. Interestingly, however, the 'peculiarity' of that mix seems no different from that of other cities, such as Wetzlar.[131] In other words, it appears as though Frankfurt was no more 'peculiar' than any other German city with a civic tradition.[132]

---

[128] N. M. Hope, *The Alternative to German Unification. The Anti-Prussian Party. Frankfurt, Nassau, and the two Hessen 1859–1867* (Wiesbaden, 1973), 20 ff.

[129] Ibid. 29 ff.

[130] Looking back, one prominent local critic of the Prussian takeover of the city in 1866 was forced to admit that before that time 'in the governing upper circles there was increasingly a political fossilization, a tendency towards a self-satisfaction which borders closely on arrogance and overestimation.' ('In den leitenden oberen Kreisen trat mehr und mehr eine politische Verknöcherung, eine Neigung zu jener Selbstgenügsamkeit ein, welche stark an Hochmut und Überschätzung grenzt.') O. Kanngießer, *Frankfurts Gegenwart und nächste Zukunft. Eine Denkschrift* (Frankfurt, 1892), 4–5. On the history of Frankfurt before 1866, see in general R. Schwemer, *Geschichte der Stadt Frankfurt am Main 1814–1866*, 3 vols. (Frankfurt, 1910–18).

[131] For a comparison of Frankfurt with other cities, see L. Gall (ed.), *Vom alten zum neuen Bürgertum. Die mitteleuropäische Stadt im Umbruch, 1780–1920* (Munich, 1991), and L. Gall (ed.), *Stadt und Bürgertum im Übergang von der traditionalen zur modernen Gesellschaft* (Munich, 1993).

[132] Despite Roth's insistence to the contrary, one is forced to wonder whether Zerback's epilogue on the Munich bourgeoisie is not similarly applicable to that of Frankfurt. Zerback emphasizes that, despite the Bavarian capital's distinctive economic, social, and political features, on a more general level the Munich bourgeoisie was similar to that in other cities in fundamental ways. Notably, Munich society displayed a distinctive mix of traditional and modern elements in economy, society, and public discourse. He also highlights the crucial importance of the period before 1848 in the formation of a bourgeois self-

The city's geographic position at the heart of Germany which enabled it to develop its own political culture, the innovations of local government and the predominant role of liberals within that government make Frankfurt an ideal case study for the motives, the limits, and the possibilities of liberals in power. Given how little we know about liberalism at the local level in Germany, and given the still prevalent assumptions about German liberals' ineptness in government, this study addresses important questions raised by historical scholarship. At the same time, while the nature of urban liberalism is very important per se, it is equally critical to ask about the implications which the nature of urban liberalism had on the character of German liberalism in general. Thus far, this issue has not been properly addressed. As we have seen, scholars like Wehler have come to accept the progressiveness of urban government, though this does not stop them from continuing to insist on the political failures of the German *Bürgertum* and the liberals at national level. Politics at the national, state, and local level continue to be regarded by many scholars as divided up into entirely separate spheres, despite the fact that voters' lives were affected at least as much by local politics as by state and national politics.

If it is the case that liberals were deeply involved in progressive local government, surely this begs the question why this endorsement of innovative solutions, and a keen, practical eye for political survival, were not passed on to liberals at the national level. The question to what extent urban liberalism stimulated liberalism at the national level is not at all fanciful, if one considers, for example, the well-known role Birmingham acquired in the late 1860s and the 1870s for defining the educational policies and the organization of the British Liberal Party. In other words, if it is possible to show that liberals had a keen political instinct at the local level, but failed to display this nationally, then a reason for this might be found not so much in the liberals' inherent failures, but in the mechanisms which made the translation from urban to national attitudes towards power so difficult.

In examining this crucial issue, then, Frankfurt offers an advantage which is probably unique, for it has an important place in the history of almost every important German liberal party. For a decade (1880–1890), it had as First Mayor perhaps the most gifted National Liberal politician, Johannes von Miquel. In Frankfurt, Miquel cemented a reputation for sound financial management and a skill in political judgement which he displayed whenever he dealt with the left-liberal council. From this position,

understanding. These conclusions for Munich are not particularly different from Roth's own observations for the Frankfurt bourgeoisie, so that it is difficult to see how Frankfurt society developed 'peculiarly'. Zerback, *München*, 296–9.

he relaunched himself into national politics, shifting his party to the right through the Heidelberg Declaration of 1884, and his crucial support for the 'Kartell' elections of 1887. On the basis of this, in 1890 he was called from his office in Frankfurt to become Prussian Minister of Finance and thus one of the few members of any liberal party to serve in a Prussian or imperial government.

It is from Frankfurt that Germany's most prominent 'social liberal', Friedrich Naumann, launched his attempt to rejuvenate German liberalism through the creation of the National Social Association in 1896.[133] In the following years, the Association continued to receive crucial financial support from some of Frankfurt's wealthy liberals with whom Naumann stayed in touch. To distinguish themselves from the Democrats, during the 1870s and 1880s the local Progressive Liberals followed faithfully Eugen Richter's hostile stance towards social reform. This stance was reversed in the 1890s, when the party began to cooperate with the Democrats. The Progressive leader, Karl Funck, was respected beyond the confines of his own party not just in Frankfurt, but also in Berlin, where he served in the Reichstag (for nearby Höchst-Usingen, 1890–3) and the Prussian *Landtag* (for Frankfurt 1892–3, 1898–1912). Most of all, it is the left-liberal Democrats who could claim a position of exceptional importance, through their role in the German People's Party. The city's most prominent Democrat, Leopold Sonnemann, was a founding member of the German People's Party in 1867. He was the party's only member in the Reichstag from 1871–4, and in the following parliament he was the unofficial leader of the small group of Democratic members.[134] Even after the Frankfurt Democrats lost the Reichstag seat to the SPD in 1884, they continued to have a disproportionate influence over the national party. It was the People's Party's best-organized and largest local branch. Frankfurt Democrats formed the People's Party's executive committee from 1873 to 1890 and again from 1898 to 1906. Perhaps even more importantly, the Democrats' importance was amplified out of all proportion by the fact that Leopold Sonnemann's newspaper, the *Frankfurter Zeitung*, was the largest and most important left-liberal newspaper south of the Main.[135] Exaggerating slightly for his own rhetorical purposes, Thomas Mann referred to it as the

---

[133] P. Theiner, *Sozialer Liberalismus und deutsche Weltpolitik. Friedrich Naumann im Wilhelminischen Deutschland, 1860–1919* (Baden-Baden, 1983).

[134] BAK, NL 20 n. 1a fo. 27. Friedrich Payer, 'Mein Lebenslauf'.

[135] J. C. Hunt, *The People's Party in Württemberg and Southern Germany, 1890–1914. The Possibilities of Democratic Politics* (Stuttgart, 1975), 36.

'Hauptorgan bürgerlicher Bildung' (central organ of bourgeois education).[136] The importance of Frankfurt left liberalism can be ascertained in 1912, when Frankfurt Democrats and Progressive Liberals occupied a pivotal position in the unification of the left-liberal parties into the German Progressive Party.

The city's importance in the history of German liberalism is unique, and second only, perhaps, to that of Berlin itself.[137] If there was any urban liberal movement that could have had an ideological and political influence on liberalism in state and nation, it was that of Frankfurt, geographically and ideologically placed between north and south. In other words, Frankfurt is ideal for a case study not only for what liberals did when they were in power, but also for the effect this had on the vitality and viability of German liberalism in general.

The following two chapters look at the first major theme of this book, what liberals actually had to do to get into power. Chapter 2 demonstrates that local government in Frankfurt had become completely politicized by the late 1870s, as a political framework had been established that was to last until the 1920s. By 1880, not only had the municipal elections become overtly political, but business inside the council, and even the selection of the *Magistrat*, was conducted according to political ground rules. A comparison with other towns suggests that Frankfurt was not the only place which saw the advent of a more vague notion of liberal politics in the 1860s, and where politicization entered a decisive stage in the 1870s. This outcome not only questions seriously the validity of the 'unpolitical' German in municipal government. It also challenges the argument that it was the 1890s which constituted the decisive phase of liberal organization. If further detailed case studies of urban liberalism confirm the findings of this book, then the 1870s deserve a critical place in an account of German liberalism not just because of the high-political drama of Bismarck's break with the liberals, but also because at the grass roots liberalism developed into the dominant force of urban government.

Chapter 3 looks at how Frankfurt liberals, now firmly in power, fended off the political challenges that developed from the 1880s. They were faced with a number of challenges from groups which employed successively new types of tactics, rhetoric, and organization. By observing them closely, and

---

[136] Mann, *Betrachtungen eines Unpolitischen*, 336.

[137] See (though all too brief) Richter, 'Zwischen Revolution und Reichsgründung', in Ribbe (ed.), *Geschichte Berlins*. ii. 676–80. Erbe, 'Berlin im Kaiserreich', ibid. 759–63.

then adapting to and integrating these new developments liberals managed successfully to maintain their political dominance until 1914 and beyond, despite strong challenges by the SPD towards the end. This chapter portrays liberals as highly versatile, responsive, and innovative. They were undoubtedly protected by a restrictive franchise, but the effects of this could be much more subtle than has been suggested before. By keeping the SPD out of the town council until 1900, liberals could concentrate on and learn from the other formidable challenges of, first, 'unpolitical' citizens' associations, and, then, of the *Mittelstand*. This gave them experience, adaptability, and flexibility in their dealings with the SPD which at the national level they may have lacked.

This study argues that throughout the period of the Empire, Frankfurt Democrats had a distinct identity and programme that set them clearly apart from the Progressive Liberals and the National Liberals. Nevertheless, the Democrats are included in this study of Frankfurt 'liberalism' because they clearly considered themselves part of a wider, 'liberal' (in the sense of *freiheitlich*) movement. Therefore, 'Democrat' measures and ideas will be referred to separately whenever this differed from those of Progressive Liberals and National Liberals. Similarly, this study refers to 'left-liberal' attitudes and policies inasmuch as they affected both Progressives and Democrats, which explains the greater usage of the term from 1890, as the two parties cooperated increasingly.

Having laid out the conditions and the ways in which liberals remained in power, the second fundamental question of this book will be discussed, about what liberals did once they were in power. Which of their ideals were they eager to put into practice, how astute were they in realizing these goals, and to what extent did they succeed in making political capital out of their achievements? This book will not consider questions traditionally associated with urban government, notably issues relating to the city's infrastructure such as the development of transport, sewage and drainage systems, and incorporations. These issues have already been dealt with extensively, both for Frankfurt and for other towns in general.[138] Despite their undoubted importance in urban government, they were not the issues that were of the greatest concern to the Frankfurt liberals themselves.

---

[138] Fischer, *Kommunale Leistungsverwaltung, passim*. J. R. Köhler, *Städtebau und Stadtpolitik im Wilhelminischen Frankfurt* (Frankfurt, 1995). Such work has been done for a host of other cities. For perhaps the best example of these, see Fisch, *Stadtplanung im 19. Jahrhundert, passim*. More recently, see H. Matzerath (ed.), *Stadt und Verkehr im Industriezeitalter* (Cologne/Weimar/Vienna, 1996). The best general overview, which sets urban planning in its proper political context, is still Ladd, *Urban Planning, passim*.

Instead, three major themes stand out which defined urban liberalism in Frankfurt above all else: education, social policy, and taxation.

Liberal attitudes and policies towards education were closely intertwined with religious commitments. For liberals had a realistic appreciation that, given their powerlessness at the state or national level, their educational policies were the most effective instrument at their disposal in their attempt to create a more tolerant, 'liberal' society. This emphasis on a tolerant society shows the overwhelming influence of Jews particularly on left liberalism. In their endeavour, they were supported by the German Catholics, another group with disproportionate influence within the Democratic Association. On the other hand, members of the Calvinist congregations had a large influence on the local National Liberal Association's commitment to the removal of religious control over schooling. The example of Frankfurt demonstrates that religion could and did have a strong influence on liberalism in Germany.[139] Furthermore, despite the differences among liberals on education, this chapter reveals a high degree of pragmatism and political cunning, as liberals coordinated and realized their policies with remarkable success, against strong misgivings from the Prussian authorities.

The connection between liberalism and municipal socialism has often been commented upon.[140] There has been an increasing trend to view the liberal realization of municipal socialism as the German counterpart of liberal social reform in other countries, such as 'New Liberalism' in Britain.[141] These observations, however, have been based largely on the measures taken by liberals in municipal government, without a corresponding analysis about the political context in which these measures were taken, or the assumptions behind them. This study shows for Frankfurt that there were three competing theories of municipal socialism. Those following the first conducted social enquiry and social policy in a non-political context. The second had a more paternalist and anti-socialist thrust and is without doubt the one which most municipal liberals in Germany subscribed to. The third was a progressive vision aiming to

---

[139] The importance of investigating the important but neglected links between religion and liberalism has been pointed out in Langewiesche, 'Liberalismus und Region', 12–14. On the importance of religion for the study of imperial Germany in general, see W. K. Blessing, 'Kirchengeschichte in historischer Sicht. Bemerkungen zu einem Feld zwischen den Disziplinen', in A. Doering-Manteuffel and K. Nowak (eds.), *Kirchliche Zeitgeschichte. Urteilsbildung und Methoden* (Stuttgart/Berlin/Cologne, 1996), 46–59.

[140] Langewiesche, *Liberalismus in Deutschland*, 210–11. Pohl, 'Liberalismus und Bürgertum', 279–83.

[141] Ibid.

integrate workers socially and politically. The last two were distinctively liberal political ideals, and reflect the main themes in discussions about social policy among liberals engaged in municipal government in Germany as a whole. Again, what stands out is the municipal liberals' innovativeness, and their pragmatic recognition that success could only be achieved with mutual support. But for Frankfurt as for Germany in general, this should not obscure the fact that different social measures had different underlying political and ideological assumptions behind them. There was no simple, linear connection between urban liberalism and social policy.

Historians have generally assumed that, because urban social policy is the area in which liberals have manifested themselves as most adaptable and pragmatic, this presented the liberals' best hope for political survival and, indeed, for political renewal. However, this book shows that there is very little evidence that this was the case. The electoral benefits of social policy were very ambiguous, as it may have offended more voters than it gained. The case of Frankfurt suggests that the crucial issue that determined liberal electoral success or failure was, in fact, taxation. Municipal finance is an area that has hitherto been virtually ignored. Interestingly, the growth in municipal expenditure and debt did not really have much impact on liberal electoral credibility, contrary to the assumptions common among contemporaries and subsequent historians. Instead, what mattered for political success was the kind of taxation liberals imposed, and whom they imposed it upon. The innovativeness of Frankfurt liberals in this regard is likely to have been exceptional, since the unique wealth of the city allowed them freedoms that most other local governments did not have. Despite the complete lack of other studies on this subject, however, the case of Frankfurt strongly suggests that generally, liberal electoral fortunes depended on how well the liberals dealt with the issue of taxation, how conscious they were of its political importance, and how they sold it to the public.

The example of Frankfurt portrays liberals in the cities as innovative, pragmatic, and politically astute. By 1914, they had contained the growth of the SPD, realized much of their educational vision, passed extensive and effective social policies, and devised an ingenious system of municipal taxation. The conclusion deals with the important question of why Frankfurt liberals were unable to pass on their vitality to their respective liberal parties at the state and national levels. After 1900, Frankfurt left liberals acted as lynchpins to left-liberal unification, owing to their good relationships in the city itself, and to the influence they enjoyed among left liberals in northern and southern Germany. Arguably, without Frankfurt left-liberals, unification would not have happened. In the couple of years after unification in 1910, Frankfurt liberals retained a strong influence on the Progressive People's Party, both formally (with two Frankfurt liberals on the party executive) and informally (through wealthy sponsors). Frankfurt liberals themselves also had a strong urge to spread their social ideals and their political values. And yet, they were unsuccessful.

It is not that liberals were inflexible, inept, or other-worldly. It is simply that even if they were innovative at the local level where they were in power, it was virtually impossible to influence liberals at the state or national levels because of the different political and social contexts in which liberalism operated at those levels. The dilemma for urban liberals was that even though by 1914 most cities were still governed by them owing largely to a restricted franchise, at state and especially at national elections, with its wider franchises, these urban seats became strongholds either for the Centre Party (as in the Rhineland) or the SPD. In state and national politics liberals had come to rely on the countryside for electoral success. Just as urban liberals gained increasing experience, confidence, and expertise in government, their position within liberalism at large became more and more marginal.

The biggest challenge for German liberalism in its efforts to maintain coherent policies and a national appeal was the federal system with its continuing regional, social, and economic identities. This diversity was expressed by a distinctiveness of the different spheres of local, state, and national politics which was underlined by vastly different electoral systems. In a recently unified country, such a 'compartmental' political structure had the advantage that it allowed liberals and other parties to address fully the local peculiarities of each constituency and each local electorate. Yet at the same time, the diversity and heterogeneity of the German polity made it inordinately difficult for liberals in local government to translate their experience and their ideas, which had proved so suitable for their own environment, to the state or the national level. In some ways, this contrasts sharply with Johannes Miquel, who as First Mayor managed to increase his standing by simultaneously encouraging left-liberal social reform in Frankfurt while prompting a shift to the right for National Liberalism nationwide. The ability of Miquel to move elegantly between different and often contrasting political communities was the secret of his success. The inability of German liberalism to do the same was the secret of its failure.

2
The Advent of Politics

2.1. Introduction

There has been a considerable debate amongst scholars of German political history about the nature and the timing of the politicization of public affairs in general, and about the development of liberal politics in particular. In an important essay Dieter Langewiesche dated the beginning of modern political parties for Germany as a whole to the 1848 Revolution. With regard to both parliamentary life in the National Assembly and the relationship of the individual parliamentary groups (*Fraktionen*) with their constituencies he recognized the beginnings of a 'modern' type of politics. Also, at the grass roots it was from this time that the four main types of socio-moral milieux originated: the workers', the democratic bourgeois, the liberal (which contained conservative elements), and the Roman Catholic milieu.[1] For the liberals in particular, the importance of the 1848 Revolution has been underlined by Lothar Gall in one of the most important historical debates of the late 1970s.[2] Gall argued that the Revolution caused a fundamental transformation of the liberal movement from one committed to the establishment of an inclusive 'classless society of citizens' to one defending the social status quo. Liberalism became overreliant on the bourgeoisie as a social base, a fact which contributed considerably to its growing vulnerability during the Empire and its inability to represent new emerging social forces such as labour from the 1860s and *Mittelstand* groups from the 1880s.[3]

[1] D. Langewiesche, 'Die Anfänge der deutschen Parteien. Partei, Fraktion und Verein in der Revolution von 1848/49', *GG* iv (1978), 324–61.
[2] For an overview which focuses particularly on this debate, see H. Brandt, 'Zu einigen Liberalismusdeutungen der siebziger und achtziger Jahre', *GG* xvii (1991), 512–30. More briefly, see Seier, 'Liberalismus und Bürgertum', 140–1, 199–202.
[3] L. Gall, 'Liberalismus und "Bürgerliche Gesellschaft". Zu Charakter und Entwicklung

Basing his work very much on that of Langewiesche and Gall, Michael Wettengel has considered not so much the Revolution itself, but its very failure, as a decisive turning point in the history of liberalism in the Rhein–Main area. At least in the region around Frankfurt it was in the 1850s that the liberals abandoned their idealism of the revolutionary era and became pragmatic and realistic. Thus, even though the Revolution created the necessary conditions for the formation of modern German parties, it was the period of reaction, in which the parties reconstituted themselves, which was crucial to the establishment of modern political parties.[4]

Other historians have emphasized the importance of the foundation of the Empire and its immediate aftermath, most notably the *Kulturkampf*, for the distinctive politicization of public life.[5] It is particularly towards the 1870s that German nationalism ceased to be an inclusive concept synonymous with liberalism, and acquired more aggressive, exclusive connotations dominated by conservatives: a development with lasting consequences beyond the end of the Empire in 1918.[6] On a more concrete level,

---

der Liberalen Bewegung in Deutschland', *HZ* ccxx (1975), 324–56. The nature of the 1848 Revolution as a watershed for German liberalism has been confirmed, for example, by H. Sedatis, *Liberalismus und Handwerk in Südwestdeutschland. Wirtschafts- und Gesellschaftskonzeptionen des Liberalismus und die Krise des Handwerks im 19. Jahrhundert* (Stuttgart, 1979). Gall's arguments unleashed a strong response in W. J. Mommsen, 'Der deutsche Liberalismus zwischen "Klassenloser Bürgergesellschaft" und "Organisiertem Kapitalismus". Zu einer neuen Liberalismusinterpretation', *GG* iv (1978), 77–90. For Gall's reply, see L. Gall, ' ". . . Ich wünschte ein Bürger zu sein". Zum Selbstverständnis des Deutschen Bürgertums im 19. Jahrhundert', *HZ* ccxlv (1987), 601–23. At the same time, it is important to note that relative to France, German liberals showed much greater integrative sophistication vis-à-vis artisans and small shopkeepers in the 1850s and 1860s. H.-G. Haupt and F. Lenger, 'Liberalismus und Handwerk in Frankreich und Deutschland um die Mitte des 19. Jahrhunderts', in D. Langewiesche (ed.), *Liberalismus im 19. Jahrhundert. Deutschland im europäischen Vergleich* (Göttingen, 1988), 305–31.

[4] M. Wettengel, *Die Revolution von 1848/1849 im Rhein–Main Raum. Politische Vereine und Revolutionsalltag im Großherzogtum Hessen, Herzogtum Nassau und in der Freien Stadt Frankfurt* (Wiesbaden, 1989), 504.

[5] This view has been confirmed recently by G. A. Ritter, 'Wahlen und Wahlpolitik im Königreich Sachsen 1867–1914', in Lässig and Pohl (eds.), *Sachsen im Kaiserreich*, 29–86, esp. 31. The importance of the *Kulturkampf* for the Centre party has been described by Olliges-Wiecsorek, *Politisches Leben in Münster*, 11, 34, 60, 73–89, and *passim*.

[6] D. Langewiesche, 'Reich, Nation und Staat in der jüngeren deutschen Geschichte', *HZ* ccliv (1992), 341–81, esp. 370–5. H. A. Winkler, 'Vom linken zum rechten Nationalismus. Der deutsche Liberalismus in der Krise von 1878/1879', *GG* iv (1978), 5–28. By contrast, to Lothar Gall the loss of the 'nation' as an exclusively liberal, and increasingly conservative, concept has its roots in the failure of the Revolution of 1848. It is at the heart of the transition of the bourgeois ideal from a 'classless society of citizens' to a bourgeois 'class society'. L. Gall, 'Liberalismus und Nationalstaat. Der deutsche Liberalismus und die Reichsgründung', in L. Gall, *Bürgertum, liberale Bewegung und Nation. Ausgewählte Aufsätze* (Munich, 1996), 190–202, esp. 199–202.

it has been argued that despite the political formations visible from 1848 onwards, the new political conditions of the Empire proved decisive for the stability and the particular shape of the German party system until well into the Weimar Republic.[7] Electoral participation increased dramatically, while the hitherto primarily local nature of politics was transformed with the development of a national perspective. Although the beginnings of both the Centre and the Socialist parties can be traced to 1848, neither movement developed a significant degree of popular support, parliamentary representation, or stable organization, before 1866.[8] Both parties benefited from the introduction of the universal male franchise, though the Centre Party's popular support was further galvanized and organized owing to the adversarial politics of the *Kulturkampf* era.[9] Perhaps less convincingly, for the liberals it has also been argued that the 1870s formed a watershed, as this was the decade when they sacrificed their political and economic liberalism for an attempt to cling on to power, which culminated in the 'second foundation of the Empire' in 1878–9.[10]

The list of 'decisive' turning points could, of course, go on. For instance, David Blackbourn and Geoff Eley have pleaded for the importance of the 1890s as the crucial turning point of liberalism, the decade in which liberals had to adapt to the advent of mass politics in the Wilhelmine era.[11] A different approach has been taken by Jonathan Sperber. While accepting the

---

[7] This assertion is a central theme in many of the works on electoral history. For a summary description of this view, see Rohe, *Wahlen*, 30ff. For the importance of social and demographic factors in the evolution of milieux, see K. Tenfelde, 'Historische Milieus— Erblichkeit und Konkurrenz', in M. Hettling and P. Nolte (eds.), *Nation und Gesellschaft in Deutschland. Historische Essays* (Munich, 1996), 247–68.

[8] Rohe, *Wahlen*, 54–6, 73–91.

[9] Sperber, *Popular Catholicism*, 253–76. It appears also that the *Kulturkampf* affected the nature of the Centre Party in a fundamental way. Upon its foundation in 1871, it was not clear to all that this would become a Roman Catholic interest party. Some leading figures such as Ludwig Windthorst had hoped for a more broadly Christian party, though these hopes were soon dashed by the defensive attitude it was forced to take up on behalf of the Roman Catholics. M. L. Anderson, *Windthorst. Zentrumspolitiker und Gegenspieler Bismarcks* (Düsseldorf, 1988), 134–42. K.-E. Lönne, *Politischer Katholizismus im 19. und 20. Jahrhundert* (Frankfurt, 1986), 151–72. At the same time, in 1871 Liberals were able to capture 37 out of 131 seats with a predominantly Roman Catholic population. W. Grohs, *Die Liberale Reichspartei 1871–1874. Liberale Katholiken und föderalistische Protestanten im ersten Deutschen Reichstag* (Frankfurt/Bern/New York/Paris, 1990), 177.

[10] Winkler, 'Vom linken zum rechten Nationalismus', *passim*. In Mommsen's view, liberal theory and practice were only undermined by the development of an industrial society, which did not commence in earnest until the early 1880s. Mommsen, 'Der deutsche Liberalismus', *passim*.

[11] Blackbourn and Eley, *The Peculiarities of German History*, 266. See also Sperber, *The Kaiser's Voters*, 287–8.

importance of the 1870s especially for the creation of political catholicism, as well as the 1890s for the growth of the Social Democrats, Sperber regards politicization and changes in electoral appeal as a long-term development with a series of sharp breaks in the electoral system as catalysts.[12]

In the context of this general debate, similar arguments have been put forward for the case of Frankfurt. In his work on Frankfurt liberalism and its bourgeoisie, Ralf Roth stresses the continuities of liberal politics by emphasizing the role of bourgeois societies and clubs as the main carriers of liberal reform both before and after 1866.[13] While this insistence on continuity might be taken to support Sperber's ideas of gradual politicization, with his focus on the social history of the Frankfurt bourgeoisie Roth's approach is entirely different. Following his teacher, Lothar Gall, he maintains that, despite its relative openness and its 'peculiar' 'modernity', ultimately the Frankfurt liberal movement remained a prisoner of its 'bourgeois milieu', unable to attract the votes of local workers.[14] In a study more directly concerned with this question of the evolution of politics in Frankfurt's local affairs, Ursula Bartelsheim has argued that it was the Revolution of 1848 itself which heralded the era of party politics in Frankfurt. By 1849, the subsequent political battle lines were drawn, as groups of conservatives, moderate liberals, and democrats had formed, which came to dominate the city's political life.[15] Elections ceased to be a matter for individual candidates, and were instead contested mainly by party slates,[16] while during the 1850s there is evidence that democrats effectively formed a party group inside the city's parliament.[17]

These conclusions about the nature and the timing of party politicization provide a striking contrast to those analyses which have been made more specifically in the context of urban history, and which argue that the cities themselves became politicized only fifty years later, around the turn of the century. These conclusions have been drawn with regard to Frankfurt, too. In his book significantly entitled *Die Macht der Honoratioren* ('The Power of Notables'), Karl Maly wrote that up until the formation of official party groups in the council after 1900, party political considerations were of minor importance in the city council.[18] In his study of Frankfurt city government from 1900 to 1918, John Rolling agreed. Whereas the liberals considered municipal administration to be a non-political affair characterized by cooperation rather than party strife, this ideal was, according to Rolling,

---

[12] Ibid. 247, 267–9.   [13] Roth, 'Liberalismus', *passim*.   [14] Ibid. 84.
[15] Bartelsheim, 'Politisierung', 53.   [16] Ibid. 57.   [17] Ibid. 56.
[18] Maly, *Honoratioren*, 14. More recently, see Fischer, *Kommunale Leistungsverwaltung*, 262.

destroyed only by the advent of the SPD in municipal politics.[19] According to these studies, Frankfurt would appear to be a perfect example to prove the general contention that the emergence of 'mass politics' was significantly retarded by the persistent dominance of the local élite in local government, and that local government became politicized only with the appearance of the SPD in the town council.[20]

In short, Frankfurt has been taken to be a perfect example for virtually every mutually contradictory theory of politicization which has been advanced for nineteenth-century Germany, a fact which makes the city particularly apt for a more thorough examination of these issues. It is clear from the arguments presented above that an analysis of the development of party politics must start at least with a brief examination of public life in Frankfurt before 1866. This will underline the main theme of this chapter, that the years 1866–1880 present a major caesura in the public life of Frankfurt am Main. While politics had evolved throughout the previous decade, political life in national, state, and not least local affairs changed dramatically during the period of the foundation of the Empire. Politics in Frankfurt became recognizably 'modern' in that a stable party system emerged which was permanent, public, and popular, and which became the decisive factor in local political life, at the expense of the city's local bourgeois clubs. In this sense, local politics emerged as the foundation of state and national politics, and came to dominate the workings of the city council. It even encroached upon the *Magistrat*, hitherto considered as a bastion of unpolitical life.

2.2. Political Life before 1866

Frankfurt's political debates until about 1845 were not marked by a particularly strong current of liberalism or radicalism. Even those who advocated liberal reform appreciated that the survival of the city's independence

---

[19] Rolling, 'Liberals', 208.

[20] W. Hofmann, 'Aufgaben und Struktur der kommunalen Selbstverwaltung in der Zeit der Hochindustrialisierung', in K. G. A. Jeserich, H. Pohl, G.-C. von Unruh (eds.), *Deutsche Verwaltungsgeschichte* (Stuttgart, 1984), iii. 610–13. H. Croon, 'Das Vordringen der politischen Parteien im Bereich der kommunalen Selbstverwaltung', in H. Croon, W. Hofmann, and G.-C. von Unruh (eds.), *Kommunale Selbstverwaltung im Zeitalter der Industrialisierung* (Stuttgart, 1971), 15–58. Pogge von Strandmann, 'Monopolies', 102 ff. Hofmann, *Stadtverordneten, passim*. Croon, 'Die Stadtvertretungen in Krefeld und Bochum', 289–306. Essentially, the argument has remained unchanged, '. . . bis zum Vordringen von Zentrum und Sozialdemokratie und vielfach auch noch danach wurden die Stadtverordneten mehr als Honoratioren denn als Vertreter einer Partei gewählt' Hardtwig, 'Großstadt', 46–7. For southern Germany, see Niehuss, 'Party Configurations in State and Municipal Elections', esp. 101–3.

remained in their best interests, as it would ensure their own relative political freedom. In any case, at least until the mid-1840s the conservative elements in Frankfurt politics and society were strong enough to block any significant measures of reform. What is significant about the attempt of a group of students and Polish officers to start a revolution in what became known as the *Wachensturm* in 1833 is less the incident itself than the ease with which it was quelled, the lack of response among the town's citizens, and its failure to have any impact on the political scene.[21] Despite the 'great upsurge' of the liberal movement which has been observed for the mid-1840s,[22] the conservatives won the 1847 elections to the Frankfurt city diet amidst fears that Jewish emancipation and the liberalization of trade were imminent.[23] As the drawn-out battle for the emancipation of the Jews shows, this conservatism was not just shared by the artisans and small tradesmen, but also by a significant part of the city's élite.[24]

This analysis is borne out by the events of the Revolution of 1848/9. Far from defining one of the 'hotbeds' of the Revolution, such as the democratic centres of neighbouring Mainz and Gießen, Frankfurt liberals and democrats were more noted for their moderation.[25] This is mainly attributable to the relative absence of a radical political climate in the city. The local élites succeeded in limiting participation and discussion in local affairs to a relatively small proportion of the population.[26] On 3 March 1848, citizens in Frankfurt were the last in the area to demand comprehensive political rights, such as freedom of assembly and of the press, the creation of a German parliament, and legal reform.[27] The Senate complied with all of

---

[21] For a contrasting view, see W. Klötzer, 'Frankfurt am Main von der Französischen Revolution bis zur preußischen Okkupation 1789–1866', in *Frankfurt am Main. Die Geschichte der Stadt in neun Beiträgen*, ed. Frankfurter Historische Kommission (Sigmaringen, 1991), 303–48, here 330–3.

[22] Roth, 'Liberalismus', 73. Roth, *Stadt und Bürgertum*, 397–8.

[23] Wettengel, *Revolution*, 59. Note also Rainer Koch's general point that increased political participation also increased reactionary tendencies against Jews. R. Koch, *Grundlagen bürgerlicher Herrschaft. Verfassungs- und sozialgeschichtliche Studien zur bürgerlichen Gesellschaft in Frankfurt am Main, 1612–1866* (Wiesbaden, 1983), 180–1.

[24] D. Preissler, *Frühantisemitismus in der Freien Stadt Frankfurt und im Großherzogtum Hessen, 1810–1860* (Heidelberg, 1989), 61–144, 256–60.

[25] Wettengel, *Revolution*, 195–212. This view is opposed to the one put forward by Ralf Roth, who is concerned to show Frankfurt's central position among 'democratic liberals' both after 1853 *and* before. ('Frankfurt entwickelte sich rasch wieder zu einem Zentrum des demokratischen Liberalismus.') Roth, 'Liberalismus', 60. According to Roth, the strength of democratic liberalism in the 1850s was the climax of a continuous development throughout the early 19th century, rather than the result of outside factors after 1849.

[26] Wettengel, *Revolution* 33.

[27] Ibid. 50 ff. Roth, *Stadt und Bürgertum*, 418.

the demands, except that for the equality of all citizens, including Jews. There followed a busy period in which associational life prospered, while political clubs split and became more diverse and difficult to control. At the same time, little further political progress was made until the September uprisings, which were caused by popular frustration with the impotence of the Frankfurt Parliament. The uprising itself was a protest about national politics, and had little to do with local affairs as such.[28] Nevertheless, it galvanized the city's various political organizations into preparing for elections of a constituent assembly a few weeks later, which were won by the democrats.

Until the early 1850s, there is nothing to suggest that Frankfurt was in any way peculiar in its political development. It was certainly not a particularly radical centre. During the Revolution, full equality of all inhabitants was achieved on 20 February 1849, while a new constitution was not finalized until 3 December 1849. These measures had come too late to force them onto a reluctant Senate, which dissolved the Constituent Assembly on 31 December 1849, and in 1852 reneged on the Revolution's only main achievement in Frankfurt, the emancipation of the Jews.[29] It was precisely because of the strength of popular conservative and moderate liberal feeling that it was so easy for the Senate to first stall, then ignore, and finally reverse the decisions forced upon it during the Revolution. If Frankfurt is associated with the Revolution of 1848, it is because of its hosting of the National Assembly, rather than its own radical political leanings.

During the second half of the 1850s, Frankfurt did develop into a centre of liberal and democratic politics. In part, of course, this was simply because out of all the states in the area, it was in the Free City that liberals and democrats had the greatest freedom for manoeuvre.[30] Democratic and liberal clubs and associations, such as gymnasts' and singing associations re-emerged and blossomed. National celebrations, such as the *Schillerfeier* of 1859 and the *Schützenfest* of 1862 were held with particular gusto, in memory of the Paulskirche assembly of 1848/9, and owing to the city's current role as host to the only pan-German institution of the German Confederation, the Bundestag. Frankfurt developed into the centre for the left wing of the *Nationalverein*,[31] and, from 1862, it was host to the *Reformverein*, the major organizational effort to mobilize resources in favour of the 'greater' German (*großdeutsch*) solution.[32]

---

[28] T. Nipperdey, *Deutsche Geschichte 1800–1866. Bürgerwelt und starker Staat* (Munich, 1983), 633–4.
[29] Bartelsheim, 'Politisierung', 27–30.　　[30] Wettengel, *Revolution*, 506.
[31] Schwemer, *Geschichte*, iii. 123–5.　　[32] Hope, *Alternative*, 20 ff.

Unlike in 1848/9, when liberals and democrats in Frankfurt were no more involved in the dealings of the National Assembly than those in other parts of Germany, in the 1860s local figures were closely involved in the various attempts by the liberals and democrats to find a solution to the German Question. As elsewhere, support for the *Reformverein* did not run neatly along political faultlines. The *Reformverein* was mainly supported by the local conservative élites in their concern that the city maintain its central position in a united Germany, free from Prussian or Austrian tutelage. Moreover, it was supported vociferously by a group around the *enfant terrible* of Frankfurt democrats, Nikolaus Hadermann.[33] By contrast, moderate liberals and most democrats, even if they were increasingly hostile to Prussia and a small German solution,[34] stayed within the *Nationalverein* to the bitter end in 1866.[35]

In contrast to the frustrations involved in formulating and realizing national political concerns, in the local arena political differences could be articulated clearly, and political activity achieved practical results.[36] Indeed, in the aftermath of the first elections to the Free City's legislative assembly which were contested by the democrats, the *Frankfurter Volksbote* admonished the various political groupings to stop wasting their time on national goals that were completely illusory anyway, and focus instead on the common weal of the city.[37] In the wake of the removal of citizenship from the Jewish population after the Revolution, the moderate liberals gained control of the legislative assembly.[38] This heralded an era of steady, moderate reform, beginning with the partial reintroduction of Jewish emancipation through the organic law of 1853. Jews were granted full equality in private law, and were given the active and passive vote, albeit with the stipulation that only four Jews could be members of the legislative assembly at any one time. The organic law of 6 February 1855 removed Senate representation in the legislative assembly, thus dividing the executive and the legislative. It also provided for a greater separation of the judiciary from the administration.[39] The debate surrounding these constitutional changes, and particularly the 1855 administrative reform, induced the democrats to resume their political activity. They contested

---

[33] For a fuller treatment of the democrats' views on unification, see Hope, *Alternative*, 24 ff. Here, see 30–1.

[34] Schwemer, *Geschichte*, iii. 121–3, 142–3, 244.   [35] Ibid. 270–2.

[36] For instance, in 1851 the newspaper *Frankfurter Volksbote* had given up reporting on national events on the grounds that these were beyond the control of the bourgeoisie anyway, and concentrated on local affairs. *Frankfurter Volksbote*, 31 Dec. 1856.

[37] *Frankfurter Volksbote*, 16 Nov. 1856.   [38] Schwemer, *Geschichte*, iii. 43.

[39] Bartelsheim, 'Politisierung', 33–4.

unsuccessfully the 1856 elections to the legislative assembly, but the following year won a majority, which they continued to hold until 1866.

It is extremely difficult to compare politics in Frankfurt to, say, those in Württemberg, one of the few states for which there are some studies of local liberal politics before 1866. In Württemberg, liberalism in the cities developed after 1830 both in opposition to the government and administration, and in cooperation with liberals in the state parliament; both these important factors were absent in the city state. Still, there was the Senate, opposition to which became a defining issue for democrats during the 1850s. Demands for the reduction in the number of senators, and the abolition of life tenure for a senator, exactly mirror the catalyst for Württemberg local liberalism before 1848, the abolition of life tenure for the local councils (*Gemeinderäte*).[40] While the Frankfurt democrats were unsuccessful in these demands, they were in a position to carry out a number of other important reforms. They introduced freedom of trade, as well as the full emancipation of Jews, in 1864, and the introduction of new, more democratic electoral laws in 1865 and 1866.[41] There is no question that in the years before 1866 significant legislative, administrative, and political progress was achieved in the Free City. However, these democratic innovations simply reflected similar legislation in other southern and western German states, and in that sense mirrored the economic and social realities of the post-revolutionary era.[42] As far as its results are concerned, it is difficult to see Frankfurt as 'peculiarly' advanced with regard to the development of liberal and democratic politics.[43]

Perhaps the most important development regarding the nature of politics after 1848 was the introduction of whole nomination lists in elections, rather than the candidacy of individuals. Increasingly, to have a realistic chance of being elected as one of the 75 members of the electoral college which then voted on its 45 representatives in the legislative assembly, a candidate's name had to appear on one of these nomination lists, which were

---

[40] Specker (ed.), *Ulm*, 296–9. Waibel, *Frühliberalismus und Gemeindewahlen*, 79–117.

[41] The 1865 electoral law was never realized. The elections of that year were held under the old franchise, as the Senate argued that it had insufficient time to prepare for the new conditions of the elections. In June 1866, the 1865 franchise was replaced by an even more generous franchise, which abolished voting in separate classes according to occupation in favour of an equal, much-extended suffrage. This law was never realized, either, as Prussian troops entered the city only days later. Klötzer, 'Frankfurt 1789–1866', 340.

[42] H.-U. Wehler, 'Die Geburtsstunde des deutschen Kleinbürgertums', in H.-J. Puhle (ed.), *Bürger in der Gesellschaft der Neuzeit* (Göttingen, 1991), 199–209, esp. 203–5.

[43] This is opposed to the line taken by Roth, who insists that Frankfurt followed 'a peculiar path to modernity' (Roth, *Stadt und Bürgertum*, *passim*).

handed out to the voters before the elections and which they put into the ballot box, usually unchanged. Indeed, once the democrats obtained a majority in the electoral college in 1857, they passed on strict instructions not to elect a moderate liberal or a conservative to the legislative assembly, so that from that point onwards support by the democrats became the sine qua non for election in both stages.

Political participation also reached new heights. Apart from 1848, the rate of electoral participation since 1816 had typically hovered between 10 and 20 per cent, while in the period 1856–66 the average was closer to 25 per cent, with the rate being unprecedented as above 30 per cent in four elections during that period.[44] Undoubtedly, higher participation was partly the result of a newspaper press which, like the *Frankfurter Journal*, had acquired regional importance. These newspapers closely scrutinized local affairs and the actions of the legislative assembly, especially at election times. Meanwhile, the liveliness of local debate was ensured by Nikolaus Hadermann's cantankerous *Volksfreund für das Mittlere Deutschland*, which pounded the political establishment and the other newspapers with abuse and charges of incompetence. This forced representatives in the legislative assembly and the newspapers supporting them to defend their actions publicly, perhaps more than they would have liked.

Finally, politics became more 'public' through an open meeting held before each election and organized by the democrats, at which members of the legislative assembly justified their actions to the electorate. In practice, of course, there was little about these meetings that was popular or democratic. Only supporters were welcome, while the main act of the meeting was an acclamation of a list already prepared in advance, of the committee which would be in charge of the elections.[45] In many ways, this was quite a sophisticated way of giving a popular gloss to the decisions and actions of a narrow social or political élite. At the same time, as voter interest subsided rapidly after 1863, the purpose of these meetings was also to whip up some enthusiasm, since low voter turnout and the absence of any opposition reduced the mandate of the legislative assembly vis-à-vis the conservative Senate.[46]

---

[44] The figures are taken from table 1 in Bartelsheim, 'Politisierung', 373.

[45] *Volksfreund*, 23 Oct. 1863.

[46] In 1863, electoral participation declined by almost one-third, and in the following two years by roughly one-half so that in 1865, only 6.3% went to the polls. Bartelsheim, 'Politisierung', 373. The function of these meetings (*Bürgerversammlungen*) as an instrument of popular political participation is expressed in *Frankfurter Reform*, 11 Oct. 1865. *Frankfurter Reform*, 8 Oct. 1865.

It is highly doubtful if these developments, which from 1856 politicized public life in Frankfurt to a great extent, really go so far as to allow public life to be termed 'political'. There were no political parties as such, with particular associations still serving as the main meeting place for politically like-minded citizens. The high membership for these associations alone suggests that the purpose of these clubs was social, so that they cannot be considered surrogate political organizations.[47] Moreover, political activity was never constant, but limited to the run-up of elections.[48] In early 1866, democrats finally got together to found a political organization, the *Frankfurter Verein*, but since democrats were unwilling to let themselves be pinned down on particular issues,[49] the association's statutes remained without any specific policy commitments.[50]

Moreover, politics, such as it were, clearly were in a state of flux. The high average political participation between 1856 and 1866 masks the fact that in this period participation reached not only all-time highs in some years (second only to 1848), but also an all-time low in 1865. The peaks of political participation were usually at times of heated political debate, such as the entry of democrats into the political fray in 1856, and the re-emergence in 1860 of a conservative list which gained a majority of votes in the third electoral class which included mainly artisans. By contrast, low levels of political participation occurred at times when there was no political contest, when a particular list faced no organized opposition. Despite the fact that elections in the Free City mattered much more than local elections elsewhere, political participation fluctuated as much as elsewhere, and reached similar levels to places like Barmen and Dortmund.[51]

---

[47] The 'Alter Bürgerverein', where most of the moderate liberals met, numbered 1,158 members in 1851, whereas the association frequented by the democrats, the 'Neuer Bürgerverein', had 971 members in 1850. Bartelsheim, 'Politisierung', 56 n. 26. In absolute number and particularly in proportion to the size of the city's total population, this was an extremely high level of membership, which was never remotely reached by the expressly political liberal organizations that emerged in the 1870s. This underlines the inherently non-political nature of the Bürgervereine.

[48] Bartelsheim, 'Politisierung', 56.

[49] This applies even to the democrats' main battle-cry of the time, the abolition of life tenure for senators. *Frankfurter Reform*, 20 Dec. 1865.

[50] Paragraph 1 of the statutes committed the members to work for a democratic and liberal (*freiheitlich*) development mainly of local affairs. Apart from this, the statutes were concerned with regulations on membership. *Frankfurter Reform*, 10 Oct. 1866.

[51] In Dortmund, electoral participation rose from 17% in 1851 to 25.7% in 1859, and as much as 42% in 1863. In Barmen, over 50% of the electorate voted in 1863. In Frankfurt, participation never reached 40% or more. If Schambach, then, comes to the conclusion that participation levels in Dortmund before 1870 were low, they were still higher than those of Frankfurt. Schambach, *Stadtbürgertum*, 327–30.

This fluidity was reflected in the variations of the general involvement in the constitutional changes, which had to be approved in a plebiscite. Only one-eighth of all citizens participated in the plebiscite on the 1853 Organic Law (the partial emancipation of Jews), while one-third of the electorate voted on the controversial 1855 Organic Law with its far-reaching administrative changes.[52] Finally, less than 9 per cent of the voters turned up for the plebiscite on the full emancipation of Jews in 1864.[53]

In other words, an ad hoc political leadership was complemented by an electorate which could be mobilized by specific issues, but whose commitment to public affairs was still only sporadic. This indicates that Frankfurt citizens became politicized in the sense of becoming open to political debate, while they were not yet 'political' in the Weberian sense of mass participation or having anything other than extremely vague ideas about German unification at large, and about 'liberal' (*freiheitlich*) progress in local affairs. In content, organization, and style, Frankfurt politics in 1856–66 were more reminiscent of the political debates that took place notably in Württemberg cities before 1848 and after than the local political framework which developed in the city during the next decade. In fact, it is this uncertain political climate, in which people had become politicized without being set in their ways in political dogma or practice, which allowed the subsequent period of the foundation of the Empire to make its fundamental political impact on the city's public affairs.

2.3. The Birth of a Liberal City

The most striking characteristic of the years immediately following the Prussian annexation of the city in 1866 was the population's extreme hostility to its Prussian rulers, which was, perhaps, greater than in neighbouring Nassau, as well as Hanover and Schleswig-Holstein, which had also been annexed.[54] At the official ceremony marking the annexation of the city, Frankfurters of all political persuasions—with one exception—refused to join in the toast to their new king.[55] In April 1868, the *Polizeipräsident* in Wiesbaden still complained that Frankfurt's high society persisted in its 'grumbling' against the Prussian administration. The Prussians living in the city were isolated socially, and the bourgeois clubs, free from police supervision, became principal centres of opposition

---

[52] Bartelsheim, 'Politisierung', 32, 34.
[53] 920 out of an electorate of almost 11,000. *Frankfurter Reform*, 5 Oct. 1864.
[54] See the account of the events of 15 to 21 July 1866 in IfSG, S3/A4.770.
[55] W.-A. Kropat, *Frankfurt zwischen Provinzialismus und Nationalismus. Die Eingliederung der 'Freien Stadt' in den preußischen Staat (1866–1871)* (Frankfurt, 1971), 23.

to Prussian rule. This attitude was not just limited to the upper echelons of Frankfurt society, but extended to the popular level, as expressed by numerous, 'almost childish' (*'fast kindischen'*) anti-Prussian demonstrations whenever the opportunity arose.[56] On the anniversary of Robert Blum's death the Prussians woke up to discover a large black flag waving from the top of the *Pfarrkirche* in the centre of the town, which the Prussian military struggled for several hours to remove.[57]

Initially, the strength of Frankfurt resentment against Prussian rule was not reflected in the city's political life. Indeed, political opposition seemed remarkably muted during the first 18 months of Prussian rule. Political life was not only relatively slow to take off, but at first the candidates operating on the basis of the new status quo were remarkably successful.[58] On 12 February 1867 the conservative Carl Meyer von Rothschild was elected the city's representative to the diet of the North German Confederation with over 90 per cent of the votes. Perhaps even more surprising is the high degree of participation in this election, which at around 35 per cent[59] was double the statewide average for the 1867 elections.[60] Similarly, in the city council elections of July 1867, around 30 per cent of eligible voters turned up to elect a city council in which left liberals in particular turned out to be noticeably absent. This underlines the twofold legacy of the decade before 1866. The citizens of Frankfurt had undoubtedly been politicized to some extent, as indicated by the relatively high rates of voter participation. At the same time, the city's democratic political climate before 1866 now proved

---

[56] HStAW 405 n. 40 fos. 47–52. *Zeitungsberichte*, Jan. to Mar. 1868. This is but one example of the police president's appreciation of the general aversion felt by the citizens to Prussian rule. In fact, it was the main theme of virtually all his quarterly reports until 1869. See e.g. the following reports of that year, HStAW 405 n. 40 fos. 75–7 and fos. 112–14. *Zeitungsberichte*, 18 May 1868 and 28 Nov. 1868. On this subject, see also Kropat, *Frankfurt*, 46–9.

[57] *Frankfurter Zeitung*, 10 Nov. 1868 (1. Blatt). *Frankfurter Journal*, 9 Nov. 1868. The radical leader of 1848, Robert Blum, came to lead the revolutionary movement in Vienna and became a martyr for the democrat cause when he was executed by Austrian troops on 9 Nov. 1848.

[58] Kropat, *Frankfurt*, 35–9, 43–53. For an account of the first council elections, see also Maly, *Macht*, 22–4.

[59] Kropat, Frankfurt, 38–9. 7,368 votes were cast, out of about 20,000 eligible voters—the latter figure is an estimate made on the assumption that the number of people eligible for the vote would be roughly proportional to the total population, which remained static from 1867 to 1871. In 1871, 20,151 were eligible to vote. Wolf, *Liberalismus*, 175.

[60] G. A. Ritter, *Wahlgeschichtliches Arbeitsbuch. Materialien zur Statistik des Kaiserreichs 1871–1918* (Munich, 1980), 142–3. Admittedly, the political participation rate for this election was below that of the neighbouring district of Wiesbaden, an area characterized by a high degree of political and confessional tension in the run up to 1866. Yet in the following elections, here, too, participation rates sank to around 30% of eligible voters. B. Liebert, *Politische Wahlen in Wiesbaden im Kaiserreich (1867–1918)* (Wiesbaden, 1988), 71, 77.

to have been unstable and transitory. Just before the first council elections the *Frankfurter Journal* lamented the widespread complacency in public affairs, especially of those hostile to the new political situation.[61]

Added to this reluctance of those resenting the new status quo was an extreme confusion about the changed political environment. For instance, perhaps the most important young democrat before 1866, Friedrich Ernst Passavant, who had led the fight for the introduction of freedom of trade, was put up as an anti-annexation candidate in the elections to the North German parliament, despite the fact that he himself had already accepted Frankfurt's new conditions.[62] Even the most astute political observer such as the *Frankfurter Zeitung* found it impossible to judge the political allegiances of the candidates for the first city council.[63] Even after the new council had met several times the newspaper remained extremely vague. It found an uncoordinated majority of between 28 and 30 councillors opposed to a better organized minority of between 16 and 18, with the members of this minority forming quite a disparate group, too. And, rather uncharacteristically, the paper was unable to say anything about the politics of either group.[64] What is particularly striking about this first city council, therefore, was the relative lack of political continuity with the former *Gesetzgebende Versammlung*, the elected body of the Free City, which had been composed entirely of candidates with democrat inclinations. Naturally, many former civic leaders became city councillors which ensured social continuity in Frankfurt local government.[65] However, the council's political composition had changed dramatically, as it included, for example, seven members of the old conservative Senate.

The political climate of 1856–66 had clearly been insufficient to establish a permanent democratic base in the city. In many ways, there is no reason why this should have been otherwise. In Württemberg, where a liberal and a democratic 'party' developed in the 1850s and 1860s in remarkably similar ways,[66] the democratic 'People's Party' was almost eclipsed by

[61] It complained of the 'indifference with regard to public affairs . . .—this dulled apathy about any events and actions, which is unmoved by success'. *Frankfurter Journal*, 30 June 1867.

[62] Passavant soon became a member of the *Magistrat* and entered the National Liberal Association, the *Wahlverein*. IfSG S2/3066. R. Jung, 'Dr. Ernst Passavant', in *Alt-Frankfurt*, i (1909), 125–8. Hope, *Alternative*, 33–4. Bartelsheim, 'Politisierung', 118.

[63] '. . . as a result of last year's events, the various liberal parties have changed so much in character that it is virtually impossible to classify people [i.e. councillors] according to their previous party label'. *Frankfurter Zeitung*, 18 June 1867 (2. Blatt).

[64] *Frankfurter Zeitung*, 29 Sept. 1867 (1. Blatt).

[65] Roth, *Stadt und Bürgertum*, 495–501, 526.

[66] The similarities were striking in that in both states, democrats adopted much more radical demands than liberals with regard to constitutional reform at home, while liberals and

unification and took about a decade to reorganize.[67] In Frankfurt, it was only the threat of a return to the city's innate conservatism of before 1856 that galvanized the city's democrats into re-establishing a popular left-liberal movement. In this they were successful, but what emerged was a Democratic movement with a new style, leadership, programme, and organization.

To re-emerge as a political force, Frankfurt's left liberals[68] had to find a way of tapping the resentment which initially had been expressed mainly in non-political terms, and of harnessing it to further their own political ends. This they managed to do with extraordinary success. First of all, there were a number of important newspapers at the left liberals' disposal.[69] The direct impact of these newspapers on their readership is, of course, extremely difficult to ascertain. Nevertheless, it is probably fair to assume that newspapers could function as an expression of their readers' opinions.[70] The considerable daily circulation of left-liberal newspapers in Frankfurt, whose readership would have been much greater than their print run, is therefore a good indicator in itself about the degree of political interest, particularly in left-liberal politics, in the city.

Even leaving aside the extent to which newspapers actually did influence (rather than reflect) the political views of their readers, what is perhaps

democrats in both states avoided open splits on the national question. The most significant difference in this context is that in Frankfurt, domestic reform was a realizable possibility, hence a truce or even a 'fusion' between liberals and democrats from the late 1850s was not realistic. Langewiesche, *Liberalismus und Demokratie*, 247–306.

[67] Langewiesche, *Liberalismus und Demokratie*, 410–23.

[68] In this section the term 'left liberal' denotes both Progressive and Democratic liberals, because until 1870 there was no clear distinction between the two sides, and even then they continued to be represented in the same political associations until 1873/4, as described below.

[69] Among the important left-liberal newspapers, there was the *Frankfurter Beobachter*, whose circulation fell from 3,229 copies in the first quarter of 1871 to 2,669 copies a year later. Of great, but also declining, importance was the *Frankfurter Journal*, which sold about 2,000 of a total circulation of over 7,000 copies in the city itself. By contrast, the increasingly important *Frankfurter Zeitung* sold less than 2,000 copies out of a total circulation of around 6,000 copies in Frankfurt. HStAW 405 n. 1066 fo. 382. *Zeitungsbericht*, 18 May 1872. HStAW 405 n. 1065 fo. 62. *Zeitungsbericht*, 19 May 1869. HStAW 405 n. 1066 fos. 197, 382. *Zeitungsbericht*, 18 Nov. 1871, 18 May 1872. Note that the only available figures for newspaper circulation have been for this period, 1869–1872. Only in one instance has a breakdown of sales within and outside Frankfurt been found, that for Feb. to Apr. 1872. The newspaper distribution in Frankfurt itself has been estimated from the ratio between town and country distribution mentioned in 1872.

[70] 'At best, people select their channel of communication, and the specific content they expose themselves to, mainly to support views which they already hold'. A. J. Lee, *The Origins of the Popular Press in England 1855–1914* (London, 1976), 18.

The Advent of Politics 53

more important is that they were perceived to be a great influence upon public opinion by contemporaries. The Prussian authorities kept a close eye on the left-liberal press, not just as an expression of public opinion,[71] but as a main element of opposition against the Prussian authorities. Indeed, sometimes the left-liberal press was held almost solely responsible for the persistence of Frankfurters in their hostility towards Prussia.[72] This view of the role of the press was shared by the newspapers themselves. After the elections to the first *Magistrat*, the *Frankfurter Zeitung* confirmed that now that left liberals were effectively in a minority in both chambers of local government, it would continue to feel obliged to subject them to public scrutiny.[73] In this capacity, the newspaper published a detailed list before the second elections to the city council showing how many times each member had been absent in the previous 42 sessions, lest the most notorious absentees be re-elected.[74] And it is no accident that in the first months after Frankfurt's annexation, the left-liberal press led the calls for the organization of political parties,[75] and became the driving force behind the foundation of the most successful 'liberal' organization, the *Demokratischer Wahlverein*.[76]

The *Demokratischer Wahlverein* was founded in Febuary 1868 in order to promote democrat ideals in local and national affairs.[77] Interestingly, however, new members had to be accepted by the committee, and the membership fee was relatively high, set at 2 Guilders per year.[78] There were only 28 founding members, and attendance at its weekly meetings remained quite low.[79] At the same time, Democrats tried to develop some popular

---

[71] See e.g. HStAW 405 n. 40 fo. 51. *Zeitungsbericht*, Jan. to Mar. 1868.

[72] HStAW 405 n. 1065 fo. 14. *Zeitungsbericht*, 28 Feb. 1869.

[73] 'Wir haben vor den Wahlen unsere Schuldigkeit gethan, wir werden jetzt, nachdem der neue Magistrat bestellt ist, die uns obliegende publicistische Controle über die Thätigkeit der beiden städtischen Corporationen ernst und nachdrücklich üben.' ('We have done our duty before the elections, and, now that the new *Magistrat* has been chosen, we will exercise our due journalistic control on both councils firmly and rigorously.') *Frankfurter Zeitung*, 21 Jan. 1868.

[74] *Frankfurter Zeitung*, 31 Oct. 1868. In principle, the *Frankfurter Journal* agreed. *Frankfurter Journal*, 19 Nov. 1868 (1. Beilage).

[75] See e.g. *Frankfurter Journal*, 7 Nov. 1867.

[76] Despite their distinctive identity and political heritage, Frankfurt Democrats described themselves or their policies intermittently as 'liberal' from the beginning. Before the first local council elections, the *Frankfurter Zeitung* described its ideal candidates as 'freisinnig' (liberal), and referred to liberals and democrats as different 'liberale Parteischattierungen' (shades of Liberalism). *Frankfurter Zeitung*, 18 June 1867 (2. Blatt).

[77] There is quite a good introduction to the *Demokratischer Wahlverein* in Wolf, *Liberalismus*, 21–5.

[78] *Frankfurter Journal*, 5 Feb. 1868.

[79] HStAW 405 n. 1065 fo. 62. *Zeitungsbericht*, 19 May 1869.

appeal. Even before the first city council elections, the *Frankfurter Zeitung* pointed out that the new franchise laws had at least the one advantage that the secret ballot would take away the power of the old 'cliques' which could no longer influence local elections. To ensure that these 'cliques' would not continue to dominate local politics by controlling which nominees were to be put on the electoral lists, it urged the formation of an assembly of all electors, one in each electoral district, in which the candidates for the entire city would be nominated 'from below'.[80] The newspaper urged a direct break with past traditions, in which the once-yearly citizens' assemblies had merely rubber-stamped the candidates chosen by the democrat élite. Instead, the *Frankfurter Zeitung* hoped that these ward meetings would be transformed into permanent institutions which would meet on a regular basis to provide public control over the entire local administration. Furthermore, the ward assemblies would serve as a school for municipal government in the same way that municipal government was a school for state politics.[81]

In many ways, the establishment of the *Bezirksvereine* was a failure. Despite a few notable exceptions the meetings were rather poorly attended, and their organization turned out to be much more cumbersome than expected.[82] Mainly, however, they failed in that many of the more conservative local notables were unprepared to subject themselves to public scrutiny. Nevertheless, the *Bezirksvereine* continued to exist, and received a new, if altered, lease of life from the city's left liberals. Despite its original self-confessed intention not to intervene,[83] in 1869, the committee agreed to Sonnemann's proposal that in future local elections the Democratic *Wahlverein* select a list of candidates which would then be approved by the *Bezirksvereine*. The Democrats had succeeded, therefore, in appropriating the wards' assemblies for their own ends; soon, their meetings became known as 'democrat' district meetings. Through the initial appeal to the 'unpolitical', therefore, Sonnemann and his colleagues had appropriated the old democratic citizens' assemblies for his own ends.

There was, then, an inextricable link between the influence of Frankfurt's left-liberal newspapers, of which the *Frankfurter Zeitung* was the most important,[84] and the emergence of a lasting Democratic party

---

[80] *Frankfurter Zeitung*, 18 June 1867 (2. Blatt). See also *Frankfurter Zeitung*, 30 June 1867 (1. Blatt).
[81] *Frankfurter Zeitung*, 8 July 1867 (1. Blatt).
[82] *Frankfurter Zeitung*, 18 Nov. 1867 (1. Blatt).
[83] *Frankfurter Zeitung*, 14 Nov. 1868.
[84] On the *Frankfurter Zeitung*, see Wolf, *Liberalismus*, 51–9.

organization. The initiative to create an organizational structure came clearly from the three main liberal newspapers, so that in November 1869 the police president correctly identified almost all of their editors and subeditors as the leaders of the Frankfurt Democrat movement ('demokratische Wortführer').[85] In fact, the advent of this new leadership marks perhaps the most significant and fundamental change in Frankfurt's political climate. Before 1866, the democrat leadership consisted not so much of one particular individual, but of a group of people whose names appeared time and again, in the attacks of their opponents, as organizers of public festivals, or as hosts to political gatherings.[86] In the vast majority of appeals signed or committees formed, Leopold Sonnemann was noticeable through his absence.[87] There is no reason why this should have been otherwise. After all, he had only moved to Frankfurt in 1849 and thus had to work his way up to achieve a certain rank in the Frankfurt social establishment, in which local family ties and intermarriage counted for so much,[88] before he could acquire a prominent political position. In this he was greatly helped, of course, by the creation of the *Frankfurter Handelszeitung* in 1856. This financial newspaper acquired a political edge in 1859, when it changed its name to *Neue Frankfurter Zeitung*, and in 1866 it increased its political content even more while continuing to give prominence to financial news, changing its name simply to *Frankfurter Zeitung*. Despite its growth, the newspaper was by no means the only, or even the main, democrat or radical liberal newspaper in Frankfurt.[89] Throughout the period 1859–66, it was the *Frankfurter Journal* which carried the baton as the most influential moderate democrat newspaper which supported the *Nationalverein*. In 1862, for instance, the *Frankfurter Journal* had a circulation of around

---

[85] HStAW 405 n. 1065 fo. 125. *Zeitungsbericht*, 18 Nov. 1869. The speakers at the weekly meetings were almost exclusively employed by the newspapers. See HStAW 405 n. 1065 fo. 62. *Zeitungsbericht*, 19 May 1869.

[86] The leadership consisted mainly of F. E. Passavant, M. Reinganum, F. Friedleben, L. Braunfels, and H. Ebner.

[87] He did, however, take part in the organization of the *Schützenfest* of 1862. K. Gerteis, *Leopold Sonnemann. Ein Beitrag zur Geschichte des demokratischen Nationalstaatsgedankens in Deutschland* (Frankfurt, 1970), 32–3.

[88] The close-knit nature of Frankfurt society is described in M. J. Bonn, *Wandering Scholar* (London, 1949), 6–9. The common bonds established through family ties and a common education at the city's *Gymnasium* feature in most biographies of the time. See, for instance, M. Flesch-Thebesius, 'Der Frankfurter Sozialpolitiker Dr. Karl Flesch', *AFGK* xlvii (1960), 78–9. By contrast, Roth emphasizes that the Frankfurt élite was surprisingly open to outsiders and newcomers. Roth, *Stadt und Bürgertum*, 135–42, 515–23.

[89] Klötzer's essay on Frankfurt during the period 1789–1866 is highly misleading in this regard, as he strongly alludes to the critical importance of Sonnemann and his newspaper before 1866. Klötzer, 'Frankfurt 1789–1866', 338–9, 342.

10,000, while that of the *Neue Frankfurter Zeitung* was 3,500.[90] The prominence of the *Journal* was best reflected in the rhetoric of its opponents, as it was the *Frankfurter Journal*, rather than the *Neue Frankfurter Zeitung*, which was the target of constant abuse from Hadermann's newspaper, the *Volksfreund für das Mittlere Deutschland*. Consequently, it was the editor of the *Frankfurter Journal*, J. A. Hammeran, rather than Sonnemann, who was part of the democratic élite.[91] Only on social matters and efforts to integrate labourers and workers into the democratic movement had Sonnemann become a recognized leader;[92] it is an interesting fact in itself that such an important role was taken up by a newcomer who was still outside the political élite.

It is only after 1866 that Sonnemann's political career experienced a meteoric rise, roughly in proportion to the growing importance of his newspaper, which increased circulation from 3,100 in 1866 to 8,500 in 1867. In 1867, he still failed to secure a nomination as city councillor, at a meeting of electors at which his suggestion for a more formalized structure for ward meetings was likewise rejected. The following year Sonnemann chaired the meeting himself, and was duly nominated and elected into the city council. The full extent of this transition of power can be seen in the fact that in 1871, Sonnemann was nominated by the city's Democrats as their candidate for the Reichstag. Within five years, Sonnemann and his newspaper had become the principal representatives of Frankfurt Democrats. This is not to suggest that Sonnemann had become all-powerful amongst Democrats, but he did acquire an importance which no single person in local affairs had had before 1866.

In addition to the creation of an institutional framework, Democratic success was grounded in its rhetoric, which was crucial in fuelling and even exploiting popular resentment against the Prussian state.

---

[90] H. Heenemann, 'Die Auflagenöhen der deutschen Zeitungen. Ihre Entwicklung und ihre Probleme', D.Phil. thesis (Berlin, 1929), 48–9. Note that this figure contrasts sharply with the newspapers' official circulation figures in the Prussian police reports, which have been mentioned earlier. On the whole, the Prussian authorities would have an interest in playing down the oppositional *Frankfurter Zeitung*'s importance, so it is difficult to say which figure is correct.

[91] For instance, he was one of the sponsors of the *Bürgerversammlungen*. See the list of signatories of the invitation, e.g. *Frankfurter Reform*, 7 Oct. 1864, 8 Oct. 1865.

[92] The best example for this is his famous verbal duel with Lassalle, held on 17 and 19 May 1863 at the invitation of the Frankfurt Workers' Education Association ('Arbeiterbildungsverein'). Gerteis, *Sonnemann*, 37–8. See also *Volksfreund*, 15 May 1863.

Our William, who art in Berlin
Perished be Thy Name
Thy kingdom become a Republic
Thy will never be done
Thou willst not give us this day our daily bread, anyway
Pay what thou owest us as we had to pay what we owed thee
And lead us not into Bismarckian Politics
But deliver us from the evil of Thy magnificence
For Thine is neither the Power nor the Spirit nor the Glory
Away with Thee for ever and ever
Amen[93]

This anti-Prussian satirical version of the Lord's Prayer which circulated in Frankfurt during the years 1866 to 1870 was written down by the Democrat Eduard Fay, who, presumably during this time, also wrote:

What is the world coming to, that a person from Schleswig-Holstein, Hanover, the Electorate of Hesse, Nassau or Frankfurt, who feels free from Prussian civil servants could desire and strive for anything but the liberation, the redemption of his native land from the hypocritical and brutal yoke of Prussiandom, that he could desire and strive for anything but the destruction and dissolution of this Hohenzollern state, the curse for his native land. The curse for the entire German *fatherland*.[94]

These two examples, one ironic and one bitter, illustrate nicely the main themes of the anti-Prussian rhetoric current in Frankfurt in the years after 1866. Frankfurters resented the annexation in principle as it broke international law (the city had never been at war with Prussia), and they resented in practice the enormous reparations Frankfurt was required to pay to the Prussians. Frankfurt's 'brutal yoke' was its uniquely rough treatment by the Prussian occupying forces and then its degradation to a mere Prussian

---

[93] 'Heiliger Wilhelm, der Du bist in Berlin | Vertilgt werde Dein Namen auf Erden. | Dein Reich werde eine Republik | Dein Wille geschehe Nimmer mehr | Unser täglich Brod gibst Du uns doch nicht | Bezahle unsere Schulden wie wir die Deinigen bezahlen mußten | Führ uns nicht in die Bismarcksche Politik | Sondern erlöse uns von dem Übel Deiner Herrlichkeit. | Denn Du hast weder Kraft noch Saft noch Herrlichkeit | Fort mit Dir in Ewigkeit. | Amen'. IfSG S1/11.4. This is only one of several versions of this satire which have survived, many of which can be found in IfSG S3/A4769.
[94] 'Was auf der Welt wird es werden, daß ein Schleswig Holsteiner [sic] ein Hanovraner [sic] ein Kurhesse [sic] ein Nassauer [sic] ein Frankfurter [sic] der sich frei fühlt von preußischen Beamten [sic] etwas anderers ersuchen und erstreben könne als die Befreiung [sic] die Erlösung seiner Heimath von dem zugleich heuchlerischen und brutalen Joches [sic] des Preußenthums, daß er etwas anderes ersuchen und erstreben könne als die Zerschlagung und Auflösung dieses Hohenzollerstaates, des Fluchs für seine Heimat. Des Fluchs für das gesammte deutsche *Vaterland*!' (IfSG S1/11).

Kreisstadt in an administrative district (*Regierungsbezirk*) whose capital became the neighbouring spa resort, Wiesbaden. Finally, there was a very strong sense of opposition to the values and characteristics associated with Prussian institutions, particularly the military, the monarchy, and the bureaucracy.

Despite the strength of this resentment, a large part of Frankfurt's articulate left-liberal opinion was surprisingly realistic in its appreciation of the new political situation. Just days after it resumed its business in Frankfurt, the *Frankfurter Zeitung* looked forward to the advantages of becoming part of the Prussian legal system, as the Frankfurt legal system had been, according to the paper, in urgent need of reform for some time. Furthermore, it welcomed the political change as far as local administration was concerned. Rather predictably, it hoped that the conservative Senate, which consisted of lifelong members, would be abolished and replaced by an elected body.[95] On the whole, the newspaper agreed with perhaps a majority of Frankfurt's citizens in welcoming the introduction of the Prussian *Städteordnung*, though with the important exception of the three-class franchise.[96] At the same time, the *Frankfurter Zeitung* was curiously reluctant to welcome some of the economic benefits of the annexation. It insisted that the city owed its prosperity to its own internal democratic reforms prior to 1866, achieved from within.[97] The newspaper was not openly hostile to Prussia on economic grounds. After all, freedom of movement and the removal of the guild system were consistent articles of faith for Frankfurt Democrats throughout. Still, it took the *Frankfurter Zeitung* several decades until it openly acknowledged Prussia's positive economic influence, for example through the introduction of the freedom of movement throughout the North German Confederation in 1867.[98]

It follows that even one of the leading voices of Frankfurt left-liberal opinion was not blind to the benefits of Prussian annexation and was, for a newspaper well-known for its *großdeutsch* tendencies, surprisingly willing in principle to give credit to Prussia where credit was due. Even though only a few instances of applause for Prussian institutions or policies can be found during those years, the *Frankfurter Zeitung* was not inherently

---

[95] *Frankfurter Zeitung*, 25 Nov. 1866 (1. Blatt).
[96] *Frankfurter Zeitung*, 3 Dec. 1866 (1. Blatt), 29 Dec. 1866 (2. Blatt).
[97] *Geschichte der Frankfurter Zeitung 1856–1906* (Frankfurt, 1906), 154. The newspaper was not alone in opposing the National Liberal contention, particularly after 1870, that Frankfurt owed its economic success to the Prussians. The emphasis on the developing internal forces of reform is taken up by Roth, 'Liberalismus', 66–7.
[98] *Geschichte der Frankfurter Zeitung*, 242.

anti-Prussian, opposing Prussia for its own sake. Yet at the same time, the newspaper went on to express and even strengthen the current anti-Prussian sentiment whenever it could get past the Prussian censors.

In 1867, the *Frankfurter Zeitung* published an article in which it defended the honour of Frankfurt against attacks from Prussian newspapers by contrasting the virtues of Frankfurt to the vices of Prussia. Whereas in Prussia the state was the ultimate end for which each individual had to be pruned and mutilated in order to fit in, in Goethe's home town the individual citizen was central and allowed to flourish. In Frankfurt, the state had granted the individual virtually everything that a modern state can and ought to grant: an independent legal system, an 'outstanding school system free from state or ecclesiastical influence', freedom of trade and relative freedom of the press.[99]

A satirical letter printed just before the 1870 municipal council elections confirmed that before the annexation Frankfurt had been 'a city blessed for so many centuries with freedom, happiness and prosperity'.[100] As has already been shown, this picture of Frankfurt is to a large extent untrue. Frankfurt did not have a tradition of freedom and tolerance for all its inhabitants.[101] A few notable exceptions apart, its schools had been of quite poor quality, the absence of state influence resulting from a refusal of the state to accept any responsibility for its schools rather than from any higher principle of non-interference. Given its earlier criticism of the city's legal system and its archaic institutions, the *Frankfurter Zeitung* knowingly participated in the creation of a popular myth of a liberal tradition.

Another important way in which Frankfurt identity was articulated and politicized was through the *Frankfurter Latern*, a popular local satirical journal founded by the local poet Friedrich Stoltze. With cartoons and articles (some of them significantly in local dialect), it lampooned the National Liberals and their allies, from local dignitaries to Bismarck himself. In one of its frequent jibes against Georg Varrentrapp, it suggested that the local National Liberal leader had just forwarded a request for a new, truly democratic franchise to Berlin. This would be a five-class franchise, devised specifically for Frankfurt conditions. The first class would be composed of residents with an honorary title, dukes and princes who happened to stay in the city, army personnel from the rank of general upwards, the police

[99] *Frankfurter Zeitung*, 16 July 1867 (1. Blatt).
[100] *Frankfurter Zeitung*, 23 Nov. 1870.
[101] In his memoirs, M. J. Bonn wrote of the independent republic before 1866: 'I doubt whether it was a model state; in fact I know it was not. It was narrow, self-sufficient, and arrogant'. Bonn, *Wandering Scholar*, 6.

president, the First Mayor, the state prosecutors, and all other residents free of Democrat inclinations and with an income above one million Marks. All other citizens would be neatly divided into the remaining four classes according to the alphabet. Only those in the first class would be entitled to vote.[102] This example is quite indicative of the *Frankfurter Latern*'s general style. National Liberals were portrayed as profoundly reactionary, as suggested by their support for a restrictive franchise. They were also considered a lost and hopeless cause without any genuine support in the local population. The list of those in the first class shows just how removed the alleged National Liberal clientele was to the 'true' Frankfurter, who would naturally be a Democrat.

The picture presented by the *Frankfurter Latern* was thus perfectly complementary to that presented by the *Frankfurter Zeitung*, and this was no accident. Many of the *Frankfurter Zeitung*'s editors contributed regularly to the *Latern*'s pages, including Theodor Curti, the chief editor of the *Frankfurter Zeitung* from 1902 to 1914, and Carl Holthoff, who became Frankfurt's representative in the Reichstag in 1877. The link was cemented by Franz Schreiber, an editor of the *Frankfurter Zeitung* who was particularly active in the local Democratic Association, and who became a dominant influence at the *Frankfurter Latern* following his marriage to Stoltze's daughter in 1886.[103] In fact, the ailing weekly *Latern* was supported throughout the period of its existence through regular financial contributions by Leopold Sonnemann. Apart from the apparent friendship between Sonnemann and Stoltze, Sonnemann clearly recognized and promoted this link which Stoltze and his journal provided, between local culture and politics.[104]

A further way in which a specific Democrat identity of Frankfurt was defined was through the democratic festivals, where in countless speeches and poems the participants would commemorate their vision of a democratic Germany against a stereotypically tyrannical Prussia. To quote an interesting passage from the report in the *Frankfurter Zeitung* of the anniversary of R. Blum's death, commemorated in the *Demokratischer Wahlverein*:

The speech closed with a glimpse from the dreary present into a distant, better future. The speaker affirmed his faith in the latter with a citation from the words of the poet:

---

[102] *Frankfurter Latern*, 25 May 1876.
[103] P. Alexandre, ' "Die Frankfurter Latern". Une Publication satirique editée par Friedrich Stoltze', Ph.D. thesis (Metz, 1980), 48–50.
[104] C. Funck, *Lebenserinnerungen. Mit einer Einführung von Ludwig Heilbronn* (Frankfurt, 1921), 53–4.

The Advent of Politics

> For the power of tyrants has limits
> When the oppressed cannot find justice anywhere
> When the burden is unbearable, he reaches
> up with confidence to the sky....[105]

These almost pathetic lines apply to the situation in Frankfurt—reminiscent as they are of the language used by Eduard Fay quoted earlier—as they do to the political situation in Germany in general. In both cases, Prussia is the tyrant who puts an end to the aspirations of Germany, which are identical with the aspirations of Frankfurt. Thus, Frankfurt's history is equated with that of democratic Germany; Robert Blum died a martyr for democratic Germany as for democratic Frankfurt. Again, the result is clear: Frankfurt became the hive of democracy which it had never been before the late 1850s.

This identification of Frankfurt's destiny with that of Germany is the principal reason why the anti-government, Democratic opposition never became 'particularist' in the sense of the Hanoverian Guelph movement.[106] Even though compared to Hanover a Frankfurt identity was much easier to define, and despite the much worse treatment suffered by the city at the hands of the Prussians, Frankfurt Democrats never really demanded the restoration of the status quo ante.[107] In part, of course, this is because any notion of a Frankfurt 'tribe' (*Stamm*) in an equal concert of German tribes alongside the Bavarians, Saxons, and other more ill-defined groups (such as the Guelphs) would have been even more ridiculous than in Hanover. Maintaining the memory of a glorified, 'democratic' and free past was in part political opportunism, but it was mostly a statement of the values a unified Germany ought to espouse. For the next fifty years, Democrats fought for these values of democracy, the rule of law, and a resistance to Prussian authoritarianism and centralization. To this end, Frankfurt Democrats

---

[105] 'Der Vortrag schloß mit einem Hinblicke aus der trüben Gegenwart in eine ferne bessere Zukunft. Den Glauben an diese bekannte der Redner in dem Zitate des Dichterwortes: Denn eine Grenze hat Tyrannenmacht, | Wenn der Gedrückte nirgends Recht kann finden, | Wenn unerträglich wirkt die Last- greift er | Hinauf getrosten Muthes in den Himmel...'. *Frankfurter Zeitung*, 13 Nov. 1868 (2. Blatt).

[106] Aschoff, *Welfische Bewegung*, 1–6. In general, see D. S. White, 'Regionalism and Particularism', in R. Chickering (ed.), *Imperial Germany. A Historiographical Companion* (Westport, Conn., 1996), 131–55.

[107] This is in sharp contrast to the Guelphs in Hanover, who aimed at the restoration of the Hanoverian monarchy and refused to accept the legitimacy of the annexation. Thus, participation in the state elections became a pivotal point of principle as it implied accepting being part of the Prussian state. By contrast, for Frankfurt Democrats, state elections involved a point of principle, too, but this concerned merely the legitimacy of the three-class franchise which they shared with most other left-liberals in Prussia. Aschoff, *Welfische Bewegung*, 85–6.

even sought to extend their influence not only within the German People's Party they had helped found, but they also advocated (on the whole, unsuccessfully) their party's extension into Northern Germany—a striking contrast to the self-imposed regionalism of the Guelphs. Particularly after 1871, but even before, a return to the previous status quo was never an issue.

Another crucial instance for the establishment of a sense of Frankfurt 'right' as opposed to Prussian 'wrong' were the emotionally charged discussions about the so-called *Rezeß*, the financial settlement between the city and the Prussian state arising from the annexation. Democrats, liberals, and conservatives were united in their opposition to the way in which Frankfurt had been treated, most notably in the payment of six million Guilders by a defeated city which had never been at war. While each camp wanted to maximize compensation for the former city state's assets that had become Prussian property, the main difference between them was the language they used. While liberals on the right appealed to the King 'in a spirit of trust and openness',[108] liberals on the left and Democrats refused to see their money 'thrown into the fiery furnace of the all-consuming Prussian military state'.[109] Beneath the rhetoric, however, Frankfurt political opinion was united in its assessment that the city had been treated harshly and unjustly by the Prussians, for which it demanded compensation.[110]

An agreement was reached in February 1869. Even though the settlement was, under the circumstances, the best the Frankfurters could possibly have bargained for, the Democrats continued their battle. The *Frankfurter Journal* characteristically rejected the compromise because it involved a denial of what was right, 'ein Aufgeben des allein correcten Rechtsstandpunctes'.[111] This was an issue about 'right', and nothing less than a repayment of the full six million Guilders would do: 'man habe nur am Recht festzuhalten'.[112] In heated debates during two overcrowded meetings, the *Demokratischer Wahlverein* only just managed to avoid a split on the issue, but in the end accepted Sonnemann's motion of censure for the council.[113]

---

[108] E. F. Souchay, *Was mag Frankfurt übrig bleiben? Nach den Mittheilungen der ständigen Bürgerrepräsentation vom 18. März 1867 beurtheilt* (Frankfurt, 1867), 3.

[109] *Die projectirte Theilung zwischen dem angeblichen Staatsvermögen und dem städtischen Vermögen von Frankfurt a. Main. Ein Beitrag zur Zeitgeschichte* (Stuttgart, 1867), 76–7.

[110] *Denkschrift der Frankfurter Bürgerschaft betreffend die Einverleibung der freien Stadt Frankfurt sammt den Namensverzeichnissen der Unterzeichner* (Frankfurt, 1866). See also the letter by J. A. Fester of 22–3 July 1866 in IfSG, S3/A4.770.

[111] *Frankfurter Journal*, 18 Feb. 1869.

[112] 'One only had to insist upon one's right'. *Frankfurter Zeitung*, 14 Nov. 1868 (2. Blatt).

[113] *Frankfurter Journal*, 14 Feb. 1869 (1. Beilage), and 19 Feb. 1869.

In the light of the assumptions of traditional historical scholarship, it would appear that the left-liberals in Frankfurt displayed the German left liberals' archetypal unworldliness, the characteristic doctrinaire rigidity which made them unable to cope with changes in the political landscape. These Democrats were quite unlike those moderate democrats of 1848 of the 'Rhine–Main area' who became increasingly pragmatic and went on to find themselves supporters of the Progressive party, willing to accept the inevitable.[114] And yet, perhaps paradoxically, it is this very unworldliness which ensured the Democrats' success in Frankfurt. Through the rhetoric of principled resistance to Prussia, they were able in only a very short period of time to exploit Frankfurt grievances and the predominant discontent for their own ends. Indeed, the success of the *Demokratischer Wahlverein* is impressive. The gatherings in February 1869 against the *Rezeß* may have been an act of resistance against the inevitable, but this was not the point: each of these meetings drew an audience of more than 1,000 people. The *Wahlverein* thus used every opportunity to 'stir up' the citizens of Frankfurt during anti-Prussian demonstrations such as these and through open election meetings, which could rally as many as several hundred people. More importantly, this strategy paid off in the elections. After successfully contesting the 1868 local elections, whereupon the *Demokratischer Wahlverein* provided twelve out of 54 town council members, the Democrats went from strength to strength until in 1876 the renamed *Demokratischer Verein* possessed an overall majority.

What is really most surprising is that the Democratic rhetoric survived the wave of patriotism that swept through Frankfurt like any other city during the war of 1870/1, and that it continued to be successful after that. In 1874, the Democrat Maximilian Reinganum insisted:

The Democrat party was the one which had conserved a pious memorial to the past . . . To his regret, the Progressive Party had formed a coalition with the National Liberals, who would prefer it more than anything else if the old citizens of Frankfurt would learn to use the words *Mir* and *Mich* grammatically. (Applause.) What used to be nice about Frankfurt charm was the little bit of particularism that existed . . .; It would not hurt to preserve a little individuality. The Frankfurter was . . . always independent and liberal-minded. These days are gone, but they should be commemorated and we should resist any attacks which threaten to take away these peculiarities one by one.[115]

[114] Wettengel, *Revolution*, 518 ff.
[115] 'Die demokratische Partei sei diejenige, welche dem, was früher gewesen, ein pietätvolles Andenken bewahrt habe. . . . Zu seinem Bedauern habe die Fortschrittspartei sich der Nationalliberalen angeschlossen, welch letztern es am allerliebsten wäre, wenn die

Democrat rhetoric had thus changed slightly in form, though not in essence. The characteristics of an old Frankfurter were his natural independence and liberalism. Being Democratic was one of the good old Frankfurt traditions, which made all the difference. Reinganum was not alone in his proclaiming this message. In 1872, the *Frankfurt Latern* reprinted a poem originally written for the first council elections in 1867. In local dialect, Stoltze warned:

> Men, we need men!
> Men of true character and blood
> Hard as iron and also stubborn
> Whenever Frankfurt is concerned
> 'Strong in its Right' and proud and solid
> Frankfurt is not a hive for rogues[116]

Again, in these lines there is the appeal for men of principle, men who are in the right. The demand for 'Männer von echtem Schroth und Korn' is one that can be found in this form in countless election speeches and even manifestos, it is one for men of genuine character and honesty—in fact, it was the description that was universally recognized as one befitting only an old Frankfurter. The stanza closes with another important theme, an appeal to Frankfurt's history, in effect to the citizens' local pride.

Therefore, after the foundation of the Empire in 1871, the excesses of anti-Prussian rhetoric were gone, even though the *Rezeß* still featured prominently in speeches and pamphlets. The essence of Democrat rhetoric remained, however, and could not be expressed more clearly than in the two examples given above. Those who loved their city, its liberal traditions, its peculiarities in language and character, were Democrats (or left liberal on the occasions when the Progressives and the Democrats cooperated). The elections were to prove that Frankfurt was a 'Democratic city'.[117] To vote Democrat, therefore, became a demonstration of local patriotism and an act of civic pride.

Altfrankfurter mit Eleganz das Mir und Mich verwechseln lernten. (Beifall.) Was früher schön an Frankfurt gewesen, sei das Bischen Partikularismus . . .; es schade nichts, wenn man ein Bischen Eigenheit behalte. Der Frankfurter sei . . . immer ein Mann, der ein unabhängiges, freisinniges Wesen in sich getragen. Das sei nun vorüber, dieser Zeit soll man aber ein Andenken bewahren und sich gegen den Anprall stemmen, der Stück für Stück diese Eigenthümlichkeiten hinwegzuschwemmen drohe.' *Frankfurter Zeitung*, 24 Nov. 1874 (Abendblatt).

[116] 'Männer, Männer thun uns Noth! | Männer ächt von Korn un Schrot | Fest wie Stahl und ääch so spred | Wann derr sich's um Frankfort dreht; | 'Stark im Recht' und stolz und fest! | Frankfort is kää Lumpenest' (*Frankfurter Latern*, 23 Nov. 1872).

[117] *Frankfurter Zeitung*, 20 Nov. 1874 (Abendblatt).

By the early 1870s, therefore, Frankfurt local politics had become clearly politicized in a way that they had not been before 1866. Of course, there were important continuities. The carrier of early liberalism in Frankfurt, the bourgeois clubs (*Vereine*), did not disappear overnight, as Roth shows, and they continued to be the most important social focal points.[118] Also, the style of left-liberal politics, for example the popular festivals, had already been developed before the 1848 Revolution.[119] Last but not least, the Democrats had become the majority party of opposition to the Senate in 1857, and there was some continuity between the left-liberal notables before and after the annexation. However, Frankfurt had become an important stronghold of liberalism compared with the surrounding area only from the late 1850s, and as the period after the annexation showed, this created a political potential which nevertheless had to be brought out into the open. This was achieved through the skilful use of rhetoric, which was facilitated by the Democrats' control over the press, and through the establishment of a popular party organization. As a result of the Democrats' success in tapping the general anti-Prussian sentiment, the city's Democrats were transformed, from one of the city's parties in opposition to the one party which alone stood for the interests of Frankfurt.

In 1872, Georg Varrentrapp was nominated for re-election by a large number of 'independent citizens', in effect National Liberals. Varrentrapp, of old Frankfurt stock whose father had been the most prominent physician of his day in the city, had distinguished himself as the driving force behind Frankfurt's drainage system, the second in Germany. And yet, his enormous social prestige and his unique achievements for his native city were not good enough for Frankfurt's Democrats. On the grounds that to support Varrentrapp would amount to a 'slap in the face of the [Democrat] programme', his nomination was almost unanimously rejected by the popular gathering.[120] Social standing was important, but politics were paramount. Thus, the importance of the bourgeois clubs became limited to their social functions.[121] Significantly, in early 1868 the police president still identified the clubs as the main centres of opposition,[122] whereas once it had been established, the president found that, of all organizations, it was the

---

[118] Roth, 'Liberalismus', 65–6.   [119] Ibid. 60–1.
[120] *Frankfurter Zeitung*, 26 Nov. 1872 (2. Blatt).
[121] The reunification in 1873 of the Casino, the city's prominent club which had split in the late 1860s over the acceptance of the Prussian annexation, is less an indicator of the underlying harmony of the liberal milieu, as Roth maintains, than of the realization of its social, rather than political, function. Roth, 'Liberalismus', 65–6.
[122] HStAW 405 n. 40 fo. 50. *Zeitungsbericht*, Jan. to Mar. 1868.

Demokratischer Wahlverein which was the centre of opposition to the Prussian government.[123]

Despite the cloak of an intransigent, stubborn rhetoric, Sonnemann's organizational drive shows that these Democrats were extremely pragmatic, and an examination of their policies will show that far from looking back, they were more than willing to tackle the problems of their day and of the future. Just as in Saxony the Conservatives were galvanized by the state's forced entry into the North German Confederation into presenting themselves as the guarantors of Saxon traditions,[124] in Frankfurt the Democrats fashioned themselves in the traditionalists' cloaks precisely because of their 'modernity'. This is particularly striking when one compares their behaviour to that of the doctrinaire '*Altdemokraten*', the motley crew of radical Democrats in the tradition of the radical Nikolaus Hadermann. Although initially more numerous and more vociferous in the city council than moderate Democrats, they resisted the lead of Sonnemann and other editors in building up a more popular base. As a result, by 1873 the *Altdemokraten* found themselves sidelined and leaderless (Hadermann had died on 11 August 1871),[125] and agreed to merge with the other Democrats into the *Demokratischer Verein*. Moreover, the *Demokratischer Wahlverein*'s success forced its political opponents to act and give up some of their notions of notable politics (*Honoratiorenpolitik*), at least in appearance. Thus, in 1873 the National Liberal *Frankfurter Wahlverein* was founded, and in 1874 the *Verein der Fortschrittspartei* followed. Both organizations were designed to hold popular meetings for the selection of candidates before local, state, or national elections, while the latter tried to follow the Democrats in holding regular public meetings even though in this it remained relatively unsuccessful. Consequently, it is the Frankfurt left liberals' rhetorical and organizational response to the changes of 1866 which transformed Frankfurt's political life, and created by 1874 the political framework of three liberal parties contending for political power, in the absence of any conservative opposition. This framework was to be in place throughout the rest of the century.

2.4. State and National Elections

The National Liberals' move for better organization was a response not just to developments in local politics. Indeed, the immediate purpose for the

---

[123] HStAW 405 n. 1065 fo. 15. *Zeitungsbericht*, 28 Feb. 1869.
[124] J. Retallack, '"Why can't a Saxon be more like a Prussian?" Regional Identities and Political Culture in Germany, 1866–67', *CJH* xxxii (1997), 28–55.
[125] *Frankfurter Zeitung*, 13 Aug. 1871 (1. Blatt).

Wahlverein's creation was to prepare the party's organization for the impending national and state elections. Moreover, the formation of a local association for the Progressives was an immediate response to their disastrous showing in the 1874 national elections, in which the Progressive candidate polled a meagre 275 votes. This raises the question about the development of liberal politics in Frankfurt with regard to state and national politics, partly because it is an important indicator of the relative strengths and weaknesses of the three liberal movements in Frankfurt during the 1870s. At the same time, it sheds some light on the relationship between politics in the different tiers of government. Virtually all studies on national politics in imperial Germany consider politics in a unitary framework, in the light of government decisions, and the response of parliamentarians and, increasingly, grass-roots organizations. Yet the question remains to what extent national politics in a recently unified, federal state can be seen in the context of a complex aggregation of hitherto independent states and relatively autonomous local communities.[126] For instance, it has been argued that it was its essential social and regional diversity, and its alliances with Guelphs, Poles, and other groups, that underpinned the Centre Party's formidable strength (and ultimate weakness).[127] This section seeks to establish in what ways national and state elections in Frankfurt were affected by the prevailing local conditions. In other words, it considers the extent to which the electorate voted in national and state elections out of local considerations, and the extent to which election results were a reflection of political events and actions outside Frankfurt.[128]

Unsurprisingly, the 1870s were a time of adjustment to the new political conditions. In Frankfurt, the National Liberals established themselves as the main party of opposition in 1874. The Progressives only managed to establish themselves as a third liberal force in 1877/8, although their support remained so small that the party generally preferred to save its

---

[126] The heterogeneity and diversity of the German political cultures in 1866/71 has been emphasized, for instance, in J. J. Sheehan, 'Nation und Staat. Deutschland als "imaginierte Gemeinschaft"', in M. Hettling and P. Nolte (eds.), *Nation und Gesellschaft in Deutschland. Historische Essays* (Munich, 1996), 33–45.

[127] W. Loth, 'Soziale Bewegungen im Katholizismus des Kaiserreichs', *GG* xvii (1991), 279–310, here 281–2.

[128] For a rare investigation into the interaction between local, state, and national politics, see, for the case of Marburg, Koshar, *Social Life*, 59–76. More generally, see A. P. Thompson's thesis, though his argument about the interconnectedness of left-liberal local, state, and national politics is confined to the period of his investigation, late Wilhelmine Germany (1907–18). Thompson, 'Left Liberals', esp. 10–11.

money and support one of the other liberal candidates (usually the Democrat) instead. Only by 1884 did the results of the elections in Frankfurt broadly mirror those of the country at large.[129] From 1871 to 1881, the share of votes for the German People's Party in general experienced a fourfold increase from 0.5 to 2.0 per cent, while in Frankfurt there was a steady decline in the Democrats' share of the vote, from 1871 to 1878. This is largely explained by the much faster growth of the Frankfurt electorate. In 1877, it was much easier for the German People's Party to double its vote nationally when it started from a dismal 0.4 per cent, than it was for the Frankfurt Democrats to maintain their share of the vote as the constituency's largest party. Still, the Frankfurt Democrats actually lost support in absolute terms, despite an increase in the number of electors by a quarter. Meanwhile, in Germany as a whole the German People's Party managed to double its support. In 1881, the Democrats increased their popularity to a lesser extent in Frankfurt than in Germany as a whole, while Progressive Liberal support in the first round masks perhaps even a stagnation in the Democrats' support.

By contrast, with the establishment of the *Wahlverein*, the National Liberals managed to rally behind them all conservative opposition in Frankfurt, so that from 1874 their performance was similar to the party's aggregate performance across Germany. It is difficult to compare the Progressive Liberal results in Frankfurt with the rest of Germany. The first election which it contested with the help of a local organization was in 1877. In 1878, its support throughout Germany experienced a slight decline, whereas in Frankfurt the number of votes polled for the party increased by almost 70 per cent, but thereafter Progressive Liberals in Frankfurt fielded a candidate of their own in national elections only in exceptional circumstances. Finally, in every national election support for the SPD in Frankfurt increased, while in Germany as a whole SPD support decreased in the 1878 and 1881 elections both in absolute and in relative terms.

These figures illustrate an important point, that during the 1870s national elections at least in Frankfurt were to a considerable extent dependent upon the evolution of political conditions at the local level. The National Liberals on the ground had to unite the local electorate supportive of the government, while the results of the Progressive Liberals were singularly subject to the will of the local party leadership to contest the elections—or not to contest them at all, as was usually the case from 1881. The SPD, too, was able to benefit from the unusual political conditions

---

[129] See the relevant tables in Appendix II.

prevailing in Frankfurt. The Democrats were outright opponents of the anti-socialist laws, hence SPD representatives were usually free to turn up and speak at their rallies. As the two parties' constituencies had a natural overlap, this meant that the SPD was able to address directly its target audience.[130] It is only from 1884 that these local peculiarities became less pronounced, as the political context within which national elections were held in Frankfurt became more stable. Another way of looking at this is that the two electoral watersheds of the 1870s (the explosion of Centre Party support in 1874 and the drastic growth of the Conservative parties in 1878) manifested themselves differently.[131] There was a sharp growth in electoral participation in 1874 and 1878, but in Frankfurt there was no Centre Party to speak of, and there were no conservative candidates. Thus in Frankfurt these elections were more notable for the growth of the socialist vote (from 6.31 per cent in 1871 to 19.56 per cent in 1874) and the decline of the National Liberals to the benefit of the two left-liberal parties in 1878. By contrast, Frankfurt formed a perfect parallel to the national electoral shift of the 1887 elections. It was in these elections that the National Liberals became the main bourgeois challenger to the SPD, a position which the party retained until the 1903 elections.

In some ways, Frankfurt's election results for the Prussian Chamber of Deputies present a diametrically opposite picture of the city's political life. Here, what is most noticeable is the strong role of the local Progressive Liberal Association, which particularly until 1888 managed to send a disproportionate number of deputies to the *Landtag*: throughout that period, a Progressive deputy was elected ten times, while a National Liberal was elected four times, and a Democrat twice.[132] This contrasts sharply not only with the relatively weak state of the Progressives in the Chamber of Deputies, but also with their strength within Frankfurt itself, as displayed by their dismal performance in the Reichstag elections. This was the logical result less of the three-class franchise as such. Rather, at fault was a first-past-the-post system without run-off elections if no candidate

---

[130] V. Eichler, *Sozialistische Arbeiterbewegung in Frankfurt am Main, 1878–1895* (Frankfurt, 1983), 81.

[131] For a description of these elections on a national level, see Sperber, *The Kaiser's Voters*, 165–79.

[132] The figure for the Progressive Liberals does not include Progressive Liberals replacing other Progressive Liberals in by-elections within one session. Of the two Democrats the first representative, Guido Weiß, only won the by-elections in 1869, subsequently representing the city for one year only. T. Kühne, *Handbuch der Wahlen zum Preußischen Abgeordnetenhaus 1867–1918. Wahlergebnisse, Wahlbündnisse und Wahlkandidaten* (Düsseldorf, 1994), 672–5. See the list of Frankfurt representatives in Appendix II.

managed to gain an outright majority.[133] Whereas at national or local elections, the Progressives usually failed to make it to the run-off elections and were forced to support one of the other liberal parties, in state elections with only one round the Progressives could capitalize on their pivotal role as a third party whose support one of the other parties needed to ensure success.[134] In fact, as the party of second best, the Progressive Liberals sometimes even managed to send both Frankfurt members to the Prussian Chamber. In 1870 their two candidates received the backing of the National Liberals on the grounds that this was preferable to the seats returning to Democratic candidates. Similarly, in 1879 they were able to field two candidates on their own with the support of the Democrats, who were just happy to break up the previous National Liberal/Progressive coalition for these elections. It was only thereafter that the supporting party would demand its due and force the Progressives to concede one seat in return for its help, as happened with the National Liberals in 1873, and the Democrats in 1882.

Apart from these tactical considerations, the local political environment clearly did play a crucial part in the development and outcome of state elections. Bearing in mind their prominence in local and national elections, the poor performance of the Democrats is at first surprising. It is conditional first and foremost upon the ideological reluctance and practical unease of the only significant branch of the German People's Party within Prussia, and its most radical at that, to participate in the Prussian state elections. As has been shown above, the basis for the Democrats' popularity within Frankfurt, indeed their *raison d'être*, was the opposition to Prussia and the autocracy which it connoted, of which the three-class franchise used in these elections was the epitome. In the wake of the tensions surrounding the *Rezeß*, they won a by-election. Unable to find a convincing candidate from their own ranks, however, the Democrats had nominated Guido Weiß, a democrat newspaper editor from Berlin.

The Democrats lost the 1870 elections, held during the Franco-Prussian War, and they did not even bother to contest the 1873 elections. It appears that the first elections the Democrats fought with a sense of gusto were those of 1876. Nevertheless, the Democratic election committee failed to

---

[133] On the effect of different electoral systems on the outcome of elections in general, see M. Duverger, 'Der Einfluß der Wahlsysteme auf das politische Leben', in O. Büsch and P. Steinbach (eds.), *Vergleichende Europäische Wahlgeschichte. Eine Anthologie. Beiträge zur historischen Wahlforschung vornehmlich West- und Nordeuropas* (Berlin, 1983), 30–84.

[134] It is only in the 1890s that the National Liberals in Frankfurt were temporarily strong enough to win state elections on their own, owing to the strength of *Mittelstand* support.

come to an agreement with the Progressive Liberals, who preferred to cooperate with the National Liberals. Despite their investment of large quantities of time and energy, the Democrats failed to mount a convincing challenge. In this as in any subsequent election, the Democrats failed to muster a second candidate, even if they fought the elections on their own. In such instances, this made their election bid look half-hearted and put them a priori at a serious disadvantage in the actual elections. The elections of 1876 looked very much like a trial run to assess how much support the Democrats could muster in subsequent state elections. Moreover, it gave added publicity and experience to the candidate, Karl Holthoff, who contested the 1877 national elections with more success.

The crucial point here is that, to a far greater extent than in national elections, state election results in Frankfurt were conditional upon the local political environment.[135] Put more bluntly, in Frankfurt, politicization at the local level occurred under the aegis of municipal politics. It is true that in Frankfurt the break in the National Liberal/Progressive coalition in 1879 was heavily influenced by national events, such as common Democrat/Progressive revulsion at Bismarck's new tariff policies, and the weak state of a divided National Liberal Party in Berlin. Yet apart from what was, after all, perhaps the most crucial political caesura in imperial Germany, there is little indication that political events at a state or even at a national level had a direct impact upon the outcome of state elections in Frankfurt. Instead, they were the result of local peculiarities, most notably the Democrats' own contradictions at this level of politics, and agreements between the various local political associations which were determined as much by the local context as by events occurring outside Frankfurt.

The importance of the nature of the local polity in state and national elections is further illustrated by the nature of the election campaigns themselves. Clearly, contemporaries considered local, state, and national elections to be closely linked. This is particularly striking when one considers the rhetoric used at the different elections, which was remarkably similar at all three levels. Until the mid-1870s, Democratic reminders about Frankfurt's treatment in 1866, and the subsequent *Rezeß* settlement

[135] This confirms Peter Steinbach's work on the relationship between regional and national politicization, and his assertion about the crucial importance of local factors in popular political behaviour in state and national elections until at least 1880, and in some ways into the 1890s. P. Steinbach, 'Politisierung und Nationalisierung der Region im 19. Jahrhundert. Regionalspezifische Politikrezeption im Spiegel historischer Wahlforschung', in P. Steinbach (ed.), *Probleme politischer Partizipation im Modernisierungsprozeß* (Stuttgart, 1992), 321–49. For a detailed analysis of this theme for the region of Lippe, see Steinbach, *Die Politisierung der Region*, *passim*.

were a staple at any election. In line with local elections, state elections were about making a statement to Prussia that Frankfurt remained the cradle of freedom against reaction, a bastion of the free-thinking bourgeoisie against the military state.[136] In the 1874 national elections, Friedrich Stoltze produced an extra edition of his satirical Democrat newspaper. It contained a poem invoking the memory of Mayor Fellner's suicide in the face of advancing Prussian troops in 1866 and of the fraternal war of that year, leaving no doubt as to whose side the Frankfurt National Liberals were on.[137]

For the National Liberals, the election rhetoric is not quite so interchangeable, since in local politics they were busy defending themselves as unpolitical, which at a state or national level they could not possibly claim after 1871. Still, in many ways the rhetoric was remarkably similar, most notably the National Liberals' image as the realists and pragmatists which the Democrats were not.[138] Hence, there was no point in harking back to the past (i.e. 1866), instead it was necessary that Frankfurt should now take its due place as one of the country's most prominent cities in fashioning the new Empire.[139] In essence, this was not much different from the National Liberal *Wahlverein* complaining that the Democrats' insistence on politics in the city council was solely responsible for its inefficiency, and the *Wahlverein*'s own emphasis on the efficiency and pragmatism of its own 'unpolitical' candidates.

In the same vein, the National Liberals tried to create an alternative vision of Frankfurt history during the 1870s. Accordingly, the imperial city of Frankfurt had been faithful to and been a central locus of the imperial crown going back to the Karolingian kingdom of Charlemagne. In modern times, the imperial idea had been resurrected through the *Sturm und Drang*, whose roots were, of course, in Goethe's native city of Frankfurt. In this

---

[136] *Frankfurter Zeitung*, 9 Nov. 1870 (1. Blatt). Note also the evocation of the legacy of Robert Blum, the anniversary of whose death coincided with the first round of the Prussian state elections of 1870. *Frankfurter Zeitung*, 6 Nov. 1870 (1. Blatt). According to the newspaper, the 1874 national elections were also about this, i.e. victory for the Democrats amounted to a moral victory of Frankfurt over Prussia. *Frankfurter Zeitung*, 17 Jan. 1874 (1. Blatt).

[137] 'Der Strick an Eures Fellners Kehle, Er ward für Euch zum Liebesband!' . . . 'Gedenk ich jener heil'gen Schmerzen, | Des Grimms, den damals ich empfand, | Als sich, gewürgt von Brüderhand, | Im Staub mein armes Frankfurt wand,— | Drängt alles Blut sich mir zum Herzen'. (The rope at your Fellner's throat, it became a ribbon of love for you!' . . . 'When I look back to those holy pains, | the fury which I then felt, | when, strangled by the brotherly hand, | my poor Frankfurt writhed in the dust,— | All blood rushes to my heart') *Frankfurter Reichstagswahl Krebbelzeitung*, 9 Jan. 1874.

[138] For the local elections, this image is developed e.g. in *Frankfurter Presse*, 27 Nov. 1872 (1. Ausgabe).

[139] Most striking in this context is perhaps a commentary on the state elections of 1876. *Neue Frankfurter Presse*, 28 Oct. 1876 (1. Blatt).

sense, Frankfurt had been a central pillar to the German unification under the guidance of the Prussian crown. Thus, the city linked Charlemagne, Friedrich Barbarossa, and Wilhelm I.[140] Unfortunately for the National Liberals, this idea of history was so out of sync with the experience of most Frankfurters who had personal memories of the annexation that it did not gain much currency among contemporaries. As a result, the National Liberals tended to avoid the Democrats' localism by focusing very much on national or state matters. The 1870s saw a focus on the 'enemies of the Empire'. Here, the National Liberals tried to make a lot of capital out of the Democrats' defence of the Roman Catholics, the Poles, and the people of Alsace-Lorraine against the excesses of official discrimination.

One would expect the Democratic Association, a local branch of a geographically confined German People's Party, and its only significant local branch in Prussia, to be much more parochial in its outlook than the *Wahlverein*, whose National Liberals were enjoying their honeymoon with Bismarck. Yet, when looked at more closely, as in local politics the Democrats' apparent parochialism turned out to be particularly suited for Frankfurt conditions. It is difficult to see how the National Liberals' diatribes against Roman Catholics or against the Democrats' defence of Alsace-Lorraine could cut any ice with most Frankfurt electors. After all, the latter accusation gave Leopold Sonnemann only a further welcome opportunity to defend his opposition to Prussian arbitrary rule, which the people of Frankfurt knew only too well.[141]

A further way in which politics at the different levels were linked was with respect to party organization. After all, the express purpose of the *Wahlverein* was the organization of elections at all levels of politics. Perhaps this is the way in which the importance of the locality for national and state elections was the greatest, and in which the example of Frankfurt is transferable most easily to other cities in the Empire. Even though in 1885 the Progressive/National Liberal alliance effectively precluded the Democrats from winning in the state elections, the Democratic leadership decided to participate in the elections solely in order not to upset the party faithful.[142] Fighting elections was what the party was all about.[143]

---

[140] *Neue Frankfurter Presse*, 18 Oct. 1877 (2. Blatt). In this way, Wilhelm was welcomed in Frankfurt not so much as the Prussian King as such, who was ultimately responsible for the city's annexation in 1866, but as German emperor who had brought about unification. In this sense, the case of Frankfurt is comparable to Hamburg. R. Hauschild-Thiessen, *Bürgerstolz und Kaisertreue. Hamburg und das Deutsche Reich von 1871* (Hamburg, 1979).

[141] *Frankfurter Zeitung*, 6 Jan. 1874 (1. Blatt). [142] *Kleine Presse*, 21 Oct. 1885.

[143] Similarly, in the former Kingdom of Hanover the dispirited Guelphs chose to contest the 1867 elections to the North German Parliament principally to facilitate and enhance their

Once again, it was the Progressive Liberals who did particularly well out of the interconnectedness of local, state, and national politics. During the 1870s, the cooperation between the National Liberals and Progressives in state elections was mirrored by cooperation in elections to the city council.[144] Before the 1876 state elections, the National Liberal leader, Georg Varrentrapp, announced to a general meeting of the *Wahlverein* that the joint election campaign between the two parties which had just been agreed upon gave rise to the hope that unity between them would be equally strong and loyal in the forthcoming city council and national elections.[145] And, indeed, agreement was quickly and effortlessly reached for the local elections a month later, and this was extended to the local and national elections in 1878.

This explains why at local level, too, Progressive Liberals were treated with disproportionate respect. The other parties were always careful not to preclude future agreements with the party whose support was necessary for success in the state and local elections. In the early 1880s, for instance, despite the cooperation between Progressives and Democrats in city council and state elections, the *Wahlverein* continued to nominate a generous number of Progressive candidates for the local council. This paid off in 1885, when the Progressives changed their allegiance once more to revert to a pact with the National Liberals. As in 1879, when the Progressives broke their coalition with the National Liberals, this shift in Progressive tactics came at the heels of a major political sea-change, in this case Miquel's Heidelberg Declaration of 1884. At first sight, it seems paradoxical that this attempt to rejuvenate the National Liberal Party by steering it to the right induced the Progressive Association in Frankfurt to break its left-liberal coalition with the Democrats. However, this can be explained by the peculiarities of the Frankfurt political environment. For to their vexation, the Democrats had been outmanoeuvred by Johannes Miquel, the city's First Mayor at the time. Miquel had clearly arranged a rapprochement between the Progressive and National Liberal leaders in the city to enable a common stance in the state elections, leaving the Democrats out in the cold.[146] Regardless of circumstances, national and state politics were always directed through the prism of local politics, which in the case of Frankfurt were extremely strong.

electoral chances for the forthcoming and much more important state and provincial elections. Aschoff, *Welfische Bewegung*, 75.

[144] The nature and extent of this cooperation is discussed below.
[145] *Neue Frankfurter Presse*, 26 Oct. 1876 (1. Blatt).
[146] See Sonnemann's detailed account of the negotiations between Democrats and

The Advent of Politics

Clearly, elections held at the different levels affected each other. After all, the very frequency of local elections compared to state and national elections suggests an important role for local politics, if only in maintaining political momentum. Similarly, with regard to the politicization of local politics through state and national elections there is no reason why Frankfurt should have been unique.[147] In Frankfurt, those most prominent in local politics were obviously also involved in state and national elections. In return, the ferocity with which they fought each other at state and national levels clearly infected the tone and style of local politics. During the 1876 campaign for the state elections, the National Liberal *Neue Frankfurter Presse* retorted angrily to the Democrats' usual accusations of servility to Prussia by charging the Democratic candidate, Holthoff, as well as Sonnemann and other leading Democrats with cowardice and treason. Instead of facing the music in 1866, it argued, they had left their home town for the safety of southern Germany, from where they blasphemed the name of their *Heimat*, their country, and their compatriots.[148] For their part, the Democrats had great fun insulting the National Liberals, most notably in Friedrich Stoltze's *Frankfurter Latern*, where they were lampooned in poems, satirical columns (notably the 'Hampelmann') and, most of all, mock reports of National Liberal *Wahlverein* meetings. Funny though these were, there is no doubt that this satire, which was not only directed at the candidates themselves, but also at other prominent and active National Liberals, was deeply offensive to the individuals concerned. Elections were deeply divisive, and often personal. It is difficult to see how local politics could possibly have maintained its unpolitical nature given the acrimonies and animosities in state and national elections.

2.5. The Politicization of Local Government

Despite the establishment of a successful party organization, one central difficulty for the Democrats to advance in local government remained. They had to convince the electorate that, contrary to the prevailing view in Frankfurt as elsewhere, politics did have its rightful place inside the town

---

Progressives, and the way in which the matter had been settled behind the scenes by an agreement between Miquel, the Progressive leader, Flinsch, and the National Liberal leader, Metzler. *Kleine Presse*, 28 Oct. 1885.

[147] In Münster, political participation in local elections shot up during the *Kulturkampf* to 80% in the first and second classes, and to over 50% in the third class. In turn, this had important politicizing effects for state and national elections, for which the city had one of Germany's lowest participation rates. Olliges-Wieczorek, *Politisches Leben in Münster*, 31–8, 324–30.

[148] *Neue Frankfurter Presse*, 28 Oct. 1876 (1. Blatt).

hall. From the very beginning, the *Frankfurter Zeitung* tried to ensure that candidates with genuine left-liberal credentials be elected. Thus, in 1868 it suggested as criteria for testing the viability of candidates that they should advocate an extension of the local franchise and the abolition of the tax on animal slaughter and flour-grinding (*Schlacht- und Mahlsteuer*)—both were blatantly left-liberal demands.[149]

On the surface, it appears that the Democrats, themselves, were ambiguous about the validity of politics in local affairs. In 1874, the Democrat Maximilian Reinganum declared that 'Even if the opposition proclaims: "No politics", every independent judge has to admit that the big parties operate even in the smallest communities. Those who insist that the local council could function without politics and party political convictions cannot be serious.'[150]

Yet only two years after Reinganum made his speech quoted above, the Democrats introduced their list of candidates, 'subordinating party political considerations to the interest of the common good, without prejudice and exclusiveness'.[151] During those elections, the *Frankfurter Zeitung* complained bitterly that the alliance of Progressive and National Liberals had drawn up its list of candidates purely out of party-political considerations, irrespective of the objective good of the city.[152] This ambiguity, which was shared by the other parties, deserves closer attention because it was one of the main features of liberal rhetoric until 1900, and because it can shed some light on the general debate to what extent—and for what reasons— local government was politicized.

There are several general reasons why Frankfurt liberals emphasized the political nature of the local elections to varying degrees, depending on the circumstances of the elections. On the whole, it is the *raison d'être* of any opposition marked by a group identity based on personal connections and shared beliefs to oppose the majority. In other words, it is natural that the Democrats, as long as they were in a minority, would emphasize the political nature of local elections to show why their candidates ought to be elected, rather than the current majority which claimed to be composed of

---

[149] These two demands were likely to be at the heart of early liberal demands in local elections throughout Prussia. This needs to be investigated much more widely, but even in Düsseldorf, a city with a vastly different history, economy, and social structure, in 1868 and 1870 the liberal 'People's Party' campaigned for the democratization of the franchise, the abolition of the flour and meat tax, and a reduction in the price of gas. Hüttenberger, 'Die Entwicklung der Großstadt (1856–1900)', 601.
[150] *Frankfurter Zeitung*, 20 Nov. 1874 (Abendblatt).
[151] *Frankfurter Zeitung*, 23 Nov. 1876 (Mittagsblatt).
[152] *Frankfurter Zeitung*, 22 Nov. 1876 (Abendblatt).

talent without regard to party. Likewise, as soon as they considered themselves on the defensive, as in 1876, they would emphasize the non-political character of their list of candidates. Conversely, against continued Democratic strength the best other political groups could do was to emphasize the non-political nature of their own lists of candidates. The protestations of the National Liberals and, later, of representatives of the *Bürgervereine* and the *Mittelstand*, that politics should be kept out of the town hall, constituted a political act in itself.[153]

A further reason why it was the Democrats who emphasized the political nature of local government was that, as has been shown above, despite their roots which went back before the 1848 Revolution, the Democrats as a 'populist' organization led by the circle around Sonnemann were a new phenomenon. As such, the emphasis on politics as well as the drawing up of firm party principles helped to cement the new party identity of the Democrats after the annexation.

Moreover, the emphasis on the unpolitical is part of a self-understanding that was inherently liberal, as part of the liberal and democrat world-view that they were representing the *Volk*.[154] Obviously, in an electoral system with universal suffrage, such an 'unpolitical' world-view was unsustainable even in the short run. Yet it is useful to remember that the liberals' ability at the local level to maintain a rhetoric of the unpolitical was perhaps less a tribute to the intrinsically different nature of local government. The more sheltered environment of local politics owing to a restricted franchise

---

[153] See e.g. an article in the National Liberal *Neue Frankfurter Presse* in which the newspaper strongly opposed the Democrats' introduction of politics not just to the elections, but to the city council itself. Yet at the same time, it insisted that voters elect the 'unpolitical' list in its entirety drawn up in opposition to the Democratic politicians. *Neue Frankfurter Presse*, 24 Nov. 1874 (1. Blatt).

John Rolling notes a similar behaviour for the emergence of the SPD from 1900, against which all liberal parties emphasized the non-political character of municipal government. J. D. Rolling, 'Das Problem der "Politisierung" der kommunalen Selbstverwaltung in Frankfurt am Main 1900–1918', *AFGK* lvii (1980), 185. Rolling echoes here Sheehan's correct observations about the motives for insisting on the 'unpolitical' with respect to the SPD. Sheehan, 'Liberalism', 135–7. However, the crucial difference is that in Frankfurt this argument was used first in the 1870s beween the various liberal and Democrat parties themselves, and that this had nothing inherently to do with keeping the SPD and all it represented out of the town council.

The politicization of the 'unpolitical' was not restricted to Frankfurt. For Saxon Conservatives the insistence on the 'unpolitical' became their most important and successful rallying cry against the National Liberals, who were portrayed as importing foreign, 'Prussian' traditions of mass politics. Retallack, 'Regional Identities and Political Culture', esp. 40.

[154] Langewiesche, *Liberalismus in Deutschland*, 111, 127. The relationship between Liberals and the *Volk* also forms a major part of the analysis in Sheehan, *German Liberalism*. See e.g. 102–7, 113–18.

simply allowed liberals to continue the pretense that public matters ought not to be subject to politics for longer than at the national level.

Finally, for the parties which made a point out of the unpolitical nature of municipal politics, this was often dictated by sheer political necessity. In a closed meeting to discuss the Progressives' tactics for the coming local elections in 1882, the chairman was asked why the party did not nominate exclusively its own candidates, rather than include members of other parties on its list of nominees. He responded with the revealing comment that, firstly, this would be too expensive for the party, and, secondly, the party was too weak to go alone and thus was forced to cooperate with other parties.[155] No matter how political the Democrats chose to call the local elections, they, too, always included a considerable number from the political opposition in their nomination lists. That this was not done out of love for a non-political ideal can be assumed from the fact that the National Liberals who found their names on Democratic nomination lists were usually nominated in areas (such as the fourth electoral district) where the Democrats did not have a chance of winning, anyway.[156] In this way, the nomination of candidates was the subject of skilful political manoeuvring from the start. In 1868, Sonnemann was elected to the city council with the help of the National Liberals, but only because they considered him an important counterweight to the more radical Hadermann. When, in 1874, the now leading Democrat insisted on being nominated in his old electoral district, National Liberals were furious at his obvious attempt to deprive them of what would otherwise have been a safe National Liberal seat.[157] Their frequent unpolitical rhetoric notwithstanding, even during the 1870s all three liberal organizations in Frankfurt competed in the local elections on a distinctly political basis.

Another aspect of the politicization of municipal politics was the development of party manifestos, and, as so often, here the Democrats were pioneers. In fact, National Liberal election manifestos did not appear for more than a decade, which was only logical given the party's customary public insistence on the 'unpolitical'. The Progressives followed whichever party

---

[155] HStAW 407 n. 150¹ fo. 126. Progressive Association meeting, 20 Nov. 1882. For the same reasons, the Progressives nominated *Wahlmänner* for the state elections only in areas where they saw chances of success. HStAW 407 n. 150¹ fos. 215–16. Progressive Association meeting, 21 Oct. 1885.

[156] See also the public meeting of 1874 in which Dr May challenged the Democrats to admit that they merely did not possess the strength to nominate their own supporters in all the wards. *Frankfurter Zeitung*, 24 Nov. 1874 (Abendblatt).

[157] *Neue Frankfurter Presse*, 24 Nov. 1874 (1. Blatt).

they happened to be allied with, and did not produce a manifesto of their own. However, even if for a long time the Democrats alone stated their policy in an election manifesto signed by the party committee and adhered to by a list of candidates, it follows that the policies mentioned were at least partly contested by the other parties—otherwise there would have been no need to mention them in the first place.

As already mentioned, the *Frankfurter Zeitung* proceeded in 1867 to demand that candidates seek a liberalization of the municipal franchise and the abolition of the *Schlacht- und Mahlsteuer*. The latter was effectively a tax on meat and flour which, to make matters worse in the eyes of the Democrats, had been imposed by the Prussians without any consultation with local representatives.[158] Upon its foundation, the *Demokratischer Wahlverein* made the *Frankfurter Zeitung*'s demands their own. In its first election manifesto, drawn up specifically for the municipal elections, the *Verein* went on to demand a more independent and rigorous line against Prussia (with particular reference to the negotiations concerning the *Rezeß*), the establishment exclusively of non-denominational schools, and the institution of municipal gasworks.[159]

During the municipal elections throughout the period under investigation, these five demands, for electoral reform, for a socially acceptable burden of taxation through the introduction of direct, progressive taxes, for the maintenance of Frankfurt's self-government against Prussia, for the principle of non-denominational schooling, and for the municipal ownership of public utilities, became the essence of Democrat policies. This programme was repeated in full for the municipal elections of 1872, adapted to demands which were more specific but which all descended from the five points.[160] Subsequent election programmes until the mid-1880s were much more modest in scope and ambition, but their main themes still relate to the original programme.[161]

These were, then, the areas in which political affiliation and conviction were perceived to be of importance in local government. Naturally, this means that the narrower questions of municipal administration, such as how many streets were going to be repaired, how to ensure an adequate

---

[158] Maly, *Macht*, 35–7.   [159] Wolf, *Liberalismus*, 133.

[160] *Frankfurter Zeitung*, 23 Nov. 1872 (2. Blatt).

[161] For example, after hints that the Prussian government might consider the introduction of the new *Städteordnung* for Frankfurt, the 1876 manifesto was exclusively concerned with the preservation of Frankfurt *Selbstverwaltung*. Maly, *Macht*, 112–13. *Frankfurter Zeitung*, 23 Nov. 1876 (Mittagsblatt). The main theme of the 1878 manifesto was fair taxation. *Frankfurter Zeitung*, 18 Nov. 1878. A lacklustre 1880 manifesto merely rallied against 'reactionary' tendencies in local administration. *Frankfurter Zeitung*, 22 Nov. 1880 (Abendblatt).

water supply or in which area to build the next school, were left out of the fold of municipal party politics.[162] In this sense, a large part of municipal administration was, indeed, 'unpolitical' until the turn of the century and even beyond. And yet, even here there were many issues with potential political implications, which were exploited to the full. Arguments about the price of theatre tickets rapidly became a political matter, as Maximilian Reinganum insisted that no Democrat would ever agree to a pricing structure which was élitist. Discussions about the future of a foundation for the support of citizens' widows, the *Katharinen- und Weißfrauenstift*, became a political issue between the parties as Democrats criticized its existing organization.[163] Yet even among those areas which were deemed intrinsically 'political', its array remains impressive and covered virtually every area of importance in municipal government: fiscal policy, social policy, economic policy, education policy, and all matters concerning the city's relationship with the state.

In marked contrast to the period 1857–1866, political life was not just restricted to election times, but flourished throughout the year,[164] in that local affairs were subject virtually all year round to public debate by the three liberal parties. Of these, the most active was, of course, the Democratic Association, which held public meetings at regular one- to three-week intervals from early autumn to late spring.[165] Unfortunately, the first police reports of the meetings that survived date from 1879, so that it is impossible to give any precise attendance figures for the early meetings of the *Demokratischer Verein*. In 1879, attendances could range from 50 to 150 people, except when a Democratic member of the Reichstag or Prussian Chamber of Deputies gave his report to his constituents: During the early 1880s, these would draw between 200 and 300 people.[166] Most meetings were held publicly. At each meeting, there were one or two speakers on various local, state, or national subjects. These public meetings encouraged

---

[162] In 1882 e.g. Heinrich Rößler emphasized the importance of politics on the issues of non-denominational schooling, the franchise, and *Selbstverwaltung*, and that in consideration of the importance of these matters it would be petty and ridiculous ('lächerlich') to apply politics e.g. to the paving of streets. *Frankfurter Zeitung*, 14 Nov. 1882 (Abendblatt).

[163] *Frankfurter Presse*, 20 Nov. 1880 (Abendblatt).

[164] To Dieter Langewiesche, the concept of politics as a broad, popular movement is a major characteristic of the advent of a 'modern' form of politics. Langewiesche, 'Anfänge', 335.

[165] Wolf, *Liberalismus*, 48–51. Wolf's number of 43 'gatherings' in 1878, taken from a report in the *Frankfurter Zeitung*, is slightly misleading, in that it is not clear what form these gatherings took. Many of these may have been just private committee meetings. The police reports from 1879 suggest that there were 23 principal gatherings that year .

[166] See e.g. HStAW 407 n. 138² fos. 55, 58–60. Democratic Association meetings in Sept. and Oct. 1882.

the individual to commit himself to political debate and to participate in local politics, even by his presence alone. More importantly, in the field of municipal politics there was a widespread perception that Democratic council members were accountable to these meetings and should take their attendants' views into consideration. In a discussion of the municipal budget, one member suggested a strong censure of the Democrat councillors, whom they referred to as their 'offspring' (*Spößlinge*), 'because they considered themselves above participating in the meetings of those who had made them what they were'.[167] Although in practice Democrat councillors took infrequent notice of these meetings, there was nevertheless the view that they ought to respect their constituents' wishes not just at election times, and that they be accountable to frequent party scrutiny throughout the year.

The *Verein der Fortschrittspartei* tried to hold monthly meetings,[168] but there is no evidence to suggest that meetings were actually held at these intervals. The main reason for the relative infrequency of meetings may not have been so much reluctance on the part of the organizers, but the persistent problem of low attendance. With a usual attendance of between 20 and 40 people, these meetings could in no way claim to be popular. But the party had a much more pressing problem in that it was not affiliated to a local newspaper, which was considered a crucial drawback.[169] It relied on the National Liberal *Frankfurter Presse* or, increasingly, on the *Frankfurter Zeitung* for publicity. The Progressive party organization was clearly not as successful as that of the Democrats, though its leaders remained nevertheless keenly aware of the importance of public opinion not just during the elections.

This was also true for the National Liberal *Wahlverein*. In its general meeting of 1878, it decided that in future it, too, would have speaker meetings and discussions and that it would use this opportunity to develop the rhetorical skills of its members. Furthermore, it established a '*Preßcomite*', whose function was to promote newspaper reports favourable to the party and to defend it quickly and efficiently against any printed attacks.[170] In summary, then, all the liberal parties in Frankfurt were in various ways and to various degrees keenly aware of the public eye, and they were willing

---

[167] HStAW 407 n. 138¹ fo. 51. Democratic Association meeting, 17 Mar. 1879.
[168] Wolf, *Liberalismus*, 61.
[169] The necessity of a party newspaper was constantly outlined as one of its most pressing issues. See e.g. HStAW 407 n. 150¹ fos. 244–6. Progressive Association meeting, 21 Mar. 1887.
[170] HStAW 407 n. 160 fo. 99. National Liberal Association meeting, Oct. 1878.

(at least in theory) to subject their own actions to public scrutiny. In 1879, the *Verein der Fortschrittspartei* had managed to organize about 259 members, the *Demokratischer Verein* had 399 members in 1880, and, loose though the affiliation may have been, 563 inhabitants (it can be safely assumed that virtually all of these would have been citizens) chose to pay the annual subscription fee of the *Wahlverein* in 1880.[171] By 1880, councillors were subject to the control of the political parties whose membership equalled 10 per cent of the total local electorate and 25 per cent of those who went to the polls for the 1880 municipal elections.[172]

2.6. Liberal Politics and Municipal Administration

Committing one's candidates to a common political platform during party meetings or before elections was one thing—getting the individual councillors to keep their common pledges once elected was quite another. On the whole, the decisions of the city council, and of the administration as a whole, appear to suggest that there was very little group loyalty inside the city council, as few of the biggest party's demands were actually enacted. From the Democrats' point of view, the most important failure was their inability to achieve any significant municipal initiative to enlarge the franchise, but there were also other ones. For example, despite several attempts the gasworks was never municipalized.

A study of the minutes of the city council certainly does suggest an absence of politics from the discussions, as individuals seemed to speak for themselves rather than for a group. However, a note of caution is appropriate here, as a comparison with newspaper reports of meetings (where available) shows that in the minutes many of the most heated discussions were not reproduced in full. Furthermore, it should be borne in mind that virtually all contentious matters were initially referred to the relevant committee usually composed of members of all parties, which would then

---

[171] HStAW 407 n. 160 fo. 112. National Liberal Association meeting, Sept. 1879. See also HStAW 407 n. 160 fos. 122–5. Membership list of the National Liberal Association, 1880. HStAW 407 n. 138² fo. 131. Memberhip statistics for the Democratic Association. By 1882, that figure had grown to 495 members according to the figures given by the Democratic Association, or 527 according to the figures of the Prussian authorities. HStAW 407 n. 150¹ fo. 5. Progressive Association meeting, 7 Jan. 1879.

[172] These are astonishing figures, by any standards. In his pioneering work on liberal party organization, Michael Ostrogorski noted for England: 'Even in places where the political pulse has beaten strongly, and where the Caucus has been a decided success, as at Birmingham, the proportion of those affiliated to the party Organizations does not exceed eight or ten per cent of the total number of electors'. M. Ostrogorski, *Democracy and the Organisation of Political Parties* (London, 1902), i. 332. The participation rates for the 1880 council elections have been taken from Wolf, *Liberalismus*, 130.

try to achieve some consensus.[173] This represents not so much the 'reign of the unpolitical', but simply the most realistic way of conducting politics under the conditions of the Prussian city ordinance. Under the Frankfurt constitution, the *Magistrat* was the executive body for the policies arrived at by the city council, but in the majority of cases both chambers had to agree to these policies, lest the Prussian authorities in Wiesbaden be called in to arbitrate.[174] Seeking to avoid at all costs Prussian interference in breach of the principle of *Selbstverwaltung*, the Democrats therefore had an interest in looking for compromise with the *Magistrat*. Furthermore, since the *Magistrat* was de facto the stronger of the two bodies,[175] it was only really possible to stand up to the *Magistrat* if the city council itself was united. Therefore, it was in the Democrats' best interests to seek political compromise, even if this meant that their policies got 'watered down' in the process.

There is considerable evidence from contemporaries that the council (*Stadtverordnetenversammlung*) did play according to political ground rules. It is interesting to note that in the 1870s, the National Liberal complaint was not so much at party political rhetoric during election time, but at the fact that matters inside the city council and its committees were subject to party considerations.[176] In his memoirs, councillor Funck noted about his environment when he entered the council in the early 1880s distinct political parties, rather than unpolitical *Honoratioren*.[177] Although the Progressives cooperated with the National Liberals during the municipal elections, once in the council they more often than not voted with the Democrats 'on political matters'. A decade later, the rules had been reversed. For the 1892 elections, the Democrats declared that they were willing yet again to set up a common list of candidates with the Progressive Party, but only on the condition that the Progressives end their alliance (*'gemeinsame Fraktion'*) with the National Liberals inside the city council.[178]

One of the best indicators of the nature and extent of politicization in the town council is the list of appointments to the various committees and the prestigious council offices, whose members were elected during the first

---

[173] See the admission of councillor Paul Zirndorfer that the real work of city government lay in the commissions. *Frankfurter Zeitung*, 1 Nov. 1902 (3. Morgenblatt).

[174] On the relationship between the two bodies in Frankfurt, see Wolf, *Liberalismus*, 109–17.

[175] Hofmann, 'Aufgaben', 616.

[176] See e.g. *Frankfurter Presse*, 27 Nov. 1872 (1. Ausgabe). *Neue Frankfurter Presse*, 24 Nov. 1874 (1. Blatt).

[177] Funck, *Lebenserinnerungen*, 144.

[178] *Frankfurter Zeitung*, 15 Nov. 1892 (2. Morgenblatt). Wolf, *Liberalismus*, 145.

council sessions of each year.[179] A look at the composition of various committees during the 1870s demonstrates clearly why National Liberals complained at the advent of party politics inside the *Stadtverordnetenversammlung*. In 1875, of the 50 posts available in altogether eight committees, 31 were occupied by Democrats, and 13 by Progressive Liberals.[180] A total of four went to the National Liberals, while one councillor without party affiliation stood on two committees. In 1877, in four newly elected committees with a total of 26 places, 12 went to Democrats, 10 to Progressives, and 4 to National Liberals.[181] The relative strength of the Progressive Liberals illustrates well their bargaining power as the party in the middle, which has been described in the previous section. During the late 1870s, politics were unquestionably the crucial factor in the composition of committees inside the council.

During the 1880s and 1890s, the allocation of party members to individual committees changed.[182] During this time, most committees had at least one member from each liberal party, while there was a much greater political balance overall. A greater sense of harmony between the parties is also conveyed by the fact that the elections to the committees were usually unanimous or virtually unanimous, which suggests that they were filled with the mutual consent of all parties concerned. After the tumultuous 1870s, in which the very concept of politics aroused fierce passions inside the council, which were whipped up further by left-liberal hostility towards the *Magistrat*, the new distribution of committee posts was a testament to the political harmony achieved under the mayorality of Johannes Miquel.[183]

In 1888, of nine members of the finance committee five were Democrats, two were Progressive Liberals, and two were National Liberals. The

---

[179] For the members of the city council, its officers and the *Magistrat*, see *Haupt-Register zu den Mittheilungen aus den Protokollen der Stadtverordneten- Versammlung der Stadt Frankfurt a.M. für die Jahrgänge 1867 bis incl. 1900, nebst einem Verzeichniß der Mitglieder des Magistrats und der Stadtverordneten- Versammlung seit dem Jahre 1867*, ed. E. Dannenberg (Frankfurt, 1902). As a supplementary source, see P. Tratnik, 'Mitglieder der Frankfurter Stadtverordnetenversammlung 1867–1933' (Frankfurt, 1984), typescript in IfSG. Party affiliations for the council members have been worked out from fragmentary membership lists, appearances of candidates in political meetings, and signatures on political pamphlets.

[180] For the composition of the various committees, see IfSG, *Mitteilungen aus den Protokollen der Stadtverordnetenversammlung der Stadt Frankfurt am Main* (*MPS*), 1875 (§§1–7).

[181] IfSG, *MPS*, 1877 (§§40–4).

[182] Information for the composition of the city council committees has been obtained from IfSG, *MPS*, 1888 (§§1–22), 1889 (§§1–12), 1892 (§§1–11), 1893 (§§1–8), 1894 (§§2–3), 1897 (§§1–5).

[183] This is discussed in greater detail below.

legal committee consisted of one National Liberal, two Progressives, and two Democrats, while the organization committee (*Reorganisations-Commission*) had three National Liberal, three Democratic, and one Progressive Liberal members. It is true that a few committees were still unbalanced, most notably the two building committees, but the lack of National Liberal participation might be largely a factor of the low prestige of these committees, and the extreme hard work that they required. In 1887 alone, the *Hochbau-Commission* was composed entirely of Democrats, and met up regularly to write 42 reports to the council, while the *Ingenieur-Commission*, which was composed of three Democrats and two Progressive Liberals, had to draw up a record 197 reports. By comparison, the finance and legal committees were among the least work-intensive committees, requiring only thirteen and four reports, respectively.

Although the overall picture appears unchanged, as Democrats gained a total of 30 out of 50 committee seats, with the two other parties gaining ten each, if one discounts the work-intensive committees, the composition of council committees was much more equal. Democrats were careful to maintain an overall majority in the committees that mattered to them, such as the school and finance committees, but otherwise they were ready to grant a fair representation especially to the National Liberals, even if that meant that in some committees, National Liberals could outvote them in conjunction with the Progressive Liberals.

During the 1890s, the number of committees and of committee posts doubled. By 1897, out of a total of 95 committee posts, 42 went to Democrats, 29 National Liberals, and 24 to the Progressives. All three parties had taken a share in the increase, but, reflecting their relative loss of seats in the council itself, the Democrats lost ground relative to the other two parties. Despite the greater political balance in committee membership, the National Liberals still displayed a tendency to sit on those committees which required less involvement. They strengthened their representation in the legal committee, which in 1896 met but twice. In 1896, both Progressive and Democrat committee members went to an average of about 15 committee meetings, while their National Liberal peers went to an average of about 11.[184]

---

[184] These figures are estimates derived from the committee members elected for 1897 and the actual times the committees met in 1896. *MPS*, 1897 (§§3–5). The figure for the National Liberals is significantly boosted by the highly energetic Adolf von Harnier, who ran as an independent but whom contemporaries counted as a National Liberal. If one did not include him in the National Liberal figure, the average would fall to nine meetings for each committee member.

Of course, if political affiliation was something like a sine qua non for working in the committees, it was by no means the only criterion. Having spare time and enthusiasm was very important, too, particularly as the administrative burden of municipal government increased over the years. Committee work could be very time-consuming and unrewarding. Finally, qualification was an important consideration. This mattered particularly for the more specialized committees. In 1897, all five members of the legal committee were lawyers themselves. Still, throughout the period under consideration, and for 30 years before the advent of the SPD in the city council, the composition of committees in the city council was sometimes the result of political rivalry (as in the 1870s), while at other times of careful political compromise.

A similar picture of the importance of party affiliation can be gained from a brief look at the distribution of the more prestigious council offices. During the 1870s, the president of the city council consistently came from the strongest party in the council, the Democrats. His deputy was a Democrat from 1871 to 1877, the post filled thereafter by a representative of a party which was not connected to the president. In 1880, the presidency went over to G. A. Humser. Admittedly, as a National Liberal he was not elected out of party considerations, but because he was a widely respected figure, even among Democrats. But under these circumstances it was a matter of course that his deputy would be a Democrat. This was indeed the case, except for one year, 1893, when the Progressives, for personal reasons, refused to elect the Democratic candidate for the post, Leopold Sonnemann. Instead, they and the National Liberals elected another Democrat, Heinrich Rößler. Out of party loyalty, Rößler refused to accept his election, so that the Progressives and National Liberals proceeded to elect a Progressive, Theodor Stern.[185] For the office of the secretary and his deputy, the same applies: until 1900, both were from opposing parties. Party politics in the council, therefore, were not strict in the sense that the majority party or the majority coalition would monopolize all offices as, in theory, it could have done. Yet municipal offices were not distributed to affiliates of either party completely at random, either. There seemed to be a genuine perception reflected in the elections to municipal offices that these prestigious and influential posts ought to reflect the relative strengths of the different parties.

In the city council, there was nevertheless a distinct lack of party unity as far as voting behaviour was concerned. At a public election rally of the

[185] Maly, *Macht*, 310.

Democratic party in 1874 attended by about 600 people, the Progressive Dr Ebner complained that in too many political decisions, Democrats had voted against their own programme and against their own professed principles.[186] It was, in fact, the same charge pounded mercilessly by the SPD against the Democrats, from the late 1890s onwards.[187] However, the lack of party discipline before 1900, and even afterwards, should not necessarily be taken as a sign of weakness. After all, party unity within elected representative bodies was never a liberal forte, neither in Germany nor, indeed, in England.[188]

And yet, there was a tremendous amount of informal discussion before council meetings took place, even in the absence of formal party groups (*Fraktionen*). From the very beginning, councillors met privately with a group of like-minded peers to discuss strategic matters for forthcoming council meetings.[189] For the 1870s, there even survive procedural rules (*Geschäfts-Ordnung*) for the '*demokratische Fraktion*'.[190] There was no party whip, and there was no means of enforcement: it was extremely rare that someone would be excluded from renomination because of his voting behaviour. What the *Geschäfts-Ordnung* does confirm, however, is that informal discussions by council members affiliated to one party did take place on a regular basis. This provides further evidence for the existence of a common identity among councillors which was based primarily on common political convictions, rather than on common ties formed by membership of the same club or profession. This common identity was initially only shared by the city's Democrats. Yet by their very exclusion from this circle, whether they liked it or not, it also became the main element of Progressive and National Liberal behaviour.

Any analysis of the political content of local administration would not be complete without a brief discussion of the relevance of politics to the *Magistrat*. In the historiography on municipal government, few claims are more common and less contested than the one that more or less throughout the Empire, the *Magistrat* remained free from political considerations. Particularly as the century drew to a close, the *Magistrat* became

---

[186] *Frankfurter Zeitung*, 24 Nov. 1874 (Abendblatt). On the liberals' undisciplined voting behaviour even as late as the 1890s, see Rolling, 'Problem', 173.

[187] This was particularly, though by no means exclusively, pronounced on the liberals' inconsistencies concerning the extension of the franchise. See e.g. Rolling, 'Liberals', 189 ff.

[188] Of all the parties in the first Reichstag, the Liberal parties were the most undisciplined. Grohs, *Die Liberale Reichspartei*, 184–95.

[189] IfSG, NL Fay, S1/11.6. Sauerländer to Fay, 23 Sept. 1867.

[190] IfSG, NL Fay, S1/11.3.

increasingly 'professionalized' as local administration became more specialized and cumbersome. A *Magistrat* initially composed of local notables gave way to one composed of professional administrators who were virtually all trained lawyers and came from outside. In either case, politics had no place in the selection of the *Magistrat*'s members (*Stadträte*).[191] This development was epitomized by the election and conduct of the president of the *Magistrat*, the mayor. The only political criterion for choosing a mayor was that of the king's right of confirmation, which had a purely negative effect in ensuring that in Prussia no Social Democrat and very few left liberals ever became mayor.[192]

Frankfurt has been considered a model example in this respect.[193] Twice, the left-liberal council elected a mayor of right-liberal, even conservative, leanings, both of whom epitomized the 'unpolitical' ethic whilst in office, to contemporaries and historians alike.[194] On this account, the office of First Mayor became politicized largely during the Weimar Republic.[195] After all, throughout the Empire, a majority of *Stadträte* sympathized with the National Liberals. Only during the first decade of the twentieth century did political considerations become an important criterion for election into the *Magistrat*.[196]

This view of the unpolitical nature of the Frankfurt *Magistrat* needs to be modified. In 1868, before the first elections to the *Magistrat*, the *Frankfurter Zeitung* expounded their political importance. The experience of other cities such as Königsberg, Berlin, Cologne, and Breslau in their dealings with the Prussian government pointed to the importance of the steadfastness of '*freisinnige*' (liberal) members of the *Magistrat*. In these cities, the newspaper concluded, there was in consequence a general awareness that the candidates' political convictions ('*Gesinnungstüchtigkeit*') were of paramount importance.[197] This was about politics: What would happen to the reputation of the democratically-minded city of Frankfurt if mostly

---

[191] This view is nicely summarized in T. Nipperdey, *Deutsche Geschichte 1866–1918*. ii. *Machtstaat vor der Demokratie* (Munich, 1992), 158–9. Hofmann, 'Aufgaben', 613–16. Fisch, *Stadtplanung im 19. Jahrhundert*, 49–50.

[192] W. Hofmann, *Zwischen Rathaus und Reichskanzlei. Die Oberbürgermeister in der Kommunal- und Staatspolitik des Deutschen Reiches von 1890–1933* (Berlin/Stuttgart/Cologne/Mainz, 1974), 44–6.

[193] Dodge, *Government*, 41–7.

[194] Sheehan, *German Liberalism*, 235. Sheehan, 'Liberalism', 126. Wehler, *Deutsche Gesellschaftsgeschichte 1849–1914*, 535.

[195] W. Hofmann, 'Oberbürgermeister als politische Elite im Wilhelminischen Reich und in der Weimarer Republik', in K. Schwabe (ed.), *Oberbürgermeister* (Boppard, 1981), 33.

[196] Rolling, 'Problem', 180.   [197] *Frankfurter Zeitung*, 19 Jan. 1868 (1. Blatt).

conservatives were elected?[198] However, the ensuing elections mirrored the conservative nature of the 1867 elections to the North German Confederation and the city council. Much to the horror of the *Frankfurter Zeitung*, four of the six paid posts were filled by members of the former conservative Senate.[199] In the following years, the Democrats continued to attack the *Magistrat* relentlessly for its general administrative incompetence[200] and, more importantly, for its servility to the state,[201] in flagrant breach of the Democrats' ideal of self-government. In the ambiguous position which the *Magistrat* held, as a link between the local community and state administration, it was the Democrats' main concern that the *Stadträte* should stand firmly on the side of the city council in all matters of dispute with the state.

It is for this principal reason that the Democrats chose to confront the *Magistrat* head on, mainly through trying with remarkable success to appoint as many Democrats to it as possible. Ursula Bartelsheim has shown in some detail how during the 1870s the relationship between the Democrats and the *Magistrat* deteriorated so far that at one point Sonnemann even hoped to increase the number of salaried *Stadträte* so as to fill the *Magistrat* with Democrats.[202] While Sonnemann failed in this specific endeavour, the Democrats nevertheless did manage to replace retiring *Stadträte* with candidates sympathetic to their own views as early as 1870 and 1871.[203]

In the 1880s and 1890s, under the leadership of Johannes Miquel and Franz Adickes, controversy between the Democrat-led *Stadtverordnetenversammlung* and the *Magistrat* virtually disappeared. In response, elections to the *Magistrat* ceased being subject to open party political conflict.[204] However, this does not mean that politics ceased to be important. As was shown above, what was paramount to Democrats was to have a *Magistrat* which did not cry to Wiesbaden at the slightest hint of trouble with the council. Instead, it should unite with the council against Prussian interference so as to retain as much self-government as possible. This was not just a fundamental principle, but was also crucial, for example, for securing a maximum degree of local independence in the administration of education. As long as these principles were violated under the leadership of mayor

---

[198] *Frankfurter Zeitung*, 21 Jan. 1868 (2. Blatt).
[199] *Frankfurter Zeitung*, 24 Jan. 1868 (1. Blatt).
[200] HStAW 407 n. 138 fo. 113. Leopold Sonnemann in a meeting of the Democratic Association, 17 Nov. 1879.
[201] This charge is most cuttingly found in successive issues of the *Frankfurter Latern*, 1872–4. See e.g. *Frankfurter Latern*, 21 Nov. 1874.
[202] Bartelsheim, 'Politisierung', ch. 3, esp. 198.   [203] Ibid. 131–2.
[204] Ibid. 212–13.

Mumm, Democrats fought the *Magistrat* at every end. Conversely, once a mayor was elected who guided the *Magistrat* towards cooperation with the council, the Democrats themselves were happy to cooperate. Hence, it did not matter much if the first *Stadtrat* with a portfolio for education, Grimm, was a National Liberal, because he was well-known to be firmly committed to the city's non-denominational schools, against the state. This is why the Democrats supported Grimm despite the fact that throughout his period of office he refused to appoint a single left liberal to the office of headmaster at any municipal primary or secondary school.[205] On another matter of political interest to the city's Democrats, social policy, the Democrats managed to get their own party member, Karl Flesch, elected for the post of *Stadtrat* for social affairs.

Seen in this light, it is indeed true that most elections to the *Magistrat* were unpolitical, in that the city's left liberals were prepared to accept a majority of National Liberal *Stadträte*. Most of these posts were, in theory as in practice, administrative ones, and the Democrats cared very little whether the *Stadtrat* responsible for municipal building projects or the sewerage system was a National Liberal or not. Prospective *Stadträte* did, however, have to fulfil certain minimum political requirements, which were quite consistent with the political programmes developed by the Democrats for the city council elections. In the enforcement of this, the Democrats were very successful. Throughout the terms of office of Miquel and the more conservative Adickes, both chambers presented a common front against the Prussian state. As a result, politics did have a role to play in the Frankfurt *Magistrat*, even if that role was much more subdued than in the municipal council.

This is particularly evident in the elections of the two National Liberal mayors whilst the Democrats were in a majority in the council. As with other commissions of the council, in 1879 Democrats made sure that they had four out of nine representatives on the nomination committee for the First Mayor.[206] And yet, in voting for Johannes Miquel, the Democrat councillors were not voting for the National Liberal leader whose policies led him, while he was mayor of Frankfurt, to be one of the driving forces

---

[205] BAK, NL 44 n. 9 fo. 7. Hermann Luppe, 'Mein Leben', part ii. Luppe's statement is confirmed by the impressive number of headmasters and head teachers who filled the ranks of the local National Liberal Association. HStAW 407 n. 160 fos. 415–26. Membership list of the National Liberal Association, 1893.

[206] Bartelsheim, 'Politisierung', 204. The committee did not even include the person most actively involved in the choice of the First Mayor, Sonnemann, so that the real weight of the Democrats was much greater than is suggested by the committee's composition alone.

behind the National Liberal swing to the right in 1884. Rather, they were voting for Miquel in his capacity as perhaps liberalism's most important advocate of local self-government!

Miquel had been an active proponent of the importance of self-government throughout his political life. In theoretical discourse, during his time as mayor of Osnabrück and in frequent parliamentary debates as a National Liberal representative in the Reichstag, Miquel continuously reiterated the liberal view that an autonomous, self-governing local government would be essential to a strong German state.[207] To Frankfurt left liberals, Miquel's credentials were further boosted by his insistence on the separation between church and state in education, and by his decided support of a locally, rather than state, administered system of education.[208] No one knew better about Miquel's views than Leopold Sonnemann, who had experienced him at first hand in parliament. Furthermore, Sonnemann, who had a pivotal role in the choice of both Miquel and Adickes, was aware that if he was to succeed in ousting the conservative Mumm as First Mayor, only a candidate with the first-class administrative skills of Miquel would do.[209]

The political character of these elections is even more clear in Sonnemann's own words to a local Democrat meeting. He praised Miquel's superior administrative talents, and pointed out his acceptability to the king. Most importantly to Sonnemann, as mayor of Osnabrück from 1865 to 1869 and again since 1875, Miquel was a fellow sufferer from Prussian annexation. As such, he had rendered great services to the maintenance of provincial and municipal autonomy in Hanover. Had Frankfurt had a mayor of similar calibre, the city would have fared much better in the *Rezeß*. With regard to his party political inclinations, it was true that Miquel was a National Liberal, but then his views were still much more to the left than those of his predecessor.[210]

Miquel's appointment was not strictly party-political. Indeed, the last assurance from Sonnemann's speech, that Miquel had already promised to abstain from any party-political involvement in the city, smacks of a deal

---

[207] See e.g. J. Miquel, 'Verfassung und Verwaltung der Provinzen und Gemeinden des Königreichs der Niederlande', *PJbb* xxiv (1869), 312–40, esp. 339–40. See also his speech on 18 Mar. 1876 on the proposed city ordinance, in *Johannes von Miquels Reden*, ed. W. Schultze and F. Thimme (Halle, 1911), ii. 302–17.

[208] Ibid. 61 ff. (Speech on Church and Education of 3 Feb. 1871) and 244–6 (Speech of 11 Mar. 1875 on 'The State and Local Secondary Schools').

[209] Sonnemann appreciated very clearly that Miquel was the only alternative to Mumm who was likely to be elected. *Frankfurter Beobachter*, 19 Nov. 1879.

[210] HStAW 407 n. 138¹ fos. 114–15. Democratic Association meeting, 17 Nov. 1879.

between the two when Miquel's coming to Frankfurt was originally discussed. Yet Miquel's election was not an unpolitical act—such an act would have secured the re-election of Mumm, in his capacity as a local notable of the highest social standing. Rather, the election of Miquel fitted the general political goals of the Democrats. Given the combination of unpolitical and political criteria outlined by Sonnemann, Miquel was the perfect choice.

Miquel's time in Frankfurt was an unmitigated success, and he exceeded virtually all expectations. The relationship between the *Magistrat* and the city council was smooth as never before or after, and upon his departure Miquel could look back on an impressive list of municipal improvements while leaving behind a balanced budget. Unfortunately, there is less evidence on the motives behind Adickes's election in 1890, but in the light of the success of Miquel's selection it would seem likely that those individuals involved, Sonnemann in particular, applied similar criteria. According to Miquel, Adickes had his experience as the mayor of another trading city, Altona, to commend him, as well as an extremely congenial manner. This was essential in a city like Frankfurt, where a mayor had to treat the different parties with respect and tact.[211] With Adickes, the Democrats made sure that not only an expert mayor was elected, but one who was a visionary in educational and social reform.[212] Against what has already been said about Miquel's election, it is also extremely likely that the Democrats made sure from the start that in disputes between the state and the city, the mayor would always take a common stand with the *Magistrat* and the city council, like his predecessor.

Therefore, Adickes's election, too, was not strictly party political, in that the Democrats again were instrumental in his selection. Still, the election was clearly a political event. So great were the internal political cleavages that no acceptable internal candidate who would be supported across party lines could be found.[213] In the selection of Adickes the Democrats made

[211] Funck, *Lebenserinnerungen*, 15.
[212] Adickes's experience and his pioneering work on social policy was the reason why he, as a right-wing liberal, could be chosen while the Frankfurt National Liberal, Adolf Varrentrapp, was unacceptable to the Democrats on political grounds. For an account of the other candidates under discussion, see Bartelsheim, 'Politisierung', 280–1.
[213] Again, see Miquel's assessment in Funck, *Lebenserinnerungen*, 15. Another example of this is the National Liberals' and most of the Progressive Liberals' reaction to Sonnemann's nomination as third candidate for the mayoralty to be presented to the king. In third place, and with Sonnemann's 'red' credentials, the nomination was a mere formality in honour of the man who had done so much for the city's common weal. Nevertheless, the majority of the liberal parties in opposition to the Democrats could not bring themselves to vote for Sonnemann's nomination, the Progressive Liberal Geiger proclaiming that this amounted to an insult to the Emperor. Maly, *Macht*, 279–80.

sure some of their important political criteria for local government were met, and in this sense, Adickes, like Miquel, was the best choice the Democrats could have made.

In a city where the king could appoint the mayor at his own pleasure, cross-party agreement on the list of nominees presented to the king was paramount. In a broader sense, however, the Democrats made sure that of all possible candidates, those were elected whose objectives were most congruent with their own aims. There were, of course, important political differences which remained. All three mayors until 1912 were opposed to the important Democrat demand for the municipalization of services. On the other hand, from 1880 onwards the Democrats were happy with the composition of the *Magistrat* as a whole, so much so that it was increasingly the Democrats, and not the National Liberals, who felt they had to defend themselves against the charge of being too servile to the *Magistrat*.[214] In sum, what was important to the Democrats was that the *Magistrat* would pursue the broad political line which they advocated. This was the sine qua non for the Democrats' support. Beyond that, they were happy to support the candidates of any party, depending on their professional qualifications.

Even though the case of Frankfurt contradicts established ideas about the role of politics in municipal government, it confirms others, namely the continued importance of *Honoratiorenpolitik* until 1900, and among the liberals even until the First World War. If one considers the social rather than political composition of the city council, there is a striking degree of continuity between the pre- and post-annexation local government bodies.[215] The free professions and merchants were over-represented,[216] and apart from the newspaper circles it is these groups which were the most influential in municipal government. Of the twenty-eight councillors who held the posts of president, secretary (*Schriftführer*), and their respective deputies, sixteen were lawyers, five were owners or chairmen of large businesses, one was a banker, one a medical doctor, and only two were smaller craftsmen—though the latter two held the relatively minor office of deputy secretary only for a total of three years. The influential councillors were part of the network of clubs and societies which continued to play an

---

[214] *Frankfurter Zeitung*, 11 Nov. 1902 (3. Morgenblatt).
[215] Roth, 'Liberalismus', 17. Roth, *Stadt und Bürgertum*, 495–501, 526. In this sense, at least, the experience of Frankfurt reflects that of other cities. For Dortmund, see Schambach, *Stadtbürgertum*, 325–7, 335–7. For Munich, Ralf Zerback has noted that the new party political rhetoric which emerged from the late 1860s largely integrated traditional bourgeois discourse. Zerback, *München*, 293–5.
[216] Wolf, *Liberalismus*, 132.

important role in municipal affairs,[217] even though their influence was declining rapidly. As a result, in Frankfurt, politics by party did not replace politics by notables: they formed perfect complements.

In his analysis of the growth of modern party organizations based on the example of England and the United States but ultimately applicable to every democracy,[218] Michael Ostrogorski showed that the establishment of 'democratic', popular party organizations does not necessarily lead to a decline of the 'wire pullers', of the politics of the few. Rather, the establishment of a wide popular party base increases the power of the few occupying the key positions in the party, as it is these who really control the nominations of candidates and the resolution of policies.[219] In the case of the English Liberal Association, the popular ward central meetings generally followed the lead of their managers, and only very rarely did they rebel against the course suggested by their leaders.[220]

The example of the English liberal caucus in the 1870s and 1880s is applicable to Frankfurt only with limitations. As opposed to the much larger franchise and party membership of the English municipal caucuses,[221] in Frankfurt, most meetings were attended by less than 100 people. In such a more intimate atmosphere 'court rebellions' occurred with slightly greater frequency. In 1890, the controversial Progressive leader Berthold Geiger was booted out of the committee in a couple of stormy meetings,[222] and in 1893 several members of the Democratic party complained bitterly against the 'tyranny' of the committee and the autocratic way in which it made its decisions.[223] Yet the fact that these members

---

[217] Roth, 'Liberalismus', 18–25. See also the Democrat leaflet of 1871 in IfSG, MA R 1130.i fo. 136.

[218] Ostrogorski, *Democracy*, vol. i, pp. liii–liv.

[219] 'In the large towns the concentration of power in the hands of a few reaches its extreme limit, in spite of the autonomist doctrine of the Caucus, and exhibits in the most striking way its tendency towards oligarchic government' (ibid. 338). More generally, see 329–70, 580 ff.

[220] H. J. Hanham, *Elections and Party Management* (London, 1959), 128 ff. For a description of the National Liberal Federation's democratic presumptions, see D. A. Hamer, *Liberal Politics in the Age of Gladstone and Roseberry* (Oxford, 1972), 46–52. For a critical summary of these first claims to democratic representation, see P. J. Waller, *Town, City and Nation. England 1850–1914* (2nd edn., Oxford, 1991), 107–14.

[221] A town like Birmingham, for example, had 421,000 inhabitants, of whom 74,167 burgesses had the vote. J. T. Bunce, *History of the Corporation of Birmingham* (Birmingham, 1885), vol. ii, p. xxx.

[222] HStAW 407 n. 150¹ fos. 343–51. Progressive Liberal meeting, 4 Oct. 1890. An example of a National Liberal 'rebellion' is in HStAW 407 n. 160 fos. 126–7. Annual General Meeting of the National Liberal Association, 19 Mar. 1880.

[223] HStAW 407 n. 161¹ fos. 356–60. Annual General Meeting of the Democratic Association, Dec. 1893.

The Advent of Politics

did complain is significant, and reveals that matters were not conducted as openly by the party committee as members may have wished. The fact that these 'rebellions' were relatively infrequent, however, shows that, on the whole, the committees were in good control of their respective parties.

In Frankfurt, the annual general meetings, at which party matters were discussed and a new committee elected, were among the least frequented of the year, with only about 20 to 30 members turning up at the annual general meetings of the Progressives, and around 50 at those of the Democrats.[224] For the annual general meetings of the Democrats, the committee normally prepared a list of 11 candidates for 11 posts, which was usually accepted.[225] Only in 1893 did several members demand to have time to nominate their own list.[226] Yet even after the proceedings had been opened up in 1895, Democratic committee elections were more an exercise of acclamation than of selection. Members still voted on a printed list of nominations which the outgoing committee had prepared, except that this time the committee was obliged to nominate 22 candidates for 11 posts, and to send out the list to all the members of the party at least eight days in advance.[227] The committee also worked out the nominees for the municipal, state, and national elections, who were usually accepted at the meetings.

Far from threatening the positions of notables in the town council the popular liberal party organizations in Frankfurt buttressed their power. This contrasts with the generally held view, perhaps first formulated in Germany by Max Weber, that popular party politics would inevitably overcome *Honoratiorenpolitik*,[228] a process which for local politics began in the late nineteenth century. In Frankfurt, too, until 1900 and beyond the municipal council was still in the hands of the social élite, while a new social group of councillors emerged with the advent of the SPD. However, a closer look at party politics in its various forms suggests a close relationship between the two 'forms' of municipal government, and that they are not necessarily mutually exclusive. In Frankfurt and elsewhere,[229]

---

[224] For example, the Progressive Liberal meeting which discussed the party's nominees for the 1882 council elections was attended by a mere 18 men. HStAW 407 n. 150¹ fos. 125–6. Progressive Association meeting, 20 Nov. 1882.

[225] The list of nominees for 1893/94 is in HStAW 407 n. 161¹ fo. 358.

[226] HStAW 407 n. 161¹ fos. 356–60. Annual General Meeting of the Democratic Association, Dec. 1893.

[227] *Wahlordnung für den Vorstand des Demokratischen Vereins* of 1895, HStAW 407 n. 161² fos. 18–19. *Kleine Presse*, 9 Jan. 1895 (1. Blatt).

[228] D. Beetham, *Max Weber and the Theory of Modern Politics* (2nd edn., Cambridge, 1985), 102–9.

[229] In one of the few studies where this phenomenon is investigated (even though she does not dwell on this further), Ilse Fischer notes for Augsburg that the advent of politics in the city

politics by notables and the popularization of politics were two sides of the same coin.

2.7. Conclusion

The decade before Frankfurt's annexation by Prussia marked an important step in the politicization of the electorate, but it is during the following decade that this potential was fully realized by the city's liberal parties. Local affairs only became dominated by the political contest between liberals and democrats in 1856. These differences became less pronounced amid the political confusion and the general condemnation of the way Frankfurt had been annexed. What emerged was a new, popular democratic movement. Despite the city's rather more conservative and illiberal traditions, Democrats managed to politicize popular anti-Prussian resentment, and present themselves as the 'indigenous' party of Frankfurt. In response, the National Liberals became the party of the new status quo. They became the party to which the Prussian administration gave its support throughout the Empire. As in the annexed province of Hanover, they became the loyalist, '*regierungstreue*' party. This ensured that, in contrast to the days of the Free City, there was no effective independent conservative opposition.[230] As other spheres of politics, local politics became sucked into this process of political differentiation. By the 1870s politics were, beyond any doubt, the main factor in the conduct of virtually all aspects of local affairs.

There is no intrinsic reason why Frankfurt should have been more politicized than many other cities. It is true that Frankfurt's loss of independence and its relegation to a Prussian provincial town was a unique stimulus to the politicization of local affairs. Yet it is not clear whether this agent of politicization was any stronger than those which affected so many other German cities, but which were notably absent in Frankfurt: there

---

council, which she dates to the 1860s, occurred while the council's social composition as a body of local notables remained unchanged. Fischer, *Industrialisierung*, 232. Interestingly, despite the relative absence of political conflict at the local level, in the Hanoverian town of Harburg participation in local élite politics required membership of the National Liberal party. Witt, 'Kommunalpolitik in Harburg', esp. 228–30.

More recently, Karin Schambach has argued for Dortmund that the continuity in the city council's social composition was unaffected by the emergence of political parties in the 1860s. Schambach, *Stadtbürgertum*, 341.

[230] For the best existing summary of Hanoverian politics, see John, 'Liberalism and Society in Germany, 1850–1880', *passim*. Of parallel significance for Frankfurt is also his emphasis on the importance of the local political milieu for the success of liberalism in the province. In Hanover, a similar cleavage developed, between the 'pro-government' camp centred around the National Liberals, on the one hand, and the anti-Prussian, particularist Guelphs, on the other.

were no significant denominational tensions between the Roman Catholic and the Protestant population in the 1860s and 1870s, nor was Frankfurt an early centre of the socialist movement. Given the absence of a particularly radical or democratic tradition before 1848, there is no reason to assume that Frankfurt was unique in the degree of its politicization. Here as in countless other cities such as Leipzig, Berlin, Düsseldorf, Dortmund, Münster, Munich, Augsburg, and Regensburg, not to mention the cities of Baden, Württemberg, and the Rhineland, politics had been established at the local level by the late 1870s.[231] Even in Hamburg, the wealthy self-contained political entity with which Frankfurt is often compared, political differentiation emerged as soon as an elected parliament (*Bürgerschaft*) was established in 1859.[232]

Despite the fact that in Frankfurt politicization occurred owing to territorial change rather than religious conflict, this study confirms Karl Rohe's emphasis on the 1870s as the crucial decade of change. In Frankfurt as in other cities, the 1850s and 1860s were an important period of political change, but it was only the foundation of the Empire which provided a stable and lasting political environment as well as providing a crucial infusion of political awareness.[233] The prevalence of politics in local affairs by the late 1870s is underlined by the interconnectedness between politics at the local, state, and national levels. The nature of politics in Frankfurt was

[231] For a comparison with Leipzig, see *Frankfurter Zeitung*, 19 Nov. 1878 (Morgenblatt). The importance of politics in the municipal affairs of Leipzig is indicated in Retallack, 'Regional Identities and Political Culture', 39. Although H. Pogge von Strandmann agrees with the prevalent view that politics did not play an important role in local government until about 1900, he includes a significant number of exceptions: Berlin, Mannheim, and the Rhenish cities (although he omits Frankfurt). Pogge von Strandmann, 'Monopolies', 102–3. Schambach, *Stadtbürgertum*, 352. Zerback, *München*, 299. Dieter Hein has described the late 1860s and early 1870s as a period of forceful party political formation. D. Hein, 'Badisches Bürgertum. Soziale Struktur und kommunalpolitische Ziele im 19. Jahrhundert', in L. Gall (ed.), *Stadt und Bürgertum im 19. Jahrhundert* (Munich, 1990), 86–7.

[232] F.-M. Wiegand, *Die Notabeln. Untersuchungen zur Geschichte des Wahlrechts und der gewählten Bürgerschaft in Hamburg 1859–1919* (Hamburg, 1987), 99–114. Since this has not been the main line of Wiegand's enquiry, the true extent of the chamber's politicization from the 1860s remains unclear. Still, for the chamber itself he notes the emergence of political debate, the formation of political groups, and the determination of seating arrangements along political lines.

[233] Similarly, in Munich, Prussia's success in 1866, and particularly the introduction of freedom of trade in 1868, sparked off a reformulation of local allegiances and the politicization of local affairs. Zerback, *München*, 285–7, 290–1. By contrast, it appears that in Augsburg denominational tensions were so strong that politics had begun to determine local affairs by the 1860s. Even in this case, however, unification in 1871 changed the political goalposts in fundamental ways. For instance, it heralded the transformation in the nature of the local National Liberal Party from a more popular, 'democratic' party to one that was dominated by the interests of the city's social and industrial élite. Fischer, *Industrialisierung*, 255–60.

shaped by local conditions, which determined not just the nature of politics in local government, but also moulded the way in which state and national politics were received in the city. National, state, and local elections were all contested by the same groups with the same organizations within the context of the same local environment. In Frankfurt as elsewhere, any distinction between 'political' state and national election contests, on the one hand, and local, 'unpolitical' contests, on the other, would inevitably be very difficult to make in practice.[234]

It is crucial to highlight just how complex politics and its reception were at the local level. Politics in local government were about much more than individual decisions by the city council, just as state and national election results were about more than Bismarck's devious plans to manipulate the electorate. Karl Rohe's insistence that people identified with a particular way of life which was common to, and felt to be important by, those embedded in it has its direct equivalent in Frankfurt, where this was defined by a common notion of peculiarity, a common dialect, a common mentality,[235] and common traditions.[236] To be successful, a party had to adapt to this particular political environment, while through time it could also help it to evolve.[237] The success of Frankfurt Democrats was not based on the brief, and in many ways ill-defined, democratic ascendancy from 1857 to 1866. Instead, it was based on the political articulation of a feeling of community and distinction, which, as a result of the events of 1866, could be formulated simply and effectively in anti-Prussian, anti-reactionary terms. Control of the newspaper press allowed the expression of this shared identity and gave rise to a particular form of popular politics at local, state, and national levels in the same way that it gave rise to those who advocated it.

By the same token, it can be highly misleading to speak of a unitary 'liberal milieu', or even of a bourgeois 'camp'.[238] Such a concept may be of

---

[234] A similar point, though without particular reference to urban history or its assumptions, about the interconnectedness between local, state, and national politics at the grass-roots level has been made by Thompson, 'Left Liberals', 10–15. More recently, Thomas Kühne has emphasized the importance of local conditions to liberal success at Prussian state elections. T. Kühne, 'Die Liberalen bei den preußischen Landtagswahlen im Kaiserreich. Wahlmanipulation, Lokalismus und Wahlkompromisse', in L. Gall and D. Langewiesche (eds.), *Liberalismus und Region. Zur Geschichte des deutschen Liberalismus im 19. Jahrhundert* (Munich, 1995), esp. 279–94.

[235] This is nicely illustrated in Bonn, *Wandering Scholar*, esp. 6–9, 28–9.

[236] Rohe, *Wahlen*, 19.   [237] Ibid. 26–8.

[238] This contradicts the view put forward by Ralf Roth, that in Frankfurt there existed a 'liberal milieu' which rendered political parties unnecessary. Roth, *Stadt und Bürgertum*, 529–42. Roth, 'Liberalismus', 30. Despite its many strengths, the loose application of the term

value in areas where liberals were pitted against Social Democrats and/or political Catholicism. In Frankfurt, the concept of a unitary bourgeois camp is belied by the development of a sophisticated political culture marked by contrasting and mutually antagonistic ideals, rival party organizations, and competing groups inside the city council. Democratic leaders and their political organization were crucial in the formation and development of this culture which secured the Democrats' own political advancement at the expense of their rivals further to the right of the liberal political spectrum.[239]

The case of Frankfurt suggests, therefore, that the creation of a national polity galvanized German politics in general, not just at state and national levels, but also at the local level. Quite apart from the importance of the political shifts of 1878 which have been rightly highlighted by historians, the period of the foundation of the Empire was fundamental in the genesis of the imperial political system. Despite the absence of denominational and social conflict in Frankfurt, a party system came into being which dominated the system of local government and the local political environment, and which was impressive, above all, because of its stability and its popularity far beyond the 1870s.

'milieu' is, perhaps, a central weakness in Roth's work. This allows him to speak interchangeably of a 'liberal milieu' and 'liberal milieux', without spending much time defining the term.

[239] The use of the term 'political culture' here in effect agrees with that of Karl Rohe, for whom it defines a particular, though evolving, world-view, a social construction of political reality which is communicated by a particular language ('politische Programmsprache'). K. Rohe, 'Politische Kultur und ihre Analyse. Probleme und Perspektiven der politischen Kulturforschung', *HZ* ccl (1990), 321–46. The importance and development of a 'political culture' at state level is the major concern of Lässig, *Wahlrechtskampf*, here 13–21.

3
The Diversification of Local Politics

3.1. Introduction

Most studies agree that towards the end of the nineteenth century, liberalism was fundamentally weakened by the 'fragmentation of the middle strata'[1] from which liberals derived their greatest support. In response to Germany's industrial progress, and particularly during the 1890s, the German bourgeoisie became more fragmented and amorphous than it had ever been.[2] This fragmentation led to the formation of particular, 'proto-political' interest groups which made increasing demands on the liberals and other parties in return for their endorsement.[3] The fate of German liberalism as of the party system in general was crucially dependent

---

[1] Thus the title of ch. 16 in Sheehan, *German Liberalism*, 239–57.

[2] On the importance of the 1890s as an ideological and cultural watershed for German liberalism, see G. Hübinger, 'Hochindustrialisierung und die Kulturwerte des deutschen Liberalismus', in D. Langewiesche (ed.), *Liberalismus im 19. Jahrhundert. Deutschland im europäischen Vergleich* (Göttingen, 1988), 193–208. For an illuminating case study of the fragmentation of the middle strata in its local setting, see Koshar, *Social Life*, 91–125. By contrast, David Blackbourn has emphasized that, this fragmentation notwithstanding, the last two decades before the Great War represented a 'golden age for the bourgeoisie' (D. Blackbourn, *The Fontana History of Germany 1780–1918. The Long Nineteenth Century* (London, 1997), 363–8).

[3] S. Mielke, *Der Hansa-Bund für Gewerbe, Handel und Industrie 1909–1914. Der gescheiterte Versuch einer antifeudalen Sammlungspolitik* (Göttingen, 1976). On interest groups in general, see the 'classic' *Sonderweg* account in D. Stegmann, *Die Erben Bismarcks. Parteien und Verbände in der Spätphase des Wilhelminischen Deutschlands* (Cologne/Berlin, 1970). By contrast, see G. Eley, *Reshaping the German Right. Radical Nationalism and Political Change after Bismarck* (2nd edn., Ann Arbour, 1991). In turn, for criticism of Eley see Coetzee, *The German Army League*, here 8–11. See also H.-P. Ullmann, *Interessenverbände in Deutschland* (Frankfurt, 1988), esp. 77–123. F. Lenger, *Sozialgeschichte der deutschen Handwerker seit 1800* (Frankfurt, 1988), 154–62. On the growing complexity of politics in the 1890s in Hanover, and the importance of the *Bund der Landwirte* for the National Liberals, see Aschoff, *Welfische Bewegung*, 185–220. See also the summary in V. R. Berghahn, *Imperial Germany, 1891–1914. Economy, Society, Culture and Politics* (Providence/Oxford, 1994), 221–40.

on its ability to respond to the emergence of new, more popular forms of agitation by adequately reforming stifling, old-fashioned party organizations which were still essentially based on notable politics.[4] While there is no doubt about the severity of the problem liberals were faced with, most modern studies agree that liberals in Germany displayed a much greater ability to maintain popular support in the face of social and political change than has previously been assumed.[5] Given the considerable dearth of detailed analyses of liberal organizations and the conduct of liberal politics at the grass roots, the precise extent of the transformation of liberal politics is still unclear. So far, the crucial role that liberals involved in local government must have had in modernizing the party, for example through their unique experience in government and the inventiveness of their ideas, has only been hinted at.[6] This chapter will show for the case of Frankfurt how the local political culture and the liberal party system which had been established by the 1870s reacted to the rising diversification of politics, through the fragmentation of middle-strata politics, which was then followed by the rise of labour.

As indicated by the relevant tables in Appendix II, the composition of the Frankfurt town council shows a remarkable level of stability throughout the 1880s. A major change that did occur was the shift in the alliance of the Progressive Liberal party in 1880. As a result of a row with the National Liberals during the 1879 state elections, the Progressives decided to carry on their cooperation with the Democrats into the 1880 local elections.

[4] H.-J. Puhle, 'Parlament, Parteien und Interessenverbände 1890–1914', in M. Stürmer (ed.), *Das kaiserliche Deutschland. Politik und Gesellschaft 1870-1918* (Düsseldorf, 1970), 340–77. J. Sheehan, 'Deutscher Liberalismus im postliberalen Zeitalter, 1890–1914', *GG* iv (1978), 29–48. T. Nipperdey, *Die Organisation der deutschen Parteien vor 1918* (Düsseldorf, 1961), esp. 393–6. D. Langewiesche, 'Liberalismus und Bürgertum in Europa', in J. Kocka (ed.), *Bürgertum im 19. Jahrhundert. Deutschland im europäischen Vergleich* (Munich, 1988), iii. 384. Koshar, *Social Life*, 48–51. Eley, 'Notable Politics', 187-216. Eley, *Reshaping*, esp. 19–40. See also the brief but excellent survey of B. Fairbairn, 'Political Mobilization', in R. Chickering (ed.), *Imperial Germany. A Historiographical Companion* (Westport, Conn., 1996), 303–42, esp. 320–34.

[5] Langewiesche, *Liberalismus in Deutschland*, 175. G. Hübinger, *Kulturprotestantismus und Politik. Zum Verhältnis von Liberalismus und Protestantismus im wilhelminischen Deutschland* (Tübingen, 1994), esp. 19, 146–9, 225–6. Hübinger, 'Hochindustrialisierung', 193–208. K. H. Pohl, 'Politischer Liberalismus und Wirtschaftsbürgertum: Zum Aufschwung der sächsischen Liberalen vor 1914', in Lässig and Pohl (eds.), *Sachsen im Kaiserreich*, 101–31, here 108. The interest groups' relative lack of effectiveness at popular level, and the (grudging) adaptability of the Wilhelmine party system to mass politics is a central theme in B. Fairbairn, 'The German Elections of 1898 and 1903', D.Phil. thesis (Oxford, 1987). For the liberals' response to the fragmentation of the middle classes, see esp. 173–8.

[6] Nipperdey, *Deutsche Geschichte 1866–1918*, ii. 535–6. Langewiesche, *Liberalismus in Deutschland*, 200–1. Langewiesche, 'German Liberalism', 227–33.

From now on, the two left-liberal parties usually cooperated during the local elections, with the notable exceptions of 1886 and 1892.[7] Throughout the 1880s, the composition of the city council was stable. In 1880, the Democrats lost a number of councillors to their new coalition partners, but on the whole the two left-liberal parties managed to keep their representation in the council roughly constant, as did the National Liberals.

This stability within the town council masks a fundamental shift which occurred outside it. For the 1880s saw a significant change in the way local elections for the town council were contested. Reflecting similar developments in other German cities, *Bezirksvereine* (district associations) began to form which were founded as clubs of citizens who met to discuss the particular concerns of their district. Although some of them had been founded earlier as mainly sociable *Bürgervereine*,[8] these associations increasingly met to discuss strictly local issues (as opposed to the greater issues of politics which were the responsibility of the parties), so that it was not long before they invariably became involved in local politics.

Other parties such as the conservatives and the Centre Party tried their luck in municipal elections, albeit without much success. Where there had been two party slates in 1880,[9] in 1882 there were ten. In 1894, this had not changed significantly: for 19 vacancies, there were 50 nominees suggested by 12 different slates. This diversification of local politics posed a tremendous challenge to the three established political parties. No longer did they merely fight against each other, but in their coalitions they had to take a number of other diverse groups into account. More significantly, this

---

[7] It should be pointed out that this 'partnership' was extremely fragile during the 1880s and the early 1890s, largely owing to the mutual aversion of their respective leaders, Sonnemann and Berthold Geiger. To the Progressives, Sonnemann epitomized the socialist tendencies among the Democrats, whilst Geiger seemed to many the archetypal 'Manchester liberal'. In addition, the two men shared an intense dislike for each other, as numerous personal battles show. The alliance grew more stable only in the course of the 1890s, when the more conciliatory Democrat Heinrich Rößler and Progressive Karl Funck took over from the 'old guard'. As a result, the two parties were very much distinct from the 1870s until the 1890s, and it is a gross oversimplification to 'lump' the two parties together, as Frankfurt's historians generally tend to do. See e.g. W. Klötzer, 'Das Wilhelminische Frankfurt', *AfGK* liii (1973), 164 (table on the city council). Roth, 'Liberalismus', 63–4. Even after 1900, despite increasing cooperation and a growing congruence of ideals, after council meetings Progressives continued to socialize with National Liberals and the *Magistrat* in one bar, while Democrats met in a different establishment. H. Luppe, *Mein Leben* (Nürnberg, 1977), 21.

[8] *Bürgerverein Sachsenhausen, 1848–1929. Festschrift zum 80-jährigen Jubiläum am 29. 9. 1929* (Frankfurt, 1929).

[9] One list of nominees was suggested by the left liberals, and one by the National Liberals and the '*Bürgerkolleg*', a collection of disgruntled Democrats who refused to join the new *Demokratischer Wahlverein* in 1873. On the *Bürgerkolleg*, see (in the absence of any secondary material) *Frankfurter Beobachter*, 18 Nov. 1880.

The Diversification of Local Politics 103

diversification signalled the emergence of 'parish pump politics', which had nothing to do with the 'political' concerns of the established political parties, but which was purely concerned with more 'sectarian' interests of different parts of the local community.

The emergence of the political *Mittelstand* during the 1890s marked a further step in the diversification of municipal politics, because for the first time a conservative political group challenged the liberals' political hegemony inside the town council.[10] Studies have concentrated on an analysis of the disparate elements that made up its various constituent groups, and there is general consent that the *Mittelstand*'s social heterogeneity made it impossible for it to organize itself into a unitary political movement with coherent objectives.[11] Yet in its local political environment, the role of the *Mittelstand* is little known. This is surprising given that the emergence of the petite bourgeoisie was, to a large degree, an urban phenomenon.[12] Also, it is at the grass-roots level that the *Mittelstand* would have the least difficulty in organizing itself. Petty-bourgeois groups were not quite as heterogeneous, simply because there were fewer of them than at the national level. At the local level it would also be much easier for a well-known local figure to unite the various factions of the *Mittelstand* and to create a potent political force. Most importantly, the fair and equal distribution of public contracts to local artisans (the *Submissionswesen*), as well as the termination of municipal and state ownership of competing businesses were of central concern to virtually all factions of the *Mittelstand*.[13] Clearly, these concerns were most relevant where they mattered most, at the local level.[14]

---

[10] For a general introduction, see G. Crossick, 'The Petite Bourgeoisie in Nineteenth-Century Europe: Problems and Research', in K. Tenfelde (ed.), *Arbeiter und Arbeiterbewegung im Vergleich. Berichte zur internationalen Historischen Forschung* (Munich, 1986), 227–77. H.-G. Haupt, 'Kleine und große Bürger in Deutschland und Frankreich am Ende des 19. Jahrhunderts', in J. Kocka (ed.), *Bürgertum im 19. Jahrhundert. Deutschland im europäischen Vergleich* (Munich, 1988), ii. 252–75.

[11] See in particular D. Blackbourn, 'The *Mittelstand* in German Society and Politics, 1871–1914', *SH* iv (1977), 409–33. D. Blackbourn, 'Between Resignation and Volatility: The German Petty Bourgeoisie in the Nineteenth Century', in D. Blackbourn, *Populists and Patricians. Essays in Modern German History* (London, 1987), 84–113. G. Crossick and H.-G. Haupt (eds.), *Shopkeepers and Master Artisans in Nineteenth-Century Europe* (London, 1984). Ullmann, *Interessenverbände*, 94–104. On the various attempts to form a coherent interest group for small shopkeepers, see R. Gellately, *The Politics of Economic Despair, 1890-1914* (London, 1974).

[12] G. Crossick and H.-G. Haupt, *The Petite Bourgeoisie in Europe 1780–1914* (London, 1995), 113.

[13] H. A. Winkler, *Zwischen Marx und Monopolen. Der deutsche Mittelstand vom Kaiserreich zur Bundesrepublik Deutschland* (Frankfurt, 1991), 29.

[14] For one of the few studies on local politics and society which considers the importance of the *Mittelstand*, see Crew, *A Town in the Ruhr*, 112–45.

The rise of the SPD has been much better charted territory than either the phenomenon of the *Bezirksvereine* or the *Mittelstand*. Until recently, there has been little argument with the contention that one of the most crucial failures of liberalism was its inability to cope with the rise of labour, either by way of integration or by transforming itself as an effective alternative to the SPD.[15] Yet in his analysis of elections in imperial Germany, Jonathan Sperber has withdrawn much of the basis for the arguments about the supposed inability of liberals to attract working-class votes. In the light of Sperber's evidence, Gall's argument that in the 1848 Revolution the liberals permanently lost their appeal to labour is clearly difficult to maintain. For during the 1870s and 1880s, the liberals actually registered a net gain of working-class voters. If anything, during these decades it was the Centre Party from 1874, and the conservative parties from 1878, which posed the greatest electoral challenge to the liberals. The liberals did not lose voters to the SPD until the 1890s, while in the 1900s, the liberals' ability to attract working-class voters from the SPD was a crucial element in their recovery at the polls.[16] Indeed, Sperber has turned Gall's argument on its head by showing that, in 1903, the liberals lost heavily among their middle-class constituency, and were saved from an electoral disaster purely because of the extent of their working-class electoral support.[17]

While much of the electoral dynamics for the city of Frankfurt differ substantially from those shown by Sperber for Germany as a whole, this book shares a wider perspective which considers the SPD only as part of a chain of political challenges to the liberals. In Frankfurt, the liberals' dominance in municipal politics was challenged by new, popular political groups already from the 1880s onwards, long before the SPD appeared on the local political scene. During the 1880s and 1890s, the left liberals in particular learned to cope with this new phenomenon flexibly and pragmatically. This experience was crucial to the liberals' ultimately successful response to the rise of labour in municipal politics after 1900, which marked not so much a new beginning, but a final stage in the politicization of local government.

---

[15] In general, see J. Breuilly, *Labour and Liberalism in Nineteenth-Century Europe. Essays in Comparative History* (Manchester, 1992). Langewiesche, *Liberalismus in Deutschland*, 187–93. See also the debate between Mommsen and Gall on the relationship between liberalism and labour: Gall, 'Liberalismus und "Bürgerliche Gesellschaft"', 324–56. Mommsen, 'Der deutsche Liberalismus', 77–90. Gall, '". . . Ich wünschte ein Bürger zu sein"', 601–23. Langewiesche, 'Frühliberalismus und Bürgertum', 122–5.
[16] Sperber, *The Kaiser's Voters*, 124–8 (esp. table 3.3a), 149–51, 281.
[17] Ibid. 238.

3.2. The Fragmentation of Middle-Strata Politics

Of the political parties contesting for power, one of the more surprising features is the extremely modest success of the Centre Party. Even though 30 per cent of Frankfurt's population was Roman Catholic,[18] the Centre managed to send only a few representatives to the town council, and this only with the help of the other groups (see the table in Appendix II). Nor was it much more successful in the national elections, in which the predominantly poorer Roman Catholic population had a fair share of the vote. Unable to nominate a well-known local candidate for the 1907 elections, the Centre Association put up Matthias Erzberger. Erzberger was elected, but in a Württemberg constituency. In Frankfurt, he managed to attract just over 7 per cent of the vote.[19]

The most important underlying reason for the Centre Party's problems is that, as far as this can be measured, Roman Catholicism was very weak in Frankfurt. A study of mixed marriages, which the local Catholic paper described as the root cause for the weakening of the faith,[20] shows that in 1864, there were 1,331 'purely' Roman Catholic to 2,171 mixed Catholic marriages.[21] By contrast, in Germany as a whole, only 5 per cent of marriages were mixed, which indicates that outside Frankfurt confessional delineations were much stronger.[22] The weakness of an endogenous Roman Catholic culture is further demonstrated by the fact that a disproportionate number of mixed marriages were concluded by couples who came from native, rather than immigrant, backgrounds. And of native Roman Catholic and Protestant couples, more than 55 per cent of children were baptized as Protestants.[23] As a result of immigration, by 1880 there were now more

---

[18] On 1 Dec. 1900, 60.9% were Protestant (Lutherans and Calvinists), 30.6% Roman Catholics, 7.6% Jews, and 0.9% Non-conformists and others. F. Adler, 'Soziale Gliederung der Bevölkerung, Verfassung und Verwaltung der Stadt Frankfurt am Main', in Schriften des Vereins für Sozialpolitik, *Verfassung und Verwaltungsorganisation der Städte. Preußen (vol. ii)*, cxvii (Leipzig, 1906), 85–148.

[19] *Volksstimme*, 26 Jan. 1907 (1. Beilage).

[20] *Katholisches Sonntagsblatt für die christliche Familie*, 23 Sept. 1900, Nr. 38, 300–1.

[21] Clearly, mixed marriages are an extremely crude indicator of religious observance, and in the case of Frankfurt it is obvious that a higher proportion of Roman Catholics married a relatively lower proportion of Protestants, simply because there were fewer Catholics than Protestants. Roman Catholic intermarriage, therefore, is not necessarily an indicator of the weakness of Roman Catholic observance, but it may lead to the speculation that Roman Catholic observance was not particularly strong. By contrast, for example, there was virtually no intermarriage between Jews and Gentiles throughout the period.

[22] G. Hübinger, 'Confessionalism', in R. Chickering (ed.), *Imperial Germany. A Historiographical Companion* (Westport, Conn., 1996), 156–77, here 159–60.

[23] *Beiträge zur Statistik der Stadt Frankfurt am Main*, ed. Frankfurter Verein für Geographie und Statistik, ii (Frankfurt, 1864–1875), 45–65.

purely Roman Catholic marriages, but nonetheless over 40 per cent of marriages involving a Roman Catholic were mixed.[24]

Owing to the relative weakness of Roman Catholic practice, a Roman Catholic 'ghetto mentality' did not develop in Frankfurt.[25] This also made it extremely difficult for a separate and sustainable Roman Catholic 'milieu' to develop. In 1848, the first Roman Catholic associations of the area did not develop in Frankfurt, but in the surrounding countryside, for example in the small towns of Limburg and Rüdesheim.[26] There is little evidence of Roman Catholic associational activity available. At the constituent meeting of the Centre Association in 1892, none of the 100 or so participants even knew whether there was a delegate of the *Volksverein für das katholische Deutschland* in Frankfurt or not.[27] The inconspicuousness of Roman Catholicism's fastest-growing and most important popular organization in Frankfurt is indicative both of the absence of a Roman Catholic culture, and of the problems faced by the new Centre Association. Despite individual efforts at creating a distinctive milieu, a self-conscious Roman Catholic culture remained relatively undeveloped before the Great War.[28] By 1911, Roman Catholic trade unions still accounted for less than 4 per cent of total trade union membership.[29]

At the same time, it is not the case that Roman Catholics were truly integrated into the Democrat political culture as it developed after 1866. This is largely because of the ongoing debates about non-denominational schooling, an issue that became a Democrat and liberal article of faith after 1866, and which led to a series of disputes between the local Roman

---

[24] *Beiträge zur Statistik der Stadt Frankfurt am Main*, ed. Frankfurter Verein für Geographie und Statistik, iv (Frankfurt, 1882–1885), 19–40, esp. 27.

[25] This conclusion is opposed by the Roman Catholic histories of the period. K. Greef (ed.), *Das Katholische Frankfurt—Einst und Jetzt* (Frankfurt, 1989), 63–4. K. Schatz, *Geschichte des Bistums Limburg* (Mainz, 1983), 216. Schatz appears to contradict himself, however, by noting the absence of a Catholic spirit of unity at all costs, while mentioning the existence of a Catholic ghetto mentality ('Ghetto-Geist') in the same paragraph. Schatz, op. cit., 245.

[26] Ibid. 216.

[27] *Kleine Presse*, 9 Apr. 1892. *Volksstimme*, 10 Apr. 1892. Both are in HStAW 407 n. 187 fo. 422. On the *Volksverein*, see H. Heitzer, *Der Volksverein für das katholische Deutschland im Kaiserreich 1890–1918* (Mainz, 1979). On Roman Catholic Associational life in general, see Winfrid Halder, *Katholische Vereine in Baden und Württemberg 1848–1914. Ein Beitrag zur Organisationsgeschichte des südwestdeutschen Katholizismus im Rahmen der Entstehung der modernen Industriegesellschaft* (Paderborn/Munich/Vienna/ Zurich, 1995).

[28] H. Blankenberg, *Politischer Katholizismus in Frankfurt am Main, 1918–1933* (Mainz, 1981), 7–12. Schatz, *Geschichte*, 245.

[29] *Statistische Jahresübersichten der Stadt Frankfurt am Main 1911/12*, ed. Statistisches Amt (Frankfurt, 1912), 82–3.

Catholic clergy and the city council throughout the period under investigation.[30] Another important indicator of Roman Catholic involvement in liberal and Democrat politics is the fact that, throughout the period, liberals and Democrats had tremendous difficulty in finding suitable Roman Catholic candidates. In 1874, for instance, there was but one Roman Catholic in the city council, which induced the Democrats to ensure that in that year's council by-elections a Roman Catholic was among their nominees.[31] During the 1880s it remained relatively difficult for a Roman Catholic to be elected to the city council. In 1886 the Democrats failed to get their one Roman Catholic candidate elected, largely, they claimed, because of his denomination.[32] Roman Catholic Democrats, even if they did enter the city council, were little more than showpieces to demonstrate a Democrat commitment to fair rights for Roman Catholics, precisely because there were so few of them around.[33]

The main reason why, during the 1870s and beyond, Roman Catholics continued to support the Democrats was their mutual hostility to the *Kulturkampf*. The *Frankfurter Zeitung* was, perhaps, the most important liberal newspaper which spoke out for Roman Catholics during that period.[34] The essential reason for Roman Catholic support, therefore, was less a positive identification with the prevalent democratic political culture, than their view of the Democrats as the lesser evil of the available political choices given the absence of a strong Catholic identity, and a consequent political organization. In 1892, the local branch of the Centre Party, the Centre Association, was refounded with the explicit aim of providing a political alternative to the 50,000 Roman Catholics in Frankfurt.[35] Even though most of these were Roman Catholic only in name (*Taufscheinkatholiken*), the Association warned the Democrats not to take the Roman Catholics' support for granted, particularly given the Democrats' hostility towards Roman Catholic primary schools. From the start, the Centre

[30] For a more detailed explanation of these disputes and the role of religion in education, see Ch. 4.

[31] *Frankfurter Zeitung*, 15 Jan. 1874 (1. Blatt).

[32] The Democrats made a particular issue out of the candidate's denomination, and consequently blamed anti-Catholic feeling among the electorate for his failure to get elected. *Frankfurter Zeitung*, 2 Dec. 1886 (2. Morgenblatt). *Frankfurter Zeitung*, 3 Dec. 1886 (2. Morgenblatt).

[33] Note, for example, the exclamation by the otherwise colourless councillor Goll at a 1906 election rally, that he supported the Democrats 'precisely because he was a Catholic'. *Frankfurter Zeitung*, 11 Dec. 1906 (3. Morgenblatt).

[34] A. Kullmann, 'Die Stellungnahme der *Frankfurter Zeitung* zum Kulturkampf', D.Phil. thesis (Würzburg, 1922).

[35] For reports about the constitutent meeting of the Centre Association, see *Kleine Presse*, 9 Apr. 1892. *Volksstimme*, 10 Apr. 1892. Both are in HStAW 407 n. 187 fo. 422.

Association suffered from the lack of support of the Roman Catholic social élites, which also deprived it of important funds. It is nevertheless significant that there was a will to create such a consciousness, despite the difficulties. Similar problems were encountered by the establishment of a Roman Catholic newspaper. After a number of bankruptcies during the 1870s and 1880s due to the lack of subscribers, it was not until 1892 that a financially viable Roman Catholic newspaper began to emerge gradually.[36]

The local Centre Association did develop into a coherent political force, though its popular support was limited to between 5 and 10 per cent of the vote. Still, whereas originally these Roman Catholics would have supported the Democrats at least in the run-off elections, after 1900 Centre Party support for Democrats could no longer be taken for granted. The Democrats realized that they had used up their political capital with the Roman Catholic vote by 1912 at the latest, when the withdrawal of Centre support in the run-off elections to the Reichstag seat was crucial in ensuring the defeat of the Democrat Rudolf Oeser against the SPD candidate, Max Quarck.[37]

Thus, it is not quite true to say that throughout the period of the Empire Roman Catholics remained committed to the prevalent liberal political culture in the city.[38] The Centre Party in Frankfurt never did manage to attract the support of the '*Taufscheinkatholiken*'. However, this was not the result of the Democrats' integrative efforts, but of the weakness of Roman Catholic practice. Nevertheless, the establishment of Roman Catholic clubs and a newspaper, the formation of the local Centre Association, and its increasingly self-confident emancipation from the tutelage of the Democrats shows that even in Frankfurt, which had been mostly unaffected by the *Kulturkampf*, the Democrats had effectively lost the committed Roman Catholic vote by 1914.[39]

If there was a group with a self-conscious siege mentality in Frankfurt, it was surely the conservatives.[40] In the early 1880s, the Conservative

---

[36] H. Heil, *Zur Entwickelung der katholischen Presse in Frankfurt am Main. Ein Beitrag zur Geschichte der 'Frankfurter Volkszeitung' anläßlich ihres 50jährigen Jubliläums am 1. Oktober 1921* (Frankfurt, 1921). This book can be found in IfSG MA T 63.i.

[37] In fact, the *Frankfurter Zeitung* proved that many Centre Party supporters voted for the SPD. *Frankfurter Zeitung*, 24 Jan. 1912 (Abendblatt).

[38] Roth, 'Liberalismus', 74–8.

[39] The loss of Roman Catholic support for the Democrats' sister party in Württemberg, the People's Party, is a central theme in Blackbourn, *Class, Religion, and Local Politics*, esp. 74–6. Interestingly, Blackbourn found that Roman Catholic support for the People's Party in Württemberg similarly ebbed away only after the *Kulturkampf*.

[40] The Conservatives' failures to organize more generally at the national level are described

Association for Frankfurt and its environs had a quite respectable membership of about 200 members who were mainly public employees (teachers, civil servants) and artisans.[41] Its meetings were usually attended by around 50 people, though attendances could be as high as 300, and one meeting was even attended by as many as 550 people.[42] Nonetheless, Frankfurt's conservatives generally resigned themselves to political impotence. When in 1895 a meeting discussed sending a motion to party headquarters in Berlin to defend the Frankfurt Lutheran pastor Friedrich Naumann against recent conservative attacks, the leader of the Frankfurt Conservative Association, Diehl, argued that this was pointless. To Conservative leaders in Berlin, he pointed out, Frankfurt was a 'Social Democratic, a Democratic, a Sonnemannistic' city so that they would continue to ignore them whatever they did.[43] For the local elections of 1882, the Conservatives endorsed four candidates in connection with the National Liberal Association as well as some ultramontane groups.[44] Curiously, the Conservative Association decided to keep this endorsement as secret as possible, away from the public eye. And henceforth, all election meetings would no longer be announced in public.[45] Clearly, the Conservative Association feared that as soon as its name would be connected to any candidate, that candidate no longer stood a chance of winning.

In 1882, one of the leading Conservatives, von Seydewitz, admitted that in the current political climate the Association led a rather moderate existence. He suggested three areas for improvement. The Association needed more members, and it needed more money, at the very least enough to pay for existing debts. But what was also wanted was courage, the courage to

in J. Retallack, *Notables of the Right. The Conservative Party and Political Mobilization in Germany, 1876–1918* (Boston, 1988), esp. 23–8.

[41] See the membership lists in HStAW 407 n. 159¹ fos. 10–12, 54, 112–14. By 1887, membership went down to 175, and on 1 Dec. 1893 the Conservative Association counted 98 Members. HStAW 407 n. 159¹ fos. 121–4, 149–50.

[42] It is questionable, however, whether these figures as recorded by the Prussian police observer present are reliable, as he would be likely to report on the meeting in a particularly favourable way. At the meeting on 'Socialism, Social Democracy and Social Policy', which was ostensibly attended by an audience of 550, the bias of the attending police officer was revealed by the unlikely observation that, in contrast to some Democratic listeners, the Social Democratic leaders present at the meetings seemed to be favourably impressed by the content of the lecture. HStAW 407 n. 159¹ fos. 65–6. Conservative Association meeting, 31 Dec. 1883.

[43] HStAW 407 n. 159¹ fo. 166. Conservative Association meeting, 27 Nov. 1895.

[44] In Württemberg, the conservatives were similarly reduced to supporting the local equivalent of the National Liberal Party, which, like in Frankfurt, acted as the main viable pro-Bismarckian alternative to the local equivalent of the Democrats, the People's Party. Retallack, *Notables of the Right*, 66.

[45] HStAW 407 n. 159¹ fos. 28–9. Conservative Association meeting, 29 Sept. 1882.

speak out openly to spread the Association's message.[46] The advice went largely unheeded, and for years the Association's aim was the cultivation of the convictions of its own members, rather than spreading the Conservative message to the public.[47]

Influenced by the number of artisans as well as the number of pastors, who often occupied leading positions in the party, the Association had strong sympathies with the plight of the *Mittelstand* and for the underprivileged, calling upon the state to protect both.[48] But the Conservative Association was also anti-Semitic.[49] This was one of the main issues which caused a split in the party around 1895/6, as those with stronger views on the social question and who rebelled against the Conservatives' anti-Semitism followed Friedrich Naumann into the 'younger branch' of the Christian Social Association which soon became the National Social Association.[50]

The development of the National Social Association in Frankfurt as well as Friedrich Naumann's political work in Frankfurt has already been illustrated by Siegbert Wolf in his study of Frankfurt liberalism, so that there is no need to describe the details here.[51] Frankfurt occupied an important place in the history of the National Social Party, not just because it hosted one of its largest local branches. It was the financial support of several rich liberal philanthropists (and Charles Hallgarten in particular), whom Naumann had met during his time in Frankfurt, which made possible Naumann's career in national politics in the first place.[52]

Despite Naumann's tireless efforts, the National Social Association faced the same problems in Frankfurt as elsewhere: trying desperately to bridge the working and the middle classes, it failed to overcome suspicions on both sides, and particularly on the side of the workers. No matter how

---

[46] HStAW 407 n. 159¹ fo. 33. Conservative Association meeting, 1882.
[47] *Wiesbadener Presse*, 2 Dec. 1895. The article is also in HStAW 407 n. 159¹ fo. 161.
[48] HStAW 407 n. 159¹ fo. 37. Conservative Association meeting, 1882.
[49] HStAW 407 n. 159¹ fos. 141–2. Conservative Association meeting, 1 Dec. 1891.
[50] HStAW 407 n. 159¹ fos. 161–3. Meetings of the National Social Association, Nov. and Dec. 1895. For the first membership list of the 'Verein Christlich-Sozialer älterer Richtung für Frankfurt a. Main und Umgegend', as well as reports of its meetings, see HStAW 407 n. 159¹ fos. 184–200. For the first membership list of the 'younger' Frankfurt National Social association, see HStAW 407 n. 159¹ fos. 210–12. On the split in general, see Retallack, *Notables of the Right*, 113–27.
[51] Wolf, *Liberalismus*, 73–81. On Naumann's social and pastoral work in Frankfurt, see M. Benad (ed.), *Gott in Frankfurt? Theologische Spuren in einer Metropole* (Frankfurt, 1987), 95–106.
[52] See Naumann's correspondence with Hallgarten, BAP 90 Na 3 n. 147 fos. 13–16, 20–1, 30. Naumann to Hallgarten, 1902–7.

much Naumann attempted to penetrate the working classes, his efforts remained sponsored by a relatively small group of the middle and upper classes in Frankfurt. Politically, the Association remained insignificant. In local politics, the best it could do was to endorse those candidates whose programmes it could agree with most.[53] National Social candidates usually had no option but to endorse the left-liberal candidates while trying to influence them as much as possible through their support. In Reichstag elections, the National Social Association put forward a candidate of its own only once (Friedrich Naumann in 1898), but since he received only 3,295 votes on that occasion the Association never tried again.[54]

In the absence of any serious challenges from other parties which competed with the liberals for votes at a state and national level, it was the *Bezirksvereine* and their encroachment into municipal politics which became a major concern for the liberals. These ward associations organized social events, days out for their members and their families, as well as discussion evenings, when a speaker would talk about the district's particular concerns. In the city centre (*Altstadt*), for example, these would be issues such as the relocation of businesses from the district westwards towards the station, or how to protect the inner city from the frequent floods of the river Main.[55] Matters discussed were often much more mundane, such as the number of postboxes needed in the district.[56]

This was precisely the kind of parochialism that the liberals, and the Democrats in particular, had tried so hard to avoid during the 1870s. Their party programmes had always emphasized general political issues. Councillors should be elected for their political competence, and the more administrative matters would be dealt with efficiently almost as an encore. Nevertheless, the liberals had to take note of the associations, which displayed an extraordinary success in mobilizing the citizens to their cause. Membership figures are scarce (as voluntary associations they did not have to record their membership or their meetings with the police), but a lecture and discussion on the cleaning and widening of streets organized by the *Bezirksverein Alt-Frankfurt* (inner city district association) drew a crowd of 300 people.[57] The association, which was undoubtedly one of the most

---

[53] HStAW 407 n. 159² fo. 270. National Social Association meeting, 22 Nov. 1901.
[54] Wolf, *Liberalismus*, 80.
[55] See e.g. *Frankfurter Nachrichten*, 24 Nov. 1888 (p. 5430), and 2 Dec. 1888 (pp. 5549–51).
[56] *Frankfurter Zeitung*, 13 Nov. 1890 (2. Morgenblatt).
[57] *Frankfurter Zeitung*, 9 Nov. 1888 (1. Morgenblatt).

active and well organized, increased its membership in 1890 from 382 to 400.[58] This represents 14 per cent of the total electorate of the area it claimed to represent (the third and fourth electoral districts), and 37 per cent of those who actually went to the polls in the 1890 local elections![59] In other words, these ward associations were really quite formidable rival mechanisms to the liberals' own party organizations, particularly when they discovered that participation in the municipal elections and the nomination of candidates was extremely popular among their members. In the year in which it first decided to nominate candidates in 1902 the '*West- und Nordwestlicher Bezirksverein*' saw an increase in membership from 270 to 378 members.[60] Only on very few occasions did these associations manage to get a candidate elected on their own, but contemporaries felt that some of them could very easily swing the balance in the elections. This gave the district associations added bargaining power on the occasions when they lobbied the city council.[61]

There was some sense of uncertainty amongst the liberals as to how to respond to the challenge of the *Bezirksvereine*. In a Progressive Liberal meeting in 1880, it was argued that the new associations were imports from Berlin and hence completely unsuited to the local conditions of Frankfurt. Against this, however, the traditional argument was used that it was only fair that these associations meddled in local affairs, since the Progressive Liberals had always held that municipal elections were not about politics.[62] There were two ways in which the liberals could respond to the challenge. They could change their rhetoric, or they could try to influence and use the associations for their own ends. In the end, they chose to do both.

From the start, Democrats had established the principle that candidates should not be obliged to reside in the districts they represented. This underlined the notion that candidates represented not their particular districts, but all citizens.[63] In practice, this made it much easier for them to shuffle their candidates between the various districts and to place them in the most strategic way. This principle was first modified in 1880. During a

---

[58] *Frankfurter Nachrichten*, 23 Nov. 1890. On the association, see Bezirksverein Alt-Frankfurt, *Jubiläumsfeiern des 25 jährigen Bestehens 1882–1907* (Frankfurt, 1907).

[59] The numbers for the electorate and electoral participation have been taken from Wolf, *Liberalismus*, 130–1.

[60] *Frankfurter Zeitung*, 8 Nov. 1902.

[61] For instance, Sonnemann attributed the council's eagerness to approve street clearances to the influence of the *Bezirksvereine*. HStAW 407 n. 161^2 fo. 13. Democratic Association meeting, 22 Nov. 1894.

[62] HStAW 407 n. 150^1 fos. 42–3. Progressive Association meeting, 21 Mar. 1880.

[63] *Frankfurter Zeitung* 30 June 1867 (1. Blatt).

Democratic-Progressive election rally in 1880, Victor Cnyrim again protested against the growing tendency towards a '*Rapunzelgäßchenpolitik*', where particular interests took precedence over the whole. It would be completely ridiculous if the associations nominated candidates themselves for their own trifling concerns. But he also conceded that it was the responsibility of the councillors to inform the administration of the respective concerns of their districts.[64] In 1882, the u-turn was complete. Jean Drill confirmed against the claims of the district associations that of course any councillor would, unless it negatively affected the community as a whole, represent the interests of his electoral district.[65]

Even more significant was the shift in rhetoric as a whole. A trend that began in 1880 established itself in 1882, when even the smallest details of municipal administration were included in the political speeches held at Democratic and Progressive Liberal rallies. In 1882 Drill commended the candidates of his party for dealing with issues such as new roads, street widenings, and street lighting. The National Liberals, by contrast, had all voted against such measures.[66] The 'Kirchturmspolitik', against which the Democrats had rallied time and again and which in theory they still opposed,[67] had become politicized by the Democrats themselves. From 1886 onwards, these concerns became an integral part of the Democrat election manifesto.

At the same time, the associations, whose very essence had been their unpolitical nature as opposed to the political parties, soon became politicized themselves. In 1886, Sonnemann accused the *Ostendverein* of being mere electoral agents for his opponents, the Progressive and National Liberals.[68] At a meeting of the *Nordendverein*, the nominations had become a straight contest between the National Liberal and the left-liberal candidates by the 1890s.[69] The most interesting association in this respect is the *Bezirksverein Alt-Frankfurt*, which claimed to represent the third and fourth electoral districts—the former being the Democrats' stronghold, the latter that of the National Liberals. For most of the time, the Democrats managed to control it, as one of the most prominent Democrats, Jean Drill,

---

[64] *Frankfurter Zeitung*, 22 Nov. 1880 (Morgenblatt).
[65] *Frankfurter Zeitung*, 21 Nov. 1882 (Abendblatt).
[66] *Frankfurter Zeitung*, 27 Nov. 1882 (2. Morgenblatt).
[67] *Frankfurter Zeitung*, 14 Nov. 1882 (Abendblatt). HStAW 407 n. 138^2 fo. 76. Democratic Association meeting, 16 Nov. 1882. *Frankfurter Zeitung*, 26 Nov. 1888 (Abendblatt).
[68] *Frankfurter Zeitung*, 25 Nov. 1886 (2. Morgenblatt).
[69] *Frankfurter Zeitung*, 17 Nov. 1894 (Abendblatt). *Frankfurter Zeitung*, 15 Nov. 1898 (Abendblatt).

was its active president. At times, however, the Democrats could be caught out. In 1898, for example, the National Liberals and the artisans had rallied their members to the annual general meeting, at which they succeeded in having their own candidates nominated.[70]

The *Bezirksvereine* were not just a necessary evil that had to be dealt with, though. Indeed, some liberals were not blind to the opportunities these associations presented. The Progressive Liberals, for example, had tried for some time to create a better organization, akin to the SPD or even the Democrats. At one stage it was planned to divide the city into 48 districts, for each of which one Progressive Liberal party member would take responsibility.[71] Ultimately this and other schemes failed, because not enough people could be found to operate the changes. As a consequence, it was suggested in 1895 that Progressive Liberal *Bezirksvereine* should be founded, but Fritz Meyer pointed out that although this was a good idea in theory, the Progressives were too weak and the existing district associations too strong. Hence it would be best if one sought to influence the associations from within, in the absence of an effective party organization.[72] As shown above, seven years later, Meyer had succeeded. As president of the *West- und Nordwestlicher Bezirksverein* he had successfully pushed his association to nominate candidates for the first time in its history. Thus, through the nominations he was able to give his ally, the Democrat Heinrich Rößler, an added boost when the latter was under strong attack from the National Liberals during the election campaign.[73]

During the 1880s, therefore, the liberals reacted to the diversification of local politics, and particularly the challenge of the emerging district associations, with suitable flexibility by appropriating the language of the associations and politicizing them, as well as their concerns. Even though politics inside the council carried on very much as before, they had changed dramatically outside as councillors were now increasingly responsible to these associations and their constituents. Councillors were for the first time not only challenged for their political opinions, as had already happened before, but now they were increasingly scrutinized for every vote they took in the council. Liberal *Honoratioren* ceased to be amongst themselves,

[70] *Frankfurter Zeitung*, 12 Nov. 1898 (Abendblatt).
[71] HStAW 407 n. 150^1 fos. 392–3. Progressive Association meeting, 26 Oct. 1891.
[72] HStAW 407 n. 150^2 fos. 16–19. Annual General Meeting of the Progressive Association, 27 Feb. 1895.
[73] *Frankfurter Zeitung*, 8 Nov. 1902. In March 1901 Simon Rosenthal asked his fellow members of the Progressive Party to become involved in the Bornheimer *Bezirksverein*, so that they might eventually gain some influence in its nominations. HStAW 407 n. 150^2 fo. 206. Progressive Association meeting, 13 Mar. 1901.

'*unter sich*',⁷⁴ as even the tiniest details of local government slowly but perceptibly ceased to be left to the good judgement of the individual notable who became more and more accountable to increasingly diverse interest groups.

During the 1890s, disparate groups which can loosely be described as the *Mittelstand* became more powerful and influential in urban life. In Frankfurt as elsewhere, these groups had little more in common than a dislike of the municipal regime. In 1880, several hundred artisans had formed a *Verein zum Schutze der Handwerke* (Association for the Protection of Crafts) to protect their interests.⁷⁵ From 1882, they participated as a separate group in the council elections, but during the 1880s their success was relatively modest. The Democrats tried to accommodate this emerging group, but ultimately the differences were too great, since the Democrats were in principle opposed to the artisans' and craftsmen's main demands for the reintroduction of guilds (*Innungen*) and restrictive trading laws.⁷⁶ During the 1890s, another, more formidable group emerged as a distinct political entity, that of the *Hausbesitzer*.⁷⁷

According to the Prussian city ordinance, at least half of all city councillors were required to be house owners, which was designed as another safeguard to ensure that property would dominate local government. Not only was this an added barrier to parties such as the SPD, which had tremendous difficulties in having enough house owners among their candidates for the city council. It also meant that the house owners were by far the most powerful interest group in local politics.⁷⁸ This acquired particular importance throughout Germany from the 1890s, when the increasing priority given to the provision of adequate housing conditions precipitated direct local government interference in the housing market.⁷⁹

---

⁷⁴ Note that for Germany in general Sheehan observed this phenomenon for the first decade of the 20th century. Sheehan, 'Liberalism', 129.
⁷⁵ HStAW 405 n. 1072 fo. 65. *Zeitungsbericht*, 10 Mar. 1881.
⁷⁶ HStAW 407 n. 138³ fo. 126. Democratic Association meeting, 13 Oct. 1884.
⁷⁷ This growth in organized *Mittelstand* groups reflected a national trend. Stegmann, *Die Erben Bismarcks*, 40–6.
⁷⁸ House owners were particularly vociferous because many of them lived off their tenants' rents, which made them particularly vulnerable to potential levies or taxes imposed by the town council.
⁷⁹ Hofmann, 'Aufgaben', 597. S. Fisch, 'Die zweifache Intervention der Städte. Stadtplanerische Zukunftsgesteltung und Kontrolle der Wohnverhältnisse um 1900', in J. Reulecke and A. Gräfin zu Castell Rüdenhausen (eds.), *Staat und Gesundheit. Zum Wandel von 'Volksgesundheit' und kommunaler Gesundheitspolitik im 19. und frühen 20. Jahrhundert* (Stuttgart, 1991), 91–104. The potential power of the *Hausbesitzer* and their *Vereine* have been

In 1905, one-quarter of Frankfurt councillors lived in their own houses, while another half of them rented out accommodation. Even though many of them remained faithful to their party in support for Adickes's far-reaching *Bodenpolitik*, which was supported in the main by the three liberal parties, the influence of house owners as an independent interest group was far from negligible.[80] In 1894, for example, the house owners managed to transform a levy for connection to the drainage system (*Kanalsteuer*) from 1 per cent of the rent levied on the owners to 2 per cent levied on the occupiers.[81] House-owners and artisans' associations were complemented in 1894 by the *Steuerwehr*, which a year later developed into the *Kommunalverein* and which in part drew its strength from house owners' support.[82] Opposed to any increase in local taxation, it sought to exploit the resentment against the new tax increases of the 1890s particularly among the *Mittelstand*.[83]

In a decade that saw substantial shifts in the nature of local taxation as a result of Miquel's tax reform of 1893, fiscal questions naturally went to the top of the political agenda. This put the liberals as the parties responsible for over two decades of city government in considerable difficulty. In the absence of any sizeable conservative or Centre party, which elsewhere in Germany were the main political allies of the emerging *Mittelstand*,[84] the National Liberals managed to make the most of the situation, as a summary of the local election results in Appendix II shows. During the 1890s, they managed to increase their total number of seats considerably and thus took full advantage of the enlargement of the council, whereas the strength of the other two liberal parties remained roughly static. To the great irritation of the two left-liberal parties, the National Liberals placed themselves as the minority party against the left-liberal coalition in the council, and hence as the party not responsible for tax increases and other policies of the city

---

strikingly described by R. J. Evans, *Death in Hamburg: Society and Politics in the Cholera Years, 1830–1910* (Harmondsworth, 1987).

[80] Adler, 'Gliederung', 115. Adler's point that a particular *Hausbesitzer* interest was negligible in the Frankfurt city council is particularly odd considering that this was written at a time when the representation of the *Verein für kommunale Wahlen* peaked to make it the second largest party in the council.

[81] The *Kleine Presse* lamented that, in this instance, the council had shown itself to be truly a parliament of house owners. *Kleine Presse*, 18 Dec. 1894 (2. Blatt). See also *Kleine Presse*, 19 Dec. 1894 (2. Blatt).

[82] In opposition to the *Kommunalverein*, the *Mietherverein* had been founded. HStAW 407 n. 150² fo. 19. Annual General Meeting of the Progressive Association, 27 Feb. 1895.

[83] On the importance of the issue of taxation for the political mobilization of the petite bourgeoisie throughout Europe, see Crossick and Haupt, *The Petite Bourgeoisie*, 131–2.

[84] Lenger, *Sozialgeschichte der deutschen Handwerker*, 156.

government.⁸⁵ They underlined this with their willingness to form coalitions with any or all of the *Mittelstand* groups particularly in the run-off elections. Thus, National Liberal strength became inflated during the 1890s until, in 1898, for the first time the National Liberals were level with the Democrats inside the city council with 23 seats each, a far cry from the relative strength of the two parties a couple of decades earlier.

Interestingly, this ascendancy of the Frankfurt National Liberals was mirrored in state and national politics.⁸⁶ In the 1887 national elections, the Democrats were, for the first time, eclipsed by the National Liberals, whose candidate, Albert Metzler, proceeded into the run-off elections with the SPD candidate, Adolf Sabor. In the case of this particular 'Kartell' election, the results were probably entirely due to national factors. Indeed, National Liberals in Frankfurt did their best to exploit the local popularity of perhaps the principal architect of the Kartell, mayor Miquel, for their own purposes.⁸⁷ Against this background, local concerns had an unusually low profile, while the Democrats had considerable difficulty in attacking Miquel for fear of offending the person they worked with so well in local matters.⁸⁸ In these elections, *Mittelstand* concerns were already a factor in the rhetoric of the liberal candidates, but the artisans officially abstained and were thus not a decisive factor.⁸⁹ Against this background, the Frankfurt Democrats lost votes, though less dramatically so than the German People's Party nationwide.

What is striking is that in the subsequent elections the Democrats' vote in the first round of the national elections stagnated. As opposed to the German People's Party nationwide, the Democrats performed dismally in 1890 and 1893, while it is impossible to say how they would have done in 1898, when all the liberal parties supported a common candidate, the Progressive Heinrich Flinsch. Despite a more than twofold increase in the size of the electorate in Frankfurt, in 1903 the Democrats polled fewer votes

---

⁸⁵ *Kleine Presse*, 15 Nov. 1896 (1. Blatt).

⁸⁶ See the summary of the results in Appendix II.

⁸⁷ 'Zur Frankfurter Wahlbewegung'. *Kleine Presse*, 6 Feb. 1887. On the elections in general, see Sheehan, *German Liberalism*, 202–3. The National Liberals, for example, reprinted ad nauseam Miquel's Neustadt speech in which he had rallied the National Liberals round the supposed defence of the fatherland.

⁸⁸ See the report on Miquel's Neustadt speech in *Kleine Presse*, 1 Feb. 1887. Note the report on the *Volkszeitung*'s comments, in which the stronger words used by the Berlin newspaper were exchanged with less controversial language. *Kleine Presse*, 3 Feb. 1887.

⁸⁹ See Sonnemann's speech in *Kleine Presse*, 16 Feb. 1887. However, in the run-off elections against the SPD the artisans officially supported the National Liberal candidate, in contrast to the Democrats, who gave their support to the SPD. See Fester's speech at the Wahlverein. *Kleine Presse*, 26 Feb. 1887.

in the first round of the elections than in 1881. By contrast, while the National Liberals could never repeat their performance of 1887, they nonetheless managed to remain (marginally) the biggest liberal party in the Reichstag elections during the 1890s. For the support which the National Liberals received at local level also translated into *Mittelstand* support for elections at national and state levels. It is this support which also enabled the National Liberals to command both seats in the Prussian Chamber of Deputies from 1888 to 1898, with the exception of a single by-election in 1892 won by the Progressive Karl Funck, who subsequently represented the city for a year. And, when the National Liberals did lose the elections to the *Landtag* in 1898, this was largely because the left-liberal Progressive/Democratic alliance was actively supported for the first and only time by the SPD.

The National Liberals benefited from the *Mittelstand* support for as long as the latter was divided, allowing the National Liberals simply to impose their own candidates on the *Mittelstand* as the lesser evil of the established parties. This pattern was challenged once the *Mittelstand* had grown so much as to enable their representatives to contest the local elections in their own right. Two issues were at the root of this development.[90] The local authorities appeared to take too little notice of *Hausbesitzer* and other *Mittelstand* concerns. Rather, under Adickes they were stepping up their regulation of the housing market, but despite these efforts rents increased dramatically so that many on both sides, property owners and tenants, were disappointed.[91] Added to these concerns was the liberals' intransigence over the principle of non-denominational education; and even though National Liberals liked to play down their commitment to the issue, they, too, were firmly committed to the ideal. The dispute between Roman Catholic and Protestant supporters of religious primary schools (*Konfessionsschulen*) and the liberal city government had escalated since the Prussian school reforms of the mid-1890s, and culminated in 1904/5 when the Prussian diet tried to intervene against the Frankfurt liberals' education policies.[92] The issue of denominational schooling mobilized important support for the *Mittelstand* through the allied Protestant *Freie evangelische*

---

[90] This was recognized, for example, by the Progressive Liberal F. Meyer. *Frankfurter Zeitung*, 23 Nov. 1898 (3. Morgenblatt).

[91] On the problems in the housing market, see e.g. *MAB*, 1899, pp. xii–xxiv. This gives also a good indication of the importance the *Magistrat* attached to the problem, as it devoted more than half of its general introductory report to the issue.

[92] For a brief introduction to the issue, see K. Schäfer, *Schulen und Schulpolitik in Frankfurt am Main 1900-1945* (Frankfurt, 1994), 76–83. The subject will be dealt with in more detail in the following chapter.

Volksvereinigung and the Roman Catholic *Wahlkomitee Frankfurter Katholiken*, and the 1904 elections were fought almost as a plebiscite on the issue.[93] In this way, the *Mittelstand* coalition came to include a sufficient number of different interest groups to enable it to compete successfully in the local elections.

After taking advantage of the *Mittelstand* in the 1890s, the National Liberals were rapidly marginalized after 1898. In 1903 the National Liberals were unable to prevent the coalition of Democrats and Progressives from winning the state elections. In the national elections of that year, for the first time since 1884 the Democrats managed to overtake the National Liberals to reach the run-off elections against the SPD. As can be seen from the relevant table in Appendix II, this was caused less by their own sterling performance, than by the National Liberal loss of about 2,000 votes to the anti-Semites. Led by the agitator Hermann Laaß, the *Mittelstand* attracted just 500 fewer votes than the National Liberals. Finally, in the elections to the city council the following year, the *Mittelstand* completed its ascendancy by eclipsing the National Liberals to become the second largest political group inside the council.

The growth of the *Mittelstand* during the 1890s presented the left liberals with problems of their own. The *Mittelstand* groups brought with them an unprecedented hostility and negativity to the current political debate, which the left-liberal parties never quite managed to counter. As the parties perceived to be in power, they had to defend themselves against charges such as the squandering of public funds, the occasional embezzlement of considerable sums by local government employees, and even the misconduct of individual councillors.[94] The most contentious of these issues was the debate about the *Submissionswesen*, about how local government ought to invite tenders for its public contracts, whether these ought to go to big or small businesses and whether or not they ought to be restricted to Frankfurt firms. Entangled with this central question for the Frankfurt *Mittelstand* was the issue of whether councillors should be allowed to compete for

---

[93] Although as usual many other issues were involved, the issue of denominational schooling was time and again singled out as the central issue of the campaign. See e.g. the left-liberal manifesto in *Frankfurter Zeitung*, 27 Nov. 1904 (3. Morgenblatt), and Wedel's opening speech at a left-liberal election rally in *Frankfurter Zeitung*, 28 Nov. 1904. See also e.g. *Frankfurter Zeitung*, 29 Nov. 1904 (3. Morgenblatt).

[94] For example, on the 'Affäre Fischer', see *Frankfurter Zeitung*, 13 Nov. 1894 (2. Morgenblatt). This was the most spectacular of all cases, as *Stadtkassierer* Fischer had embezzled 850,000 Marks over a period of more than ten years. He committed suicide in 1894 in the fear that he would be discovered. *MAB*, 1894/95, p. x.

municipal contracts, and accusations that councillors had used their position of influence to further their own private businesses in the past.

In reaction to the new tone which the *Mittelstand* brought into the political debate, the Democrat and Progressive Liberal parties changed tactic. This is already apparent in the common left-liberal election manifesto. In 1888, for example, it included some aims of municipal policy, but these were still altogether vague. The issue of the municipalization of the tramway was to be resolved in a socially acceptable way, and the desires of individual districts were to be taken account of. Otherwise, the appeal was mostly concerned with chivalrous promises to defend the municipal constitution from all 'assaults'.[95] In 1896, by contrast, the manifesto included specific demands for the municipalization of tramways, the development of the municipal electrical power station, the building of cheap flats, public reading rooms (*Lesehallen*), and the development of the successful public lecture series organized jointly by liberals and Social Democrats.[96] In addition, demands such as the one for a *Submissionswesen*[97] more favourable to local interests or the insistence on fair and open competition for offices in local government were clearly a concession to the *Mittelstand* and the National Liberal opponents.

More specific demands in social policy were enabled by the fact that since Karl Funck had taken over from Berthold Geiger as the Progressive 'leader', the party had moved more closely towards the Democrats' social policies.[98] Still, the fact that they could be more specific on social matters does not explain why they chose to be so in practice. After all, in Württemberg the Democrats' sister party, the People's Party, refused to abandon its laissez-faire policies on social issues in response to the *Mittelstand*.[99] Clearly, the left liberals were out to attract the small but growing number of SPD voters, at least for the run-off elections. This was put succinctly in a leader of the *Kleine Presse*. In it, the newspaper lamented the complete lack of principle ('*Rückgrad- und Prinzipienlosigkeit*') of the National

[95] *Frankfurter Zeitung*, 28 Nov. 1888 (2. Morgenblatt).
[96] *Frankfurter Zeitung*, 10 Nov. 1896 (2. Morgenblatt). In later election campaigns, the manifestos' demands were very similar in kind, only progressively more detailed. See e.g. *Frankfurter Zeitung*, 15 Nov.1898 (2. Morgenblatt).
[97] Liberals were extremely lukewarm about the contentious issue and were in no doubt that the only reason why they had to advocate change was that otherwise they would lose votes. *Frankfurter Zeitung*, 30 Nov. 1894 (2. Morgenblatt).
[98] In an extremely illuminating public speech Funck tried to draw the lessons from the recent left-liberal defeat in the state elections for his party, urging the Progressives to develop in their social policy to bring them more into line with the Democrats. HStAW 407 n. 150¹ fo. 500 (newspaper report from the Progressive/Democrat meeting of 18 Nov. 1893).
[99] Blackbourn, *Class, Religion and Local Politics*, 145–8.

Liberals which had been revealed by their alliance with the 'fanatics' of the *Mittelstand* ('*Kommunalvereinler*') and even the anti-Semites. It reiterated an earlier comment by the SPD newspaper that the party would prefer a Democrat as the least of all evils, since both parties were for an extension of the franchise.[100] Henceforth, a distinction was made between the 'left' and the 'right', '*Fortschritt*' and '*Rückschritt*'.[101]

As a result of this juxtaposition, the Democrat party rhetoric, which the Progressives appeared happy to adopt, gained an interesting twist. Rather than identifying the act of voting Democrat just as an act of local patriotism, as had happened before, now there was a reinforced message that Frankfurt was a progressive, 'fortschrittlich' city—a term that could include the SPD. At a rally in 1902 Rudolf Oeser, in contrasting *freisinnige* (liberal) tendencies with the 'Mischmasch zünftlerisch-reaktionärer Observanz' appealed that: 'Our bourgeoisie is . . . liberal . . . take care that on 12 November [polling day] no liberal-minded person stays at home, so that Frankfurt may remain what it always has been: an ornament to the cities, the pride of the Empire!'[102]

The National Liberals in their support for particular interests such as those of the artisans, of religious groups, or of the *Mittelstand* groups in general now became decried as 'particularists', in contradistinction to their behaviour in national politics.[103] By contrast, voting for the left, and for the left liberals in particular, became an act of patriotic duty, against the particularism of all the parties on the right.[104] The left liberals had managed, therefore, to turn their particularist image of the 1860s and 1870s into one of true patriotism, whereas the National Liberals, once the party of unification, were now the party of true particularism.[105]

---

[100] 'We should have thought that this would still be the case today, precisely because the Democrats are in favour of the extension of the local franchise, whereas the parties on the right have nothing to offer on this issue.' (*Kleine Presse*, 15 Nov. 1896 (1. Blatt)).

[101] In the words of Heinrich Rößler, 'Man wird also die Sachlage dahin zusammenfassen können, daß bei uns alle vorwärtsstrebenden Richtungen sind, im gegnerischen Lager aber alle rückläufigen.' (In summary, all progressive elements are in our camp, whereas the opposition unites those that are backward-looking.)*Frankfurter Zeitung*, 11 Nov. 1898 (Abendblatt).

[102] 'Unser Bürgertum, . . ., ist freigesinnt . . . sorgen Sie dafür, daß am 12. November kein freigesinnter Mann zu Hause bleibt, auch [*sic*] das Frankfurt bleibt, was es stets gewesen ist: Der Städte Zierde und des Reiches Stolz!' (*Frankfurter Zeitung*, 1 Nov. 1902).

[103] *Kleine Presse*, 15 Nov. 1900 (2. Blatt).

[104] *Frankfurter Zeitung*, 11 Nov. 1902 (Abendblatt). Voting against the particularists became an act of 'patriotischer Pflicherfüllung', National Liberal behaviour simply being 'unpatriotic'.

[105] This also explains the rather bizarre exchange betwen the *Frankfurter Zeitung* and the *Kreuzzeitung*, at which the former protested against the latter's claim that on his recent visit to the city's electrotechnical exhibition the Emperor had refused to shake Sonnemann's hand. By

Instead of the outright opposition which saw Leopold Sonnemann refuse even in 1883 to decorate or light his house for the passing emperor during his procession through the city,[106] Democrats started to contribute increasingly to national celebrations, though in their own inimitable style. On the twenty-fifth anniversary of German unification in January 1896, the pacifist guest speaker Ludwig Quidde confirmed to an audience of 500 that the days of particularism were over. He summed up his speech, however, by demanding 'that the politics of rape be replaced by the politics of understanding'.[107] The Democrats then chose to make another celebration, on 19 March 1896, out of the twenty-fifth anniversary of the opening of the Reichstag. In a room whose only special decoration consisted of a large black, red, and golden banner, the Democrats could not resist measuring the imperial parliament against the first German parliament of 1848.[108] Democrats, then, continued to celebrate their democratic traditions. Put differently, they no longer opposed a borussian, militarist nationalism outright, but instead the Democrats tried to fill it with their own, federalist, content.[109] Their positive national commitment and even the language of patriotism would have been inconceivable twenty years earlier.

Despite early attempts at some form of cooperation between the SPD and the left-liberals during the 1880s,[110] frictions between the parties were the

---

contrast, Sonnemann's papers insisted that he had shaken the Emperor's hand not just once, but twice. The initial reports of the Kaiser's visit by the *Kleine Presse*, the *General-Anzeiger*, and the *Frankfurter Zeitung* of 10/11 Oct. 1891 are in HStAW 407 n. 99¹ fo. 257. For the *Frankfurter Zeitung*'s refutation of the *Kreuzzeitung* of 15 Oct., see HStAW 407 n. 99¹ fo. 253. See also *'Eine neue Zeit . . .!' Die Internationale Elektrotechnische Ausstellung 1891*, ed. Historisches Museum Frankfurt am Main (Frankfurt, 1991), 40–1.

[106] HStAW 405 n. 1199 fo. 66. *Zeitungsbericht*, 11 Dec. 1883. Nevertheless, Sonnemann was the only one reported to act in such a way, which shows that support for these 'particularist' manifestations was ebbing away.

[107] 'daß die Politik der Vergewaltigung ersetzt werde durch die Politik der Verständigung' (HStAW 407 n. 161² fos. 82–7). Democrat commemorative meeting on the 25th anniversary of the foundation of the German Empire, 18 Jan. 1896.

[108] HStAW 407 n. 161² fo. 102. Democrat commemorative meeting on the 25th anniversary of the opening of the Reichstag, 19 Mar. 1896. This is also in *Frankfurter Zeitung*, 20 Mar. 1896 (4. Morgenblatt).

[109] On the two competing concepts of the German nation, see D. Langewiesche, 'Kulturelle Nationsbildung im Deutschland des 19. Jahrhunderts', in M. Hettling and P. Nolte (eds.), *Nation und Gesellschaft in Deutschland. Historische Essays* (Munich, 1996), 46–64.

[110] The SPD put up candidates for the council for the first time in 1882. Eager to please his 'working class' Reichstag constituency, Sonnemann urged his party to support a socialist candidate. In 1886, the Democrats finally heeded Sonnemann's demand, with much reluctance. *Frankfurter Zeitung*, 21 Nov. 1882 (Abendblatt). *Frankfurter Zeitung*, 19 Nov. 1886 (2. Morgenblatt). *Frankfurter Zeitung*, 23 Nov. 1886.

norm throughout the 1890s, when the question of the extent to which the left-liberal parties should cooperate with the SPD recurred at every local election. At the root of the tension was essentially the same charge made by the SPD about the left liberals' lack of principles and of genuine commitment to their ideals. Central to the SPD's complaints against the left liberals was, of course, the franchise issue, which appeared to epitomize left-liberal ambiguity about their own ideals.[111] For despite minor improvements in the franchise which Heinrich Rößler managed to wrestle from the council and the *Magistrat* in 1895,[112] the franchise law remained essentially unchanged until the end of the Empire. The Progressive Liberals remained uneasy about changing the franchise throughout the period, and even some Democrats were unsupportive about the issue as it became increasingly apparent that the SPD would be the net beneficiaries of the change.[113]

For their part, the Democrats found it difficult to cope with the SPD's aggressive and negative language on many issues, which was extremely similar in style to that employed by the *Mittelstand*[114]—after all, the SPD was, like

[111] It seems that throughout Germany, SPD charges against liberal reluctance to widen the franchise was one of the party's most effective vote-winners at grass-roots level. See, for instance, M. Hurd, 'Tale of Two Cities. Socialists, Liberals and Democracy in Hamburg and Stockholm 1870–1914', in Bo Stråth (ed.), *Language and the Construction of Class Identities* (Gothenburg, 1990), 95–126. On franchise restrictions in Hamburg, see also R. J. Evans, '"Red Wednesday" in Hamburg: Social Democrats, Police and *Lumpenproletariat* in the Suffrage Disturbances of 17 January 1906', in R. J. Evans, *Rethinking German History. Nineteenth-Century Germany and the Origins of the Third Reich* (London, 1987), esp. 282–3. More generally, see Ritter, 'Wahlen und Wahlpolitik im Königreich Sachsen', esp. 71–9. Sheehan, *German Liberalism*, 269. C. Schorske, *German Social Democracy, 1905–1917. The Development of the Great Schism* (2nd edn., Cambridge, Mass., 1983), 171–80. On the liberal ambiguity on the franchise, see W. Gagel, *Die Wahlrechtsfrage in der Geschichte der deutschen liberalen Parteien 1848–1918* (Düsseldorf, 1958), 143–9, 159–62.

[112] At long last, the *Bürgerrechtsgeld* was abolished and people were enfranchised who paid taxes for an income of over 1,200 Marks, but who were pushed below the tax barrier by the receipt of other benefits (e.g. for their children). *Frankfurter Zeitung*, 25 Sept. 1896 (3. Morgenblatt). Wolf states that as a result of this, 2,600 men were enfranchised, but he omits to point out that most of this increase would have been the result of a natural increase which occurred at every election. The net effect of the change in regulations alone would be more likely to be around 1,000 new voters, out of a total of 17,500 electors. Wolf, *Liberalismus*, 148.

[113] The importance of a restrictive franchise to the fortunes of Frankfurt's liberal parties in city government has been emphasized in C. Rohr, 'Kommunaler Liberalismus und bürgerliche Herrschaft in den Städten Frankfurt am Main und Leipzig 1900–1924', *JLF* vi (1994), 167–77. This will be explored in greater detail in C. Rohr, 'Kommunaler Liberalismus zwischen Kaiserreich und Weimarer Republik. Frankfurt am Main und Leipzig', D.Phil. thesis (Frankfurt, forthcoming). The debates about the extension of the municipal franchise have often been discussed, and there is no need to go through the minute steps of the debate here. See Rolling, 'Liberals', 189–208. Wolf, *Liberalismus*, 98–109.

[114] The SPD had as much to complain about municipal charges and the 'inefficiency' of the council as the *Mittelstand*. See e.g. Quarck in *Frankfurter Zeitung*, 16 Nov. 1894 (3. Morgenblatt).

various groups on the right, another party representing a particular interest. The narrow class interests of the SPD, as the Democrats saw it, were revealed, for example, whenever the SPD chose not to support them in the run-off elections. Just because in theory the two parties were closest to each other, SPD support could not be taken for granted, and for tactical reasons the SPD on one occasion even chose to support a candidate of the *Mittelstand*.[115]

Nevertheless, the left liberals continued to woo the SPD vote throughout the 1890s. Perhaps the most remarkable aspect of left-liberal political speeches and manifestos of the time is the surprisingly muted tone of the criticism of the SPD.[116] An important reason is that the SPD was clearly not perceived as a threat during this decade. This is revealed by the naive and patronizing attitudes many left liberals continued to have towards the socialists. Some were prepared to welcome two or three Social Democrat councillors so that they would, in the words of B. Geiger, stop 'whingeing' all the time and 'shut up and realise some of the real issues involved'.[117] Another recurrent theme was that a couple of SPD representatives would act as a 'safety valve' against socialist attempts to realize their goals by other means. Only the most progressive Democrats argued that the SPD would add to the quality of the council and that, for example, their input to social matters would be most valuable.[118]

More important were tactical considerations. The Democrats needed all the support they could muster against the *Mittelstand*, whilst the SPD, still in need of a bourgeois ally to get into the council, was most likely to find support from the Democrats, given their traditional involvement in workers' issues. Indeed, the ideological closeness between the two parties was demonstrated repeatedly during the contests for the Reichstag elections.[119] There, during the period of the anti-socialist laws and at times of nationalist hysteria such as the 1887 Kartell elections, Democrats were perhaps the greatest bourgeois champions of SPD rights. In most elections, what distinguished the two parties was less their stance on national politics, than their view of local politics and the nature of Frankfurt's interests in the

---

[115] *Frankfurter Zeitung*, 30 Nov. 1902 (5. Morgenblatt). *Frankfurter Zeitung*, 8 Nov. 1904 (Abendblatt).
[116] This includes even the National Liberals! Before the 1896 run-off elections, for example, the *Kleine Presse* positively contrasted the 'principled' SPD to a National Liberal party characterized by lack of substance. *Kleine Presse*, 15 Nov. 1896 (1. Blatt).
[117] HStAW 407 n. 150^2 fos. 146–7. Progressive Association meeting, 10 Nov. 1898.
[118] *Frankfurter Zeitung*, 15 Nov. 1898 (3. Morgenblatt).
[119] This is not to deny the heterogeneity of the SPD in Frankfurt, or the importance of its Marxist wing. However, in the national and later in the council elections, the candidates each

Empire. This ideological closeness was not just rhetorical. In all three run-off elections between the SPD and the National Liberals, the Democrats supported the SPD candidate, which was crucial to the SPD victory in 1887, and made it all but certain in 1890 and 1893. For their help, the Democrats were rewarded in the 1898 state elections, which the left liberals won on account of SPD support. Ultimately, there was a clear perception in the SPD, too, that of all the parties, the left liberals and particularly the Democrats had the greatest ideological affinity to the SPD. Moreover, the SPD, too, had reason to be opposed to the property owners and guild interests of the *Mittelstand*.

From the turn of the century, the SPD became an increasingly important threat to the liberals' hegemony inside the city council.[120] In this situation, one might have expected the left liberals' commitment to the 'progressive bloc' to have been severely tested. Still, the left liberals left no doubt that they preferred the rise in municipal politics of the SPD to the 'reactionary mishmash'. From 1901, when the first SPD member, Max Quarck, entered the city council the left-liberal councillors assured their own party members and their constituencies that Quarck was, despite his disagreeable personality and his offensive behaviour in the council, preferable to any member of the *Mittelstand*. Once elected, the latter did not do any work inside the council, whereas Quarck at least had convictions and worked hard.[121]

The 1906 elections proved a watershed, as in many districts the liberals fought a genuine two-front battle against the SPD on the left and the *Mittelstand* on the right. Thus threatened, the liberals agreed with the SPD for mutual support in the run-off elections against the *Mittelstand*. Whereas before the left liberals had had enormous trouble in rallying their electors in support of the SPD, the Socialists for the first time acknowledged that left-liberal help had been decisive in securing the election of two of their candidates.[122] As a result, the *Mittelstand* did not get a single candidate elected. It lost 7 councillors, almost half of its total strength in the council.

---

time came from the party's reformist camp. G. Mai, 'Konservative Stabilisierungsstrategien im Kaiserreich. Zur Praxis des Sozialistengesetzes in Frankfurt/M. 1878-1890', *JHL* xxxiv (1984), 193–206. Stübling, *Die Sozialdemokratie in Frankfurt am Main, passim*.

[120] See e.g. the post-election analysis in *Frankfurter Zeitung*, 13 Nov. 1902 (3. Morgenblatt).
[121] HStAW 407 n. 161^4 fos. 55–6. Democratic Association meeting, 25 Nov. 1901. HStAW 407 n. 150^2 fos. 231–2. Progressive Association meeting, 26 Mar. 1902. *Frankfurter Zeitung*, 1 Nov. 1902 (3. Morgenblatt). Councillor Zirndorfer at a joint Democratic/Progressive election rally, 31 Oct. 1902.
[122] *Volksstimme*, 13 Dec. 1906 (1. Beilage).

The *Mittelstand* never recovered from this. In 1908 it split on the issue of the anti-Semitism among some of its more radical members, so that in the municipal elections of that year it only salvaged three seats, helped by SPD support against the liberals. In subsequent years, *Mittelstand* representation in the council dwindled into insignificance. Furthermore, the National Liberals had learnt from their previous election defeat that they badly needed a change of tactics if they were to survive against the *Mittelstand*. Henceforward, until the outbreak of the First World War they entered an informal coalition inside the council, and established ad hoc agreements during national and local elections, with the Progressive Liberals and the Democrats, as well as the National Social party. Therefore, in 1906 there occurred yet another shift in Frankfurt municipal politics, as politics became polarized between the combined forces of the liberals, on the one hand, and the SPD, on the other.

3.3. The Rise of the SPD

The liberals were in no doubt about the potency of the socialist challenge.[123] Firstly, the SPD was likely to profit from the 'natural' increase in those entitled to vote in municipal elections. Particularly thanks to a rapidly expanding party organization which managed to mobilize this new pool of voters much more effectively than the liberals could, the number of SPD votes increased from 2,500 in 1902 to just under 4,500 in 1904, and to 6,500 in 1906.[124] By contrast, the total vote for the left liberals increased from 1902 to 1904 by a mere 3,000 votes to 17,067.[125] The natural increase of the franchise by itself became particularly problematic for the liberals from 1906. Previously, the voting restrictions which enfranchised only those with taxable incomes above 1,200 M. had excluded about two-thirds of those entitled to vote in the Reichstag elections under universal male suffrage. As a result of inflation and the relatively high wages paid in the Frankfurt area, between 1906 and 1910 this census restriction ceased to be effective in excluding skilled and semi-skilled workers from the vote. From

---

[123] In this context, see an extremely illuminating article in 1904 which proves that contemporaries were very aware of the seriousness of the SPD threat. It was appreciated that the growth of the municipal electorate as a result of endogenous and exogenous increases in voters benefited chiefly the SPD. *Frankfurter Zeitung*, 10 Nov. 1904 (3. Morgenblatt).

[124] *Volksstimme*, 23 Nov. 1906 (1. Beilage).

[125] In these crude estimates it is only possible to reproduce the total vote by party slate. As a result, it is not possible to calculate a figure for the exact increase of left-liberal votes in 1906, as in that year they shared the party slate with the National Liberals, whereas before they had a choice between a National Liberal and a left-liberal list. The votes from 1902 and 1904 have been compiled from *Frankfurter Zeitung*, 13 Nov. 1902, and *Frankfurter Zeitung*, 10 Nov. 1904 (3. Morgenblatt).

about 1910, more than two-thirds of the Reichstag electorate was included in the equal local franchise, and most of this increase was the result of rising incomes just beyond the required threshold of 1,200 M., which the SPD regarded as their natural constituency.[126]

Secondly, the SPD stood to gain from an imminent reallocation of council seats which became inevitable as a result of the increasing size of the outer, densely populated districts at the expense of the inner city areas, the traditional liberal strongholds. In 1906, for example, 2,489 electors in the third district (*Altstadt*), who usually returned Democrat councillors, were represented by six councillors, whereas in Bockenheim, the first district to elect a Social Democrat, 3,566 voters were represented by five councillors.[127] The new electoral districts of 1910 resulted in a much fairer ratio of councillors to electors. Despite the efforts of the *Magistrat* to redraw the boundaries of the wards in the interests of the *Bürgertum* as far as this was feasible,[128] this was bad news for the liberals as the more populated industrial areas became better represented.[129]

Last but not least, the SPD stood out to gain from Adickes's incorporation programme. Industrial Bockenheim, incorporated in 1895, was the electoral home of Frankfurt's first socialist councillor elected in 1900. By 1906 it would have been clear to those involved in municipal government that the incorporation of the rest of the Frankfurter *Landkreis* was not far off in conclusion to Adickes's plans, and as a logical inference of the *Magistrat*'s steady acquisition of land in these areas.[130] When the last remnants of the *Landkreis* were finally incorporated in 1910, the SPD gained five seats and the left liberals the remaining two, one of these with a margin of only one vote.[131] The benefit which the SPD was bound to derive from the demographic and social changes of Frankfurt's population and the resulting increase in the municipal franchise was multiplied by the formidable socialist party organization, which was the envy of every liberal party.[132]

---

[126] The figures for the size of the local and national franchise, 1871–1918, are in Wolf, *Liberalismus*, 175.

[127] M. Fleischer, *Das Frankfurter Stadtparlament* (Frankfurt a.M., 1907), 23.

[128] At least in two instances the *Magistrat*'s efforts were rewarded by liberal victories in areas previously represented by a socialist candidate. Rolling, 'Liberals', 206.

[129] *Frankfurter Zeitung*, 15 Nov. 1912 (3. Morgenblatt).

[130] D. Rebentisch, 'Industrialisierung, Bevölkerungswachstum und Eingemeindungen. Das Beispiel Frankfurt a.M. 1870–1914', in J. Reulecke (ed.), *Die deutsche Stadt im Industriezeitalter* (Wuppertal, 1978), 108–10.

[131] Wolf, *Liberalismus*, 163–4. Rolling, 'Liberals', 132–3.

[132] For praise from the Progressives, see HStAW 407 n. 150¹ fo. 346. Progressive Association meeting, 4 Oct. 1890.

The Democrats realized that the SPD could make good use of its voter potential thanks to a permanent, efficient, and reckless party organization.[133] The remainder of this chapter will analyse liberal attempts to meet this compounded challenge, which brought popular politics to a new level.

Since only those with incomes over 1,200 M. per annum had the vote in municipal elections, the SPD aimed to appeal to workers as well as the 'small man', a term that included the petty bourgeoisie (lower-paid state officials and white-collar workers) and large sections of the *Mittelstand*.[134] In Frankfurt, the SPD could point from 1906 to the electoral pacts between left liberals and National Liberals as proof that the left liberals had now shifted to the right and no longer represented the interests of the 'small man'. Frankfurt left liberals had now aligned themselves with the millionaires from the National Liberal party, and were thus increasingly out of touch with the concerns of most electors.[135] Interestingly, the SPD adopted part of the Democrat rhetoric to appeal to precisely the same groups which the left liberals vied for. Accordingly, in their drift to the right to accommodate the National Liberals the left liberals increasingly betrayed the principles which they had advocated during their 'golden age' in the past. Now the SPD promoted itself as the true bearer of the Democratic values and traditions.[136] In language that was clearly borrowed from the Democrats, for the 1907 Reichstag elections the SPD promoted its candidate, Max Quarck, 'for freedom of speech, for tolerance in every sphere of life and for the democratic development of our entire constitution'.[137]

The SPD, of course, had a point, in that their municipal programme very much resembled that of the left liberals, except that it was more radical. Thus, the SPD duly exploited the left-liberal ambiguity about their traditional demand, electoral reform.[138] In Frankfurt as anywhere else, as SPD

---

[133] *Frankfurter Zeitung*, 10 Nov. 1904 (3. Morgenblatt).

[134] *Volksstimme*, 17 Nov. 1906. At the local level, therefore, the SPD was forced to react to the growing fragmentation of a *Mittelstand* earlier and much more forcefully than at national level. M. Prinz, 'Wandel durch Beharrung. Sozialdemokratie und "neue Mittelschichten" in historischer Perspektive', *AfS* xxix (1989), 35–73, esp. 42–60.

[135] O. Zielowski, *Die Millionärswirtschaft auf dem Frankfurter Rathause. Ein Rückblick für die Stadtverordnetenwahlen auf die städtische Verwaltung in den Jahren 1900 bis 1904* (Frankfurt, 1904). *Volksstimme*, 17 Nov. 1906.

[136] *Sozialdemokratie und Stadtverwaltung in Frankfurt a.M. Zugleich Rechenschaftsbericht der sozialdemokratischen Stadtverordneten-Fraktion zu den Stadtverordnetenwahlen 1906*, ed. Sozialdemokratischer Verein (Frankfurt, 1906), 79–80, 83. Also, see e.g. *Volksstimme*, 4 Nov. 1908.

[137] *Volksstimme*, 4 Feb. 1907.

[138] On liberal attitudes towards the franchise in general, see Gagel, *Die Wahlrechtsfrage*, *passim*.

strength increased, the left liberals' commitment to universal manhood suffrage became increasingly hollow.[139] Similarly, the SPD was staunchly in favour of the municipalization of services, but it could contrast its principled, coherent stance with that of the weak, wavering left liberals. In particular, the SPD mounted a large propaganda effort after many left-liberals once again submitted to the First Mayor's opposition to the municipalization of the gasworks in 1909.[140] Finally, the SPD could out-manoeuvre the liberals on virtually every aspect of social policy, since the SPD had little to lose by demanding ever-greater municipal expenditure on social services. Whereas the SPD could continue to ask for better and safer working conditions to be introduced for all municipal contractors, liberals were not particularly keen on the issue since their ranks included many of those employers who would be affected. A similarly thorny question for the liberals concerned the pay and conditions of municipal employees. The SPD took up the issue as often as it possibly could, partly because of the city's duty to be a 'model employer' whose employment conditions would influence those in the private employment sector. But in addition, through styling themselves as the representatives of municipal employees of the lower and middle ranks, SPD councillors were clearly aiming for the vote of this workforce, most of whom had incomes above 1,200 M.[141] Liberals, on the other hand, had to balance their policy towards municipal employees with their overall responsibility for municipal spending, and with many liberal councillors' private positions as employees in their own right. The SPD was quite aware of these liberal problems and contradictions, and did its best to exploit them.[142]

Finally, in its rhetoric the SPD could and did exploit the weaker party discipline of the liberals. For every left liberal who had voted for sweeping

[139] *Sozialdemokratie und Stadtverwaltung* (1906), 11–14. Rolling, 'Liberals', 201–2.

[140] *Sozialdemokratie und Stadtverwaltung in Frankfurt am Main. Ein Rückblick auf zehn-jährige Tätigkeit. Zugleich Rechenschaftsbericht der sozialdemokratischen Stadtverordnetenfrak-tion für die Jahre 1909/10 zu den Stadtverordnetenwahlen 1910*, ed. Sozialdemokratischer Verein (Frankfurt, 1910), 37–61. *Volksstimme*, 26 Feb. 1909, 3 Mar. 1909. Both articles are in HStAW 407 n. 43⁵ fos. 78–80.

[141] *Beiträge zur Statistik der Stadt Frankfurt am Main. Untersuchung über den Stand der Lohn und Arbeitsverhältnisse der Arbeiter und Unterangestellten der Stadt Frankfurt a.M. im Juli 1907*, ed. Statistisches Amt (Frankfurt, 1909), esp. 17–20. In 1906, for example, the city had 10,359 employees. *Statistische Jahresübersichten der Stadt Frankfurt am Main 1906/07*, ed. Statistisches Amt (Frankfurt, 1908), i. 123. Paul Mombert states the number of municipal employees for 1906 as 10,430. P. Mombert, 'Die Gemeindebetriebe in Deutschland', in Schriften des Vereins für Sozialpolitik, *Gemeindebetriebe*, i. *Neuere Versuche und Erfahrungen über die Ausdehnung der kommunalen Tätigkeit in Deutschland und im Ausland*, cxxviii (Leipzig, 1908), 6.

[142] *Sozialdemokratie und Stadtverwaltung* (1906), 79–82.

social or political reform, the SPD could always point out another who had opposed it. For example, the party was fond of quoting the statement of the Democrat councillor May in 1904, that it was not too much work which ruined workers, but their slovenliness, their uncontrolled drinking habits, and their presumptuousness.[143] In 1903, one of the Democratic leaders, councillor Rößler, severely reprimanded some of his colleagues for not voting for an extension of the local franchise. But when challenged by the Social Democrat present, Max Quarck, about what sanctions the Democratic leadership proposed to impose upon the rebellious councillors, Rößler was forced to defend his colleagues in the interests of the party.[144] Although from 1901 there were now distinct, official party groups inside the council, there was still no way for the liberals to enforce the official party line, in contrast to the Social Democrats whose votes were virtually always unanimous inside the council.

The rise of the SPD led to a change in liberal tactics. The strength of the SPD combined with the electoral system meant that in most districts the left liberals could no longer win on their own, and they now needed the support of as many other political groups as possible. This became especially important in run-off elections, which involved the two highest-polling candidates when neither had won an absolute majority in the first ballot. As a result, the National Liberals became marginalized in local politics and, from 1906, usually formed a coalition with the left liberals, though clearly as a junior partner.[145] Now that the political power of the *Mittelstand* had been broken, the SPD joined the left liberals in courting the support of this important marginal group. The left liberals were also happy to accept the support of the Conservatives in the 1910 run-off elections, and of the growing Centre party in the local elections of 1912.[146]

Frankfurt left liberals had to find a language which at least did not alienate all these different groups. Continuing emphasis on their 'progressiveness' would have been both offensive to them, and futile in the face of SPD opposition. But having previously undergone the transformation from the party of Frankfurt particularism to one of patriotism, it was but a small step for Frankfurt left liberals to see themselves as the party of the Frankfurt citizenry (*Bürgerschaft*). Appealing to their audience's sense of

---

[143] *Volksstimme*, 11 Nov. 1908.
[144] *Volksstimme*, 17 Feb. 1903. The article is in HStAW 407 n. 161⁴ fo. 122. Democratic Association meeting of 16 Feb. 1903.
[145] An exception to this were the municipal elections held in the newly incorporated suburbs in summer 1910.
[146] Rolling, 'Liberals', 136, 139.

civic pride, left liberals noted that to vote SPD would be to desire a break with the city's organic development, as all that Frankfurt was and stood for was the result of its sense of civic pride and independence, its *freier Bürgersinn*.[147] The city's liberal development was juxtaposed with the possibility of narrow SPD class rule.[148] To go to the polls and to vote liberal thus became a citizen's duty, and those who did not vote were not 'good citizens'.[149] According to the official liberal election appeal, 'Love for our beautiful city and joy at its prospering cannot be better expressed than in caring about a good result in the election.'[150]

During the 1900s, an integral part of liberal rhetoric was social reform. But whereas the SPD could outbid the left liberals on virtually any aspect of social reform,[151] the left liberals could emphasize their dedication to social reform in conjunction with a commitment to keeping taxation to a minimum in order to justify not going as far as the SPD.[152] The addressee of the liberals' messages was primarily the *Mittelstand*, white-collar employees, and lower civil servants. Thus, alongside measures for the improvement of municipal and other workers, the liberal programme of 1908 promised, for example, an old people's home, efforts to promote the city's trade, and the facilitation of cheap credit.[153]

The liberals emphasized their appeal to those groups which did not consider themselves part of the working classes, but rather part of the city's bourgeoisie, by their commitment to sound financial management. Despite previous increases in the tax burden they were able to point to the SPD as the party of high taxation and financial irresponsibility, which the party had demonstrated, for example, in their campaign for the municipalization of the gasworks in 1909 which would have led to higher taxation. And, in their rejection of the 1910 budget, the SPD not only showed that they were unfit to govern, but they also, through their actions, invited the intervention of the state government which would have stepped in had the budget not been carried by liberal votes. This would have been a blatant rejection of the

[147] Councillor Rumpf in Sachsenhausen, *Frankfurter Zeitung*, 11 Oct. 1910 (3. Morgenblatt).
[148] For example, see the speeches at the main liberal electoral rally in *Frankfurter Zeitung*, 10 Nov. 1910 (3. Morgenblatt).
[149] 'Vor den Stichwahlen'. *Kleine Presse*, 28 Nov. 1910.
[150] *Frankfurter Zeitung*, 19 Nov. 1906 (Morgenblatt).
[151] This was as true in the locality as it was at national level. Fairbairn, 'The German Elections of 1898 and 1903', 190.
[152] *Kleine Presse*, 26 Nov. 1910 (4. Blatt), 17. *Frankfurter Intelligenzblatt (Frankfurter Journal)*, 8 Nov. 1908, 35–6.
[153] *Frankfurter Intelligenzblatt (Frankfurter Journal)*, 8 Nov. 1908, 35–6. *Frankfurter Zeitung*, 8 Nov. 1908 (3. Morgenblatt).

cherished principle of self-government, striking at its very nerve, the city's financial autonomy.[154]

Even though the liberals realized that they could never reach the organizational perfection of the SPD,[155] they did their best to try. The first all-out effort of the liberals against the SPD, after the SPD-liberal coalition in the 1906 run-offs for the city council elections, were the Reichstag elections little more than a month later, in early 1907. For the first time since 1880, the left liberals managed to send their candidate into the Reichstag. The outcome in Frankfurt was, of course, nothing unusual given that during these emotionally charged 'Hottentot' elections, the SPD had lost almost half of its seats nationwide, even though in Frankfurt as elsewhere, the SPD had actually managed to increase its support in absolute numbers.[156] Nonetheless, the elections had an important impact on Frankfurt left liberalism. This was not so much because of the outcome of the run-off elections, in which the left-liberals' candidate was supported by virtually all other non-Socialist parties, but because of their extraordinary success in the first round of the elections, which they fought unsupported by any electoral agreements. In that round, the left liberals secured 17,687 votes against opposition from the SPD, the National Liberals, and the Centre Party, more than 10,000 more than in the previous election. Indeed, this was a greater increase than even the Social Democrats managed.[157] This was achieved through unprecedented electoral organization which caught even the masters of the game, the SPD, completely by surprise.[158] According to the SPD newspaper, the Democrats worked as though their life depended on the outcome of the elections. From the first to the last, well-organized groups of liberal helpers went out to guide potential voters to the polls. New pamphlets were distributed hourly and liberal agents

---

[154] Councillor Gehrke in *Frankfurter Zeitung*, 10 Nov. 1910 (3. Morgenblatt).
[155] Commentary in *Frankfurter Zeitung*, 15 Nov. 1912 (3. Morgenblatt).
[156] For the election results nationwide, see Ritter, *Wahlgeschichtliches Arbeitsbuch*, 41. In preparation for the 'Bülow Bloc', Chancellor Bülow had managed to persuade a coalition ranging from the left liberals to the conservatives to rally together behind the government against the SPD and the Centre. Active government intervention, which castigated the two latter parties as being opposed to the national interest, produced an unprecedented turnout at the elections. Of the liberals, the left liberals did particularly well out of this arrangement, as they increased their strength from 36 to 49 seats. Nipperdey, *Deutsche Geschichte 1866–1918*, ii. 729–31.
[157] F. Specht and P. Schwabe, *Die Reichstagswahlen von 1867–1907* (Berlin, 1908), 157, Appendix, 45.
[158] Interestingly, despite the different context in which they operated, National Liberals in Saxony were similarly catapulted into the age of modern, 'mass' electioneering during these elections. Pohl, 'Politischer Liberalismus und Wirtschaftsbürgertum', 109–10.

commuted between electoral districts to ensure the smooth running of the liberal electoral machine. Its efficiency was greatly enhanced by the use of the motor car.[159] The effect of the 1907 elections on Frankfurt's left liberals was that it proved that if only they could mobilize their voters enough, they could even beat the SPD.[160] This impression was confirmed by the 1908 local elections which, from the liberals' point of view had been rather lacklustre, and in which the SPD made major gains.[161] The left-liberal loss of nine seats and a corresponding gain by the SPD was a luxury that the left liberals could henceforward no longer afford.

It is interesting to note that the improvements in Democratic organization and rhetoric were almost concurrent at national and local levels. The shift in Democrat rhetoric against the growing *Mittelstand* came in response to its threat both in local and national elections from 1900. At the same time, there is no doubt that the Democrats' election performance in 1907, even in the first round, benefited enormously from the peculiarity of the Bülow Bloc. In these elections, for the first and only time, the anti-government camp was not divided between the SPD and Democrats, in other words the Democrats could now appeal to voters who felt strongly about social and political reform, but were uneasy about supporting a party hostile to the government. Nevertheless, what was also required to realize this potential was a sterling organization, and this had been built up by Democrats at the grass roots, and had developed over time, and since the turn of the century in particular. In national elections, Frankfurt Democrats had done badly against the SPD since 1884. This leads to the conclusion that it was only once the Democrats were threatened in the local sphere as well that they were galvanized into aggressive campaigning in both local and national elections. The growing approximation of the extent of the local and national franchise before 1914 made liberal political organization and rhetoric even more interconnected.

Aided by the new possibilities of electioneering and party organization afforded by the new associational law of 1908,[162] and revitalized by their

[159] *Volksstimme*, 26 Jan. 1907.

[160] This confirms Jonathan Sperber's view for Germany as a whole that it was in 1907 that the liberals and conservatives were, for the first time, able to match the election agitation of the Centre Party and the SPD. Sperber, *The Kaiser's Voters*, 247.

[161] In particular, the liberals lost heavily in the run-off elections to the SPD and the *Mittelstand* candidates, at an average voting participation of 65%. By contrast, the left liberals emerged victorious from the industrial suburb Bockenheim, where voter participation had been around 90%. Wolf, *Liberalismus*, 162–3. *Frankfurter Zeitung*, 1 Dec. 1908 (3. Morgenblatt).

[162] E. L. Turk, 'German Liberals and the Genesis of the German Association Law of 1908', in K. H. Jarausch and L. E. Jones (eds.), *In Search of a Liberal Germany. Studies in the History of German Liberalism from 1789 to the Present* (Oxford, 1990), 257–60.

134   *The Diversification of Local Politics*

unification of 1910 the left liberals fought the last two municipal elections before the war with tremendous tenacity.[163] In addition to the methods of electioneering applied in the 1907 elections, liberals became increasingly appreciative of the importance of women as helpers to the liberal cause,[164] as well as of liberal youth organizations.[165] Following the example of the SPD there were now liberal campaigns to register new voters,[166] and the various liberal parties held an increasing number of simultaneous electoral meetings in different voting districts.

Improvements at party organization were closely paralleled by the growth in the diversity and the quality of the newspaper press. Again, Sonnemann's newspapers kept abreast of the changes, and retained, if not extended, their influence over the Democratic Association in Frankfurt, and even the German People's Party as a whole. The efficacy of Sonnemann's *Kleine Presse*, which sold 30,000 copies per day to a local and regional audience, can be gauged from the irritation and abuse it attracted from Social Democrats. The newspapers influenced local party politics in a number of more direct ways, too. Throughout the period under investigation, the editors of the *Kleine Presse* and particularly of the *Frankfurter Zeitung* were the most frequent speakers at Democratic Association meetings, and a majority of the Democratic deputies to the Prussian state parliament as well as all the Democratic Reichstag members were closely linked to the *Frankfurter Zeitung*.[167] It was thus no accident that Heinrich Rößler,

---

[163] In fact, the dynamism during these elections came almost exclusively from the left liberals, but all their efforts were supported by the National Liberals with whom they formed an alliance during the main elections of 1910 and 1912.

[164] Councillor Bruck at a liberal assembly in Bockenheim, *Frankfurter Zeitung*, 11 Nov. 1908. Altogether more than 200 women were active on the two election days for Rudolf Oeser. C. Klausmann, 'Politik und Bewegungskultur. Bürgerliche und proletarische Frauenbewegung in Frankfurt am Main 1876 bis 1914', D.Phil. thesis (Tübingen, 1995), 250. This dissertation has been published as C. Klausmann, *Politik und Kultur der Frauenbewegung im Kaiserreich. Das Beispiel Frankfurt am Main* (Frankfurt, 1997).

[165] Councillor Gehrke in *Frankfurter Zeitung*, 14 Nov. 1910 (Morgenblatt).

[166] Rolling, 'Liberalism', 153.

[167] Of the five Democrat deputies to the Prussian *Abgeordnetenhaus*, two (Carl Sänger and Karl Flesch) had no connection to the *Frankfurter Zeitung*. Guido Weiß, elected in 1869, was a journalist from Berlin and a close political friend of Sonnemann, and worked as an editor at the *Zeitung* from 1872 to 1873. Both Josef Stern and the Democrats' longest serving deputy in Berlin, Rudolf Oeser (elected in 1901, 1903, and 1913), were editors of the newspaper. For the Frankfurt deputies to the *Abgeordnetenhaus*, see T. Kühne, *Handbuch der Wahlen zum Preussischen Abgeordnetenhaus*, 672–5.

The newspaper's proprietor, Leopold Sonnemann, was a member of the Reichstag from 1871 to 1876, and from 1879 to 1884. Karl Holthoff, Democrat member of the Reichstag from 1876 to 1869, had been an editor of the *Frankfurter Zeitung* from 1864 to 1871. Finally, from 1907 to 1912 the Democrat member of the Reichstag was the editor Rudolf Oeser. For a

who was undoubtedly the city's most influential and respected Democrat second only to Sonnemann himself, became chairman of the newspaper's board of governors after Sonnemann's death in 1909.[168]

After 1906 the Democrats turned away some of their attention from the organized *Mittelstand* to increase their appeal to workers. No longer were the majority of Democrats resigned to leave the workers to the SPD. In the admittedly rather unsuccessful left-liberal attempt to promote the link between liberalism and workers through the *Reichsverein der liberalen Arbeiter und Angestellten*, Frankfurt could nevertheless boast the largest local membership of this liberal workers' association with 208 members (out of a total of 4,307) by May 1914.[169] In 1910, Frankfurt liberals could announce that their candidates truly represented all sections of Frankfurt society, including a worker—the secretary of the local Hirsch-Duncker trade union, who was duly elected in the run-off elections.[170] The liberals contrasted this to the exclusivity of the SPD list of candidates, which included virtually no 'real' workers, anyway, as the vast majority on the list were either paid party officials or employees of the party newspaper.[171] In addition, the liberals also became quite keen on presenting representatives of various trades or professions as well as workers to underline this image that the liberal parties were there for everyone, including the workers. At one electoral rally, for example, the post office clerk Bechstedt emphasized the allegiance of public officials and teachers to the liberal regime in Frankfurt, and tramway worker Göbel spoke for his fellow employees to the same effect.[172] In this new spirit, one liberal councillor even went so far as to claim that it was the liberals who were the representatives of the working classes, not the Social Democrats.[173]

The consequence of this increased liberal effort was a remarkable increase in electoral participation to over 70 per cent in both 1910 and 1912. Indeed, those two elections became public festivals in their own right. On the news that the fourteenth district had been carried by the liberals, there

more detailed description of the relationship between the various editors and the *Frankfurter Zeitung*, see *Geschichte der Frankfurter Zeitung*, esp. 139–40, 393, 574.

[168] *Heinrich Roessler, 1845–1924. Ein halbes Jahrhundert DEGUSSA-Geschichte*, ed. DEGUSSA AG (Frankfurt, 1984), 63.

[169] BAP 60 Vo 3 n. 52 fo. 198. Membership list of the *Reichsverein der liberalen Arbeiter und Angestellten*, 11 May 1914.

[170] See the meeting of the local Liberal Workers' Association in *Frankfurter Zeitung*, 11 Nov. 1910 (3. Morgenblatt).

[171] *Frankfurter Zeitung*, 7 Nov. 1910 (Abendblatt).

[172] Electoral assembly in the north and northeastern district, in *Frankfurter Zeitung*, 12 Nov. 1910 (3. Morgenblatt).

[173] Councillor Lönholdt in Bockenheim, ibid.

were reports of happy crowds in the streets. In a triumphant procession, the victorious candidate was carried through the streets by his supporters, who were not content until he had addressed them four times.[174] Descriptions of public excitement at these elections were rivalled only by those of the Reichstag election of 1907. It is difficult to accept the view that local government had become a forum of activity for middle-class liberals who preferred the 'quieter municipal stage' to the mass politics at the national level.[175]

The overall effectiveness of this liberal response to the rise of the SPD is extremely hard to ascertain. It cannot be judged through an analysis of the growth and the composition of party membership, because in Frankfurt as elsewhere in Germany liberals continued to rely mostly on informal social links and a network of clubs and associations.[176] Moreover, an analysis of liberal electoral strength by 1912 bears conflicting messages. One interpretation is that the liberals did surprisingly well given the changes in the nature of the electorate and the nature of the political challenges they faced. From 1902 to 1910, the number of votes cast trebled. Even though liberals could not possibly hope for their share of the vote to keep constant under those circumstances, votes cast for their candidates nevertheless doubled.[177] The left liberals lost their overall majority in the council in 1910, but together with the National Liberals they still had a comfortable majority in 1912. With a net increase in the number of council seats of only one, it appeared as though the SPD advance in the council was brought under control by 1912. In addition, a look at the national election results for Frankfurt in 1912 shows a further dramatic increase in the number of voters in the first round, even discounting the support of the National Liberals for the Democratic candidate, Oeser.[178] As shown above, the failure of the Democrats to recapture the seat in the run-off elections was not so much the result of their own failure to mobilize support, but of their tactical inability to secure the support of the Centre Party.[179]

---

[174] *Frankfurter Zeitung*, 15 Nov. 1912 (3. Morgenblatt).

[175] Blackbourn, *The Fontana History of Germany*, 423.

[176] Rolling, 'Liberalism', 154. See in general Thompson, 'Left Liberals', esp. 352–6 on the example of Schleswig-Holstein.

[177] The number of eligible voters rose by 220%, with participation rising from 50% to 75% Rolling, 'Liberalism', 178.

[178] See the general election results in Appendix II.

[179] *Frankfurter Zeitung*, 23 Jan. 1912 (Abendblatt). Again, while the local Centre Party Association clearly followed instructions from the national party, its compliance was enabled by local factors, notably the destruction of the Centre Party sympathy for the Democrats during the disputes about non-denominational education in 1904. Hitherto, the Centre Party

Conversely, it was equally true that, in terms of the total number of votes cast, the SPD had become the most popular local party in Frankfurt, and that the liberals had come to rely for their predominance in the council on the support of other groups in the run-off elections, notably the *Mittelstand* and the increasingly important Centre Party, which in the 1912 local elections attracted just under 9 per cent of the votes. In a way, left-liberal dependence on electoral pacts should not be overemphasized, as in this period, in virtually any election at any level, success in run-off elections became the bread-and-butter of liberal representation throughout Germany.[180] And in Frankfurt, the ability of left liberals to appeal to potential SPD voters while also appealing to the National Liberals without alienating the Centre and the *Mittelstand* was clearly a sign of political skill and maturity. Still, left-liberal support became increasingly volatile as soon as any one of these groups endorsed the SPD for the run-off elections, as happened in 1908, when the liberal alliance only managed to win three out of eleven seats.

It is worth pointing out that the political optimism which many left liberals felt as a result of left-liberal unification in 1910 throughout Germany was also noticeable in Frankfurt.[181] In Frankfurt, it is unclear how much this was the result of the completion of liberal unification. Rather, it seemed to stem from the growing appreciation that the liberals were not powerless to stop the rise of the SPD. For despite the accelerating strength of the latter, there were at least signs that not all workers were permanently lost to the SPD. In 1908, the liberals managed to win the seats in Bockenheim, the industrial suburb which had been the first district to return a Social Democrat councillor, Max Quarck, in 1901. According to the SPD newspaper, against the trend in the 1908 elections even many workers had voted for the liberal candidate there, as this true Bockenheimer had campaigned tirelessly for a whole year through speeches and appearances at public festivals to secure popular support.[182] Two years later, the SPD won the two seats vacant for the suburb, but Frankfurt's bourgeoisie was jubilant when the liberals, supported by all other 'bourgeois' groups including the Centre Party, managed to reclaim the district in 1912, beating

---

had often defied the national leadership to support Democrats in run-off elections, for the last time in 1903. See the election analysis in *Kleine Presse*, 27 June 1903.

[180] Thompson, 'Left Liberals', 17. Fairbairn, 'The German Elections of 1898 and 1903', 167–8, 170–1.

[181] This optimism is a central theme in S. T. Robson, 'Left-wing Liberalism in Germany, 1900–1919', D.Phil. thesis (Oxford, 1966). See also Thompson, 'Left Liberals', chs. 3, 6.

[182] *Volksstimme*, 1 Dec. 1908 (1. Beilage).

the Social Democratic leader, Quarck himself, into second place. Here, it was particularly gratifying for the liberals that this success had been made possible through the active support of the largest group of municipal employees, the tramway workers,[183] whose interests the liberals had keenly promoted in the city council.[184] At the liberal election party where the day's election results were announced and celebrated, the choir of the tramway workers appeared and surprised the gathering with a serenade on Frankfurt, the 'queen of German cities'.[185] Furthermore, in the first round of the 1912 elections the liberals managed to capture the council seat for Niederrad, whose electoral sociology was among the most unfavourable of all voting districts for a liberal victory.[186]

With regard to the advent of the SPD within the council, the image of the SPD introducing politics from 1901, and of the party strife that began in the council as a result, has been exaggerated by Rolling and others. There is no doubt that the tone inside the town council changed from 1901 and that the council became 'more' politicized, but the difference in the council's conduct was more one of degree than of kind. There was never a solid liberal hostility against Quarck and his colleagues inside the council, and Quarck often found allies for his petitions, either from representatives of the *Mittelstand* or from liberal councillors or both. It is true that Quarck's abrasive and provocative manner was never much liked by his liberal colleagues. It was this personality, rather than disagreements on policy principles, which led to the animosity between Quarck and the leading

---

[183] *Frankfurter Zeitung*, 15 Nov. 1912 (3. Morgenblatt).

[184] *Sozialdemokratie und Stadtverwaltung in Frankfurt am Main. Zugleich Rechenschaftsbericht der sozialdemokratischen Stadtverordneten-Fraktion für 1907/08 zu den Stadtverordnetenwahlen 1908*, ed. Sozialdemokratischer Verein (Frankfurt, 1908), 31–3. Municipal employees and lower public officials were one of the most contested groups of electors between the SPD and the Liberals not just in Frankfurt. See Christoph Nonn, 'Soziale Hintergründe des politischen Wandels im Königreich Sachsen vor 1914', in Lässig and Pohl (eds.), *Sachsen im Kaiserreich*, 371–92. Lenger, *Sozialgeschichte der deutschen Handwerker*, 157–9. K. H. Pohl, *Die Münchener Arbeiterbewegung. Sozialdemokratische Partei, Freie Gewerkschaften, Staat und Gesellschaft in München 1890-1914* (Munich/London/New York/Paris, 1992), 143–7, 298, and esp. 439–41.

[185] *Frankfurter Zeitung*, 15 Nov. 1912 (3. Morgenblatt).

[186] According to the occupational classifications of voters established for each voting district by J. Rolling, only 1.5% were tradesmen or merchants, 2.9% were free professionals or directors in industry and commerce, and 17.7% were white-collar employees, technicians, etc. By contrast, 29.4% were unskilled manual workers, messengers, porters, and street peddlars, while 48.5% were skilled manual workers, lowest public officials, office-helpers, police-patrolmen, and clerks with a minor office. Rolling, 'Liberals', Tables iii.6a, iii.6b, 183–4. For the result of the Oberrad (14th district) elections, see *Frankfurter Zeitung*, 15 Nov. 1912 (3. Morgenblatt).

left-liberal reformer, Karl Flesch.[187] Moreover, his sour personal relations with Sonnemann which he did his best to publicize did not help his prospects among many Democrats.[188] Liberals found such offensive behaviour very hard to cope with, but they did not object to this only when it came from a Social Democrat. The veteran Progressive leader, Berthold Geiger, had similar personal attributes, and until Quarck's arrival there is no doubt that he was the least liked person in the council. In 1892, Geiger's insults had so offended the Democrats that they could not bring themselves to support his candidacy for the council, which destroyed the prospects of an electoral agreement with the Progressives in that year.[189]

It is important to remember that the liberals, and the left liberals in particular, were not a monolithic bloc, particularly in their approach to the SPD inside the council. As noted above, even before the advent of the SPD there were liberals who were sympathetic to many of the SPD's grievances. Likewise, despite their hostile rhetoric, many leading representatives of the SPD maintained their links with liberals inside and outside the council. For all his personal enemies, for example, Quarck remained in close contact with the philanthropist Wilhelm Merton and the Democratic leader Heinrich Rößler over the issue of social reform. When Merton founded his journal for social reform, the *Blätter für Soziale Praxis*, Quarck became one of its two founding editors.[190] There were other Social Democrats with whom many liberals were happy to and did cooperate. Even though he was never a member of the city council, Ludwig Opificius, a Social Democrat employee of Heinrich Rößler, was central in all the major social reform initiatives undertaken by the liberals such as the industrial tribunals, the hugely popular 'people's lectures', and the social congress of 1893.[191] The Democrats at least treated the SPD Reichstag member for Frankfurt from 1889 to 1907, Wilhelm Schmidt, with much more respect even when they opposed his candidacy than they had treated many a National Liberal nominee for the Reichstag. And among councillors, liberals got on well with Heinrich Hüttmann, although to their regret there were few other SPD councillors like him.[192]

[187] Luppe, *Mein Leben*, 18.
[188] M. Quarck, *Zur Naturgeschichte der Frankfurter Zeitung und der bürgerlichen Demokratie* (Frankfurt, 1896).
[189] See in particular a letter signed 'Veritas' in *Kleine Presse*, 19 Nov. 1892, 4.
[190] K. Gniffke, 'Max Quarck (1860–1930): Eine sozialdemokratische Karriere im Deutschen Kaiserreich. Zum Aufstieg eines bürgerlichen Akademikers in der Arbeiterbewegung im Spannungsfeld von revolutionärer Theorie und reformistischer Praxis', D.Phil. thesis (Frankfurt, 1992), 126–34, 269.
[191] Eichler, *Sozialistische Arbeiterbewegung*, 421–2.
[192] *Frankfurter Zeitung*, 28 Nov. 1908 (3. Morgenblatt).

John Rolling has described how more and more liberals learned to work constructively with the SPD inside the town council as well as outside. Left liberals and the SPD led protestations against the Prussian state franchise inside and outside the council, culminating in a public demonstration of 30,000 people in the streets of Frankfurt on 27 February 1910.[193] Together with their liberal colleagues, SPD councillors worked to enact practical social reform such as of housing policy and tramway fares.[194] By 1914 it was increasingly the case that to be successful, most social reform initiatives from the liberals as well as from the SPD needed mutual support if they were to succeed.[195] Finally, in the last days before the beginning of the First World War liberals and socialists established local unemployment insurance which had been discussed and promoted by left-liberal circles since the mid-1890s, but which had had no chance of being passed by the *Magistrat* under the leadership of Adickes. Discussions between liberal and socialist council members were not nearly as hostile in private as they were in public. As one liberal remarked in the heat of the 1912 elections, under the exclusion of the public eye some SPD councillors were quite affable: after all, the decisions of the city council committee on social policy, in which there were several SPD councillors, were usually unanimous.[196] Logic dictated that the main battle for the voters in the public sphere should be between the two biggest local parties, the SPD and the left liberals. Logic similarly dictated that inside the town council, the two parties should increasingly cooperate, given that they were in total agreement on the ideal of self-government and on many aspects of social policy as well as education.

The years 1912 to 1914 brought to a climax the fundamental political realignment that had started in 1901. This was triggered by three interdependent factors. The first was, as described above, the advent of the SPD in local politics and the liberal need to react to it. The second was the declining influence and prestige of Franz Adickes, Frankfurt's First Mayor. This was partly the result of his outright hostility to the SPD. Indeed, the First Mayor was the only political element in Frankfurt that was actually politicized by the advent of the SPD, for despite his frequent protestations that local politics ought to be unpolitical, his actions after 1901 were steeped in

---

[193] Rolling, 'Liberals', 202–4.   [194] Rolling, 'Liberals', ch. 5.
[195] The relationship between the various liberal parties and the SPD on the issue of social reform will be discussed in greater detail in Ch. 5.
[196] Karl Funck in *Frankfurter Zeitung*, 12 Nov. 1912 (Drittes Morgenblatt).

hostility towards socialists. Adickes's grip on local politics was also weakened by the realization that his extravagant and highly interventionist *Bodenpolitik* through municipal purchases of land and the zoning of the city had failed to reduce house prices.[197] This, together with his highly autocratic style of government, brought him an increasing number of critics amongst the ranks of the left liberals. Thirdly, the *Magistrat* became less subservient to Adickes, largely as a result of rising hostility among its paid officials and their appreciation that, in the long run, Adickes's policies were becoming untenable.[198]

An important signal that Adickes's halcyon days were over was the election of Hermann Luppe to a position in the *Magistrat*. Luppe was a left liberal with strong convictions who since his arrival in Frankfurt had worked closely with Karl Flesch. During that time, he had gained not only the respect of the left liberals but also that of the Social Democrats, and it was the latter who became his strongest backers for his promotion to the *Magistrat*. When Luppe was first a candidate in 1905, Adickes had destroyed his chances by spreading the rumour that Luppe had embezzled 150 M.[199] A year later, support for Luppe had grown so much that Adickes could only prevent Luppe's candidacy for a vacancy through threatening to resign if Luppe were elected. By 1909, left liberals could no longer be intimidated or outmanoeuvred by Adickes. Together with staunch SPD support, Luppe was duly elected into the *Magistrat*.[200]

In 1912, Adickes resigned, mainly for health reasons, but presumably also because he realized he was losing his battle against the Social Democrats as increasingly they, and not he, received the support of the left liberals in the municipal council. As his successor, the left liberals and Social Democrats elected the left-liberal Georg Voigt, a remarkable choice given Frankfurt's previous selection of mayors. The most extraordinary conclusion of the relationship between liberals and the SPD before the war, however, was the election in 1914 of Prussia's first SPD *Stadtrat*, with left-liberal support.

3.4. Conclusion

The advent of the SPD in the town council marked an important step in its politicization, but it did not initiate it. The rise of the SPD was but part of a

---

[197] Adickes's *Bodenpolitik*, which was the most central issue upon which his reputation was based, will be discussed in greater detail in Ch. 5.
[198] BAK, NL 44 n. 8 fos. 199, 208. Luppe, 'Mein Leben'.
[199] BAK, NL 44 n. 8 fos. 137–9. Luppe, 'Mein Leben'.
[200] Luppe, *Mein Leben*, 19–22.

process of politicization which had been continuously developing since the annexation of the city, and in particular of the process of the diversification of local politics that set in about 1880. Whereas the *Mittelstand* had challenged the liberals in their marked disunity and negativism, the SPD was threatening because of its very unity and efficiency, inside and outside the council. If it really had been the case that Frankfurt's municipal affairs had been politicized only from 1901, then such a quick and effective response first to the *Mittelstand* and then to the SPD in only one decade would have been almost inconceivable. If those sitting in the municipal council had been merely notables, it would have taken them years to adapt to the idea of politics inside the town council, and their response particularly to the rise of the SPD would have been slow and cumbersome. Instead, they managed to bring their former enemies into their fold. This was particularly true for the *Bezirksvereine*,[201] but it was also valid for the *Mittelstand*. Having perceived the latter as their biggest threat until 1906, once they had relegated it to the political sidelines the left liberals were happy to enjoy its endorsement in the local elections of 1910 and 1912.

The liberals' responsiveness to the various changes in the political landscape from the 1880s is best portrayed in their changing rhetoric. Left liberals had converted the hostile, particularist, anti-Prussian rhetoric, which was still very much in evidence in 1880, into a positive language of local patriotism as well as of a specific national patriotism for a 'democratic' Germany by the late 1890s. The National Liberals had thus been forced in the opposite direction, from the party of German unification to a party that stood for particular interests such as the *Mittelstand*. The left liberals were thus able to style themselves, after 1906, as the party of the *Bürgertum*, whose values and efforts had made Frankfurt the pride of German cities. It was a rhetoric that National Liberals could happily join in with, and which could even be supported by other political groups. The crucial legacy of the decades of politicization before the advent of the SPD, therefore, was a remarkable degree of political flexibility and professionalism, marked by a considerable absence of ideological rigidity. This was why in Frankfurt the left liberals were ultimately so much more successful than National Liberals who increasingly could not function without left-liberal support. But it was also the central reason why the left liberals, supported by other parties and groups, had managed to bring the SPD advance in the municipal council to a virtual standstill by 1912.

[201] See also Rolling, 'Liberals', 155–6.

In the light of this analysis the almost paradoxical conclusion comes as no surprise that during the last few years before the First World War, at a time when local political diversity and thus the challenge to the city's liberal hegemony was greatest, Frankfurt left liberalism had reached its zenith, and the left liberals were stronger than ever before. Democrats had always defined their *raison d'être* vis-à-vis the Progressive Liberals with regard to the importance of social policy, and the rise of municipal socialism vindicated them at last. The rise of the SPD was a serious challenge to left liberalism, but at least the left liberals were the only ones who were strong enough to lead an independent defence against the rise of socialism. This new strength gave them increasing self-confidence and political cunning. By 1914, with Voigt as First Mayor and Luppe as his deputy, the left liberals were finally fully in control of municipal policy, and they were able to cooperate with either the SPD or the National Liberals whenever it suited them to translate their policies into practice. Unfortunately, the outbreak of the First World War precludes any knowledge of whether the left liberals' new control of municipal politics would have translated into victory at the polls.

Frankfurt liberals were no different from liberals elsewhere in that their success was conditional upon a restricted franchise. In the long run, the importance of the restricted franchise was not so much in preventing the emergence of the SPD or other political groups in municipal politics.[202] By 1912, the Frankfurt franchise extended probably to a majority of male workers. However, it did mean that the rise of first the *Mittelstand* and then the SPD was a gradual process. Rather than being overwhelmed by the emergence of mass politics during the 1890s, Frankfurt liberals had the time and the freedom of manoeuvre to adjust to new political developments. Even though the Frankfurt franchise was relatively uncommon, the effect of the three-class franchise would have been similar in all the cities where the SPD (or the Centre Party) had no problem gaining the vote in the third class, and where the second class became increasingly contested between the (usually) ruling liberals and their more popular challengers. Liberals in Frankfurt used the diminishing security which the franchise allowed them with no less sophistication than liberals in Britain or other countries who were similarly shielded by a diminishingly restricted franchise. For liberals in the cities, survival was therefore not conditional upon a restrictive franchise as such, but upon the way in which they reacted to its increasing porosity.

[202] Sheehan, 'Liberals', 132.

Chapter 2 exposed the limitations of analysing Frankfurt politics in terms of one 'national' camp ('*Lager*'), or even of a single liberal milieu. Despite the absence of political Catholicism and Social Democracy, confrontational politics developed which can only be explained by the rivalry between liberals and Democrats themselves. Yet even when Social Democrats emerged as a significant force in local politics in the 1890s, an analysis in terms of a single camp still appears misplaced. Despite their political rivalry, Democrats felt throughout that they had much more in common with Social Democrats than with the political *Mittelstand*. While in some ways the city's political history especially from 1900 can be described in terms of the competition between left-liberals and Social Democrats, this should not mask the many personal links that existed between their leaders. Nor should it obscure the ideological closeness between Democrats and Social Democrats, which was buttressed by actual cooperation in run-off elections and on specific issues. This result cannot be generalized for Germany as a whole, as Rohe's analysis of competing political camps appears to have been confirmed only recently by an analysis of the confrontational politics which developed in Saxony during the early 1870s.[203] Yet Frankfurt was no exception, either, as the less rigid nature of its politics was mirrored elsewhere, especially in southern Germany.[204] While in Freiburg, for instance, three distinctive camps appear to have existed, their divisions were never rigid, while cooperation on social and other policies became increasingly common.[205]

For Frankfurt, the sombre conclusions of scholars led by Thomas Nipperdey that liberalism ultimately had not managed to adapt itself to more modern forms of politics and society, are incorrect, because of the Democrats' continued organizational efforts there as well as the prevalence of an adapting left-liberal political culture.[206] And yet, these verdicts have been made largely, if not exclusively, with state or national politics in mind. When Nipperdey concludes, therefore, that German political parties

[203] Ritter, 'Wahlen und Wahlpolitik im Königreich Sachsen', 31. For doubts about this approach, see Retallack, 'Die "liberalen" Konservativen', 147–8, and, more forcefully, Nonn, 'Soziale Hintergründe des politischen Wandels im Königreich Sachsen', esp. 378–9.

[204] Ritter, 'Wahlen und Wahlpolitik im Königreich Sachsen', 35. Pohl, *Die Münchener Arbeiterbewegung*, esp. 518.

[205] Haumann et al., 'Industriestadt oder "Pensionopolis"?', 178–9, 205, 235–8. It should be noted, however, that this subject needs more detailed attention. Despite the general tenor of cooperation between the parties and their 'milieux', the authors state that from the 1880s three separate and distinct camps formed. Ibid. 231.

[206] Nipperdey, *Organisation*, 395–6. Sheehan, *German Liberalism*, 271. Nipperdey, *Deutsche Geschichte 1866–1918*, ii. 535.

reflected the social and political realities of the Second Empire,[207] then this is also true for liberals in Frankfurt am Main. Through their organization and their rhetoric, Frankfurt liberals managed to react appropriately and dynamically to the evolving social and political conditions in which they operated. Evidently, it is impossible to generalize from the experience of Frankfurt, as too little is known, for example, about the organizational efforts of liberals in other cities. However, this and the previous chapters have argued that there were a host of other cities in which the liberals had to cope with even greater political challenges to their political hegemony than in Frankfurt, because of the strength of the Centre Party even before 1900. Also, Frankfurt was not the only city with a proud civic tradition that could be invoked by a liberal milieu, and it is unlikely that by 1914, Frankfurt was particularly unique in appealing to the *'Bürgersinn'*, the sense of civic responsibility, to protect the proud *Vaterstadt* against the assault of a narrow section of society represented by the SPD. In fact, the case of Frankfurt indicates that civic pride became the ideological foundation to liberal politics in the cities throughout Germany. For instance, in Düsseldorf liberalism stood for a dynamic, 'modern', and industrial development of the city,[208] whereas in Dortmund liberals tapped into local pride by highlighting the city's proud medieval Hanseatic tradition.[209] The case of Frankfurt suggests that it was at the level of local government that German liberals made the most concerted and thorough efforts at political renewal, precisely because it was here that social change was most apparent, and it was only at this level that liberals, rather uniquely, were in positions of government which enabled them to respond effectively to the social fragmentation of the middle strata and the rise of labour.

Having considered how liberals got into power, it is now necessary to investigate what they did once they were in power. At a left-liberal election rally in 1904, the city's leading Democrat, Heinrich Rößler, proclaimed that at the German *Städtetage* it was recognized that thanks to liberal city government, Frankfurt was leading the field in the three important areas of policy: education, social policy, and finance.[210] These three areas occupy most of the arguments in speeches and at election rallies, and no other area received nearly as much attention over the years. This is hardly surprising, since

[207] Nipperdey, *Organisation*, 395.
[208] Hüttenberger, 'Vom ausgehenden 19. Jahrhundert', 42–68.
[209] G. Luntowski, 'Das Jahrhundert der Industrialisierung (1803 bis 1914)', in *Geschichte der Stadt Dortmund* (Dortmund, 1994), here 340–1.
[210] *Frankfurter Zeitung*, 8 Nov.1904 (3. Morgenblatt).

education and social policy, loosely defined (e.g. including municipal services, street clearances, and other housing schemes), constituted the brunt of the activity of local government, and consumed an ever-increasing share of municipal expenditure. This also explains the importance of municipal finance. Even though it has thus far been completely neglected by historical scholarship, through taxation and charges the financing of spiralling municipal expenditure had a direct impact on every person's life in Frankfurt, more so than any other area of municipal government.

4

Liberals and Education

4.1. Introduction

Since the idea of *Bildung*,[1] of which a crucial part consisted of education in the widest sense, was critical to the definition and self-understanding of the German *Bürgertum*,[2] it is not surprising that education was a central concern to liberals in the cities. For a start, education was closely tied to the liberal ideal of individual self-improvement which had been central to liberal thought since the days of Adam Smith.[3] In Germany, the ideal of *Bildung* played a particularly important role in the way liberals sought to bring about their goal of a 'classless bourgeois society', at least until the Revolution of 1848.[4] It appears to be the case that from the mid-nineteenth century onwards liberals increasingly lost sight of this ideal of universal *Bildung*, once so eloquently proposed by Humboldt,[5] as part of their effort

---

[1] The German term *Bildung* is used here because it denotes not just education, but comprehensive scholarliness and cultivation.

[2] J. J. Sheehan, 'Wie bürgerlich war der deutsche Liberalismus?', in D. Langewiesche (ed.), *Liberalismus im 19. Jahrhundert. Deutschland im europäischen Vergleich* (Göttingen, 1988), 30–4. W. Conze and J. Kocka (eds.), *Bildungsbürgertum im 19. Jahrhundert. Teil 1. Bildungssystem und Professionalisierung im internationalen Vergleich* (Stuttgart, 1985), esp. 11.

[3] J. S. Shapiro, 'Was ist Liberalismus?', in L. Gall (ed.), *Liberalismus* (Königstein, 1980), 20–36, esp. 27, 35. For Prussia, see F. Harkort, *Die preußische Volksschule und ihre Vertretung im Abgeordnetenhause von 1848–1873* (Hagen, 1875). K.-E. Jeismann, 'Volksbildung und Industrialisierung als Faktoren des sozialen Wandels im Vormärz. Dargestellt am Beispiel der Forderungen Friedrich Harkorts zur Bildungsreform', *Zeitschrift für Pädagogik*, xviii (1972), 315–37. In general, see L. Gall and R. Koch (eds.), *Der europäische Liberalismus im 19. Jahrhundert. Texte zu seiner Entwicklung*, 4 vols. (Frankfurt, 1981).

[4] M. Kraul, 'Bildung und Bürgerlichkeit', in J. Kocka (ed.), *Bürgertum im 19. Jahrhundert. Deutschland im europäischen Vergleich* (Munich, 1988), iii. 45–73. Gall, 'Liberalismus und "Bürgerliche Gesellschaft" ', 324–56. Sheehan, *German Liberalism*, 32–3.

[5] For an introduction to the concepts behind the reformer's educational reforms, see C. Menze, *Wilhelm von Humboldt* (Sankt Augustin, 1993).

to preserve the current social status quo and to keep *Bildung* open only to those that were currently part of the educated bourgeoisie.[6] Unfortunately for our understanding of German liberalism, historians of education have carried out a similar debate, about the intended and actual social stratification of secondary education through the course of the Empire, without any apparent concern for the political implications which this had for liberal assumptions of a *bürgerliche Gesellschaft*, a society of citizens.[7]

The growing liberal appreciation of the role of education in maintaining and preserving the social structure of Germany, and especially in preserving the character of the bourgeoisie against other emerging sections of society was given further impetus in 1890 as an integral part of Emperor William II's 'New Course'. According to the Emperor, German schools had in the past failed to educate 'true Germans', and henceforth he regarded school education as a central element in combatting the SPD.[8] In the absence of any monographs on the subject,[9] the changing attitudes of liberals towards education remain open to speculation. However, it would appear likely that liberals shared the central ambiguity of the German

---

[6] This effort to maintain an ideal of 'bourgeois universality' through *Bildung* was already being undermined by the social changes which made the bourgeoisie increasingly heterogenous as early as the 1850s. See, e.g. Sheehan, *German Liberalism*, 169–71.

[7] Among the central works which discuss the issue of social stratification in secondary education are D. K. Müller, *Sozialstruktur und Schulsystem. Aspekte zum Strukturwandel des Schulwesens im 19. Jahrhundert* (Göttingen, 1977). D. K. Müller and B. Zymek, *Datenhandbuch zur deutschen Bildungsgeschichte*. ii. *Höhere und mittlere Schulen*. Teil 1. *Sozialgeschichte und Statistik des Schulsystems in den Staaten des Deutschen Reiches, 1800–1945* (Göttingen, 1987). F. K. Ringer, *Education and Society in Modern Europe* (Bloomington, Ind., 1979). F. K. Ringer, 'Bildung, Wirtschaft und Gesellschaft in Deutschland 1800–1960', *GG* vi (1980), 5–35. J. C. Albisetti, 'The Debate on Secondary School Reform in France and Germany', in D. K. Müller, F. K. Ringer, and B. Simon (eds.), *The Rise of the Modern Educational System: Structural Change and Social Reproduction 1870–1920* (Cambridge, 1987), 181–96. J. C. Albisetti, 'Systematisation: A Critique', in Müller, Ringer, and Simon (eds.), op. cit., 210–16. For a local case study on Minden, see P. Lundgreen, M. Kraul, and K. Ditt, *Bildungschancen und soziale Mobilität in der städtischen Gesellschaft des 19. Jahrhunderts* (Göttingen, 1988).

[8] C. Führ, 'Die preußischen Schulkonferenzen von 1890 und 1900. Ihre bildungspolitische Rolle und bildungsgeschichtliche Bewertung', in P. Baumgart (ed.), *Bildungspolitik in Preußen zur Zeit des Kaiserreichs* (Stuttgart, 1980), 189–223, esp. 210. J. A. Nichols, *Germany after Bismarck. The Caprivi Era 1890–1894* (Cambridge, Mass., 1958), 88–90, 97–101. On the limits of Prussian attempts to transform the primary school into a bulwark against Social Democracy, see M. Wölk, *Der Preussische Volksschulabsolvent als Reichstagswähler 1871–1912. Ein Beitrag zur historischen Wahlforschung in Deutschland* (Berlin, 1980).

[9] Curiously, historians of education appear to have largely ignored the political dimension of their subject, whereas political historians, too, appear to have failed to notice the centrality of the issue for state politics. For an illustration of this, see Nipperdey's summary of the history of late 19th-century education in T. Nipperdey, *Deutsche Geschichte 1866–1918*. i. *Arbeitswelt und Bürgergeist* (Munich, 1990), 531–61.

bourgeoisie towards *Bildung*, appreciating on the one hand its integrative function in a society marked by social strife, and on the other its importance in defending the *Bürgertum*'s intellectual and social properties against encroachment from other aspiring social groups.

A second, central reason why education was a primary liberal concern was that it touched a raw nerve among liberals through the issue of religion.[10] Across Europe, in places where schools did exist in the early nineteenth century, the vast majority were denominational schools, either run directly by the church, or with the resident clergy having at least an important say in the syllabus.[11] During the second half of the nineteenth century, once in power, liberals across Europe embarked on a programme of separation of Church and State, which affected particularly the area of education. Encouraged by an increasingly secular perception of the state, education became seen as a state matter.[12] The debate about secular or clerical control of education became one of the most controversial issues in late nineteenth-century European politics.[13] The significance of the *Kulturkampf* as a determinant of the official Protestant character of the German nation in general, and German liberalism in particular, has been increasingly emphasized.[14] By contrast, the precise impact of religion, and particularly of Protestantism, on German liberalism is still largely unknown.[15]

[10] For the best description of the general friction between German liberalism and religion, see Langewiesche, *Liberalismus in Deutschland*, 180–2. On the importance of the concept of *Bildung* in the *Kulturprotestantismus*, see Hübinger, 'Confessionalism', 172–3.

[11] This was the case even in Prussia, the state with one of the first universal education systems. See A. Mächler, 'Aspekte der Volksschulpolitik in Preußen im 19. Jahrhundert. Ein Überblick über wichtige gesetzliche Grundlagen im Hinblick auf ausgewählte Gesichtspunkte', in P. Baumgart (ed.), *Bildungspolitik in Preußen zur Zeit des Kaiserreichs* (Stuttgart, 1980), 224–41.

[12] The pivotal importance of education for the dissemination of secularism, national allegiance, and cultural values is the central theme in W. K. Blessing, *Staat und Kirche in der Gesellschaft. Institutionelle Autoriät und mentaler Wandel in Bayern während des 19. Jahrhunderts* (Göttingen, 1982).

[13] H. McLeod, *Religion and the People of Western Europe 1789–1970* (Oxford, 1981, reprinted 1990), 15–21. G. M. Luebbert, *Liberalism, Fascism or Social Democracy. Social Classes and the Political Origins of Regimes in Interwar Europe* (New York, 1991), 56–7.

[14] Nipperdey, *Deutsche Geschichte 1866–1918*, i. 487–91. H. W. Smith, *German Nationalism and Religious Conflict. Culture, Ideology, Politics, 1870–1914* (Princeton, 1995), esp. 21–37, also 51–2, 121. From the point of view of the Centre Party and its relationship with liberalism, see D. Blackbourn, 'Progress and Piety: Liberals, Catholics and the State in Bismarck's Germany', in D. Blackbourn, *Populists and Patricians. Essays in Modern German History* (London, 1987), 143–67. See also Sheehan, *German Liberalism*, 135–7. Note, however, that popular, cultural perceptions of the German nation were distinctly Protestant in character, and this pre-dates the foundation of the Empire (and the *Kulturkampf*) itself. Langewiesche, 'Kulturelle Nationsbildung', esp. 61–3.

[15] For a first attempt to investigate the nature of political Protestantism, see H. Gollwitzer,

So important and sensitive was the issue of education that it remained on the political agenda long after the end of the *Kulturkampf*. Despite a number of attempts by various Prussian ministers of education to introduce a statewide education bill, each abortive attempt fostered such strong and resourceful liberal opposition in the Prussian Chamber of Deputies that by 1914, no statewide education bill had been passed. These attempts triggered particularly strong and united resistance from liberals at the grass-roots level, and from liberals in the cities in particular.[16]

Another reason why these liberals had such strong views on this matter is that education touched upon a third liberal preoccupation and one that was central particularly for urban liberalism, that of self-government. For an important aspect of education was that it was part of the prerogative of local government, a role that was increased by the inability of many states to pass any statewide education laws.[17] Local government had the strongest influence on primary education, which affected over 90 per cent of the population. In Prussia, state and local government roughly shared their responsibilities according to the principle that the former was responsible for 'inner' school administration, whereas the latter was in charge of 'outer' school administration.[18] Rather conveniently for the Prussian state, this meant that local government was primarily responsible for the construction and maintenance of school buildings, as well as the payment of teachers, whereas the state determined the qualitative content of education such as the syllabus (including its religious content).[19] By and large, this system in which the locality paid for education, and the state directed it, applied not just to primary, but also to secondary schooling. Notable exceptions to this were the classical neo-humanist state *Gymnasien*, which in Prussia were under the direct supervision of the Ministry of Education and whose teachers were state civil servants.

Vorüberlegungen zu einer Geschichte des Protestantismus nach dem konfessionellen Zeitalter (Opladen, 1981). With reference to the *Kulturkampf*, see esp. 32.

[16] On the two most notable attempts at drawing up a statewide education law, see F. Meyer, *Schule der Untertanen. Lehrer und Politik in Preußen 1848–1900* (Hamburg, 1976), 167–83. For the cities' opposition, see 176.

[17] P. von Gizyki, 'Das Volksschulwesen', in W. Lexis (ed.), *Das Unterrichtswesen im Deutschen Reich.* iii. *Das Volksschulwesen und das Lehrerbildungswesen im Deutschen Reich* (Berlin, 1904), 1–232, here 3.

[18] For a critical discussion of the legal basis of this practice, see H. Preuß, 'Die staatliche Bestätigung der Mitglieder städtischer Schuldeputationen nach preussischem Recht', *AfR* xv (1900), 202–25, esp. 209 ff.

[19] E. N. Anderson, 'The Prussian *Volksschule* in the Nineteenth Century', in G. A. Ritter (ed.), *Entstehung und Wandel in der modernen Gesellschaft. Festschrift für Hans Rosenberg zum 65. Geburtstag* (Berlin, 1970), 265–6. This also weakened liberal demands in the Prussian Chamber

The principle that local government should merely pay for, but have no say in, professional matters concerning primary and secondary education should not be overemphasized. As will be shown in Chapter 6, in Frankfurt as elsewhere spending on education took up the most significant share of ordinary public expenditure. More importantly, all the running and maintenance costs of schools as well as some of the cost of school buildings could not be met by loans, but had to be borne directly by the tax- and fee-paying electorate. As a result, liberals in the cities had to be particularly careful in justifying their expenditure in this area, and this alone encouraged them to get involved in educational policy. The cities thus developed into centres for educational reform in primary and secondary education during the Empire, as this chapter will demonstrate. If liberals in the cities staunchly defended their ideal of local self-government, education was perhaps its most central purpose. For only a truly liberal education, which in a conservative state like Prussia could only be sustained through local self-government, could ensure that German society would be permeated by liberal ideals of self-fulfilment and religious tolerance.

4.2. Liberalism and Religion

By the time the Prussians annexed the city of Frankfurt, its education 'system' had two central characteristics. Firstly, it was denominational. The city's Roman Catholic *Domschule* was founded in the ninth century, and the first school for girls was founded by an English order of nuns (*Englische Fräulein*) in 1749.[20] There were two important Jewish secondary schools, the reformist *Philanthropin* and the orthodox *Realschule der Israelitischen Religionsgesellschaft*. But for the notable exception of the grammar school, all Frankfurt schools were staffed by teachers from one denomination only, and were supervised by a denominational school board.[21]

Secondly, the standard of public education in Frankfurt was low. Frankfurt may have had a better education system than the Hanseatic free

---

of Deputies for greater resources in primary education, since the state could insist that this was a matter for local government. P. M. Roeder, 'Gemeindeschule in Staatshand. Zur Schulpolitik des Preußischen Abgeordnetenhauses', *Zeitschrift für Pädagogik*, xii (1966), esp. 547–50.

[20] P. Maué, 'Die Englische Fräulein-Schule', in *Zu den öffentlichen Prüfungen in der katholischen höheren Töchterschule, genannt Englische Fräulein-Schule* (Frankfurt, 1869), 4–7. Hermann Herterich, 'Aus der Geschichte der Domschule', in *Handbuch*, ed. Vereinigung ehemaliger Domschüler Frankfurt a.M. (Frankfurt, 1929), 5–12.

[21] The *Philanthropin* was a partial exception to this. Even though it was funded entirely by the local Jewish community, in the pursuit of its aim to further religious harmony it employed Christian teachers in addition to trying to attract Christian pupils.

cities, but compared to Prussian or southern German cities with a system of universal primary education, Frankfurt was notably backward. And even in the schools that existed, headmasters appointed from outside and other observers were shocked at the prevailing standards. In 1868, out of 21 teachers of the *Philanthropin*, only nine had received an academic education of any kind. Of these, only two had been trained for teaching in secondary education, and four for teaching in primary education.[22] In all existing Frankfurt schools after the annexation the curriculum was radically improved in order to advance to Prussian levels of education, efforts which rather predictably triggered local opposition to this introduction of 'Prussian militarism' into the schools.[23]

Upon annexation, Frankfurt's entire school system had to be reorganized, since before 1866 schools had been subject to denominational boards and had been financed by the state of Frankfurt.[24] Now that the state had ceased to exist, the city of Frankfurt had to define a new relationship with its schools according to Prussian law. If the Frankfurt schools already had difficulties in coping with demand before 1866, pressure on the education system increased exponentially as a result of an increase in population and particularly of the introduction of universal education.[25] The reorganization of Frankfurt's education system was not completed until 1872, and even this was only the result of intense pressure from the Prussian authorities.[26] Two new supervisory bodies were set up, a municipal board for secondary education (*städtisches Curatorium für höhere Schulen*),[27] and a school deputation (*Schuldeputation*) which oversaw municipal primary

[22] *Festschrift zur Jahrhundertfeier der Realschule der israelitischen Gemeinde (Philanthropin) zu Frankfurt am Main 1804–1904* (Frankfurt, 1904), 121–2.

[23] *Festschrift zur Hundertjahrfeier der Musterschule in Frankfurt am Main, 1803–1903* (Frankfurt, 1903), 136–40. For the suspicion aroused by the Prussian headmaster Tycho Mommsen in the Frankfurt *Gymnasium*, see O. Körner, *Erinnerungen eines deutschen Arztes und Hochschullehrers 1858–1914* (Munich/Wiesbaden, 1920), 19. For another anecdotal account of the clash between Prussian and Frankfurt educational attitudes, see Bonn, *Wandering Scholar*, 28–9.

[24] F. C. Paldamus, 'Zur Lage des Frankfurter Schulwesens', in *Einladungsschrift zu den am 29., 30., 31. März und 1. April 1871 stattfindenden öffentlichen Prüfungen an der höheren Bürgerschule* (Frankfurt, 1871), 13.

[25] Ibid. 3–5.

[26] A. Anderhub, *Verwaltung im Regierungsbezirk Wiesbaden 1866–1885* (Wiesbaden, 1977), 115–19.

[27] Schools of 'higher' education were the *Realschule* (secondary modern school), the *Oberrealschule* (upper secondary modern school), the *Realgymnasium* (an intermediate school between the upper secondary modern school and the grammar school), and the *Gymnasium* (grammar school). Liberal attitudes to these various schools will be discussed later in the chapter.

education.[28] In different compositions,[29] they comprised members of the *Magistrat* and council, as well as from the major religious denominations.[30]

The set-up of the administration of schooling was Rudolf Gneist's ideal of self-government as a link between state and society in action. In contrast to the previous denominational school boards, the city acquired a much more direct control over the running of its schools' affairs. Yet at the same time, it is characteristic that the two new supervisory bodies, each of whose majority consisted of local government representatives of city council and *Magistrat*, were directly responsible not to local government, but to the Prussian authorities in Kassel (in the case of the *Curatorium*) and Wiesbaden (for the deputation). In addition, of course, members of the *Magistrat* were also directly responsible to the state in their usual role as *Stadträte*. In theory, this left little scope for independent action on educational matters by the local government of Frankfurt.

The most important matter that emerged after the reorganization of the city's school administration was the question of whether new schools erected by the municipality would in principle be denominational or not. This was a debate that started with the opening of the *mittlere Bürgerschule* in 1860/1, but was conducted with more intensity during the general reorganization of the school system after the annexation.[31] By 1872, both *Magistrat* and city council had decided that all new schools established by the city government would be non-denominational. In this decision, Frankfurt liberals followed the mainstream of liberal opinion during the *Kulturkampf* until 1879. The central arguments put forward by Frankfurt liberals are well summed-up in a motion introduced by Carl Wilhelm Nolte in the city council in 1869.[32] Nolte brought forward the classic liberal argument that denominational control over schooling would impede progress which was why a progressive city which Frankfurt aspired to be needed non-denominational

---

[28] The school deputation was responsible for all *Volksschulen* (primary schools), *Bürgerschulen* (citizens' schools), and *Mittelschulen* (middle schools). See below for liberal policies towards these schools.

[29] The *Curatorium* comprised three members each of the *Magistrat* and of the city council respectively, as well as representatives of each main Christian denomination (Roman Catholic, Lutheran, and Calvinist). The *Schuldeputation* consisted of three members of the *Magistrat*, three members of the city council, one Protestant and one Roman Catholic minister, and another representative of each of the main Christian denominations.

[30] As the two Jewish schools of higher education did not receive any municipal funding they were directly supervised by the provincial school authorities in Kassel.

[31] The debate that surrounded the restructuring of the local school administration can be found in IfSG, AS 1312.

[32] IfSG, AS 1312 fos. 40–3. Motion by W. Nolte: 'All municipal schools to be founded from henceforth are *non*-denominational', Jan. 1869.

schools in which religious education would be treated like any other subject. To liberals in Frankfurt as elsewhere, the secularization of schooling became a yardstick for cultural progress in a modern state.³³

Implicit in Nolte's statement was another point often made in this context, that denominational schools would be impractical in a city that showed an unusual degree of confessional variety, for not only was there a significant Jewish minority, but there was also a small, but nonetheless unusual, number of other confessions in the city.³⁴ Given the absence of a tradition of non-denominational schooling in the city, it is interesting to observe how liberals fashioned this into a central Frankfurt peculiarity. Nolte dwelt at length on the conditions in the neighbouring Duchy of Nassau where a comprehensive system of non-denominational schools had been established since 1817. Over the next decades Frankfurt liberals approximated the Nassau tradition of non-denominational schooling ever more closely to the Frankfurt educational system, so that Frankfurt schools of this kind became simply referred to as 'unsere nassauer Simultanschule'.³⁵ Moreover, such schools had also been established in the Grand Duchy of Hesse, as well as in cities across Southern Germany, notably in Baden, Bavaria, and Austria. If backward, denominational schools were obviously the norm in the old Prussian provinces, it is clear that these were inappropriate for the liberal, progressive city of Frankfurt. Finally, Nolte pointed out that denominational schools were unlawful even according to Prussian laws. This argument was based entirely on Rudolf Gneist's arguments in *Die confessionelle Schule*, a book which Gneist had published only days before Nolte's motion. Gneist argued that with the introduction of compulsory education in 1717 by the head of state, King Frederick William I, education had effectively become a state concern.³⁶

---

³³ See also e.g. the speech of the Democrat Wedel in the city council on 16 Mar. 1905, reprinted in E. J. Müller, *Aufklärungen über den Schulkampf im Jahre 1904 und 1905 in Frankfurt am Main* (Frankfurt, 1905), 63. For the importance of the removal of the clerical influence over schooling for German liberals in general, see the summary in Hübinger, 'Confessionalism', 159, 162–4.

It is worth remembering that the law that officially sparked off the *Kulturkampf* was the Prussian Law of School Supervision (*Schulaufsichtsgesetz*) of 11 Mar. 1872. F.-M. Kuhlmann, 'Niedere Schulen', in C. Berg (ed.), *Handbuch der Deutschen Bildungsgeschichte*, iv. *1870–1918* (Munich, 1991), 179–228, here 184.

³⁴ In 1880, there were 1,057 'Dissident Confessions' in Frankfurt which amounted to less than 1% of the total population. Of these, 446 were members of the German Catholic/Free Evangelical Church. Frankfurt was unusual in that it had an Anglican congregation (which numbered 40), and there were 44 Baptists in the city. *Beiträge zur Statistik* (1882–5), 34–5.

³⁵ See e.g. *Frankfurter Zeitung*, 6 Nov. 1904 (Drittes Morgenblatt).

³⁶ R. Gneist, *Die confessionelle Schule. Ihre Unzulässigkeit nach preußischen Landesgesetzen und die Nothwendigkeit eines Verwaltungsgerichtshofes* (Berlin, 1869). It is interesting to note

These arguments which Nolte put forward so comprehensively in 1869 were used time and again by Frankfurt liberals whenever they were called upon to defend their stand on the issue of denominational schooling. Until 1880, Roman Catholic and Protestant schools were scaled down in size while all new schools that were built were non-denominational. By 1880, as many as half of all Roman Catholic children in Frankfurt were educated in non-Catholic schools.[37] Thus far, Frankfurt liberals had behaved rather predictably, and apart from the particular Frankfurt rhetoric in which the debate was carried out there was probably little difference between left- and right-liberal opinion on the role of religion in education in Frankfurt and elsewhere in Germany.

Until the end of the *Kulturkampf*, it was relatively easy for Frankfurt liberals to put their policies into practice, since the state undertook little to hinder them in their educational zeal.[38] With the end of the *Kulturkampf* and Bismarck's partial reconciliation with the Centre Party,[39] it was bound to become much more difficult for Frankfurt's schooling authorities to pursue the ideal of non-denominational schooling against the conservative inclinations of the Prussian educational authorities. Furthermore, until 1879 there was little that Frankfurt's Roman Catholic community could do to stop liberal educational policy as it would not dare to affront Frankfurt left liberals and their newspapers, which did so much to condemn the excesses of the *Kulturkampf*. After 1879, Frankfurt Catholics were no longer bound by such tactical considerations, and from then on they fought bitterly to preserve Frankfurt's tradition of denominational schooling. It was under these conditions after 1879 that the Frankfurt liberals' commitment to the principle of non-denominational education was truly tested, and it is the extraordinary tenacity with which Frankfurt liberals almost

that it was because of this argument, on the issue of education, rather than on self-government, that Gneist became by far the most frequently quoted academic on any subject by Frankfurt left liberals.

[37] E. F. A. Münzenberger, *Der stille Culturkampf auf dem Gebiet des Frankfurter Schulwesens* (Frankfurt, 1880), 10, 22.

[38] It is always important to remember that even during the *Kulturkampf* the conservative Prussian state never actively promoted non-denominational schooling in any way. During this time it was merely the case that the Prussian state would do nothing to hinder the establishment of non-denominational schools. Indeed, the emphasis of the controversial Minister of Education, Adalbert Falk, lay on the appointment of secular state school supervisors to replace the clergy currently in charge of the task. M. Lamberti, 'State, Church and the Politics of School Reform during the Kulturkampf', *CEH* xix (1986), 63–81.

[39] E. L. Evans, *The German Center Party 1870–1933. A Study in Political Catholicism* (Carbondale/Edwardsville, Ill., 1981), 80–2.

unanimously clung to this ideal that is a truly remarkable feature of Frankfurt liberalism. The ferocity of Frankfurt liberal educational policy can best be illustrated by two examples of clashes between the Frankfurt school authorities and the state authorities in Wiesbaden. Together they reveal the limits of local self-government in education in the case of Frankfurt, and they demonstrate that explanations other than the *Kulturkampf* are needed to account for the extraordinary commitment of Frankfurt liberals to this ideal of non-denominational education.

The main bone of contention between the Catholic community and the Frankfurt school authorities was whether, as a result of the compensation settlements for the secularization of Church property in 1803, the city was legally obliged to maintain a confessional system of education as then existed, or whether it was simply obliged to the upkeep of the few denominational schools expressly mentioned in the treaty. The Prussian authorities in Wiesbaden established the principle that the city of Frankfurt was obliged to establish new denominational schools in proportion to demand. Unimpressed by admonitions from Wiesbaden to respect the wishes of those parents who wanted a Roman Catholic education for their children, the city council continued to deny the establishment of new denominational schools until matters came to a head from 1882 to 1886. Countermanding the city government's efforts to transform the Protestant *Bürgerschule* in the recently incorporated suburb of Bornheim into a non-denominational school, the Wiesbaden authorities ordered not only that the *Bürgerschule* remain Protestant, but also that the new primary school that was to be opened in that area would become a Roman Catholic school.[40] The city refused to acquiesce, so that by February 1885 Wiesbaden's patience had run out and it insisted that it alone had the legal right to establish the denominational character of a school, even without the consent of the local authorities.[41] The council remained unimpressed. It pointed out that the authorities could only make the new primary school into a Roman Catholic one once it had been opened. Therefore, the council refused to hand over the new buildings for their use as a school. To the council, this also settled the question of the *Bürgerschule*, since its Protestant character was tied to the opening of the Roman Catholic primary school in the district. And, for a time, the council even refused to pay the salaries of

---

[40] IfSG, AS 1173 fos. 3–7. Printed documents on confessional schooling in Frankfurt, Oct.–Dec. 1882.

[41] Anderhub, *Verwaltung*, 242.

teachers of the *Bürgerschule* who did not declare their support for non-denominational schools.[42]

Ultimately, this was a conflict that the council could not win, particularly because it did not enjoy the full support of the *Magistrat* which in its dual function as a local body and as an administrative arm of the state was rather less keen on a head-on confrontation with the state authorities.[43] In the face of *Magistrat* pressure,[44] the council had no option but to give in. Still, principle had to be maintained. From now on, each annual budget passed by the council contained the amendment first introduced on 2 March 1886 that the funding of the Bornheim school and other denominational schools in no way implied an acceptance of the principle of denominational schooling in Frankfurt. This result was more a compromise than a defeat. For whereas the city could no longer take its autonomy on educational matters for granted, the Prussian state had to concede that the recently established non-denominational schools would be there to stay. During the course of the conflict in the early 1880s it had to promise that non-denominational schools, once thus established, would not be changed in character.[45]

Subsequently, before the opening of every school a tussle ensued between the city council, the school administration in Wiesbaden, and the Roman Catholic parishes in Frankfurt to determine the confessional character of the new school. With regard to existing schools, the council took full advantage of Wiesbaden's promise not to change the character of any non-denominational school. Thus, the council would usually enlarge a non-denominational school so that it became a *Doppelschule*, that is a school in which there were two separate classes in every year. If it was the case that the school building became too small in the process, the council would grant new funds for another building which then functioned as an extension of the old school. After a few years, this new wing would become a separate new school, and only then could Wiesbaden step in to transform the school into a denominational one. However, the Prussian authorities were now presented with a fait accompli, so that in practice they could do little to avert the non-denominational character of the new school. By

---

[42] IfSG, AS 1173 fo. 20. School Commission of the city council on the proposed budget of 1885/6, Mar. 1885.

[43] On the conflict between the council (through its School Commission) and the *Magistrat*, see e.g. IfSG, AS 1173 fos. 15–17. School Commission to *Magistrat* on a *Magistrat* proposal of 9 Jan. 1885. IfSG, AS 1173 fo. 23. *Magistrat* to city council, 20 Mar. 1885.

[44] IfGS, AS 1173 fo. 23. *Magistrat* report, 20 Mar. 1885. IfGS, AS 1173 fos. 44–8. *Magistrat* to city council, 24 May 1886. IfGS, AS 1173 fos. 49–52. School Commission to *Magistrat*, 23 Dec. 1886.

[45] This dispute is also described in Anderhub, *Verwaltung*, 238–42.

contrast, the council usually refused any funds for denominational schools to become a *Doppelschule*, as it was usually careful to restrict their size to minimal levels.[46] Another favourite method employed by the city council was that of delaying replies to Wiesbaden for as long as possible, and never giving out more information than requested. Through the tactics thus employed, definite orders by Wiesbaden, for example for the establishment of more denominational classes,[47] sometimes arrived after the start of the new academic year, by which time they had become redundant. In response, the central Roman Catholic parish council sent a letter to the Minister for Education urging the authorities in future only to communicate to the Frankfurt city council by telegraph, to speed up communication between the parties involved.[48]

In the two decades from 1886 to 1906, only two out of the 19 schools which were founded were Roman Catholic, the rest were non-denominational.[49] The second Roman Catholic school had been opened in 1906, eleven years or so after the city had been prompted to do so by the Ministry of Education in Berlin.[50] The establishment of a non-denominational system of education is all the more remarkable when considered next to the fate of non-denominational education elsewhere in Prussia. In the years 1886 to 1906, about 90 per cent of Roman Catholic and 95 per cent of Protestant children received their education in denominational schools in Prussia.[51] By 1906, out of 37,761 publicly funded primary schools, only 900 were non-denominational. Of these, the vast majority were in Posen and West

[46] This method is described e.g. in J. A. Kunz, *Entstehung und Durchführung des Simultanschulsystems in Frankfurt a.M.* (Frankfurt, 1927), 5–9. By 1909, all single-sex non-denominational schools in Frankfurt had at least two classes in every year (i.e. a total of at least 16 classes), whereas all those that were denominational had a single tier of classes (i.e. a total of 8 classes). *Führer durch das Städtische Schulwesen von Frankfurt am Main.*, ed. Städtische Schulbehörden (Frankfurt, 1909), 10.

[47] Actually, in this instance the council had successfully denied Wiesbaden the right to impose the ad hoc institution of new denominational classes. For this controversy, see IfSG, AS 1173 fos. 93–111.

[48] The complaint of the Roman Catholic Parish Council to the Prussian Minister for Education, 18 Apr. 1896, is in IfSG, AS 1173 fos. 104–9.

[49] The city of Frankfurt did, however, have to accept the denominational character of the schools in those areas which were incorporated into the city in 1895 and 1900, respectively. Of nine such schools, six were denominational (four were Protestant and two Roman Catholic) and only three were non-denominational. These figures have been compiled from the table in *Führer durch das Städtische Schulwesen*, 10–11.

[50] Letter from the Prussian Minister for Education from 29 June 1895 to Wiesbaden, which was then forwarded to the city. IfSG, AS 1173 fos. 76 ff. According to Kunz, the legitimacy of the Roman Catholic claim for the building of this school in the west of the city had been recognized by the Ministry as early as 1883. Kunz, *Entstehung*, 9.

[51] Gizyki, 'Das Volksschulwesen', 60–1. Kuhlemann, 'Niedere Schulen', 185.

Prussia,⁵² while 119 were in the governmental district of Wiesbaden which included the Duchy of Nassau, where non-denominational schools continued to be the norm throughout the period of the Empire.⁵³ Considering how few non-denominational schools had survived by 1906, particularly in areas where there had been no tradition of them before the *Kulturkampf*, the establishment of such a comprehensive system of non-denominational primary schools in Frankfurt was an astonishing achievement of Frankfurt liberal policy.

There was, of course, disagreement about how far non-denominationalism should go. Liberals on the right aimed at preserving the current status of Frankfurt's non-denominational schools in which children of all denominations were taught in the same classroom, except for religious education, which continued to be denominational.⁵⁴ Non-denominational schools would thus promote true religiousness through promoting harmony between those of different faiths, in preparation for adulthood.⁵⁵ Most Frankfurt left liberals, on the other hand, increasingly saw the current non-denominational schools as a first step towards a school where religion would be excluded from the classroom altogether.⁵⁶ The latter view was also taken unanimously by the SPD, which espoused the liberal view that religious influence on schools impeded progress and hindered workers from improving their situation. Naturally, it was also very suspicious of denominational primary education which was regarded by the Prussian government as a bulwark against socialism.⁵⁷

These differences were, however, secondary in the fight against the Prussian school authorities, and to achieve their aims as far as possible the liberal parties rallied around the lowest common denominator, the National Liberal view of non-denominational schools. So important was this issue to Frankfurt liberals that this became a party-political issue right from the start. In 1882, the Frankfurt Democrats refused to nominate

---

⁵² M. Lamberti, *State, Society, and the Elementary School in Imperial Germany* (New York/Oxford, 1989), 95–7, 109–53.

⁵³ E. Loening, 'Die Unterhaltung der öffentlichen Volksschulen und die Schulverbände in Preussen', *JöR* iii (1909), 68–138, here 110.

⁵⁴ See the affirmation at a meeting of Frankfurt's National Liberal party that they were not against religion as such, but that they merely wanted religion to take its rightful place in education. *Frankfurter Journal*, 2 Feb. 1892 (Abendblatt), also in IfSG, S2/381.

⁵⁵ *Stadtrat* Grimm on 20 Jan. 1897, in C. Bartscher, *Zur Fünfzigjahrfeier der Gellertschule 1884–1934* (Frankfurt, 1934).

⁵⁶ See e.g. the speech by Karl Funck at a Progressive Liberal meeting, 13 Dec. 1889. HStAW 407 n. 150¹ fo. 294. See also Müller, *Aufklärungen*, 16–19.

⁵⁷ M. Quarck, *Kommunale Schulpolitik. Ein Führer durch die Gemeindetätigkeit auf dem Gebiete der Volksschule* (Berlin, 1906), 67–70.

any candidate for the city council elections who had not committed himself against denominational schooling.[58] Still, given the general agreement on this issue, it was difficult for left liberals to gain any political capital out of their resolute stance, except perhaps on occasions when the National Liberals accepted the support of the Centre Party in local council elections such as in 1898.[59] The policy of non-denominational education was, therefore, the one issue around which Frankfurt liberals of all parties could unite. It also offered grounds for cooperation between liberal and Social Democrat councillors: any support was welcome, including from the SPD.[60]

If the motives that have been outlined above can explain why Frankfurt liberals and democrats, like their liberal counterparts elsewhere, favoured non-denominational education during the period of the *Kulturkampf*, it is doubtful that these alone are sufficient to explain the sheer resolve and determination of Frankfurt liberals to fight for the principle of non-denominational education. After all, after 1879 this was in blatant opposition to the policies of the Prussian Ministry of Education.[61] In fact, there was one particular reason which strengthened Frankfurt liberal resolve to fight against denominational schools more than any other motive, and this was the overwhelming influence over Frankfurt liberalism exercised by the city's religious groups, of which the Jewish were most important.

Frankfurt was the German city with the highest proportion of Jews among its inhabitants. In 1871, 10,000 Jews lived in the city, making up 11 per cent of the population. That figure declined marginally to 9.7 per cent by 1890,[62] and, as a result of subsequent incorporations of rural and industrial suburbs as well as of largely non-Jewish immigration, it shrank to a still considerable 6.3 per cent in 1910.[63] Jews in Frankfurt were highly self-conscious and articulate, in part the natural result of the incessant debate about emancipation during the first half of the nineteenth century in which full emancipation had been granted twice (1811 and 1848) before being taken away again. From the late eighteenth century Frankfurt had developed into

---

[58] *Frankfurter Zeitung*, 22 Nov. 1882 (Abendblatt).
[59] On the other hand, Ch. 3 has shown that this did not prevent the left liberals from incurring heavy losses against the coalition of National Liberals, *Mittelstand*, and Centre Party.
[60] *MPS*, 15 Mar. 1906, §298, 139–40. In contrast, note Quarck's public rhetoric of condemnation of lax liberal policy on the issue in Quarck, *Kommunale Schulpolitik*, 71–2.
[61] Lamberti, *State, Society, and the Elementary School*, esp. 3, 95–7.
[62] *Statistisches Handbuch der Stadt Frankfurt am Main*, ed. Statistisches Amt (Frankfurt, 1907), 37.
[63] *Statistische Jahresübersichten* (1912), 21.

a centre for Jewish reform, epitomized by the development of the *Philanthropin* school in the quest for 'humanism and enlightenment'.[64] This development did not meet with universal acclaim, so that in 1851 a small group of orthodox Jews formed a breakaway Jewish community, the *Israelitische Religionsgesellschaft*.[65] Their new rabbi, Samson Raphael Hirsch, became the leading figure in German Jewish modern orthodoxy,[66] not least because of his foundation, in 1853, of the very successful *Realschule der Israelitischen Religionsgesellschaft*, an orthodox counterpart to the *Philanthropin*.[67] Jewish self-consciousness was heightened further by the tensions between the two communities. In 1869, the Jewish orthodox community lamented that since the start of the nineteenth century, it had been 'persecuted' and 'suppressed' by the 'fanaticism' of the reformist majority. As a result, it argued that the split between the two communities was now much deeper and more divisive than those between the various Christian denominations.[68]

Especially for the period after 1866, the argument that has been advanced for Frankfurt, that liberalism was sustained by all denominations (including Jews, Roman Catholics, and Calvinists) in roughly equal measures, needs to be corrected.[69] During the period 1866 to 1914, particularly

[64] F. Michel, 'Jahrhundertfeier der Emanzipation der jüdischen Bewohner Frankfurts', in *Philanthropin. Realschule und Lyzeum der israelitischen Gemeinde zu Frankfurt a.M. Programm Ostern 1912* (Frankfurt, 1912), 35–49, here 48. A. Galliner, 'The Philanthropin in Frankfurt. Its Educational and Cultural Significance for German Jewry', *YLBI* iii (1958), 169–86. I. Schlotzhauer, *Das Philanthropin 1804–1942. Die Schule der Israelitischen Gemeinde in Frankfurt am Main* (Frankfurt, 1990).
[65] In general, see R. Liberles, *Religious Conflict in Social Context. The Resurgence of Orthodox Judaism in Frankfurt am Main 1838–1877* (Westport/London, 1985).
[66] In fact, Hirsch was the founder of German Jewish modern orthodoxy. M. A. Kaplan, *The Making of the Jewish Middle Class. Women, Family, and Identity in Imperial Germany* (New York/Oxford, 1991), 146. Liberles, *Religious Conflict*, 18.
[67] The school was successful at least as far as numbers were concerned. It had been founded with 84 students, and five years later that number had increased to almost 200. *Festschrift zur Jubiläumsfeier des 50 Jährigen Bestehens der Unterrichtsanstalten der Israelitischen Religionsgesellschaft zu Frankfurt a.M.* (Frankfurt, 1903).
[68] Declaration of the Council of the *Israelitische Religionsgesellschaft* from 11 Feb. 1868, in *MPS*, 1869, §74. In 1876 Rabbi Hirsch demanded a separate cemetery for the Jewish orthodox community with the words 'Lieber in Sachsenhausen christlich beerdigt sein, als zusammen mit jenen' ('Better to be buried Christian in the suburb of Sachsenhausen than be buried with those [the reformist Jews])', in P. Arnsberg, *Die Geschichte der Frankfurter Juden seit der Französischen Revolution* (Darmstadt, 1983), i. 853. On the split between the two Jewish communities, see 'An den Hohen Senat der freien Stadt Frankfurt auf die hochverehrlichen Rathschlüsse vom 15. Januar und 13. April 1858. Gehorsamster Bericht und Bitte von Seiten des Vorstandes der israelitischen Gemeinde dahier. Das Verhältnis der Mitglieder der Religionsgesellschaft zur israelitischen Gemeinde betreffend.', in IfSG, AS 1,312 fos. 63–73.
[69] Roth, *Stadt und Bürgertum*, 534–42. Roth, 'Liberalismus', 71–8.

162 Liberals and Education

Frankfurt left liberals, but also National Liberals, were overwhelmingly influenced by Jews. As far as the Prussian authorities were concerned, for example, Frankfurt left liberals and Jews were synonymous.[70] In 1881, the Frankfurt police president noted with regret that Sonnemann's election to the Reichstag had been made possible through the unanimous support of Frankfurt Jews.[71] But in the wider public, too, left liberals were identified with the Frankfurt Jewish community, a perception which in the early years the Democrats even encouraged publicly,[72] and which was strengthened by the fact that some of the left liberals' most visible public figures such as Sonnemann and Geiger, were Jewish. At an election meeting of the *Mittelstand* parties in 1904, for example, the reporter of Sonnemann's *Kleine Presse* was thrown out at the start of the proceedings with the universal chorus of 'schmeiße 'mer 'n 'naus, den Juddebub', even though the reporter himself was Protestant.[73] To the great irritation of the *Frankfurter Zeitung*, even the Protestant party which had been set up to defend denominational schooling in alliance with the *Mittelstand* came to refer to the left liberals as the 'jüdisch-demokratisch-fortschrittliche Partei'.[74]

In practice, the public perceptions about the Jewish character of the city's left liberals were largely correct. For it is not just that so many prominent left liberals were Jewish, or that the city's left-liberal press was largely in Jewish hands,[75] but it also seems that the most active members at the grass roots were of that faith. Time and again the Prussian police officer's report on the regular Democrat party meetings showed that the officer present was struck by the number of Jews present. At an election rally for the Imperial parliament in 1890, the officer noted that the audience consisted of 450 to 500 Jews.[76] At a meeting in 1884, of the 308 men present, most were Jewish,[77] while at another meeting the officer present was struck

---

[70] See e.g. the Prussian report that the only ones not to cheer the current Prussian victories against France were the 'Jews', a statement that equates ostensible Jewish hostility towards Prussia directly with that of the city's Democrats. HStAW 405 n. 1065 fos. 268–9. *Zeitungsbericht*, 19 Nov. 1870.

[71] HStAW 405 n. 1072 fos. 292–3. *Zeitungsbericht*, 12 Dec. 1881.

[72] See the anonymous letter 'Zur Stadtverordnetenwahl' in *Frankfurter Zeitung*, 23 Nov. 1870 (1. Blatt).

[73] 'Let's throw him out, the Jewish rogue'. *Frankfurter Zeitung*, 6 Nov. 1904 (Drittes Morgenblatt).

[74] The 'Jewish Democratic Progressive Party'. *Frankfurter Zeitung*, 29 Nov. 1904 (3. Morgenblatt).

[75] On the importance of the *Frankfurter Zeitung* to German Jewry, see E. Kahn, 'The Frankfurter Zeitung', *YLBI* ii (1957), 228–35.

[76] HStAW 407 n. 161^1 fo. 107. Democratic Association meeting, 3 Feb. 1890.

[77] HStAW 407 n. 138^3 fo. 108. Democratic Association meeting, 13 Oct. 1884.

by the fact that the 110 people present were 'almost exclusively Jews'.[78] At another gathering, in 1879, the officer present was even more specific, as he reported that the meeting in question was attended by nine Christians and 43 Jews.[79]

In the German Empire, Jews tended to support liberalism, and left liberalism in particular, at first because of a genuine convergence of aims, and then for want of a better alternative.[80] Given the absence of political alternatives, what is interesting in Frankfurt is not the Jewish support for the liberal parties as such,[81] but the quality of that support, as Jews provided both liberal leadership and grass-roots activism. As a consequence, the Jewish sections of the Frankfurt population had a crucial influence in shaping liberal policies. This can be shown on a number of issues. The issue of Sunday closing, for example, which was important in local politics in Frankfurt and elsewhere, brought Frankfurt left liberals into particular disarray. It was a matter of great concern especially for practising Jews, because Sunday closing meant Jewish shopkeepers would have to keep their shop closed on Sunday on top of the *Shabbat*. By contrast, opposition to Sunday trading would lose them considerable *Mittelstand* support. Yet it is the liberals' policies on education, and their insistence on non-denominational education in particular, which was most clearly and successfully influenced by their Jewish supporters.

The Jewish communities were connected with the issue of non-denominational schooling in two ways. First, it was argued by the local Roman Catholic hierarchy that, since the Jews were freely allowed to run their own schools, the Roman Catholic church should be allowed to do so, too. But to liberals, this was precisely the point. After centuries of ill-treatment by the Frankfurters, fairness demanded that if Jews were required to pay for their own schools, then the Roman Catholics should

---

[78] HStAW 407 n. 138² fos. 68–72. Democratic Association meeting, 14 Oct. 1882

[79] HStAW 407 n. 138¹ fo. 108. Democratic Association meeting, 17 Nov. 1879. Interestingly, the Progressive Liberals appear to have been identified with Frankfurt's Jewry in similar ways and to a similar degree. See e.g. HStAW 407 n. 150¹ fos. 159–61. Progressive Liberal meeting, 29 Mar. 1884. See also the following report in HStAW 407 n. 150¹ fo. 172.

[80] P. Pulzer, *Jews and the German State. The Political History of a Minority, 1848–1933* (Oxford, 1992), 88–90, 121–47. W. E. Mosse notes that even the Jewish economic élite, most of whom were conservative before 1868, gradually shifted towards liberalism as they became unwelcome in an increasing number of parties. W. E. Mosse, *The German-Jewish Economic Elite 1820–1935. A Socio-Cultural Profile* (Oxford, 1989), 226–32.

[81] For the similar case of the city state of Hamburg, where the debates about Jewish emancipation 1860/4 paralleled those in Frankfurt, and where Jews were also predominantly Jewish, see H. Krohn, *Die Juden in Hamburg. Die Politische, Soziale und kulturelle Entwicklung einer jüdischen Großstadtgemeinde nach der Emanzipation* (Hamburg, 1974).

have to do so, too. The city did not mind Roman Catholic schools as such, so long as these schools were paid for by the Roman Catholic church, and not by the city.[82] In response, Roman Catholic advocates tried to show how they, in turn, were disadvantaged by the city vis-à-vis the Jews,[83] for example in the provision of religious education in non-denominational schools, or by the anti-Catholic, but never anti-Jewish, content of some of the textbooks used there.[84]

There was another way in which Jews influenced the debate about education, and this was really the heart of the matter. In virtually any liberal public statement on the issue, be it in the council, at election rallies or at party meetings, it was emphasized how non-denominational education was instrumental in creating a tolerant society. In this way, the liberals' fight against the excesses of the *Kulturkampf* had been closely linked to an awareness of the implications excessive state power might have on their Jewish supporters.[85] Denominationalism and anti-Semitism became inextricably linked to ultramontanism,[86] so that the growing use of anti-Semitic language at local Centre Party meetings came as no surprise.[87]

---

[82] See e.g. councillor Wedel in *MPS*, 1906, §298. *Frankfurter Zeitung*, 28 Nov. 1904 (Morgenblatt). Karl Funck in HStAW 407 n. 161⁴ fo. 166. Joint meeting of the Democratic and Progressive Associations, 2 Nov. 1903.

[83] See in general E. F. A. Münzenberger, *Die Entwicklung des Frankfurter Schulwesens im letzten Jahrzehnt* (2nd edn., Frankfurt, 1880), 62–75. Ernst Münzenberger was the resident Roman Catholic priest of the central Frankfurt parish (*Stadtpfarrer*), between 1871 and 1890.

[84] Münzenberger, *Der stille Culturkampf*, 14, 22. On the relationship between the disadvantaged Roman Catholic and Jewish minorities within imperial Germany in general, see D. Blackbourn, 'Catholics, the Centre Party and Anti-Semitism', in D. Blackbourn, *Populists and Patricians. Essays in Modern German History* (London, 1987), 168–87.

[85] See the passionate speech on non-denominational schooling by the Democratic and Progressive Liberal candidate for the Prussian Chamber of Deputies in 1882, Josef Stern, in which he explicitly linked this issue to his own Jewish heritage, and his commitment to overcome discrimination against '*any* estate and denomination'. See the report in *Frankfurter Zeitung*, 17 Nov. 1882, which is also in HStAW 407 n. 138² fo. 76. For an analysis of the link between the *Kulturkampf* and anti-Semitism, see U. Tal, *Christians and Jews in Germany. Religion, Politics and Ideology in the Second Reich, 1870–1914* (Ithaca, NY, 1975). D. Blackbourn, 'Roman Catholics, the Centre Party and Anti-Semitism in Imperial Germany', in P. Kennedy and A. Nicholls (eds.), *Nationalist and Racialist Movements in Britain and Germany before 1914* (Basingstoke, 1981), 106–29.

[86] Ralf Roth has correctly pointed out that the Frankfurt liberals' and democrats' aversion to the *Kulturkampf* was closely linked to the memory of discrimination against Jews before 1864. However, it is important to go further than that, since denominationalism endangered the ideal of tolerance just as much as excessive state power. The dispute over denominational schooling was thus not simply the only incident of dissent between liberals and democrats, on the one hand, and many Roman Catholics, on the other, as Roth maintains. Rather, it was the key component in their relationship, and the reason for their increasing divergence and the formation of a local branch of the Centre Party. Roth, *Stadt und Bürgertum*, 527–39.

[87] *Frankfurter Zeitung*, 11 Nov. 1902 (3. Morgenblatt).

Liberals and Education 165

The importance of Jewish political participation in local politics relative to national or state government is, of course, nothing new.[88] Yet the example of Frankfurt shows that for the 'Jewish élite' participation in local government could be motivated by more than the simple desire to 'find the enhanced status and public esteem which some of them craved, an outlet for their public spirit, and a degree of influence on the conduct of public affairs'.[89] For Jews in Frankfurt, participation in liberal municipal politics simply offered the best hope in their fight against discrimination and anti-Semitism.[90] Given that the German Jewish population was largely urban, in an increasingly anti-Semitic national social and political environment, participation in local government as liberals (and Democrats) offered the most effective and realistic way of resisting this national trend. In this sense, active participation in, and the extension of, local self-government became a matter of vital self-interest for Jews living in Germany during the course of the Empire.[91]

The strength of anti-Semitic feeling in Frankfurt is not quite clear. In her study of anti-Semitism in Frankfurt, Inge Schlotzhauer shows that, with a number of notable exceptions, political anti-Semitism was never a viable political force in Frankfurt politics and was, for most of the time, dependent on outside help for its survival.[92] Indeed, anti-Semitic groups were somewhat ambiguous in their anti-Semitism. In 1908 the *Mittelstand*, which included the city's most engaged anti-Semite, Hermann Laaß, among its ranks, successfully nominated the practising Jew Josef Fromm for the Ostend ward where the electorate was 35 per cent Jewish.[93] And there are other indications which show that anti-Semitism in Frankfurt was relatively restrained. Despite considerable controversy, Germany's first

---

[88] In general, see S. Wenzel, *Jüdische Bürger und kommunale Selbstverwaltung in preussischen Städten, 1808–1848* (Berlin, 1967).

[89] Mosse, *The German-Jewish Economic Elite*, 222.

[90] In the same vein, Donald Niewyck has argued that Jews largely considered activity in defence of liberal values to offer the most realistic way to combat the anti-Semitism of the Weimar Republic. D. L. Niewyk, *The Jews in Weimar Germany* (Baton Rouge, La., 1980).

[91] Compared to Werner Blessing's book on education in Bavaria, the more careful assessment in this study about the possibility of education to influence social and cultural attitudes may simply be the result of the Frankfurt liberals' attempts to work against, rather than complement, current cultural trends. For instance, the success of primary education in the dissemination of 'national' values was decidedly more limited in agricultural areas still dominated by the sceptical Roman Catholic church than in the more secular cities. Blessing, *Staat und Kirche*, esp. 165–75.

[92] I. Schlotzhauer, *Ideologie und Organisation des politischen Antisemitismus in Frankfurt am Main 1880–1914* (Frankfurt, 1989).

[93] Arnsberg, *Geschichte der Frankfurter Juden*, ii. 484. It is equally telling, however, that once inside the council, Fromm moved over to join the left liberals.

statue of Heinrich Heine was erected in Frankfurt in 1913.[94] In his memoirs, Selmar Spier wrote that the continuing tensions between orthodox Jews living in the East of the city (close to the synagogue) and reformist Jews aspiring to live with the gentile social élite in the West end, was itself much greater that any tension between Jews and gentiles.[95]

Nonetheless, it would be surprising if there were no anti-Semitism in the city with the highest proportion of Jewish inhabitants in Germany. After all, until 1864 anti-Jewish feeling was still strong enough to prevent full Jewish emancipation, though this was largely for economic reasons.[96] If there are personal accounts which testify for the absence of anti-Semitism in Frankfurt, there are also those which demonstrate the opposite. In Wilhelmine Frankfurt there was a story current which, to contemporaries, epitomized Frankfurt peculiarity, but which is equally revealing about attitudes towards Jews in Frankfurt. A local builder threw a brick at a Jew who came from outside Frankfurt. The Jew ducked, and the brick flew past him and destroyed a window pane. The Jew brought the matter to court, but the official (*Amtmann*) declared, 'First of all, we are dealing with a Jew; and even with a Jew from out of Frankfurt. What did the Jew have to duck for? Had he not ducked, the window pane would still be in one piece. So the Jew will be punished in this matter.'[97]

Furthermore, despite Schlotzenhauer's conclusions she herself devotes much of her analysis to the 'Deutscher Hof' hotel, whose notoriety derived from the fact that it was perhaps Germany's only 'Jew-free' hotel.[98] The fact that the hotel was a great commercial success,[99] and that its proprietor,

---

[94] Rohr, 'Kommunaler Liberalismus', 168–70. Schlotzhauer, *Ideologie*, 263–94.

[95] S. Spier, *Vor 1914. Erinnerungen an Frankfurt geschrieben in Israel* (2nd edn., Frankfurt, 1968), 39, 56–7, 83.

[96] For a description of the overwhelming popular hostility towards Jews in Frankfurt during the first decades of the 19th century as reflected in the curtailment of Jewish rights after 1815, see I. Schlotzhauer, 'Die bürgerliche Gleichstellung der Frankfurter Juden im Urteil zeitgenössischer Schriften', *JHL* xxxiv (1984), 129–62. Preissler, *Frühantisemitismus, passim*. Note that Preissler's title of 'early anti-Semitism', though, is misleading, as he himself shows that this form of anti-Jewishness was not so much shaped by any ideology or programme, but was determined by fears of economic rivalry among particular trades and professions threatened by Jewish competition. On the distinction between this earlier anti-Jewishness and anti-Semitism which developed from the 1870s, see P. Pulzer, *The Rise of Political Anti-Semitism in Germany and Austria* (2nd edn., London, 1988), esp. p. ix.

[97] 'Erschtens ämol hawwe mers mit eme Judd zu dhu; un sogar mit eme auswärtige Judd. Was hat sich dann der Judd aach zu bicke. Hett der sich net gebickt, do wer die Scheib heut noch ganz. Do werd der Judd in der Sach gestroft.' G. W. Pietzsch, 'Erinnerungen eines Lehrers', ed. W. Klötzer, *AFGK* xlix (1965), 5–78, here 35.

[98] Schlotzhauer, *Ideologie*, 192 ff., here 208.

[99] Ibid. 205–6.

Hermann Laaß, was a city councillor from 1905 to 1910 indicates that, however much it was hidden behind other *Mittelstand* concerns, there was a strong anti-Semitic undercurrent among sections of the Frankfurt population.[100] This was recognized explicitly by Charles Hallgarten, the Jewish philanthropist. Having travelled widely around the world and in Europe, he was forced to conclude that anti-Semitism was no less of a problem in his native Frankfurt than it was elsewhere.[101] In practice, even the Frankfurt liberals had to take account of the anti-Semitic undercurrent in their political considerations. Left liberals in the city had to accept that the successful capture of the Reichstag seat in the 1907 election was only made possible because the Democrats had consciously nominated a Christian, rather than Jewish, candidate in order to avoid opposition from anti-Semitic circles in the run-off elections.[102]

It is ultimately impossible to conduct a fair comparison between anti-Semitism in Frankfurt and in other cities. Public anti-Semitism was relatively muted compared to Leipzig or Berlin, but that may simply have been the result of the city's relatively low intake of East European Jewish refugees.[103] Even if anti-Semitism remained politically and socially unacceptable throughout the period, there was a considerable current of anti-Semitic feeling in Frankfurt as in other cities of the Empire, which Frankfurt liberals had every reason to be extremely concerned about, particularly since so many of them were Jewish themselves.[104]

The Jews were not the only religious community with close links to and influence in the Frankfurt political arena. The other religious minority that exercised a disproportionate influence on the Democrats was the Free Church of the German Catholics. Founded in Frankfurt on 1 June 1845, it was one of a host of Free Churches that were created in Germany in the

---

[100] For an example of the quite considerable anti-Semitic literature on Frankfurt, see [Germanicus], *Die Frankfurter Juden und die Aufsaugung des Volkswohlstandes* (Leipzig, 1890). Anti-Semitic pamphlets and reports of anti-Semitism in Frankfurt are in HStAW 407 n. 187.

[101] C. Hallgarten, *Neues über den Antisemitismus* (Frankfurt, 1897), 9–10.

[102] Pulzer, *Jews and the German State*, 186–7.

[103] J. Wertheimer, *Unwelcome Strangers. East European Jews in Imperial Germany* (New York/Oxford, 1987), here table IIb. On the effects of the influx of Eastern European Jews on anti-Semitism, see also S. E. Aschheim, *Brothers and Strangers. The East European Jew in German and German Jewish Consciousness, 1800–1923* (Madison, 1982), 35–79.

[104] For a different interpretation which emphasizes the 'largely successful political and social integration of the Jewish population', see Rohr, 'Kommunaler Liberalismus', 169–70. Roth, 'Liberalismus', 72–4. By contrast, see S. Jersch-Wenzel, 'Minderheiten in der bürgerlichen Gesellschaft. Juden in Amsterdam, Frankfurt und Posen', in J. Kocka (ed.), *Bürgertum im 19. Jahrhundert. Deutschland im europäischen Vergleich* (Munich, 1988), iii. 392–420.

mid-1840s, in reaction to what they considered the superstition and intolerance of the Protestant and Roman Catholic Church establishments.[105] According to the revised principles of the Frankfurt German Catholics of 1892, Christ was respected simply as the 'greatest Reformer in religious and moral terms' (Art. III). The community strove for an improvement and enlightenment of the earthly life alone (Art. V), leaving to individual members the belief in an afterlife if they so desired.[106]

It is highly illuminating that the German Catholic leader, Carl Sänger, went out of his way to emphasize the community's belief in a higher, mysterious force,[107] and in its political neutrality,[108] precisely because the Church's history and practice would suggest opposite conclusions. In 1854, the congregation was refused the further use of the Lutheran church of St Peter's because of its preacher's insistence that the future of religion belonged not to Christianity, but to humanitarianism (*Humanität*).[109] In 1876, under the brief leadership of a radical faction the German Catholic community severed any remaining links with spirituality and devoted itself purely to the pursuit of science and rationality.[110] The more traditional elements of the community quickly reasserted the leadership of the congregation. Nevertheless, a sect which rejected any articles of faith and dogma that contradicted modern science, logic, and reason was inevitably at great pains to find a convincing *raison d'être* for the supernatural.

Similarly, even though the Frankfurt German Catholics were non-political in theory, their beliefs inevitably predisposed them towards a particular political direction. After all, the movement's creation was itself inseparable from the political desire for emancipation and national unity during the *Vormärz* period. From the beginning, its humanitarian influences, democratic (self-governing) organization, and associational structure emphasized the importance of each individual.[111] Before and

---

[105] F. W. Graf, *Die Politisierung des religiösen Bewußtseins. Die bürgerlichen Religionsparteien im deutschen Vormärz: Das Beispiel des Deutschkatholizismus* (Stuttgart, 1978), 26–66. C. Sänger, *1845–1895. Geschichte der freireligiösen Bewegung und der deutschkathol. (freien religiösen) Gemeinde zu Frankfurt a.M. Festschrift zur Feier des fünfzigjährigen Bestehens der Gemeinde* (Frankfurt, 1895).

[106] 'Grundsätze der Deutschkatholischen (freien religiösen) Gemeinde zu Frankfurt a.M.', in *Satzungen der im Jahre 1845 gegründeten Deutchkatholischen (freien religiösen) Gemeinde mit dem Sitze in Frankfurt a.M.* (Frankfurt, 1901), 21–2. A copy of this is also in IfSG, S3/H2923.

[107] C. Sänger, *Fest-Predigt gehalten bei der Einweihung des neuen Andachts-Saales der Deutschkatholischen (freien religiösen) Gemeinde zu Frankfurt a.M.* (Frankfurt, 1892), 10.

[108] Sänger, *Geschichte*, 30.

[109] H. Dechent, *Kirchengeschichte von Frankfurt am Main seit der Reformation* (Leipzig/Frankfurt, 1921), ii. 449–50. Sänger, *Geschichte*, 25.

[110] Sänger, *Geschichte*, 27.

[111] Graf, *Die Politisierung des religiösen Bewußtseins*, esp. 101–19.

during the 1848 Revolution, there were close ties between democrats and German Catholics, while the reverence with which the 'martyr' Robert Blum was regarded by many German Catholic communities was highly reminiscent of Democrat folklore in Frankfurt.[112]

Despite subsequent changes in the movement's ideas largely due to the fusion of the German Catholic and the Free Protestant communities in 1858,[113] the political implications of its theology remained clear. The absence of any focus on an active God, and the subsequent lack of any particular covenant with God or the expectation of life after death, put a special emphasis on the ideal of 'love thy neighbour'. With the value of human life being entirely this-worldly, this ideal was one of the few clear practical principles of the community.[114] To Carl Sänger, the giving of alms was insufficient. Human dignity, indeed the reason for human existence, lay in knowledge. What was important was to create conditions for everybody to live in dignity, which by implication meant to give everyone the opportunity to gain an education. It was a universalist, even pacifist message as it considered one of the most important duties of the community that of enlightening all those whose minds were taken up by discord between peoples, and who did not see the inherent equality of all humankind.[115] These were ideas any Democrat could subscribe to.

Another characteristic which the German Catholics shared with the Democrats was the experience of being a small group outside the establishment which fought vociferously for its own full equality. Frankfurt German Catholics were at one with Jews and Democrats in their fight for religious toleration and against prejudice and discrimination.[116] The German Catholics' emphasis on education, and their fight for equal treatment, also made them outright opponents of the established denominations' hold over primary and secondary schools. Indeed, the president of the German Catholic community, Ferdinand Richard, even argued in 1892 that it was the recent school bill, which aimed to reintroduce universal Church supervision for primary schools, which was the German Catholics' main *raison d'être*.[117]

Naturally, the influence of a small community whose full membership fell sharply from 743 in 1853 to 154 in 1876,[118] reaching more than 800

---

[112] Ibid. 132–41.   [113] Sänger, *Geschichte*, 19–22.
[114] 'Grundsätze der Deutschkatholischen (freien religiösen) Gemeinde zu Frankfurt a.M.', in p. 22 (Art. VI).
[115] Sänger, *Fest-Predigt*, 14–17. C. Sänger, 'Einleitung', in M. Henning (ed.), *Das freie Wort. Eine Auswahl von Beiträgen aus den beiden ersten Jahrgängen der Zeitschrift 'Das freie Wort'* (Frankfurt, 1903), 5.
[116] Sänger, *Fest-Predigt*, 10–11.   [117] Ibid., preface, 4.
[118] *Gemeindebericht* 1876 in IfSG, S3/H2923. Freireligiöse (deutschkatholische) Gemeinde.

members only in 1900, was extremely limited.[119] In addition, its membership did not extend to the upper echelons of Frankfurt society. Still, it had a disproportionate influence over the city's Democrats, mainly owing to the influence which Carl Sänger came to exercise over the party. Having moved to Frankfurt in 1884 to become the German Catholics' preacher, he joined the Democrats and became one of their most active members until his early death in 1901. Of 18 Democrat meetings between January 1895 and February 1896,[120] Sänger presided over six, while being a speaker at one further meeting against state efforts to protect and encourage religious observance.[121] His political activities grew with the introduction of the party's discussion evenings. In 1898, he presided over six party meetings out of eighteen, convening another two meetings, and speaking on two more occasions.[122] In late 1897, Sänger gave a talk on the subject most dear to the Democrats, social policy. Emphasizing the responsibility of local government in the face of the national government's passivity, he advocated generous social policies which would ensure the physical but also the spiritual welfare of all inhabitants.[123]

Apart from Heinrich Rößler, Sänger had clearly advanced to become the most active and influential Democrat who was not linked to the *Frankfurter Zeitung* in any way. He became the Democrats' nominee for the 1898 state elections, and, together with Karl Funck, he broke the National Liberals' hold over the constituency. Sänger's political activities were strongly encouraged by the German Catholic community. Far from fearing a conflict of interest, the community expressly commended his appeal in the Chamber of Deputies for the rights of Dissidents to withdraw their children from religious education in schools.[124] Finally, Sänger advanced his inseparable religious and political views through the journal he created in 1901, *Das freie Wort*.[125] For instance, in a telling article on the German

---

[119] For the membership figures, see Dechent, *Kirchengeschichte*, ii. 451. *55. Jahresbericht der Deutschkatholischen (freien religiösen) Gemeinde zu Frankfurt a.M.* (Frankfurt, 1901), 2.

[120] HStAW 407 n. 161.2 fos. 18–97. Democratic Association meetings, Jan. 1895 to Feb. 1896.

[121] In line with his Democrat and German Catholic convictions, he outlined the futility of any state efforts to enforce religiosity. If the state wanted to overcome socialism, this would be done much more effectively through social legislation. HStAW 407 n. 161.2 fo. 23. Democratic Association meeting, 25 Jan. 1895.

[122] The convenor was responsible for the organization of the meeting, e.g. the notification in advance to the police. HStAW 407 n. 161.3 fos. 18–82. Democratic Association meetings, 1898.

[123] HStAW 407 n. 161.3 fos. 6–9. Democratic Association meeting, 15 Dec. 1897.

[124] *55. Jahresbericht der Deutschkatholischen (freien religiösen) Gemeinde*, 4–11.

[125] Norbert Schlossmacher has identified *Das freie Wort* as one of the principal mouthpieces of the internal Catholic resistance to ultramontanism. However, this undermines his own

bourgeoisie he reflected on its perceived powerlessness which it had just demonstrated in the debates about the building of the *Mittellandkanal*. However, in his view this spinelessness against agricultural interests and the government was not the result of its intrinsic aversion to politics, or even a 'feudalization', but the consequence of its own moral corruption, of bourgeois strivings for money and selfish short-term gains.[126]

It is difficult to determine exactly the extent to which through Sänger German Catholic ideas entered the ideas of Frankfurt Democrats at large. Since their aspirations were often identical with those of Frankfurt Jews, German Catholics certainly supported the Democrat position that religious influence over education fostered backwardness and intolerance. Moreover, the speeches on education and religious matters given by 'Pfarrer' Sänger gave the Democrats added authority in these areas. Education was just one of many issues on which Democrats and German Catholics intrinsically shared opinions. Another issue was the introduction of cremation, an issue which was debated with great ferocity in local politics from the turn of the century.[127] In many ways, to German Catholics as to Democrats it epitomized the struggle of reason against superstition, of individual freedom of conscience against overbearing traditional religious authority. German Catholicism in Frankfurt was in many ways the perfect spiritual complement to the Democrats' political ideals.

The other, more established faiths also had political connections. The relationship between Roman Catholicism and Frankfurt liberalism, and the Democrats in particular, has already been described in Chapter 3. Of the Protestant communities, the groups with the clearest political connections, this time with the National Liberals, were the Calvinist groups, of which

---

argument, because despite the journal's willingness to publish a wide variety of views, ultimately its purpose was to further progress through the promotion of knowledge and human dignity. *Das freie Wort* was clearly an organ of the German Catholic community in Frankfurt. The necessity to publish in a journal that was allied to a movement with very dubious links to Roman Catholicism, not to mention Christianity, highlights how very difficult it was for opponents to ultramontanism to air their views. N. Schlossmacher, 'Der Antiultramontanismus im Wilhelminischen Deutschland. Ein Versuch', in W. Loth (ed.), *Deutscher Katholizismus im Umbruch zur Moderne* (Stuttgart/Berlin/Cologne, 1991), 164–98, here 177–8.

[126] C. Sänger, 'Regierung und Bürgertum', in M. Henning (ed.), *Das freie Wort. Eine Auswahl von Beiträgen aus den beiden ersten Jahrgängen der Zeitschrift 'Das freie Wort'* (Frankfurt, 1903), 37–40.

[127] R. Weigt, 'Die Stellung der Kirche zur Feuerbestattung', in M. Henning (ed.), *Das freie Wort. Eine Auswahl von Beiträgen aus den beiden ersten Jahrgängen der Zeitschrift 'Das freie Wort'* (Frankfurt, 1903), 58–62. See also G. Wolff, 'Leichenverbrennung und Körperbestattung in Geschichte und Vorgeschichte unserer Gegend', in *Alt-Frankfurt*, ii (1910), 101–8.

there were two in Frankfurt, the German Reformed Church, and the French Reformed Church.[128] The two communities descended from several waves of immigrants, who had made their way to Frankfurt from Switzerland and the Austrian Netherlands after 1554, and from France after 1685. In theory, throughout the period of consideration both congregations were open to new members. In practice, the persistent use of French as the *lingua franca* in all Church matters kept the French Reformed congregation élitist, undiluted, and inward-looking. All Reformed newcomers to Frankfurt, the majority of whom were baptized into the Prussian United Church, had to be cared for by the German Reformed Church, which in some aspects changed beyond recognition as a result.[129] In 1864, there were officially 6,624 Calvinists who were assigned to the German Reformed Church.[130] By 1905, the German Reformed Church was responsible for most of the 18,600 people who described themselves as Calvinists throughout Frankfurt, although those who were registered as full members of the Church numbered 2,014.[131] Clearly, the community failed to keep up with its new responsibilities. With an average Sunday attendance of 430 (or just over 2 per cent of official members), active participation was extremely low, even in relation to other major commercial or industrial cities across Germany.[132] It is not surprising that the dramatic change in scale and quality of the work of the German Reformed Church was not reflected in the parish leadership. The council of elders (*Presbyterium*) continued to consist largely of those whose families had been with the parish for generations, many of whom were part of the city's social élite. One of the most prominent elders was Gustav Humser, the much-respected National Liberal who had been supported as leader of the city council even by the left-liberal majority for 25 years until his retirement in 1904. Of the fourteen members of the *Presbyterium* in 1893, five were National Liberals (including the Pastor, R. Ehlers), and one was a conservative.[133] In 1905, of the 61 members of the great council of elders (*großes Presbyterium*), twelve were

---

[128] An introduction into the history and the culture of the French Reformed community is in *400 Jahre Französisch-Reformierte Gemeinde, Frankfurt am Main*, in IfSG, S3/H14.691.

[129] Dechent, *Kirchengeschichte*, ii. 503–5.

[130] *Beiträge zur Statistik*, ii (1864–1875), 55.

[131] Of the 18,600, the number of people in the care of the French Reformed Church numbered no more than 1,000. *Die 350 jährige Gedenkfeier der deutschen evangelisch-reformierten Gemeinde zu Frankfurt am Main* (Frankfurt, 1906), 31.

[132] Ibid. 31–5. For the general context, see also Smith, *German Nationalism and Religious Conflict*, 87–92.

[133] Deutsche evangelisch-reformierte Gemeinde zu Frankfurt a.M., *Zur Erinnerung an die Jubiläumsfeier* (Frankfurt, 1893), 6.

Liberals and Education

also members of the National Liberal Association.[134] Of the seventeen representatives from the more socially elevated French Reformed Church to the newly established Frankfurt Reformed Synod in 1900, three were National Liberals. A fourth was Eduard von Harnier, an energetic member of the council until 1900 who was without formal party allegiance, but whom contemporaries considered to be a National Liberal.[135] By contrast, only two German Reformed elders were members of the Progressive Liberal Association, though one of those was the influential Albert Helff who served as deputy secretary to the council from 1900 to 1904.[136] It was not possible to attribute Progressive Liberal membership to any leading representative of the French Reformed community. Owing to the absence of Democrat membership lists during the 1890s and 1900s, it is impossible to come to definite conclusions about Democrat political activity among Frankfurt Calvinists, but it does not appear as though there was a prominent Democrat in the council of elders in either Reformed Church.

Clearly, there was a great, disproportionate congruence between membership of the National Liberal Association, and active membership of the Reformed Churches. The Calvinist influence over the National Liberals explains why these liberals on the right were also such staunch defenders of a non-denominational system of education. For central to the self-understanding of both Calvinist communities was the memory of, first, persecution and, then, the discrimination which they had endured until the early nineteenth century. At the centenary celebrations of the inauguration of their first church, Pastor Ehlers reminded his congregation that for two centuries, the German Reformed community had been forced to worship outside the city walls. His colleague, Heinrich Bauer, chose to preach on the sentence 'Wherever I cause my name to be invoked, I will come to you and bless you' (Exodus 20: 24). He explicitly likened the Calvinists' long persecution and discrimination before and after their arrival in Frankfurt with that of the Israelites in Egypt. Just as the Israelites' suffering had come to an

---

[134] The most recent available National Liberal membership list dates from 1893. If anything, therefore, this figure underestimates the true National Liberal membership, since it is more likely that in the following twelve years additional members would have entered the party, in line with its general growth in membership. The two lists are in HStAW 407 n. 160 fos. 415–25. Membership List of the National Liberal Association of 13 May 1893. *Bericht des Presbyteriums der deutschen evangelisch-reformierten Gemeinde über seine Tätigkeit im abgelaufenen Kirchenjahr* (Frankfurt, 1905). This can be found in the library of IfSG.

[135] IfSG, S2/H2291, fo. 228. Minutes or the great council of elders of the French reformed congregation, 16 Feb. 1900: elections to the Synod.

[136] HStAW 407 n. 150.2 fos. 103–12. Membership list for the Frankfurt Progressive Liberal Association, 1897.

end only when they were able to build the Lord a temple in Jerusalem, so the building of the church in Frankfurt marked the end of religious persecution there.[137] Hence the building was to be understood principally as a memorial to 'denominational harmony and peace', to 'true Christian acceptance [*Weitherzigkeit*] and evangelical tolerance, which give justice to those of different faiths'.[138] In this spirit, politically active Calvinists had every reason to support the Jews in their quest for a tolerant society through non-denominational education.

The close Calvinist involvement with the National Liberals at the same time explains why they could never be as radical as the Democrats on this issue. There had always been some Protestant opposition to denominational schooling, though this had little impact.[139] Yet at the height of the controversy before 1906, the liberal and Democrat consensus on non-denominational education led a prominent elder from the German Reformed congregation, Ernst Julius Trommershausen, to lead the fight against non-denominational schooling on the Protestant side. To this end, in 1903 he founded the *Freie evangelische Vereinigung*, an association to promote a popular revival of established Protestantism through the principal medium of Protestant primary school education.[140] In complete contrast to the Democrats' localist aims and rhetoric, Trommershausen demanded a Protestant education which alone could raise a Christian, 'national' German youth. Central to his message was also the language of 'struggle', as only spiritual, moral, and religious confrontation could lead to the renewal of the country.[141] Clearly, his views represented everything the Democrats and liberals tried to fight against, namely nationalism, intolerance, and (only thinly disguised) anti-Semitism.

Supported by the leader of the combined Frankfurt Protestant synods,[142]

---

[137] 'Festpredigt von Pfarrer Ehlers', in Deutsche evangelisch-reformierte Gemeinde, *Erinnerung an die Jubliäumsfeier*, 7.

[138] 'Ein Wahrzeichen konfessioneller Eintracht und Friedfertigkeit'. 'So erhebt sich dies Bethaus vor unseren Augen als Denkmal ächter christlicher Weitherzigkeit und evangelischer Duldsamkeit, welche auch dem Andersgläubigen sein Recht wiederfahren läßt.' Bauer, 'Bericht über die Geschichte der Kirche', in Deutsche evangelisch-reformierte Gemeinde, *Erinnerung an die Jubliäumsfeier*, 23.

[139] The most vociferous Protestant opponent of the denominational school in the 1870s was Friedrich August Finger, a rather conservative acting head teacher at the *Mittlere Bürgerschule*. F. A. Finger, *Ausgewählte pädagogische Schriften* (Frankfurt, 1887), esp. i. 212–14, 231–4, 272–300.

[140] Dechent, *Kirchengeschichte*, ii. 533.

[141] E. Trommershausen, *Über protestantische Erziehung* (Saarbrücken, 1904), 7, 18.

[142] 'Rede des Herrn Professor Dr. Trommershausen in der Stadtverordnetenversammlung am 9. Januar 1905' (Frankfurt, 1905). This pamphlet has been added to the copy in IfSG of Trommershausen, *Über protestantische Erziehung*.

Trommershausen led the *Freie evangelische Vereinigung* into an alliance with the Roman Catholics and the *Mittelstand* to form the *Verein für kommunale Wahlen* (Association for Local Elections), which contested the 1904 elections. As shown in the previous chapter, in these elections, which were fought on the single issue of non-denominational schooling, this loose electoral alliance was so successful that it eclipsed the National Liberals to become the second largest group in the city council. There is no doubt that Trommershausen split the Protestant vote and thus contributed to this result. He led the Association's campaign in the prosperous Westend (fourth electoral district), which was normally safe National Liberal territory. This time, Trommershausen and the Association's other two nominees were elected, together with the allied anti-Semite leader, Hermann Laaß. Not one National Liberal was returned.

Once in the city council, Trommershausen never held back his aggressive rhetoric that was more alien to the liberal and Democrat establishment than that of the Social Democrats. However, even though he became a principal target for left-liberal attacks, the National Liberals could not afford to marginalize him completely. Following a compromise achieved in 1908 by the Prussian authorities, whereby out of ten new primary schools, three were to be denominational, the question of religion in education became less prominent.[143] It was thus possible to overcome the overt political split in Protestant ranks, and convince Trommershausen to stand for the 1910 municipal elections as a National Liberal.

In contrast to the Roman Catholics, the Calvinists who broke with the liberal parties were not endorsed by any of the four reformed ministers. Their breakaway did not lead to the creation of a separate milieu, while their success in the 1904 elections was mainly based on the ability to provide that extra proportion of votes needed to win against the National Liberals. In short, amongst Frankfurt National Liberals the relatively smaller Jewish influence (which was still important) was compensated for by the Calvinist influence which was motivated by that community's own memory of persecution and intolerance. However, since that experience was essentially

---

[143] This compromise followed the 1906 *Volksschulunterhaltungsgesetz*, which gave the Minister for Education much greater powers vis-à-vis the localities. J. Freiherr von der Goltz, 'Die Entwicklung der Selbstverwaltung innerhalb der staatlichen Verwaltung der öffentlichen Volksschule in Preußen', D.jur. thesis (Greifswald, 1914), 76–86. In response, even many left liberals, led by Karl Funck, accepted the compromise in order to settle the issue. This did not stop the liberals and Social Democrats from converting two of these newly opened Roman Catholic schools to non-denominational schools in 1913, at a time when education had moved from the Prussian political agenda. Maly, *Das Regiment der Parteien*, 117–20. Schäfer, *Schulen und Schulpolitik*, 76–84.

limited to Frankfurt, Frankfurt Calvinists who integrated a growing number of immigrants could never be as insistent upon issues such as non-denominational education as Jews, whose experience of suffering was universal.

This book argues that by 1866 Frankfurt had not become an unusual hive of progressive reform. The best example of this is the fate of the city's Lutheran Churches. In desperate need of reform in 1866, the Prussian authorities accepted the majority's plea not to interfere with the Lutherans' traditional and peculiar Church organization. In the following decades, the Lutheran Churches struggled on, until state pressure forced a reorganization in 1900. Until then, Frankfurt was in the peculiar situation of having no real parish organizations. Frankfurt Lutherans could attend and be a member of any church within the city. In marked contrast to the two Reformed congregations with their distinct identities, there was very little sense of a Lutheran Church or parish community. There was thus no structure for integrating new Lutheran arrivals into parish life. Such a system may just have been viable in an independent Free City without freedom of movement, but it was completely unsuited for the mass mobility of industrial Germany. Even more importantly, without clear demarcation lines, decisions were cumbersome and slow, as responsibilities were shifted from one church to the next. This had the astonishing consequence that despite the growth of the Lutheran population from 53,621 in 1864 to 123,538 in 1895, and to around 135,000 in 1900,[144] not a single new Lutheran church had been built during this period or indeed since the Reformation.[145]

One problem which Lutherans and Calvinists shared was that most of the Protestants new to the city came from areas which adhered to the Prussian Union of Lutheran and Reformed Churches. Indeed, so lax was Church affiliation that in the 1895 census, almost 40 per cent of all Protestants stated that they belonged to the Union without being aware that it did not even exist in Frankfurt.[146] Clearly, these people had no connection at all to either of the two Reformed congregations or to the one Lutheran 'super'

---

[144] For the 1864 figure, see *Beiträge zur Statistik*, ii (1864–1875), 55. E. Trommershausen, 'Beitrag zur Geschichte des landesherrlichen Kirchenregiments in den evangelischen Gemeinden zu Frankfurt a.M.', in *Programm des Lessing-Gymnasiums zu Frankfurt a.M.* (Frankfurt, 1897), 5. The 1900 figure is derived by substracting the 11,129 registered Calvinists from the total number of Protestants. *Die 350 jährige Gedenkfeier der deutschen evangelisch-reformierten Gemeinde*, 31. *Statistisches Handbuch der Stadt Frankfurt am Main*, ed. Statistisches Amt (Frankfurt, 1907), 37.

[145] Dechent, *Kirchengeschichte*, ii. 487.

[146] This ratio would undoubtedly have been much higher had the question on religious affiliation actually listed the Union alongside the categories 'Reformed' and 'Lutheran'. Trommershausen, 'Beitrag zur Geschichte des landesherrlichen Kirchenregiments', 8–9.

parish.¹⁴⁷ In the end, the impetus for the reorganization came from the increasing need for funds. Since a Church tax of 10 per cent of income tax could not be raised without state approval, the Lutherans had to bow to state pressure and accept a new structure based on individual parishes.¹⁴⁸ In the process, the city acquired its own, distinct Protestant *Landeskirche*, which consisted of three synods, a Lutheran synod for the city, a Lutheran synod for the outer parishes, and one Reformed synod.¹⁴⁹

The absence of a transparent organizational structure until 1900 makes it extremely difficult to gain any clear view about the political preferences and ideals of Lutherans. If anything, the majority of Lutherans probably supported the liberals and Democrats in their pursuit of religious tolerance.¹⁵⁰ By contrast to those active in the Reformed Churches, however, Lutheran support for religious tolerance was not the result of religious conviction, but, as the Calvinist pastor Rudolf Ehlers argued, of the overwhelming religious indifference which appeared to have been the pervasive feature of Lutheran life as early as 1868.¹⁵¹ Even though Frankfurt's small churchgoing population consisted overwhelmingly of women which reduced even further the pool for communicant Lutherans engaged in municipal politics,¹⁵² there were, of course, a number of more or less active Lutheran men in the political élite. Despite the relative preponderance of Calvinists, the membership of the local Gustav-Adolf-Foundation for the support of Protestantism included a significant number of Lutherans from both liberal and Democratic parties.¹⁵³ Still, it is difficult to come to the

---

¹⁴⁷ Ibid. 8–9.

¹⁴⁸ H. Bauer, *Ueber den Entwurf einer Kirchengemeinde- und Synodial-Ordnung für Frankfurt am Main* (Frankfurt, 1897), 5–6.

¹⁴⁹ Dechent, *Kirchengeschichte*, ii. 483–6. This decentralized, 'democratic' system of organization is itself testimony of the liberal character of Frankfurt Protestantism. On church organization in general, see Nipperdey, *Deutsche Geschichte 1866–1918*, i. 480–1. Hübinger, *Kulturprotestantismus*, 8, and esp. 42–3, where he describes the system's ideological affinity to liberal concepts of self-government.

¹⁵⁰ *Die protestantischen Gemeinden der Stadt Frankfurt in Preußen* (Frankfurt, 1868), 5. This booklet was published anonymously by Eduard Franz Souchay.

¹⁵¹ *Zur Verständigung über die Frankfurter Kirchenfrage. Für und gegen die Schrift: 'Die protestantischen Gemeinden der Stadt Frankfurt in Preußen* (Frankfurt, 1868), 3–4. This was published anonymously by Pastor Ehlers.

¹⁵² In Frankfurt, 70% of the Protestant congregation was female, an unusually high number in the national context. This figure is likely to have been higher among Lutherans, given that the Reformed communities, and esp. the French Reformed Church, had a core of (male) members who still considered active membership an integral part of their social and cultural position. In general, see Smith, *German Nationalism and Religious Conflict*, 89.

¹⁵³ Members of the Association included such local political leaders as Franz Adickes and Heinrich Rößler. *Jahresbericht und Rechnungs-Ablage des Haupt-Vereins der evangelischen Gustav-Adolf-Stiftung für das Jahr 1906* (Frankfurt, 1907).

conclusion that Lutheran faith in Frankfurt influenced political behaviour in a positive way. In many ways, this is unsurprising, because minority faith groups, particularly if they had been disadvantaged for a long time, had a particular incentive to define themselves clearly and sharply against the (silent) majority. As a result, it is rather more difficult to judge conclusively what the majority stood for, especially if it was characterized by heterogeneity and relative indifference.

It follows that the group that can be determined with some precision is one of a small but vociferous minority within Lutheranism. For in Frankfurt, too, there was a nationalist brand of Protestantism.[154] Ironically, this was led by the Pastor of the Paulskirche, the former assembly of the revolutionary Frankfurt Parliament in 1848/9, Julius Werner. Werner used his platform with enthusiasm, preaching time and again about the importance of Christianity for the greatness of the German nation.[155] More importantly, his stance had clear political implications, as he held that Pastors should not shy back from giving political advice and guidance. He urged support for parties that stood for the interests of Protestantism, and in Frankfurt he explicitly supported Trommershausen's party.[156] In general, Werner urged support for the 'national' wing of the National Liberals and all parties to its right.[157] The penetration of the Democrats by the Jewish reform movement, on the other hand, meant that they were to be opposed at all cost.[158] Similarly, Protestants should support only those newspapers which were explicitly Christian in outlook, i.e. those sponsoring 'Christianity, Germanness, monarchy and social reform'. The rejection of the *Frankfurter Zeitung* or any other left-liberal newspaper in Jewish hands could have been hardly more explicit.[159] Once again, it is difficult to know how much effect these words had in Frankfurt itself. Still, they serve as an important reminder about the illusory nature of a unitary 'bourgeois milieu', and the fact that there could be drastic conflicts within what is usually oversimplistically summarized as 'Protestantism' at the grass roots.

In contrast to the solidity of the Jewish and German Catholic support for

---

[154] See the definition of 'national Protestantism' in Gollwitzer, *Vorüberlegungen*, 26–9. On the 'Pastorennationalismus', see Nipperdey, *Deutsche Geschichte 1866–1918*, i. 501.

[155] J. Werner, *Deutschtum und Christentum. Gedenkreden* (Heidelberg, 1906).

[156] J. Werner, *Der deutsche Protestantismus und das öffentliche Leben* (Hagen i.W., n.d.), 83–4.

[157] Ibid. 96–7.   [158] Ibid. 99.

[159] Ibid. 87–9. On the dominance of the liberal press by 1914, see Wehler, *Deutsche Gesellschaftsgeschichte 1849–1914*, 1241–3. Nipperdey, *Deutsche Geschichte 1866–1914*, i. 802–3.

the Democrats, the existence of a hostile minority demonstrates that there were limits to the Calvinist and Lutheran enthusiasm for a tolerant society. In some ways, this confrontation is reminiscent of that described by Hübinger between *Kulturprotestantismus*, on the one hand, and national Protestantism with its organizational background in the Evangelical League (*Evangelischer Bund*), on the other.[160] The difference is, firstly, that in Frankfurt it is too simplistic to speak of 'Protestantism' in general without reference to the very different historical backgrounds and cultural attributes of the various denominations. Secondly, with the support of Calvinists and some Lutherans the emphasis of Frankfurt liberals and Democrats was on a tolerant society. Undoubtedly because of the strong Jewish political influence, the assumption of German political culture as having a Protestant character was absent from most leading Protestant and liberal élites, as was the expectation of Jewish assimilation.[161] Finally, noting the coincidence between the ascendancy of *Kulturprotestantismus* and a reviving left liberalism, Hübinger is, perhaps, a little too quick to connect the two. The example of Frankfurt, with its vociferously hostile national Protestant movement, emphasizes that Protestant influence on liberalism could be a source of conflict and division as much as of strength.[162]

Ultimately, the extent to which certain Protestant movements strengthened particular types of liberalism was highly dependent on the strength of individual religiosity. This point seems banal, but Frankfurt liberals and Democrats could only make a successful stance for non-denominational education because this was an article of faith. Indifference would have dictated a more opportunistic policy which would not cause offence for many national Protestants and the seclusion of the Roman Catholic community. Similarly, this explains the effective weakness of national Protestantism in Frankfurt. Since most of the active faithful men were firmly ensconced in the Democratic and National Liberal camps, Trommershausen and Werner only had those left to appeal to who were not active church-goers and to whom, by definition, the question of denominational

---

[160] Hübinger, *Kulturprotestantismus*, 237–50. Gollwitzer, *Vorüberlegungen*, 26–33. Hübinger, 'Confessionalism', 167–8. On the Evangelical League, see Smith, *German Nationalism and Religious Conflict*, esp. 127–38.

[161] Hübinger, *Kulturprotestantismus*, esp. 233–50, 264–75.

[162] This argument goes one step further than that presented by Harry Liebersohn, who has shown how a common interest of the educated bourgeoisie in the social question, derived from a common Protestant faith, could not be synthesized into a common programme of views or actions. H. Liebersohn, 'Religion and Industrial Society: The Protestant Social Congress in Wilhelmine Germany', *Transactions of the American Philosophical Society*, lxxvi, Part 6 (Philadelphia, 1986).

schooling was less relevant. Protestantism influenced and reinforced political consistency and coherence, but it is not clear that it attracted popular support to a persistent and significant degree.

4.3. Education and Self-Government

There was another major motive for the Frankfurt liberals' resistance to Prussian efforts at reintroducing denominational education in the city, but in this respect Frankfurt liberals and Democrats were fully representative of urban liberals elsewhere. For in Frankfurt as anywhere else, educational battles between the city and the state struck at the heart of the liberal concern of local self-government. Frankfurt liberals declared that they were happy to bear the tremendous financial burdens which education imposed upon the local budget, but at the very least they demanded a say in how their schools were run.[163] In recent years, Frankfurt schools had flourished because of the principle of self-government, so while nobody would challenge the supervisory role of the state it was clear that the quality of education in Frankfurt was directly linked to the amount of self-government left to Frankfurt on educational matters.[164]

The Frankfurt liberals' and Democrats' emphasis on the intimate connection between education and local self-government were reflected by liberals in local government throughout Germany. The connection between local self-government and education had great currency in German liberal thought through the writings of Rudolf Gneist. To Gneist, extensive and effective local government over schools was the best way of ensuring the funding and the commitment for education. After all, at state level, parliament was showing itself to be completely unable to pass a statewide education law. By the same token, such an education system would complement the aim of self-government of realizing stable local communities loyal to the state. Administrative reform, enhanced local government principally in the rural areas, and improved education went hand-in-hand.[165]

As ever, with his insistence on local government Gneist was primarily

---

[163] *Frankfurter Journal*, 2 Feb. 1892 (Abendblatt), also in IfSG, S2/381.
[164] See the speech by the Frankfurt *Stadtrat* responsible for school affairs, Otto Grimm, on the eve of his by-election victory to the Prussian Chamber of Deputies in *Frankfurter Journal* 17 Dec. 1891 (Beilage), also in IfSG, S2/381. This point was also made by the Democrat Heinrich Rößler in *Frankfurter Zeitung*, 14 Nov. 1882 (Abendblatt). In general, left liberals conveyed this message in much stronger language, as state intervention was decried as an 'act of violence' and 'amounting to rape'. HStAW 407 n. 161³ fo. 234. Democrat deputy Sänger on 11 Apr. 1900. Democrat councillor Wedel in *MPS*, 1908, §168, p. 194.
[165] R. Gneist, *Die Selbstverwaltung der Volksschule. Vorschläge zur Lösung des Schulstreites durch die preußische Kreis-Ordung* (Berlin, 1869). Goltz, 'Die Entwicklung der Selbstverwaltung', here esp. 59–64.

concerned about the rural areas of Prussia. While his views were undoubtedly received by liberals in the cities at the time, it was not until the explosion of municipal spending (on education in particular) in the 1890s and the corresponding increase in municipal assertiveness which is described in Chapter 6 that liberals in the cities became more insistent on the relationship between education and self-government. Education became the principal area in which the ideals of the state and of local self-government clashed.[166] A state which demanded greater municipal financial contributions without granting local government correspondingly greater rights offended the very principle of self-government.[167] In his speech to mark the 100th anniversary of the Prussian city ordinance of 1808, the Mayor of Halle, Richard Robert Rive put forward this view succinctly. Speaking about the local school in general, he highlighted the contradiction that in school administration, self-government had been most curtailed, although it was in school administration that self-government had the greatest potential. This was why, despite all restrictions imposed from outside, local government was determined to make any sacrifice to turn municipal education into the 'finest creation of culture'.[168] Rive was not alone in this view. When he had elaborated this particular line of argument at a previous meeting of the Prussian city congress in 1904, his view had been supported by a near unanimous vote (one delegate was opposed, none abstained).[169]

At another conference of the Prussian city congress in 1906 to discuss the Prussian finance bill for education (*Schuldotationsgesetz*), the Mayor of Breslau emphasized the unique position of education in local self-government. At a time of social, political, and religious strife, education was the one issue over which local parties could unite in their endeavour to achieve the highest standards.[170] The rather more conservative Mayor of

---

[166] Preuß, 'Die staatliche Bestätigung', 202.

[167] Hugo Preuß in A. Wagner and H. Preuß, *Kommunale Steuerfragen* (Jena, 1904), 56–9. H. Preuß, *Das Recht der städtischen Schulverwaltung in Preußen* (Berlin, 1905), esp. 93.

[168] 'Its image is a peculiar one within the framework of self-government. In it the rights of self-government have been developed the least, yet in it the ability of self-government celebrates its proudest triumph. The cities have upheld material generosity and idealistic enthusiasm in order to make urban education into the finest creation of culture, notwithstanding all formal limitations' (R. R. Rive, 'Die Entwicklung der preußischen Städte seit dem Erlaß der Städteordnung von 1808', in *Verhandlungen des Sechsten Preußischen Städtetages am 5. und 6. Oktober 1908 zu Königsberg* (Königsberg, 1908), 29–36, here 34–5.

[169] For Rive's speech, see *Verhandlungen des Vierten allgemeinen Preußischen Städtetages am 6. und 7. Dezember 1904 zu Berlin* (Berlin, 1905), 24–8. For the vote on the motions based on Rive's talk, see 35.

[170] *Verhandlungen des Fünften allgemeinen Preußischen Städtetages am 15. Januar 1906 zu Berlin* (Berlin, 1906), 28.

Kiel, Fuß, pointed out that the cities were 'historically developed individual organs' whose growth would be hampered through undue state interference, to the detriment of the state itself.[171]

At the same time, the concern of German liberals in the cities for self-government with regard to education did not arise out of an obsession with *Selbstverwaltung* for its own sake. Concluding his views on the importance of self-government in education in 1908, Rive exclaimed: 'Thus the municipal development of culture permeates the entire life of the people. Education of the young for life, the vivid realization of the ideals of *Bildung*, raising the people to moral, spiritual, and economic power and, above all, a fresh breeze of eternally young, true art: this is the social and idealistic content of municipal work in education.'[172]

This view was supplemented, also to universal acclaim, by the Mayor of Breslau, who emphasized that, more than any other task, it was school administration which led people to make sacrifices for the community, to the benefit of the school, the community, and the state.[173]

Local school administration epitomized, therefore, the true values of self-government, for not only did it fulfil its immediate task, the most efficient and effective imparting of knowledge, but it would ultimately lead to the moral, and spiritual improvement of the community. Local self-government in education alone could lead the individual towards the higher values of true culture, morality, and self-sacrifice. This was in complete agreement with the faith which Frankfurt liberals placed in the local administration of education. According to the Democrat leader Rößler, education should not be dominated by the spirit of sectarianism, but by scientific and enlightened education.[174] For the natural sciences, 'unconditionally rational and scientific thinking' alone could liberate permanently the German people from superstition and prejudice.[175] Moreover, left liberals held that it was the free development of schools (i.e. under the auspices of local government) which was the foundation of 'the most important cultural properties' of the people.[176] As has been shown, the

---

[171] *Verhandlungen des Fünften Preußischen Städtetages (1906)*, 22.
[172] *Verhandlungen des Sechsten Preußischen Städtetages (1908)*, 35.
[173] *Verhandlungen des Fünften Preußischen Städtetages (1906)*, 28.
[174] Quoted in Müller, *Aufklärungen*, 91.
[175] *Heinrich Rößler. Sonderabdruck des Physikalischen Vereins* (Frankfurt, 1924), 4. Also in IfSG, S2/1054.
[176] See the left-liberal resolution of 4 June 1904, carried by all against one vote, printed in Müller, *Aufklärungen*, 16.

whole point of the Frankfurt liberals' insistence on non-denominational education was to create a free and tolerant society, with a particular though by no means exclusive thrust against anti-Semitism, at least for the community of Frankfurt.

For the liberals in Frankfurt, as in other cities, self-government in education was, perhaps, the most important concern of practical politics. For they were highly aware that education was the 'key to the future', that it was perhaps the best way to influence generations of people, and particularly the young. True to its ideal, self-government in education was the best way of overcoming the conflicts within, and the fragmentation of, society which contemporaries were so worried about. Doubtless many liberals on the right (though not necessarily in Frankfurt) accepted the government's stance that primary schools had a particular role to play in combating Social Democracy.[177] However, whereas the government held that this could be best achieved through uniform emphasis on religious and moral teaching, liberals in the cities, if they believed in it at all, maintained that this could only be done by schools which were organized and financed by the community and which thus bound the community together.

It is doubtful if in their aspirations for self-government in education liberals stopped there. For surely, by the 1900s control over local education was the most important means left at the liberals' disposal to liberalize German society. Increasingly marginalized in national and state politics, education was the most potent way left for those liberals who were still largely in control of the cities to try to reverse the withdrawal of their ideals in German society. Frankfurt liberals were in no doubt about the crucial role of education in the shaping of society. According to Frankfurt liberal doctrine, confessional discord and intolerance destroyed the foundations of Frankfurt's economic and social welfare, as well as the principles of culture, philanthropy, and harmony upon which Frankfurt society was founded. Only non-denominational schooling could prevent a spiritual and material decline, the return to backwardness and small-mindedness. Education was thus the key to Frankfurt's position as a model of German self-government and the preservation of liberal values, of everything that Frankfurt stood for.[178] Not surprisingly, it was liberals in the cities who led the opposition

---

[177] Of the three denominational schools to be opened in 1908, the Prussian Minister of Education ordered two to be established in predominantly industrial areas. See Quarck's complaint in *MPS*, 1908, §168, 191–203.

[178] See the left-liberal programme for the 1904 elections in *Frankfurter Zeitung*, 27 Nov. 1904 (3. Morgenblatt).

against the school bill compromise of 1904.[179] On account of schools controlled by liberals, future generations, infused with the virtues of tolerance, morality, and self-denial, would perhaps be less susceptible to conservative ideals drenched in Prussian militarism, and more open to liberalism.[180]

4.4. The Quality of Primary Education

If Frankfurt liberals considered themselves extremely progressive on account of their success in the introduction of non-denominational schools, the quality of primary education was otherwise surprisingly poor particularly in the first decades after the annexation. The basic schools frequented by children of better-off parents, the *Bürgerschulen*, charged 18 M. per annum, and, in the early 1880s, had an average class size of 45. By contrast, the primary schools (*Volksschulen*) for the poorer children still cost 6 M. per annum, but their classes contained between 60 and 70 pupils,[181] and in some there were over 100.[182] In 1886, Frankfurt was the only city with over 100,000 inhabitants which still had primary schools with only four grades, so that pupils would be stuck in each grade for two years.[183] By contrast, the local *Bürgerschulen* had seven grades (pupils would move up each year from grade seven to grade one, in which they would remain for two years).

Only as a result of growing protests by the local teachers' association from the mid-1880s did the Democrats end their lethargy on this matter and demand an end to the neglect of the quality of primary schools. The final decision for reform, however, did not come from the city's liberal/Democrat government, but was forced upon the city by the statewide abolition of fees for all types of primary schools in 1888.[184] From

---

[179] Lamberti, *State, Society, and the Elementary School*, 197–8.

[180] For example, Frankfurt left liberals liked to emphasize that their primary aim was to educate not Protestant or Catholic Prussians, but Frankfurters. Councillor Rößler in *Frankfurter Zeitung*, 14 Nov. 1882 (Abendblatt).

[181] See e.g. the annual school reports of the *Magistrat*, here *MAB*, 1883/4, pp. 152–4, *MAB*, 1885/6, pp. 184–7, *MAB*, 1886/7, pp. 197–200. In 1880/1 there were ten *Bürgerschulen* with 4,859 pupils compared with three primary schools with a total of 2,112 pupils. *Sozialdemokratie und Stadtverwaltung* (1906), 71.

[182] *MAB*, 1887/8, p. 199.

[183] For a general overview, see the summary of primary school conditions in various German big cities in Vorstand des Lehrer-Vereins zu Frankfurt a.M. (ed.), *Herr Direktor Dr. Georg Veith und die vierklassigen Volksschulen zu Frankfurt a.M. Eine pädagogische Abfertigung* (2nd edn., Frankfurt, 1887), 56–65. This demonstrates clearly the backwardness of the Frankfurt system of primary schools.

[184] In Frankfurt itself, owing to Democrat pressure, the issue was considered by the council from March 1887 onwards, but the *Magistrat* remained resolutely opposed to any change in the dual primary school system. *Sozialdemokratie und Stadtverwaltung* (1906), 71.

April 1889, therefore, all Frankfurt primary schools were free and had seven grades.[185] Within the next few years, Frankfurt caught up with the quality of primary schools in other cities. A relatively high number of pupils managed to reach the final seventh year compared to other German cities, and the city was able to afford the highest teachers' salaries in Prussia by 1903. At the same time, compared to other cities, with an average class size of 51 pupils, with 14 per cent of pupils in classes of 60 or more,[186] Frankfurt's primary schools were rather average.[187]

For children from more privileged backgrounds, there were still the more advanced primary schools, the *Mittelschulen*, with a school fee of originally 36 M. and which taught compulsory French and optional English on top of the usual primary school curriculum. These schools were later heavily criticized by the SPD since the relatively high school fee effectively barred children of industrial workers or other sections of the population with small incomes.[188] Presumably, it is for this reason also that the right of existence of the city's *Mittelschulen* was never questioned, or even considered to be a problem, by the liberals. They were extremely popular among a large proportion of Frankfurt's *Mittelstand*, and especially its poorer sections such as the lower civil servants, white-collar workers, and small shopkeepers and artisans.[189]

More contentious than the *Mittelschulen* were the local preparatory schools to which those who aspired to attend the local grammar school usually went for three years in order to avoid having to spend the first years in a primary school. These *Vorschulen* were attached to the secondary schools and charged the same exorbitant fees, and it is these preparatory schools in particular which remained bastions of social exclusiveness.[190] They were welcomed by liberals on the right and especially in the *Magistrat*, but as these schools of a particular 'estate' (*Standesschule*) contradicted the very

---

[185] *MPS*, 1889/90, pp. 232–3.   [186] *MPS*, 1898/9, p. 449.

[187] Gizyki, 'Das Volksschulwesen', 204–13. Gizyki points out that the number of children reaching the highest primary school grade is a factor not only of the quality of education, but also of parents' income and the corresponding need for the children to work in their spare time, as well as general health conditions.

[188] *Sozialdemokratie und Stadtverwaltung* (1906), 71.

[189] Amongst liberals there was the widespread conviction that 'standesbewußte' ('estate-conscious') parents who sent their children to the middle schools would want to pay school fees as part of this consciousness. For the views of the *Stadtrat* responsible for schools, Ziehen, and the Democrat leader Rößler, see Schäfer, *Schulen und Schulpolitik*, 45–6, 50.

[190] The other great advantage of the preparatory schools, esp. from the point of view of the less intellectually versatile children of the wealthier citizens, was that after three years its pupils would progress to the secondary school automatically, without entrance exams and with little regard for the pupils' merits.

principle of popular primary schools, they came under periodic Democrat attack from 1892.[191] In response to SPD pressure, for Democrats it became a matter of social justice that all groups of society should initially go to the same primary school,[192] and eventually the National Liberals in the council gave in. From 1909 this liberal/SPD consensus was strong enough to challenge a reluctant *Magistrat* to abolish the preparatory schools. Nonetheless, *Vorschulen* were not abolished until 1926 (although this had been in preparation since 1917).[193]

After a period of relative neglect, therefore, from the 1890s onwards the quality of Frankfurt's primary schools received more political attention and was improved accordingly, largely for three reasons. Firstly, it was the result of the genuine social political concerns of left liberals who demanded the abolition of preparatory schools or even the introduction of free school materials (*Lernmittelfreiheit*). The motivation was less a general struggle to avoid the spread of socialism, than an understanding that an improvement of education for the poorer classes of society formed part of their responsibility towards the common weal of the Frankfurt community.[194] For the most part, however, men like Rößler were in a minority, and even when, as in the case of the preparatory schools, they were successful in persuading the council, they still had to encounter the hostility of a rather more conservative *Magistrat* under the leadership of Adickes.[195]

The second factor that led to the improvement of the primary schools was the work of individual philanthropists and of voluntary associations. Typically, specialist schools of various kinds would be founded by private associations or individual philanthropists and would, if proven successful, be taken over or at least supported by the city. Thus, the city's schools of trade and commerce went back to private foundations. According to this pattern, Frankfurt could boast of one of the country's leading institutes for the deaf and dumb in the country,[196] an institute for the mentally ill from

---

[191] See the speech by the Democrat Wedel in *Kleine Presse*, 23 Nov. 1892.

[192] See Heinrich Rößler's speech in HStAW 407 n. 161⁴ fo. 75. Democratic Association meeting, 17 Feb. 1902.

[193] Schäfer, *Schulen und Schulpolitik*, 83–93.

[194] Apart from Rößler's speech in HStAW 407 n. 161⁴ fos. 75–7 (Democratic Association meeting, 17 Feb. 1902), see also headmaster Dörr in a speech delivered to the Frankfurt Democrats in HStAW 407 n. 161⁴ fo. 40. Democratic Association meeting, 29 Apr. 1901. See also Eduard Jungmann in *Frankfurter Zeitung*, 11 Nov. 1902 (3. Morgenblatt).

[195] The differing views on social policy between *Magistrat* and various city councillors will be discussed in the following chapter.

[196] Chosen to represent Prussian deaf and dumb institutions, it received the great prize at the world exhibition in St Louis in 1904. Haux, 'Die Taubstummen-Erziehungs-Anstalt zu Frankfurt a.M.', in *Deutsche Taubstummenanstalten, -Schulen und -Heime in Wort und Bild*

the late 1880s, and a school for children with learning difficulties from 1889.[197] Apart from the benefit which accrued to primary schools from these efforts by taking children with special needs out of their care, primary schools benefited from Frankfurt philanthropic efforts also in much more direct ways. By 1914 pupils had the opportunity to attend summer camps and various other school trips,[198] there were substantial scholarships for needy primary school pupils, and a warm breakfast was distributed to poor children every day.[199]

Third, and most importantly, at a time when even the Emperor had underlined their principal importance in the educational system, primary schools now became a matter of local prestige, of civic pride. The buildings of Frankfurt's first primary schools had been rather makeshift and completely inadequate for the number of pupils that attended them,[200] but by 1914 Frankfurt liberals prided themselves in the quality of their primary school buildings. New school buildings were designed according to newly accepted hygenic standards to provide the minimum quantities necessary of 'light, air, and sun',[201] so that from 1906 even the SPD no longer complained that they were inadequate. Instead, the socialists admitted that at long last the standard of primary school buildings had started at least to approximate to that of secondary school buildings.[202]

Impressive though the change of emphasis and the improvement in the quality of primary school education were, they were but part of a general phenomenon in Germany which saw a fundamental change in the way the role of education and of the primary school in particular was perceived from the 1890s onwards. It was during this decade that it became clear that repressive legislation had failed to contain the SPD, and that it was no longer a political option given the intense unpopularity of the *Umsturzvorlage* of 1895 and the *Zuchthausvorlage* of 1899. As it was evident that the 'social question' would get more, not less, pronounced following another

(Halle, 1915), 1–12. For the innovativeness of the institute, see also C. Perini, *J. Vatter und die Taubstummen-Anstalt zu Frankfurt a.M.* (Friedberg, 1910).

[197] This school was particularly promoted by the philanthropist Charles Hallgarten, 'Die Hilfsschule in Frankfurt a. M.', in *Deutsche Hilfsschulen in Wort und Bild* (Halle, 1913), 3–10.

[198] *Frankfurter Ferienwanderungen*, ed. Centrale für private Fürsorge (Frankfurt, 1911).

[199] A compilation of these private efforts is in Herber, *Vom Volksschulwesen Frankfurts* (Berlin, 1914), 24–35.

[200] F. Poppe, *Meine Erfahrungen an einer Simultanschule in Frankfurt am Main. Ein kritischer Beitrag zur Lösung der Simultanschulfrage* (4th edn., Frankfurt, 1880), 6.

[201] See e.g. *50 Jahre Günthersburgschule 1906–1956. Festschrift* (Frankfurt, 1956), 13.

[202] *Sozialdemokratie und Stadtverwaltung* (1906), 72.

industrial take-off from the mid-1890s, the German state, as well as bourgeois social reformers, turned their attention to the primary schools and all matters concerning the education of the country's youth. Beyond the traditional role of primary education imparting bourgeois values of thrift, diligence, and sobriety,[203] social reformers became interested in the 'moral' and physical health of the young as this was affected not just by the primary school itself, but also by the domestic and social environment. Social reformers therefore undertook to improve the health of the primary pupils through immediate care by municipally employed doctors, through the sponsorship of popular leisure and sport activities, and through the provision of recreational school trips to the countryside.[204] It is this national phenomenon of a rising concern for the education and the upbringing of the sons (and increasingly also the daughters) of the less well-off which manifested itself in the actions both of the Frankfurt municipal government as well as of local philanthropists and various societies to improve primary school buildings, to provide medical care for primary school pupils, and to organize school trips to the surrounding countryside with increasing frequency.

By 1914, therefore, primary schools had improved considerably in Frankfurt, though there is little evidence to suggest that they in any way surpassed the standard of schools in other large German cities. If anything, in the early years the standard of primary schools in Frankfurt was appalling when compared to other schools in cities of similar size. If, therefore, Frankfurt liberals prided themselves in the fact that 'the schools of Frankfurt are at the top of the entire Prussian school system' with reference to their primary schools,[205] it is evident that this could only apply to the non-denominational system, where Frankfurt liberals were, indeed, in the forefront of the fight against denominational schooling. In some ways, the success of the non-denominational system of education made other improvements in the quality of education much less pressing. For to

---

[203] J. Reulecke, 'Bürgerliche Sozialreform und Arbeiterjugend im Kaiserreich', *AfS* xxii (1982), 304–10.

[204] A. Gräfin zu Castell Rüdenhausen, 'Die Überwindung der Armenschule. Schülerhygiene an den Hamburger öffentlichen Volksschulen im Zweiten Kaiserreich', *AfS* xxii (1982), 201–26. See also P. D. Stachura, *The German Youth Movement 1900–45. An Interpretative and Documentative History* (London, 1981). The growing concern for the young at this time was not just a German phenomenon. J. Springhall, *Youth, Empire and Society. British Youth Movements 1883–1940* (London, 1977). M. Mitterauer, *A History of Youth* (Oxford, 1992), esp. 151–2, 182–225.

[205] Deputy Sänger at a Democratic Association meeting in Apr. 1900. HStAW 407 n. 161³ fo. 234.

liberals, the removal of clerical influence was in itself the most important (and the cheapest!) contribution they could make towards a good education.

4.5. Secondary Education[206]

As one of Germany's principal cities engaged in international commerce and trade, in Frankfurt there was an unusually large demand for modern languages to be taught in its secondary schools, instead of the otherwise prevalent Latin. In the early 1870s, therefore, the majority of pupils in secondary education were taught in four secondary modern schools without Latin, while the city's neo-humanist *Gymnasium* and one secondary modern school taught Latin as the second language. In subsequent decades, the *Gymnasium* became increasingly popular, since it was the only school whose final examinations were a qualification for the study of any subject at university. Nonetheless, by 1890, only 27.7 per cent of pupils in secondary education went to the neo-humanist grammar schools (compared to 59.2 per cent in Prussia), 21.3 per cent went to other secondary schools with Latin, the *Realgymnasium* (compared to 24.9 per cent in Prussia), while the majority of Frankfurt pupils engaged in secondary education, 51 per cent, went to non-Latin teaching secondary schools, the *Oberrealschulen* (compared to 15.9 per cent in Prussia).[207]

Ever since the establishment of secondary modern schools with an emphasis on modern languages and science in Prussia in 1859, there was a growing debate about the extent to which the final examinations of these *Realschulen* should be a qualification to university admission. From 1870, graduates of the latter schools were entitled to study mathematics, sciences, and modern languages, but they were still barred from the important

---

[206] There were two kinds of secondary schools throughout the period. From 1882, there were a number of *Realschulen*, which pupils would attend for six or seven years following the preparatory schools. The second type of school consisted of the *Gymnasium*, the *Realgymnasium*, and the *Oberrealschule*, which children could attend for a maximum of nine years after leaving the preparatory schools. This section will discuss exclusively the development of the latter type of schools, since these schools occupied the prominent position in local and national debates about secondary education. A good introduction to the different types of schools in a complex school system is in D. K. Müller and B. Zymek, *Datenhandbuch zur deutschen Bildungsgeschichte*. ii. *Höhere und mittlere Schulen*. Teil 1. *Sozialgeschichte und Statistik des Schulsystems in den Staaten des Deutschen Reiches, 1800–1945* (Göttingen, 1987), 35–48.

[207] P. Bode, 'Die Entwicklung des lateinlosen höheren Schulwesens in Frankfurt a.M.', in *Programm der Adlerflychtschule zu Frankfurt am Main* (Frankfurt, 1901), 20–7. Bode's figures for Prussia are virtually identical to those given in Müller and Zymek, *Datenhandbuch zur deutschen Bildungsgeschichte*, 55 (table 3.2).

subjects of law and medicine.[208] This was only in part a debate about how education could best reflect, and prepare its students for, a dynamic, industrializing society. Opening up Germany's universities to graduates of the country's *Realschulen* would have implied opening up higher education to the sons of the commercial bourgeoisie and even the lower middle classes, who tended to frequent those schools. This not only called into question the homogeneity of Germany's social élite, the *Bildungsbürgertum*, whose main defining feature was a common classical education at a neo-humanist grammar school as well as a university education, at a time when its ideals and values had already come under increasing attack.[209] More importantly, it was also a debate about the homogeneity of Germany's ruling élite, whose members had almost all passed through Germany's universities, usually through the faculty of law.[210] As a result, the battle lines in this debate were complex and interwoven, but as the century drew to its close it became increasingly difficult for Prussian policy-makers to ignore the calls for secondary school reform coming not only from industry and commerce, but also from the army, and, after 1888, from the Emperor himself.[211]

---

[208] Moreover, until 1887 for graduates of the *Realschulen* the entitlement to read for a degree entailed the restriction that those who wanted to obtain a teaching degree in these subjects could only look for employment at *Realschulen* and were barred from teaching at the *Gymnasium*.

[209] This argument should be treated with caution, however, as Jürgen Kocka has cast doubt over the existence of a *Bildungsbürgertum* with a recognizable degree of cohesion and common identity. J. Kocka, 'Bildungsbürgertum—Gesellschaftliche Formation oder Historikerkonstrukt?', in J. Kocka (ed.), *Bildungsbürgertum im 19. Jahrhundert. Politischer Einfluß und gesellschaftliche Formation* (Stuttgart, 1989), iv. 9–20.

[210] On the crucial social and political function of the *Bildungsbürgertum*, see K. H. Jarausch, *Students, Society and Politics in Imperial Germany. The Rise of Academic Illiberalism* (Princeton, 1982), esp. 8–11. The conservative desire to preserve the social and educational cohesion of a small ruling élite was also considered to be a crucial issue of the debate at the time. See e.g. the reformist article by F. Paulsen, 'Der Sieg der Einheitsschule oder das Ende des klassischen Gymnasiums. Item: das Ende des Realgymnasiums', *PJbb* lxviii (1891), 866–75, esp. 871, as well as the conservative Hans Delbrück's revealing reply in *PJbb* lxviii (1891), 875.

[211] On the complex high political debates surrounding school reform, and the aspirations and fears of their participants, see J. C. Albisetti, *Secondary School Reform in Imperial Germany* (Princeton, 1983). J. C. Albisetti and P. Lundgreen, 'Höhere Knabenschulen', in C. Berg (ed.), *Handbuch der deutschen Bildungsgeschichte. iv. 1870–1918* (Munich, 1991), 229–50. For greater detail, see W. Lexis (ed.), *Die Reform des höheren Schulwesens in Preußen* (Halle a.S., 1902).

It is worthy of note that the Prussian army, of all bodies, was one of the most vociferous proponents of school reform, out of its need to recruit officers capable of dealing with new technologies in warfare. In 1901, it appointed the Frankfurt school reformer Julius Ziehen as director of education at its military academy in Berlin. Likewise, the army's support was pivotal in swinging the balance at the 1900 school conference which paved the way for university admission for all secondary school graduates. Ludwig Ziehen, 'Julius Ziehen', 42, in IfSG, S2/2107. M. Messerschmidt, 'Schulpolitik des Militärs', in P. Baumgart (ed.), *Bildungspolitik*

The teaching plans of 1882 and the school conference of 1890 had reduced somewhat the distinctiveness of the *Gymnasium* with its heavy bias towards Latin and Greek. The teaching of Latin was reduced from 86 hours to 62 hours per week,[212] while the teaching of modern languages, sciences, and German was increased. By contrast, in those secondary modern schools that included Latin in their curriculum, the teaching of Latin was increased by 20 per cent. Reflecting their hybrid status between *Oberrealschulen* and the *Gymnasien*, they were now called *Realgymnasien*. Still, to the dismay of mostly the commercial bourgeoisie in the cities, the 1890 conference left the *Realgymnasien* rather dead in the water.[213] On the crucial issue of qualification for higher education, those graduating from the *Realgymnasium* were still not allowed to study law and medicine. At the same time, graduates of the *Oberrealschulen* were now entitled to study for the same degrees as those of the *Realgymnasium*, with the exception of modern languages. To the concern of the supporters of the *Realgymnasium* was added those who saw the essence of the neo-humanist grammar school threatened by the drastic decline of the classical languages.[214]

As in any other large Prussian city, the outcome of the school conference in December 1890 caused much concern in Frankfurt. The decision not to give graduates of the *Realgymnasium* the same general access to university as those of the *Gymnasium* affected a quarter of all students engaged in secondary education, in all about 1,000 pupils. On 11 January 1891, Franz Adickes became First Mayor of Frankfurt. Before, as Mayor of Altona, he had become interested in and enthused by the 'Altonaer System', an educational trial introduced in 1878 which established the same curriculum for the first three years of two different types of secondary modern school (*Oberrealschule* and *Realgymnasium*). Only then would the pupils have to decide whether to continue their education at a secondary modern school with Latin as the third language, or one which taught French instead.[215]

---

in Preußen zur Zeit des Kaiserreichs (Stuttgart, 1980), 242–55. This confirms Geoff Eley's arguments against the Kehrite school's belief in the exclusively reactionary tendencies of the military. G. Eley, 'Army, State and Civil Society: Revisiting the Problem of German Militarism', in G. Eley, *From Unification to Nazism. Reinterpreting the German Past* (2nd edn., London, 1992), 85–109.

[212] This figure denotes the total hours per week for a student's entire school career.
[213] P. Cauer, 'Das Ergebnis der Schulkonferenz', *PJbb* lxvii (1891), 88–98.
[214] The details of the curricula of 1882 and 1892, as well as the 1890 school conference, are summarized in M. Kraul, *Das deutsche Gymnasium 1780–1980* (Frankfurt, 1984), 90–4, 100–8. Führ, 'Die preußischen Schulkonferenzen', 204. For contemporary criticism, see P. Cauer, 'Die neuen Lehrpläne', *PJbb* lxix (1892), 256–79.
[215] As a result of neighbouring Hamburg's strong trading links with English-speaking countries, the first modern foreign language taught in Altona (as in Hamburg) was English,

The advantage of this system was that pupils no longer had to decide about their future career at the age of 9, but could postpone that decision until they were 12 years old.

Given the unusually high proportion of the city's élite whose sons did not attend a neo-humanist grammar school, but rather the other forms of high school with greater emphasis on modern language and science teaching, Frankfurt was a fertile ground for school reform. In the aftermath of the December conference of 1890, Adickes quickly seized the initiative in Frankfurt to establish the 'Frankfurt system'. In less than a year, the Prussian ministry had given its approval to the scheme, so that the new curriculum could be introduced by Easter 1892.[216] The Frankfurt system was based on the same principle as that of Altona, with the important difference that a common curriculum for the first three years was not only introduced for the two types of *Realschulen*, but for the grammar school as well. Like the secondary modern schools, the *Gymnasium* now started with French as a foreign language, and only after three years did its curriculum start to differ as it introduced Latin with ten hours per week. By contrast, students of the *Realgymnasien* were taught Latin for eight hours per week, with stronger emphasis on French.

There were two major benefits of the Frankfurt system. Firstly, it gave the vast number of children who attended one of the *Realschulen* at least the theoretical opportunity of switching to the *Gymnasium* until they reached the age of 12. Secondly, it gave a new lease of life to Frankfurt's *Realgymnasien*. If the effect of the new curricula of 1892 had been to stress the difference between the curriculum of the *Realgymnasium* and that of the *Gymnasium* across Prussia,[217] the Frankfurt system re-emphasized the similarity of those two types of schools, thus giving added weight to reformist efforts at opening up Prussia's universities to the graduates of secondary modern schools. What is striking about the Frankfurt system is that it provided a direct response to the Emperor's three central criticisms of the current system of secondary education. At the expense of Latin and Greek, there was a significant increase in the teaching of German and history, a relatively small increase in the teaching of mathematics, and an overall reduction in the number of teaching hours, reflecting Kaiser

---

not French. K. Reinhardt, 'Die Reformanstalten', in W. Lexis (ed.), *Die Reform des höheren Schulwesens in Preußen* (Halle, 1902), 331.

[216] *Festschrift zu der am 7. Januar 1897 stattfindenden Einweihung des Goethe-Gymnasiums in Frankfurt a.M.* (Frankfurt, 1897), 4.

[217] Kraul, *Das deutsche Gymnasium*, 105.

Wilhelm's concern for the students' health endangered by 'excess of mental work'.[218]

Frankfurt thus became a centre for educational reform during the 1890s. By 1901, there were thirty-seven reformed systems of higher education in Germany, of which twenty-six were modelled on the Frankfurt system, and eleven on the Altona system. Of these, a total of eight were in Prussia. The 1890s were still a period during which the system was on trial, but even by 1913 there were only twenty-three grammar schools which taught the Frankfurt curriculum, out of a total of 364 grammar schools.[219] The repercussions of the Frankfurt trial were nonetheless enormous. The Frankfurt example demonstrated that Latin was not essential to the nature of the neo-humanist grammar school, that, just as in other secondary schools, the teaching of Latin could wait until the fourth year, well after the introduction of a modern foreign language. If the supporters of the classical neo-humanist *Gymnasium* needed any evidence of the severity of the threat which the traditional concept of the grammar school faced, it was surely this. Their apprehension was confirmed by the attention received in 1898 by a petition from Adickes, three Frankfurt *Stadträte*, and a further forty-six lawyers, calling for the admission of graduates from the *Realgymnasium* to read law.[220] So intense had the debate become that another conference was convened in 1900, and this time the dispute was resolved successfully. In principle, the right of graduates of all three types of secondary school to study any subject at university was accepted. In a way, this decision made the Frankfurt system redundant since it took the urgency out of the choice of schools. This is precisely why the result was accepted by the supporters of the neo-humanist *Gymnasium*, because this was seen as the only way of avoiding the general introduction of the Frankfurt system in Prussia.[221]

Considering the importance of the Frankfurt system, it is curious that there was so little debate among the various liberal parties about the issue. It confirms Albisetti's view that secondary school reform was not a party-political issue, in marked contrast to questions concerning primary education.[222] At the same time, the Frankfurt debate highlights a number of important aspects of municipal politics in general, and of the Frankfurt polity in particular. The introduction of the Frankfurt system

---

[218] Albisetti, *Secondary School Reform*, 3. K. Reinhardt, *Die Frankfurter Lehrpläne* (Frankfurt, 1892), 37.
[219] K. Groh, *Ist der Versuch der Preußischen Unterrichtsverwaltung, den Frankfurter Lehrplan auf das Gymnasium zu übertragen, geglückt?* (Gütersloh, 1915), iv. 63–72.
[220] Führ, 'Die preußischen Schulkonferenzen', 207.   [221] Ibid. 208–10.
[222] Albisetti, *Secondary School Reform*, 60–1.

demonstrates, perhaps better than any other issue in Frankfurt municipal politics, the potential for action of an enterprising and resourceful mayor. This was very much Adickes's project. He managed to inspire the member of the *Magistrat* responsible for education, Otto Grimm, by his idea, with which he found himself in total agreement with the headmaster of the municipal *Gymnasium*, Karl Reinhardt.[223] These three people worked out the project almost amongst themselves.

The issue also shows the relative unimportance of the city council, and with it the concept of self-government in education, once qualitative matters, rather than budgetary concerns, were under discussion. In this case, it was much more important for Adickes and other members of the school board to find agreement with the ministry than with the city council, as the latter's support was not strictly necessary.[224] Another reason why the issue did not feature heavily in political debate was that in a narrow sense this was a debate about educational theory. In Karl Reinhardt and Julius Ziehen, the city had two gifted academics who engaged in debates with other leading educational theorists at the time. Reinhardt not only developed the curriculum, he also devised new textbooks to include new teaching methods as a necessary complement to the reform, while Ziehen led the ensuing debates through countless speeches, pamphlets, and books in defence of the system.[225] This was a debate in which academics had a very important role. Finally, the school reforms were discussed and introduced in Frankfurt at precisely the time when the liberal councillors were concentrating on attacking the education bill for primary schools. This made left-liberal initiatives for secondary school reform extremely awkward, since the introduction of the Frankfurt system depended upon the goodwill of the very same minister for education, Count von Zedlitz und Trützschler, whom the liberal parties otherwise so bitterly opposed on the question of primary education.

Nonetheless, left liberals welcomed Adickes's efforts. In 1884 the *Frankfurter Zeitung* had led demands for a common curriculum for

---

[223] K. Reinhardt, 'Goethe-Gymnasium', in *Festschrift zu der am 7. Januar 1897 stattfindenden Einweihung des Goethe-Gymnasiums in Frankfurt a.M.* (Frankfurt, 1897), 3–5.

[224] On the good relationship between the Prussian minister of state for education responsible for the universities, Althoff (1897–1907), and Adickes, and their discussions on the subject of school reform, see F. Adickes, *Persönliche Erinnerungen zur Vorgeschichte der Universität Frankfurt a.M. zum 18. Oktober 1914* (Frankfurt, 1915), 7–8.

[225] Reinhardt, 'Die Reformanstalten', 328–42. J. Ziehen, *Der Frankfurter Lehrplan und seine Stellung innerhalb der Schulreformbewegung* (Leipzig/Frankfurt, 1900). J. Ziehen, *Aus der Werkstatt der Schule. Studien über den inneren Organismus des höheren Schulwesens* (Leipzig, 1907). J. Ziehen, *Schulpolitische Aufsätze* (Frankfurt, 1919). See also the impressive catalogue of Ziehen's publications in IfSG, S2/2107.

secondary schools based on the introduction of the more useful French and English as first foreign languages. Not only was such a system more responsive to local needs, but it was also a step towards the diminution of class differences,[226] since at least for a time students from a large number of schools, frequented by children from a greater variety of social backgrounds, would be taught the same subjects.[227] When the Frankfurt system was finally introduced in a slightly less radical form than that suggested by the *Frankfurter Zeitung*, Frankfurt liberals supported the moves for two principal reasons. Frankfurt left liberals had no pretensions that their policies with regard to secondary education were anything other than *Mittelstandspolitik*, because it was clear that it was the *Mittelstand* who were the principal users of Frankfurt's secondary modern schools.[228] Moreover, the idea of Frankfurt's leading role in educational reform agreed very much with the left-liberals' own vision of Frankfurt as a beacon of liberal educational values, and with their civic pride in general.[229]

In fact, civic pride was pivotal in the way Frankfurters viewed their secondary schools. Finding resources had never been a problem for the long-established *Gymnasium* or *Musterschule*. The schools that emerged from 1890, however, were nothing short of lavish. The *Lessing-Gymnasium* was opened with a rich endowment of prints and copies of paintings by German and especially by Frankfurt artists.[230] For the new building of the *Goethe-Gymnasium*, the city council granted 90,000 M. to be spent on the beautification of the building.[231] City councillors were aware of the fact that the

---

[226] *Frankfurter Zeitung*, 9 Nov. 1884 (Morgenblatt).

[227] By contrast, Detlev Müller has argued rather controversially that the principal aim of school reform was to maintain the social hierarchies that were endangered by social and geographical mobility. Müller, *Sozialstruktur*, esp. 55–60, 287–97.

[228] HStAW 407 n. 161⁴ fo. 72. Democratic Association meeting, 10 Feb. 1902. Therefore, there were few considerations at the time to make secondary education accessible to children of the poorer sections of the population, and even discussions about the number of scholarships available were essentially led for the benefit of the poorer sections of the middle classes. For the relationship between education and the *Mittelstand* in general, see Ludwig von Friedeburg, *Bildungsreform in Deutschland* (Frankfurt, 1989), 173–9. For the increasing importance of the *Gymnasium* to the *Mittelstand*, see Bernd Schönemann, *Das braunschweigische Gymnasium in Staat und Gesellschaft. Ein Beitrag zur Schulgeschichte des 19. Jahrhunderts* (Cologne/Vienna, 1983), 167–98, esp. 195–8.

[229] HStAW 407 n. 161¹ fo. 272. Democratic Association meeting, 19 Feb. 1902. Note that in contrast to the issues of non-denominational as well as universal primary education this subject was discussed at least with some contention. In other words, at no time did the reform of secondary education become an article of faith for Frankfurt left liberals.

[230] Paul Ankel, 'Die künstlerische Ausschmückung eines humanistischen Gymnasiums', in *Frankfurter Zeitung*, 18 Oct. 1902 (1. Morgenblatt). The article is also in BAK, NL 20 n. 20 fo. 97.

[231] Part of the cause for this expense was the fact that the architect insisted on using differently coloured stone for the building. *MPS*, 1894, §657, pp. 400–2.

new building would accommodate a school whose progress would receive national and international attention, hence this building was an opportunity to show what Frankfurt could do.[232] The school, in turn, was conscious of what it owed the city for its generosity. At the inauguration of the new building, the headmaster, Karl Reinhardt, pointed out:

On the front of the speaker's desk are the initials of the old words: 'Senatus populusque Francofurtanus.' Whenever our young people see these initials, may they always remember that it is their home town, that it is this great community, to which they owe the precious gift of this school building; may they be strengthened by this thought in the joy of their surroundings [*Heimat*] and the love of their home town and fatherland.[233]

This building was a memorial to the generosity of the people of Frankfurt, and students were to be aware that they owed their gratitude first and foremost to their *Heimat*, the community of Frankfurt. This confirms Celia Applegate's masterful study of the concept of *Heimat*, in which she pointed out the mutually reinforcing compatibility of *Heimat* and nation.[234] In Frankfurt, this term inevitably had different connotations than in other areas such as the Palatinate.[235] The appeal to the *Heimat* (in this case the city) was a clear statement of the kind of society and nation Frankfurters wished to have, that is one characterized by tolerance, generosity, and humility.

The distinctiveness of these educational goals is illustrated by a comparison with the ideals behind the first state *Gymnasium*, the *Kaiser-Friedrichs-Gymnasium*, opened in 1888. As made clear by the first headmaster in the opening ceremony, and repeated later by his successor, the school's endeavour was to serve God, King, and Country ('Gott, König und Vaterland'). It was essential to educate the pupils strictly, in 'Zucht und Ordnung', in order: 'to inflame the holy fire of enthusiasm for the highest

---

[232] See the photographs of this magnificent building, which are printed in *Programm des Goethe-Gymnasiums in Frankfurt a.M.* (Frankfurt, 1897).

[233] 'An der Stirnseite dieses Rednerpultes stehen die Initialen des alten Wortes: "Senatus populusque Francofurtanus." Unsere Jugend möge, wenn sie diese Zeichen sieht, stets des eingedenk sein, daß es ihre Vaterstadt, daß es das große Gemeinwesen ist, dem sie die kostbare Gabe dieses Schulhauses verdankt; sie möge sich dadurch bestärken lassen in der Freude an ihrer schönen Heimat und in der Liebe zu ihrer Vaterstadt und ihrem Vaterlande'. *Programm des Goethe-Gymnasiums* (1897), 6.

[234] C. Applegate, *A Nation of Provincials. The German Idea of Heimat* (Berkeley, 1990), esp. 85–6.

[235] For *Heimat* interpretation of German culture in the Palatinate, see C. Applegate, 'Localism and the German Bourgeoisie: The 'Heimat' Movement in the Rhenish Palatinate before 1914', in Blackbourn and Evans (eds.), *The German Bourgeoisie*, 224–54, here 233–42.

goods in life and to arouse a sense for one's own people's past and custom, to tender the love for *Heimat* and fatherland, for whose protection and defence, if need be, we must all be prepared to shed our heart's blood gladly.'[236]

Frankfurt educational values were thus directly opposed to those of the Prussian educational system. Education was perhaps the clearest manifestation in practice of the self-definition of 'Frankfurt values' which the Democrats had established successfully after 1866.

Debates about secondary education were conducted with much less ferocity and passion than those about primary education, as all parties approved of the Frankfurt system. There were other significant and rather crucial differences in the way in which Frankfurt liberals approached primary and secondary education. Most obvious of all was the difference in funding. Even after various cuts in the building estimate, the city granted almost 440,000 M. for the building of the *Goethe-Gymnasium* in 1894. By contrast in 1906, for example, the *Günthersburg* primary school was opened, at a cost of 325,000 M.[237] The *Goethe-Gymnasium* was built for a total of 9 classes, one class in each year,[238] each of which was to contain about 30, or at most 40, students. The primary school, on the other hand, was designed for 16 classes and opened with 17, each consisting of an average of 50 pupils.[239] This example highlights the quantitative difference in resources which were employed in primary and secondary education. These differences are essentially due to the fact that liberals were well aware that secondary education was a central concern of their own constituency, the middle classes, whereas until the mid-1900s only a few of those who sent their children to primary schools had enough income to qualify for the local franchise. It is no accident that the quality of primary schooling became a central concern for the left liberals only after the turn of the century.

Underlying the various qualitative and quantitative differences in the Frankfurt liberals' approach to primary and secondary education, however,

---

[236] '"das heilige Feuer der Begisterung für die höheren Lebensgüter zu entzünden und den Sinn zu erwärmen für des eigenen Volkes Vergangenheit und Art, zu pflegen die Liebe zu Heimat und Vaterland, zu dessen Schutz und Schirm, wenn es gilt, wir alle freudig unser Herzblut zu vergießen bereit sein müssen"'. R. Busse, *Kaiser-Friedrich-Gymnasium. Rückblick auf die ersten 25 Jahre der Anstalt* (Frankfurt, 1913), 7. See also 4. Busse is here repeating the words of his predecessor made at the opening of the school in 1888, which make them directly comparable to those of Reinhardt.

[237] *50 Jahre Günthersburgschule*, 12.

[238] See the meeting of the *Magistrat* on building extensions to the grammar school of 29 Apr. 1902, in IfSG, AS 978.

[239] *50 Jahre Günthersburgschule*, 14. For an instructive overview, see A. Koch, *Die neueren Schulgebäude der Stadt Frankfurt a.M.* (Frankfurt, 1904).

were the same assumptions about tolerance and religious freedom.[240] Interestingly, after naming the city's first grammar school after their favourite son, Goethe, the municipal authorities chose to name the second local grammar school founded in 1897 after Lessing, the enlightened neo-humanist friend of Moses Mendelssohn, who was best remembered for his fight for Jewish emancipation through his work 'Nathan der Weise'. This point was not lost on the representative of the Prussian educational authorities, who at the inauguration of the new school buildings in 1903 urged the school to become a true cradle of tolerance in the spirit of Lessing.[241] Moreover, despite qualitative differences, from the 1890s the education system in general was subject to intense local, civic pride.

The study of liberal attitudes to primary and secondary education confirms Lothar Gall's view that liberals had abandoned their earlier ideal of creating a 'classless society of citizens', at least through the obvious medium of education.[242] Liberals were concerned about high school fees or the number of scholarships available to poor but gifted students, but this was entirely seen to be in the interest of the *Mittelstand*. Little attempt was made to make education for the *Mittelstand* available to children from poorer backgrounds. What is striking is that it appears as though the Frankfurt SPD was not primarily interested in this liberal ideal either, for it completely accepted the fact that secondary education was a prerogative of the middle classes. The party was largely interested in secondary education as it drained away resources from primary education, which affected the overwhelming majority of its own constituency.[243] At least in Frankfurt, therefore, the liberal abandonment of the ideal of a 'classless society of citizens' in the realm of education is unlikely to have made a great political impact since both liberals and the SPD accepted the social assumptions that underlined the current education system.

---

[240] Religion in secondary schools was never directly subject to debate, because, unless they were religious foundations, all secondary schools were (traditionally) non-denominational.

[241] 'Thus it [this institution] will instil respect for the honest conviction of one's neighbour and that noble tolerance which does not cause dispute or hatred, but which promotes peace and reconciliation and which in mutual discourse does not emphasize what separates, but what unites'. *Programm des Lessing-Gymnasiums zu Frankfurt a.M.* (Frankfurt,1903), 7.

[242] Gall's argument about the transition in 1848/9 of the bourgeois ideal from a 'classless society of citizens' to a 'bourgeois class-society' has been presented in Ch. 2.

[243] See e.g. *Sozialdemokratie und Stadtverwaltung* (1906), 66–75, *Sozialdemokratie und Stadtverwaltung* (1908), 10–15, *Sozialdemokratie und Stadtverwaltung* (1910), 116. The fact that the vast majority of workers and of lower civil servants and white-collar workers (*Angestellte*) sent their sons to primary schools was by no means unusual. For the case of Minden, see Lundgreen, Kraul, and Ditt, *Bildungschancen*, 78.

Moreover, there is no evidence, at least for Frankfurt, that liberals instead reverted to the opposite goal of trying to prevent any encroachments into their bourgeois society from aspiring outsiders, for example through positively barring upward social mobility. It is simply that from the 1870s liberals in Frankfurt had different priorities. The priority was no longer the creation of an harmonious society through changes in the social structure. During the Empire, it became much more important to establish and defend liberal values in society as a whole, both against encroachments of socialism and from Prussian conservative values. The emphasis had shifted, therefore, from the mid-nineteenth-century ideal of classic, humanist *Bildung* to one which emphasized the aim of science and rationality not only as a preparation for a modern world of industry and commerce, but also as a defence of core liberal social and political values of religious tolerance and self-government.

4.6. Conclusion: The Establishment of the Civic University of Frankfurt

In 1914, Germany's first civic university, a university entirely funded not by the state but through individual donations and subscriptions, was opened in Frankfurt. This university has rightly been regarded as the epitome of the civic spirit that prevailed in the city of Frankfurt. Described by Franz Adickes as a testament to Frankfurt's *Bürgersinn*,[244] this was also the view taken by Paul Kluke in his study of the history of the university. Its foundation was not so much a response to any particular need which other universities could not satisfy: it was simply the product of a self-satisfied, affluent bourgeoisie whose actions turned out to be their swansong.[245] Beneath the surface, however, there were rather more complex reasons behind the foundation of the civic university, and these reasons sum up nicely the central themes of liberal attitudes towards education in Frankfurt which have been discussed in this chapter.

As with the establishment of the Frankfurt system of secondary education, the university could never have been established but for the energy and the ambition of the First Mayor, Franz Adickes.[246] During the last years of his mayoralty, few wealthy individuals or corporations could hope for any favourable assistance from the city without making a donation to

---

[244] L. Heilbrunn, *Die Gründung der Universität Frankfurt a.M.* (Frankfurt, 1915), 85.
[245] P. Kluke, *Die Stiftungsuniversität Frankfurt am Main 1914–1932* (Frankfurt, 1972), 21.
[246] On Adickes's easy relationship with Prussian government officials ranging from Bismarck to Althoff, see Adickes, *Persönliche Erinnerungen*, 1–9.

Adickes's pet project.[247] Equally important were Adickes's conservative credentials in Berlin which ultimately overcame conservative fears about the potential danger of establishing a university in that centre of left liberalism, Frankfurt.[248] This shows once again the liberal councillors' impotence when it came to positive educational initiatives, because the initiative for drastic change could only come from the city's executive body, the *Magistrat*. By the same token, it highlights the central importance of the mayor, which lay precisely in the ambiguous position of this office between local politics and state administration.[249] The more this ambiguity could be utilized, the more local government could thrive.[250] This is why the left liberals' choice of two right-liberal mayors in succession, far from being a contradiction in terms, was the most consistent choice given the parameters of local government.

The liberal aim of creating a more enlightened society infused with liberal values also lay behind the foundation of the university. The university had emerged to a significant degree from the *Institut für Gemeinwohl*, founded by the philanthropist William Merton in 1896, which later developed into the *Akademie für Handels- und Sozialwissenschaften*.[251] These institutes endeavoured to study the social and economic environment, with

---

[247] Adickes's increasingly aggressive (and, indeed, corrupt) methods for obtaining donations for 'his' university are well described in BAK, NL 44 n. 8 fos. 216–20. Luppe, 'Mein Leben'.

[248] Compare the hostility of the conservative and even National Liberal parties in the Prussian Chamber of Deputies with the positive and encouraging tone of Adickes's discussions with the Prussian Minister for Education and his bureaucrats. Heilbrunn, *Gründung*, 88–90, 123–8. It is also interesting to note that among the most vociferous defenders of the university in Berlin were the current Minister of Education, von Trott zu Solz, as well as the erstwhile promoter of the Frankfurt system during his tenure as Minister for Education, Zedlitzch von Trützschler. Adickes, *Persönliche Erinnerungen*, 54.

[249] Equally, the maintenance of the non-denominational school system after the *Kulturkampf* owes a great deal to Miquel, who, as First Mayor, also made full use of the ambiguities of his office. Openly, he was fully supportive of the council's grievances against the Prussian school authorities, and yet it was under his direction that the *Magistrat* became less than resolute against Prussian help for the denominational schools. On the other hand, Miquel did nothing to discourage the impression among Prussian authorities that as long as he was in charge of Frankfurt, the local education system would be spared the worst excesses of left-liberal policies; hence the authorities refrained from an all-out effort to refashion Frankfurt's schooling system along confessional lines. Anderhub, *Verwaltung*, 238–42. Miquel's report of 31 May 1880 to the Wiesbaden education authorities in which he summarized—deferentially, but firmly—the position of Frankfurt liberals on denominational schooling and which subsequently became one of the cornerstones of the Frankfurt liberals' defence of their position, is reprinted in Müller, *Aufklärungen*, 82–5.

[250] In general, see Matzerath, *Urbanisierung in Preußen*, 350–2.

[251] See also R. Wachsmuth, *Die Gründung der Universität Frankfurt* (Frankfurt, 1929), 46–60.

a particular emphasis on linking up academic theory and practical reform, and on disseminating the results to a large audience.[252] When the academy was integrated into the university, Germany's first independent faculty of economic and social sciences was established.[253] In similar vein, Merton established Prussia's first chair of educational theory (*Pädagogik*) in 1915, with the express aim of linking academic research and practical work, on the general questions of the relationship between education and economic and social conditions.

Merton hoped for academic input on questions such as the social usefulness of scholarships and the promotion of gifted people. It is no accident that Frankfurt's first professorship of educational theory was awarded to the ardent promoter of the Frankfurt system, Julius Ziehen.[254] Therefore, there was a clear aim that the university should further the general education of society, creating a more enlightened community, which would be more harmonious and less riven by social conflict. In the same way that state universities functioned as the 'pride of the nation', and as seedbeds of patriotism devoted to a Protestant culture,[255] Frankfurt's civic university was created to disseminate civic values of a 'common weal', of tolerance and scientific progress, not only in Frankfurt itself, but also far beyond the city limits.[256]

The foundation of the university was closely intertwined with the Jewish population in Frankfurt. Indeed, this was one of the principal objections from Prussian conservatives to the foundation of the university, as newspapers such as the *Kreuzzeitung* feared that a university in a city like Frankfurt would inevitably become infused with the 'Jewish Democrat spirit' prevalent in the city.[257] And, indeed, the university was predominantly funded by donations from Jews. The baptized Jew William Merton donated more than 4 million Marks to the university, and the Jewish couple

---

[252] Kluke, *Die Stiftungsuniversität*, 34.

[253] Elsewhere, chairs in national economy were part of faculties of philosophy or law. Ibid. 92.

[254] G. Böhme, 'Schulpolitik, Volkserziehungswissenschaft und Universitätspädagogik— Aus Anlaß des 60. Todestages von Julius Ziehen (1864–1925)', in G. Böhme (ed.), *Geistesgeschichte im Spiegel einer Stadt. Frankfurt am Main und seine grossen Persönlichkeiten* (Frankfurt, 1986), 122–39, esp. 128. J. Ziehen, 'Schulpolitik und Pädagogik', *Zeitschrift für lateinlose höhere Schulen*, xvii (1906), 33–48.

[255] N. Hammerstein, *Antisemitismus und deutsche Universitäten. 1871–1933* (Frankfurt/ New York, 1995), 15, 40–1, 60–7.

[256] With its new subjects and the absence of a faculty of theology, the university did indeed prove to be a pariah in an increasingly nationalist and conservative university culture, esp. during the Weimar Republic. Ibid. 78.

[257] Kluke, *Die Stiftungsuniversität*, 66.

Georg and Franziska Speyer donated another 4 million Marks. Of the capital of 14.6 million Marks which had been provided by the time of the opening of the university,[258] more than 8 million Marks came from Jews or baptized Jews.[259] Frankfurt became the first university without either a Protestant or a Catholic faculty of theology.[260] And it became something of a sine qua non for the university that the donors secured a guarantee in the university statutes that all appointments were to be made without regard to creed.[261] For even though at the time it was perfectly possible for a Jew to occupy a chair at any German university, in practice Jews were still very much discriminated against in university life.[262] None other than the Nobel Prize winner Paul Ehrlich was led to accept Althoff's and Adickes's invitation to move his Institute for Vaccine Research from Berlin to Frankfurt by the fact that the academic establishment of the capital still refused to offer him an ordinary chair on account of his being Jewish.[263] Here was at last an opportunity to make sure that there was at least one university in Germany which would not discriminate against Jews.[264]

The most contentious issue surrounding the proposed university from its inception was that of self-government. Given the peculiar German university system in which the most important examinations, for instance for the subjects of law and medicine, were examined by the state, it was inconceivable for the Prussian Ministry of Education and for Adickes that the new university should be anything other than a state university. On the other hand, the university's civic founders demanded a say in its running, if only to make sure that the university respected their ideals of religious

---

[258] Wachsmuth, *Die Gründung*, 80. Merton's overall donation of about 4 million M. went to his institutes which then formed part of the university, so that these donations are not part of the 14.6 million M. necessary for the actual foundation. However, Merton did pledge further funds for the opening itself, and continued to donate money to the university after 1914.

[259] See the overview of Jewish donations to the university in Arnsberg, *Geschichte*, ii. 292–9.

[260] J. Conrad, 'Allgemeine Statistik der Deutschen Universitäten', in W. Lexis (ed.), *Die Deutschen Universitäten* (Berlin, 1893), 115–70. Here see e.g. table x, 156–7.

[261] Kluke, *Die Stiftungsuniversität*, 90.

[262] With regard to pursuing an academic career, Max Weber noted 'If he is a Jew, of course one says *lasciate ogni speranza*'. M. Weber, 'Science as a Vocation', in H. H. Gerth and C. Wright Mills (eds.), *From Max Weber: Essays in Sociology* (reprint, London, 1993), 134. Hammerstein, *Antisemitismus und deutsche Universitäten*, 11–12, 19–20, 42–3, 68–75. S. Volkov, 'Soziale Ursachen des Erfolgs in der Wissenschaft. Juden im Kaiserreich', *HZ* ccxlv (1987), 315–42, here 329–33.

[263] Wachsmuth, *Die Gründung*, 38–9. Heilbrunn, *Gründung*, 57–9. Kluke, *Die Stiftungsuniversität*, 54–5, esp. 103 n. 8. Hammerstein, *Antisemitismus und deutsche Universitäten*, 68–9.

[264] Kluke, *Die Stiftungsuniversität*, 85. Hammerstein, *Antisemitismus und deutsche Universitäten*, 76–8.

toleration. In addition to the university's private sponsors, the city's left-liberal councillors also wanted to establish some guarantee of municipal influence over the university's affairs.[265] This was particularly important for them in order to escape the logic of the Social Democrats' arguments. Stealing the left liberals' clothes, as guardians of self-government, the socialists pointed out that it was neither the job of the city nor of the citizens of Frankfurt to donate a university to the Prussian state over which the original donors would exercise virtually no control.[266]

Consequently, the concessions made by the state were considerable. The university received an unprecedented organization through the creation of a grand council, made up of representatives of the donors and of the city, which then elected an executive organ, the *Kuratorium* (committee), from its members.[267] These bodies were largely responsible for all matters financial, but the *Kuratorium* even had the right to interfere in the curriculum of individual faculties by suggesting a curriculum of its own. Frankfurt liberals had thus achieved for their university the kind of influence which they had consistently but unsuccessfully craved for in primary and secondary education. This further emphasizes the importance of the ideal of self-government in education which could acquire a kind of momentum of its own. It was the enabler of the liberals' educational drive, with regard both to Adickes's positive innovations and to the liberals' negative resilience against the state about primary education. Yet it was also their intermediate aim. For it was through the liberals' attempt at increasing, or at least at marking clearly, the boundaries of self-government in education against the state that they could hope to create a truly liberal society, at least within Frankfurt, a city characterized by tolerance, culture, and true learning.

The political effects of liberal educational policies in Frankfurt were ambiguous. Whereas they did unite the liberals at crucial moments and provided important rallying cries for their supporters, it is unclear whether

---

[265] It should be noted that even though this was a civic university, and even though the city made very few direct monetary contributions to it, the city had always been heavily involved in the promotion of higher education through the provision of cheap municipal land and/or buildings as well as of direct grants to various institutions which would form the nucleus of the university. Therefore, the city was also recognized as one of the university's principal founders. The sheer scale of municipal financial involvement, esp. in the purchase of sites and the construction of the university buildings, which ran into several million Marks, is hinted at in BAK, NL 44 n. 8 fo. 197. Luppe, 'Mein Leben'.

[266] Heilbrunn, *Gründung*, 161–75. Many left liberals asked themselves, too, whether it was sensible to surrender the fruits of old-Frankfurt civic spirit to reactionary Prussia. Kluke, *Die Stiftungsuniversität*, 77.

[267] In 1914, 16 out of 38 members of the grand council, and 8 out of 21 members of the *Kuratorium*, were Jewish or of Jewish origin. Arnsberg, *Geschichte*, ii. 295.

their rigid hostility to denominational education was of electoral benefit to them. After vociferously defending Roman Catholics against the excesses of the *Kulturkampf*, Frankfurt left liberals lost their political capital with many of the city's Roman Catholic population through their stubborn discrimination against denominational schools. Given the liberals' educational aims, it is ironic that this policy became the catalyst for the denominalization of local politics through the foundation of separate Roman Catholic and Protestant parties during the 1890s and 1900s, and the gradual emergence of the Centre Party as a local political force by 1914.

Moreover, the impact of their educational policies on the liberals' electoral fortunes in relation to the SPD is difficult to ascertain. Unlike secondary and tertiary education, liberals clearly failed to create a model system of primary education. Demands, for instance for free school materials, were usually refused by the *Magistrat* with reference to an ostensible lack of resources. Given the city's ability, however, to establish an entire university through fundraising and direct public contributions amounting to millions of Marks, liberals clearly could have improved the quality of primary education beyond recognition had they truly wanted to.

At the same time, the political failures of liberal educational policies should not be exaggerated. Their policies were distinct from those of the SPD more in degree than in kind. Both largely agreed on the fundamental necessities of non-denominational education and local self-government. Liberals began to take up SPD demands for the abolition of preparatory schools, and they displayed increasing willingness to invest in primary education after 1890. Liberals and Social Democrats in Frankfurt even came to agree on the social assumptions that lay behind the educational system, and neither fundamentally questioned the fact that primary education provided for the education of poorer employees' and workers' offspring, whereas secondary education was largely a prerogative of the middle classes.[268] Education was not just a unifying goal for the liberals and the Democrats, it also brought them into considerable agreement with the Social Democrats.

As a result of the Jewish influence on Frankfurt liberalism, it is likely that liberal insistence on local self-government in education and the ideals of a tolerant society were more pronounced in Frankfurt than elsewhere.[269]

[268] It appears that cooperation between liberals and Social Democrats on education occurred not just in Frankfurt. For the case of Saxony, see K. H. Pohl, 'Sachsen, Stresemann und die Nationalliberale Partei. Anmerkungen zur politischen Entwicklung, zum Aufstieg des industriellen Bürgertums und zur frühen Tätigkeit Stresemanns im Königreich Sachsen vor 1914', *JLF* iv (1992), 211–13.

[269] Still, the Jewish influence on local liberalism is clear with regard to Breslau. Hettling, 'Von der Hochburg zur Wagenburg', 269. More surprisingly, the importance of Jews to

Nonetheless, the general thrust of Frankfurt liberal educational policy is unlikely to have been unique. The fact that Frankfurt was one of the few places where liberals succeeded in setting up non-denominational primary schools should not hide the fact that most liberals in the cities probably harboured this ideal, as is revealed by their attempts during the *Kulturkampf*.[270] If Frankfurt liberals were more successful, this is the result of a voiceless Roman Catholic minority and the unusual strength of Jewish and Protestant support. Moreover, even if Frankfurt was the first city to establish a civic university, preparations for civic universities were also underway in Cologne and Hamburg.[271]

Overall, the minutes of the Prussian *Städtetag* show an impressive degree of liberal unanimity with regard to the aims and ideals of education. Indeed, the quality of a city's schools became central objects of civic rivalry throughout the country. With dwindling political influence at the state and national levels, and given the general liberal perception that Bismarck's break with the liberals in 1879 instigated not only a political, but also a fundamental economic, social, intellectual, and moral shift towards conservatism,[272] control over local education became the liberals' best hope of re-creating a liberal society in Prussia, at least within the cities. Indeed, this goal, whether it was ultimately realized or not, took clear precedence over party-political efforts to meet some of the SPD's demands for practical improvements in primary education.[273] This chapter has thus shown that liberals in Frankfurt as elsewhere came to develop a distinctive vision of education, which emphasized standards of academic rigour, tolerance, and individuality, and this was not only a crucial element of their self-understanding. It was this vision of liberals in the cities which became a fundamental determinant of the quality and the nature of Prussian education during the Empire.

---

liberal politics in Düsseldorf has been suggested in Hüttenberger, 'Vom ausgehenden 19. Jahrhundert', 168.

[270] Lamberti, *State, Society, and the Elementary School*, 62–72.

[271] On the similarity in aims and purpose of the civic universities, see Hammerstein, *Antisemitismus und deutsche Universitäten*, 76–81.

[272] D. Langewiesche, 'Bildungsbürgertum und Liberalismus im 19. Jahrhundert', in J. Kocka (ed.), *Bildungsbürgertum im 19. Jahrhundert. Politischer Einfluß und gesellschaftliche Formation* (Stuttgart, 1989), iv. 95–121, esp. 100–1. This contemporary liberal view has been, of course, deeply influential in the subsequent historiography. For doubts about its validity, see K. D. Barkin, 'The Second Founding of the Reich: A Perspective', *GSR* x (1987), 219–35.

[273] To Frankfurt left liberals, a tolerant and progressive society was the central aim which would, in itself, improve the position of the workers. *Frankfurter Zeitung*, 27 Nov. 1904 (Drittes Morgenblatt).

5
Liberal Social Policies

5.1. Introduction

Throughout Europe, the crucial determinant of liberalism's viability as a modern political force in the twentieth century was whether it could face up to the 'social question', that is, whether it was able to formulate a political programme which could address the economic and political aspirations of the growing proletariat while at the same time satisfying the increasingly heterogeneous middle classes. Put differently, the challenge was whether an ideology dominant in the middle of the nineteenth century which believed in market capitalism and individualism, one which set the political and ideological framework for industrialization to happen in the first place, could reinvent itself successfully enough to solve the problems largely created by industrialization, for instance problems of urban squalor, poverty, and unemployment.[1]

German liberals had tremendous problems in adapting their ideologies to this process of social change. Compared particularly to the British Liberal Party,[2] German liberals failed to articulate and represent adequately

---

[1] R. Bellamy, *Liberalism and Modern Society. An Historical Argument* (Cambridge, 1992). Luebbert, *Liberalism*, 15–109. Specifically for urban society, Lothar Gall has characterized this problem as one about the changing nature of *Herrschaft*, the extent to which this was caused by forces from within urban society, and the extent to which it was the result of complex changes in the external environment. Put differently, it was a question of how power relations changed over the century, and what part did social, economic, and constitutional factors play in this change. Gall, 'Stadt und Bürgertum', 1–18, esp. 5–12.

[2] The question why in Germany liberals did not manage to contain labour until the twentieth century, in marked contrast to Britain, was a central issue in the *Sonderweg* debate. See in particular J. Breuilly, 'Liberalism or Social Democracy? Britain and Germany, 1850–1875', in J. Breuilly, *Labour and Liberalism*, 115–59. S. Berger, *The British Labour Party and the German Social Democrats, 1900–1931* (Oxford, 1994). For a survey of the literature, see C. Eisenberg, 'The Comparative View in Labour History. Old and New Interpretations of the English and German Labour Movements before 1914', *IRSH* xxxiv (1989), 403–32.

the social and economic demands of the emerging labouring classes, which responded to this failure with the establishment of an independent labour movement during the 1860s.[3] Moreover, in subsequent decades German liberals seemed largely unable to adapt their programme of reform developed in and for the 1850s to a rapidly industrializing society.[4] Many leading liberals took part in current debates about social policy,[5] especially in the *Centralverein für das Wohl der Arbeitenden Klassen*, founded in 1844, and later in the *Verein für Sozialpolitik*. Yet the liberals' very involvement in these associations, which acted largely as forums for intellectual debate composed of conservatives as well as liberals,[6] epitomizes the liberals' failure to find a common, coherent approach to social policy that was unequivocally liberal in character. These problems were compounded during the 1880s, when they failed to find a uniform response to Bismarck's social insurance legislation.[7]

If social policy received more attention from national politicians during the 1880s, the response to the 'social question' became a matter of critical importance from the 1890s onwards. For it is now that the liberals' failure to address the concerns of the working classes and, even more importantly, of the lower middle classes, translated into a large-scale defection of voters.[8]

---

[3] T. Offermann, *Arbeiterbewegung und liberales Bürgertum in Deutschland, 1850–1863* (Bonn, 1979). For a case study which highlights the liberal failure to appeal ideologically and organizationally to the workers in the most rapidly industrializing German state, Saxony, see R. J. Bazillion, 'Liberalism, Modernization, and the Social Question in the Kingdom of Saxony, 1830–90', in K. H. Jarausch and L. E. Jones (eds.), *In Search of a Liberal Germany. Studies in the History of German Liberalism from 1789 to the Present* (Oxford, 1990), 87–110. By contrast, around the turn of the century Saxon liberals displayed considerable skill in reinventing themselves. Retallack, ' "What is to be done?" ', 271–312.

[4] R. Aldenhoff, 'Das Selbsthilfemodell als liberale Antwort auf die soziale Frage im 19. Jahrhundert. Schulze-Delitzsch und die Genossenschaften', in K. Holl, G. Trautmann, and H. Vorländer (eds.), *Sozialer Liberalismus* (Göttingen, 1986), 57–69.

[5] Donald G. Rohr, *The Origins of Social Liberalism in Germany* (Chicago, 1963).

[6] R. vom Bruch (ed.), *Weder Kommunismus noch Kapitalismus. Bürgerliche Sozialreform in Deutschland vom Vormärz bis zur Ära Adenauer* (Munich, 1985), 11–13. R. vom Bruch, 'Gesellschaftliche Funktionen und politische Rollen des Bildungsbürgertums im Wilhelminischen Reich—Zum Wandel von Milieu und politischer Kultur', in J. Kocka (ed.), *Bildungsbürgertum im 19. Jahrhundert. Politischer Einfluß und gesellschaftliche Formation* (Stuttgart, 1989), iv. 179.

[7] Liberal inability to develop a coherent approach to social reform was a striking contrast to the long tradition of conservative state reform in Prussia, of which Bismarck's social legislation can be considered a climax. On the history of the most important of Bismarck's social reforms, the 1883 sickness insurance law, see U. Frevert, *Krankheit als Politisches Problem 1770–1880. Soziale Unterschichten in Preußen zwischen medizinischer Polizei und staatlicher Sozialversicherung* (Göttingen, 1984). In general, see G. A. Ritter, *Social Welfare in Germany and Britain* (Leamington Spa, 1986), 17–130.

[8] In 1890, support for the liberals among the Protestant workers halved from its 1887 level. It remained low throughout the 1890s, but recovered in the following decade. Liberal

The 1890s witnessed the emergence of the most dramatic industrial and economic boom of imperial Germany,[9] which caused social problems of extraordinary scale and quality. Chapter 3 has already highlighted that this presented the liberals with the fragmentation of their major social base, the bourgeoisie. To make matters worse, from 1900, SPD and particularly 'free' trade union membership exploded, with the result that by 1912 the SPD had become the largest party in the Reichstag.[10] Therefore, liberals were caught between placating demands from labour on the one hand and from the 'new' *Mittelstand* on the other, and the more they were seen to appease one group, the more they offended the other.[11] Finally, historians have been struck by the relative absence of new intellectual approaches shown by the main liberal parties to the social problems that resulted from Germany's economic and social change during those years. It is true that liberal politicians, such as Friedrich Naumann, or liberal academics, such as Lujo von Brentano, Hugo Preuß, and Max Weber were concerned about these issues, but in practice they exercised little influence on the major liberal parties.[12]

The implications of these debates for local government have so far been largely neglected, even though it was in the cities where the social problems of a rapidly industrializing and urbanizing society were most pressing. Among the reasons for this is, firstly, that the effect of the state's social legislation during the nineteenth century was a gradual erosion of local social responsibilities towards the poor. This was partly because freedom of movement overburdened the poor relief budgets of local authorities with the influx of the migrating agrarian poor, and partly because the social problems of a national industrializing economy required social provisions

---

support among the Protestant middle class declined by one-third in 1893, and by one-quarter in 1898, at which low level (29 per cent of the Protestant middle class) it stabilized. Sperber, *The Kaiser's Voters*, 364–7 (tables A.27–A.34).

[9] See e.g. the summary of Germany's industrial output in Berghahn, *Imperial Germany*, 298–9.

[10] In 1912, the number of trade union members was more than half of the total number of votes cast for the SPD in the Reichstag elections of that year. Berghahn, *Imperial Germany*, 335–7.

[11] R. Koch, 'Liberalismus und soziale Frage im 19. Jahrhundert', in K. Holl, G. Trautmann, and H. Vorländer (eds.), *Sozialer Liberalismus* (Göttingen, 1986), 29–30. Langewiesche, 'Bildungsbürgertum', 95–121. Langewiesche, 'Liberalismus und Bürgertum in Europa', 376. Sheehan, *German Liberalism*, 233–57. Sheehan, 'Wie bürgerlich war der deutsche Liberalismus?', 36–7.

[12] G. Trautmann, 'Die industriegesellschaftliche Herausforderung des Liberalismus. Staatsintervention und Sozialreform in der Politikökonomie des 18./19. Jahrhunderts', in K. Holl, G. Trautmann, and H. Vorländer (eds.), *Sozialer Liberalismus* (Göttingen, 1986), 34. Theiner, *Sozialer Liberalismus und deutsche Weltpolitik*, passim.

on a national scale.¹³ Secondly, at least since 1848 the state recognized that the growing number of urban poor could pose a potential political threat to the existing order.¹⁴ Thirdly, historians analysing liberalism for its innovative attitudes towards labour have often concentrated on comparing German 'social liberalism' with the ideas of English 'New Liberalism'. This shifted their focus to the social interventionist policies of the state, rather than the locality.¹⁵ This is unfortunate, since one crucial reason why a viable social liberalism at national or state level could not develop was because in Germany, in contrast to England, liberals were not in government and were thus unable to link social reform to any effective finance reform.¹⁶ Effective social reform through a 'People's Budget' was thus never an option for German liberals. Only at the local level, where liberals were in control of both, did liberals have the opportunity to come up with a viable programme of social policy. And, indeed, during the Empire the cities were major centres of social reform.¹⁷ Yet following the conclusions of urban historians sceptical of party politics in the local sphere, the cities' efforts at social reform have been largely seen as products of an enlightened local bureaucracy headed by an innovative mayor, in the face of stubborn resistance of local councils full of reactionary house owners seeking only their own immediate benefit.¹⁸

Even if the initiative for social policy mostly came from the *Magistrat*, it was the city councils which put the individual *Stadträte* into office in the

---

¹³ C. Sachse and F. Tennstedt, *Geschichte der Armenfürsorge in Deutschland. Vom Spätmittelalter bis zum 1. Weltkrieg* (Stuttgart/Berlin/Cologne/Mainz, 1980), 196–218.

¹⁴ F. Tennstedt, *Sozialgeschichte der Sozialpolitik in Deutschland. Vom 18. Jahrhundert bis zum Ersten Weltkrieg* (Göttingen, 1981), esp. 84 ff. This continued to be a major motive of the state's social legislation, e.g. under Bismarck. Tennstedt, op. cit., 222.

¹⁵ See the definition of social liberalism in K. Holl, 'Überlegungen zum deutschen Sozialliberalismus', in K. Holl, G. Trautmann, and H. Vorländer (eds.), *Sozialer Liberalismus* (Göttingen, 1986), 229.

¹⁶ G. Schmidt, 'Liberalismus und soziale Reform: Der deutsche und der britische Fall, 1890–1914', *TAJG* xvi (1987), 228–32. In contrast to Holl's exclusive focus on state policies of social interventionism, Gustav Schmidt has argued convincingly that the structure of the state, i.e. the relationship between locality, state, and nation was a central difference with regard to why liberals were so much more successful in addressing the social question in England than they were in Germany. Schmidt, op. cit., 228–9.

¹⁷ W. R. Krabbe, 'Munizipalsozialismus und Interventionsstaat. Die Ausbreitung der städtischen Leistungsverwaltung im Kaiserreich', *GWU* xxx (1979), 265–83. Krabbe, *Die deutsche Stadt*, 121–6.

¹⁸ F. Tennstedt, *Vom Proleten zum Industriearbeiter. Arbeiterbewegung und Sozialpolitik in Deutschland 1800–1914* (Cologne, 1983), 573–95. Hardtwig, 'Großstadt', 19–64. J. Reulecke, 'Bildungsbürgertum und Kommunalpolitik im 19. Jahrhundert', in J. Kocka (ed.), *Bildungsbürgertum im 19. Jahrhundert. Politischer Einfluß und gesellschaftliche Formation* (Stuttgart, 1989), iv. 138–44.

first place. Moreover, as social policy initiatives invariably cost money, the city council at the very least had to approve of the *Magistrat*'s initiatives. Since most councils were dominated by liberals, it seems reasonable to conclude that innovative urban social policies mainly emanated from urban liberals. Thus, the municipal strand of social liberalism invariably has to be taken into account in any evaluation of liberal approaches towards social policy before the First World War.[19] Langewiesche's views are confirmed by the example of Frankfurt. Far from considering social policy to be their Achilles heel, the issue on which they were bound to fail whatever they did, Frankfurt liberals viewed their achievements in the area of social policy with pride.

5.2. Liberal Policies after the Annexation

In a brief address on his local political life during the celebrations of his seventieth birthday, Leopold Sonnemann singled out one personal political achievement which stood above all others. This was to have directed the Frankfurt citizens' attention to questions of social policy from the 1860s onwards.[20] Indeed, there can be no doubt as to Sonnemann's commitment to improving the social conditions of the growing proletariat from the very start of his career. Sonnemann was the driving force behind a final liberal effort to articulate workers' issues through the *Vereinstag der deutschen Arbeitervereine* from 1863, and in subsequent years he did everything he could to keep the gap between workers and the bourgeoisie from widening.[21] Even after the Eisenach congress of 1869, Sonnemann never gave up hope. Against the instincts of most of his southern German colleagues, he managed to include a commitment to social justice as a central demand in the programme of the German People's Party when it was founded in 1868. The view that social and political justice formed two sides of the same coin became the Democrats' central article of faith,[22] and the major distinguishing feature against the Progressive Liberals, along with their differing

---

[19] Langewiesche, 'Deutscher Liberalismus im europäischen Vergleich', 17. For a summary of liberal involvement in urban social reform, see Langewiesche, *Liberalismus in Deutschland*, 200–11. Karl Heinrich Pohl has recently claimed that 'In the localities dominated by liberals we find the distant forerunner of the social welfare state [*Sozialstaat*] of the late twentieth century' (Pohl, 'Politischer Liberalismus und Wirtschaftsbürgertum', 123–4).

[20] *Leopold Sonnemann's siebzigste Geburtstagsfeier* (Frankfurt, 1901), 7.

[21] August Bebel, *Aus meinem Leben* (Stuttgart, 1910), i. 82–8, 102–13, 194–5. See also BAP, 90 Kn 1 n. 13 fo. 137. Sonnemann to Knorr, 4 July 1865. See also *Bericht über die Verhandlungen des ersten Vereinstages der deutschen Arbeitervereine. Abgehalten zu Frankfurt a.M. am 7. und 8. Juni 1863*, ed. Ausschuss des Vereinstages (Frankfurt, 1863).

[22] See e.g. councillor Paul Holdheim in HStAW 407 n. 138^2 fo. 6. Democratic Association meeting, 9 Jan. 1882. On Sonnemann's and the Frankfurt Democrats' leading role with regard

views about the nature of the federal state.²³ The German People's Party's economic and social programme included the commitment to a form of neo-corporatism (*Genossenschaftswesen*), the abolition of all privileges and monopolies, the establishment of technical schools (*Fortbildungsschulen*), and the abolition of indirect taxation in favour of progressive direct taxation.²⁴

By contrast, while it has been noted earlier that in the local sphere the Democrats demanded the abolition of the indirect tax on meat and flour, as well as better housing provisions by the municipality,²⁵ these policies did not feature prominently among the Democrats' goals after 1875. By that time, the question of indirect taxation had been resolved, and municipal involvement in housing gave way to a greater emphasis on public thrift and economy as the growing indebtedness of the city at the end of the *Gründerzeit* featured prominently in the public mind. Moreover, the Democrats' adamant and consistent demands for the municipalization of gas and water were undoubtedly progressive. Yet these were not social policies as such, that is policies directed at social reform in order in some way to solve the 'social question'.²⁶ Nor were they intended to be such by contemporary Democrats, who emphasized time and again the general benefit of these policies for the entire community.²⁷

Democrats were peculiarly unconcerned about the traditional areas of municipal welfare policy and poor relief, and in particular about the complete disarray of municipal policy towards the poor before 1883. And when they finally realized that an efficient system of poor relief needed to be established, this was motivated primarily by the need to reduce the spiralling cost of poor law provision, rather than by genuine concern for the welfare of the poor.²⁸ Therefore, while at the national level Democrats, and Sonnemann in particular, actively promoted social policies such as

to social justice within the German People's Party as a whole, see Gerteis, *Sonnemann*, 41–54, esp. 47–8. *Geschichte der Frankfurter Zeitung*, 159–63, 168–73. Hunt, *The People's Party*, 24–5, 111–19.

[23] See e.g. Sonnemann's speech to the Frankfurt Democratic Association on the relationship between Democrats and Progressive Liberals in *Frankfurter Zeitung*, 15 Oct. 1890 (1. Morgenblatt). The article is also in HStAW 407 n. 161¹ fo. 130.

[24] *Frankfurter Journal*, 15 Oct. 1873, in IfSG, S3/015.102.

[25] *Frankfurter Zeitung*, 15 Nov. 1872 (2. Blatt). Wolf, *Liberalismus*, 36.

[26] See George Steinmetz's definition of 'social policy' in G. Steinmetz, *Regulating the Social. The Welfare State and Local Politics in Imperial Germany* (Princeton, 1993), 67–9.

[27] See e.g. *Frankfurter Zeitung*, 23 Nov. 1872 (2. Blatt). *Frankfurter Zeitung*, 18 Nov. 1878 (Abendblatt).

[28] See the Democrat councillor Martin May on the reform of Frankfurt's provisions for the poor in HStAW 407 n. 138² fos. 19–21. Democratic Association meeting, 23 Jan. 1882.

Bismarck's social legislation, at the local level they tended to promote progressive policies aimed not so much at any particular group, but at improving social welfare in general.

Instead, perhaps the prominent proponent for municipal social reform in Frankfurt at the time was the physician Georg Varrentrapp. As a city councillor from 1867 until his death, Varrentrapp was the city's leading National Liberal who was twice selected as the party's candidate for the Reichstag elections. He was perhaps the first person in Frankfurt to recognize in 1860 that the supply of cheap, affordable housing became an increasing problem for families with low incomes. He thus became the driving force behind Frankfurt's first charitable building society which had built its first flats by 1868.[29] Much more importantly, as the chief protagonist of public hygiene in Frankfurt, it was Varrentrapp who lobbied hard and successfully for the establishment of a sewage and drainage system, the second in Germany, which had been under discussion since 1854 and the building of which finally began in 1867.[30] He was also the moving spirit behind the municipal takeover of the provision of water with the help of reservoirs from the nearby Vogelsberg mountain range in 1875.[31] Even though these policies were supported by many Democrats around Sonnemann, it was largely as a result of Varrentrapp's efforts that the city caught up with and surpassed most other German cities in the provision of public hygiene.

Varrentrapp's reputation as one of the leading experts on public sanitation in Germany and his local standing as the son of Frankfurt's leading physician in his day, from old Frankfurt stock,[32] gave his arguments about the urgency of sanitary reform important weight. Nevertheless, other arguments weighed more heavily in the minds of many of those who actually approved the considerable sums involved in these projects. Instead of being anxious about sanitation as such, most were concerned with the loss of revenue from the visitors and delegates of the Bundestag now that the German

---

[29] Henriette Kramer, 'Die Anfänge des Sozialen Wohnungsbaus in Frankfurt am Main, 1860–1914', *AFGK* lvi (1978), 123–90, esp. 134–7.

[30] E. Marcus, 'Dr. Georg Varrentrapp', in *Jahresbericht über die Verwaltung des Medizinalwesens der Stadt Frankfurt a.M.* (1886), 268. The article is also in IfSG, S2/796.

[31] *MAB*, 1874, p. v.

[32] They were described as 'Pettenkofer der Begründer der wissenschaftlichen Hygiene in Deutschland, Varrentrapp der Vater der praktischen Hygiene' (A. Spiess, 'Georg Varrentrapp. Gestorben am 15. März 1886', in *Deutsche Vierteljahresschrift für öffentliche Gesundheitspflege*, xviii (Brunswick, 1886), pp. iii–xxiv, quotation at p. xv. The article is also in IfSG S2/796. It is likely that Spiess slightly overrated Varrentrapp's importance, given that as Frankfurt's municipal physician he owed his job to him. Nevertheless, Varentrapp was a key figure in the German public health movement. Ladd, *Urban Planning*, 38–9.

Confederation had ceased to exist. Providing for a cleaner and healthier city was one way of attracting more visitors (*Fremdenverkehr*).³³ The First Mayor's explicit goal was to develop the city into a geographical and cultural centre of world standing, in order to attract a wealthy élite.³⁴ For once, the left-liberal Otto Kanngießer agreed. While usually never missing an opportunity to criticize the excessive spending of the city as he saw it, he advised in 1877 that comprehensive municipal expenditure was necessary to develop the city, and should be regarded as investment capital.³⁵

These arguments also provided the rationale behind most of the other improvements made to the city: the planning and construction of a new central railway station, the construction of several new streets through the crowded inner-city area and finally the building of a new opera house which, as a result of inept financial management, brought the city close to financial ruin in the late 1870s. Even though many of these policies had their origins in the last few years before the city's annexation, the strength and extent of this feeling largely derived from the Prussian takeover of the city, which spurred many Frankfurters into action to make up for the losses they perceived the annexation to entail.³⁶

Naturally, this expansion of municipal activity was not without opposition. At first, this came largely from the group of councillors around Nikolaus Hadermann, and, after his death in 1871, around Otto Volger.³⁷ These 'old Democrats' were opposed to the 'modern' organization and programme of Sonnemann's Democrats, and they tried to prevent, for example, the city's economic (and in particular its industrial) expansion after 1866.³⁸ More important than this relatively small group which merged into the Democratic Association in 1873 was the hostility of those who formed the Progressive Liberal Association in 1874. In the council, Berthold Geiger quickly proceeded to become their most prominent spokesman, and with his colleagues he offered firm resistance to any proposals for increased municipal provisions. Rigorously opposed to any form

---

³³ W. Forstmann, 'Frankfurt am Main in Wilhelminischer Zeit', in *Frankfurt am Main. Die Geschichte der Stadt in neun Beiträgen*, ed. Frankfurter Historische Kommission (Sigmaringen, 1991), 376.

³⁴ *Neue Presse*, 26 Jan. 1957, in IfSG, S2/3052.

³⁵ O. Kanngießer, *Geschichte der Eroberung der Freien Stadt Frankfurt durch Preußen im Jahre 1866* (Frankfurt, 1877), 447–8.

³⁶ For instance, in its first day of publication after the annexation, the *Frankfurter Zeitung* argued that the building of a drainage system and other improvements in municipal hygiene and the construction of the theatre were the expression of one and the same aim, namely to 'preserve the prosperity of the city'. *Frankfurter Zeitung*, 16 Nov. 1866 (2. Blatt).

³⁷ HStAW 405 n. 1066 fos. 294–5. *Zeitungsbericht*, 18 Feb. 1872.

³⁸ Wolf, *Liberalismus*, 28.

of municipalization of private monopolies, the Progressives were fiercely critical of lavish municipal spending on civic buildings.[39] They were thus essentially opposed to municipal intervention with the aim of raising the welfare of Frankfurt's citizens as a whole, and they were even more hostile to suggestions that the city intervene in favour of any particular group. In response to proposals for the creation of a shelter and a soup kitchen for the homeless following the examples set by Paris and London, it was noted at a Progressive Liberal meeting that such institutions brought more harm than good, and that it was inappropriate for the city's coffers to be thus 'exploited'.[40] This Progressive Liberal attitude to the municipal provision of welfare persisted in subsequent decades, and remained a strong minority position within the party even after the moderate Karl Funck took over from Geiger in leading the party during the 1890s. At the same time, under Funck the majority was increasingly willing to compromise with the social policy of the Democrats, and from the 1890s the social policy of this section of the Progressives gradually came to resemble that of the Democrats.

Despite Sonnemann's claims to have directed his fellow citizens' attention to social policies from the 1860s, no party in Frankfurt developed any consistent municipal social policy during the 1870s. It appears that during this time Sonnemann and his political friends focused their attention on the social policy of the Empire rather than of the city, which is hardly surprising given Sonnemann's intensive involvement in national politics at this point. Although the abolition of local indirect taxation was a local matter, it is likely that the Democrats proposed it with more than one eye turned to the national elections, since the main beneficiaries of this measure did not even have the municipal vote. Instead, the Democrats around Sonnemann and the National Liberals shared a commitment to raising the general welfare of the community through municipal policies, such as the provision of minimum standards of hygiene. In the former independent Free City, with its patrician and civic traditions, such a view of the role of local government was nothing new. What was new was the sheer scale of that provision. There were, of course, important differences between the views of left- and right-liberals about which policies were considered legitimate for the cities to conduct in the general interest. Whereas the Democrats largely shared the National Liberals' concern for civic building and public hygiene, the National Liberals remained at best cautious about the municipalization of private enterprises. Nevertheless, with the significant

[39] See e.g. HStAW 407 n. 150¹ fos. 12–13. Progressive Association meeting, 10 Feb. 1879.
[40] HStAW 407 n. 150¹ fo. 15. Progressive Association meeting, 10 Feb. 1879.

exception of the Progressive Liberals, the city's liberals were in considerable agreement about the principle of expansive municipal activity, not out of a commitment to a particular section of the city's society, or as part of a programme of social reform, but simply for the common weal.[41]

5.3. Frankfurt under Miquel: The Origins of 'kommunale Daseinsfürsorge'[42]

During the 1880s, social policy in Frankfurt underwent a dramatic change. Where there had been no consistent concern for municipal social policy among any of the political parties or the local administration before, both the administration and the Democrats developed theoretical and practical models of social policy of unusual sophistication. This sea-change in attitudes was the result of a number of interdependent factors. One element was the increasing attention paid by the Democratic leadership to matters of social policy. The early 1880s saw the rise to prominence within the party of Karl Flesch, who, upon finishing his degree in jurisprudence started to work as a lawyer in his home town in 1880.[43] Flesch started to publish on the problem of social policy, and put forward his views at a number of meetings of the Democratic Association.[44] Furthermore, during the 1880s Sonnemann himself started to shift some of his attention from imperial to municipal social policy, even though the effect of this was most clearly manifested during the 1890s, once he had given up all hope of ever re-entering the Reichstag. His first mention of social policy in the municipal context appears to have been made during the hotly contested 1884 election campaign for the Reichstag, in which he called for a municipal social policy to help a particular section of society, the artisans and craftsmen, for example through municipally subsidized credit.[45] Perhaps most importantly

---

[41] On the evolution of welfare provision in local government in the 19th century in general, see W. R. Krabbe, 'Die Entfaltung der modernen Leistungsverwaltung in den deutschen Städten des späten 19. Jahrhunderts', in H. J. Teuteberg (ed.), *Urbanisierung im 19. und 20. Jahrhundert. Historische und Geographische Aspekte* (Cologne/Vienna, 1983), 373–92.

[42] 'Kommunale Daseinsfürsorge' denotes a city government's provisions for the common weal, a term that evoked traditional notions of civic responsiblities for all those living within the city area. Langewiesche, *Liberalismus in Deutschland*, 201–4.

[43] Flesch-Thebesius, 'Der Frankfurter Sozialpolitiker Dr. Karl Flesch', 78.

[44] For an example of his speeches in 1882–3, see HStAW 407 n. 138^2 fos. 2–7. Democratic Association meeting, 9 Jan. 1882. HStAW 407 n. 138^2 fos. 144–8. Democratic Association meeting, 6 Mar. 1883.

[45] HStAW 407 n. 138^3 fos. 108–19. Democratic Association meeting, 13 Oct. 1884. The meeting was summarized in the *Frankfurter Zeitung*, which is in HStAW 407 n. 138^3 fo. 126. Sonnemann repeated his views on this question in HStAW 407 n. 138^3 fo. 137. Democratic Association meeting, Oct. 1884.

for Democratic attitudes towards social policy was the emergence during this decade of Heinrich Rößler as the party's most respected and influential leader, second only to Sonnemann himself.[46] Rößler's advance was in part the result and in part the cause of the growing social political consciousness of the Democrats. For Rößler was a strong authority on matters of social policy. In the year that he took over at the newly created *Deutsche Gold- und Silber-Scheideanstalt* (DEGUSSA) in 1873, he created a pension fund for his employees, and in 1884 he introduced the eight-hour day for his workers.[47] Such was his commitment to social policy that despite political differences he was on good terms with the local representatives of the SPD throughout his life, so that he was usually exempt from Social Democratic criticism of Democrat policies.[48] Rößler soon found that cooperation with workers' representatives not only enhanced the quality of life for his workers, but also the efficiency of his company. Given the strong hostility of the chemical industry to free trade unions in general, his public defence of their usefulness and their positive influence on the chemical industry demonstrates particularly well Rößler's genuine concern for social policy.[49]

Naturally, the transition of the Democrats' commitment towards a progressive social policy did not happen overnight, nor was this process complete by 1890. In 1902 Rößler himself admitted that it had taken some time and effort by the party leadership to arouse social-policy concerns among the rank and file.[50] The nature of this transition which occurred largely during the 1880s is well illustrated by the 1886 municipal election campaign, during which matters of social welfare found an unusual amount of attention. The official Democrat programme was still concerned with poor

---

[46] During the start of the decade, Rößler was far from prominent in the debates of the Democratic Association, neither was he a member of the party committee. For a list of the committee in 1882 and 1883, see HStAW 407 n. 138² fo. 108. By the end of the decade, Rößler was, alongside Sonnemann, the most frequent speaker at the Democratic Association, with four out of seventeen speeches in 1889/90 given by each. *Frankfurter Zeitung*, 15 Oct. 1890 (1. Morgenblatt). The article of the Annual General Meeting of the Democratic Association is also in HStAW 407 n. 161¹ fo. 130.

[47] See in general *Heinrich Rößler 1845–1924*, 44–61.

[48] In a debate on the crucial issue of the extension of the municipal franchise, for example, in his accusations against the Democrats Max Quarck acknowledged that Rößler was a 'white raven among the black' (*Volksstimme*, 17 Feb. 1903, in HStAW 407 n. 161⁴ fo. 122). See also Rößler's obituary in the SPD organ *Volksstimme*, 17 Apr. 1924. This article is also in IfSG, S2/1054.

[49] See Rößler's speech in 1905 on 'Was kann der Arbeiter zur Lösung der Frage [Bekämpfung von Giftgefahren] tun?', in IfSG, S1/6.

[50] H. Rößler, 'Die Sozialpolitik in unserem Gemeinwesen. Vortrag, gehalten im Demokratischen Verein', in *Gemeinnützige Blätter für Hessen und Nassau. Zeitschrift für soziale Heimatkunde*, iv (1902), 49–56, here 49–50.

relief mainly in order to reduce its cost to the city, with Sonnemann summarizing what he called 'social reform' as 'economic' matters. With the traditional commitment to the common weal, he demanded technical education and the establishment of municipal electricity works and housing.[51] Yet another Democratic candidate, Franz Wirth, already pledged a specific commitment to raise standards amongst working and artisanal classes. To him, technical education, the provision of electricity, and the improvement of poor relief and health, as well as the improvement of housing, were policies that were designed to benefit these particular sections of the population above all others.[52] This change of semantics is important, for it indicates a careful transition, which was still ambiguous in 1886, from a commitment towards the general welfare of the city to an overt social policy which was primarily directed towards the poorer sections of society.

Another crucial change that occurred during the 1880s was the appointment of Karl Flesch as a salaried *Stadtrat* and chairman of the *Armenamt*, for Flesch not only inspired the city's practical social policies from 1884 onwards: he also provided a theoretical foundation for them. In fact, he was one of the first social reformers to appreciate the fundamental difference between social policy and poor relief.[53] The entire justification of the former was to make the latter redundant.[54] The core of Flesch's theory was that traditional legal theories of contract failed to take account of the social realities of the time.[55] Hence, Flesch was part of a wider movement which criticized legal positivism's notions of equal treatment before the law. Spearheaded by academics, such as Gierke, it argued instead that the social question be taken into the civil code, especially given the de facto superiority of association over individuals, creditors over debtors, and rich over poor.[56] Flesch translated such concerns to the sphere of municipal government. Individual contracts of employment or housing were never agreed between equal partners. In the first case, there was a discrepancy between current wage arrangements, which simply provided the minimum needed by the worker to continue in his work, and the actual minimum needed by the individual not only to sustain himself and his family, but also to participate in culture and public life. The latter included the cost of living, as well as the cost of education, of going to the theatre, of visiting art galleries, and

---

[51] *Frankfurter Zeitung*, 23 Nov. 1886 (Abendblatt).
[52] *Frankfurter Zeitung*, 2 Dec. 1886 (1. Morgenblatt).   [53] Luppe, *Mein Leben*, 16.
[54] Weitensteiner, 'Karl Flesch', 46–7.
[55] H. Sinzheimer, *Der Sozialpolitiker Karl Flesch und seine literarisch-wissenschaftliche Tätigkeit* (Frankfurt, 1915), 9–10.
[56] John, *Politics and the Law*, 108–11, 114–15.

so forth. The other fundamental problem with current contracts of employment was that the individual worker had almost no protection against breach of contract by the employer.[57]

Flesch supported all efforts at social enquiry which could highlight the precise extent of these problems. By the end of the decade, Flesch was able to prove that despite the relatively high wage of Frankfurt workers, they could only make ends meet with the help of charity, even if they displayed the highest amount of thrift and diligence.[58] The Democrats thus came to believe that the 'social question' could only be solved if the community, and the municipality in particular, took measures to improve general real wage levels. This should be done through subsidized municipal services, generous terms of employment in municipal enterprises, cheap access to cultural events and, perhaps above all, cheap rents in healthy and adequate accommodation.[59] Flesch's views were a radical departure from traditional liberal beliefs in education and self-help. Important as these were,[60] the central thrust of Flesch's policies was to affect the individual's disposable income directly. This was clear interference in the labour market, and became a central objective of the Democrats' social policy.[61] Flesch's ideas were bound to become extremely influential among the city's left liberals, not only because he continued to propagate his views in speeches to the gatherings of the Democratic Associations at regular intervals after his appointment. His views were profoundly based on and appealed to Democratic values, notably the inalienable link between social and political freedom.[62] Likewise, even though most Democrats held no particular views on municipal social policy until the 1880s, Flesch's view that it was the duty of municipal self-government to become involved in areas where the state and even the Empire failed could not fall on deaf ears in a party with such passionate beliefs in the value of local self-government.[63]

The third factor which led to a fundamental change in municipal social

[57] K. Flesch, 'Zur Kritik des Arbeitsvertrages', in K. Flesch, *Karl Flesch's soziales Vermächtnis* (Frankfurt, 1922), 15–44.

[58] K. Flesch (ed.), *Frankfurter Arbeiterbudgets. Haushaltsrechnungen eines Arbeiters einer Königl. Staats-Eisenbahnwerkstätte, eines Arbeiters einer chemischen Fabrik und eines Aushilfearbeiters* (Frankfurt, 1890).

[59] K. Flesch, 'Wohlfahrtseinrichtungen für Arbeiter und deren Familien', in Flesch, *Karl Flesch's soziales Vermächtnis*, 63–100.

[60] Sinzheimer, *Der Sozialpolitiker Karl Flesch*, 7.

[61] Flesch himself used the slogan 'Wohnfrage ist Lohnfrage' (housing is a function of pay). Karl Flesch, 'Sozialpolitik in der Gemeinde und im Erwerbsleben', in K. Flesch, *Karl Flesch's soziales Vermächtnis* (Frankfurt, 1922), 100–23, here 112.

[62] Sinzheimer, *Der Sozialpolitiker Karl Flesch*, 4.

[63] Weitensteiner, 'Karl Flesch', 225.

policy during the 1880s was the social policy concerns of Frankfurt's First Mayor, Johannes Miquel. Miquel's period of office has been commonly characterized as one in which Miquel successfully balanced the budget after the poor financial management of his predecessor, but in which he failed to have the vision of his successor in responding to the challenges of modern city government.[64] Put more positively, the 1880s are often seen as a precondition for the activity and drive of Franz Adickes, First Mayor from 1890 to 1912.[65]

It is true that Miquel's most lasting contribution in social policy, the reorganization of poor relief in 1883, had an extremely redeeming effect on the municipal budget. Following the introduction of freedom of movement in 1867, private poor relief could no longer provide for the influx of the poor into the wealthy city of Frankfurt, particularly after the depression set in during the mid-1870s.[66] The situation was made worse by the fact that this private relief was not coordinated with the new municipal relief, which often resulted in payments by both bodies to the same recipients. Even worse, the private system enabled many paupers to stay in Frankfurt after their arrival until they were eligible to receive municipal support. Miquel responded by introducing the well-proven Elberfeld system of poor relief,[67] and by the coordination of private and public poor relief by the *Armenamt*, so that in effect the private bodies were subsidizing public poor relief.[68] Miquel's reorganization of poor relief was a phenomenal success, as

---

[64] The *Frankfurter Nachrichten* wrote on the death of Adickes: 'Adickes folgte dem ängstlichen Miquel, dem rechnenden Finanzmanne, der stetes im Banne des Ausgleichs seines Budgets lebte, der an neue Aufgaben erst herantrat, wenn die Notwendigkeit des Augenblicks sie forderten.' ('Adickes succeeded the anxious Miquel, that calculating man of finance, who constantly lived under the spell of his balanced budgets, who approached new tasks only when they became inevitable.') *Frankfurter Nachrichten*, 4 Feb. 1915 (Mittagsausgabe). See also Julius Rothenberger, 'Von Miquel bis Adickes (1880–1912)', in *Jahrbuch der Frankfurter Bürgerschaft* (1926), 126.

[65] G.-C. von Unruh, 'Bürgermeister und Landräte als Gestalter kommunaler Leistungsverwaltung', in H. H. Blotevogel (ed.), *Kommunale Leistungsverwaltung und Stadtentwicklung vom Vormärz bis zur Weimarer Republik* (Cologne/Vienna, 1990), 48. Klötzer, 'Das Wilhelminische Frankfurt', 172.

[66] For the general impact of the freedom of movement on municipal poor relief, see Steinmetz, *Regulating the Social*, 112–18.

[67] Codified in Elberfeld in 1853, this was a decentralized system of poor relief which enlisted a large number of volunteers to supervise each recipient of poor relief personally and to encourage each pauper to become self-reliant. The Elberfeld system is described in Steinmetz, *Regulating the Social*, 158–60.

[68] From 1876 to 1881, per capita expenditure on municipal poor relief doubled. M. Büttel, *Die Armenpflege zu Frankfurt a.M. mit besonderer Berücksichtigung der Kinderpflege im 18. und 19. Jahrhundert bis zum Eintritt der neuen Armenordnung im Jahre 1883* (Frankfurt, 1913), 108–17. According to the actuary Ebeling, the municipal poor relief budget rose from

per capita spending on poor relief continued to fall throughout the 1880s.[69] However, this was more than an act of economic prudence. The reorganization of poor relief was the first recognition by a city which until 1866 had had no system of poor relief at all, and which had grudgingly granted the statutory provisions of poor relief subsequently imposed by Prussian state laws, that the municipality had an obligation to provide for all the poor in the community.[70] In appreciation of this new obligation, the *Magistrat* also decided to employ the first municipal medical doctor in Germany, Dr A. Spiess, almost immediately after the reorganization of poor relief had come into effect on 1 April 1883.[71]

Miquel's most important contribution to the 'social question' lay in his support for, and substantial identification with, the programmes of Flesch. Indeed, Flesch's very appointment to the *Magistrat* in 1884 deserves attention, and not simply because he was only 30 years old at the time of his appointment. As shown above, he was an outspoken Democrat who by that time had already pronounced many of his views on the social question, some of which he had published.[72] It is simply inconceivable that Miquel could have appointed the left liberal had he not at least partially agreed with his views.[73] This agreement is best illustrated by their shared view that the lack of adequate housing was central to the 'social question'. In 1883, Miquel was the moving spirit behind an inquiry of the *Verein für Sozialpolitik* into the housing question, which was published in 1886 and

---

3,636 M. in 1870 to 202,500 M. in 1877. HStAW 407 n. 138¹ fo. 31. Democratic Association meeting, 24 Feb. 1879. Büttel's and Ebeling's figures do not add up, which may be explained by different measures of accounting for total poor relief expenditure. For the reorganization of the system of poor relief, see *MAB*, 1882/83, pp. 109–15, and *MAB*, 1883/84, pp. 155–60. For the new Frankfurt system of poor relief relative to its Elberfeld model, and for the theoretical underpinnings of Miquel's reform, see P. Stein, 'Das Verhältnis der freiwilligen und zwangsgemeinschaftlichen Körperschaften in der Wohlfahrtspflege', in Schriften des Vereins für Sozialpolitik, *Gemeindebetriebe*. i. *Neue Versuche und Erfahrungen über die Ausdehnung der kommunalen Tätigkeit in Deutschland und im Ausland*, cxxviii (Leipzig, 1908), 427–40.

[69] Weitensteiner, 'Karl Flesch', 44.

[70] This was recognized at the time. Karl Flesch wrote that the 'introduction and realization of the system of poor relief . . . signifies nothing less than a break with all principles and customs which had traditionally dominated our poor relief . . .'. K. Flesch and H. Bleicher, *Beiträge zur Kenntnis des Armenwesens in Frankfurt am Main und zur Armenstatistik* (Frankfurt, 1890), 1.

[71] *MAB*, 1883/84, p. 9.

[72] See the list of Flesch's publications in K. Flesch, *Karl Flesch's soziales Vermächtnis* (Frankfurt, 1922), 226–32.

[73] It is likely that Adickes, for example, would never have appointed Flesch. As late as 1906, the Mayor managed to prevent the election of Flesch's right-hand man, Hermann Luppe, to the post of a salaried *Stadtrat* despite (and also because of) Luppe's left-liberal and SPD support. Luppe, *Mein Leben*, 20.

discussed at a conference in Frankfurt in September of the same year. The importance of this investigation for housing reform throughout Germany can hardly be overestimated, for it ended over a decade of silence and public inactivity on the issue and provided the basis for subsequent discussions. It was the first time that details concerning the extent and the nature of the housing question had been brought into the public sphere.[74] Miquel's initiative is even more remarkable considering that he did not react strictly to demand. It may be true that the First Mayor had gained a valuable insight into the defects of the Frankfurt housing market during his reorganization of the city's system of poor relief,[75] but during the 1880s Frankfurt could boast the best housing conditions of any large city in Germany.[76] Moreover, by 1885, housing conditions had actually seen a marginal improvement over the previous two decades.[77]

What appears to have galvanized Miquel into action, apart from his own concern for the social question, was Flesch's concern for housing and insistence on the importance of social enquiry. Flesch's influence on Miquel's views is only too evident in the latter's introduction to the report of the *Verein für Sozialpolitik*. His article was an exposition about the various ways in which current laws failed to take account of current realities in the housing market. The tenant had little or no protection against breaches of contract by the owner, and there was little that the individual tenant could do against financial exploitation. In this sense, the weaknesses of current tenancy agreements were directly analogous to the problems inherent in employment contracts. As a remedy, he demanded an imperial housing law which gave the municipalities extra powers to enforce certain hygiene standards and to protect the tenants from breaches of contracts.[78] Clearly, Miquel's insight about the inadequacy of the law in failing to

[74] Bullock and Read, *The Movement for Housing Reform*, 63–70. On contemporary perceptions of the lack of housing as the central problem of urbanization, see also H. J. Teuteberg, 'Historische Aspekte der Urbanisierung. Forschungsstand und Probleme', in H. J. Teuteberg (ed.), *Urbanisierung im 19. und 20. Jahrhundert. Historische und Geographische Aspekte* (Cologne/Vienna, 1983), esp. 8–11, 19–22.

[75] Bullock and Read, *The Movement for Housing Reform*, 64–5.

[76] H. Lindemann (C. Hugo), 'Wohnungsstatistik', in Schriften des Vereins für Sozialpolitik, *Neue Untersuchungen über die Wohnungsfrage in Deutschland und im Ausland*, lxiv (Leipzig, 1901), 285, 290–1, 331–2, 340.

[77] E. Klar, 'Die Entwicklung des Wohnungswesens von 1870–1914', in *Das Wohnungswesen der Stadt Frankfurt a.M.* (Frankfurt, 1930), esp. 58–9.

[78] J. Miquel, 'Einleitung', in Schriften des Vereins für Sozialpolitik, *Die Wohnungsnoth der armen Klassen in deutschen Großstädten und Vorschläge zu deren Abhilfe*, xxx (Leipzig, 1886), pp. ix–xxi.

take into account current social political realities was entirely borrowed from Flesch.[79]

The combination of these factors, the growing Democratic awareness of social policy through its leadership, Flesch's appointment to the *Magistrat*, and Miquel's own concerns, produced quite dramatic results in Frankfurt during the 1880s. In 1887 and 1889, the city council agreed to the building of a number of flats for municipal civil servants.[80] Modest though the scale of this building was, it was nevertheless the first time the municipality built houses on its own. And in January 1890, the *AG für kleine Wohnungen* whose purpose was the building of small, adequate, and hygienic flats, was founded. Miquel became the president of the company, and, most remarkably, he did not resign his post when he left Frankfurt but kept it until his death in 1901. And as member of the board, Flesch undertook the effective running of the company. Again, these were only beginnings, as at the outset there was no public money involved in the company. Yet it is important to note that Frankfurt's most successful charitable housing company was founded with the active support and encouragement of Flesch and Miquel.[81] In the realm of education, 1889 saw the establishment of a school for children with special needs (*Hülfsschule*) to cater for those children who could not follow the lessons in ordinary schools.[82] More importantly, in 1890 the city finally established a *gewerbliche Fortbildungsschule*, a technical school for those craftsmen and apprentices who required particular skills in their employment such as reading, writing, or arithmetic.[83] Thus a demand which the Democrats had campaigned and lobbied for had come to fruition.[84]

Finally, at least as significant as Miquel's and Flesch's housing initiatives were their attempts to redress the legal insecurity of the worker. Flesch created the *gewerbliche Schiedsgericht*, an industrial tribunal which proved to be a cheap and efficient way of settling outstanding disputes between employers and employees. As a result of Miquel's backing, the Frankfurt tribunal became the model for the nationwide *Gewerbegerichtsgesetz* in

---

[79] See also Flesch's own contribution to the inquiry. K. Flesch, 'Die Wohnungsverhältnisse in Frankfurt a.M.', in Schriften des Vereins für Sozialpolitik, *Die Wohnungsnoth der armen Klassen in deutschen Großstädten und Vorschläge zu deren Abhilfe*, xxx (Leipzig, 1886), 57–91.

[80] Maly, *Macht*, 237–8, 265.

[81] Kramer, 'Anfänge', 148–51. *70 Jahre Aktienbaugesellschaft für kleine Wohnungen Frankfurt a.M., 1890–1960* (Frankfurt, 1960).

[82] *MAB*, 1889/90, p. 235.   [83] *MAB*, 1889/90, p. v. *MAB*, 1890/91, pp. 254–6.

[84] *Kleine Presse*, 23 Oct. 1889. See also HStAW 407 n. 161¹ fo. 28. Democratic Association meeting, 21 Oct. 1889.

1890.⁸⁵ Finally, the pioneering idea of a municipal labour exchange, which was eventually established in 1895, also had its origins in the deliberations of Miquel and Flesch.⁸⁶

At first sight, Miquel's enthusiasm for social policy in Frankfurt is as puzzling as it is unexpected. To begin with, his policies in Frankfurt were diametrically opposed to those he had advocated in Osnabrück in the late 1860s and late 1870s. In Osnabrück Miquel's social concern led him to cushion the blow which the introduction of the freedom of trade had dealt to the city's craftsmen by reintroducing a modified guild system on a voluntary basis.⁸⁷ Yet even before his appointment to Frankfurt, Miquel was left in no doubt that such a policy of supporting a guild system would be unwelcome in Frankfurt, even if it was associative and rested on a voluntary membership.⁸⁸ Frankfurt left liberals considered guilds to be restrictive and backward, and an impediment to Frankfurt's unfettered economic progress.⁸⁹

What is most striking is that through the introduction of the industrial tribunal Miquel pursued a policy which brought him into direct confrontation with the city's guild associations (*Innungen*). For the industrial tribunal was an intervention into the guilds' affairs, and if there was to be a court that was to decide on disputes between an employer and an employee, the guild associations preferred to introduce their own tribunals which would be free from outside interference and composed in the employers' favour. By contrast, the municipal tribunal's independence was central to its existence, hence Miquel and Flesch vigorously defended the principle of parity in the composition of the court, that is of equal representation for employees and employers with a municipal appointee as chairman having the casting vote.⁹⁰ Miquel also seemed to contradict his own views stated in the Heidelberg Declaration of 1884, which showed great concern for the more traditional demands of the *Mittelstand*.⁹¹ In Frankfurt Miquel did not

---

⁸⁵ Weitensteiner, 'Karl Flesch', 123–39.
⁸⁶ R. Roth, *Gewerkschaftskartell und Sozialpolitik in Frankfurt am Main. Arbeiterbewegung vor dem Ersten Weltkrieg zwischen Restauration und liberaler Erneuerung* (Frankfurt, 1991), 159–60.
⁸⁷ Herzfeld, *Miquel*, i. 389–403.   ⁸⁸ Ibid. 511–12.
⁸⁹ Despite the political challenge of the *Mittelstand*, liberals never budged from their conviction that guilds were synonymous with 'medieval institutions'. Yet in practice, the dividing line between voluntary guilds, on the one hand, and artisans' associations to which the left liberals had no objections on the other, was very unclear. Heinrich Rößler in *Frankfurter Zeitung*, 15 Nov. 1898 (Morgenblatt).
⁹⁰ Weitensteiner, 'Karl Flesch', 120–3.
⁹¹ *Frankfurter Zeitung*, 28 Mar. 1884 (Morgenblatt). For a more recent example of the view that the Declaration was more concerned about the *Mittelstand* than about the plight of

hesitate to engage in long negotiations with workers' representatives, an act which gave them added legitimacy and a further public sphere to operate in, thus undermining Bismarck's anti-socialist laws which Miquel himself had supported.[92] Indeed, Miquel tried his very best to convince the Prussian authorities first in Wiesbaden and then in Kassel to allow the tribunal to halt its operations during strikes in order to preserve its neutrality.

It would be easy to explain these apparent contradictions with the traditional argument that Miquel's policies at the state and national levels were different from those at the local level because at the local level Miquel's activities portray a mayor who acted 'above' politics. That certainly could explain why Miquel was largely in agreement with Frankfurt Democrats in his social policies while steering his party to the right in national politics at the same time. However, it fails to take into account the apparently different policies Miquel pursued as mayor of Osnabrück and as mayor of Frankfurt. Moreover, with Miquel it is particularly difficult to define the point at which he stopped acting 'unpolitically' as Mayor and started acting politically as a national politician. For example, as the moving spirit behind the Association for Social Policy's housing investigation Miquel based his authority on his experience as a mayor, but his central demand was for an imperial law which could help the localities solve the housing problem.

Instead, Miquel's various actions in national, state, and local politics reveal him as the expert and professional politician that he really was. Underlying his activities was a deep commitment to social reconciliation in a rapidly evolving industrial society which was one of German liberalism's core concerns. To distinguish between the 'political' and 'unpolitical' ways in which he pursued this central liberal goal misses the point. Moreover, Miquel combined this aim with a sharp awareness of political realities.[93] In Osnabrück, Miquel presided over a city with deep and overlapping social, political, and confessional tensions and a still powerful guild system which during the 1860s made it extremely hard to find any form of governing

---

industrial workers and employees, see Nipperdey, *Deutsche Geschichte 1866–1918*, ii. 329–30. It should be noted, however, that in contrast to contemporary and later interpretations of the Heidelberg Declaration, a disproportionate attention to the plight of the *Mittelstand* at the expense of the working classes is not evident from its actual wording. Instead, the Declaration was largely aimed at satisfying the demands of the southern German agricultural constituencies of its signatories. The Declaration is printed in D. S. White, *The Splintered Party. National Liberalism in Hessen and the Reich, 1867–1918* (Cambridge, Mass., 1976), 238–9.

[92] Beacuse of these negotiations, Miquel also prevented the expulsion of these socialist leaders from the city for their socialist activities. Weitensteiner, 'Karl Flesch', 116.

[93] In assessing Miquel's move from Mayor of Frankfurt to the Prussian government, Hofmann comes to a similar conclusion. Hofmann, *Zwischen Rathaus und Reichskanzlei*, 180–1.

consensus.[94] In this situation, he placated a strong artisanate, but he also showed an awareness of the social problems of workers. Thanks to his efforts the city built the first houses for miners working for the municipality.[95] By contrast, Miquel's *Mittelstand* policies had no chance of political support in Frankfurt, so he did not even try. This did not mean that Miquel's interest in the social question receded. On the contrary, it made sense for him to support the innovative policies of the Democrats. They might just work, though given their local nature he had little to lose if they did not.

Miquel's political actions in state and national politics have to be judged against the fact that at that level he had to appeal to a different constituency than existed in predominantly liberal Frankfurt.[96] The breakaway of the Secessionists from the National Liberal Party in 1880 and the results of the elections prior to the Heidelberg Declaration had made it abundantly clear that the National Liberals' constituency was in small towns and in the countryside, and it was to these areas that he had to appeal for political survival.[97] And yet this did not stop him from consistently lobbying for social reform at national level, too, even if his demands were rather more careful and conservative as he adapted them to a national constituency.[98] In the same way, Miquel's social policies in Frankfurt demonstrate that he was an astute politician concerned with, and able to adapt his political ideals to, the political environment in which he operated.

For Frankfurt, the 1880s, and more specifically the years 1883 and 1884, marked the beginning of progressive municipal social reform. Despite the critical importance of Flesch and Miquel in this outcome, it would be mistaken to absolve the city council from any responsibility for the municipal social policies that emerged during the 1880s. Under the leadership of Rößler and Sonnemann, the Democratic Association became a firm supporter of these policies. The new municipal *gewerbliche Fortbildungsschule* was a demand for which Democrats had campaigned and lobbied for some time.[99] The Democratic Association also supported the creation of the

---

[94] Lembke, *Johannes Miquel*, esp. 8–10. John, 'Kultur, Klasse und regionaler Liberalismus', 184–6.

[95] Lembke agrees with Herzfeld's assessment that Miquel's concern for the artisans was the cornerstone of his policies in Osnabrück, but then his discussion of Miquel's 'social policy' shows the mayor to be surprisingly progressive. Lembke, *Johannes Miquel*, 65 ff.

[96] A good example of this is that in the Heidelberg Declaration, he called for higher taxes on stock exchange transactions, a demand that was completely opposed to the interests of the city of Frankfurt and which could not even be contemplated in the local context.

[97] White, *The Splintered Party*, 84–122, esp. 105–7, 112–13.

[98] Nipperdey, *Deutsche Geschichte 1866–1918*, ii. 330.

[99] *Kleine Presse*, 23 Oct. 1889, also in HStAW 407 n. 161[1] fo. 28. Democratic Association meeting, 21 Oct. 1889.

charitable building company *AG für Kleine Wohnungen*, with Sonnemann even suggesting a municipal subsidy for the company, at a time when the company had not even been founded.[100] That Rößler was closely in tune with the First Mayor's ideas on housing is shown by the pivotal role he played later in the creation of the 'Association Imperial Housing Law' through which he lobbied hard for the creation of a national housing law largely along the lines suggested by Miquel.[101] Rößler was also very involved in the creation of the industrial tribunal. Together with the Democrat entrepreneur Schmidt-Knatz, he persuaded the employers to agree to an equal franchise for the elections to the tribunal.[102] This is not to deny that scepticism about this progressive form of social policy among councillors was generally still quite strong, much stronger, in fact, than in subsequent decades. Also, Democratic house owners could vote for their personal interest in precedence to their party allegiance in the 1880s just as they could in subsequent decades. Nonetheless, a progressive city council was an absolute prerequisite for a municipal social policy.[103] The gradual change in social-policy views of Frankfurt's Democrats in particular was a precondition of the change in attitude towards social policy that occurred during the 1880s. This change, together with the rise to prominence of Karl Flesch and Miquel's term of office, ultimately caused the introduction of a progressive social policy in the 1880s. These factors were interdependent. Flesch was a Democrat through and through, and Miquel not only had similar social-policy aims, but he also needed the Democrats' support for the reforms which he pioneered in association with Flesch. Social policy in Frankfurt am Main was not the result of some bureaucrats' actions, but was embedded in the evolving political environment of the city.

5.4. Social Policies in Wilhelmine Frankfurt

During Adickes's term of office, social policy in Frankfurt expanded dramatically, both in quality and in scope. The archetypal 'unpolitical' National Liberal mayor of this era,[104] Adickes has been regarded as one of the pioneers of municipal socialism in Germany,[105] and even his opponents

---

[100] HStAW 407 n. 161¹ fos. 51–2. Democratic Association meeting, 11 Nov. 1889.
[101] H. Rößler, 'Die Aufgaben von Reich und Staat in der Wohnungsfrage', in A. Damaschke and H. Rössler, *Der Kampf gegen die Wohnungsnot* (Frankfurt, 1903), 7–23. On the *Verein Reichswohnungsgesetz (e.V.)*, see Bullock and Reid, *The Movement for Housing Reform*, 255–67.
[102] Weitensteiner, 'Karl Flesch', 115.
[103] H. Rößler, 'Sozialpolitik in der Gemeinde', in IfSG S1/6 fo. 28.ii.
[104] Thompson, 'Left liberals', 45.
[105] Notably by Frankfurt's First Mayor during the period of the Weimar Republic, Ludwig Landmann, in E. Adickes (ed.), *Franz Adickes. Sein Leben und sein Werk* (Frankfurt, 1929), p. viii.

could not but testify to the breadth of his vision.[106] Together with Miquel, Adickes, whom Sheehan has described as 'the ideal mayor in the late imperial period', is generally regarded as one of the leading mayors in the German Empire.[107] In contrast to Miquel, however, Adickes never had any designs to enter state or national politics, so that Adickes's career was, more typically, entirely devoted to local government.[108] As a result, Adickes did not so much adapt himself to the Democrats' vision of social policy, but he came to Frankfurt with a social-policy agenda of his own. In fact, Adickes was one of the first mayors in Germany to develop a holistic, comprehensive concept of municipal social policy, where social policy was the essence of municipal government in its classic liberal aim of contributing to a harmonious society.[109]

An important concern for the left liberals and especially of Adickes, who came to articulate and represent National Liberal opinion on social policy,[110] was a commitment to the city's *Mittelstand*. The demand for technical education undoubtedly formed the most consistent and often repeated Democratic social policy initiative in favour of the *Mittelstand*, along with the favourable system of taxation discussed in the following chapter. During the 1900s, this was complemented by calls for an exhibition hall in which small craftsmen and artisans could sell their work at low cost,[111] for the provision of cheap credit by the municipality, and for the realization of other *Mittelstand* concerns such as the building of an old people's home.[112]

---

[106] BAK, NL 44 n. 21 fo. 2. 'Franz Adickes, sein Leben und sein Werk'. Book review by H. Luppe, typescript.

[107] Sheehan, 'Liberalism', 126. See also H. Delvos, 'Oberbürgermeister einst und heute', in *Frankfurter Allgemeine Zeitung*, 11 Mar. 1964. The article is also in IfSG, S2/649.iii.

[108] Even at the level of state politics, as a member of the Prussian upper chamber, the *Herrenhaus*, Adickes remained an authority first and foremost on matters concerning local government. See in general W. Klötzer, 'Franz Adickes, Frankfurter Oberbürgermeister 1891–1912', in K. Schwabe (ed.), *Oberbürgermeister* (Boppard, 1981), 39–56, esp. 40. See also the biographical article by Alfred Hugenberg, leader of the DNVP in the Weimar Republic, who was, interestingly, Adickes's son-in-law. A. Hugenberg, 'Franz Adickes als Staatsmann und Politiker', in Adickes (ed.), *Franz Adickes*, 233–52. Unsurprisingly, however, the article tends to exaggerate Adickes's influence in state politics. BAK, NL 44 n. 21 fo. 3. 'Franz Adickes, sein Leben und sein Werk'. Book review by H. Luppe, typescript.

[109] Adickes and Beutler, *Die sozialen Aufgaben*, 12.

[110] The Democrats liked to mock the National Liberals about the odd member who was sometimes caught by a brief social political urge ('ein sozialpolitischer Raptus'), and might even be serious about social policy, but who would never go further than 'Uncle Adickes' would allow. Councillor Zirndorfer in *Frankfurter Zeitung*, 1 Nov. 1902 (3. Morgenblatt).

[111] *Frankfurter Zeitung*, 19 Nov. 1906 (Morgenblatt).

[112] *Frankfurter Zeitung*, 8 Nov. 1908 (3. Morgenblatt).

Their overall central concern for the middle classes notwithstanding,[113] the principal aim of left- and right-liberal social policy was to 'protect the weak, to constrain the reckless, to confront the overpowering might of capital and to reduce social conflict through raising the unpropertied classes'.[114] To Heinrich Rößler, the spiritual and physical well-being of the lower sections of society was the prerequisite of a 'blossoming, great community'.[115] For a reconciliation of all sections of society, social policy had to be primarily directed towards the poorer sections of society.

The centrepiece of Adickes's social concern, in line with most other social reformers in Germany during the last two decades before the First World War, was land policy, a comprehensive effort to create not only sufficient, affordable housing, but also a clean and aesthetically pleasant municipal environment.[116] Adickes pursued these aims in three ways. In his attempt to put an end to the speculation in building land and thus reduce the price of land and ultimately of housing, Adickes introduced a building ordinance. This imposed strict requirements on the building of new flats, and standardized the building regulations in all parts of the city.[117] Furthermore, it introduced the principle of 'zoning', whereby the city was divided into different zones, so that, for example, industrial buildings could only be constructed in a zone designated for that purpose.[118] His efforts to circumscribe the housing market by building regulations climaxed with the famous *Lex Adickes*, which was first introduced in the Prussian Parliament in 1893, but which was not passed until 1901, curtailed in its application to Frankfurt alone.[119] The *Lex* introduced the principle of '*Umlegung*' which meant that private owners of land could be forced to exchange their land for an equivalent plot elsewhere if this was deemed necessary, for example for the building or widening of streets.

A second strand of Adickes's housing policies was his drive for incorporations to create more space for the city and thus to reduce the price of land. Whereas up to 1890 there had only been one reluctant incorporation

---

[113] Frankfurter Zeitung, 8 Nov. 1908 (3. Morgenblatt).
[114] Adickes and Beutler, *Die sozialen Aufgaben*, 10.
[115] H. Rößler, 'Sozialpolitik in der Gemeinde', in S1/6 fo. 28.i.
[116] Under Adickes, Frankfurt became 'the generally acknowledged pioneer in German housing reform'. See in general Ladd, *Urban Planning*, 139–85, here 167.
[117] Adickes's concern to avoid Berlin-style 'Mietskasernen' is highlighted in R. Koch, 'Franz Adickes', in G. Böhme (ed.), *Geistesgeschichte im Spiegel einer Stadt: Frankfurt am Main und seine grossen Persönlichkeiten* (Frankfurt, 1986), 112–13.
[118] *MAB*, 1891/92, pp. x–xii.
[119] A. Sutcliffe, *Towards the Planned City. Germany, Britain, the United States and France, 1788-1914* (Oxford, 1981), 37. This book is also a good introduction into the surrounding debates on urban planning in Germany and elsewhere at the time.

(of Bockenheim in 1877),[120] there followed three 'bursts' of incorporation in 1895, 1900, and 1910, by which time the entire Frankfurt *Landkreis* had been incorporated into the city and Frankfurt had become the largest German town in terms of area.[121] The *Magistrat* pursued the policy of buying large tracts of land in the areas it had targeted for incorporation. This was doubly beneficial as the existence of Frankfurt as the biggest landowner in these communities added pressure for incorporation, and it meant that the city could acquire a lot of land cheaply before speculation set in as a result of incorporation.[122]

By 1914 the city of Frankfurt was perhaps the largest municipal owner of land within its city limits in Germany. Yet it soon became clear that the municipal ownership of land in itself did not automatically lead to an improvement of the housing market. If the municipality sought to influence the price of land through selling its land cheaply, it could lead to speculation as those who bought the land could resell it at market price for a quick profit. Conversely, if the municipality decided to hold on to its land, it effectively reduced the supply of land on the market, thereby increasing the price of available land even further. In response, to provide municipal land cheaply while seeking to prevent its use for speculative purposes, Adickes pioneered for Germany the idea of the *Erbbaurecht*, the system whereby the municipality would lease out its lands for extremely low fees to those who wanted to build houses. And, to facilitate conditions for private building even further, Adickes set up a municipal bank which could provide second loans to families and charitable building companies with little starting capital.[123]

The third important strand of Adickes's *Bodenpolitik*, and one closely linked to his policy of incorporation, was his support for the improvement of the city's infrastructure. Cheap and efficient transport by municipal tramways enabled workers to live further away from their workplace where living conditions were better. Parks were layed out to improve the living

[120] Maly, *Macht*, 104–9.
[121] D. Rebentisch, 'Politik und Rauplanung im Rhein-Main Gebiet. Kontinuität und Wandel seit 100 Jahren', *AFGK* lvi (1978), 195–6 and, more elaborately, Rebentisch, 'Industrialisierung', 90–113. W. Hofmann, 'Oberbürgermeister und Stadterweiterungen', in R. Dietrich and G. Oestreich (eds.), *Forschungen zu Staat und Verfassung. Festgabe für Fritz Hartung* (Berlin, 1958), 59–90. See also W. Seitz, 'Kommunale Wohnungspolitik im Kaiserreich am Beispiel der Stadt Frankfurt am Main', in H. J. Teuteberg (ed.), *Urbanisierung im 19. und 20. Jahrhundert. Historische und Geographische Aspekte* (Cologne/Vienna, 1983), 393–428.
[122] Rebentisch, 'Industrialisierung', 109.
[123] W. Bangert, 'Baupolitik und Stadtgestaltung in Frankfurt a.M. Ein Beitrag zur Entwicklungsgeschichte des deutschen Städtebaus in den letzten 100 Jahren', Ph.D. thesis (Technische Hochschule Berlin, 1936), 55–60.

conditions for those who stayed in the city.[124] Finally, Adickes promoted a large number of street clearances in the inner-city area, partly to reduce congestion through the building of large streets and boulevards, and partly to improve the city aesthetically, by following Stübben's ideas, for example, on the desirability of wide-open spaces from which the city's landmarks such as the cathedral could be seen.[125]

With these ideas on the housing question, Adickes achieved national prominence, largely for two reasons. Firstly, he occupied something of a half-way house between two opposite poles in the debate. His highly interventionist housing policies satisfied housing reformers for whom the extortionate prices for small flats were rooted in supply-side problems such as speculative behaviour.[126] Yet Adickes was heavily interventionist in every aspect of the housing market save the actual building of housing. This gave him something to offer to those who considered the price of housing a direct result of excess demand, and who therefore emphasized the need for 'laissez-faire' in the market.[127] The second reason for Adickes's prominence in the housing debate was that he put into practice what legal experts considered to be traditional 'Germanist' solutions to the social problem. Indeed, municipal socialism was a way of adapting notions of medieval, financially independent, and socially benevolent city government to modern conditions. Thus it could play a crucial part in reconciling the various classes which had grown apart even further since the industrial revolution.[128] Adickes's policies were the direct answer to Gierke's attempts to construct a German 'social law' to mediate between public and private law

---

[124] *Monographien Deutscher Städte*, vii. *Frankfurt am Main*, ed. E. Stein and G. Voigt (Oldenburg i. Gr., 1914), 106–12. Bangert, 'Baupolitik', 41. For a rare overview, see D. Hennebo, 'Öffentlicher Park und Grünplanung als kommunale Aufgabe in Deutschland', in H. H. Blotevogel (ed.), *Kommunale Leistungsverwaltung und Stadtentwicklung vom Vormärz bis zur Weimarer Republik* (Cologne/Vienna, 1990), 169–82.

[125] Josef Stübben was the architect of the Cologne *Neustadt* and of a large number of other city-planning projects in Europe. An admirer of Haussmann's Paris, he was the most influential advocate of the building of wide and spacious streets, and of creating 'air and light' around important monuments and civic buildings to enhance their aesthetic effect. Ladd, *Urban Planning*, 96–103. Bangert, 'Baupolitik', 38–47.

[126] For example, Adickes's programme was the answer even to the more radical demands of a Friedrich Naumann. F. Naumann, *Die Wohnungsnot in unserer Zeit. Vortrag auf dem 6. Verbandstage Deutscher Mietervereine in Cassel* (Leipzig, n.d.).

[127] For a summary of the economic background to the 'housing problem', see R. Tilly, 'Cyclical Trends and the Market Response: Long Swings in Urban Development in Germany, 1850–1914', in W. R. Lee, *German Industry and German Industrialisation. Essays in German Economic and Business History in the Nineteenth and Twentieth Centuries* (London, 1991), 148–84. Seitz, 'Kommunale Wohnungspolitik', 402–4.

[128] K. Bücher, *Die wirtschaftlichen Aufgaben der modernen Stadtgemeinde* (Leipzig, 1898), esp. 3–11.

which combined guarantees for individual freedom with collective social responsibility, in contrast to Roman law which sought to guarantee only the former, and to socialism, which sought to guarantee only the latter. In particular, Gierke emphasized that property carried with it rights as well as duties to the community. Gierke called on public law to enforce the 'proper' use of land, and this was precisely the point of Adickes's policies such as the *Erbbaurecht* and the *Lex Adickes*.[129]

Even though the city's left liberals by and large supported Adickes in his endeavours, they had substantial misgivings about important areas of his policies. Not surprisingly, large sections of the Progressive Liberal Association were opposed to the more interventionist and costly policies through which Adickes proposed to regulate the housing market.[130] But the Democrats also showed considerable unease, for example, at Adickes's expensive street clearance projects.[131] Many Democrats considered the *Lex Adickes* at best 'superfluous', and at worst a 'barbarian' intervention into the rights of the citizens.[132] Eight years later in 1901, when the law was again under discussion, Democrats were slightly more welcoming to the proposals, yet they were still hostile to the wide powers of expropriation which it offered to housing authorities, and they preserved a considerable scepticism as to how much of a solution the law would actually be.[133] The left-liberal rank-and-file regarded the *Lex Adickes* with considerable suspicion, notwithstanding the support Adickes received from left-liberal prominence including Flesch, Rößler, Funck, and Oeser.[134]

Beneath these more predictable arguments, there were two fundamental reasons for left-liberal scepticism about Adickes's policies of housing reform. The first was that there was doubt as to whether Adickes's policies were actually working, and, as has been shown in Chapter 3, that doubt increased during his last years in office. Adickes's peculiar policy of interfering with every aspect of the housing market save the building of

---

[129] O. von Gierke, 'Die soziale Aufgabe des Privatrechts', in E. Wolf (ed.), *Quellenbuch zur Geschichte der Deutschen Rechtswissenschaft* (Frankfurt, 1949), 478–511. John, *Politics and the Law*, 108–11, 120–2. M. John, 'Constitution, Administration, and the Law', in R. Chickering (ed.), *Imperial Germany. A Historiographical Companion* (Westport, Conn., 1996), 203–4. On Gierke's social thought, see G. Dilcher, 'Genossenschaftstheorie und Sozialrecht: Ein "Juristensozialismus" Otto v. Gierkes?', *Quaderni Fiorentini per la storia del pensiero giuridico moderno* iii/iv (1974/5), 319–65.
[130] See e.g. HStAW 407 n. 150² fo. 215. Progressive Association meeting, 28 Oct. 1901.
[131] See e.g. HStAW 407 n. 161⁴ fo. 53. Democratic Association meeting, 11 Nov. 1901.
[132] HStAW 407 n. 161¹ fos. 323–7. Democratic Association meeting, 27 Mar. 1893.
[133] HStAW 407 n. 161⁴ fos. 37–8. Democratic Association meeting, 13 Apr. 1901.
[134] HStAW 407 n. 161⁴ fo. 92. Democratic Association meeting, 7 Apr. 1902. HStAW 407 n. 161⁴ fos. 26–7. Democratic Association meeting, 4 Mar. 1901.

municipal housing itself, and in particular his enthusiasm for buying up as much land as possible without interfering in the market directly, was self-contradictory and achieved the worst of both worlds. By 1907, around 49 per cent of all the land within the city limits was directly owned by the municipality, and a further 19 per cent was owned by charities controlled by the city.[135] If the private provision of housing was the answer, therefore, Adickes's policies were perhaps the main contributor to the shortage of housing through the withdrawal of 68 per cent of land from the market.

Indeed, the city frequently pushed up the price of land available on the private market directly by buying land for considerably above the current price.[136] Given the sheer amount of land in municipal ownership, the most efficient way of providing cheap housing would have been for the city to take a more active part in the building of flats. As it was, Adickes's efforts at encouraging the less well-off (though not industrial workers) to build their own homes through the *Erbbaurecht* and cheap credit met only with partial success. It did enable the foundation of many new charitable building societies which could make extensive use of the *Erbbaurecht* through the building of housing with little starting capital of their own. By contrast, Frankfurt's largest housing charity, the *AG für kleine Wohnungen*, made little use of the system since in the long run it had much to gain from the increasing value of its land.[137] Furthermore, the system was little used by individual families, who were put off by the idea that they would not own the land for posterity.[138] Finally, despite his ambitious and expensive street clearances, Adickes failed to solve the city's traffic problems.[139] His obsession with building wide streets aroused frequent complaints,[140] because again it reduced the amount of land available for building and hence increased prices.[141]

---

[135] H. Silbergleit, *Preussens Städte. Denkschrift zum 100 jährigen Jubiläum der Städteordnung vom 19. November 1908* (Berlin, 1908), 174–7.

[136] Bangert, 'Baupolitik', 53–4. BAK, NL 44 n. 8 fos. 197–9. Luppe, 'Mein Leben'.

[137] According to the data given by Kramer, less than one-third of all flats built by charitable housing trusts were built by taking advantage of the *Erbbaurecht*. Kramer, 'Anfänge', 143–8, 174–6. Note that the figure she gives for the number of flats built by charitable housing trusts by 1914 on p. 179 (6,512) contradicts the figure for the same item given on p. 178 (5,507).

[138] Bangert, 'Baupolitik', 56–8.

[139] BAK, NL 44 n. 8 fos. 191–2. Luppe, 'Mein Leben'. Bangert, 'Baupolitik', 39–44.

[140] HStAW 407 n. 161³ fos. 173–4. Democratic Association discussion group, 15 Nov. 1899. See also the complaint by the National Liberal teacher Martell in HStAW 407 n. 161⁴ fos. 37–8. Democratic Association meeting, 13 Apr. 1901. See also E. L. Hinderliter, 'Worker Protection in Imperial Germany. The Example of Frankfurt am Main 1869–1914', Ph.D. thesis (Providence, RI, 1977), 60–1.

[141] Bangert, 'Baupolitik', 39. BAK, NL 44 n. 8 fo. 189. Luppe, 'Mein Leben'. In addition to increasing the scarcity of land available for building, house-owners had to contribute significantly to the cost of the streets which served their property.

If the left liberals were increasingly sceptical about the actual benefits of Adickes's wide-ranging policies, the second, crucial disagreement was over his motives. Although Adickes was undoubtedly interested in providing healthy and cheap living conditions for those on moderate incomes, he was more concerned about the provision of housing for the *Mittelstand* than for industrial workers.[142] The former, not the latter, were the principal beneficiaries of the *Erbbaurecht* and the cheap municipal credit facilities.[143] Moreover, for Adickes the provision of cheap housing was always secondary to creating a city which would remain attractive to its wealthy inhabitants. Even though Adickes supported a number of charitable building initiatives, by and large he and his right-liberal supporters remained hostile to charitable housing.[144] For if charitable housing trusts offered flats at below the market price, it would distort and disrupt the private housing market.[145]

The underlying motive of Adickes's housing policies was diametrically opposed to that of the left liberals. Certainly, left liberals would not have argued with the First Mayor's efforts at attracting the wealthy or supporting the *Mittelstand*. However, whereas Adickes was concerned to ensure that the private market would work without distortions from either speculation or underpriced housing, the Democrats followed the ideal of Karl Flesch, the point of whose social policy in housing was precisely to distort the market, in favour of those with lower incomes. Democrats supported the cheap provision of municipal land for building purposes,[146] as well as

---

[142] Adickes and Beutler, *Die sozialen Aufgaben*, 41. Adickes's building plan of 1890 for Altona, for instance, clearly intended to prevent the growth of more crowded accommodation from the poorer sections of the city to its affluent areas. H. Böhm, 'Bodenpolitik deutscher Städte in der Zeit vor dem Ersten Weltkrieg', in J. Reulecke (ed.), *Die Stadt als Dienstleistungszentrum. Beiträge zur Geschichte der 'Sozialstadt' in Deutschland im 19. und frühen 20. Jahrhundert* (St Katharinen, 1995), 38. Moreover, Adickes tried hard to avoid as much as he could incorporations which extended to predominantly industrial areas, as he feared an increase in the SPD electorate. As a result, he strove to incorporate Schwanheim while refusing to contemplate the incorporation of neighbouring Griesheim and Nied, in BAK, NL 44 n. 8 fos. 218–20. Luppe, 'Mein Leben'.

[143] Bangert, 'Baupolitik', 57.

[144] BAK, NL 44 n. 8 fos. 192–3. Luppe, 'Mein Leben'. On the National Liberals' general lack of enthusiasm for the building of small flats, see the left-liberal Paul Zirndorfer's accusations in *Frankfurter Zeitung*, 1 Nov. 1902 (3. Morgenblatt). Adickes's concern for the welfare of the city's wealthy inhabitants was born partly out of his conservatism, but partly also out of the realistic assessment that the city was heavily dependent on their income tax for its revenue.

[145] This was precisely why Adickes opposed any municipal subsidies for charitable building trusts. Kramer, 'Anfänge', 142–3. Bangert, 'Baupolitik', 61.

[146] HStAW 407 n. 161² fos. 31–2. Democratic Association meeting, Jan. 1895. *Frankfurter Zeitung*, 8 Nov. 1904 (3. Morgenblatt). *Frankfurter Zeitung*, 19 Nov. 1906.

the *AG für kleine Wohnungen* and other charitable building societies.¹⁴⁷ In the light of Adickes's opposition to direct intervention in the housing market, this was the best Democrats could do. Indeed, the *AG für kleine Wohnungen* was extremely successful, for it had built by far the largest number of flats relative to any other charitable building company by 1914.¹⁴⁸ It provided the cheapest housing in Frankfurt, well below the market rate, and pioneered tenants' representative councils and communal facilities for entertainment and education. In 1914, as many as 65 per cent of its tenants were unskilled workers, which means that the *AG* housed a considerably higher proportion of unskilled workers than even the Socialists' own *Volks- Bau- und Spargesellschaft*.¹⁴⁹ While its aims were diametrically opposed to those of Adickes, the left-liberal programme of housing reform was different from that of the SPD more in degree than in kind.¹⁵⁰

The different perception of the purpose of social policy between Adickes and the Frankfurt Democrats became apparent in another area which they all considered to be essential for solving the social question: the realm of education. After a number of early unsuccessful attempts by Sonnemann and others to organize public lectures for workers,¹⁵¹ in 1890 Karl Flesch, Heinrich Rößler, and the left-liberal philanthropist Charles Hallgarten created a committee for popular lectures.¹⁵² In close cooperation with the Social Democrats,¹⁵³ they organized an extremely popular annual lecture series during the winter months.¹⁵⁴ Adickes supported such left-liberal

---

[147] This is not altered by the fact that, on occasion, Democrat house owners defied party principles to vote down proposals for municipal subsidies for the *AG für kleine Wohnungen*. Weitensteiner, 'Karl Flesch', 23–4. Flesch's frustration at the house owners' rejection of the subsidies was shared by other Democrats. *Kleine Presse*, 30 Oct. 1896.

[148] By 1914, 1,636 flats were in the hands of the *AG*, whereas Frankfurt's second biggest charitable building societies, the socialist *Volks- Bau- und Sparverein* had built 794 flats by 1914. Kramer, 'Anfänge', 174–5.

[149] Ibid. 152–3, 163.

[150] Rolling, 'Liberals', 262–3. Rolling rightly comments on the differences between Adickes and 'bourgeois' left-liberal reformers, but he still sees the fundamental difference in approach to social policy as between liberals and socialists. However, his summary of SPD attitudes towards social policy presents them as being no different from those of Karl Flesch, for example.

[151] On the Frankfurt Workers' Association, founded in 1861, see the reports of the annual meetings in *Frankfurter Zeitung*, 11 Dec. 1866 (1. Blatt), 16 Oct. 1868 (2. Blatt), 2 Dec. 1868 (2. Blatt). 1874 saw the foundation of the Association for the Dissemination of Popular Education, again with the cooperation of some workers' representatives. Eichler, *Sozialistische Arbeiterbewegung*, 356.

[152] On Hallgarten, see R. Hallgarten, *Charles L. Hallgarten* (Frankfurt, 1915). Hallgarten's enthusiasm for social welfare and philanthropy had their roots in his Jewish identity. Hallgarten, *Neues über den Antisemitismus*, 15–17.

[153] Most notable amongst these was Rößler's employee Ludwig Opificius.

[154] *Heinrich Rößler, 1845–1924*, 57–8. Eichler, *Sozialistische Arbeiterbewegung*, 356–61.

initiatives, as there was little argument between himself and the Democrats about efforts to promote general access to the city's museums, cheap popular theatre, and concert performances, and compulsory technical education for primary school leavers.[155] Whilst there was general agreement that the 'lower classes' were 'hungry' for education, Adickes feared that if this hunger were not satisfied by the municipalities these groups would seek their satisfaction from other, 'foul' sources, in other words the SPD.[156] This is the origin of Adickes's support for popular 'cultural' entertainment, whilst in the realm of education Adickes was otherwise chiefly concerned about the contribution a well-educated, successful *Mittelstand* could make to the international competitiveness of the German economy.[157]

By contrast, the Democrats were as happy as Adickes to carry out any educational policy that would benefit the *Mittelstand*.[158] They agreed with the First Mayor that the 'lower classes' had a great desire for education, but they drew entirely different conclusions from this. Education was a crucial part of the social question in that it was greatly responsible for the gulf that separated the social classes.[159] *Bildung* had become a preserve for the wealthy, for a relatively small social group that had enough spare time and money to make use of cultural and educational facilities. And yet, *Bildung* was public property by right, hence it was the duty of social policy to ensure equal and universal access to it.[160] More significantly, the importance of cooperation between all sections of society in the organization of public lectures or concerts was explicitly recognized. Finally, during the 1890s Democrats came to appreciate that this commitment to universal education included the demand for free and universal primary education, as discussed in the previous chapter,[161] an issue that met with the strict opposition of Adickes.[162] Therefore, even in the area where there was greatest agreement on practical matters, there was a fundamental disagreement in the underlying vision of social policy. Whereas the point of Adickes's social policies in education was to combat Social Democracy, the aim of left-liberal social policies in education was to reduce class tensions through cooperation with the Social Democrats.

---

[155] Adickes and Beutler, *Die sozialen Aufgaben*, 41–2. *Frankfurter Zeitung*, 1 Apr. 1912 (1. Morgenblatt). E. Adickes (ed.), *Franz Adickes*, 197.
[156] Adickes and Beutler, *Die sozialen Aufgaben*, 43.   [157] Ibid. 41–3.
[158] Rößler, 'Sozialpolitik in der Gemeinde', in IfSG S1/6 28.iv. In this speech to the German People's Party, Rößler showed himself in substantial agreement with the ideas of Flesch.
[159] Karl Flesch, 'Die Bildungsfrage als soziale Frage', in Flesch, *Soziales Vermächtnis*, 154–71, here 162.
[160] Ibid. 156–61.   [161] Rößler, 'Sozialpolitik in der Gemeinde', in IfSG, S1/6 28.iv.
[162] Adickes, *Die sozialen Aufgaben*, 53–4.

While Adickes's social policy was largely centred primarily on *Bodenpolitik*, and then on education, the city's left liberals' approach to social policy was significantly more diverse. They continued to support Flesch in his efforts to improve the labour market, notably through the institution of a labour exchange whose organization would again be based on the principle of parity, with equal representation of workers and employers on the board.[163] In contrast to his predecessor, Adickes showed only lukewarm support for Flesch's efforts. Indeed, Adickes publicly denounced Flesch's vision that the labour exchange could become a nucleus of an employment office (*Arbeitsamt*) which could regulate all matters concerning the labour market, from the placement of labour to the collection of statistical data.[164] Despite the fact that the protracted negotiations which led to the eventual creation of the municipal labour exchange in 1895 and the first 17 years of its operation fell during the mayoralty of Adickes, it was Miquel, and not his successor, who was officially remembered as one of the personalities who, next to Flesch, 'left his mark' on the labour exchange.[165] Left-liberal support of and commitment to the exchange was epitomized by the fact that their leader, Rößler, took over the running of the exchange after Flesch's death in 1915.

Democrats took their commitment to labour one step further. From the mid-1890s Leopold Sonnemann began to campaign tirelessly amongst his party colleagues in Frankfurt and throughout southern Germany for the idea of unemployment insurance. In October 1896 the Democratic Association showed general agreement with Sonnemann's view that, since social policy had come to a standstill at national level, unemployment insurance would have to be a local matter. The municipal tribunals and the labour exchange were regarded as ideal foundations for municipal unemployment insurance. Democrats were agreed that municipal unemployment insurance was both necessary and desirable.[166] By contrast, the Frankfurt Democrats had considerable difficulties in making themselves heard on the issue within the German People's Party. It required several years of lobbying by Sonnemann, as well as his boycott of the 1898 party congress for the first time since the party's foundation, to move the German People's Party to accept as official party policy the demand for an imperial law which

---

[163] On the Frankfurt labour exchange, see in general Roth, *Gewerkschaftskartell*, 158–70.
[164] Adickes and Beutler, *Die sozialen Aufgaben*, 28.
[165] P. Schlotter, 'Fünfundzwanzig Jahre städtisches Arbeitsamt', *Frankfurter Wohlfahrtsblätter*, xxiii (1920), 11–16, here 12, 16. This is also in BAK, NL 44 n. 20 fos. 73–5.
[166] *Frankfurter Zeitung*, 20 Oct. 1896 (3. Morgenblatt). The article is also in HStAW 407 n. 161² fo. 109. Democratic Association meeting, 19 Oct. 1896.

would give the municipalities greater freedom in devising a system of unemployment insurance.[167]

In a country which was peculiarly reluctant to introduce any form of national unemployment insurance scheme,[168] the attitude towards unemployment was, perhaps, the touchstone for the progressiveness of municipal social reformers. This became clear in the discussions during the third national *Städtetag* in 1911. A substantial minority there, including the mayors of Cologne, Strasbourg, and Schöneberg, agreed with the Frankfurt Democrats that it was the municipality's duty to organize unemployment insurance.[169] Clearly, together with social reformers elsewhere Frankfurt Democrats were very much on the progressive frontline in Germany. However, the discussions at the municipal congress also showed that there was still a majority of municipal representatives who believed that, if at all, it was the duty of the national government to provide such an insurance, and that all the cities could do was to wait for imperial legislation on the matter. Unfortunately for the Frankfurt Democrats, the spokesman for the latter view was Franz Adickes.[170] Adickes denied the magnitude of the problem of unemployment, and was resolutely opposed to the principle of any public support for people who were not working.[171] As a result of Adickes's fundamental disagreement with progressive social reformers, it was clear that any attempt to pursue the insurance in Frankfurt would be met by the First Mayor's fierce resistance. As a result, unemployment insurance was introduced in Frankfurt only in 1914, although by this time there were still only relatively few cities in Germany which had established a system of unemployment insurance.[172]

Liberals in power could be extremely effective and innovative in their response to the social question. What this section has shown, however, is that it is highly misleading to speak of one 'liberal' social policy. Adickes's social policies were impressive in their scope and ingenuity, but he was still

---

[167] HStAW 407 n. 161³ fos. 65–6. Democratic Association meeting, 4 Oct. 1898. BAK, NL 20 n. 8 fos. 42–51. Hunt, *The People's Party*, 114.

[168] Ritter, *Social Welfare*, 98–103.

[169] On the introduction of municipal unemployment insurance, see H. Henning, 'Arbeitslosenversicherung vor 1914: Das Genter System und seine Übernahme in Deutschland', in H. Kellenbenz (ed.), *Wirtschaftspolitik und Arbeitsmarkt* (Munich, 1974), 271–87. Steinmetz, *Regulating the Social*, 203–13.

[170] See the debate in *Verhandlungen des Dritten Deutschen Städtetages am 11. und 12. September 1911 zu Posen* (Berlin, 1911), 24–57. For Adickes's speech, see *Verhandlungen des Dritten Städtetages (1911)*, 28–40.

[171] *Verhandlungen des Dritten Städtetages (1911)*, 29, 31–3.

[172] For a more detailed discussion of the issue of unemployment in Frankfurt politics, see Rolling, 'Liberals', 332–95.

very much in the Bismarckian mould as a reformer. In contrast to Miquel,[173] Adickes had little real sympathy for the concerns of the working classes. By contrast, cooperation with labour became the fundamental tenet of left-liberal social policy. Whereas Adickes's social policy was based on traditional liberal values of self-improvement and thrift, the Democrats explicitly recognized that social policy was in effect about the redistribution of wealth.[174] In other words, Adickes tried to respond to the problems of a rapidly changing urban environment with mid-nineteenth-century assumptions of thrift, self-responsibility, and a hierarchical order of estates. By contrast, the left liberals tried, with considerable success, to find entirely new ways of responding to the social problems of their day.[175] Rather than any individual measure of reform, it is this conceptual advance of social policy which was the real breakthrough in which the cities led the German state.[176]

5.5. Politics and Social Reform

The preceding two sections, which show the progressiveness and modernity of liberals in power both in theory and practice, beg the obvious question about the extent to which the liberals' social policies were motivated by, and helped them in their fight against, the emerging Social Democrats. As described in the introduction to this chapter, the inability of the liberals to develop a coherent and persuasive 'social liberalism' has been considered to be one of the root causes of the liberals' failure to respond to the political challenges of the Wilhelmine period. For the local level, historians have adopted a different framework of interpretation. Some historians have argued that at this level, social reforms were conducted in a 'political vacuum' by bourgeois or even liberal social reformers, simply as a response to the needs of their environment.[177] Others have been more willing to acknowledge the political implications of the liberals' progressive

---

[173] See the speech by the Democrat councillor Paul Zirndorfer in *Frankfurter Zeitung*, 1 Nov. 1902 (3. Morgenblatt).

[174] Rößler, 'Sozialpolitik in der Gemeinde', in IfSG, S1/6 28.ii.

[175] This study, therefore, confirms observations by George Steinmetz about the changing views of social policy, from one that worked against the trade unions to one that cooperated with them. In the case of Frankfurt, it is striking how these two different notions of social policy matched the political fault lines between right- and left-liberal attitudes to social policy. Steinmetz, *Regulating the Social*, esp. 42–4.

[176] D. Langewiesche, ' "Staat" und "Kommune". Zum Wandel der Staatsaufgaben in Deutschland im 19. Jahrhundert', *HZ* ccxlviii (1989), 621–35.

[177] See e.g. W. R. Krabbe, *Kommunalpolitik und Industrialisierung. Die Entfaltung der städtischen Leistungsverwaltung im 19. und frühen 20. Jahrhundert* (Stuttgart/Berlin/Cologne/Mainz, 1985), 85. Reulecke, *Geschichte der Urbanisierung*, 125.

social policies in the city, which leads to the conclusion that social liberalism was most progressive not at state or national levels, but in the city.[178] Unfortunately for the liberals there, however, the political benefits of developing a comprehensive social policy at the municipal level were nullified by the liberals' counterproductive refusal to remove or reduce municipal franchise restrictions. Social progressiveness was cancelled out by political regressiveness.[179] By contrast, the general phenomenon of progressive municipal socialism, on the one hand, and a restrictive franchise, on the other, has led to the speculation by Dieter Langewiesche that liberal social policy was not contrary to, but conditional upon, a restrictive franchise. According to this view, the reason why liberals were only able to develop a coherent social policy at a local rather than a national level was that at the local level liberals did not feel beleaguered and threatened by the Social Democrats.[180] In this way, liberals were free to carry out social policies when it coincided with their own self-interest, regardless of political consequences.[181] This latter interpretation has the obvious shortcoming that by 1914 local liberal élites were already challenged by the Social Democrats to a considerable extent.[182]

In contrast to Langewiesche, George Steinmetz has argued that, crucially, at the national level the government was much less, rather than more, dependent upon popular politics since the national government was not elected. As a result, government at the national level could afford a more distant perspective on the increasing social pressures, and therefore on the rise of the SPD, than at the local level.[183] Municipal social policies were a function partly of the strength of the SPD, but also of the nature of the bourgeoisie in charge of local government, and of the wealth of the city. For instance, poor relief was shaped by bourgeois attitudes and was dependent upon the city's wealth, but it was negatively affected by a strong local SPD membership which suggested to local élites that poor relief was unlikely to

[178] J. Reulecke, 'Stadtbürgertum und bürgerliche Sozialreform im 19. Jahrhundert in Preußen', in L. Gall (ed.), *Stadt und Bürgertum im 19. Jahrhundert* (Munich, 1990), 171–97, here 196–7.

[179] Even though Reulecke finds that substantial aspects of municipal socialism were consciously conducted outside the realm of party politics (p. 125), this does not stop him from pointing out the adverse effect which liberal insistence on a restrictive franchise had on liberals in the cities who might otherwise have reaped the political rewards from their social policies. Reulecke, *Geschichte der Urbanisierung*, 138–9. Sheehan, 'Liberalism', 136–7.

[180] Langewiesche, 'Deutscher Liberalismus im europäischen Vergleich', 17. Langewiesche, 'German Liberalism in the Second Empire', 231.

[181] Langewiesche, *Liberalismus in Deutschland*, 210–11.

[182] Sheehan, 'Liberalism', 129–30.

[183] Steinmetz, *Regulating the Social*, 108–57, esp. 144, 154.

improve social order.[184] By contrast, for the introduction of a system of municipal unemployment insurance it was crucial that SPD presence in the city council was strong, but not threatening to local élites.[185] Steinmetz's analysis, which is based on a statistical aggregation of the causes and effects of municipal social policies, cannot take account of the full complexity of social and political relations within a single community like Frankfurt. Therefore, the rest of this chapter will test the general and often contradictory assumptions that have been made with regard to the relationship between liberal municipal social policy and the ascendancy of the SPD in municipal politics.

There is no doubt that the advent of the SPD in Frankfurt municipal politics had a significant impact on municipal social policy. The liberals were the first to admit this. According to Franz Adickes, bourgeois social reform developed as an answer to the emergence of socialism.[186] The left liberals recognized this just as clearly. Heinrich Rößler argued that the greater interest in social questions of all parties since the 1890s was partly due to the enlightened efforts of leading bourgeois social reformers, but admitted that it was primarily the result of the growth of Social Democracy which had sharpened the general social consciousness.[187] Karl Flesch anticipated, and indeed urged, SPD participation in local politics from as early as 1878, in an anonymous article addressed to the SPD, written together with Carl August Schmidt and Eduard Bernstein.[188]

At the same time, the question of the extent to which liberals were prompted to social policy by the rise of the SPD is more complex than might at first sight appear to be the case, and not only because there were in the case of Frankfurt broadly two liberal approaches to social policy. As has been pointed out in the previous chapter with regard to education, the increased liberal attention to social policy was part of a general shift of, and increase in, an awareness of social policy that began during the 1890s. In addition, Bismarck's social insurance laws had left many areas of welfare, such as poverty or the growing phenomenon of unemployment, untouched.[189] As a result, there were a considerable number of social

---

[184] Steinmetz, *Regulating the Social*, 154–76.   [185] Ibid. 203–13.
[186] Adickes and Beutler, *Die sozialen Aufgaben*, 9, 26.
[187] Rößler, 'Die Sozialpolitik in unserem Gemeinwesen', 49–50.
[188] 'Rückblicke auf die sozialistische Bewegung in Deutschland, kritische Aphorismen von ***', *JSS* i (1879), 75–96. On the authorship of the article, see Tennstedt, *Vom Proleten*, 381–3, 573.
[189] D. J. K. Peukert, *Grenzen der Sozialdisziplinierung. Aufstieg und Krise der deutschen Jugendfürsorge von 1878 bis 1932* (Cologne, 1986), esp. 49–62.

policies in which no connection with political expediency can be detected whatsoever. For instance, Karl Flesch was deeply influenced by Pastor von Bodelschwingh in Bethel in his concern for people with physical disabilities or those fighting addictions.[190] As a result, Frankfurt became one of the pioneers for finding ways of employment for people with disabilities by expanding the existing system of labour exchanges to bring these people into the labour market.[191] Concern for handicapped people is unlikely to have generated many votes for the liberals. Instead, this concern shows that the Democrats' efforts at improving the labour market formed a genuine attempt to deal imaginatively with all aspects of the problem, even if they were unlikely to yield any immediate political benefits.[192] One of the reasons for the Democrats' social policy, therefore, lies in the self-image which the Democrats had of their own role as a socially progressive party, quite apart from immediate political expediency.[193]

Where the left-liberal social policy did respond to the demands of labour and the SPD, the relationship between social policy and electoral appeal could be very ambiguous indeed. This can be demonstrated best by the issue of municipalization. This was an issue through which the Democrats could appeal particularly well to the potential electorate of the SPD, since it has always been a central issue of the Democratic programme, long before the SPD could make it into a demand of its own.[194] During the discussions about the municipalization of the first labour-intensive service, the tramways, it was quickly realized that one of the central tasks of the

[190] Flesch-Thebesius, 'Der Frankfurter Sozialpolitiker Dr. Karl Flesch', 80.
[191] H. Luppe, 'Arbeitsnachweis für Erwerbsbeschränkte', in *Der Arbeitsmarkt* (1907/8), 37–40. The article is in BAK, NL 44 n. 32 fo. 2.
[192] Similarly, the left liberals' concern for the homeless cannot be explained by political expediency, because by definition these did not meet the residence requirement necessary for the franchise. The motivation for this concern did not come out of an aesthetic desire to take the homeless off the streets. Rather, it was argued that it was intolerable that a wealthy city such as Frankfurt could not provide sufficiently for its poor. Josef Balzer in *Frankfurter Zeitung*, 12 Nov. 1910 (3. Morgenblatt). See also Ludwig Heilbrunn in *Frankfurter Zeitung*, 10 Nov. 1910 (3. Morgenblatt).
[193] Unfortunately, in his concern to systematize the 'bourgeois' response in municipal government to the advent of the SPD, George Steinmetz fails to take into account the possibility of social policy based on genuine political conviction.
[194] On the Social Democratic attitude towards municipalization, see H. Lindemann (C. Hugo), *Arbeiterpolitik und Wirschaftspflege in der Deutschen Städteverwaltung. Zweiter Band: Wirtschaftspflege* (Stuttgart, 1904). H. Lindemann (C. Hugo), *Die städtische Regie* (Berlin, 1907). Lindemann's ideas are more far-reaching than those of the Democrats, i.e. in his view that profits from municipal services amounted to an indirect tax and should thus be avoided through lower prices. On the principle and the benefits of municipalization, however, his arguments are virtually indistinguishable from those of the Democrats or of many liberals in other cities.

municipal owner would be to introduce model working conditions which would set an example for the entire community. This triggered a very small but resolute opposition within the Democrat party which objected to the cost of the introduction of such working conditions.[195] The problem in cases where the city was called upon to ensure good working conditions either in its own companies or the companies to which it contracted out services was that many liberal councillors were employers themselves. As such, they were worried that working conditions among their employees might have to be improved according to the municipal example.

Usually, only a small minority of left liberals voted against party principle, but it did lay the left liberals open to the SPD charge of half-heartedness in social policy, and of not going far enough. Even though left liberals advocated a much more progressive municipal employment policy than the *Magistrat*, it was inevitable that they would be much more moderate on these issues than the SPD, both because of individual self-interest, and because they had to keep their *Mittelstand* constituency in mind.[196] In other words, municipal socialism could yield potential electoral benefits as it was popular with the electorate which usually enjoyed better services at lower prices, and could potentially bind municipal workers to the parties in power who were responsible for enlightened employment policies. But at the same time, municipal companies could be a tremendous political liability as they constantly exposed the liberal city government to the charge of not doing enough for its employees.[197]

Of all Frankfurt liberals, it was the ostensibly 'unpolitical' First Mayor who recognized the political dangers inherent in municipal socialism most clearly. He warned that municipal corporations were particularly prone to 'popular demands for dangerous price reductions', and that they could easily lead to the use of the city council for workers' agitations, the more so with the presence of SPD representatives inside the council. This is why in principle Adickes preferred private stock companies to municipal ones, even though in practice he accepted the need, for example, for the municipalization of tramways.[198]

---

[195] HStAW 407 n. 161¹ fos. 188–91. Democratic Association meeting, 13 Apr. 1891.
[196] Virtually all debates of the last decades before the Great War about municipal employment practices tend to show this pattern. See e.g. *MPS*, 20 Oct. 1908 and 27 Oct. 1908, pp. 979–1010.
[197] In Munich, for instance, municipal employees were characterized by a high degree of socialist trade union membership. With over 3,000 members by 1912, the municipal workers' association had advanced to become the seventh largest body within the Munich trade union movement. Pohl, *Die Münchener Arbeiterbewegung*, 441–5.
[198] Adickes and Beutler, *Soziale Aufgaben*, 29–30. See also 27.

Similarly, Ralf Roth has described in some detail how some of the more progressive left-liberal social policies such as the creation of a labour exchange, despite their goal to reduce social tension, could actually lead to tremendous hostility between the municipal authorities and the official representatives of labour. This was not so much because of left-liberal inconsistency or half-heartedness, but because Social Democrats had every reason to fear the effect that these liberal initiatives of social reconciliation could have on the 'socialist' resolve of their followers.[199] Unless SPD predominance was ensured in these municipally-sponsored institutions, the SPD was more keen to establish organizations such as a labour exchange of its own. Therefore, many left-liberal social policy initiatives became subject to constant barrages of hostile propaganda from the SPD, so that in the medium run the liberals' political disadvantages probably outweighed their political benefits.[200] Also, the principle of parity for institutions such as the industrial tribunal meant that their boards consisted of elected representatives, chosen equally from employers and from employees. To the SPD, this presented another opportunity for political agitation, so that for most of the period the majority of the board of the industrial tribunal consisted of representatives of the SPD.[201]

If active involvement in municipal socialism was a double-edged sword for liberals, this was also true for the Social Democrats. On the one hand, the SPD could benefit from it politically as it could point to the inadequacy of 'bourgeois' municipal socialism if left to its own devices, which could in turn lead to a greater demarcation between liberals and Social Democrats.[202] On the other hand, participation in liberal social policy could lead

[199] The importance of these tribunals for the resolution of conflict and the political and social integration of labour in Germany (and in Munich in particular) has been described in Pohl, *Die Münchener Arbeiterbewegung*, 295–304.

[200] On the problems of the municipal labour exchanges, see in general Roth, *Gewerkschaftskartell*, 158–70, and esp. Weitensteiner, 'Karl Flesch', 176–224.

[201] The reason for SPD predominance in the tribunal, even though half of the representatives were chosen from the employers, was that the party could muster a relatively steady number of small employers to vote for its list. Until the system of proportional representation was introduced in 1904, this meant that if the non-socialist employers were badly organized, or if they boycotted the elections, the SPD could catch all of the seats under the first-past-the-post system which applied for the entire list. The SPD favoured the system of proportional representation, however, because its majority amongst the employees was larger than its minority amongst the employers so that its majority was guaranteed in any case. Roth, *Gewerkschaftskartell*, 130–3.

[202] To the evidence presented in this chapter can be added Adelheid von Saldern's study of the SPD in Göttingen, where the little notice the party took of local affairs was usually restricted to hostility in the area it was competent in, social policy. A. von Saldern, *Auf dem Wege zum Arbeiter-Reformismus. Parteialltag in sozialdemokratischer Provinz Göttingen*

to the loss of the party's radical, 'social' edge, the increase of its progressive, 'reformist' wing, and, ultimately, to the liberals and the Social Democrats moving closer together.[203] The example of Frankfurt shows that these two results were not necessarily contradictory, as the Frankfurt Social Democrats showed no signs of lessening their rhetoric assaults against the liberal councillors before the First World War while steadily improving their relationship with at least the left liberals inside the town council. At the same time, the fierceness of the SPD rhetoric against the liberals itself was an admission of vulnerability, a tacit appreciation that both the SPD and the left liberals were fighting for the same pool of voters.

There was no necessary and direct relationship between general social policy and electoral benefit. There is no doubt that social policy could and did yield electoral benefits, at least in the sense that it made the Frankfurt left liberals less vulnerable to attacks by other emerging parties. This is especially true for the more particular social policies which the left liberals adopted in response to pressure from the *Mittelstand* (for example the municipal assistance for artisans and craftsmen in selling their products at municipally sponsored exhibitions) and from the SPD (such as the provision of free school materials and free breakfasts for poor school children or the municipal provision of free or cheap milk and meat).[204] Yet the more fundamental left-liberal social policies which attempted to remove some of the injustices of the capitalist economy could also yield direct benefits. The case of Frankfurt's labour exchange shows that ultimately tenacity could pay off for the liberals, since after a long struggle the socialist trade unions had to admit defeat and accept that they could not run an independent labour exchange against the municipal institution. It has been shown in Chapter 3 that in the realm of municipalized services, despite considerable SPD pressure, the liberals did appear to have won the allegiance of the municipal tramway workers by 1914. Political support in return for

(1870–1920) (Frankfurt, 1984), 119–22. Stefan Berger has argued that in Germany, as in England, the 'growing class consciousness of the working class can be perceived especially on the local level of politics'. By contrast, his examples of liberal and socialist cooperation are taken from state and national politics. Berger, *The British Labour Party*, 46–8, quotation on 47.

[203] D. Rebentisch, 'Die deutsche Sozialdemokratie und die kommunale Selbstverwaltung. Ein Überblick über Programmdiskussion und Organisationsproblematik, 1890–1975', *AfS* xxv (1985), 1–20. Koch, 'Liberalismus und soziale Frage', 29–30. This is one of the central themes in Pohl, *Die Münchener Arbeiterbewegung*, e.g. 441–65. Simone Lässig has confirmed this view for the state level, by establishing that even in the 'red kingdom' of Saxony, labels such as 'left', 'right', 'radical', and 'reformist' became irrelevant at the practical level, as evidenced by the discussions about mass protest. Lässig, *Wahlrechtskampf*, here 254.

[204] These particular demands are all taken from the left-liberal election programme of 1906, in *Frankfurter Zeitung*, 19 Nov. 1906 (Morgenblatt).

social policy could be extremely slow to materialize, and it could never be taken for granted.

This leaves the question of the precise relationship between a progressive social policy and a restrictive municipal franchise. This connection has not just been made by historians: contemporaries were only too aware that the two were closely linked, and that one was in contrast to the other. It was the politically astute Franz Adickes whose views on this subject resemble most closely the analysis of subsequent historians like Dieter Langewiesche. For Adickes, social reform could be carried out most easily at the local level, because, compared to the other levels of government, local government represented a 'neutral realm of peace' in which decisions were not subject to political conflict, but to political cooperation. Adickes referred, of course, to the non-political ideal of local government, even though by 1903 this was well and truly buried throughout Germany.[205] Still, it is clear that Adickes held a restricted franchise at least partly responsible for this unique non-political sphere. Adickes staunchly defended the German model of liberal social progressiveness in a restricted franchise by claiming that what was important was not the form of politics but the actual results, so that as long as liberals in the cities carried out their social and other policies successfully, there was no need for a liberalization of the franchise.[206] In this sense, there was no contradiction between Adickes's rather more conservative views on social policy and his paternalistic attitude towards political representation.[207]

Adickes's views contrasted sharply with those of Frankfurt's Democrats. Whereas the Progressive Liberals were at best lukewarm in following the Democrats' lead for an extension of the franchise,[208] it is striking that those Democrats who were the most progressive in their views on social policy were also those who were the most consistent and progressive on municipal franchise reform. Flesch conceded that the absence of labour representatives in the councils could to some extent be compensated by progressively-minded individual liberals,[209] but he was adamant that truly progressive municipal social reform was inextricably linked to a

---

[205] Adickes and Beutler, *Die sozialen Aufgaben*, 65.   [206] Ibid. 59–63.

[207] Adickes's views expressed here and elsewhere may have been unusual in their sophistication, but they were far from unique in substance. For similar attitudes towards social policy and the question of political rights, see the section on Göttingen liberals and their Lord Mayor, Georg Friedrich Calsow, in A. von Saldern, *Vom Einwohner zum Bürger. Zur Emanzipation der städtischen Unterschicht Göttingens, 1890–1920. Eine sozial- und kommunalhistorische Untersuchung* (Berlin, 1973), 227–35.

[208] See e.g. HStAW 407 n. 150² fos. 51–3. Progressive Association meeting, 29 Jan. 1896.

[209] Flesch, 'Sozialpolitik in der Gemeinde', 101–2.

progressive, that is universal, municipal franchise.[210] Put it in a nutshell, 'Social and political progress must always go hand in hand, they must permeate and complement each other. No political freedom can exist without social reforms; no social reform has any value without the most extensive implementation of the self-government of the people.'[211] Self-government, social reform, and political freedom were intertwined. Without the realization of at least a universal male franchise, all other efforts at reconciliation between workers and the bourgeoisie were futile.

In addition, Rößler and Flesch campaigned for the use of proportional representation instead of the traditional first-past-the-post system.[212] In this demand, Frankfurt Democrats took up a fundamentally liberal idea. John Stuart Mill had already realized that in an equal democracy, the first-past-the-post system would lead to that liberal fear, the tyranny of the majority, whereas proportional representation would at least ensure that the minority would be represented in proportion to its numerical strength.[213] Ironically, for this reason, proportional representation was increasingly being welcomed as the best form of equal franchise by Prussian conservative and liberal opponents to a democratic franchise. To them, it seemed to offer the best guarantee for the preservation of at least a strong conservative and liberal minority against a likely SPD predominance in the state.[214] If, therefore, Frankfurt left liberals were successful in their campaign that the Reichstag allow in principle the introduction of proportional representation for elections to the industrial tribunals, and if a city like Frankfurt was allowed to go ahead with this in 1904, then the reason was not the persuasiveness of the Democrats' arguments. Rather, it allowed at least a minority of Christian and liberal trade union representatives to be elected to the tribunals' board.[215] This explains why the Democrats successfully pioneered proportional representation in Germany when at the same time

---

[210] Weitensteiner, 'Karl Flesch', 23–4.

[211] 'Soziale und politische Fortschritte müssen stets Hand in Hand gehen und sich gegenseitig durchdringen und ergänzen. Keine politische Freiheit kann bestehen ohne soziale Reformen; keine soziale Reform hat Wert ohne die weiteste Durchführung der Selbstverwaltung des Volkes.' Flesch quoted in Sinzheimer, *Der Sozialpolitiker*, 4.

[212] Rößler, 'Sozialpolitik in der Gemeinde', in IfSG, S1/6 28.ii. See also Rößler, 'Die Sozialpolitik in unserem Gemeinwesen', 55–6. Weitensteiner, 'Karl Flesch', 142–61, 155–9.

[213] J. S. Mill, *Considerations on Representative Government* (London, 1861), ch. 8. This is reprinted in J. S. Mill, *Utilitarianism, On Liberty, Considerations of Representative Government*, ed. H. B. Acton (reprint, London, 1991), 277–98.

[214] D. J. Ziegler, *Prelude to Democracy. A Study of Proportional Representation and the Heritage of Weimar Germany, 1871–1920* (Lincoln, Nebr., 1958).

[215] Weitensteiner, 'Karl Flesch', 154–6.

they failed in their attempt to promote beyond the confines of Frankfurt the women's active vote, which they had managed to introduce for the elections to the local industrial tribunal.[216]

There is no need here to recount in detail the futile Democrat efforts at the introduction of an extended municipal franchise.[217] Rößler and his fellow left-liberal leaders once even managed to impose strict party discipline not just over Democrat, but also over the much more sceptical Progressive Liberal councillors, so that in 1901 Rößler's motion to increase the municipal franchise to all income tax payers was accepted by a considerable margin. However, given that many Progressive Liberals were usually more inclined to side with their National Liberal colleagues in order to preserve the current franchise, this majority was too fragile to be able to overcome Adickes's hostility to the measure. This liberal ambiguity over an extension of the franchise to the poorer male population mirrors the liberals' extremely lukewarm support for the introduction of the women's franchise in national and local elections. That particular stance is unlikely to have lost them many votes given the extreme caution with which this idea was embraced by liberals throughout Germany,[218] while their ambiguities left sufficient room for the important practical support at election times of the German Association for the Women's Franchise, which had its largest local branch in the city.[219]

By contrast, there is no doubt that no other single issue did the Democrats' credibility as much damage as their inability to realize an extension of the franchise for the male population.[220] It left the left liberals totally vulnerable to charges of inconsistency and betrayal,[221] and the SPD exploited this to the best of its ability.[222] However, it is important to point out that

---

[216] Ibid. 117–19.

[217] Wolf, *Liberalismus*, 98–109; Rolling, 'Liberals', 189–200.

[218] There is no evidence that this issue played any noticeable part in the election contests before 1914.

[219] On the activities of the Frankfurt women's movements for the franchise, see Klausmann, 'Politik und Bewegungskultur', 242–90.

[220] Rolling, 'Liberals', 210–14.

[221] Rößler, 'Die Sozialpolitik in unserem Gemeinwesen', 51.

[222] See e.g. the summary of left-liberal failures in this respect in *Sozialdemokratie und Stadtverwltung* (1906), 5–14. The SPD frequently juxtaposed their own steadfastness to this left-liberal inconsistency ('Halbheit', 'Rückhaltlosigkeit'). More importantly, the SPD used particularly the Democrats' failure to realize franchise reform as proof that there was no difference between left- and right-liberals, that they were all blind followers of the conservative Adickes. See e.g. *Volksstimme*, 17 Nov. 1906, 20 Nov. 1906. Unsurprisingly, at almost every Social Democrat electoral rally, the franchise issue was brought up. See e.g. the report of various rallies in *Volksstimme*, 20 Nov. 1906 (1. Beilage). See also *Volksstimme*, 20 Nov. 1906 (Wahlbeilage).

Democrat attempts to increase the franchise were not merely cosmetic,[223] nor were they signs of ideological half-heartedness. By 1900, the ideological commitment to social and political progress and reconciliation was directly challenged by the fact that any extension of the franchise would have largely benefited the Democrats' political opponents, the SPD. As Wolfgang Hardtwig has pointed out, liberals then, as historians now, could not have it both ways. It is simply impossible to accuse German liberals of a lack of political realism and to expect those liberals who actually were in power, in the cities, to relinquish it for their ideals.[224] If even the Frankfurt Democrats, despite the strength of their convictions, did not pursue their goal of a municipal franchise too vigorously, this is not so much a sign of their inconsequence or weakness as a demonstration of their political maturity.

This section disproves at least for Frankfurt that there was a positive link between a restriction of the franchise and municipal social reform. Even the most conservative municipal liberals such as Adickes were driven to defend themselves against the charge that both were linked precisely because they accepted the contradictions inherent in social progressiveness and political conservatism. Indeed, in Frankfurt there was a clear negative link between the two issues, as the city's most innovative social reformers on the left were also progressive, and indeed innovative, about electoral reform as they pleaded for universal suffrage and proportional representation. On the other hand, it would be oversimplistic to argue that social policy was a direct response to a changing political environment and the emergence of the SPD in municipal politics. As this section has pointed out, there were undoubtedly many left-liberal social policies which constituted a direct response to the demands of the SPD. Yet there were also a number of social policies which proved to be deeply divisive, at least in the medium run. In these instances, the limited electoral franchise, as well as the fact that the day-to-day running of these policies was left to the politically more detached *Magistrat*, were undoubtedly of great advantage for the feasibility of these policies in the long run. Despite the evidence of considerable left-liberal success in halting the advance of the SPD by 1912, this was not inevitably the outcome of left-liberal social policy in Frankfurt am Main.

---

[223] Rolling, 'Liberals', 200.

[224] Hardtwig, 'Großstadt', 64. For instance, for Saxony Karl Heinrich Pohl has judged the liberals' active involvement in franchise reform with a view to strengthen their own position at the expense of the conservatives as manifestations of naked egoism ('nackter Egoismus'). In his view, this highlights not so much the liberals' political maturity and pragmatism, but the persistence of a 'retarding', backward streak. Pohl, 'Politischer Liberalismus und Wirtschaftsbürgertum', 116–17.

5.6. Conclusion

This chapter has contradicted much of current historiography in its claim that the growth of municipal socialism is largely attributable to the rise of the bureaucrats from the 1890s onwards, rather than to the liberal politicians in the cities themselves. This crucial role of the municipal bureaucracy has also been attested for Frankfurt, where the leading role of bureaucrats such as Georg Varrentrapp, Alexander Spiess, Karl Flesch, Hermann Luppe, Johannes Miquel, and Franz Adickes has been emphasized.[225] Yet at the same time, these names serve as perfect proof that this bureaucracy was, in fact, deeply involved in the local political milieu. Georg Varrentrapp was the city's most prominent National Liberal politician during the 1870s, while Alexander Spiess's appointment as Germany's first municipal physician and the extent to which he was endowed with particular powers were deeply political decisions at the time. As this chapter has shown, Karl Flesch was not only a lifetime member of the Democrats, but he bore the most decisive influence over the development of the Democrats' approach to municipal social policy from the 1880s, surpassing even the influence of Sonnemann in this particular aspect. Flesch crucially depended not only on the support of his political colleagues, but also on the opportunity to disseminate his views through, for example, the *Frankfurter Zeitung* and the Democratic Association. His later deputy, Hermann Luppe, thrived on left-liberal and Social Democrat support which alone saved his career against the hostility of Adickes.[226] While Miquel's political astuteness is beyond doubt, of all Frankfurt liberals it was Adickes who displayed the most acute sense of political realism and cunning. This clearly revises the general view about Adickes that 'the ideal mayor of the late imperial period . . . resolutely avoided any relationship to a political party'.[227] If Adickes, of all mayors, depended for his success on his relationship to the cities' political parties, this challenges more generally the view of the 'unpolitical' nature of German mayors, the standard-bearers of the unpolitical ideal.[228]

The sheer quantity and the innovative character of the social policies that emanated from Frankfurt show that municipal bureaucrats, important

---

[225] Roth, *Gewerkschaftskartell*, 83–91. The inclusion of Georg Varrentrapp in this list seems an odd choice since Varrentrapp was a physician at the local hospital and not directly employed by the city. IfSG, S2/796.

[226] Luppe, *Mein Leben*, 19–20. BAK, NL 44 n. 8 fos. 126–7. Luppe, 'Mein Leben'.

[227] Niehuss, 'Party Configurations in State and Municipal Elections, 101.

[228] In addition to the references cited perviously, see also Matzerath, *Urbanisierung in Preußen*, 352.

though they were, could only realize their goals if they were supported by a broad political consensus among the politically active population and in the municipal council itself. While circumstances were different in every German city, there is no reason why the basic assumptions and goals which lay behind social policy in Frankfurt should have been different in other cities that were similarly self-consciously progressive and innovative in their social policy, such as Mannheim, Freiburg, Strasbourg, Berlin, Munich, or Cologne.[229]

This chapter has also addressed two mutually contradictory views of current historical scholarship—that social reform was carried out despite the franchise restrictions, and that both were complementary. These views reflect the differences between Frankfurt liberals on the matter. Democrats, such as Flesch, Rößler, and Sonnemann, saw a clear contradiction between a limited franchise and social reform, but were powerless to do anything about this contradiction. By contrast, for Adickes it was perfectly possible to carry out municipal social reform in a system of a restricted municipal franchise. Thus, historians have not taken into sufficient account that views on a restricted franchise and social reform were, in fact, subject to distinct liberal approaches to municipal social policy. For the case of Frankfurt am Main demonstrates that it is a gross oversimplification to speak of liberal social policy as a relatively uniform phenomenon.[230] In that city alone there were two separate liberal approaches to municipal social policy with different policy goals, and with contrasting underlying assumptions.

The direct political impact of these liberal social policies is difficult to judge, because of the ambiguity with which they were received at popular level. And yet, the liberal optimism at being able to stem the political advance of the SPD and the concurrent realization that liberals could also win votes from the working classes which has been described in Chapter 3 came at precisely the time when trade union resistance to liberal policies of social reform, and the labour exchange in particular, ran out of steam.[231] Equally important is the fact that left-liberal social policy in Frankfurt was undoubtedly a fundamental factor in buttressing the increasing

---

[229] Adickes's *Bodenpolitik* was exemplary, but by no means unique. Böhm, 'Bodenpolitik', esp. 31. In addition to the literature quoted earlier, for Strasbourg, see A. Dominicus, *Straßburgs deutsche Bürgermeister Back und Schwander 1873–1918* (Frankfurt, 1939).

[230] This view for Frankfurt has been confirmed for Mannheim and Baden in general, albeit with emphasis on the diverse Protestant approaches to liberal social policy, by Hübinger, *Kulturprotestantismus*, 105–13.

[231] Roth, *Gewerkschaftskartell*, 198–215, esp. 210.

cooperation between left liberals and the SPD inside the city council in the years leading up to the First World War.[232] By contrast, the SPD never softened its hostility to Franz Adickes and his social policies.[233] Again, this demonstrates the need to distinguish carefully between the different liberal approaches to social policy. It is not true that 'a' liberal social policy, and Adickes's *Bodenpolitik* in particular, encouraged the SPD to become more reformist.[234] This was achieved alone through left-liberal cooperation with the SPD, for example in the organization of public lectures or the provision of cheap housing.[235]

This study's emphasis on the existence of two distinct liberal social policies in Frankfurt am Main should not cloud the fact that it was precisely this diversity in approaches which was responsible for the extraordinary scale of liberal social policies in this city. In the immediate aim to reduce class tension the supporters of each liberal approach tolerated the other. Flesch and Adickes may have had contrasting views about the nature of social policy, but what is remarkable is that despite these fundamental disagreements they did little to hinder each other in practice. Also, despite the fact that this chapter has concentrated on the political aspects of social policy, it must not be forgotten that both political approaches could count on a third, strictly non-political approach to social policy, sponsored by the philanthropist William Merton, whose central aim was to create a better understanding of the problem itself by conducting enquiries and research into the social question. For this purpose Merton founded the *Institut für Gemeinwohl* (Institute for Common Welfare). In 1892, it became responsible for editing the '*Blätter für Soziale Praxis*', which from 1897 was edited in Berlin as the nationally influential '*Soziale Praxis*'.[236] In conjunction with other social organizations, the institute was also willing to sponsor practical social policy initiatives.

The institute's endorsement of both left- and right-liberal social policies was possible because Merton and other philanthropists saw this private commitment to social welfare as complementary to, but nonetheless

---

[232] See Ch. 3.

[233] This is nicely illustrated by the socialist *Volksstimme*'s comment on Adickes's retirement, in *Volksstimme*, 1 Apr. 1912. See also Adickes's obituary in *Volksstimme*, 10 Feb. 1915. Both articles are in IfSG, S2/649.ii.

[234] Koch, 'Liberalismus und soziale Frage', 29.

[235] It appears that at least in southern Germany, Frankfurt was more a norm than an exception. For Munich, K. H. Pohl has also emphasized the importance of popular evening classes and public lectures in reducing the tensions between the bourgeoisie and Social Democracy. Pohl, *Die Münchener Arbeiterbewegung*, 368–82.

[236] H. Achinger, *Wilhelm Merton in seiner Zeit* (Frankfurt, 1965), 128.

separate from, municipal or state social policy.[237] They were enthusiastic supporters of Adickes's policies of town planning, but unlike Adickes they were also happy to support initiatives based on the concept of equal cooperation with the SPD. Ultimately, the Institute's support was vital to the pursuit of policies which could not find a majority inside the city council. For instance, from 1897 the Institute for Common Welfare sponsored a legal advice bureau for women organized by the German Women's Association (*Allgemeiner Deutscher Frauenverein*), at a time when these ideas were still scoffed at amongst the Frankfurt bourgeoisie at large. The legal advice bureau proved extremely successful. From 1908, its increasing need for money was met by a municipal subsidy, and on 1 April 1918 it became a municipal agency.[238]

The existence of a non-political agency of social reform also had the effect of making the left liberals' social policies less dependent on the support of Adickes and the National Liberals, and vice versa. This renders any description of 'bourgeois liberal' reform meaningless, as there were not only different liberal approaches to social policy, but there was also a conscious difference between private, 'bourgeois' efforts at social reform and those of the liberals engaged in municipal government. At the same time, none of the different 'parties' of social reform could be successful if their policies were boycotted by the others. Therefore, Frankfurt's position as a centre of municipal liberal reform was achieved precisely because of the variety of approaches to social reform, which were separate, distinct, and even opposed to each other in nature but which nonetheless tolerated and encouraged each other in practice.

Municipal social reform was based on entirely different parameters from social policy at a national level. For example, Flesch's concept of parity, of realizing social reform in partnership with representatives of labour, was much easier to carry out at the local level, where the leading socialist representatives were known, and sometimes even trusted, by the bourgeois politicians on a personal level. Frankfurt Democrats were in a position to know that the socialist leaders, such as Quarck, Hüttmann, or Zielowski were not interested in revolution. In comparison, the distance between an unelected national government and the SPD grass roots were all the greater. As for liberals at the national level, they had to focus on the social

---

[237] Nathanael Brückner, *Die öffentliche und private Fürsorge. Gemeinnützige Thätigkeit und Armenwesen mit besonderer Beziehung auf Frankfurt am Main* (Frankfurt, 1892), vol. i, p. viii. According to Merton's biographer, the anonymous introduction to what was the Institute's first publication was from William Merton himself.
[238] Klausmann, 'Politik und Bewegungskultur', 72–9.

and economic demands of their main constituency, farmers and small-town artisans.[239]

For their part, liberals in the cities were concerned first and foremost with reducing social tension in the cities, even if they were keen to realize their ideas at the national level. As a result, they devised institutions of social policy which were suited to the particular municipality in which they operated in the first instance, and then to other German cities in general. For such measures, the best liberals could do in the Empire or in the individual states was to create the legal framework in which the liberals in the cities were able to carry out their measures in *Bodenpolitik* or labour relations. Yet this heterogeneity also meant that it was extremely difficult to translate municipal social policy into a coherent and effective liberal policy at the national or state level.

As a result, liberal *kommunale Daseinsfürsorge* was neither the German answer, nor was it the alternative model, to social liberalism as it occurred in liberal movements at the national level, most notably in England.[240] Liberal social reform in the German city was progressive, innovative, and comprehensive, but overall it hardly constituted a great advance over municipal liberal social policy initiatives in that archetypal country of comparison, England.[241] After all, even the term with which contemporaries, starting with the conservative liberal Adickes, and historians have commonly described these policies, namely 'municipal socialism', was invented in England. In both countries, it was equally difficult to transform local liberal social policies such as town planning or labour exchanges into

---

[239] Eley, 'Notable Politics', 195, 207. For evidence of liberal presence in agricultural areas, see the German electoral map of 1912 in Ritter, *Wahlgeschichtliches Arbeitsbuch*, 46–7. Thus it can be explained that, when on the national stage Miquel championed Frankfurt's industrial tribunals for adoption in all German cities, this was ardently supported by the national SPD, to whom on aggregate this presented an opportunity for greater political influence in the locality. By contrast, it was strongly opposed by the Frankfurt SPD, which feared a loss of influence in its particular circumstances. Weitensteiner, 'Karl Flesch', 127–39.

[240] For this reason, Frankfurt was certainly not the 'centre of a German version of the pact between Liberals and Labour'. Roth, *Stadt und Bürgertum*, 649 n. 1334. Roth, 'Liberalismus', 85 n. 116. In general, see D. Langewiesche, 'The Nature of German Liberalism', in G. Martell (ed.), *Modern Germany Reconsidered, 1870–1945* (London, 1992), here 106. D. Langewiesche, 'German Liberalism in the Second Empire, 1871–1914', in K. H. Jarausch and L. E. Jones (eds.), *In Search of a Liberal Germany. Studies in the History of German Liberalism from 1789 to the Present* (Oxford, 1990), 230.

[241] For a contemporary outline of municipal social reform in England, see H. Lindemann (C. Hugo), *Städteverwaltung und Munizipal-Sozialismus in England* (Stuttgart, 1897). For more recent studies, see Waller, *Town*, 298–316. A. Briggs, *History of Birmingham*, ii (Oxford, 1952). A. Briggs, *Victorian Cities* (reprint, Harmondsworth, 1990). D. Fraser (ed.), *Municipal Reform and the Industrial City* (Leicester, 1982).

liberal policies at a national level, simply because these policies were naturally most effective at the local level. Yet the difference remains, as in Britain social liberalism developed over and above liberal social reform at the local level, whereas in Germany it appears that this process did not occur.

The occurrence of innovative and diverse liberal social policies in the municipality, which is unlikely to have been restricted to Frankfurt, by no means indicates that German liberals in general were socially more aware, or had made greater moves to develop a peculiar German form of social liberalism, than had previously been thought. What this does show is how innovative and progressive German liberals were in response to the social challenges with which they were presented when they actually were in government, at the local level. The example of Frankfurt highlights, therefore, not only the diversity of liberal assumptions which resulted in a great variety and number of liberal measures of social reform, but it also points to the central reasons why municipal social reform could not be translated to liberal policies at the national level. Only at the local level were liberals actually in a position to carry out their policies which were tailored to a particular urban constituency, through trying to solve problems that were particular to a rapidly urbanizing and industrializing community. It was difficult for liberal municipal social reform to influence national liberal approaches to social policy in any country, but this was made almost impossible in the case of Germany, where in addition urban liberals' attitudes towards social reform had to transcend and be applicable to three peculiarly distinct levels of government.

6

Liberalism and Municipal Finance

6.1. Introduction

Perhaps the subject most indicative of liberal assumptions about politics in general, and about the nature and role of the state in particular, is public finance. For the British Liberal Party during the second half of the century the budget epitomized its ideals about the social, political, and economic role of the state.[1] In Prussia and Germany, too, the deliberations on the annual budgets, when the Prussian Chamber of Deputies and the Reichstag wielded the most power vis-à-vis the government, were the catalysts which forced the liberals time and again to define their policies and their relationship with the state. In fact, the centrality of the question of finance to German political life was even more pronounced than in Britain precisely because of the parliaments' weakness in other political matters.[2] The most glittering examples of this are the Prussian constitutional crisis of 1862 to 1866, and the liberal split, ostensibly over the issue of tariffs, in 1880. But in the absence of clear principles of state finance as they had emerged in England, ultimately every budget, and particularly those concerned with military spending, was about liberal visions of the relationship between state and parliament, about liberal ideals of politics and social welfare, and about liberal concepts of the federal nature of the German state.[3]

Just as Prussian or German liberalism cannot be properly evaluated

---

[1] H. C. G. Matthew, 'Disraeli, Gladstone, and the Politics of Mid-Victorian Budgets', *HJ* xxii (1979), 615–43.

[2] H. Preuß, *Reichs- und Landesfinanzen* (Berlin, 1894), 15–18.

[3] Hugo Preuß pointed out the paradox that it was precisely the lack of any principled policy of finance which led to constant arguments about principle among German parties. Ibid. 18. The best account of the implication of the constitutional crisis and the tariff issue for liberalism is in Langewiesche, *Liberalismus in Deutschland*, 93–104, 170–80. See also the implications, for example, of the 1874 budget, ibid. 167–70.

without an understanding of its ideas on financial policy,[4] so urban liberalism cannot be understood without an appreciation of liberal views on municipal finance. This is particularly the case since liberals had much greater influence over the budget at local than at the state or the national levels. In the latter cases, the liberals were but one part of a parliament which could amend, reject, or accept the budget. In the cities, liberals were more often than not able to draw up budgets themselves, and they were mostly in control of the municipal councils which had to deliberate on those budgets. Control over municipal budgets not only forced the liberals to make up their minds about their policies, but was also a crucial factor determining their attitude to the state. It was the financial constraints put upon them by the state governments that set the limits to their freedom of manoeuvre in city government. In other words, the size and nature of municipal budgets determined the extent of local self-government.[5]

TABLE 6.1. *Relative public expenditure of local, state, and national government in Prussia/Germany, 1881–1913*

	Share of government expenditure (in %)			
	Local	State	National	Total government share of GDP
1881	26.30	44.40	29.30	10.00
1891	25.40	40.70	33.90	13.20
1901	29.50	36.10	34.40	14.90
1907	32.90	32.30	35.20	16.50
1913	32.90	31.80	35.30	17.70

Source: T. Köster, *Die Entwicklung kommunaler Finanzsysteme am Beispiel Großbritanniens, Frankreichs und Deutschland 1790–1980* (Berlin, 1984), 171. On the growth of government expenditure in general, see S. Andrich and J. Veverka, 'The Growth of Government Expenditure in Germany since the Unification', *FA*, Neue Folge xxiii (1963/4), 169–278.

---

[4] A discussion, therefore, of the way in which the extent and the nature of taxation affected the relationship between the bourgeoisie and the German state (presumably defined, in this case, as an aggregate of local, state, and national governments) misses the point. There cannot have been a more political issue than that of finance in general, and of taxation in particular (as this chapter shows). Hence, taxation and public finance affected not so much national or regional loyalties, but party allegiances. Hans-Peter Ullmann, 'Die Bürger als Steuerzahler im Deutschen Kaiserreich', in M. Hettling and P. Nolte (eds.), *Nation und Gesellschaft in Deutschland. Historische Essays* (Munich, 1996), 231–46.

[5] The essential connection between self-government and municipal finance has been recognized, but its political implications never followed up. H. Matzerath, '"Kommunale

Liberalism and Municipal Finance

Another important reason for studying liberal attitudes towards municipal finance is the importance of local government finance relative to state and national finance. As Table 6.1 illustrates, local government expenditure increased during the last decades of the Kaiserreich relative to state and national public expenditure until they were roughly of the same size. The relative growth of the importance of municipal budgets is even more impressive when it is borne in mind that it concurred with a general increase in public expenditure, whose share of the GDP rose by 77 per cent in the years 1881 to 1913. Furthermore, the average relative growth of local government expenditure conceals the extraordinary growth of the most vibrant cities in Prussia. For example, in the period 1875 to 1908, municipal expenditure in Berlin increased by 478 per cent, in Cologne by 1,071 per cent, in Düsseldorf by 2,020 per cent, and in Charlottenburg by 9,616 per cent.[6] This extraordinary increase in the importance of municipal finance is a good indicator of the growing importance of municipal government in German public life. Hence the phenomenon of the evolution of municipal finance, and the assumptions of the liberals in the cities who guided it, are important points of investigation in themselves.

There is a third reason why an investigation into municipal finance is crucial for an understanding of urban liberalism. As will be shown later in this chapter, the main reasons for the increase in municipal spending resulted largely from a growing imperative to provide better schooling, infrastructure, and municipal services, all of which bore some relation to a better provision of public welfare. Liberal municipal budgets are the supreme test of the liberal commitment to social welfare, and, in fact, to all the policies they openly advocated, because in the budget hard decisions had to be made about priorities, and how policies were to be paid for. This point was made by the national economist Adolph Wagner at a controversial address to the *Verein für Sozialpolitik* in 1877. Speaking on local taxation, he pointed out that in no other area of policy was it more feasible to meet the demands of socialism. Social reform through taxation was not so

Leistungsverwaltung". Zu Bedeutung und politischer Funktion des Begriffs im 19. und 20. Jahrhundert', in H. H. Blotevogel (ed.), *Kommunale Leistungsverwaltung und Stadtentwicklung vom Vormärz bis zur Weimarer Republik* (Cologne/Vienna, 1990), 11. G.-C. von Unruh, 'Die normative Verfassung der kommunalen Selbstverwaltung', in K. G. A. Jeserich, H. Pohl, and G.-C. von Unruh (eds.), *Deutsche Verwaltungsgeschichte* (Stuttgart, 1984), iii. 561. Perhaps the best introduction to local finance is Matzerath, *Urbanisierung in Preußen*, 361–71.

[6] Silbergleit, *Preussens Städte*, 480–1. The actual figures given by Silbergleit should be treated with care, as it was not possible to see how he compiled the figures that he gives for Frankfurt municipal expenditure, for example. This does not invalidate the general pattern of the growth of local government expenditure for individual cities which is evident from his analysis.

much a question of practicality or feasibility, as a question of political will.⁷ Urban liberalism cannot be properly understood without an examination of liberal policies towards the budget, because the municipal budget represents the point of transition between liberal theory and liberal practice.

6.2. Local Government Finance in Prussia

To appreciate fully the financial policies and aims of Frankfurt liberals and Democrats, it is first necessary to discuss briefly the evolution of municipal finance in general. During the second and third quarters of the nineteenth century, Prussian municipal taxation had evolved slowly but steadily towards a system that was overwhelmingly based on local supplements to the state income tax, instead of direct taxation on property or indirect taxation on goods.⁸ As Table 6.2 shows, in 1869, 65 per cent of local taxation in Prussian cities was direct, and the remaining 35 per cent were raised through indirect taxation. In the former category, 84.4 per cent of all direct taxes were levied as personal income taxation, and only 15.5 per cent as taxation on property. The relationship between these two forms of taxation remained roughly similar until Miquel's local tax reforms came into effect in 1895.⁹

After the tax laws of 25 May 1873 improved the efficiency of the income tax, extending it to those with incomes below 3,000 M., and abolished the indirect state tax on meat and flour, the trend towards local supplements on direct taxation was even accelerated, so that by 1883/84, 95 per cent of all local taxes in Prussian cities were raised in the form of direct taxation.¹⁰ In that year, about 79 per cent of all local taxes were paid through direct personal taxation, whereas the figure for 1869 had been a still considerable 55 per cent. The rapid increase in personal direct taxation as the main form

---

⁷ A. Wagner, *Die Communalsteuerfrage. Ausarbeitung eines Referats im Verein für Sozialpolitik* (Leipzig/Heidelberg, 1878), 44.

⁸ On the development of, and the principles behind, income taxation, see F. J. Neumann, *Die Progressive Einkommensteuer in Staats- und Gemeindehaushalt. Gutachten über Personalbesteuerung auf Veranlassung des Vereins für Sozialpolitik* (Leipzig, 1874, reprint 1904).

⁹ 1883/84 the relationship between taxation on property and personal taxation was 16.4 per cent to 83.6 per cent, in 1894/95, 16.3 per cent to 83.7 per cent. R. von Kaufmann, *Die Kommunalfinanzen. Großbritannien, Frankreich, Preußen*, 2 vols. (Leipzig, 1906), ii. 351.

¹⁰ W. Klose, 'Die Finanzpolitik der preußischen Großstädte', D.Phil. thesis (Halle, 1907), 35. Despite the improvements of the 1873 laws, the system of local and state taxation remained cumbersome and slow. To name but two important examples, the assessment of the so important income tax remained deeply flawed until 1891, and in a fast-changing world the assessment rates for taxation on property were estimated only every 15 years. For contemporary criticism of the Prussian system of taxation, see G. Cohn, 'Die Fortführung der preußischen Steuerreform', *JGVV* xvi (1892), 271.

of local government income is all the more impressive if one considers that at the same time total taxation almost doubled, from 6.47 M. per head in 1869 to 11.42 M. per head in 1883/84.[11] Numerically, the decline of local indirect taxation was directly offset by the absolute increase in property taxation.[12] This means that virtually the entire growth in municipal spending was raised through direct personal taxation. The rise in the sheer volume of local taxation, as well as the shift towards one particular form of local taxation was bound to generate attention. For in the years 1869 to 1876, municipal expenditure rose from 100 million M. to 178 million M., and during the depression years until 1883/84 it rose still further to 213 million M. To many, therefore, the local system of taxation seemed in crisis, because it appeared unlikely that a municipal tax system that was so overwhelmingly based on just one particular form of taxation would be able to cope with the increasing demand on the municipal budgets.

TABLE 6.2. *Local taxation in Prussia, 1869 and 1883/1884* (in Marks)

	1869	1883/4
Property taxation		
land tax	—	1,993,381
building tax	2,437,086[a]	7,217,597
business tax	210,462	1,307,769
other	2,169,507	6,313,005
TOTAL	4,844,055	16,831,752
Personal taxation[b]		
income tax	20,984,094	73,642,521
other	5,239,032	12,112,227
TOTAL	26,223,126	85,754,748
Total direct taxation	31,067,181	102,586,500
Indirect taxation	16,812,171	5,512,465
Total local taxation	47,879,352	108,098,965

[a] This figure is for building and land tax combined.

[b] Note that in 1869, most of the personal taxes were still raised by separate local taxation, whereas by 1883/4, 67% of personal taxation was raised through supplements on state taxes.

Source: Kaufmann, *Die Kommunalfinanzen*, ii. 352–62.

[11] The figures given in this paragraph have been summarized from Kaufmann, *Kommunalfinanzen*, ii. 358.

[12] Note, however, that, despite the numerical relationship, it is almost impossible to prove conclusively that one tax was purposefully used to offset the other.

No state or municipal tax reform had been enacted by 1890. The introduction of a stop-gap *Kommunalsteuernotgesetz* (Emergency Local Tax Act) of 1885 aimed to alleviate some of the worst financial difficulties that many cities found themselves in.[13] Still, it was clear that no thorough reform of municipal or state taxation could be enacted while Bismarck remained Prussian Minister President: he was vehemently opposed to the introduction of a modern, progressive income tax and was solely interested in the reduction of land taxation for property and the lowering of school fees to help the lower classes.[14]

TABLE 6.3. *State and local direct taxation in 1883/1884* (in 1,000 Marks)

	State taxation	Local taxation[a]
City communities	74,787	116,936
Village communities	55,421	91,839
TOTAL	130,208	208,775

[a] This figure includes taxation raised by all local government bodies, the province, the *Kreis*, churches, and schools. Taxation by these bodies was negligible in the cities, but it was all the more important in the countryside.

Source: A. Wagner. *Finanzwissenschaft*, iv. *Specielle Steuerlehre (Praxis der Besteuerung). Die deutsche Besteuerung des 19. Jahrhunderts* (Leipzig, 1899), 88–9, table 13.

Meanwhile, the crisis of municipal finance deepened. As Table 6.3 indicates, in 1883/84 local direct taxation was a greater financial burden than direct state taxation. This imbalance was greatly increased if one bears in mind that, as we have seen, in the municipalities the lion's share of this direct tax burden was raised through supplements to the state income tax, whereas only 42 per cent of direct state taxation was levied through the income tax itself.[15] In other words, even though direct personal taxation was in essence a state tax, it had in practice, through the sheer volume of local financial requirements, become primarily a local tax.

Matters did not improve until the end of the decade. In 1892/93, local

---

[13] The 1885 Act made 'non-physical persons' such as share companies and non-resident owners of property liable to local taxation, after they had already been made subject to state taxation in 1873. For a summary of Prussian financial policies from 1873 to 1890, see Klose, 'Finanzpolitik', 35–6, 46–9.

[14] Herzfeld, *Miquel*, ii. 146–51, H.-H. Kramer, 'Die Entwicklung der Preussischen Steuerverfassung im 19. Jahrhundert', D.jur. thesis (Kiel, 1970), 112–13.

[15] Wagner, *Finanzwissenschaft* (1899), 88–9, table 13.

supplements to direct personal taxation in all cities above 10,000 inhabitants averaged 190 per cent, or 164 per cent on income tax supplements alone.[16] In particular, of the 205 cities in question, 58 raised a supplement on income tax between 200 and 300 per cent, and in 13 cities the supplement was even higher.[17] Cities had become exceedingly reliant on the single source of personal direct taxation, which in 1891/92 accounted for 81.4 per cent of local tax returns, while only 13.1 per cent were raised through taxation of property. Other forms of taxation had become almost meaningless, accounting for a mere 5.5 per cent of local taxation.[18]

Clearly, local government finance was in desperate need of reform, now with greater urgency than ever. And yet it is doubtful whether this crisis would have been addressed without the general change in the political climate as a result of Bismarck's departure and the beginning of Caprivi's 'New Course'. For the centrepiece of this new policy was to 'rule with conciliation and good will', 'to gather together all the elements that support the state', in order 'step by step to satisfy the justifiable demands of the working classes and in that way even to cooperate with them',[19] as Miquel summarized and influenced the essence of the 'New Course'.[20] As a former mayor of Frankfurt, where local taxation was already used as an instrument of social policy (as will be shown below), Miquel clearly appreciated the political importance of an efficient, fair system of taxation not only to government finance, but also as a means of ensuring social justice. Moreover, as a principal author of the Heidelberg Declaration he had shown himself sensitive to the needs of (at least southern) agriculture and its recurrent demands for lower taxes.[21] A tax reform offered Miquel the opportunity to kill two birds with one stone, both the appeasement of the working classes, and the relief of agriculture.[22]

The two phases of the tax reforms had distinct but connected aims. The first reform of 1891 was aimed at making the tax system more efficient by simplifying the state's tax structure. In an attempt to reverse the previous

---

[16] Ibid. 91, table 16. Direct personal taxation included a tax on income as well as a tax on rent.

[17] Kaufmann, *Kommunalfinanzen*, ii. 299.   [18] Ibid. 297.

[19] Miquel to General von Waldersee, 6 Mar. 1890, quoted from the translation in Nichols, *Germany after Bismarck*, 87.

[20] Nipperdey, *Deutsche Geschichte 1866–1918*, ii. 699.

[21] White, *The Splintered Party*, 100–5.

[22] For an impressive case study of the burden of the pre-1891/93 system of taxation on agriculture and its central demands, see W. Pyta, *Landwirtschaftliche Interessenpolitik im deutschen Kaiserreich. Der Einfluß agrarischer Interessen auf die Neuordnung der Finanz- und Wirtschaftspolitik am Ende der 1870er Jahre am Beispiel von Rheinland und Westfalen* (Stuttgart, 1991), esp. 39–44.

trend whereby the income tax had increasingly been hijacked by local government, a reformed personal income tax now became the core of the state tax system. Incomes over 100,000 M. per annum were to be taxed at a top rate of 4 per cent, for incomes below that the rate would be progressively reduced:[23] incomes above 9,500 M. per annum would be taxed at 3 per cent, down to less than 1 per cent for incomes in the lowest taxable group, 900 to 1,050 M. per annum.[24] Interestingly, for incomes below 3,000 M. per annum, taxable income was to be reduced by 50 M. for every dependent member of the family. Perhaps the most important innovation introduced was that of self-declaration of income. Many conservatives still felt that this was immoral and tempting for the individual to break the law,[25] but on the whole it was accepted that this was necessary for improving the efficiency of the income tax.[26]

It is certainly correct to point out that the reforms of 1891 contained little that was new, and that Miquel's major contribution had been to steer the measure through the two chambers of parliament.[27] However, from the outset Miquel regarded the 1891 reforms as part of a general reform of state and local taxation which, for pragmatic reasons, had to be carried out separately.[28] It was this second part of Miquel's tax reform, the reform of local taxation, which was truly innovative for a Prussian finance minister.[29]

Miquel's local tax reforms had two aims. Firstly, he wanted to create

[23] Note that contemporaries were extremely touchy about whether an income tax rate should be progressively reduced (*Degression*) or progressively increased (*Progression*). Miquel chose the less controversial former method, because this put an upper limit on the rate of taxation. Many feared that progressive taxation offered no safeguards against further increases in the rate of taxation for higher incomes.

[24] Nichols, *Germany after Bismarck*, 91. As explained in the previous footnote, however, Nichols is technically wrong to describe the income tax as progressive. See also Herzfeld, *Miquel*, ii. 231 ff. It is interesting that the tax rates were not just subject to fiscal and social considerations. Miquel had originally fixed the top rate at 3%, but since wealth was shifting already away from agriculture towards industrial wealth, the conservatives pushed through the higher rate of 4% so that the balance of taxation would shift a little more towards industry. Nichols, *Germany after Bismarck*, 92.

[25] H. Delbrück, 'Politische Correspondenz', *PJbb* lxvi (1890), 637–40.

[26] For a summary of the development of Prussian state taxation since 1815, as well as Miquel's reform of 1891–3, see D. E. Schremmer, 'Taxation and Public Finance: Britain, France and Germany', in P. Mathias and S. Pollard (eds.), *The Cambridge Economic History of Europe*. viii. *The Industrial Economies: The Development of Economic and Social Policies* (Cambridge, 1989), 315–494, esp. 418–53.

[27] Nichols, *Germany after Bismarck*, 91.

[28] Ultimately, Miquel sought to complement his efforts on tax reforms with a thorough reform of imperial taxation, but without success. W. Gerloff, *Die Finanz- und Zollpolitik des Deutschen Reiches nebst ihren Beziehungen zu Landes- und Gemeindefinanzen vor der Gründung des Norddeutschen Bundes bis zur Gegenwart* (Jena, 1913), ch. 29.

[29] The reforms have been described as 'The only modern and pioneering model tax reform during the imperial period'. Volker Hentschel, 'German Economic and Social Policy,

clear distinctions between state and local taxation, and, secondly, he intended to set up clear principles and guidelines for local government taxation which were to be applied, for the first time, throughout the state. As a result, general expenditure, particularly when it was fulfilling a duty imposed upon the locality by the state (e.g. primary schools, poor relief), was to be met by a universal tax. Expenditure which increased the quality of life (e.g. technical schools, lunatic asylums (!)), thus attracting more business and increasing the value of property, should be met by owners of property. Finally, expenditure on streets, pavements, parks, secondary schools, etc. primarily benefited property and should thus be borne, in the first instance, by property-owners and businesses.[30] The application of these principles marked an important shift in the practice of taxation in Prussia. For whereas since 1891 the state system had been firmly rooted in the principle of ability to pay, local taxation was subsequently based on the benefit derived from local government activities, as a return for actual services received (*Leistung und Gegenleistung*).[31] For the first time during the nineteenth century, the Prussian state explicitly acknowledged that local government was not just an arm of state government, but that it had a separate sphere, with different functions and objectives.

Paragraph two of the Local Taxation Act (*Kommunalabgabengesetz*) of 14 July 1893 stipulated that the primary source of taxation was to be the city's income from its own assets. This could be levied through charges (*Gebühren*), which were a regular charge levied for a particular service (such as drainage), or through fees (*Beiträge*), which were raised on a one-off basis, whenever a particular benefit could not be evaluated (such as connection to the sewage system, road building, etc.). The latter could only be

---

1815–1939', in P. Mathias and S. Pollard (eds.), *The Cambridge Economic History of Europe*. viii. *The Industrial Economies: The Development of Economic and Social Policies* (Cambridge, 1989), 778. A detailed account of the individual measures of the reforms is in F. Adickes, *Studien über die Weiterentwicklung des Gemeindesteuerwesens. Auf Grund des Preussischen Kommunalabgaben-Gesetzes vom 14. Juli 1893* (Tübingen, 1894). See also H. Führbaum, 'Die Entwicklung der Gemeindesteuern in Deutschland (Preußen) bis zum Beginn des 1. Weltkriegs', Ph.D. thesis (Münster, 1971).

[30] *Denkschrift* of 2 Nov. 1892, in *Drucksachen des Abgeordnetenhauses 1892/93*, Nr. 8. The above principles are also summarized in Kaufmann, *Kommunalfinanzen*, ii. 304. See also the ministerial directive in E. Scholz, 'Das heutige Gemeindebesteuerungssystem in Preußen. Unter besonderer Berücksichtigung des Westens der Monarchie', in: Schriften des Vereins für Sozialpolitik, *Gemeindefinanzen*, i. *System der Gemeindebesteuerung in Hessen, Württemberg, Baden, Elsaß-Lothringen, Bayern, Sachsen, Preußen*, cxxvi (Leipzig, 1908), 286–7.

[31] P. Gerstfeld, *Städtefinanzen in Preussen. Statistik und Reformvorschläge* (Leipzig, 1882), 3. Wagner, *Finanzwissenschaft* (1899), 79.

applied to property owners and businesses.[32] Once the local community had exhausted the income derived from its assets, the next preferred income was that of indirect taxation. Save for a number of indirect taxes which were raised by the Empire, local communities were free to raise any kind of indirect tax, subject to state approval. Only once these two sources of income had been exhausted was it possible for local government to raise direct taxation.

In return for the reaffirmation of income tax as a principal state tax, direct taxation of property (*Realsteuern*) by the locality was given a much more prominent role than before. As shown above, *Realsteuern* were now expected to apply to all those who directly benefited from local expenditures, i.e. men of property and business. Local communities had considerable freedom in raising taxation on property and business according to a number of criteria, whichever suited them best. By contrast, local personal taxation was effectively limited to surcharges on the state income tax.[33] As the former First Mayor of Frankfurt was only too aware of the difficulties in inducing city councils to vote for taxes on property,[34] Miquel added a final safeguard to ensure that the full potential of the *Realsteuern* was realized. The ratio of direct personal taxation to direct property taxation was to be calculated on a range from 1:1 to 1:1.5. In other words, if a locality raised local personal taxation equivalent to 100 per cent of the state income tax, ideally local taxation raised through direct property taxation should amount to about 150 per cent of state income tax. If local taxation supplements needed to be increased beyond these rates, they required approval by the Prussian state authorities. Only if local needs for revenue continued to grow was it permissible to raise personal income taxation disproportionately, since anything above a 200 per cent levy of personal property taxation relative to state taxation was deemed unacceptable.[35]

The Act of 1893 was certainly not without its faults. As the left liberals were quick to point out, the handing-over of the property tax by the state to the localities was not just done for the good of local government, but it was also a considerable sweetener for the Prussian conservatives. For it effectively meant that many Junkers, who were in charge of their own local districts, were now in the position to tax themselves, on their own property.[36] Hence, left-liberal opposition was perhaps strongest with respect to the new property tax, which was also considered to be regressive as it was feared

[32] Scholz, 'Gemeindebesteuerungssystem', 283–4.   [33] Ibid. 284–5.
[34] Herzfeld, *Miquel*, i. 517–19. On the power of property owners to prevent property taxes, see Klose, 'Finanzpolitik', 46.
[35] Kaufmann, *Kommunalfinanzen*, ii. 349–50.   [36] Herzfeld, *Miquel*, ii. 258–9, 269.

that the new system of property taxation would not be efficient enough. Furthermore, the promotion of indirect taxes was resented.[37] Finally, Miquel had yielded to agrarian interests in handing over responsibility for tax collection to the *Landrat*, who was at least in part responsible to the agrarian community, rather than to officials of the Prussian Ministry of Finance.[38] Nonetheless, it is interesting to note that the left liberals disagreed more with the details of the law than with the principles that lay behind it.

For the conservatives, the main obstacle was the introduction of the supplementary tax (*Ergänzungssteuer*), which was synonymous with a wealth tax to supplement the income tax. This was introduced to compensate for the abortive inheritance tax two years previously. However, conservatives soon became aware that, even though the new tax was an invasion of privacy, this was bearable given that it would weigh more heavily on mobile (industrial and commercial) than immobile (agricultural) capital.[39] Welcoming the additional sweetener of the property tax for the Junkers, and considering that for voting purposes they were still classed as though they payed that property tax which maintained their voting influence under the three-class franchise, the conservatives gave their necessary agreement to the reform.[40]

Miquel's local tax reforms were clearly a child of liberal ideals of local finance, and, ultimately, of liberal attitudes towards local self-government. These attitudes rested on visions of a careful interplay between state supervision, on the one hand, and local government initiative, on the other. Hence emerges the apparent paradox that while local government was given wider scope to raise its own taxation, state supervision was also increased. As long as state interference was muted enough to allow local initiative to prosper, the increase of state supervision was not a problem. Even though the extent of state supervision was often resented,[41] it also helped local taxation to achieve its full potential, as will be shown in the case of the introduction of property taxes.

---

[37] See e.g. the speeches of Rickert, *SPAH*, 3. Sitzung (18 Nov. 1892), 38–40. Richter, *SPAH*, 4. Sitzung (19 Nov. 1892), 68–80, esp. 69, 73, 77.

[38] P.-C. Witt, 'The Prussian Landrat as Tax Official, 1891–1918. Some Observations on the Political and Social Function of the German Civil Service during the Wilhelmine Empire', in G. Iggers (ed.), *The Social History of Politics. Critical Perspectives in West German Historical Writing since 1945* (Leamington Spa, 1985), 137–54.

[39] See Delbrück's initial hostility, and then his 'conversion', in H. Delbrück, 'Politische Correspondenz', *PJbb* lxix (1892), 711, and *PJbb* lxx (1892), 506–7.

[40] Richter, *SPAH*, 4. Sitzung (19 Nov. 1892), 68. Herzfeld, *Miquel*, ii. 270–1.

[41] Scholz, 'Gemeindebesteuerungssystem', 289–91.

One of the more constant charges which the Progressive leader, Eugen Richter, made against Miquel was that he had devised his reform like a 'textbook of financial theory',[42] and that in the interest of theoretical purity Miquel had lost any touch with what was really needed, or with what the real consequences of his laws would be.[43] Indeed, one of the reform's most significant shortcomings was that as a statewide law, it consequently failed to take any account of the substantial local variations between the cities. Of course, this had been one of Miquel's guiding principles—that this should be a national reform rather than one applying to certain regions only. Yet the reforms of the former mayor of pre-industrial Osnabrück and of that wealthiest of Prussian cities, Frankfurt, turned out to be rather better suited for prosperous cities such as Berlin, Kassel, and Wiesbaden than for the new industrial centres of Solingen, Königshütte, or Viersen. For in the spirit of the reforms, the former cities could afford to reduce their income tax supplements to below 100 per cent because of their high yield in property taxation, whereas the industrial cities had so little resident wealth that their income tax supplements, even in the year of the reform's introduction, were above 200 per cent.[44]

The failure to take account of such differences was not merely an important failure on Miquel's part, however, but it was a contradiction inherent in most liberals' view of self-government. The problem was not so much that the finance reform created relative winners and losers, which in itself was inevitable. Rather, the difficulty was the complicated system of personal and property local taxation, and the amount of state supervision introduced to monitor its application, which constrained the cities in their ability to adapt the system of taxation to their individual circumstances. These checks and balances were crucial, of course, to keep in check local assemblies still dominated by the propertied *Bürgertum* as well as local property owners. Just as before 1893 property taxation had failed because the house owners' majorities in the city councils had refused to tax themselves, so it had to be ensured that, now that all property taxation had been handed over to the local communities, these majorities had to accept a minimum level of property taxation.

The only real solution was for the state to allow an extension and equalization of the franchise, and the removal of the requirement that at least

---

[42] Richter, *SPAH*, 4. Sitzung (19 Nov. 1892), 69.   [43] Ibid. 74.
[44] H. Lücker, *Gemeindefinanzen*, ii, part 3. *Die Entwicklung und die Probleme des Gemeindeabgabenwesens in den Städten und großen Landgemeinden der preußischen Industriebezirke*, Schriften des Vereins für Sozialpolitik, cxxvii (Leipzig, 1910).

50 per cent of councillors be house owners.⁴⁵ Since the Prussian state (and, least of all, Miquel) was unwilling to contemplate such a radical proposal, the ironic result was that only detailed and principled state interference in municipal finance guaranteed the greatest realization of self-government in the cities. The price of this was an increasing differentiation in municipal wealth, and ultimately in the quality of life for the German urban population. This was only properly taken account of in 1920, with the introduction of Matthias Erzberger's finance reforms.⁴⁶

Despite this criticism, it is equally the case that the 1893 local tax reform was a remarkable practical acknowledgement by the Prussian state that local self-government had a distinct role to play in the interest of efficient and innovative government in general, and of state government in particular. As a result, local government in the two decades or so after the reforms came into effect in 1895 achieved a role greater than ever before or after, with its distinct sphere of activity financed through its own, distinct sources of revenue.

The theoretical implications of Miquel's tax reforms are, of course, only one side of the coin, because for their complete evaluation it is necessary to consider briefly their actual effect on municipal income and expenditure. It is difficult to imagine that even Miquel could have believed that property taxation would be able to overtake personal income taxation as the local community's main source of income from direct taxation. After all, the local income tax was supposed to cover those items of expenditure on which the community was spending in the interest of the state, in particular primary schools and poor relief. These also happened to be some of the biggest spending items in any local budget.⁴⁷ Nevertheless, as Table 6.4 shows, the 1893 reforms did result in a significant switch from personal to property taxation.⁴⁸ Even though soon after the switch in 1895 personal taxes began to grow faster than property taxes again, this relative growth was only slight, and the ratio stayed at about 60:40 until 1911.⁴⁹ Clearly, Miquel's

---

⁴⁵ Hugo Preuß in Wagner and Preuß, *Kommunale Steuerfragen*, 44–9.
⁴⁶ For a brief introduction, see Krabbe, *Die Deutsche Stadt*, 165–8.
⁴⁷ J. Bolenz, 'Wachstum und Strukturwandlungen der kommunalen Ausgaben in Deutschland 1849–1913', D.jur. thesis (Freiburg, 1965), 165, 168.
⁴⁸ Unfortunately, it is difficult to say whether the total property tax burden increased as a result of the changes, because there seems to be no available statistic which shows state property tax payments just for *Gemeinden* (local communities, cities) before 1895, which could then be compared to the available data on local property tax payments after the introduction of the reform.
⁴⁹ Krabbe, *Die Deutsche Stadt*, 160. According to Krabbe's data, the ratio between property and personal local taxation was 42.6:57.4 (1895/96), 40.0:60.0 (1900), 39.9:60.1 (1911).

safeguards were sufficient to ensure that house owners and businesses could not avoid the local tax in the way they had been able to before.

TABLE 6.4. *Proportion of property and of personal (income) taxation in % of total local direct taxation, 1869–1900*

	Property taxation	Personal taxation
1869	15.6	84.4
1883/4	16.4	83.6
1894/5	16.3	83.7
1895/6	44.0	56.0
1899/1990	41.6	58.4

Source: Kaufmann, *Kommunalfinanzen*, ii. 351.

The preferred indirect taxes had a less happy fate. As Table 6.5 shows, indirect taxation doubled when the local tax reform came into effect in the financial year 1895/96, but it still amounted to less than 10 per cent of total taxation, and during the next few years the proportion remained relatively constant. This is presumably because this new emphasis on indirect taxes in the mid-1890s came at a time when the SPD, whose constituents were hardest hit by the tax, was waiting in the wings to challenge bourgeois domination of the city councils in most areas. As a result, this regressive form of taxation could not be introduced quite as freely as in previous decades. In any case, local indirect taxation was made all but redundant by the imperial law of 1902, to take effect on 1 April 1910, which turned all the major indirect taxes into imperial ones and explicitly rejected local supplements to these.[50] As a result, from 1902 local indirect taxation dwindled into insignificance, though none of this could, of course, have been foreseen by Miquel at the time. In the immediate aftermath of the reform, however, the increase in local property taxation more than compensated for the decrease in personal taxation, and, together with a doubling of indirect taxation, from one year to the next local tax revenues increased by 17.3 per cent.

---

[50] For an excellent account of the introduction of the 1902 taxes, their implication for local self-government, and the cities' reaction, see H. Beckstein, *Städtische Interessenpolitik. Organisation und Politik der Städtetage in Bayern, Preußen und im Deutschen Reich 1896–1923* (Düsseldorf, 1991), 147–53. Gerloff, *Finanz- und Zollpolitik*, 385–8. A. Günther, 'Die Belastung kleinerer und mittlerer Einkommen durch Verbrauchsabgaben seit Geltung des Zolltarifs vom 25. Dezember 1902', in Schriften des Vereins für Sozialpolitik, *Die Neuordnung der deutschen Finanzwirtschaft*, ed. H. Herkner, clvi (Munich/Leipzig, 1918), ii. 189–268.

TABLE 6.5. *Local taxation in Prussian cities of over 10,000 inhabitants* (in Marks per head)

	1876/7	1883/4	1891/2	1894/5	1895/6	1899/1900
Indirect taxes	0.95	0.81	0.88	1.05	2.09	2.57
Income taxes	10.19	11.51	12.53	12.67	9.56	12.04
Property taxes	1.83	2.03	2.02	2.30	7.35	8.39
Charges and Fees				2.32	2.64	3.43
TOTAL	12.97	14.35	15.42	18.35	21.63	26.43

Source: Kaufmann, *Kommunalfinanzen*, ii. 365.

Table 6.5 shows a slow, but steady rise in municipal income through charges and fees. Contemporaries and historians alike have argued frequently that the tax reform's changed emphasis on charges and fees, not all of which were subject to state sanction, produced a large incentive for cities to increase their spending on municipal services in order to increase their non-taxed income.[51] Very often, this assessment was based on the extraordinarily high growth-rates for municipal income at that time without discounting the fact that the vast majority of this income went to servicing the debt which had to be incurred to municipalize services in the first place. The actual net income from municipal assets was relatively small,[52] so that it is highly doubtful whether it was the prospect of fees and charges that spurred urban governments into action to increase their revenue. Furthermore, it should be borne in mind that Miquel's prioritization of income from municipal assets was nothing new. The 1808 city ordinance had already introduced the principle that taxation be raised only for local expenditure that went over and above the city's non-taxed income. The one change introduced by the 1893 reform was that charges could now be levied in such a way as not only to cover all the costs, but also as to make a profit, the extent of which was not specified.[53] As a result, it was natural that fees and charges went up, but it is questionable whether they were responsible for a sea-change in municipal finance which led to a large increase in municipal assets.[54]

---

[51] Lindemann, *Die städtische Regie*, 34–5. Bolenz, 'Wachstum', 189.
[52] Scholz, 'Gemeindebesteuerungssystem', 281–318, esp. 298.
[53] Klose, 'Finanzpolitik', 53.
[54] O. Landsberg, 'Die Entwicklung des Gemeindeabgabenwesens in den preußischen Städten unter der Herrschaft des Kommunalabgabengesetzes mit besonderer Berücksichtigung der östlichen Provinzen', in Schriften des Vereins für Sozialpolitik, *Gemeindefinanzen*, ii, part 1. *Einzelfragen der Finanzpolitik der Gemeinden*, cxxvii (Leipzig, 1910), 3–5.

TABLE 6.6. *Expenditure of Prussian cities, 1869–1913* (absolute and per head)

	Expenditure, in M.	Expenditure per head, in M.	% increase per head	Average annual % increase (on base year), per head
1869	100.50	13.00		
1876	176.80	20.10	54.62	7.80
1883/4	212.70	21.93	9.10	1.30
1891/2	314.90	26.27	19.79	2.47
1895/6	394.80	30.47	15.99	4.00
1899/1900	553.00	38.22	25.43	6.36
1907	907.70	51.26	34.12	4.27
1913	1328.10	65.67	28.11	4.69

Source: Bolenz, 'Wachstum', 55.

The question about the importance of the cities' own income touches on the remaining important issue to be considered in an evaluation of the effect of Miquel's tax laws. Having considered their effect on local taxation, it is now necessary to turn to their role in affecting local government expenditure. Table 6.6 shows the increase in overall spending of all Prussian cities between 1869 and 1913. It shows that the boom years until the mid-1870s were followed by a period of fiscal consolidation. Not only was the average spending increase minimal, but a comparison with Table 6.5 shows also that during this period, income from taxation grew marginally faster than expenditure. As for Prussia's large municipal cities with a population over 100,000, Table 6.7 shows even a reduction in total spending over the period up until 1883. Thereafter, Table 6.6 indicates an increase in average municipal expenditure per head, and it is, indeed, true that the largest boom in municipal spending took place in the interval immediately following the establishment of Miquel's local finance reforms between the years 1895 and 1900. Hence, Miquel's laws did have an effect on local public spending, even though the increase in those years was quite exceptional, and after 1900 the increase in local spending was less, though still more than 4 per cent per annum.

In order to locate the precise effect of Miquel's reforms on local spending, however, it is useful to look at the detailed breakdown of local public spending in Table 6.7. It shows municipal spending by area, as it has been generally recognized that it was in the big cities where financial problems were the worst, and thus any effect of Miquel's reforms would be most

TABLE 6.7. *Municipal expenditure in cities with a population of over 100,000, by item of expenditure in Prussia, 1869–1911 (in Marks per head)*

Number of cities	Year	Administration	Education	Public welfare	Transport	Municipal enterprise	Debt servicing	Total spending
4	1869	4.62	4.18	4.36	4.27	2.35	2.35	22.13
6	1876	8.30	9.32	5.14	13.68	12.54	5.32	54.30
7	1883/4	6.88	9.37	6.54	7.08	14.45	4.00	48.32
16	1891/2	5.83	10.02	7.23	8.74	21.50	5.25	58.57
13	1911	13.51	21.52	18.65	19.82	22.08	31.66	127.24

Source: Köster, *Entwicklung*, 185.

visible here. Indeed, it is evident that in many cities public spending per head was at times more than double the national average as shown in Table 6.6. It is unfortunate that there are no data for the interval 1891/1892–1911, but following the general trend evident from Table 6.6 it is safe to assume that a disproportionate increase in municipal spending took place after the coming into effect of the local tax reform in 1895.

Two important facts emerge from this analysis. First, per capita spending on municipal services increased most during the affluent years of the period of the foundation of the Empire, the *Gründerzeit*. It increased only slightly during the next two decades as the large cities were anxious to reduce the burden of their debts. This was followed by another substantial increase in spending on municipal services until 1891/92. Even though in the following period spending on this item remained high, there was virtually no increase in expenditure for the next twenty years. Taking into account the enormous increase in municipal spending during the period from 1891 to 1911, the share of municipal spending on the cities' own assets halved from 36.7 per cent in 1891 to 17.4 per cent in 1911. This is not to diminish in any way the significance of municipal enterprises for local government,[55] which has attracted the attention of contemporaries and historians alike. It is merely to point out that this wave of municipalizations started in the mid-1880s, before Miquel's reforms.[56]

It is, therefore, not the case that Miquel's tax reforms led to an increase in municipal business through the ability to raise more charges and fees, because of the two items of expenditure which were affected by these revenues, expenditure on municipal services remained more or less stagnant, and the share of spending on transport showed only a 1 per cent increase in the twenty years before 1911.

The second striking feature of Table 6.7 is the extraordinary rise of municipal public debt in the two decades before 1911. Having been held more or less constant in the years 1869 to 1891, and making up less than 9 per cent of total spending in the years 1883 to 1891, municipal expenditure on debt servicing rose by 600 per cent over the next 20 years, to become the single biggest item of municipal expenditure at 24.9 per cent of

---

[55] It is quite possible that this is simply the result of separate budgets being introduced for municipal enterprises around the turn of the century, and that, as will be described below, the city of Frankfurt may not have been the only city where most of the spending on municipal enterprises was no longer accounted for by general budget expenditure.

[56] Thus, for the municipalization of gas, the last 15 years of municipalization have been described as the 'second phase of municipalization'. H.-D. Bunckhorst, *Kommunalisierung im 19. Jahrhundert dargestellt am Beispiel der Gaswirtschaft in Deutschland* (Munich, 1978), 222–5.

the total. This change can be explained by the fact that before 1891, most of the spending on municipal services could be financed through current income. During the last decades before the Great War, however, municipal expenditure on other areas increased so much that all of current income was used up to finance these, so that most of the spending on municipal businesses was now financed through debt. This was encouraged by the reluctance of the state to approve of any municipal debt that was taken to finance recurrent, 'ordinary' (*ordentlich*) expenditures, such as on schools or roads, and by the ease with which debts for 'extraordinary' (*außerordentlich*) projects such as municipalization or particular municipal building projects were approved.[57]

As a result, municipal debt increased to almost unimaginable proportions. In 1913, 50 Prussian cities with a population over 50,000 inhabitants were faced with a total debt of 3,066 billion M.[58] In 1905, debts of over 300 M. per head were not uncommon in large Prussian municipalities.[59] Yet this debt should not be overdramatized, neither in theory nor in practice, because it was perfectly reasonable to have improvements in municipal services or items such as school buildings paid for not just by current taxpayers, but by future generations which would also benefit from these institutions.[60] And in practice, Prussian administrators were not too worried about municipal debt as long as the municipalities were backed up by sufficient assets.[61]

Yet, it is also possible to say that, since spending on municipal services remained more or less constant over the period, this means that the large increase in debt servicing, and the correspondingly large increase in municipal debt, were effectively necessary to pay for the increases in the other areas of municipal spending. Put more poignantly, while providing some badly needed income for local governments immediately after its introduction, the 1893 local tax reform failed to provide the means or the

---

[57] Krabbe, *Die deutsche Stadt*, 163–4. Whereas in England, for example, it took an Act of Parliament for a municipality to take up debts, in Prussia taking up debt was merely subject to approval by the next higher level of administration, in the case of the cities the *Bezirksausschuß*. This was subject to guidelines from the Interior Ministry. These concerned mainly the nature of debts that could be incurred, as well as the period over which the debt had to be reserviced. Debt could be taken up, subject to approval by the authorities, for anything that was in the interest of the common weal, a stipulation that was interpreted increasingly liberally. Kaufmann, *Kommunalfinanzen*, ii. 477–80.

[58] Krabbe, *Die deutsche Stadt*, 164.

[59] Krabbe, *Kommunalpolitik und Industrialisierung*, 361.

[60] On the current theory of municipal debt, see Kaufmann, *Kommunalfinanzen*, ii. 437–48.

[61] Krabbe, *Die deutsche Stadt*, 163–5.

necessary mechanisms for local government to cope with the fast-rising demands and strains on local government resources, and thus taking up debt remained the only alternative. Again, it is important to keep a regional perspective of this problem. For the amount of debt, large as it undoubtedly was, was never really a problem for well-off cities, such as Frankfurt, Bonn, or Cologne, where there would always be sufficient assets to balance the debt. But it was a tremendous problem for some of the poorer new industrial cities and the smaller cities, where propertied wealth had little presence. These found it almost impossible to finance even the spiralling ordinary spending on roads, education, and other items through current income, without taking up debt.[62]

It remains to be explained what caused the significant increase in municipal spending that occurred. From 1876 to 1891, municipal spending increased by an overall 108 per cent, yet in the following two decades, public spending on administration, education, public welfare, and transport each increased by over 200 per cent. One general explanation which covered all of these areas in some way or another was that the state tried to shift some of its administrative burdens onto the locality. The state had often used the rivalry between local governments, for example, to move out to cities prestigious government offices which would raise the municipal profile while shifting a significant part of the cost to these municipal governments—often, the highest bidder won.[63] Another general trend which affected all areas of municipal government was that towards 'scientific' municipal government. This is evident, for example, in the mushrooming of various city congresses (*Städtetage*) on a regional, provincial, state, and even national level, and in the publication of municipal journals such as the *Städte-Zeitung*, and its aim of promoting good, scientific, and enlightened city government.[64] One of the most obvious examples of this trend is the rise of

---

[62] See e.g. the report of the Lord Mayor of the Upper Silesian Town of Gleiwitz, Menzel, 'Die Überbürdung der oberschlesischen Industriestädte mit Schullasten', *Städte-Zeitung*, 10 Nov. 1905, No. 3, 59–62, continued in *Städte-Zeitung*, 24 Nov. 1905, No. 4, 91–3. *Städte-Zeitung*, 8 Dec. 1905, No. 5, 117–18.

[63] There are several examples of this with regard to Frankfurt alone. See e.g. Frankfurt's successful bid for the *Oberlandesgericht* and the positive impact the Prussian authorities judged this to have on the population of the city. Maly, *Macht*, 171. HStAW 405 n. 1071 fos. 208–10. *Zeitungsbericht*, 11 Mar. 1879. For Germany in general, see W. H. Dawson, *Municipal Life and Government in Germany* (London, 1914), 358–9.

[64] O. Ziebill, *Geschichte des Deutschen Städtetages. Fünfzig Jahre deutsche Kommunalpolitik* (Stuttgart, 1955), 10–37, esp. 35. A good example of the growing 'science' in all areas of local government is a series of articles on gardening whose range includes a minute description of the type of trees recommended for various purposes as well as the type of fence suggested to

town planning as a 'science'. If the first stages of urbanization occurred largely uncontrolled and in an ad hoc manner, municipal expansion became increasingly trammelled, first by the need to improve hygienic standards, and then by a whole catalogue of considerations including technology, aesthetics, hygiene, social policy, and economics. In addition to this, town planning was supposed to represent and underline the cultural spirit (*Selbstverständnis*) of the city.[65]

More specifically with regard to individual areas of expenditure, the rise in educational expenses can be explained by new demands made upon local government to improve the education system (for example the introduction of technical schools) without providing adequate means to pay for the changes. Also, as a rare measure to further equity between local communities and large cities, the 1897 Education Act, for example, introduced the principle that all communities which employed more than 25 teachers were wealthy enough to pay for them without state grants.[66] But there were other, less tangible reasons. As has been discussed earlier, these included insights into the importance of (costly) sanitary provisions ('space, light, and air') for new school buildings, better pay for teachers as local authorities competed with the state, and with each other, for the best teachers, and efforts to reduce class size and make schooling generally more effective through the provision of school meals.

The rising administrative cost of municipal government can be explained not only by the increase in the sphere of local government activities. It is also likely that this increase in administrative duties led to diseconomies of scale as the size of the burden of administration increasingly meant that it could only be carried out by professionals rather than by the voluntary work of the citizen. Also, whereas most municipal enterprises before 1890 were capital-intensive (such as gas- or waterworks), many enterprises that were municipalized after that date were rather more labour-intensive, such as tramways. As a result, there was a large increase in the number of municipal employees particularly from about 1890 onwards.[67]

---

protect public parks. Tapp, 'Städtische Gartenanlagen', *Städte-Zeitung*, 18 Jan. 1907, No. 8, 192–4. See also Hennebo, 'Öffentlicher Park und Grünplanung', esp. 176–8.

[65] R. Baumeister, 'Grundsätze des Städtebaus', *Städte-Zeitung*, 18 Jan. 1907, No. 8, 189–92. Ladd, *Urban Planning*, chs. 3–4. This was, of course, an international phenomenon. C. E. Schorske, *Fin-de-Siècle Vienna. Politics and Culture* (New York, 1985). A. Sutcliffe (ed.), *The Rise of Modern Urban Planning 1800–1914* (London, 1984).

[66] Lücker, 'Entwicklung', 37.

[67] Mombert, 'Gemeindebetriebe', 4–7. In general, see Dawson, *Municipal Life*, 359. Matzerath, *Urbanisierung in Preußen*, 353–6.

The rise in public welfare spending after 1891 may be attributed to changing attitudes towards social policy, in particular an emphasis on preventive and scientific social work, as well as on 'proto-corporatist' social policy, directed at a malfunctioning labour market.[68] It was also an inevitable reaction to the process of urbanization which posed unprecedented challenges to scientists and local politicians alike. After the pioneering efforts of some cities to create a healthy urban environment inasmuch as that was possible, other cities followed suit in an effort to improve not just overall physical but also moral health, as the two came to be seen as inextricably linked.[69] Finally, added burdens on local government under the amended Social Insurance Law show that here, too, local government was required to bear increasing general government responsibilities.[70]

Perhaps the most important determinant of the increase in municipal transport expenditure was the wave of incorporations (*Eingemeindungen*) which set in around 1900. In extending their city limits to the surrounding areas and communities large municipalities hoped to create space for better and cheaper housing, away from the congested city centres. The problem with this was that the new villages or areas that were incorporated were often without adequate road or drainage systems, all of which now had to be financed by the municipal government after the takeover.[71] Also, these measures could only relieve the municipal housing market if the city spent considerable sums on creating sufficient and cheap transport facilities through road building and the extension of tramway lines.

None of the increases in these areas of municipal expenditure appear to be related, or in any way connected, to Miquel's finance reforms. Yet even the above cursory survey of the reasons for the growth of municipal spending on transport, education, and public welfare shows that a crucial factor in this increase was a new awareness of the means required to alleviate current social (and ultimately political) problems caused by urbanization and industrialization, and of the importance of the city in this endeavour. As demonstrated by the works of Rudolf Gneist, the role of local self-government in mediating between a changing society and the state has long

---

[68] Steinmetz, *Regulating the Social*, 188–214.
[69] J. Reulecke, 'Von der "Hygienisierung" der Unterschichten zur komunalen Gesundheitspolitik', in J. Reulecke and A. Gräfin zu Castell Rüdenhausen (eds.), *Stadt und Gesundheit. Zum Wandel von 'Volksgesundheit' und kommunaler Gesundheitspolitik im 19. und frühen 20. Jahrhundert* (Stuttgart, 1991), 11–14.
[70] Dawson, *Municipal Life*, 359.
[71] Reulecke, *Geschichte der Urbanisierung*, 78–86. Rebentisch, 'Industrialisierung', 90–113, esp. 104–6.

had an important role in liberal ideals. Never before, however, had there been such an acknowledgement of the pioneering role of local government in addressing current social questions, and hence in its overall importance in the German system of government.

This increased municipal self-confidence was reflected at various levels. In the academic debate, the left-liberal student of Gierke, Hugo Preuß, started to challenge Gneist's accepted wisdom that self-government was part of the hierarchical state by arguing that both local government and the state were parts of an unbroken ascending chain of human communities, so that local self-government, rather than the state or the monarchy, became the foundation of the body politic.[72] At a different level, Prussian cities became political actors in their own right. In 1896 the Prussian *Städtetag* (city congress) was formed.[73] And, during the controversy surrounding the 1891/92 school bill, the Prussian Ministry of Education was inundated with petitions from ostensibly non-political local governments and their representatives. Some observers perceived this increased municipal self-consciousness, translated into rivalry between the different municipalities, to be directly responsible for some of the tremendous increases in municipal spending before the First World War.[74]

It is undeniable that the 1893 tax reforms failed to provide local self-government with adequate means to raise sufficient income in order to meet spiralling local expenditure during the last two decades before the Great War. Yet since debts were seen as a perfectly legitimate way of financing certain activities of local government, the debt crisis was, although existent, not quite as dramatic as it may first appear. More important than this was the failure of Miquel's reforms to take any account of the extraordinary variety of cities that were affected by his general reforms. There could be little self-government in communities where income was so low that expenditure on education alone took two-thirds of total ordinary expenditure.[75] For most of the larger Prussian cities, however, Miquel's reforms, which were the practical manifestation of the liberal ideal of self-government and the confirmation of the distinct role of local self-government in the Prussian governmental structure, confirmed and emphasized the growing sense of self-importance felt by Prussian municipalities.

Whereas there was a certain stimulus to expenditure through a number of concrete changes in local taxation, the most significant impact of Miquel's

---

[72] See e.g. H. Preuß, *Staat, Recht und Freiheit. Aus 40 Jahren Deutscher Politik und Geschichte* (Tübingen, 1926), 25–102.
[73] Ziebill, *Geschichte des Deutschen Städtetages*, 20 ff.
[74] Lücker, 'Entwicklung', 35.   [75] Ibid. 38. Croon, 'Aufgaben deutscher Städte', 60.

tax reforms on local finance was more intangible, in that they furthered the cities' awareness of the worth of self-government. Because Miquel's reforms had introduced the important principle that local government was primarily responsible for the welfare of the local community, local government began to take a long-term view that it should invest for that purpose. That Miquel's reforms did strengthen municipal self-government effectively is demonstrated by the emergence of some formidable threats to the ideal of local self-government by 1914, which were the result of this very success. On the one hand, municipal government was so effective in raising revenue and in administration itself that the states found it increasingly expedient to shift some of their financial and administrative burdens onto the cities. Yet this happened at the same time that municipal financial autonomy was being challenged for the first time by the imperial state, as was the case with the Empire's appropriation of indirect taxation on consumption from 1910. In a similar vein, the Empire tried to appropriate the unearned increment tax in 1911, just after the cities had pioneered this new tax with great success.[76] In that case, the Empire was not quite so successful in its endeavour,[77] but both instances demonstrate that in the last years before the Great War municipal government was threatened with becoming the victim of its own success, through increasing financial and administrative burdens and diminishing means of raising revenue. Miquel's tax reforms, therefore, were a precondition for the ensuing 'golden age of municipal life',[78] as they were a product of, and a main influence on, changing attitudes about the role of self-government in public life which became evident with the increase in spending on municipal businesses since the mid-1880s.

Having explored the attitudes of liberal academics and politicians active at the state or national level towards municipal finance, the remainder of this chapter seeks to analyse how these assumptions of liberals 'at the top' translated into grass-roots liberal perceptions of the increasing size and the changing function of municipal finance. Naturally, in this case study of liberal attitudes towards municipal finance in Frankfurt, allowances have to be made for the fact that Frankfurt was Germany's richest city with a strong civic tradition as a result of its former independence and wealth.[79] It would

---

[76] Dawson, *Municipal Life*, 397–9. On the problems of imperial finance in general, see P.-C. Witt, *Die Finanzpolitik des Deutschen Reiches von 1903 bis 1913. Eine Studie zur Innenpolitik des Wilhelminischen Deutschland* (Lübeck/Hamburg, 1970).
[77] Dawson, *Municipal Life*, 399–400 n. 1. [78] Krabbe, *Die deutsche Stadt*, 165.
[79] In 1876, Frankfurt had by far Prussia's highest per capita yield of the state income tax. Gerstfeld, *Städtefinanzen*, 42–9, table iii. In fact, in 1889 Frankfurt's total local tax yield per

be misguided to try to investigate the hardships caused by Miquel's finance reform. New industrial cities, such as Solingen or Barmen would be much better suited for an investigation of this kind. Moreover, the citizens of the former Imperial City of Frankfurt were more used to the idea of the city being the focal point of the common weal, so that it was likely that the change in attitude about the role of municipal government manifested in the budget was going to be less pronounced than in newer industrial cities in the Ruhr basin or elsewhere. Yet the fact that Frankfurt was Prussia's wealthiest city also has advantages for an investigation of this kind. For Frankfurt's wealth meant that perhaps in no other city were the opportunities for realizing the goals of municipal self-government as great as here. If one contemporary argument against a particular item of municipal expenditure did not stick here in contrast to other communities, it was the excuse of having no money. The relative absence of budgetary constraints makes Frankfurt an extremely illuminating case for the way in which liberals in local government appreciated and used municipal finance for the realization of their ideals and political aims.

6.3. Municipal Expenditure[80]

An evaluation of Frankfurt liberal attitudes towards municipal finance must begin with a brief examination of the actual development of Frankfurt municipal expenditure during this period. Figure 6.1 depicts the growth of

capita outstripped that of any other large German city by at least 20%. Adickes, *Studien über die Weiterentwicklung des Gemeindesteuerwesens*, 6.

[80] Throughout the chapter, figures and graphs represent nominal values both in order to enable a comparison with the general statistical data for municipal finance given above, and because the precise amount of inflation during the period is not yet clear. Furthermore, whereas for the actual effects of expenditure, income, and debt, the figures given have to be discounted by the rate of inflation, in any five-year average prices were never below 75% and never above 106% of 1913 prices. Indeed, over the entire period from 1871 to 1913 inflation was minimal, if it existed at all. Whereas there does appear to be a period of modest inflation from about 1896 to 1913, inflation during that period averaged at about 1% per year which does little to change the overall growth pattern of municipal expenditure in Frankfurt as evidenced in Figure 6.1. (From 1896 to 1912, nominal municipal expenditure in Frankfurt rose by an average of over 22% per year.) Finally, available statistics on inflation or deflation have been compiled on a national basis, whereas a completely accurate compilation of real values of expenditure, income, and debt would have to take into account price changes in Frankfurt alone. For a summary of various analyses of price changes in Germany during the period, see F. B. Tipton, Jr., *Regional Variations in the Economic Development of Germany during the Nineteenth Century* (Middletown, Conn., 1976), 41–2, 82–3. For a comparative set of data, see B. R. Mitchell, *European Historical Statistics, 1750–1975* (2nd edn., London, 1981), 779–80. For an analysis of German inflation during the Empire, and esp. from the 1890s, see N. C. Ferguson, *Paper and Iron. Hamburg Business and German Politics in the Era of Inflation, 1897–1927* (Cambridge, 1995), 20–7.

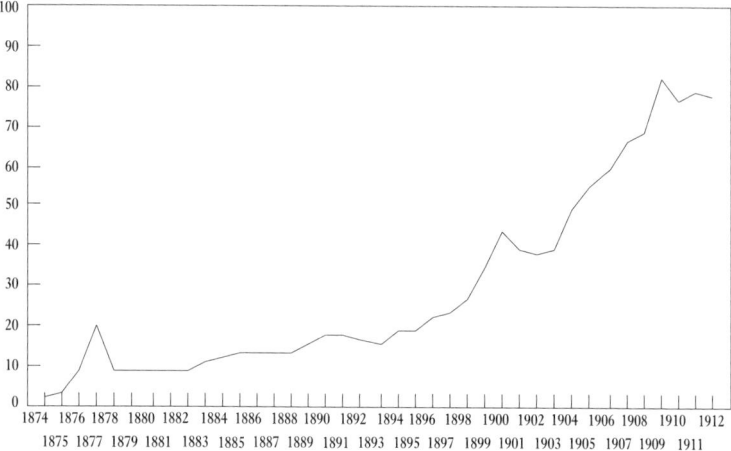

FIG. 6.1. General budget expenditure in Frankfurt am Main, 1874–1912 (in million Marks)
MAB, 1874–1912. For the data summarized in this graph, see Table A in Appendix I.

general budget expenditure from 1874 to 1912. The figures show that Frankfurt municipal expenditure rose in bursts similar to municipal budgets elsewhere. In the initial boom until about 1876, expenditure rose by over 400 per cent in the three years of 1874 to 1876 alone. Subsequently, more careful budgeting to recover from this initial burst of activity, as well as Miquel's prudence after 1880, led to relatively moderate increases of a little over 200 per cent in budget expenditure in the next 20 years. 1895 formed a watershed in Frankfurt fiscal policy too, because the following years witnessed an extraordinary rise in municipal expenditure, which more than quadrupled in the years 1895 to 1911. By 1910 Frankfurt liberals noted with pride that the size of Frankfurt's ordinary expenditure surpassed that of no less than 18 states.[81]

In consideration of the amount spent on various broad categories, a comparison between Table 6.8 and Table 6.7 shows that Frankfurt differed from the aggregate of Prussian cities in its relatively high spending on municipal services from as early as the 1870s.[82] Even in that decade it was

[81] See the speech by L. Heilbrunn, *Frankfurter Zeitung*, 10 Nov. 1910 (3. Morgenblatt).
[82] In Table 6.8, the summary of individual spending items into several broad categories essentially involves certain subjective criteria which are not always unambiguous. For example, expenditure on the sewage and drainage systems is linked to road improvements as well as improvements in public health. Nonetheless, since the city's eagerness to expand the systems is primarily connected with their ultimate financial rewards, they have been

TABLE 6.8. *Municipal expenditure in Frankfurt, 1879–1905, by item of expenditure* (in Marks)

	Administration	Education	Public welfare	Transport	Municipal enterprise	Debt servicing	Ecclesiastical affairs	Other	Total expenditure
1879	1,045,507	1,223,388	1,023,362	1,796,805	2,894,745	1,422,258	344,155	1,723	9,751,943
1884	1,011,492	2,384,269	1,562,775	1,989,549	4,035,847	1,970,516	99,747	91,544	13,145,739
1889	1,347,794	2,490,039	1,378,118	4,239,848	4,159,892	3,215,826	129,985	156,062	17,117,564
1894	1,777,739	3,338,836	2,663,737	2,319,792	5,946,766	3,160,022	309,745	41,031	19,557,668
1896	2,186,796	4,226,867	2,170,305	3,386,880	6,017,020	4,206,219	104,543	325,831	22,624,461
1905	5,451,115	8,383,929	5,288,808	10,078,482	15,193,021	8,061,599	100,443	4,283,419	56,840,816

Note: In 1889 the figure for debt servicing is unusually high because it includes a one-off payment for debt servicing that year.

Source: MAB, 1879/80, pp. 6–12. *MAB*, 1884/85, pp. 16–32. *MAB*, 1889/90, pp. 22–53. *MAB*, 1894/95, pp. 22–56. *MAB*, 1896/97, pp. 30–68. *MAB*, 1905, pp. 4–34.

282   *Liberalism and Municipal Finance*

one of the few cities to invest heavily in expensive drainage and sewage systems, and throughout the period the city spent large sums on the purchase of property. The significant fact to emerge from the data presented in Table 6.8 is, in short, the constantly high investment of the city in municipal services, and the relatively steep rise of expenditure on transport and education over the period.

Correspondingly, expenditure on the servicing of the municipal debt was relatively high during the early years to finance many of these municipal services such as the sewage and drainage systems, whereas it was relatively low in 1905. The main reason for the low figure in 1905 is that, from 1898 onwards, most of the income and expenditure on municipal services was administered in a separate budget, true to the principle that, ideally, current income from municipal services should exceed and provide for all related current expenditure and debt-servicing on this item.

The existence of an entirely separate budget for municipal services already shows that the ordinary budget itself is by no means a complete indicator of municipal financial activity, as from 1897/98 the method of accounting for municipal financial transactions grew increasingly complex.[83] The general budget consisted mainly of two parts, the ordinary budget (*Ordinarium*) and the extraordinary budget (*Extraordinarium*). Whereas the former included all regular items of income and expenditure such as spending on schools, salaries, debt-servicing, etc., the latter was composed of those items which were non-recurrent such as particular buildings, parks, and transactions regarding municipal property. This distiction had practical consequences, as it was generally held that all current expenditure on regular items in the ordinary budget should be covered by the city's own income, and that it could only raise debts for expenditure in the extraordinary budget.[84] From 1897, a supplementary budget (*Neben-Verwaltung*) was separated from the general budget, which again consisted of largely two components. The first denoted direct income and expenditure on municipal services (again divided into ordinary and extraordinary transactions), whereas the second (*Nebenkassen und Fonds der Nebenverwal-*

accounted for under 'Municipal Enterprise'. As a result, comparisons of the ratios between the items of expenditure for Frankfurt in Table 6.8 with those for Prussian cities in general in Table 6.7 can only be made with great caution.

[83] *MAB*, 1897/8, pp. 32–3. Also Maly, *Macht*, 357.

[84] It is against this background that the amount of debt servicing in Table 6.8 has to be evaluated. For even though expenditure on the servicing of the municipal debt and corresponding interest payments never exceeded 15% of the total general budget, they fluctuated between 20% and 25% of all regular budget expenditure which had to be financed through taxes and other means of income.

tung) described funds which provided the capital stock for the foundation and improvement of municipal enterprises and other major capital outlays such as schools and roads (here, the single biggest budgetary item, the fund for debts, accounted for over 60 per cent of expenditure and income). Finally, a third separate account existed for the movement of public capital (e.g. transfers of capital with the municipal bank or money transfers between the various municipal offices) and interest-yielding assets.[85] This was the 'extrabudgetary account' (*außeretatsmäßige Rechnung/Stammrechnung*), which formed the large bulk of what has been summarized in Table 6.9 as 'other financial transactions'.[86]

Table 6.9 shows the complete growth in municipal transactions from 1899 to 1912. It demonstrates just how much local financial activity extended beyond general budget transactions. The growth of municipal budget activity, which is impressive enough when considering the general budget alone, rises quite dramatically after 1895 in complexity and size. Nonetheless it is important to recognize that these figures belong to two quite different categories. Whereas expenditure on the general budget and on municipal services was actual, expenditure on supplementary funds and other financial transactions recorded money transfers between different funds and departments and included such items as debts and direct taxes which were collected for the state.

Naturally, the general budget remains of greatest importance, since it included all municipal income resulting from taxation and the expenditure relating to it, so it is this budget which was of overriding concern to policy-makers and the public alike. But for a fair assessment of the actual development of municipal expenditure, without capital transfers or funds, expenditure on the general budget, as well as on municipal services once these were listed separately, has to be added. Figure 6.2 shows the actual municipal expenditure and demonstrates the extraordinary rise in municipal activity after 1895. After an average increase by 977,127 M. per annum during the years 1874 to 1896, municipal expenditure increased by an average of 10.9 million M. per annum in the period 1896 to 1912. The increase was strongest during the years 1896 to 1900 and 1904 to 1909, when municipal spending increased by an annual average of 15,032,989 M. and 12,550,014 M., respectively.

---

[85] Originally in 1897, it also included *Nebenkassen und Fonds der Nebenverwaltung*, but soon this was accounted for as supplementary budget expenditure. Compare *MAB*, 1897/8, pp. 110–11 to *MAB*, 1899, pp. 106–9.

[86] The other, albeit relatively insignificant, item of expenditure consisted of transactions to private welfare foundations.

TABLE 6.9. *Public expenditure in Frankfurt am Main, 1899–1912* (in Marks)

| | General budget expenditure | Supplementary budget expenditure | | Other financial transactions | Total municipal budget expenditure |
		(a) Municipal services	(b) Supplementary funds		
1899	37,964,204	27,574,874	68,187,675	53,396,830	187,123,583
1903	42,286,448	44,236,384	94,539,496	93,384,395	274,446,723
1905	58,468,089	58,696,994	105,363,593	117,691,809	340,220,485
1908	72,885,562	74,973,328	148,109,544	188,248,256	484,216,690
1911	84,590,046	111,331,917	124,104,973	230,441,383	550,468,319
1912	83,999,170	113,990,229	91,583,003	252,454,354	542,026,756

Note: The figures are for the financial year, from 1 April to 31 March of the following year.

Source: *MAB*, 1899, pp. 106–7. *MAB*, 1903, p. 177. *MAB*, 1905, p. 163. *MAB*, 1908, p. 73. *MAB*, 1911, p. 74. *MAB*, 1912, p. 78.

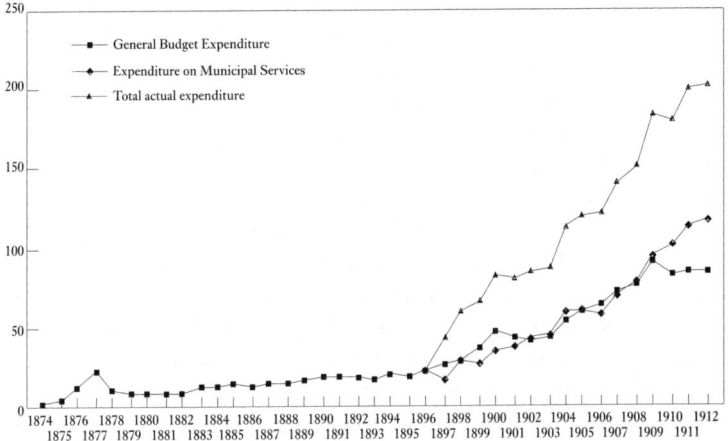

FIG. 6.2. Actual public expenditure in Frankfurt am Main, 1874–1912 (in million Marks)
MAB, 1874–1912. For the data summarized in this graph, see Tables A and B in Appendix I.

This brief survey of Frankfurt municipal expenditure speaks for itself in at least one respect, that municipal finance grew extremely complex from the 1890s onwards. It is also obvious that municipal expenditure, regardless of its type, rose to extraordinarily high levels from the 1890s and particularly during the 1900s until about 1909. From 1910 to 1912 the growth slowed down considerably, although it is not possible to say whether municipal expenditure would not have picked up again but for the war.

What is most surprising in a study of minutes of council debates or political rallies is the lack of political debate whenever the issue of spending was discussed. It would appear to be reasonable to expect the various liberal parties to fight over each item of expenditure: after all, municipal spending was the most effective way of realizing the parties' various political goals, such as education reform or social justice. Also, governments which hand out money are usually more popular than governments which are seen to take money away, so that it would seem likely that the parties tried to seize in the best possible way the opportunity of appearing to be the responsible driving force behind particular items of municipal expenditure. Naturally, there were certain basic political decisions to be made, such as the construction of a drainage and sewage system or the priority that should be given to the building of schools. Yet once these parameters on spending had been set, for most of the period no party had a comprehensive political agenda for municipal spending. It would be impossible to consider Table 6.8, for example, in a party-political light, as for the most part liberal politics was not responsible for the composition and the amount of municipal spending.

One important reason why these issues remained largely outside the political debate is that with regard to spending, the *Magistrat* was in a much stronger position than the city council. For even though every item of expenditure had to be sanctioned by the council, it was only the members of the *Magistrat*, who were charged with the day-to-day running of the administration, who were really in the know about the necessary expenditure for each item. It was in control of daily expenditure and had to consult the city council only when actual spending diverged significantly from planned expenditure. It was up to the *Magistrat*, in consultation with the council, to determine fees and prices for municipal services, and to determine conditions of pay and employment with the growing number of municipal employees.[87] Most councillors, by contrast, were rather ill-qualified to judge the necessity of measures such as individual street improvements and so on. In Frankfurt, the city of finance and trade, this problem was certainly less pronounced than elsewhere, as members of the social élite continued to be recruited into the council until 1914 and beyond.[88] Nonetheless, the council's finance commission, which had the task of scrutinizing the *Magistrat*'s suggestions for each budget, frequently complained at not having enough information, or that the budget became too complicated for any amateur to follow.[89]

The other reason why politics seemed to play such a minor role when it came to municipal expenditure lies in the nature of the expenditure itself. In the area of administration, municipal expenditure only aroused the interest of the electorate in particular circumstances, for example when a local official had embezzled funds or when a local councillor was awarded municipal contracts.[90] Yet apart from these instances, it appears that during the election campaigns the liberals were not often required to defend

---

[87] H. Luppe, 'Der städtische Haushaltsplan 1912/13', in *Frankfurter Zeitung*, Jan. 1912. The article is in BAK, NL 44 n. 19 fo. 1.

[88] This is in marked contrast to other cities. See e.g. Croon, 'Die Stadtvertretungen in Krefeld und Bochum', 304. Croon, 'Das Vordringen der politischen Parteien', 38. Reulecke, *Geschichte der Urbanisierung*, 135–6.

[89] See the urgings of the finance commission for more transparency in the budget reports drawn up by the *Magistrat*, e.g. *MPS*, 1877, §189, p. 158. *MPS*, 1894, §166, pp. 95–6, *MPS*, 1900, §282, p. 136, §1273, p. 556. In 1902, the budget proposals had a volume of no less than 848 pages. *MPS*, 1903, §282, p. 129. This was a general problem faced to a greater or lesser extent by all cities. Luppe, 'Der städtische Haushaltsplan 1912/13', BAK, NL 44 n. 19 fo. 1.

[90] These issues have been discussed above in Ch. 3.

themselves against *Mittelstand* attacks on the issue of general municipal expenditure on administration.

Given the importance of the issue of education to Frankfurt liberals, it is not really surprising that there was plenty of controversy about expenditure on schools, and particularly about teachers' pay. Indeed, of all municipal employees, the teachers were the most numerous, the best-organized, and the most vociferous group. They took an active part in the initial diversification of municipal politics in 1882, as they formed a teachers' committee to oversee the election of their 'teacher's candidate'. The nominee, Harnischfeger, was convinced that even if his candidature was not successful this time, his nomination would mean that at least in the future the municipal council would have to take note of the teachers' plight.[91] Even though on this occasion Harnischfeger was endorsed also by the National Liberals, it was usually the Democrats and the Progressives who competed for the support of municipal teachers, and especially of primary school teachers.[92] Addressing themselves as the true champions of the teachers' interests, they targeted this profession in ways in which they addressed no other occupational group, and in contradistinction to their usual rhetoric about representing the interests of the community of Frankfurt citizens as a whole.[93] At the same time, these debates reveal more about the way in which liberals conducted politics and their realism in appreciating the potential benefits of the allegiance of such a large pool of voters, than about the liberals' financial considerations, even though these were sometimes invoked as an argument.

The brunt of expenditure on public welfare was spent on necessities such as poor relief and the municipal hospital. More interesting items from a

---

[91] *Frankfurter Zeitung*, 21 Nov. 1882 (Morgenblatt).

[92] Unfortunately, the Democrats did not state occupation in their membership lists so that it is difficult to compare the proportion of teachers in liberal party membership. Progressive and National Liberal parties had a similar proportion of teachers among their members (7–8%), the crucial difference being that a majority of National Liberal teachers were better-paid teachers such as *Oberlehrer*, secondary school teachers and headmasters, whereas with one exception Progressive Liberal teachers universally came from the lower ranks of the profession. The membership lists for 1893 are in HStAW 407 n. 160 fos. 415–25 (National Liberal Association) and HStAW 407 n. 150^1 fos. 466–77 (Progressive Liberal Association).

[93] It appears that the Progressive Liberals were more successful than the Democrats at courting the teachers' vote. The inadequacy of municipal teachers' pay was a frequent topic in the meetings of the Progressive Liberal Association, and there are indications that their meetings were disproportionally well attended by teachers. HStAW 407 n. 150^2 fos. 3 (Progressive Association meeting, 9 Jan. 1895), 37–8 (Progressive Association meeting, 15 Nov. 1895), 99 (Progressive Association meeting, 22 Nov. 1895), 222 (Progressive Association meeting, 3 Feb. 1902). For an example of the Democrats trying to outdo the Progressives in their fight for the teachers' vote, see the letter to the editor in *Kleine Presse*, 19 Nov. 1892.

political point of view such as the *Gewerbegericht* (an industrial tribunal for the arbitration of trades disputes) and the *Arbeitsnachweisstelle* (labour exchange) made up only a tiny fraction of overall spending on welfare.[94] And in their hostility towards parish pump politics, most liberals found it hard to consider the issue of street pavements or street clearances in a political light. Of course, there were individual contentious issues to be dealt with, such as the building of a bridge over the Main which turned into a battle of principle between *Magistrat* and city council,[95] but these were not principled political debates over the amount of spending to be devoted to each project as such.

The one item of expenditure which was subject to considerable political controversy was municipal services. Throughout, liberals across party lines agreed that municipal services were justified if they were beneficial to the local economy. This was notably the case with the decision to go ahead with the establishment of the local drainage system in 1867, but this argument was also the main driving force behind all other larger municipal projects, such as the building of a disastrously expensive theatre, or the lavish rebuilding of the burnt-out cathedral.[96] These decisions were by no means uncontentious and sparked off considerable grass-roots opposition, usually among left liberals. Yet ultimately, the Democratic leadership, and particularly the Democratic councillors, were in favour of these projects, and it was they, after all, who were in control of Democratic municipal policy.[97]

Much more contentious was expenditure on municipal enterprises, that is the municipalization of businesses with the express primary motive of making profits for the city treasury. Of these businesses, the municipal provision of water was obviously the least contentious, because it was quite obviously a sanitary measure.[98] By contrast, Frankfurt was one of the few German cities where the provision of gas was still in private hands by 1914,[99] even though the Democrats wanted to municipalize gas throughout the Empire. If this was not achieved, it was certainly not because of

---

[94] In 1896, for example, both cost the city about 25,500 M., which was just over 1% of the city's total welfare expenditure that year. *MAB*, 1896/97, p. 51.

[95] Maly, *Macht*, 85–7.   [96] *MPS*, 1867/68, §331, pp. 293–302. *MPS*, 1869, §486, p. 550.

[97] See e.g. HStAW 407 n. 138¹ fos. 44–6. Democratic Association meeting, 10 Mar. 1879. HStAW 407 n. 138¹ fos. 48–51. Democratic Association meeting, 17 Mar. 1879.

[98] It is interesting to note that in marked contrast to England, German cities never saw anything wrong in making profits from the sale of water. Even though they saw it as a basic utility, lower costs did not lead to reductions in the price of water, but rather to increased profits. Mombert, 'Gemeindebetriebe', 24–31.

[99] By 1914, of cities over 100,000 population, 80.5% possessed municipal gasworks. Krabbe, *Die deutsche Stadt*, 121.

Democratic half-heartedness or lack of effort. To convince the *Magistrat* to municipalize gas in 1869, the Democrats even started a campaign for potential customers to sign up for their custom of municipal gas in advance, in order to prove to the *Magistrat* that municipalization carried minimal financial risk.[100] Yet at that time the idea seemed too novel and risky to the *Magistrat* which, after all, had just commissioned the building of the extensive drainage system two years earlier, whereas in 1883, when the issue was again under debate, the plans did not agree with Miquel's ideas of strict financial discipline.[101] It is only in the 1890s that the attitude of the *Magistrat* changed as more and more other enterprises were municipalized. But by then, it was too late. The city did build a municipal gasworks for some of its newly incorporated suburbs after 1900, but the fact that the Frankfurt Gas Company's concession to supply gas did not run out until 1959 meant that any municipalization would involve an extortionate mark-up for the company's shareholders. Along with other cities in similar situations,[102] the city decided that this would be an irresponsible squandering of public funds and concentrated instead on the improvement of the existing contract.[103]

During the 1890s, the city's Democrats, and an increasing number of Progressive Liberals, started to make their case for the municipalization of enterprises more successfully. The issue that brought about a change was the municipalization of electricity in Frankfurt. The fact that electricity was municipalized so successfully was due overwhelmingly to the Herculean efforts of Leopold Sonnemann, who led private campaigns to promote the issue from the late 1880s and who, when he saw that he was getting nowhere, organized an international electricity fair which took place in 1891. The purpose of this exhibition was to establish, once and for all, which form of electrical transmission was preferable, direct or

[100] On the Democratic campaign, see *Frankfurter Journal*, 14 Jan. 1870, 19 Jan. 1870, 25 Jan. 1870, 27 Feb. 1870, 17 Apr. 1870.

[101] On the intermittent tug-of-war between the Democrats and the *Magistrat* over the issue, see Wolf, *Liberalismus*, 37–8. Maly, *Macht*, 47–8, 194–5. Even though as mayor of Osnabrück Miquel had actively promoted municipal ownership of enterprises, the *Gründerkrach* had sharpened Miquel's awareness of the financial risks involved in municipalization. Lembke, *Johannes von Miquel*, 47.

[102] Swimming against the tide with regard to municipalizations, another pioneer in social reform, Strasbourg, took pride in the fact that, in a similar situation, it had avoided the waste of public funds on buying the local electricity works and achieved terms of contract with the private operator which had made this arrangement preferable to municipalization. Dr Leoni, 'Die Verbindung von Städten und Privatkapital für wirtschaftliche Unternehmungen', in *Verhandlungen des Vierten Deutschen Städtetages (1914)*, 46–56. See also H. Croon, 'Aufgaben deutscher Städte im ersten Drittel des 20. Jahrhunderts', in W. Rausch (ed.), *Die Städte Mitteleuropas im 20. Jahrhundert* (Linz, 1984), 47.

[103] *MAB*, 1909, pp. xix–xx.

alternating current. It was at this fair that the superiority of the alternating current was finally established, which solved the problem not only for the Frankfurt city government, but for municipal authorities around the world.[104] Despite all these efforts, Sonnemann was only able to convince the *Magistrat* and some doubtful councillors by conceding that initially the plant would be operated through a private firm, the Swiss BBC. The plant started operation on 1 January 1895, and was only brought under full municipal control on 1 April 1899.[105]

The next municipal acquisition came in the late 1890s, when there was general agreement to municipalize the local tramway system. Having refused to municipalize the system in 1890, the change of ownership followed directly from the municipal production of electricity, which could now be used to switch to an electrified tramway system. Compared to earlier battles, this municipalization was relatively uncontentious, because it fitted directly with Adickes's land policies and his ideas about how the pressure on inner-city housing might be relieved. Even so, in principle Adickes believed that ultimately private corporations were more efficient and responsive to market needs than municipalized companies, which explains why private gasworks continued to exist in the city during his mayorality. Therefore, even though in the city council the general support of Democrats, Social Democrats, and most Progressive Liberals for municipal enterprises became overwhelming, there was an element of ambiguity in the liberal city government's approach to the issue.

It has been noted in Chapter 2 that municipalization was an integral part of the Democrat programme. To achieve their goal, they fought with determination and ingenuity. Yet despite this, the *Magistrat* had the upper hand most of the time in that the left liberals never managed to insist on municipalization against the intentions of the *Magistrat*. This confirms the latter's strong position with regard to expenditure. Through its technical know-how and its knowledge of financial details it was in a uniquely strong position which it could use very effectively as soon as there were disagreements with the city council. Hence, even in the few areas of expenditure where party political concerns did exist, it was extremely difficult for city councillors to realize their own political agenda.

[104] On the history of the establishment of an electrical power station, see *MPS*, 1892, §656, pp. 291–308. See also *'Eine neue Zeit . . .!'*, esp. 11–12, 18–20. See also Hermann Schaefer, '"New Industries" and the Role of the State: The Development of Electrical Power in South Germany from *c*.1880 to the 1920s', in W. R. Lee (ed.), *German Industry and German Industrialisation. Essays in German Economic and Business History in the Nineteenth and Twentieth Centuries* (London, 1991), 200–19, esp. 203.

[105] *Geschichte der Frankfurter Zeitung*, 760. Maly, *Macht*, 287–90.

Municipal expenditure moved into the political debate only gradually, especially after 1900. One reason for this was the appearance of the SPD in the council, which did not leave many items of spending unchallenged, even though it usually did not get very far. Added to this was the rapidly increasing number of municipal employees, so that the battles about municipal spending on pay became much more intense. After all, previously the battles for the sympathy of municipal employees had been confined to the teachers. With the emergence of other municipal employees in the municipal services, the issue of working conditions for municipal employees became more important and complex. And after 1900 the SPD brought the issue of municipal employees constantly to the attention of the council, thus emphasizing, to the chagrin of the liberals, the SPD's claim to represent the municipal workers.

Yet despite this relatively late surge in the political debate about municipal expenditure, by and large the city council accepted the yearly increases in budget spending as inevitable, and there was enough evidence to show it that this was true. In a speech to the *Bezirksverein Ostend*, the Progressive Liberal Geiger pointed out that every increase in the population by 10,000 automatically led to an increase in municipal spending by one million marks per year (through the provision of extra schooling, etc.) without a corresponding increase in income tax revenue.[106] And it is true that each year the highest increases in ordinary budget expenditure went on schools, followed by items such as road building and debt-servicing.[107] Therefore, with the exception of municipalization of enterprises liberals in Frankfurt never had a clear political agenda on municipal expenditure, which was both the result and the cause of the *Magistrat*'s strong position in determining the size and the composition of municipal expenditure. Although liberal political awareness about spending on social matters

---

[106] *Frankfurter Zeitung*, 22 Nov. 1904 (3. Morgenblatt). In 1906, to justify the tax increases Ernst Ladenburg pointed out in an election rally that in the five years before 1904, the population had increased by 16%, whereas taxes had risen only by 5%. The figures are incorrect, but nevertheless in the period 1900 to 1904, population increased by 11% while taxation increased by just over 5%. During the same period, expenditure increased by 12%. *Frankfurter Zeitung*, 16 Nov. 1906 (Drittes Morgenblatt).

[107] In 1900, for example, the highest increase in expenditure in the ordinary budget was on schools (434,000 M.), followed by road building (136,000 M.) and debt servicing (102,700 M.). *MPS*, 1900, §1273, pp. 556–7. In 1905, expenditure on schools witnessed the highest increase again (180,000 M.), while road building and street improvements necessitated an increase of 111,000 M. *MPS*, 1905, §29, p. 13. There has always been an assumed correlation between population growth and municipal expenditure. Moreover, Jürgen Bolenz has demonstrated just how close the correlation was between average income of the population and municipal expenditure. Bolenz, 'Wachstum', 215–25.

changed somewhat after 1900, liberals in Frankfurt had few political qualms about the extraordinarily rapid growth of municipal expenditure from the 1890s, or the overall composition of that expenditure. Rather, it was accepted as an inevitable corollary of good municipal government.

6.4. Municipal Debt

The developments in municipal expenditure outlined above raise the question of how the increases in municipal spending were financed. A large part of municipal spending was, of course, matched by corresponding income, such as fees for the drainage and sewage systems, income from municipal property, and so on. To fund the difference between income and expenditure, there were two sources of finance, debt and taxation. Figure 6.3 charts the development of the municipal debt from 1873, when all debts were remnants of pre-Prussian times, to 1913. In Figure 6.4, the increasing value of municipal assets has also been added from when they became published, and the difference between assets and debts results in the figures for net municipal wealth.

Even a brief glance at the increase in municipal debt reveals that the increase in municipal spending described above was accompanied by an increase in municipal debt which was no less dramatic. Municipal debt increased by almost 50 million M. in the two decades from 1873 to 1894,

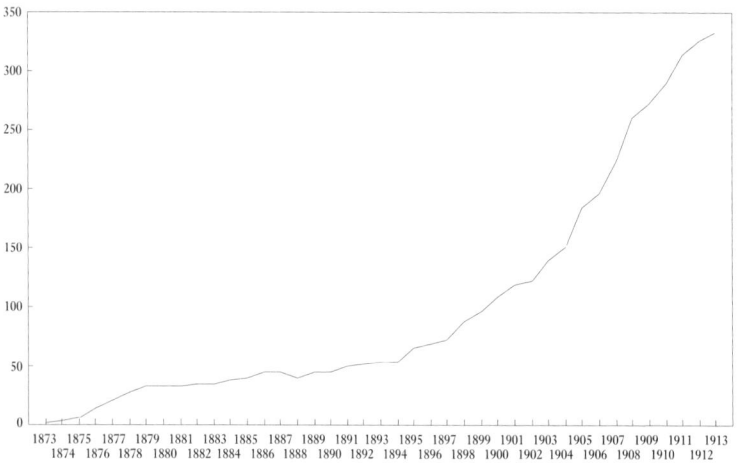

FIG. 6.3. Municipal debt in Frankfurt, 1873–1913 (in million Marks)
MAB, 1874–1914. For the data summarized in this graph, see Table C in Appendix I.

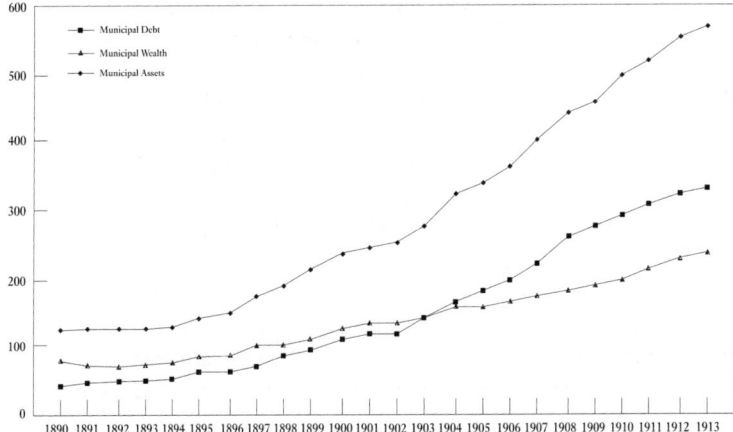

FIG. 6.4. Municipal wealth in Frankfurt am Main, 1890–1913 (in million Marks) *MAB*, 1890–1914. For the data summarized in this graph, see Table C in Appendix I.

and by roughly the same amount in the following six years until 1900. The truly dramatic increase, however, came between 1902 and 1911, when municipal debt rose by 190,274,545 M., or by an average of over 21 million M. per year. Whereas between 1872 and 1913 Prussian per capita public debt increased by about 450 per cent, the per capita increase in Frankfurt municipal debt from 1873 to 1913 was nearer to 3,500 per cent.[108] By 1910 Frankfurt liberals pointed out with considerable municipal pride that there were only eight German states whose debts were higher than those of the city of Frankfurt.[109]

Compared to other German cities, Frankfurt's municipal debt, and its growth, was high, but not extraordinarily so.[110] It is precisely this increase in municipal debt in the years after 1895, and particularly from about 1900 onwards, which was so alarming to contemporary observers of Frankfurt municipal finance and of Prussian cities in general. However, as Frankfurt liberal policy-makers were quick to point out, debt could not be seen in

---

[108] For Prussian public debt, see Schremmer, 'Taxation and Public Finance', 454.
[109] See Ludwig Heilbronn's speech in *Frankfurter Zeitung*, 10 Nov. 1910 (3. Morgenblatt).
[110] By 1907, the size of Frankfurt's debts and their growth since 1897 was fourth to those of Berlin, Munich, and Cologne. O. Most, *Gemeindefinanzen*, ii, part 2. *Die Gemeindefinanzstatistik in Deutschland. Ziele, Wege, Ergebnisse*, Schriften des Vereins für Sozialpolitik, cxxvii (Leipzig, 1910), 207. Note that Most's figures for Frankfurt are different from the ones given in this chapter, but the scale and the rate of growth are similar.

isolation from municipal assets, for which the debt had been incurred in the first place. As Figure 6.4 illustrates, despite the phenomenal increase in debt, municipal wealth unburdened by debt increased steadily because of the increase in assets as well as debts. Unfortunately, not all municipal assets were disposable, for the figure, though correct in a statistical sense, included, for example, schools and other public buildings. Frankfurt liberals must also have been concerned by the fact that debts grew faster than municipal assets, so that from 1904 onwards the value of Frankfurt's municipal debts was higher than that of its net municipal assets.[111]

The amount of municipal debt was hardly ever an election issue in Frankfurt because liberals of all parties agreed in their assessment of the significance of this debt. Their attitude was brilliantly summarized by the Frankfurt *Stadtrat* Wilhelm Woell in a speech on the role of credit in municipal budgets, delivered to the second German municipal conference in Munich in 1908.[112]

Woell distinguished between debts for three types of expenditure. Debts incurred for municipal enterprises which would provide the servicing of the debt out of their own income were unproblematic: indeed they were a sign of progressive local government. Debts incurred for other assets such as drainage, sewage, and other provisions which would provide for their servicing through fees fell into the same category of economic advancement. Hence it was only debts incurred for regular, ordinary expenditure which were dependent on the tax base of each municipality. Here, Woell recommended the hoarding of investment funds for large, regular expenditures such as the building of schools, roads, etc., to avoid having to make large interest payments. Debts should only be incurred for those expenditures which could not wait and which did not recur periodically. Woell concluded that, based on the meagre data that was available at the time, in German cities, about 75 per cent of all debts that were incurred fell into the first two categories. Of the 25.25 per cent that was spent for unproductive purposes, 23.25 per cent was spent on administrative duties and school-building, items that were generally regarded as *Staatsaufgaben*, duties

---

[111] In Frankfurt, there was thus no correlation between the élite's desire for a lower tax burden, and municipal socialism, since the latter proved so costly, and profitable only over generations. R. H. Tilly, 'Städtewachstum, Kommunalfinanzen und Munizipalsozialismus in der deutschen Industrialisierung: eine vergleichende Perspektive 1870–1913', in J. Reulecke (ed.), *Die Stadt als Dienstleistungszentrum. Beiträge zur Geschichte der 'Sozialstadt' in Deutschland im 19. und frühen 20. Jahrhundert* (St Katharinen, 1995), 125–52.

[112] W. Woell, 'Der Kreditbedarf im Haushalt der Städte', in *Verhandlungen des Zweiten Deutschen Städtetages am 6. und 7. Juli 1908 zu München* (Berlin, 1908), 8–14.

which local government undertook in lieu of the state. Hence, only 2 per cent was spent on such luxuries as fire services, welfare, and cultural services. Woell concluded that 'The increasing use of municipal credit is therefore nothing reprehensible. Rather, it is an indispensable, significant means of municipal progress.'[113]

Woell's optimistic assessment was shared by Frankfurt liberals throughout most of the period under investigation. If anything, what is striking is the absence of any controversy in the municipal council when new debts were incurred.[114] And even at a time when the *Magistrat* tried to keep debts in check during the 1880s, there were many who doubted the wisdom of this, arguing that this led to a disproportionate burden on the present generation for benefits which would accrue to present and future generations. There was, after all, no need to panic about the municipal debt because of the enormous value of the assets which counterbalanced it.[115] Also, in Frankfurt, most of the municipal debt was serviced not by the taxpayer but by the municipal enterprises which had incurred these debts in the first place. Throughout the years of spiralling debt, municipal assets serviced around 70 per cent of the municipal debt.[116]

This Frankfurt view of municipal debts as expressed by Woell is quite representative of other cities. At the 1908 municipal convention, the motions which summarized his ideas were carried without much criticism from the representatives of other cities. At the following municipal congress in 1911, the Lord Mayor of Dessau, Ebeling, spoke again about the question of municipal debt in the light of the availability of further data. He confirmed that in Prussian cities of over 25,000 inhabitants, over half of all debts were raised for municipal enterprises. Also, municipal wealth had increased faster than municipal debt, and furthermore in recent years there had been a significant accumulation of assets through the establishment of municipal funds. Finally, it was pointed out that German municipal taxation per head was in line with that of other countries (as far as this could be compared given the differences in administrative structures between

---

[113] 'Die zunehmende städtische Kreditbenutzung ist danach nichts Tadelnswertes; sie stellt sich vielmehr als ein unentbehrliches bedeutsames Mittel des kommunalen Fortschritts dar.' Ibid. 14.

[114] For 1875, when the first major debt was incurred, see the small note in *Frankfurter Beobachter*, 10 Nov. 1875. See also the council minutes when debts of 27 million M. each were approved, *MPS*, 1900, §1096, pp. 484–5. *MPS*, 1900, §1223, pp. 538–40. *MPS*, 1903, §341, pp. 205–7.

[115] See e.g. the discussion in the Democratic Association on the municipal budget of 1883 in HStAW 470 n. 138² fos. 150–3. Democratic Association meeting, 12 Mar. 1883.

[116] See e.g. the tables in *MAB*, 1905, p. 38, and *MAB*, 1908, p. 76.

them), and that overall taxation was still much lower in Germany than in either England or France.[117] Ebeling confirmed Woell's assessment that the growth of municipal debt as such was justified, and that it was nothing wrong. What did cause controversy at these municipal conventions was rather the problem that the growth of municipal debt entailed, namely the increasing difficulty of obtaining cheap credit. For the growth of imperial and state debts of similar magnitudes led to a scarcity of capital, and it was this lack of cheap credit, rather than the need or desire of municipalities to finance many of their activities through debts, which was of such concern to liberals in the cities.[118]

Liberals wholeheartedly supported the growth of municipal expenditure and the corresponding increase in municipal debt. In their assessment of their own cities' financial situation liberals in Frankfurt, as well as in many other cities represented at the *Städtetag*, saw the growth in municipal financial activity as nothing extraordinary. In this, they were quite aware that they were not always in agreement with contemporary observers. Woell noted, for example, that the view put forward by Frankfurt liberals and agreed to by the *Städtetag* about the desirability of funds differed from many academic treatments including Richard von Kaufmann's and Walter Klose's studies of municipal finance. For while the latter maintained that the accumulation of funds imposed financial obligations on the present generation for the benefit of future generations, Woell and others maintained that the laws of *Leistung und Gegenleistung*, of return on investment,

[117] Ebeling, 'Bericht des Vorstandes über die Prüfung der Kreditverhältnisse der Deutschen Städte (auf Beschluß der Hauptversammlung in München 1908)', in *Verhandlungen des Dritten Deutschen Städtetages (1911)*, 7–15, esp. 8–10. According to Ebeling, total German debt in 1907 accounted for 407 M. per head, of which 66 M. was incurred by the Empire, 220 M. by the various states, and 121 M. by local government. (The low figure for local government is due to the inclusion not just of municipal government, but also of local government in the countryside in this average figure.) By contrast, in France total public debt was at 718 M. per head, and in England 557 M. Ibid. 8.

[118] In 1914, of 29 billion M. of public debts, 7.5 billion M. were incurred by the municipalities, 16.3 billion M. by the individual states, and 5 billion M. by the Empire. Reulecke, *Geschichte der Urbanisierung*, 111. Inevitably, this shortage of capital led to an increase in the cost of borrowing. The problem was compounded by the fact that municipal bonds (*Obligationen*), through which some 80% of debt was raised, had to be sold at a higher price than state or imperial bonds, since the latter were considered to be a more secure investment by the market. Mitzlaff, 'Die Formen und Wege zur Befriedigung des Kreditbedarfs der Städte', in *Verhandlungen des Zweiten Deutschen Städtetages (1908)*, 14–23, esp. 18–19. For details of municipal debts (including the source, interest rate, and rate of debt servicing), see Most, 'Gemeindefinanzstatistik', 208–12. For a summary of the ways in which debts could be incurred, see J. Wysocki, 'Kommunale Investitionen und ihre Finanzierung in Deutschland 1850 bis 1914', in W. Rausch (ed.), *Die Städte Mitteleuropas im 19. Jahrhundert* (Linz, 1983), 174–9.

did not apply. It was a citizen's duty to provide all he could for the common welfare of his community.[119]

On the whole, liberals in the cities were quite right in congratulating themselves on good financial management, as they increased their net wealth which enabled them not only to provide for the duties imposed upon them as a tier of the German administrative structure, for example the provision of schooling, but also to become more independent and self-conscious centres of local self-government. This link between financial expansion and self-government was only too clear to the representatives of the *Städtetag*. Echoing Woell's remarks, the Mayor of Munich, Borscht, pointed out in his opening speech to the congress in 1908 that the size of the current municipal debt of a total of 4 bn. M. was nothing negative:

> but is a clear sign of ascending development, not a proof of financial mismanagement, but, on the contrary, an expression of rare willingness to make sacrifices. At a time when there are calls for relief almost everywhere and individual states have no scruples about claiming the compliance of the cities to fulfil their own obligations, it seems appropriate to highlight that it is precisely the German cities that have been unanimous in never trying to reduce their own obligations.[120]

To liberals in the cities, therefore, the expansion of municipal financial activity was the essence of self-government, and in this they agreed with liberal theory. Indeed, this explains why, in the case of Frankfurt as in the case of the debates in the municipal conferences, there was so little difference in opinion between left-liberal and right-liberal, or even civic leaders of other parties, on the growth of municipal expenditure. For liberals and other municipal leaders at the grass roots shared the academic consensus on the value of local government, to which ideas about municipal finance were inextricably linked, in high-political debates as well as in the cities themselves. This could not have been put more succinctly by the Mayor of Munich in his speech to the 1911 municipal congress, in which he justified the enormous municipal debt:

> If one recalls that it is precisely due to the generosity and far-sightedness of the German bourgeoisie that the most valuable cultural assets of the German people

---

[119] Woell, 'Kreditbedarf', 11–12.

[120] 'sondern ein sicheres Kennzeichen emporsteigender Entwicklung, nicht ein Beweis finanzieller Mißwirtschaft, sondern im Gegenteil der Ausdruck seltener Opferfreudigkeit ist. In einer Zeit, in der fast überall der Ruf nach Entlastung ertönt und einzelne Staaten kein Bedenken tragen, für die Erfüllung ihrer eigenen Obliegenheiten die Mitwirkung der Städte in Anspruch zu nehmen, erscheint es wohl veranlaßt, hervorzuheben, daß gerade die deutschen Städte ohne Unterschied das Maß ihrer Verpflichtungen niemals einzuschränken versuchten.' *Verhandlungen des Zweiten Deutschen Städtetages (1908)*, 7.

have benefited from such tremendous promotion and enrichment, then one also realizes the justification of the desire of these municipal corporations to be appreciated and treated by the state authorities as they deserve to be, as powerful and selfless bearers of the public, social welfare system, as pillars of the state.[121]

6.5. Municipal Taxation

If Frankfurt liberals were in broad agreement about financial policy with regard to municipal expenditure and municipal debt, this was not the case with regard to taxation. On 16 November 1884, Leopold Sonnemann delivered a speech to the Frankfurt Democratic Association to mark the fifteenth anniversary of its foundation in which he gave a critical assessment of the party's history and its future prospects. In his speech he considered it necessary to deal not only with high politics, but also with the party's involvement in local politics. For, according to Sonnemann (as recorded by the police inspector present at the meeting):

Whoever wants reform should start in his own backyard. The Democratic Association may look back on its activities over the past fifteen years with satisfaction. This is true namely for the local tax system, which is unlike that of any other city in Prussia or Germany. Just now Berlin is seeking to imitate our tax system. The speaker illustrates further the local system of taxation and comes to the conclusion that the entire burden of taxation rests only upon the shoulders of a small number of wealthy individuals.[122]

This quotation not only illustrates the close links that the Democrats perceived between local, state, and national politics. More importantly in this context, Sonnemann singled out the establishment of Frankfurt's system of local taxation as the most important Democratic achievement in local politics. The crucial significance of the issue of taxation for the self-understanding of Frankfurt's left liberals has already been noted in

[121] 'Vergegenwärtigt man sich, . . . welch eine ungeheure Förderung und Mehrung die höchsten kulturellen Güter des deutschen Volkes gerade durch die Opferwilligkeit und den Weitblick des deutschen Bürgertums erfahren haben, . . . dann begreift man aber auch, wie wohlberechtigt der Wunsch dieser städtischen Gemeinwesen ist, von der Staatsgewalt so gewürdigt und behandelt zu werden, wie sie es als mächtige und uneigennützige Träger der öffentlichen Wohlfahrtspflege, als Grundpfeiler staatlicher Ordnung verdienen.' *Verhandlungen des Zweiten Deutschen Städtetages (1908)*, 7.
[122] 'Wer reformieren wolle, müsse zunächst in seinem eigenen Hause beginnen. Der democratische Verein dürfe mit Befriedigung auf seine 15 jährige Wirksamkeit zurückblicken. Es sei dies namentlich in Bezug auf das Steuerwesen der Fall, welches hier wie in keiner anderen preußischen oder deutschen Stadt geregelt sei. Grade jetzt werde von Berlin gesucht, unsere Steuereinrichtungen nachzuahmen. Redner erläutert näher das hiesige Steuersystem und kommt zu dem Schluß, daß die ganze Steuerlast nur auf einer kleinen Zahl von Schultern der Reichen ruhe.' HStAW 407 n. 138³ fo. 80. Democratic Association meeting, 16 Sept. 1884.

Chapter 2, when it was shown that just after the annexation, hostility to the imposed indirect tax on meat and flour (*Schlacht- und Mahlsteuer*) served as one of the first rallying cries of a forming left-liberal opposition. This was all the more effective since opposition to this Prussian tax served as a reminder that the tax burden had doubled as a result of the annexation.[123] Taxation was an issue over which Democrats had come to define themselves, but it was also regarded as one of their biggest vote-winners.[124]

On the whole, there were two basic tenets to the Democrats' views on taxation. The first was that taxation should be according to the principle of ability to pay, so that those with lower incomes should pay less. The second was that local taxation was the enabler of effective local self-government, hence local fiscal autonomy should be guarded as much as possible. Interestingly, of these two principles, the former appears to have been considered more important than the latter. In their attempt to have the tax on meat and flour abolished, the democratic veterans of 1848, Hadermann and Wolschendorff, noted that one of the evils of the tax was that it had been simply imposed upon the city by the Prussian state, without any prior consultation. But the emphasis in this question had to lie in a just distribution of the tax burden and in the subsequent relief of the poorer classes of the population. Given this priority it even had to be accepted that the Prussian state would benefit from the proposed substitution of the purely local tax by the Prussian class tax.[125]

Hadermann and Wolschendorff failed to bring about the abolition of the hated meat and flour tax in 1868, and the Frankfurt Democrats, who were still in the minority in the city council, had to wait for the abolition of the tax by the Prussian state in 1873, due to take effect from 1 January 1875. In 1874 the city council's finance commission debated the adjustments that would have to be made in response to the abolition of the meat and flour tax. Whereas the majority published its report recommending further indirect taxes (such as a special local tax on meat), Sonnemann wrote a minority report of his own. In it he proposed the abolition of all indirect taxation and an increase in the local tax supplement on the class and income tax.

---

[123] Kropat, *Frankfurt*, 63–4.

[124] See also e.g. the Democratic petition against the threat of new taxes in the North German Confederation in *Frankfurter Zeitung*, 27 May 1869 (2. Blatt). In early 1879, a public petition to the Prussian Diet taking issue with current discussions about changes in the system of local taxation was used quite obviously as a publicity drive by the party to recruit new members. HStAW 407 n. 138¹ fos. 9–13. Democratic Association meeting, 28 Jan. 1879.

[125] *MPS*, 1867/68, §82, pp. 95–6. The secondary importance of the role of Prussia is all the more notable considering that these two Democrats were among the most vociferous opponents of Prussia, at a time when the *Rezeß* had not yet been settled.

Furthermore, this local tax supplement was to be reduced for people on middle and lower incomes.[126] This was one of Sonnemann's finest hours in local politics. With his report, he had caught his fellow councillors (though perhaps not his political friends) completely unawares, and after a heated discussion Sonnemann's motion was carried.[127] Henceforth, the conviction that all taxes including local income tax supplements ought to include a progressive element became generally accepted in Frankfurt municipal politics.

In consequence, in 1890, 31 per cent of income tax payers were in the lowest tax band, providing 7.59 per cent of taxable income. Yet they paid only 1.45 per cent of local income tax revenue. By contrast, 88 individuals (out of 60,300 income tax payers) in the highest tax band had 25.69 per cent of all taxable income, but they contributed 35.73 per cent to local income tax revenue.[128] These figures not only demonstrate the effect of Frankfurt's progressive legislation, but they also show that the Frankfurt progressive tax system was made possible through the extraordinary wealth of a small number of individuals. Indeed, Frankfurt defied ordinary tax logic that an increase in the tax on the poor yields more revenue than a tax on the rich. When in 1892 the city council discussed new local surcharges for the state income tax rates in response to Miquel's tax reform, in addition to the degression which was built into the state tax the *Magistrat* itself proposed a further degression of the local surcharge, from 100 per cent of the state income tax for all incomes above 9,000 M., down to a rate of 85 per cent for all incomes below 3,000 M. Against this proposal, the council's finance commission, of which Sonnemann was a member, suggested that the rate of degression should be reduced still further, from a surcharge of 100 per cent for incomes up to 10,500 M. down to a rate of 70 per cent for all incomes below 3,000 M. One of the most compelling arguments of the commission was that the further reductions were significant for those who benefited from them, whereas the extra revenue lost amounted to barely 4 per cent of that paid by the wealthy citizens with an income over 10,500 M. Partly as a result of this argument, the proposals of the finance commissions were accepted unanimously in the council.[129] The local tax rates were based on the state income tax and were levied in addition. The effect of the new Frankfurt local income tax rate was, therefore, to increase the progressive

---

[126] From a full local tax supplement of 100% for incomes over and including tax band 11 (mean income 13,200 M. p.a.), the supplement was progressively reduced to 23% for those with the lowest taxable incomes (mean income 540 M. p.a.). *Anzeige-Blatt der städtischen Behörden zu Frankfurt am Main*, 31 Dec. 1874.

[127] IfSG, AS P 854 (1874), §277, fos. 529–74. City Council meeting, 15 May 1874. AS P 855 (1874), §655. City Council meeting, 31 Oct. 1874. Maly, *Macht*, 94–5.

[128] *MPS*, 1890/91, p. 74.   [129] *MPS*, 1892, §206, pp. 96–9.

impact of total income taxation. Incomes in the lowest tax band from 900 to 1,050 M. had to pay 6 M. per annum in state income tax, and a local income tax supplement of 70 per cent (4.20 M.), which amounted to a total annual income tax of about 1 per cent, or 10.40 M.[130] By contrast, a person with an income of over 100,000 M., who was paying the highest state income tax rate at 4 per cent was, with a local income tax supplement of 100 per cent, subject to a total income tax burden of 8 per cent.

The relative ease with which progressive local taxation could be carried out in Frankfurt should not distract attention from the fact that Frankfurt's income tax was grounded upon firm political principles. Hence, despite rapidly rising expenditure in the 1890s and 1900s, income tax revenue rose slowly and naturally, and despite frequent suggestions to the contrary the local tax rate was never increased above 100 per cent of the state income tax rate after 1892.[131] Frankfurt left liberals appreciated that Miquel had only given permission for Frankfurt's peculiarly progressive tax system, despite personal misgivings, because of his personal connections with the city. At the time, he had made clear that any change of the tax rate would necessitate a review of the whole system, and Frankfurters were in no doubt that any increase above 100 per cent of the top rate of the local income tax supplement would lead to the abolition of the city's progressive tax system (and an infringement of municipal freedom).[132]

The fact that Frankfurt Democrats in particular could (justifiably) call themselves the party of progressive taxation is, in fact, a decisive factor in explaining their popularity in the Frankfurt municipal elections. For it must be remembered that whereas the abolition of indirect taxation in 1874 was a measure designed to benefit especially the working classes, progressive income taxation was not. Especially from 1883, when those with incomes below 900 M. were exempt from paying income tax, it was not really the poor who benefited from progressive income tax rates. In 1890, when old class taxes (*Klassensteuer*) were still levied on all incomes above 420 M. per year, almost 60 per cent of those taxpayers earned incomes

---

[130] *Anzeige-Blatt der städtischen Behörden zu Frankfurt am Main*, 3 May 1892, also *MAB*, 1892/93, pp. 63–4.

[131] In the 1904 municipal tax reform, each rate of the income tax was raised by 5%. This was possible, since previously the overall local income tax supplement (a top rate of 100% and progressive reductions to 70%) amounted to an aggregate supplement of 95% of the state income tax. A rise by 5% in 1904 brought the aggregate rate of the local income tax supplement up to 100% and meant that no further municipal tax increases were possible without state approval. See the tax reform proposals for 1904 in *MPS*, 1903, §1270, esp. pp. 609, 621, 629–30.

[132] *MPS*, 1895, §361, pp. 222–3. *MPS*, 1903, §1270, p. 612. *MPS*, 1904, §19, p. 17.

below 900 M. Only in subsequent decades (and especially from 1900 onwards) did an increasing number of workers earn more than 900 M. and hence benefit from the system of progressive local income tax supplements.

When the system was conceived in the early 1890s it was clearly the *Mittelstand*, that is small shopkeepers, artisans, and other groups with small incomes between 900 and 3,000 M., that benefited most, with a smaller benefit extending to the quite well-to-do with incomes up to 10,500 M. There is nothing coincidental about this, since a large majority of those with incomes above 900 M. had the vote.[133] The most tenacious opponent of the tax system, councillor Caspari, was right to object to the fact that, if the aim of progressive taxation was to relieve those on lower incomes, it was absurd to class those with earnings between 5,000 and 7,000 M. among them.[134] Yet Democrats were well aware of this. In a report on various forms of direct taxation, the minority of the council's finance commission (yet again including Sonnemann) argued successfully against the majority of the commission and the *Magistrat* that of all taxes, the progressive income tax was crucial to Frankfurt's well-being. For a trading city like Frankfurt, it was particularly important to cultivate a thriving *Mittelstand* which was the primary beneficiary of the changes.[135] This explains the stubbornness with which left liberals clung to the ideal of progressive income taxation, and why the SPD representative in the council, Max Quarck, was quite prepared to consider a revision of the local income tax if that meant that other direct taxes and charges levied on all citizens such as the hated tax on rents could be dropped.[136] For the Democrats and their left-liberal allies, therefore, progressive income taxation was an ingenious device which enabled them to carry out an effective *Mittelstandspolitik*, on the one hand, while enabling them to maintain a rhetoric of social justice for all.

Figure 6.5 illustrates the steady growth of income tax in Frankfurt and shows its importance relative to all other taxes. Frankfurt liberals on the left and on the right were generally ambiguous about the second pillar of the tax system until 1895, the rent tax. On the one hand, liberals such as Sonnemann never tired of pointing out that it was, at least, a highly pro-

---

[133] *MAB*, 1893/94, pp. 78–9. *MAB*, 1890/91, p. 74. Note that the figure given in both accounts for the same tax year 1890/91 differs slightly.

[134] *MPS*, 1904, §85, p. 44.

[135] *MPS*, 1894, §177, pp. 109–10. See also A. Meyer's speech on the budget to the Democratic Association, in *Frankfurter Zeitung*, 8 Mar. 1894 (2. Morgenblatt). The article is also in HStAW 407 n. 161¹ fo. 266.

[136] *MPS*, 1903, §282, p. 156.

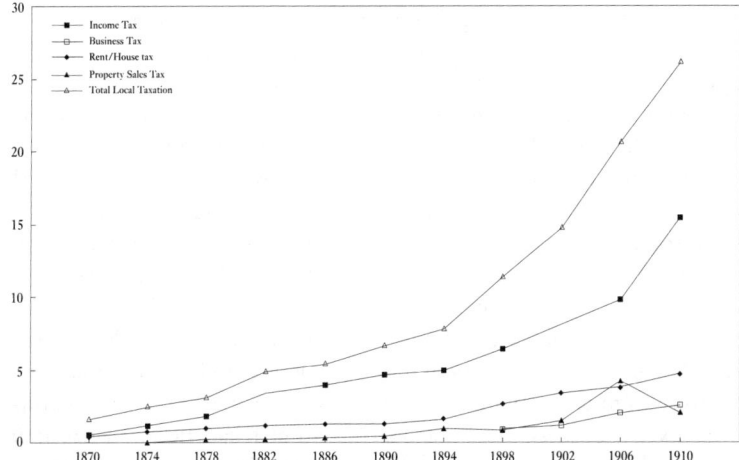

FIG. 6.5. Local taxation in Frankfurt am Main, 1870–1913 (in million Marks) These figures do not account for revenue from fees such as the *Kanalgebühr*, which were accounted for separately. *MAB*, 1874–1914. For the data summarized in this graph, see Table D in Appendix I.

gressive tax which at one time ranged from 0.5 to 15 per cent of rentable value.[137] As an old local tax which had been in operation for half a century it was the only direct tax which Frankfurt could raise independently from the state. On the other hand, while it taxed property it did tax the occupiers rather than the owners of accommodation. Also, ever since Frankfurt's loss of independence its citizens had lost the ability to control immigration into the city. Therefore, particularly in the years before the reform of the system of poor relief in 1883, Frankfurters were aware that the system of taxation offered the best way of preventing large-scale migration of the poor into the city.[138] It is tempting to assume, therefore, that even Sonnemann, who had been responsible for abolishing indirect taxation in 1873, was quite content to keep this tax which did affect the poor and which made sure that there

---

[137] *Frankfurter Zeitung*, 8 Mar. 1892 (2. Morgenblatt), in HStAW 407 n. 161¹ fo. 266.
[138] Kropat, *Frankfurt*, 64–8.
[139] Sonnemann's dialectical approach to taxation was not necessarily a contradiction. The abolition of indirect taxation in 1873 could be presented to his working-class constituents as a significant victory, while Sonnemann had to be careful not to be too radical for his other Reichstag and municipal council electors. After 1884 Sonnemann lost the working-class votes to the SPD, so that from now on he had to concentrate on appealing primarily to those who were wealthy enough to qualify for the municipal franchise.

were at least some remaining deterrents for poor migrants into the city.[139]

Another reason for Sonnemann's enthusiasm for the tax was that, once again, it benefited the *Mittelstand*, in the sense that local businesses only paid a uniform rate of 2 per cent,[140] which was less than a state tax with a local supplement added on to it. Ultimately it was state interference which brought this tax to an end. Miquel's local tax reforms stipulated that all local rent taxes had to be abolished by 1900.[141] The Frankfurt rent tax was thus gradually phased out after 1895 and replaced by a house tax, an adapted version of the building tax which had just been transferred from the state to local government.

Most other local taxes and fees that were raised were similar to those raised in other Prussian cities, and, as elsewhere, local legislators met fierce hostility from property owners with every proposition of levying a property tax (*Realsteuer*). As First Mayor, Miquel had never managed to increase the burden of the *Realsteuer* to relieve the income tax against opposition from both Democrats as well as from property owners, as the latter were committed to keeping their tax burden as low as possible.[142] Property owners continued to exert a powerful influence in the city council, for example when they managed to transform the proposed sewage fee from a fee of 1 per cent of property value to be paid by the owner to one of 2 per cent of rentable value to be paid by the occupier.[143] Nevertheless, Miquel had learnt his lesson, and the imposition of tighter government restrictions on municipal taxation in 1893, even if liberals concerned about the sanctity of self-government objected to them, did have the desired effect. Thus, for the 1904 municipal tax reform the *Magistrat* made it clear that the authorities would authorize no further tax increases unless most of these were increases in *Realsteuern*, since these were underdeveloped in Frankfurt and had not yet reached the desired 150 per cent of income tax revenue.[144]

Apart from the local income tax, there was one other tax which formed

---

[140] *MPS*, 1894, §177, p. 106. To the above percentage rates a further uniform rate of 1 per cent of rentable value has to be added, the *Laternengeld*.

[141] See Sonnemann's announcement of this fact in the council and his plea, supported by the *Magistrat*, in favour of the tax. Nevertheless, Sonnemann did not lose much time in becoming an open critic of the tax, taking pride in the fact that he had opposed it ostensibly ever since the 1870s. *MPS*, 1893, §306, pp. 155–6. It is illuminating to compare this to Sonnemann's speech in HStAW 407 n. 161² fo. 10. Democratic Association meeting, 8 Oct. 1894.

[142] Herzfeld, *Miquel*, i. 516–19. This is perhaps the best printed summary of financial policy in Frankfurt during the 1880s.

[143] *Kleine Presse*, 19 Dec. 1894 (2. Blatt).

[144] See the proposal of the *Magistrat* for a tax increase with its frequent reference to the obligations imposed by the local tax reform of 1893. *MPS*, 1903, §1270, pp. 609–30. See also Adickes's plea for the *Magistrat*'s suggestions, §1270, p. 648.

the basis of Frankfurt left liberals' pride in having the most progressive system of local taxation in Germany with regard to social policy.[145] This was the *Wertzuwachssteuer*, a levy imposed on the value of property every time it was sold and which progressively taxed the speculative gain on the value of property. The local authorities had wanted to introduce it in 1895, but this had been rejected by the Prussian authorities, presumably because the proposed tax on the sale of land was deemed too high.[146] In a subsequent more successful attempt, Frankfurt was the first city in Germany to introduce such a tax in 1904. It was based on an already existing property sales tax (*Währschaftssteuer*), and introduced a supplementary tax on the sale of buildings if they were resold within 10 years or on the sale of land if it was resold within five years, and for both categories if their value had increased by more than 30 per cent during that period.[147] As Figure 6.5 shows, the increased tax rates as well as the new supplement brought substantial new revenue to the city coffers. More importantly, the tax translated liberal theory directly into liberal practice, for, ever since Henry George, liberals, not only in Germany, but notably also in England, were concerned to tax the unearned increment on land, which became perceived as the major root of high rents.[148] But the tax had obvious political merits, too. Given that some new revenue had to be found, this tax had the greatest potential, since it combined the social instincts of Adickes, one of whose primary concerns was a municipal policy to realize affordable housing, with the policy aims of Frankfurt left liberals to stand for the interests of 'small men'. The *Wertzuwachssteuer* thus gave new credence to the old left-liberal claim that one of the most significant achievements of Frankfurt left liberals was the creation of a progressive, pioneering, and social system of taxation;[149] a claim that was made all the more important in the face of constant SPD

---

[145] Speech of councillor Funck in *MPS*, 1904, §19, p. 17. Frankfurters were flattered by the suggestion of a Prussian *Ministerialrat* that the Frankfurt tax system was, in effect, a Social Democratic one. *Frankfurter Zeitung*, 27 Nov. 1904 (3. Morgenblatt).

[146] For the original proposals, see the 'Steuerordnung das Währschaftsgeld in Frankfurt a.M. betr.', in *MPS*, §733, pp. 445–6. Kaufmann noted that initially the Prussian authorities were reluctant to allow any differential treatment between land and buildings, and to allow rates above 1% of their value. Kaufmann, *Kommunalfinanzen*, ii. 320.

[147] A good summary of the terms of the tax, also in the context of the general trend in Germany to introduce such a tax, is in Kaufmann, *Kommunalfinanzen*, ii. 327–9.

[148] Ladd, *Urban Planning*, 177–8. A. Offer, *Property and Politics 1870–1914. Landownership, Law, Ideology and Urban Development in England* (Cambridge, 1981), esp. 184–200. Waller, *Town*, 259. Sutcliffe, *Towards the Planned City*, 39.

[149] See the statement of Emil Ladenburg at an electoral rally in the run-up to the local elections, which demonstrates how these two taxes—income tax and the property sales tax—were at the heart of liberal social policy in Frankfurt. *Frankfurter Zeitung*, 16 Nov. 1906 (3. Morgenblatt).

attacks against the bourgeois coalition of property owners who acted only in their own self-interest.[150] Frankfurt Democrats had created a system of taxation which was uniquely progressive, and innovative. Indeed, Frankfurt had the lowest incidence of local supplements to direct state taxation of all Prussian cities.[151] In the end, municipal taxation remained one of the few areas in which SPD attacks remained rather vague and ill-defined, precisely because the left-liberals had created a system of taxation whose main principle of social justice seemed so closely to match their own.

6.6. Conclusion

In Frankfurt as elsewhere, the last two decades before the First World War were in many ways the epitome of the liberal ideal of self-government, as local government fulfilled its administrative obligations dutifully and efficiently, and as it expanded its sphere of activity, particularly in the economic sector. At the same time, it is beyond doubt that local government was living beyond its means. Only a few liberals involved in local administration started to appreciate the dangers inherent in spiralling municipal debt just before the war, as municipal budgets became inevitably very sensitive to outside influences on the interest rate. On the whole, it was only during the shortages and financial difficulties of the First World War that many liberals in the cities started to appreciate the precariousness of the cities' financial position.[152] Ultimately, the fact that liberal self-government can be judged a success has much to do with the fact that the German cities' astronomical debts were all but wiped out in the inflation of 1923.[153] German cities thus never had to live with the negative long-term consequences of their financial expansion before 1914.[154]

Given the momentum of municipal fiscal activity, and the enthusiasm with which liberals incurred ever-greater debts, it is striking how difficult it was for liberals to make political capital out of the flurry of municipal activ-

---

[150] *Volksstimme*, 17 Nov. 1906. [151] Most, 'Gemeindefinanzstatistik', 218.

[152] O. Most, 'Die Gemeindefinanzen nach dem Kriege', in Schriften des Vereins für Sozialpolitik, *Die Neuordnung der deutschen Finanzwirtschaft*, ii, ed. Heinrich Herkner, clvi (Munich/Leipzig, 1918), 291–355. Most's gloomy assertion about a universal acceptance of the need for local finance reform before the war (ibid. 293–5) contrasts with his own statement in 1913 that German local government had proven wrong concerns about excessive municipal spending. O. Most, *Die deutsche Stadt und ihre Verwaltung. Eine Einführung in die Kommunalpolitik der Gegenwart*, 3 vols. (Berlin/Leipzig, 1913), ii. 18.

[153] This was certainly the case for Frankfurt. BAK, NL 44 n. 8 fo. 199. Luppe, 'Mein Leben'. For municipal finance during the Weimar Republic in general, see Krabbe, *Die deutsche Stadt*, 165–75, here 168–9.

[154] This is not to say that inflation and hyperinflation did not create a whole range of new, equally formidable financial problems for local government in the Weimar Republic.

ity. In this 'golden age' of local government, this 'epoch of liberal debt management',[155] the growth of municipal expenditure and debt, while becoming more contentious from the 1900s, was surprisingly muted in the political debate at the time. The main reason for this is that the vast majority of municipal spending was directed to areas from which the largely middle-class electorate drew disproportionate benefit, such as preparatory and secondary schools, or clean and wide streets to benefit property owners. Until the turn of the century, the actual amount devoted to social policy or education for the benefit of those without the franchise was relatively low. As has been shown in the previous chapter, the system of poor relief was reformed out of a desire to make economies, while major social policy initiatives such as the industrial tribunals cost very little to run indeed. Moreover, it is only from the 1890s that the cities took seriously the provision of good basic primary education. Since municipal expenditure was heavily biased towards the existing franchise, it can thus be of little surprise that this only became a major political issue with the advent in local politics of the SPD, that self-proclaimed champion of the non-enfranchised workers.[156]

When municipal expenditure did become subject to public attention and debate, liberals more often than not found themselves on the defensive against the SPD. As shown in the previous chapter, liberals had difficulties in reaping the political benefits of the relatively generous municipal employment contracts, cheap water and gas bills, and other benefits which municipal socialism entailed. Instead, they were frequently barraged by the SPD for not going further. Indeed, it is ironic that, during the decades which in many ways saw the fulfilment of a liberal ideal of self-government with regard to local autonomy, this ideal became less identifiably liberal as it was fully accepted, for instance, by the reformist wing of the SPD.[157]

'There is scarcely any public matter which does not begin or else end in a tax.' De Tocqueville's observation about the pivotal importance of taxation in politics was well recognized by English liberals and became the cornerstone of their politics.[158] In a similar way, taxation was the key to politics in Frankfurt am Main. As illustrated in Figure 6.6, from 1868 to 1913, local taxation per head grew more than fourfold, a large increase in

---

[155] Reulecke, *Geschichte der Urbanisierung*, 111.
[156] H. Lindemann (C. Hugo), *Steuern und Gebühren* (Berlin, 1906), 34–5.
[157] See the various works by Hugo Lindemann, the main SPD authority on the subject of local self-government. Note, for instance, his description of the relative nature of locality and state, and his insistence that both were essentially the same ('wesensgleich'). Lindemann, *Steuern und Gebühren*, 3–8.
[158] Matthew, 'Disraeli', 615–16.

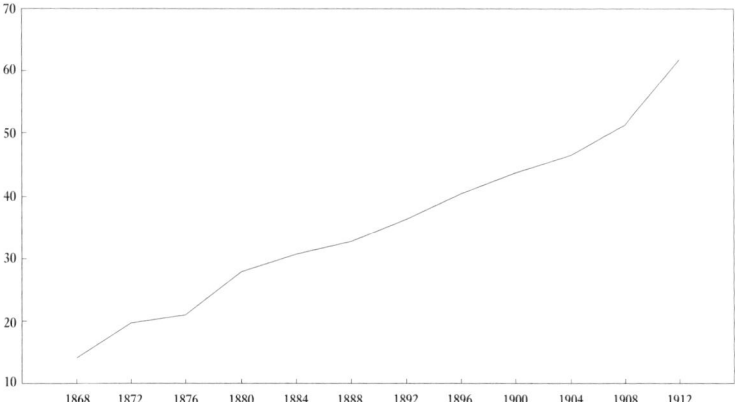

FIG. 6.6. Local taxation in Frankfurt am Main, 1868–1913 (in Marks per head)
For the data summarized in this graph, see Table D in Appendix I.

the tax burden of the individual even allowing for the fact that average wages during this period may have as much as doubled.[159] This explains the paradox that, even though it was municipal expenditure which grew so dramatically in Frankfurt, it was municipal taxation with its relatively modest and steady growth which caused such political controversy.

The political attention devoted to taxation rather than other aspects of municipal finance was given added impetus by the relative roles of council and *Magistrat*. If the latter body, in charge of the day-to-day administration, was much more competent to argue about municipal expenditure, the former, elected body representative of the people of Frankfurt had much more authority when it came to the taxation of its constituents.

The example of Frankfurt shows how throughout the period, in one of the cities with the highest public expenditure per capita, it was the issue of taxation which continued to be the most sensitive political issue. The left liberals' success in creating a policy which was clothed in the rhetoric of social concern, but which was effectively one designed to support those with middling incomes, who formed the bulk of the municipal electorate, was at the very core of the left liberals' appeal throughout the period under investigation. This is the most crucial factor in explaining the liberals' success in rallying behind it a fragmented bourgeoisie despite threats from a rebellious *Mittelstand* movement, and in using this position of strength to respond successfully to the challenge of a growing SPD.

[159] Tipton, *Regional Variations*, 83. A. V. Desai, *Real Wages in Germany, 1871–1913* (Oxford, 1968), esp. 34–8. Mitchell, *European Historical Statistics*, 194.

To generalize with confidence from Frankfurt, it would be necessary for further studies on the financial policies of liberals in other cities to be conducted. In Frankfurt, as increasing numbers qualified for the franchise, the liberals managed to stem the SPD's advance with surprising success. Clearly, this is mainly the result of their policies of taxation, rather than of 'municipal socialism'. Even if, with hindsight, the overall incidence of taxation on the *Bürgertum* was relatively low,[160] what clearly mattered was the perception of unprecedented levels of taxation. This suggests that in other cities, too, the success of urban liberalism was crucially dependent on whether liberals there appreciated (more clearly than subsequent historians) the importance of taxation rather than municipal socialism as a tool for electoral success.[161]

This chapter has also demonstrated that liberal attitudes towards municipal finance were not simply a response to increasing burdens imposed upon them by the rapid pace of urbanization. Underlying their financial attitudes in theory as well as in practice was a clear consciousness that the question of municipal finance was inextricably linked to the question of local self-government. The positive view which so many liberals shared about the growth in municipal debt is by no means self-evident. It contrasts sharply, for example, with the gloom felt by many in English cities after the turn of the century who were ever more conscious of the financial burdens of self-government.[162] The system of grant-in-aid, which became ever more important for municipal finance from the 1880s onwards,[163] and Lloyd George's social legislation were clear admissions of the limits of the ideal of local self-government.[164]

In England, of course, parliament was an assembly of local interests. Since local and national government were thus closely intertwined, the growth of national government at the expense of the localities mattered less in principle. In Germany, by contrast, liberals in the cities had every interest to defend and even expand their powers vis-à-vis an authoritarian,

[160] Ullmann, 'Die Bürger als Steuerzahler', 241.

[161] It appears, for instance, that in Münster, low taxation quickly replaced the defence of Roman Catholic interests in the *Kulturkampf* as the central electoral appeal of the all-powerful 'Christian-conservative electoral committee' in 1880. Olliges-Wieczorek, *Politisches Leben in Münster*, 336. This chapter has thus underlined the point made by Richard H. Tilly, that a city's political environment was a crucial determinant of its political economy. Tilly, 'Städtewachstum, Kommunalfinanzen und Munizipalsozialismus', 152.

[162] Note e.g. Charles Vince's sombre assessment in 1902 of municipal government in Birmingham, home to the optimism surrounding the 'municipal gospel' just three decades earlier. C. A. Vince, *History of the Corporation of Birmingham*, iii (Birmingham, 1902), p. iv.

[163] Waller, *Town*, 263–72.

[164] J. Harris, 'The Transition to High Politics in English Social Policy, 1880–1914', in M. Bentley and J. Stevenson (eds.), *High and Low Politics in Modern Britain* (Oxford, 1983), 60, 73–7.

conservative national government dominated by landed interests. That is why, increasingly, unemployment insurance was embraced by liberals in local government at a time when in Britain it was realized that, like other social legislation, this was a national concern. Local government was therefore not just a sop which compensated liberals for their loss of influence at the national and (at least in Prussia) at the state level. Its growing share in total public spending meant that through it, liberals could actually increase their influence on everyday life. Local government finance was not just the determinant of liberal popularity at local level, it was also the underpinning of the relative and absolute growth of local government activity, and with it of liberal power before the First World War.

7

Conclusion

This book has sought to disprove the existence of the 'unpolitical German' in charge of local government. The notion that politics had no place inside the city council is not just an invention of historians. It is a rhetoric to which most contemporaries, in Frankfurt as elsewhere, subscribed. Closer examination of the case of Frankfurt shows that this was precisely what it was: all rhetoric, but little substance. Naturally, this study of one city cannot establish conclusively the reign of party politics inside local government for all of Germany. It is true that the precise way in which Frankfurt politics developed in response to its historical and social circumstances was unique to the city, just as politics in any other German city had to engage with that city's peculiar economic, social, religious, and historical background. At the same time, it is unlikely that Frankfurt was atypical in the importance of politics for local government with regard to public debate, the city council, the *Magistrat*, and the relations to the state authorities. Moreover, the rhetoric of municipal pride, which was so crucial to the Frankfurt left liberals' success in local politics, was an important element in the public discourse in all German cities. Before 1866, certainly in comparison with local government in Baden, Württemberg, the Rhineland, and a host of towns from Osnabrück and Münster in the north, to Augsburg in the south, Frankfurt politics did not stand out as being peculiarly advanced. In fact, in Frankfurt the conditions for the politicization of local government were relatively unfavourable, given the absence of an early labour movement and of confessional conflict. There is no reason why Frankfurt should have been unusual in the establishment of a definite political framework for local government by the late 1870s. Similarly, towards the end of the Empire, there is no doubt that in its politics the city was progressive, but it was no more progressive than a host of other cities across Germany.

Always bearing in mind, then, that this study is an in-depth analysis of liberals in power in one city, its observations about the nature and extent of politicization in local government lead to important general conclusions. Perhaps the most significant of these is the overwhelming importance of local identity, which throughout the period of the Empire was the prism through which politics were received. In the first years after the annexation of Frankfurt, this could, perhaps, be expected, given that local resentment against the city's treatment was running high. Soon after 1871, however, Frankfurters became reconciled with the newly created German Empire. In subsequent decades, local identity changed in nature, but not in importance. For any political party, it remained critical to address local peculiarities and perceived traditions. This was done in public meetings and popular festivals, in the rhetoric that was used, and even in the language that was employed (i.e. local dialect). Moreover, local peculiarities determined political programmes at large, as visions of education and finance, but also of the social question, reflected and in turn affected the liberals' perception of Frankfurt's role in the Empire. Leopold Sonnemann for one proudly referred to Frankfurt as an 'oasis in the desert'.[1] The exact ways in which notions of the locality, of the '*Heimat*', affected politics was, by definition, unique to Frankfurt. Yet by 1914 the appeal to civic pride had become a staple of every liberal city government in Germany. The appeal of urban liberals to the weal of the local community at large is an application to the local level of the liberals' claim at national level to represent the whole *Volk*. Whereas at the national level, this concept lost its persuasiveness from the 1880s, at the local level the liberal appeal to civic pride was more pervasive. It was much more convincing in that liberals actually had the power in the cities, in most cases right up to 1914.[2] Moreover, an appeal to local identity was much more effective, in that this could include local distinctivenesses and peculiarities with which people could identify more easily. Put differently, with reference to Benedict Anderson, the nation was clearly an imagined, if not artificial, community, whereas this was less clear about a local community with which people readily and naturally identified.[3] Local identity, then, was a crucial factor in the development of politics in a newly created federal Germany, and it was an indispensable element in the evolution of liberal politics in local government.

This leads to a second important result of this study, as the late 1860s and early 1870s come into focus as an era of fundamental political change in the

---

[1] For the full quotation, see Roth, 'Liberalismus', 42.
[2] Sheehan, 'Liberalism', 131–2.
[3] B. Anderson, *Imagined Communities* (London, 1983).

cities. Without denying the achievements or the importance of urban history, it is time to consider politicization in the cities as a process not distinct from, but intimately connected to, the evolution of politics in other political spheres. Previously, Frankfurt had been held up as an example of the reign of the 'unpolitical' in local government until 1900, in contrast to the importance of liberal politics at the state or national levels. On closer inspection this study has found little evidence for such a view. It is difficult to see why politics at the local level should be regarded as being separate from the state or national level, when it was conducted by the same organizations and parties, with the same language, by the same people.

In Frankfurt, the period of the foundation of the Empire led to the establishment of a system of three essentially liberal parties: a loosely organized National Liberal Party which rallied all pro-government groups, a small Progressive Liberal Party which learnt to exploit its pivotal role as the third party, and a 'home-grown', Democrat party. An adversarial political system had thus developed which consisted entirely of liberals of different political complexions. The case of Frankfurt suggests that the politicization of local government did not occur as a result of the rise of the SPD at this level from 1900 onwards. Instead, local politics in Frankfurt (and without doubt in other cities) developed as a response to the new political and national environment which liberals in the city experienced after 1866. The example of Frankfurt highlights the importance of the period of the foundation of the Empire as a crucial time of political change. The emergence of politics before that time was important, but it was only after 1866 that politics took its final shape which lasted in its essentials well into the Weimar Republic. And without wanting to slight the impact on liberalism of Bismarck's second foundation of the Empire in 1879, or the emergence of mass politics in the 1890s, liberals in the cities encountered these crises in the political environment created in the decade after 1866.

In Frankfurt the emerging liberal parties were clearly distinctive in their policies and aims, as well as in their religious profile, their rhetoric, and their organization. This suggests further that it can be highly misleading to assume a single bourgeois 'camp' (*Lager*). For liberal political parties to emerge in local government, challenges from the SPD or the Centre Party were not a sine qua non: each other's company could be quite sufficient. In Frankfurt, there emerged from the late 1860s different and rival liberal conceptions in many areas of social policy, the municipalization of services, and education. The fact that liberals chose to compromise and cooperate in practice on some of these issues speaks more for their political realism and astuteness, than for their actual similarities. After all, so bad were relations between the National Liberals and the Democrats that in Reichstag elections the latter lent consistent support to the SPD in run-off elections against the National Liberals. Similarly, before 1914 the Democrats were happy to accept SPD support against the National Liberals and Adickes when it suited them. By the same token, the National Liberals had no qualms about cooperating with the main enemies of the Democrats, the *Mittelstand*.

Naturally, the Frankfurt party system did not remain static. Most important to the relationship between the three liberal parties was the gradual shift of the Progressive Liberals from their initial alliance with the National Liberals to their eventual merger with the Democrats in 1910. Ultimately, as in national politics at large, success in local politics depended on how well the parties responded to their changing political environment. A restricted franchise at the local level prolonged the period of adjustment, but did not prevent the need for adaptation as such. The strength of the Frankfurt Democrats in particular lay not only in their creation of a political culture in the first place, but also in their sophistication at changing and adapting it to the evolving cultural and political climate such as the reconciliation of Frankfurt with the Empire, or the diversification of politics. The flexibility and the astuteness with which particularly Democratic liberals dealt with the growth of the *Bezirksvereine* in the 1880s, and the *Mittelstand* during the 1890s, gave them the necessary experience to cope successfully with the Social Democrats as they emerged in local politics from the mid-1890s onwards. In Frankfurt, the election of the first SPD councillor in 1900 did not form a watershed: it simply marked another stage in the growing complexity of local politics.

The politicization of local affairs in the late 1860s and early 1870s did not leave out the town hall. The persistence of an unpolitical urban bureaucracy, for which Frankfurt has often been held up as a model, has been perhaps the most persistent claim of urban historians. In the light of the evidence presented in this book, this view is difficult to maintain. In the city council itself, the all-important committees where the real decisions were made were composed primarily according to party affiliation. Despite the absence of official party groups until 1901, since the 1870s councillors more often than not voted with their party colleagues. The political nature of the *Magistrat* was less pronounced, but nonetheless real. During the 1870s, Democrats fought it and the First Mayor tooth and nail, and only when Miquel took control from 1880 did the relationship between council and *Magistrat* improve markedly. True, Miquel and most of the *Magistrat* were National Liberal, but that was a secondary issue. What was crucial was that they accepted the Democrats' main tenets of local government, i.e. the importance of self-government, and the ultimate goal of a harmonious, tolerant society in Frankfurt, notably through non-denominational education. Party politics in the strict sense were not a factor between 1880 and 1900, but politics remained important nonetheless.

Moreover, it is no accident that the city's most seasoned left-liberal politician, Leopold Sonnemann, effected the selection of two prominent and pronounced National Liberals as First Mayor. The reason for this was not an ideal of the 'unpolitical', which in Sonnemann's case would be extremely unconvincing. Nor was it primarily a fear that only National Liberals would be accepted by the king. Rather, a mayor whom the Prussian government trusted but who had nevertheless committed himself to the Democrats' main goals of local government gave Frankfurt the greatest possible freedom for manoeuvre. Assured by Miquel's and Adickes's presence in charge of this hive of left-liberal activity, the Prussian authorities were prepared to allow the council its experiments in education and social policy which otherwise would have been much more difficult to realize. Only Miquel could have prevented the expulsion of the Frankfurt socialist leaders at the time of the anti-socialist laws because their goodwill was crucial to the success of the industrial tribunals.[4] Only Miquel could achieve a compromise on non-denominational education with the state authorities which effectively guaranteed its survival in Frankfurt. And Adickes's conservative credentials alone assuaged Prussian fears about the civic university's potential left-wing and Jewish nature. Left-liberal relations to the *Magistrat*, therefore, were not so much a manifestation of the 'unpolitical' in local government. Politics in this realm were more subtle, and this was fully appreciated by Frankfurt left liberals; an important example of the political sophistication of which liberals in power were capable.

Further to an analysis of how liberals gained political control and what forms that control took, this study of local government highlights what liberals did when they were in power. An issue of overriding and fundamental importance to liberals in Frankfurt as elsewhere was education. It was primarily through education that municipal liberals hoped to realize a 'liberal', meritocratic society distinguished by mutual tolerance and scientific endeavour. Of course, there were important disagreements about the resources devoted especially to primary education (from the 1890s), or the extent to which clerical influence ought to be removed from schools. But in their underlying vision for education, liberals were in agreement with each other, and even with the SPD.

[4] Weitensteiner, 'Karl Flesch', 116.

Frankfurt is a particularly good example of the importance which the goal of a liberal, tolerant, and educated society had for urban liberals, owing to the perhaps unusual influence of the previously disadvantaged religious minorities, notably the Jews, the German Catholics, and the Calvinists. What is surprising is less the importance of the Jews to the various liberal parties themselves, which has been shown in many other instances already. What is new is that their influence can be traced to particular policies pursued by the liberals, the most important of which was the non-denominational system of education. Also of particular significance is the importance of the relatively small group of German Catholics in Frankfurt, and their links with the Democrats. This connection was personified by Carl Sänger, the German Catholic Pastor in the 1890s, and the second senior non-Jewish Democrat after Heinrich Rößler. Even more significant is the fact that in 1914, Heinrich Rößler himself became the President of the 'Weimar Cartel', the federation of all German 'free-thinking' and 'free-religious' organizations, which had its headquarters in Frankfurt. This link reinforced further Democrat insistence on non-denominational education and other policies designed to improve rational, scientific conduct free from prejudice, such as the introduction of cremations. National Liberals, too, had strong connections to non-Jewish religions. Their acceptance of non-denominational education also can only be explained by this being an article of faith for the city's Calvinist and Lutheran establishment. While the connection between liberalism and religion is still one of the most underresearched subjects in imperial German history, this book has illustrated the importance and fruitfulness of its investigation at the grass roots.

Given the paucity of research in this area, it is impossible to say whether Frankfurt was unique in the influence of religion upon its liberal movements. Still, the concern for a tolerant society, although perhaps particularly evident in Frankfurt, was central to all liberals in Germany. In his attempt to define and describe the nature of German liberalism, Friedrich Naumann noted that the most fundamental shortcoming of German society in comparison with society in England or the United States was a fundamental lack of popular appreciation for individual freedom and a traditional tendency to welcome authority. Hence, what was needed most was a comprehensive education of society in liberal values.[5] At least in

---

[5] BAP 90 Na 3 n. 193 fos. 1–3. Friedrich Naumann, 'Deutscher Liberalismus'. Naumann was not the only prominent left liberal to believe in the power of education to renew German society. Right until the end of the war, for example, Hugo Preuß held up education as an effective antidote to the virtual military dictatorship in place by 1917. C. Applegate, 'Democracy or Reaction? The Political Implications of Localist Ideas in Wilhelmine and Weimar Germany',

Prussia, it was the liberals in the cities who had the greatest opportunity for realizing this ideal.

Liberals in Frankfurt pursued this goal with a single-mindedness and perseverance which more often than not stood up successfully against the reservations of the Prussian authorities. With non-denominational primary schools, the introduction of what became known as the 'Frankfurt system' of secondary schools, and the establishment of Germany's first 'civic' university by 1914, Frankfurt liberals came as close as they possibly could towards creating a truly 'liberal' system of education. However, against an increasing nationalist rhetoric of chauvinism and *Weltpolitik*, it is not clear whether the liberals' trust in changing society 'from the bottom up', through education, was justified. Given the city's wealth and its international trading links, Frankfurt society was likely to be relatively open and tolerant in any case. Over and above this, there is simply not enough evidence to suggest that the city became more tolerant as a result of more than forty years of liberals in power.

Still, liberals did their best to try, despite the political cost of their attempts to create a 'tolerant' education system, namely the loss of the committed Roman Catholic and, at least temporarily, Protestant, vote. What is striking is less the question of whether the liberals' ideals were practical and realistic in the long run, but the tenacity and success with which liberals realized their immediate goals. The introduction of a non-denominational system of education, despite the national trend, was the result of peculiar local circumstances, i.e. a weak, at first voiceless, Roman Catholic minority, the strength and influence of Jews, and, more importantly, the convictions of the city's leading Protestants. Still, it is a tribute to the efficiency and cunning that German liberals were capable of given the right cause and the chance to pursue it.

This sense of purpose and ingenuity was also abundant in social policy. Frankfurt liberal and bourgeois reformers pioneered a number of measures, notably industrial and trade tribunals, labour exchanges, and *Bodenpolitik* to improve the housing market. In smaller ways, the promotion of charitable housing, the establishment of popular lectures, and higher spending on primary schools underline the innovativeness, diversity, and importance of the measures through which liberals in power responded to their rapidly changing environment. It has been well-known among contemporaries and historians alike that Frankfurt was a pioneer in social

in L. E. Jones and J. Retallack (eds.), *Elections, Mass Politics, and Social Change in Modern Germany* (Cambridge, 1993), 257.

policy. Yet it is important to acknowledge that this concern for social policy was deeply embedded in the local political structure. Not only did all municipal reform have to be approved by a *Magistrat* and a city council, but the city's main innovators in social policy were important and influential political leaders in their own right, even if many of them were employed by the city.

It should come as no surprise that underneath this flurry of social activity there were fundamental differences about its nature and objectives. Adickes had the paternalistic instincts of a Bismarckian reformer, while the Democrats aimed at the emancipation and inclusion of the working classes into society. This explains why the political effects of municipal socialism are complex and ambiguous. It is far from clear that these policies contributed significantly to the liberals' political success before 1914. Given the initial hostility of the Frankfurt labour movement to the industrial tribunals, this remarkable instrument of conciliation is more likely to have increased the hostility of labour in the medium run. It is not at all evident that, once these problems were overcome and the tribunals were an obvious success, labour support for the liberals increased to make up for the initial losses. In general, liberal social policies did win over working-class support (e.g. of municipal employees), but it equally highlighted the ostensible half-heartedness towards the social question of the liberals relative to the SPD. If the political effects of the Democrats' social policies were ambiguous, it is doubtful whether the paternalist policies of Adickes gained one single working-class vote. Moreover, through inflated house prices and growing tax requirements, Adickes's *Bodenpolitik* ultimately made life difficult even for those it was intended to benefit, the middle and lower middle classes. The innovative policies of Frankfurt liberals are indicative of the agility and the 'modernity' of which German liberals were capable given half a chance of being in power. Yet they also demonstrate the limitations and the problems of even the most responsive and flexible liberal movement when trying to compete against a well-organized political labour movement with a much more clearly defined constituency. Even in Frankfurt there was no clear positive correlation between political progressiveness and electoral success.

In the end, the key to liberal electoral fortunes lay with the middle classes. They were the liberals' original constituency, and even by 1914 they still formed the majority of electors. Any efforts to attract the support of workers were ultimately supplementary to the need to maintain the support of the increasingly heterogenous middle classes. The fate of liberals in Frankfurt as elsewhere depended on how keenly they appreciated this fact. This is why the Frankfurt liberals' willingness to spend more on schools frequented by the middle classes than on the basic primary schools was not so much ideological inconsistency, but political realism.

What cannot be emphasized enough given the dazzlement of contemporaries and historians alike of the liberal achievements under the guise of 'municipal socialism', is this study's findings that neither the liberals' pet projects on education, nor their social policies, appear to have been decisive in electoral terms. There is no reason why Frankfurt should have been exceptional: municipal socialism was not the principal determinant of liberal political success. Instead, the example of Frankfurt highlights the crucial importance of municipal finance. Frankfurt was one of the most active cities in a municipal environment already characterized by accelerating municipal spending and debt. Municipal spending was of disproportionate benefit to those of middling and upper income who had the vote, and not only in Frankfurt. In another city which liked to think of itself in the vanguard of municipal socialism, Breslau, spending on 'social policy' took up most of the municipal budget. Yet in 1908, 85 per cent of that expenditure was on primary schools, the financing of which was one of the main functions of local government anyway. By contrast, 0.02 per cent of 'social policy' spending was devoted to industrial tribunals. Public reading halls took up 0.6 per cent, and public provision of breakfast for poor school children accounted for a further 0.09 per cent of the social policy budget.[6] In real terms, municipal socialism was politics for the middle classes (*Mittelstandspolitik*) in thin disguise, and of very little material benefit to the working classes.

Since municipal spending benefited largely the middle classes, and because day-to-day spending was effectively controlled by the *Magistrat*, expenditure was not a matter of public debate until the turn of the century. It was only with the advent of the SPD in local politics that municipal spending became an issue. Even so, it is striking how little controversy individual items of expenditure caused. What mattered instead was taxation. This was the make-or-break issue for the liberals. The growth of the political *Mittelstand* in the 1890s was triggered to a large extent not by municipal spending, but by increased fees, charges, and taxes. Its most important components included the 'tax defence association' and the house-owners' association. By the same token, taxation ultimately ensured

---

[6] G. Sonnenberg, *Deutschlands sozialpolitische Einrichtungen im Budget des Reiches, dreier Einzelstaaten, Preußen, Bayern, Baden, und dreier Großer Städte, Berlin, Breslau, Köln* (Berlin, 1912), 191–2.

the left-liberals' success against the political *Mittelstand*, and even against the SPD. Not unlike education and social spending, the tax system was highly favourable to those on middling incomes (and who qualified for the local franchise). At the same time, its progressive aspects made it extremely suited for a rhetoric of social justice which could appeal to the working classes, especially those whose incomes were around the 1,200 M. threshold for the municipal franchise. Naturally, the success of Frankfurt left liberals, and the Democrats in particular, was the result of a complex variety of factors, originating in their ability to address and profit from local peculiarities and particularities. Of all the elements that determined the Democrats' success throughout the period, however, it was taxation, not social policy, which sustained and even increased left-liberal popularity.

It has already been pointed out above that a restrictive franchise helped the liberals adapt to political and social change, but it did not in itself guarantee liberal predominance in the city council. This point cannot be emphasized enough, for too often is a restricted franchise being pointed out as the principal factor in maintaining liberal supremacy in local government. Clearly, throughout Germany the importance of this contributor to liberal predominance varied according to the extent of the franchise's limitations. The underlying problem with this argument is the assumption that those who did not qualify for the local vote would vote for the SPD, while a largely middle-class electorate is likely to vote overwhelmingly for the liberals. Yet at least for the national level, Jonathan Sperber has shown that, by 1912, liberal voters would include almost as many Protestant workers as members of the Protestant middle classes. In numerical terms, the erstwhile bedrock of liberal support, the Protestant middle classes, were more likely to vote SPD than liberal.[7] Protestant working-class support for the SPD, and Protestant middle-class support for the liberals, simply cannot be taken for granted in the decade before the First World War. This is confirmed by the experience of Frankfurt, where liberals became very good at addressing the concerns of workers while never losing sight of the importance of maintaining middle-class support. At the local level, liberals could be much more resolute in their concerns for their urban electorate, in the way that liberals at the state and national levels, who constantly had to balance urban and agricultural interests, could not.[8] The case of Frankfurt

---

[7] 29% of the Protestant middle classes voted liberal, and 44% voted SPD in 1912. In that year, 26% of Protestant workers voted liberal, and 54% voted SPD. Sperber, *The Kaiser's Voters*, 367 (table A.34).

[8] Sperber attributes the liberal electoral weakness in the 1890s to the liberals' inability to speak out clearly against tariffs for fear of offending their rural voters, and he argues that their

shows, therefore, that liberals did not just remain in control of local government throughout Germany because they were shielded by a restrictive franchise; the principal reason for their success was their response to, and successful articulation of, social and political change in the urban environment.

The example of Frankfurt confirms that the old debate about whether the state or the locality should be the focus of the body politic was over.[9] By the turn of the 1890s, it appeared to many contemporaries that the bourgeoisie had not become more self-conscious or influential, but rather the contrary. The traditional argument that local government was merely a good preparation (or for some liberals on the right a good substitute) for bourgeois participation in and liberalization of state and national politics had become outdated.[10] According to Frankfurt liberals themselves, the bourgeoisie was lacking in self-confidence and self-assurance, so that it became the primary function of local government to lift up the bourgeoisie and infuse it with liberal values.[11] Hence the city became important in its own right.

It is too simplistic to conclude that local government became important to liberals as they were marginalized at other levels of government. The cities were more than just a refuge for liberals disillusioned with the advent of mass politics at the state and national levels.[12] There were positive reasons why the cities became so much more important to liberals towards the end of the Empire. It was during this period that the idea of local self-government gained added impetus through a new generation of left-liberal writers such as Josef Redlich and Hugo Preuß, who broke with the consensus established by Gneist and Gierke a generation earlier that local government, important though it was, was subordinate to the state. Instead, they argued that local government was equal to the state in essence, as the state was but an aggregation of local communities.[13]

---

strength in 1907 and 1912 was the result of their much more resolute stand against agricultural interests, in favour of their urban constituencies. Ibid. 232–3, 236–8, 254–8.

[9] R. Koch, 'Staat oder Gemeinde? Zu einem politischen Zielkonflikt in der bürgerlichen Bewegung des 19. Jahrhunderts', *HZ* ccxxxvi (1983), 73–96.

[10] The *Frankfurter Zeitung*, too, had subscribed to the view that local government was a 'preparatory school' for state government. *Frankfurter Zeitung*, 8 July 1867 (1. Blatt).

[11] See esp. Karl Funck's speech in *Frankfurter Zeitung*, 16 Nov. 1906 (3. Morgenblatt).

[12] Sheehan, 'Liberals', esp. 131–7.

[13] Preuß, *Die Entwicklung des Deutschen Städtewesens*. i. *Entwicklungsgeschichte der Deutschen Städteverfassung* (Leipzig, 1906), 378–9. Preuß, *Gemeinde, Staat, Reich als Gebietskörperschaften*. Bücher, *Die wirtschaftlichen Aufgaben*, esp. 8–11. J. Redlich and F. W. Hirst, *Local Government in England*, 2 vols. (London, 1903). This book corrected many of the false

The revival of the academic liberal debate about the nature and the value of local self-government was matched by a growing liberal consciousness of the importance of the city at the level of practical politics. For liberals who considered themselves to be essentially bourgeois, it was natural to turn to where the *Bürgertum* was, the cities. Similarly, if education was so important to them, then local government was the only way for liberals to gain any influence in the way primary and secondary schools were run, or in the way that education was expanded, for example, to the creation of compulsory technical schools. To prove their political ability the left liberals in Prussia were eager to point away from their negative role in the Prussian chamber of deputies to their positive achievements in municipal government, such as the 'beautiful and well-equipped' schools as well as the general quality of education in many large cities which they considered to be the pride of progressive liberal city government.[14]

The growing importance of local government in the body politic was not just a liberal illusion, but was reflected in the increasing financial weight of local government vis-à-vis the state, and the spiralling local government expenditure. Local government came to affect all walks of life. Following the reluctance of the Empire and the states to respond adequately to the social question during the 1890s and 1900s, liberals in local government took up the challenge, however imperfectly, with ingenuity, zeal, and conviction. Considering the steady increase of local government activity in German public life, by 1914 the futility of liberal confidence in the growing importance of local self-government was by no means clear.[15]

Far from seeking to retreat from the national stage, urban left liberals in Frankfurt used their acquired local political strength not just to carry out their policies in Frankfurt itself, but also as a springboard for national and state politics. The *Frankfurter Zeitung*, which was directly linked to almost all Democratic representatives in Berlin, was one of the main German newspapers to lead the extra-parliamentary opposition to any repressive legislation, militarism, and anti-Semitism.[16] Moreover, Frankfurt

---

notions of English local government current in Germany since they had been established by Rudolf Gneist. For a conservative assessment of the importance of the cities in the East in promoting German culture, see Menzel's article in *Städte-Zeitung*, 24 Oct. 1904, 91–3. The argument that an emphasis on local government did not necessarily entail backwardness and being old-fashioned has been made in Applegate, 'Democracy or Reaction?', esp. 247–57.

[14] P. Scheven, *Die Nationalsozialen und die volkstümlichen Parteien*. i. *Der Freisinn und die Nationalsozialen*, in BAP 90 Na 3 n. 285.

[15] See also John, 'Constitution, Administration, and the Law', 199–200.

[16] A. Eigenbrodt, *Berliner Tageblatt und Frankfurter Zeitung in ihrem Verhalten zu den nationalen Fragen 1887–1914. Ein geschichtlicher Rückblick* (Berlin-Schöneberg, 1917).

Democrats continually tried to increase their influence within the German People's Party, an enthusiasm rewarded with Frankfurt serving as the party headquarters for most of the party's existence.[17] Rather less successful were their efforts in the 1880s to extend the German People's Party into northern Germany, which made for bad relations with the Progressive Liberals in northern Germany, and their suspicious Württemberg colleagues in the south.[18]

The importance of Frankfurt left liberalism for its respective national political movements was further underlined and increased by its pivotal role in the process of left-liberal unification from about 1903 to 1910.[19] This influence rested on the close relationship which the left-liberal leaders, particularly the Progressive Liberal Funck and the Democrat Rößler, had developed in the sphere of local politics, where both had been active for two decades. Also, it rested on the close relations which the Frankfurt representative to the Prussian chamber of deputies, Funck,[20] and Democrats such as Rößler and Rudolf Oeser had with their colleagues in state and national politics.[21]

Frankfurt left liberals were on good terms not only with the two larger left-liberal parties, the *Deutsche Volkspartei* and the *Freisinnige Volkspartei*, but also with Theodor Barth and Friedrich Naumann of the *Freisinnige Vereinigung*, with whose programmes of social and political reform they largely agreed.[22] In particular, Barth and Naumann placed similar emphasis on the reform of the Prussian three-class franchise. And their insistence

---

[17] For example, Württemberg Democrats were constantly irritated by the *Frankfurter Zeitung*'s hostility to their left-liberal 'sister party', the Progressive Liberals, which was the direct result of Sonnemann's personal feud against the Progressive Liberal leader Eugen Richter. BAK, NL 20 n. 4 fo. 174. Payer to Sonnemann, 13 June 1891.

The fact that Frankfurt was the seat of the party headquarters for most of the period is in itself a demonstration of the vitality of Frankfurt liberalism, as the duties of the party executive were extremely burdensome and thus unpopular. BAK, NL 20 n. 3 fos. 261–4. Württemberg party secretary to Dr Prior (Frankfurt), 3 July 1889 and 17 Aug. 1889.

[18] Hunt, *The People's Party*, 38.

[19] For a general account of the moves towards left-liberal unity in 1910, see Theiner, *Sozialer Liberalismus und deutsche Weltpolitik*, 140–55. K. Simon, *Die württembergischen Demokraten. Ihre Stellung und Arbeit im Parteien- und Verfassungssystem in Württemberg und im Deutschen Reich 1890–1920* (Stuttgart, 1969), 81–92.

[20] Karl Funck was Frankfurt's Progressive Liberal deputy from 1892–3, and 1898–1913.

[21] It was vital that Funck enjoyed not only the trust and friendship of the German People's Party's leaders Friedrich Payer and Konrad Haußmann, but, in contrast to other Frankfurt left liberals, he was also on good terms with the difficult Progressive leader, Eugen Richter. Funck, *Lebenserinnerungen*, 23–5.

[22] The close relationship which the left-liberal leaders Rößler, Oeser, and Funck had with Barth and Naumann is evident from BAP 90 Na 3 n. 211.

that the most important goal of social policy should be the transformation of workers' rights to equal those of their employees was perfectly reminiscent of the social policy which Frankfurt Democrats had pursued for decades.[23] Almost from the beginning of the negotiations about the fusion of the *Freisinnige Vereinigung* and the National Socials, Barth had kept Sonnemann informed about their progress. Once the fusion was announced, the *Freisinnige Vereinigung* could count on the steadfast and enthusiastic support of the *Frankfurter Zeitung*.[24] In 1908 the Frankfurt Democrats offered Barth the chance to become a Prussian deputy for the safe seat of Frankfurt, though Barth declined and Karl Flesch went to Berlin instead.[25] Finally, the Frankfurt left-liberal philanthropist Charles Hallgarten was perhaps the single largest financial benefactor of Friedrich Naumann's activities.[26]

Given the additional benefit that as a meeting-point Frankfurt was an ideal compromise for the predominantly Prussian *Freisinnige Volkspartei* and the People's Party with its electoral base south and west of the Main, it is questionable whether the left-liberal unification of 1910 could have occurred without the energy and the unique position of Frankfurt left liberals.[27] The ability of Frankfurt liberals to 'pull the cart of left-liberal unity', as Barth put it in a letter to Naumann,[28] was primarily based on their personalities, their support from the *Frankfurter Zeitung* (whose offices served as an important meeting place for the various liberal representatives), and their individual enthusiasm for the cause. At the same time, there is no doubt that the foundation of their influence lay in their experience and their success in local politics which provided them with the necessary support and authority. Otherwise, the role of someone like

---

[23] K. Wegner, *Theodor Barth und die Freisinnige Vereinigung. Studien zur Geschichte des Linksliberalismus im wilhelminischen Deutschland (1893–1910)* (Tübingen, 1968), 24–5.

[24] Ibid. 94.

[25] Rößler's offer to Barth is in BAP 90 Na 3 n. 211 fos. 63–4. Rößler to Barth, 12 Mar. 1908.

[26] Naumann's relationship with Hallgarten is evident from BAP 90 Na 3 n. 147. For the relative importance of Hallgarten's donations to Naumann's political activities, see e.g. BAP 90 Na 3 n. 147, fos. 15–16. Naumann to Hallgarten, 29 Oct. 1903. See also BAP 60 Vo 3 n. 5/1 fos. 21–3. Minutes of the Progressive People Party's executive meeting, 27 Feb. 1906.

[27] There is also an extremely valuable (handwritten) account of the negotiations between the representatives of the various parties, written by Heinrich Rößler in 1909 in IfGS, S1/6.

[28] Commenting on the recent Munich party congress of the People's Party, Barth wrote 'Wir müssen, wie ich meine, jetzt unsere Frankfurter Kompagnons vor den Einigungswagen spannen, *unsere Wahlrechtspläne darauf packen* [sic] und den Versuch machen, das Gefährt mitsamt der Ladung in Bewegung zu setzten'. ('In my opinion, we must now span our Frankfurt colleagues before the cart of unity, load it with our plans for electoral reform, and make the attempt to set the vehicle with its cargo in motion.') BAP 90 Na 3 n. 211 fo. 27. Barth to Naumann, 3 Oct. 1906.

Heinrich Rößler would be incomprehensible, as the highest political position he ever occupied was that of a deputy chairman of the Frankfurt city council—he was never a member of either the Prussian chamber of deputies or the Reichstag. Furthermore, it was in cooperation in local politics that individual Progressive Liberals such as Funck gained the trust and the friendship of the Democratic leadership which subsequently became indispensable to the single-minded pursuit of liberal unity by Frankfurt left liberals. This is not to deflect from perhaps the central reason why left-liberal unity became possible, which was the death of Eugen Richter in 1906 who had obstinately refused to compromise on social policy issues and attitudes towards the state.[29] Nonetheless, the importance of Frankfurt left liberalism particularly in this process of left-liberal unification deserves to be emphasized. After all, during the 1880s and early 1890s it was the Frankfurt Democrats who, as a result of their strong commitment to social policy and because of their sometimes rocky relationships with the local Progressive liberals, vetoed any attempt made by the German People's Party as a whole to move closer to Richter's Progressive Liberals.[30] Put more poignantly, one important reason why German left-liberal unification could not happen one or two decades earlier was that the older generation of Frankfurt left-liberal leaders, the Progressive Berthold Geiger and the Democrat Leopold Sonnemann, detested each other.[31]

As a result of their position during the process of left-liberal unity, Frankfurt left-liberals were in an unusually influential position within the

---

[29] B. Heckart, *From Bassermann to Bebel. The Grand Bloc's Quest for Reform in the Kaiserreich, 1900–1914* (New Haven, 1974), 26–33. Wegner, *Theodor Barth*, 104–10, and *passim*.

[30] In 1885, the Frankfurt Democrats' insistence on extending the German People's Party to northern Germany in direct opposition to the Progressive Liberals threatened a split within the party, though ultimately the Württemberg section of the party, which was more interested in maintaining good relations with Richter, prevailed. Hunt, *The People's Party*, 37–8. In 1891, Friedrich Payer was forced to decline an invitation issued by Karl Funck to address the national party conference of the Progressive Party in Frankfurt that year as a result of the Frankfurt Democrats' outrage. The latter objected to Payer thus supporting their political opponents, as they had been let down too often by the Frankfurt Progressives in the city council to consider them political friends, despite their frequent cooperation in municipal elections. BAK, NL 20 n. 4 fos. 167–9. Louis Hamburger for the Frankfurt Democratic Association to the Committee of the German People's Party in Stuttgart, 11 May 1891. See also the interesting letter from Payer to Funck of 12 May 1891, in which he declines Funck's offer. It is marked by a warmth which is conspicuously absent in the correspondence between Payer and Sonnemann during these years and until Sonnemann's death. BAK, NL 20 n. 4 fo. 171.

[31] Sonnemann's strong dislike not only of the locally prominent Geiger, but also of Eugen Richter, was one of the causes of the Democrats' strong aversion to the Progressive Liberal Party, much to the dismay of their southern German party colleagues.

new party from 1910 onwards. Karl Funck, who was the first chairman of the central committee of the new Progressive People's Party, and Heinrich Rößler, the committee's other influential member from Frankfurt, continually tried to raise the party's awareness of social questions. In particular, they attempted to muster up official party support for the Imperial Insurance Law (1910/11) as well as Flesch's ideas for a reformulation of employment contracts.[32] The last decade before the Great War marked the zenith of Frankfurt left-liberal influence not only in local politics, but in state and national politics through their position in Progressive Party politics as well.

This study has consistently argued that the political nature of liberal local government, and the problems and challenges it faced, were far from unique to the city of Frankfurt. By contrast, the particular position of Frankfurt Democrats and later of Frankfurt liberals more generally in their respective national parties really was quite extraordinary. The strong links between Frankfurt left liberals and the various German left-liberal parties constituted, perhaps, the central peculiarity of Frankfurt liberalism during the Empire. Yet despite the inventiveness and the energy with which Frankfurt liberals pursued the policies that mattered to them, what is most striking is how little success they had in translating these policies to state or national party politics. This calls to mind the success with which the most influential urban liberal movement of the 1870s in England, that of Birmingham, managed to export not only its 'municipal gospel', but also to attract national attention for its ideas on party organization and education. It is thus not inconceivable that Frankfurt liberals, with exceptional ideas and outstanding connections to liberals in other levels of government, could have influenced German liberalism similarly. Why, then, did the ideas and the success of liberalism at local level, as in Frankfurt, have so little repercussions on German liberalism in general?

In fact, in a larger, unified national party after 1910 it was more difficult for Frankfurt to pull its weight, particularly as the *Frankfurter Zeitung* now had to share its position as the leading left-liberal party newspaper with the formerly Progressive Liberal *Vossische Zeitung* and the *Berliner Tageblatt*.[33] Still, its influence was remarkable. For instance, the left-liberal attempt to form links with the working classes through the *Reichsverein der liberalen Arbeiter und Angestellten* was congruent with the social demands of Theodor Barth, on the one hand, and the Frankfurt Democrats, on the

---

[32] See the Frankfurt Petition for social policy from Nov. 1910 in BAP 60 Vo 3 n. 37 fos. 184–90.

[33] Nipperdey, *Deutsche Geschichte 1866–1918*, i. 799–803.

other, that the relationship between employer and employee be transformed from a relationship ruled by force to one determined by the law.[34] Yet this counted for little given the reluctance of leading Progressive and Democratic liberals from outside Frankfurt to take any notice of this organization or its aims.[35] The failure of the *Reichsverein* at the national level shows precisely how difficult it was to translate the liberal experience in Frankfurt to the national level.[36]

Even before 1910, despite the disproportionate influence of Frankfurt Democrats within the German People's Party, there were severe constraints to Frankfurt left-liberal influence. After bitter struggles, Sonnemann and the Frankfurt Democrats did largely get their way in emphasizing the party's commitment to social policy. Nonetheless, the practical effect of this was minimal, as from about 1890 national policy was practically determined by the group of German People's Party's members of the Reichstag, and by their leaders Payer and Haußmann in particular. Despite Frankfurt's influence, the People's Party was still essentially at home in Württemberg, the state which contained two-thirds of the party's total membership and whose state parliament was the one national or state assembly in which the party exercised considerable political influence. There, however, the party was reliant on a large rural constituency, which made Frankfurt concerns about urban poverty and the plight of the working classes much more remote.[37] Even though on several occasions Sonnemann may have won the commitment of his party on paper, it is doubtful that by his tactics, and through the implicit threat of using the *Frankfurter Zeitung* for his own ends, he won over the hearts of his Württemberg party friends.

The failure of Frankfurt left-liberal urban social reformers, despite their important and unusual influence over the left liberals at national level,

---

[34] BAP 60 Vo 3 n. 52 fo. 300. *Reichsverein der liberalen Arbeiter und Angestellten*, Leipzig, 1912.

[35] For the relationship between the *Reichsverein* and the central committee of the Progressive People's Party, see BAP 60 Vo 3 n. 52.

[36] A consideration of the *Reichsverein*'s treatment by the Progressive People's Party makes it difficult to accept Sperber's view that the liberals were, in some sense, aware of their own success among the working classes. Sperber, *The Kaiser's Voters*, 149–50. To the contrary, given the apparent working-class support for the left liberals in 1912, the left liberals' failure to respond to working-class concerns and the marginalization of the *Reichsverein* is very striking indeed.

[37] Simon, *Die württembergischen Demokraten*, 39–42, 47. See also K. Simon, 'Die soziale Struktur der württembergischen Volkspartei und ihre Auswirkung auf Programm und Politik der Partei (1882–1914)', in G. A. Ritter (ed.), *Die deutschen Parteien vor 1918* (Cologne, 1973), 224–42, esp. 236.

illustrates very neatly the extraordinary difficulty of translating policies from one level of government to another. The social question was naturally a burning issue for liberals in the cities in Frankfurt as elsewhere, but it was an issue with entirely different connotations for the national political aspirations of the German People's Party, which depended crucially on the rural and small-town constituencies of southern Germany for the election of its representatives to the Reichstag.[38] The same was true for the stronghold of left liberalism, Prussia, where, despite the fact that left liberals derived a great proportion of their support from urban voters, by 1912 left-liberal strength in the Reichstag was crucially dependent on rural and small-town votes, as a result of the overwhelming urban support for the SPD.[39] The liberals' predominant reliance on the countryside for electoral support in state and national elections, then, points to the most important shortcoming of urban liberalism. For however much contemporary urban liberals put their hope in a liberal revival of German politics and society in the cities, based on the vitality, the sophistication, and the innovative nature of urban liberal policy and organization, this hope would necessarily be futile as long as the liberals' political survival outside the level of urban government depended on the countryside. For urban left liberals, party unity in 1910 reinforced this problem, since the extended party's agricultural concerns were proportionately reinforced. For the specific case of Frankfurt, this meant that left liberals there not only had to contend with the priority concern given to southern agriculture, as with the old German People's Party. In the new party, they had to accept in addition the overriding importance of the party's constituencies in the northern and eastern German countryside.

If translating policies from urban to national level proved extremely difficult with regard to the social question, this proved impossible in

---

[38] See the results of the 1898 imperial elections in Württemberg where average support for the People's Party diminished roughly in inverse proportion to the size of the locality. Ritter, *Wahlgeschichtliches Arbeitsbuch*, 113. Simon, *Die württembergischen Demokraten*, 25–36, 42.

[39] In 1912, the Progressive People's Party gained one seat in Berlin, whereas Berlin's other five seats went to the SPD. By contrast, the left liberals fared much better in the districts of Liegnitz (5 out of 10 seats), Schleswig-Holstein (7 out of 10), and Stralsund (2 out of 2). Ritter, *Wahlgeschichtliches Arbeitsbuch*, 67–83. For the example of Schleswig-Holstein, see esp. Thompson, 'Left liberals', 347–402. The dependence on the countryside was not unique to left liberals, as the strength of the SPD or the Centre parties in the cities increased the importance of the countryside to the National Liberals, too. For the most recent study of National Liberal politics in one of their most important rural strongholds, see John, 'Kultur, Klasse und regionaler Liberalismus', 161–93. The need for National Liberals to respond differently to different types of constituencies has been highlighted in Eley, 'Notable Politics', 187–216.

education. For one thing, education was not a primary issue in national politics, as it was a state matter. Even though, as this study has shown, education was a critical factor of unity and purpose for liberals in the city, it was simply impossible for this to spill over to the liberals at the national level. Yet even had education been a national concern, it is unlikely that liberals in the cities could have made a great impact at that level. As the debates surrounding various Prussian education bills show, liberals in the cities, especially in the National Liberal party, were unable to make themselves heard at state level. Too large were the differences between cities and the countryside, confessional faultlines, and varying degrees of religious observance. The best illustration of this is the 1906 school finance bill, which urban left- and right-liberals throughout Prussia opposed with one voice. And yet, this was a bill which had originated not with the government, which would have been content to leave the issue of denominational education well alone, but with the National Liberal (and Conservative) representatives in the Prussian chamber of deputies, in their concern for the tremendous burden which financing the rural primary school placed upon the poorer agricultural and small-town areas.[40] Instead of being the great unifying and galvanizing force of liberalism, in which urban liberals could play an important and progressive part, in Germany education became a source of fundamental contradiction and division between liberals in the city and liberals at state level.

The relationship between liberals at the local, state, and national levels on the issue of finance is rather more complex. Unlike in education and, to some extent, in social policy, liberals in the city had vastly different views about municipal finance themselves, as they operated in very different circumstances according to the social, industrial, and historical composition of their urban environments. Still, Miquel's local finance reform of 1893 provided liberals in the cities with the wherewithal to expand, and, despite creating relative winners and losers, it gave urban liberals a tremendous boost in self-confidence and importance vis-à-vis the state. Despite problems, then, local government finance had effectively and comprehensively been addressed, at least for Prussia. Yet if after 1893 self-government was encouraged, as urban liberals could raise taxation which was specific to local government, it diverted their attention away from issues of national and state finance. Liberals in the cities may have become increasingly sophisticated at the implementation of property taxation, as is shown by Adickes's pioneering efforts in taxing profits on land speculation. This gave them

[40] Loening, 'Die Unterhaltung der öffentlichen Volksschulen', 90–1.

little to say, however, about taxation at the state or national level. And yet, it was the much-needed imperial finance reform that occupied leading liberal academics and politicians since 1906 more than any other issue, save, perhaps, the reform of the Prussian franchise.[41] Liberals in the cities could have little to say about this, except that in Prussia they became but one other interest group lobbying for the retention of their particular rights against encroachment from the imperial state. In Germany, any national finance reform undertaken by a government and political parties overwhelmingly dominated by agricultural interests was almost bound to be opposed to the aspirations of liberals in the cities. Despite their best intentions, and despite their innovativeness in the field of municipal finance, education, and social policies, the federal nature of the German polity made it all but impossible for liberals in the cities to make a significant contribution to liberalism in state or national politics.

There was, of course, a lively interchange of ideas between urban liberals themselves. Other cities could and did adopt the Frankfurt system in secondary schools, in the same way that Frankfurt liberals took inspiration from the technical schools pioneered in Munich. As with social or financial policies, the most effective way for urban liberals to influence education elsewhere was by lobbying state authorities to allow cities the freedom to introduce individual innovations themselves. Helped by annual gatherings such as the *Städtetag*, the best liberals in the cities could achieve was to extend their ideas to each other, and to preserve their achievements as best they could against governments at the state and national levels, and often also against the various liberal parties operating at those levels.

The failure of Frankfurt's left liberals to translate their ideas and their experience of being in power to the state or national levels stands in stark contrast to the success of Johannes Miquel in moving effortlessly from local politics to national politics, and on to state government. Ironically, during the 1890s the best hope for the locally dominant Democrats to achieve some of their aspirations on a wider level rested on their unique access to Miquel in Berlin. Yet apart from Miquel's undoubted ingenuity, there was an important reason for his success. To move between the various levels of politics, Miquel was forced to be extremely Janus-faced which only his

---

[41] On the inability of the German Empire to reform its finances in the run-up to the First World War, see N. Ferguson, 'Germany and the Origins of the First World War: New Perspectives', *HJ* xxxv (1992), 725–52. N. Ferguson, 'Public Finance and National Security: The Domestic Origins of the First World War Revisited', *PP*, no. 142 (1994), 141–68. On the abortive negotiations for an imperial finance reform up to spring 1909, see Witt, *Die Finanzpolitik*, 17–58.

secure position in local government as First Mayor could allow him to do. During the 1880s, Frankfurt Democrats watched with indignation at Miquel's role in shifting the National Liberal Party to the right at the national level. Yet at no time did Miquel rely on the popular Frankfurt vote. When he decided to stand for the Reichstag in the 1887 elections, he stayed well clear of Frankfurt and stood for the seat of Kaiserslautern, where he got duly elected. This ideological flexibility was a luxury that urban liberals could ill afford. For in their aspirations for political influence beyond the urban environment, they nevertheless had to be mindful first and foremost to their urban constituencies at home.

This study has demonstrated for the case of Frankfurt am Main that Germany was not an inherently illiberal society, and neither were the cities bastions of 'the unpolitical German', if he ever existed. German liberals were neither intrinsically possessed by dogmatic rigidity, nor were they political amateurs who in their naivety completely failed to recognize the growing complexities of German politics and society. A study of liberal politics at the local level of government, which was, after all, the only level of government at which liberals across Germany had any real political power throughout the Empire, shows how sophisticated, dynamic, and pragmatic German liberals could be, given half a chance of being in power. This study's findings about how liberals coped when they were actually in control of the executive confirms more recent arguments, that the central 'peculiarity' of German liberalism relative to liberal movements in other countries was the lack of parliamentary government in Germany. If Frankfurt Democrats, once they had a majority in the council, guaranteed their survival in a changing political environment through their popular budgets and rates of taxation, the inability of liberals at the state and national levels to do the same appears all the more critical. Without the ability to introduce and pass a 'People's Budget', there could be no German equivalent of the English 'New Liberalism'.

Moreover, this problem of the absence of parliamentary government cannot be seen in isolation to the challenge which the federal nature of Germany presented to the liberals. Unlike the Centre Party or the SPD, German liberals could not count on the solid support of relatively well-defined confessional or social groups. Their central problem was how to find a consistent appeal to the electorate in three different polities which differed vastly in the number and social composition of the electorate, their political traditions, and the function of their legislative bodies. In a country so recently united, it is not surprising that a precondition for liberal success at a local or regional level was the ability to appeal to and then shape the local political culture.[42] Across Germany, local patriotism became the essential ingredient of liberal rhetoric and electoral appeal. In Frankfurt, liberals constantly needed to appeal to the local peculiarities in the city's culture and history. Yet if liberals recognized this basic fact of German political life, then their responsiveness to regional peculiarities made the achievement of nationally consistent and unambiguous policies which satisfied every regional liberal movement almost impossible. The diversity of their various local and social constituencies may not be the least of reasons why liberal unity proved impossible to achieve during the Empire. Moreover, the need to operate in vastly different political environments in federal Germany made it so difficult for municipal liberalism to transmit some of its experience of being in the executive, its energy, and its innovative character to liberals at the national level, and made urban liberal hopes at a liberalization of German society from the grass roots so unrealistic. By 1914, despite the urbanization of German society, much of the parliamentary support of German left- and right-liberalism at the state and national levels rested with the countryside. This is precisely why liberals found it so difficult to come out unambiguously for the urban consumer on the issue of tariffs, and this is why urban liberals had such trouble getting themselves heard at the national and state levels. German liberals were not 'peculiar', for the example of Frankfurt shows that they could be as pragmatic and sophisticated as any liberal movement in late nineteenth-century Europe. What was pecu-liar, and what presented German liberalism with almost insurmountable difficulties, was the constitutional environment in which it operated.

---

[42] This is in striking contrast to Eugenio Biagini's conclusion for liberalism in Britain that despite the regional and local diversity in which liberals operated there, too, there was a remarkable cultural homogeneity which was conducive to the development of a popular, united liberal movement, at least until the 1880s. E. F. Biagini, *Liberty, Retrenchment and Reform. Popular Liberalism in the Age of Gladstone, 1860–1880* (Cambridge, 1992).

Appendix I

Unless indicated otherwise, the figures for the following tables have been compiled from the annual administrative reports of the *Magistrat* to the city council. See *MAB*, 1874–1914. It is important to note that the years denote financial, rather than actual, years. Until 1876, the financial year ended on 31 December, whereas from 1877 the financial year carried on from April to March (the financial year of 1877 consisted of fifteen months).

Figures for municipal assets were only included in the printed reports of the *Magistrat* from 1890. The earliest figure for municipal assets in this period appears to be from 1882. However, the definition of what constituted municipal assets changed over the years, and was only conclusive once all municipal property was properly recorded and evaluated, from 1893. Figures in Table C before then should be treated as estimates rather than actuals. IfSG, AS A 47 fo. 25 f. *MAB*, 1891/2, p. 16.

TABLE A.   *General public expenditure in Frankfurt am Main, 1874–1912* (in Marks)

Year	Amount	Year	Amount
1874	2,132,073	1894	19,921,988
1875	3,448,016	1895	20,012,264
1876	9,005,974	1896	23,628,865
1877	21,481,195	1897	25,579,738
1878	10,180,773	1898	29,026,743
1879	9,751,943	1899	37,964,204
1880	8,939,979	1900	47,068,341
1881	8,853,591	1901	42,267,235
1882	9,662,445	1902	41,323,465
1883	11,915,595	1903	42,286,448
1884	13,622,739	1904	53,597,155
1885	14,664,721	1905	58,468,089
1886	14,173,161	1906	63,923,020
1887	14,303,701	1907	70,845,172
1888	15,033,689	1908	72,885,562
1889	17,117,564	1909	87,229,571
1890	19,116,464	1910	80,871,728
1891	19,423,187	1911	84,590,046
1892	18,363,703	1912	83,999,170
1893	16,939,446		

The figures are the sums of ordinary (recurrent) and extraordinary (one-off) budget expenditures in Marks and include expenditure in the *Reste-Verwaltung* which consisted of unspent funds from the previous year. (On account of the latter, the figures given here slightly differ from figures for total expenditure 1894–1906 given in Table 6.9 in Ch. 6, which exclude the *Reste-Verwaltung*.)

The 'blip' in 1877 is a mistake of accounting, for it includes a loan of 16 million Marks, whereas usually loans were recorded through annual repayments of debts and interest charges.

TABLE B. *Actual public expenditure in Frankfurt am Main, 1895–1912* (in Marks)

	General budget expenditure	Expenditure on municipal services	Total actual expenditure
1895	20,012,264		20,012,264
1896	23,628,865		23,628,865
1897	25,579,738	17,837,834	43,417,572
1898	29,026,743	30,201,854	59,228,597
1899	37,964,204	27,574,874	65,539,078
1900	47,068,341	36,692,480	83,760,821
1901	42,267,235	37,457,460	79,724,695
1902	41,323,465	42,942,771	84,266,236
1903	42,286,448	44,236,384	86,522,832
1904	53,597,155	58,918,344	112,515,499
1905	58,468,089	58,696,994	117,165,083
1906	63,923,020	56,338,168	120,261,188
1907	70,845,172	67,817,311	138,662,483
1908	72,885,562	74,973,328	147,858,890
1909	87,229,571	92,675,680	179,905,251
1910	80,871,728	97,772,583	178,644,311
1911	84,590,046	111,331,917	195,921,963
1912	83,999,170	113,990,229	197,989,399

Appendix

TABLE C. *Municipal debts and assets in Frankfurt am Main, 1873–1913* (in Marks)

	Total debts	Total assets	Municipal wealth
1873	2,114,228		
1874	4,072,885		
1875	6,570,485		
1876	13,437,556		
1877	24,213,746		
1878	28,861,319		
1879	30,344,742		
1880	33,073,260		
1881	33,840,908		
1882	34,436,431	70,936,035	
1883	34,764,260		
1884	37,285,488		
1885	41,297,602		
1886	43,043,602		
1887	43,066,002		
1888	41,928,316		
1889	42,826,973		
1890	43,407,869	121,958,632	78,550,763
1891	48,700,915	122,617,240	73,916,325
1892	51,997,920	126,579,527	74,581,607
1893	51,704,344	127,203,115	75,498,771
1894	51,802,961	130,291,481	78,488,519
1895	64,067,439	146,207,580	82,140,141
1896	65,552,279	150,464,961	84,912,681
1897	70,874,651	176,785,111	105,910,460
1898	84,947,672	191,542,130	106,594,458
1899	94,026,958	208,080,809	114,053,850
1900	106,918,667	233,564,971	126,646,304
1901	116,337,872	245,260,293	128,922,421
1902	122,155,131	256,024,115	133,868,983
1903	138,189,569	277,830,305	139,640,735
1904	166,326,297	323,019,054	156,692,756
1905	182,581,723	341,683,113	159,101,390
1906	196,329,683	365,479,646	169,149,963
1907	222,947,688	397,676,161	174,728,472
1908	259,214,027	438,232,193	179,018,165
1909	271,101,420	457,960,814	186,859,393
1910	288,023,051	490,954,292	202,931,240
1911	312,429,676	523,779,815	211,350,138
1912	322,247,186	548,474,046	226,226,860
1913	327,896,274	565,157,118	237,260,893

TABLE D. *Local taxation in Frankfurt am Main, 1868–1913 (in Marks)*

	Income tax	Rent/house tax	Property sales tax	Business tax	Other	Total	Per head
1868	383,407	414,586			338,235	1,136,228	14.20
1869	417,588	429,210			386,953	1,233,751	14.85
1870	503,414	445,906			513,961	1,463,281	16.96
1871	521,117	449,120			477,427	1,447,664	16.14
1872	601,511	560,419			645,353	1,807,283	19.48
1873	985,995	556,945			668,880	2,211,820	23.09
1874	1,140,059	691,968			492,512	2,324,539	23.57
1875	1,268,812	737,527	359,174		50,692	2,416,205	23.73
1876	1,167,400	803,000	246,599		53,130	2,270,129	21.57
1877	1,492,218	1,063,160	367,825		95,398	3,018,601	24.91
1878	1,668,300	917,659	219,395		73,800	2,879,154	23.22
1879	2,118,748	957,572	158,173		70,966	3,305,459	25.89
1880	2,503,690	1,001,352	165,326		71,634	3,742,002	28.00
1881	2,933,700	1,017,897	235,122		122,510	4,309,229	30.92
1882	3,165,903	1,039,112	234,516		120,480	4,560,011	31.41
1883	3,355,973	1,060,573	211,877		112,088	4,740,511	31.78
1884	3,380,155	1,089,915	219,007		115,929	4,805,006	30.99
1885	3,497,739	1,112,690	219,224		116,446	4,946,099	30.90
1886	3,561,685	1,147,688	263,318		107,380	5,080,071	31.43
1887	3,778,477	1,181,913	297,969		113,660	5,372,019	32.01
1888	3,948,243	1,249,287	422,356		120,914	5,740,800	32.97
1889	4,177,499	1,187,838	497,631		127,734	5,990,702	35.03

Year						
1890	4,379,599	1,225,207	443,453		177,967	6,226,226	34.72
1891	4,501,719	1,310,701	480,451		167,093	6,459,964	34.53
1892	4,765,639	1,358,983	494,291		243,959	6,862,872	36.89
1893	4,714,638	1,499,004	755,653		233,649	7,202,944	37.71
1894	4,647,565	1,529,811	852,705		284,385	7,314,466	36.79
1895	4,948,365	2,313,289	592,251	834,346	418,192	9,106,443	40.21
1896	5,151,559	2,518,071	589,308	889,157	311,791	9,459,886	40.95
1897	5,603,428	2,470,290	873,227	920,519	432,710	10,300,174	43.19
1898	6,073,334	2,425,144	761,268	906,224	512,522	10,678,492	43.51
1899	6,771,509	2,596,491	1,583,363	1,031,353	420,907	12,403,623	48.19
1900	7,335,398	2,745,477	1,114,376	1,101,479	420,089	12,716,819	44.62
1901	7,776,686	3,008,800	1,270,925	1,130,896	449,613	13,636,920	46.38
1902	7,658,663	3,209,600	1,359,962	1,114,136	473,236	13,815,597	45.75
1903	7,587,386	3,365,878	1,922,530	1,020,716	481,534	14,378,044	46.38
1904	7,747,085	3,152,070	1,999,372	1,448,656	539,194	14,886,377	46.88
1905	8,464,212	3,350,469	3,801,135	1,737,345	734,707	18,087,868	53.67
1906	9,149,377	3,567,284	3,967,373	1,863,137	798,146	19,345,317	56.40
1907	10,010,151	3,736,788	2,486,081	1,997,424	762,233	18,992,677	53.95
1908	10,199,598	3,963,898	1,532,019	2,027,851	681,069	18,404,435	51.12
1909	12,265,543	4,127,212	1,564,603	2,282,390	688,491	20,928,239	56.71
1910	14,574,220	4,456,555	1,931,824	2,390,443	1,164,004	24,517,046	59.13
1911	15,174,392	4,599,769	1,840,472	2,405,537	1,141,551	25,161,721	59.88
1912	16,309,006	4,790,036	1,963,941	2,557,921	1,275,171	26,896,075	62.27
1913	16,939,601	4,981,810	1,905,562	2,624,203	1,197,741	27,648,917	62.51

Appendix II

The main sources for this table are the reports in the *Frankfurter Zeitung* of each council election result. The difficulty is that the party of the individual councillor is only stated a few times. More often, party strengths are given for each party coalition, which does not allow for a discrimination between, say, the Democrats and the Progressive Liberals. Unfortunately, the most common practice for the newspaper was to reveal the success of party lists, which is a nice rhetorical way of hiding the real results of the election as they included members of all parties. In this way, for example, the Democrats could claim victory for 'their' list during almost each election in the fourth electoral district, even though the candidates were almost always National Liberals. Once the ice of the newspaper's rhetoric has been cut, it is possible to determine the party composition of the city council with reasonable accuracy from 1881 onwards. The party strengths given here differ slightly from the *Frankfurter Zeitung*'s own statements in that the paper was fond of counting as its own candidates who had run as independents but whom it considered to be on the left of the political spectrum. It should be noted that for the figures given for the party composition of the council from 1875 to 1879 there is a small margin of error. This is essentially because the *Frankfurter Zeitung* could not make up its mind whether to include a handful of councillors as Democrats or not. For example, in the 1877 council the paper reported that the Democrats had 33 seats, whereas the National Liberals and the Progressive Liberals together could muster only 21 seats. In 1878, however, the newspaper was involved in a bizarre row with the National Liberal newspaper *Neue Frankfurter Presse*, as it tried to defend the Democrats over 'allegations' that they had had the majority in the city council throughout most of the 1870s. The *Frankfurter Zeitung* tried to show that from 1876 to 1878 it had never possessed a majority in the council, and denied that individual councillors such as Eduard Fay or Christian Sauerwein were Democrats (which they clearly were). For the period 1875 to 1881, therefore, the party composition is an approximation of party strength, as the party allegiance of up to four members of each council could not be determined with absolute certainty.

The party allegiance of individual members has been been compiled from party membership lists (which were of little help), petition signatures, signatures under election manifestos, appearances in election meetings, and listings in the *Frankfurter Zeitung*. The most important sources are:

Appendix

E. Dannenberg (ed.), *Haupt-Register zu den Mittheilungen aus den Protokollen der Stadtverordneten- Versammlung der Stadt Frankfurt a.M. für die Jahrgänge 1867 bis incl. 1900 nebst einem Verzeichniß der Mitglieder des Magistrats und der Stadtverordneten- Versammlung seit dem Jahre 1867* (Frankfurt, 1902).
Patricia Tratnik, 'Mitglieder der Frankfurter Stadtverordnetenversammlung 1867 bis 1933' (Frankfurt, 1984), typescript in IfSG.
Geschichte der Frankfurter Zeitung 1856–1906 (Frankfurt, 1906), 566.
Frankfurter Zeitung, 5 Dec. 1876 (Morgenblatt), 22 Nov. 1878 (Abendblatt), 24 Nov. 1878 (Morgenblatt), 29 Nov. 1878 (Morgenblatt), 29 Sept. 1879 (Morgenblatt), 28 Nov. 1882 (Morgenblatt), 5 Dec. 1882 (Morgenblatt), 28 Nov. 1884 (Morgenblatt), 5 Dec. 1884 (Morgenblatt), 26 Nov. 1886 (2. Morgenblatt), 3 Dec. 1886 (2. Morgenblatt), 29 Nov. 1888 (2. Morgenblatt), 25 Nov. 1890 (2. Morgenblatt), 1 Dec. 1892 (Abendblatt), 23 Nov. 1894 (2. Morgenblatt), 27 Nov. 1894 (Abendblatt), 13 Nov. 1896 (3. Morgenblatt), 20 Nov. 1896 (3. Morgenblatt), 18 Nov. 1898 (3. Morgenblatt), 25 Nov. 1898 (3. Morgenblatt).

The party composition from 1900 is well-known and is given in Patricia Tratnick's study as well as in John Rolling, 'Liberals', 180. Rolling also notes the council's composition by party group for 1898, but his figures for that year contradict those given by the *Kleine Presse* (whose figures are adopted here). *Kleine Presse*, 24 Nov. 1900.

Distribution of seats in the Frankfurt City Council, 1877–1913

	1877	1879	1881	1883	1885	1887	1889	1891	1893	1895
Democrats	32	30	29	28	27	29	28	28	27	26
Progressive Liberal Association	10	8	11	14	14	13	14	14	12	15
National Liberal Association	11	12	12	11	13	12	13	13	14	19
SPD										
Mittelstand										
Centre Party										
Others	1	7	5	4	3	3	2	2	4	1
TOTAL NUMBER OF SEATS	54	57	57	57	57	57	57	57	57	61

	1897	1899	1901	1903	1905	1907	1909	1911	1913
Democrats	27	23	23	23	23	24	17	34	32
Progressive Liberal Association	14	13	11	12	12	13	12		
National Liberal Association	19	23	20	20	11	13	10	12	12
SPD			1	1	3	6	15	22	23
Mittelstand		1	6	8	15	8	8	3	3
Centre Party			2						1
Others	1	1	1				2		
TOTAL NUMBER OF SEATS	61	61	64	64	64	64	64	71	71

The Prussian State Elections in Frankfurt am Main[a]

Candidates elected successfully[b]		Unsuccessful candidates	
1867	Schiele (PL), Ebner (PL)[c]	Scharff (C)	
	Kugler (PL)		
1869	Weiß (D)[d]	Kugler (PL)	Passavant (NL)
1870	Kugler (PL)	Richter (PL)[e]	
	Vogtherr (PL)	Weiß (D)	
1872	Flinsch (PL)[f]	Prior (D)	
	Schrader (PL)[g]	Marti (D)	
1873	Schrader (PL)		
	Lasker (NL)	Virchow (PL)	
1876	Schrader (PL)	Holthoff (D)	
	Lasker (NL)		
1878	Lucius (NL)[h]	Götz-Rigand (PL)	
1879	Labes (PL)	Lasker (NL)	
	Traeger (PL)	Janssen (Z)	
1882	Flinsch (PL)	Metzler (NL)	
	Stern (D)		
1885	Flinsch (PL)	May (D)	
	Metzler (NL)		
1888	Metzler (NL)	Flinsch (PL)	
	Hergenhahn (NL)		
1891	Grimm (NL)[i]	Funck (PL)	
1892	Funck (PL)[j]	Grimm (NL)	
1893	von Rath (NL)	Horckheimer (PL)[k]	
	Oswalt (NL)		
1898	Funck (PL)	Oswalt (NL)[l]	
	Sänger (D)	von Rath (NL)	
1901	Oeser (D)[m]	von Rath (NL)	
1903	Funck (PL)	Quarck (SPD)	
	Oeser (D)	Hüttmann (SPD)	
1908	Funck (PL)	Quarck (SPD)	Ladenburg (NL)
	Flesch (D)	Hüttmann (SPD)	Hamecher (Z)
1913	Flesch (D)	Quarck (SPD)	Varrentrapp (NL)
	Oeser (D)	Hüttmann (SPD)	Kleinschmidt (NL)

[a] T. Kühne, *Handbuch der Wahlen zum Preußischen Abgeordnetenhaus 1867–1918. Wahlergebnisse, Wahlbündnisse und Wahlkandidaten* (Düsseldorf, 1994), 672–5. Years printed in bold denote general state elections.

[b] PL = Progressive Liberals. NL = National Liberals. D = Democrats. C = Conservatives. SPD = Social Democrats. Z = Centre Party.

[c] Schiele refused to accept his election, Ebner was elected instead.

[d] Weiß replaced Kugler.

[e] Eugen Richter was nominated by the Democrats in the hope to split the official local Progressive Liberal ticket.

[f] Flinsch replaced Vogtherr.   [g] Schrader replaced Kugler.

[h] Lucius replaced Schrader.

[i] Grimm replaced Hergenhahn.   [j] Funck replaced Grimm.
[k] Horckheimer was the common candidate for the Democrats and the Progressive Liberals.
[l] After the elections of electors produced an overwhelming victory for the supporters of the left-liberal candidates, the National Liberals recommended that their electors stay away from the actual polls.
[m] Oeser replaced Sänger.

National General Elections in Germany, 1871–1914 (in %)

	1871	1874	1877	1878	1881	1884	1887	1890	1893	1898	1903	1907	1912
German People's Party	0.5	0.4	0.8	1.1	2.0	1.7	1.2	2.0	2.2	1.4	1.0	1.2	
National Liberal Party	30.1	29.7	27.2	23.1	14.7	17.6	22.3	16.3	13.0	12.5	13.8	14.5	13.6
German Progressive Party	8.8	8.6	7.7	6.7	12.7	17.6	12.9	16.0	8.7	7.2	5.7	6.5	12.3
Liberal Association					8.4				3.4	2.5	2.6	3.2	
Social Democratic Party	3.2	6.8	9.1	7.6	6.1	9.7	10.1	19.7	23.3	27.2	31.6	28.9	34.8
Centre Party	18.6	27.9	24.8	23.1	23.2	22.7	20.1	18.6	19.1	18.8	19.7	19.4	16.4
Anti-Semites							0.2	0.7	3.4	3.7	2.6	2.2	2.5
Conservatives	14.1	6.9	9.7	13.0	16.3	15.2	15.2	12.4	13.5	11.1	10.0	9.4	9.2
Free Conservatives	8.9	7.2	7.9	13.6	7.4	6.9	9.8	6.7	5.7	4.4	3.5	4.2	3.0
Others	15.8	12.4	12.6	11.8	9.1	8.7	8.3	7.6	7.7	11.2	9.5	10.4	8.2
TOTAL	100.0	100.0	100.0	100.0	100.0	100.0	100.0	100.0	100.0	100.0	100.0	100.0	100.0

Source: Ritter, *Wahlgeschichtliches Arbeitsbuch*, 38–42.

National General Elections in Germany, 1871–1914 (in 1,000 votes)

	1871	1874	1877	1878	1881	1884	1887	1890	1893	1898	1903	1907	1912
German People's Party	19	22	45	66	103	96	89	148	167	109	91	139	
National Liberal Party	1,171	1,543	1,470	1331	747	997	1,678	1,178	997	971	1,313	1,637	1,663
German Progressive Party	342	448	418	385	649	997	973	1,160	666	558	543	736	1,497
Liberal Association					429				258	196	243	359	
Social Democratic Party	124	352	493	437	312	550	763	1,427	1,787	2,107	3,001	3,259	4,250
Centre Party	724	1,446	1,341	1328	1,183	1,283	1,516	1,342	1,469	1,455	1,875	2,180	1,997
Anti-Semites							12	48	264	284	245	249	300
Conservatives	549	360	526	749	831	861	1,147	895	1,038	859	948	1,060	1,126
Free Conservatives	346	376	427	786	379	388	736	482	438	344	333	472	367
Others	613	643	681	679	464	491	627	549	590	869	903	1,172	1,007
TOTAL	3,888	5,190	5,401	5761	5,097	5,663	7,541	7,229	7,674	7,752	9,495	11,263	12,207

Source: Ritter, *Wahlgeschichtliches Arbeitsbuch*, 38–42.

National General Elections in Frankfurt a.M., 1871–1914 (in %)

	1871	1874	1877	1878	1881	1884	1887	1890	1893	1898	1903	1907	1912
German People's Party	43.20	41.51	32.08	35.61	46.20	33.62	27.93	20.47	22.75		18.46	28.85	42.31
National Liberal Party	2.61	36.03	30.31	23.83	8.58	16.41	37.91	23.65	23.57		12.41	8.61	
German Progressive Party	8.77	2.28	9.72	13.11				8.15		30.77			
National Social Party										8.36			1.74
Social Democratic Party	6.31	19.56	22.48	21.19	27.83	36.30	34.08	42.29	43.68	50.82	49.39	47.08	48.23
Centre Party	3.22		5.34	5.14	6.31	6.16		5.33	5.24	6.07	8.69	7.18	7.71
Anti-Semites									4.69	3.94	11.03	8.25	
Conservatives	35.86			1.06	10.96	7.30							
Others	0.03	0.63	0.07	0.07	0.14	0.21	0.08	0.11	0.07	0.04	0.02	0.03	0.01
TOTAL	100.00	100.00	100.00	100.00	100.00	100.00	100.00	100.00	100.00	100.00	100.00	100.00	100.00

National General Elections in Frankfurt a.M., 1871–1914 (in number of votes cast)

	1871	1874	1877	1878	1881	1884	1887	1890	1893	1898	1903	1907	1912
German People's Party	3,060	5,016	4,920	6,858	7,810	7,378	7,081	6,126	7,020		7,543	17,692	31,306
National Liberal Party	185	4,353	4,648	4,589	1,450	3,601	9,609	7,078	7,274		5,068	5,280	
German Progressive Party	621	275	1,491	2,524				2,438		12,123			

National General Elections in Frankfurt a.M., 1871–1914 (in number of votes cast)

	1871	1874	1877	1878	1881	1884	1887	1890	1893	1898	1903	1907	1912
National Social Party										3,295			1,289
Social Democratic Party	447	2,363	3,448	4,080	4,704	7,965	8,640	12,653	13,482	20,019	20,178	28,869	35,686
Centre Party	228		819	989	1,066	1,352		1,594	1,617	2,391	3,551	4,405	5,708
Anti-Semites									1,448	1,551	4,506	5,056	
Conservatives	2,540			204	1,852	1,602							
Others	2	76	11	14	23	46	20	34	22	14	8	17	8
TOTAL	7,083	12,083	15,337	19,258	16,905	21,944	25,350	29,923	30,863	39,393	40,854	61,319	73,997
Electoral Participation (in %)	35.2	60	56.2	66	54.6	64.4	70.4	72.8	64.2	65.9	55.9	79.6	83.8

Conservatives: 1871: Freikonservative, 1878: Deutschkonservative, 1881: Konservative

Source: 'Ergebnisse der Wahlen in Frankfurt am Main 1871–1933', ed. Statistisches Amt und Wahlamt Frankfurt (Frankfurt). See also Specht and Schwabe, *Reichstagswahlen*, 157, 45.

Run-off Elections in Frankfurt a.M., 1871–1914

	1871	1874	1877	1878	1881	1884	1887	1890	1893	1898	1903	1907	1912
German People's Party	3,758	7,185	10,329	12,489	9,146	10,777							
National Liberal Party		5,685	7,339	5,556			12,687	10,567	11,266		21,796	33,695	35,686
Social Democratic Party					8,602	12,166	12,876	18,088	17,180		23,581	30,778	39,233
Conservatives	3,679												

Bibliography

A. ARCHIVAL SOURCES

Institut für Stadtgeschichte, Frankfurt am Main (IfSG)
S1 – Nachlässe
S2 – Personen
S3 – Ereignisse, Parteien, Vereine, etc.
AS – Akten der Stadtverordnetenversammlung
AS P – Protokolle der Stadtverordnetenversammlung
ASA – Akten des Statistischen Amts der Stadt Frankfurt am Main
MA – Akten des Magistrats

Hessisches Hauptstaatsarchiv, Wiesbaden (HStAW)
Abt. 405 – Regierungspräsidium Wiesbaden (Zeitungsberichte)
Abt. 407 – Polizeipräsident Frankfurt am Main

Bundesarchiv Koblenz (BAK)
NL 20 – Nachlaß Friedrich Payer
NL 44 – Nachlaß Hermann Luppe

Bundesarchiv Potsdam (BAP)
Reichsamt des Innern. Centralbüreau
60 Vo 3 – Fortschrittliche Volkspartei
90 Ba 4 – Nachlaß Theodor Barth
90 Sta 1 – Nachlaß Franz August Schenk von Stauffenberg
90 Na 3 – Nachlaß Friedrich Naumann
90 Br 3 – Nachlaß Max Broemel
90 Do 2 – Nachlaß Karl E. Doepler
90 Kn 1 – Nachlaß Julius Knorr

B. PRINTED SOURCES

i. Municipal Government in Frankfurt am Main

Anzeige-Blatt der städtischen Behörden zu Frankfurt am Main (1867–1914).

Berichte des Magistrats, die Verwaltung und den Stand der Gemeinde-Angelegenheiten am Schlusse des Etatsjahres . . . betreffend (Frankfurt, 1871–1914).
Bürgerbuch (Sammlung von Verordnungen) der Stadtgemeinde Frankfurt am Main. Amtliche Ausgabe 1912 (Frankfurt, 1912).
Haupt-Register zu den Mittheilungen aus den Protokollen der Stadtverordneten-Versammlung der Stadt Frankfurt a.M. für die Jahrgänge 1867 bis incl. 1900, nebst einem Verzeichniß der Mitglieder des Magistrats und der Stadtverordneten-Versammlung seit dem Jahre 1867, ed. Ernst Dannenberg (Frankfurt, 1902).
Mitteilungen aus den Protokollen der Stadtverordnetenversammlung der Stadt Frankfurt am Main (Frankfurt, 1867–1914).
TRATNIK, PATRICIA, 'Mitglieder der Frankfurter Stadtverordnetenversammlung 1867–1933' (Frankfurt, 1984). Typescript in the Institute for Local History (the Frankfurt City Archives).

ii. Statistical Sources

Beiträge zur Statistik der Stadt Frankfurt am Main, ed. Frankfurter Verein für Geographie und Statistik, ii (1864–1875).
Beiträge zur Statistik der Stadt Frankfurt am Main, ed. Frankfurter Verein für Geographie und Statistik, iii (1876–1880).
Beiträge zur Statistik der Stadt Frankfurt am Main, ed. Frankfurter Verein für Geographie und Statistik, iv (1882–1885).
Beiträge zur Statistik der Stadt Frankfurt am Main, ed. Frankfurter Verein für Geographie und Statistik, v (1890).
Beiträge zur Statistik der Stadt Frankfurt am Main, ed. Statistisches Amt (Frankfurt, 1895).
Beiträge zur Statistik der Stadt Frankfurt am Main. Untersuchung über den Stand der Lohn und Arbeitsverhältnisse der Arbeiter und Unterangestellten der Stadt Frankfurt a.M. im Juli 1907, ed. Statistisches Amt (Frankfurt, 1909).
Beiträge zur Statistik der Stadt Frankfurt am Main, ed. Statistisches Amt (Frankfurt, 1909).
Statistisches Amt und Wahlamt, 'Ergebnisse der Wahlen in Frankfurt am Main 1871–1933. Eine Zusammenstellung aus früheren Veröffentlichungen' (unpublished typescript, Frankfurt University Library, Frankfurt Collection).
Statistisches Handbuch der Stadt Frankfurt am Main, ed. Statistisches Amt (Frankfurt, 1907).
Statistische Jahresübersichten der Stadt Frankfurt am Main 1906/07, ed. Statistisches Amt (Frankfurt, 1908).
Statistische Jahresübersichten der Stadt Frankfurt am Main 1907/08, ed. Statistisches Amt (Frankfurt, 1908).
Statistische Jahresübersichten der Stadt Frankfurt am Main 1909/10, ed. Statistisches Amt (Frankfurt, 1910).
Statistische Jahresübersichten der Stadt Frankfurt am Main 1911/12, ed. Statistisches Amt (Frankfurt, 1912).

Statistische Jahresübersichten der Stadt Frankfurt am Main 1913/14, ed. Statistisches Amt (Frankfurt, 1915).

Statistisches Handbuch der Stadt Frankfurt am Main. Zweite Ausgabe enthaltend die Statistik der Jahre 1906/07 bis 1926/27, ed. Statistisches Amt (Frankfurt, 1928).

iii. Newspapers

Frankfurter Beobachter, 1875–1888.
Frankfurter Intelligenzblatt, 1864.
Frankfurter Intelligenzblatt (Frankfurter Journal), 1900–1914.
Frankfurter Journal, 1856–1878.
Frankfurter Latern, 1872–1877.
Frankfurter Nachrichten, 1888–1908.
Frankfurter Presse, 1870–1873, 1880.
Frankfurter Reform, 1864–1866.
Frankfurter Volksbote, 1856.
Frankfurter Zeitung, 1866–1914.
Katholisches Sonntagsblatt für die christliche Familie, 1894–1900.
Kleine Presse, 1885–1914.
Neue Frankfurter Presse, 1873–1878.
Städte-Zeitung, 2 (1904)–4 (1907).
Volksfreund für das Mittlere Deutschland, 1857–1866.
Volksstimme, 1906–1909.

iv. Other Sources

Stenographische Berichte über die Verhandlungen des Preußischen Abgeordnetenhauses (1867–1908).

C. PRINTED PRIMARY SOURCES

50 Jahre Günthersburgschule 1906–1956. Festschrift (Frankfurt, 1956).

55. Jahresbericht der Deutschkatholischen (freien religiösen) Gemeinde zu Frankfurt a.M. (Frankfurt, 1901).

70 Jahre Aktienbaugesellschaft für kleine Wohnungen Frankfurt a.M., 1890–1960 (Frankfurt, 1960).

150 Jahre Elisabethenschule 1803–1953. Festschrift (Frankfurt, 1953).

ADICKES, FRANZ, *Studien über die Weiterentwicklung des Gemeindesteuerwesens. Auf Grund des Preussischen Kommunalabgaben-Gesetzes vom 14. Juli 1893* (Tübingen, 1894).

—— *Persönliche Erinnerungen zur Vorgeschichte der Universität Frankfurt a.M. zum 18. Oktober 1914* (Frankfurt, 1915).

—— and BEUTLER, GUSTAV OTTO, *Die sozialen Aufgaben der deutschen Städte. Zwei Vorträge, gehalten auf dem ersten deutschen Städtetage zu Dresden am 2. September 1903* (Leipzig, 1903).

ADLER, FRANZ, 'Soziale Gliederung der Bevölkerung, Verfassung und Verwaltung der Stadt Frankfurt am Main', in *Schriften des Vereins für Sozialpolitik*,

Verfassung und Verwaltungsorganisation der Städte. Preußen (vol. ii), cxvii (Leipzig, 1906), 85–148.

BARTSCHER, CHRISTIAN, *Zur Fünfzigjahrfeier der Gellertschule 1884–1934* (Frankfurt, 1934).

BAUER, HEINRICH, *Ueber den Entwurf einer Kirchengemeinde- und Synodal-Ordnung für Frankfurt am Main* (Frankfurt, 1897).

BEBEL, AUGUST, *Aus meinem Leben*, i (Stuttgart, 1910).

Bericht des Presbyteriums der deutschen evangelisch-reformierten Gemeinde über seine Tätigkeit im abgelaufenen Kirchenjahr (Frankfurt, 1905).

Bericht über die Verhandlungen des ersten Vereinstages der deutschen Arbeitervereine. Abgehalten zu Frankfurt a.M. am 7. und 8. Juni 1863, ed. Ausschuss des Vereinstages (Frankfurt, 1863).

Bezirksverein Alt-Frankfurt, *Jubiläumsfeiern des 25 jährigen Bestehens 1882–1907* (Frankfurt, 1907).

BODE, P., 'Die Entwicklung des lateinlosen höheren Schulwesens in Frankfurt a.M.', in *Programm der Adlerflychtschule zu Frankfurt a.M.* (Frankfurt, 1901), 14–27.

BONN, MORIZ J., *Wandering Scholar* (London, 1949).

BRÜCKNER, NATHANAEL, *Die öffentliche und private Fürsorge. Gemeinnützige Thätigkeit und Armenwesen mit besonderer Beziehung auf Frankfurt am Main*, 2 vols. (Frankfurt, 1892/3).

BÜCHER, KARL, *Die wirtschaftlichen Aufgaben der modernen Stadtgemeinde* (Leipzig, 1898).

Bürgerverein Sachsenhausen, 1848–1929. Festschrift zum 80-jährigen Jubiläum am 29.9.1929 (Frankfurt a.M., 1929).

BUSSE, ROLF, *Kaiser-Friedrich-Gymnasium. Rückblick auf die ersten 25 Jahre der Anstalt* (Frankfurt, 1913).

CAUER, PAUL, 'Das Ergebnis der Schulkonferenz', *Preußische Jahrbücher*, lxvii (1891), 88–98.

—— 'Die neuen Lehrpläne', *Preußische Jahrbücher*, lxix (1892), 256–79.

COHN, GUSTAV, 'Die Fortführung der preußischen Steuerreform', *Jahrbuch für Gesetzgebung, Verwaltung und Volkswirtschaft im Deutschen Reich*, xvi (1892), 267–76.

CONRAD, J., 'Allgemeine Statistik der Deutschen Universitäten', in Wilhelm Lexis (ed.), *Die Deutschen Universitäten* (Berlin, 1893), 115–70.

DELBRÜCK, HANS, 'Politische Correspondenz', *Preußische Jahrbücher*, lxvi (1890), 637–40.

—— 'Politische Correspondenz', *Preußische Jahrbücher*, lxvii (1891), 103–9.

—— 'Politische Correspondenz. Das Volksschulgesetz', *Preußische Jahrbücher*, lxix (1892), 280–9.

—— 'Politische Correspondenz', *Preußische Jahrbücher*, lxx (1892), 504–7.

Denkschrift der Frankfurter Bürgerschaft betreffend die Einverleibung der freien Stadt Frankfurt sammt den Namensverzeichnissen der Unterzeichner (Frankfurt, 1866).

Deutsche evangelisch-reformierte Gemeinde zu Frankfurt a.M., *Zur Erinnerung an die Jubiläumsfeier* (Frankfurt, 1893).

Die 350 jährige Gedenkfeier der deutschen evangelisch-reformierten Gemeinde zu Frankfurt am Main (Frankfurt, 1906).

'Die Hilfsschule in Frankfurt a.M.', in *Deutsche Hilfsschulen in Wort und Bild* (Halle, 1913), 3–10.

Die projectirte Theilung zwischen dem angeblichen Staatsvermögen und dem städtischen Vermögen von Frankfurt a. Main. Ein Beitrag zur Zeitgeschichte (Stuttgart, 1867).

Die protestantischen Gemeinden der Stadt Frankfurt in Preußen (Frankfurt, 1868).

'Die Taubstummen-Erziehungs-Anstalt zu Frankfurt a.M.', in *Deutsche Taubstummenanstalten, -Schulen und -Heime in Wort und Bild* (Halle, 1915), 1–12.

DIETZ, ALEXANDER, *Frankfurter Bürgerbuch* (Frankfurt, 1897).

DODGE, MARTIN HERBERT, *The Government of the City of Frankfort-on-the-Main* (New York, 1920).

Festschrift zu der am 7. Januar 1897 stattfindenden Einweihung des Goethe-Gymnasiums in Frankfurt a.M. (Frankfurt, 1897).

Festschrift zur Hundertjahrfeier der Musterschule in Frankfurt am Main, 1803–1903 (Frankfurt, 1903).

Festschrift zur Jahrhundertfeier der Realschule der israelitischen Gemeinde (Philanthropin) zu Frankfurt am Main 1804–1904 (Frankfurt, 1904).

Festschrift zur Jubiläumsfeier des 50 Jährigen Bestehens der Unterrichtsanstalten der Israelitischen Religionsgesellschaft zu Frankfurt a.M. (Frankfurt, 1903).

FINGER, FRIEDRICH AUGUST, *Ausgewählte pädagogische Schriften*, 2 vols. (Frankfurt, 1887).

FLEISCHER, MAX, *Das Frankfurter Stadtparlament* (Frankfurt a.M., 1907).

FLESCH, KARL, 'Die Wohnungsverhältnisse in Frankfurt a.M.', in Schriften des Vereins für Sozialpolitik, *Die Wohnungsnoth der armen Klassen in deutschen Großstädten und Vorschläge zu deren Abhilfe*, xxx (Leipzig, 1886), 57–91.

—— (ed.), *Frankfurter Arbeiterbudgets. Haushaltsrechnungen eines Arbeiters einer Königl. Staats-Eisenbahnwerkstätte, eines Arbeiters einer chemischen Fabrik und eines Aushilfearbeiters* (Frankfurt, 1890).

—— *Karl Flesch's soziales Vermächtnis* (Frankfurt, 1922).

—— 'Zur Kritik des Arbeitsvertrages', in Karl Flesch, *Karl Flesch's soziales Vermächtnis* (Frankfurt, 1922), 15–44.

—— 'Wohlfahrtseinrichtungen für Arbeiter und deren Familien', in Karl Flesch, *Karl Flesch's soziales Vermächtnis* (Frankfurt, 1922), 63–100.

—— 'Sozialpolitik in der Gemeinde und im Erwerbsleben', in Karl Flesch, *Karl Flesch's soziales Vermächtnis* (Frankfurt, 1922), 100–23.

—— 'Die Bildungsfrage als soziale Frage', in Karl Flesch, *Karl Flesch's soziales Vermächtnis* (Frankfurt, 1922), 154–71.

—— and BLEICHER, HEINRICH, *Beiträge zur Kenntnis des Armenwesens in Frankfurt am Main und zur Armenstatistik* (Frankfurt, 1890).

Frankfurter Ferienwanderungen, ed. Centrale für private Fürsorge (Frankfurt, 1911).
Führer durch das Städtische Schulwesen von Frankfurt am Main, ed. Städtische Schulbehörden (Frankfurt, 1909).
FUNCK, CARL, *Lebenserinnerungen. Mit einer Einführung von Ludwig Heilbronn* (Frankfurt, 1921).
Gerhard-Hauptmann-Schule 1861–1961 (Frankfurt, 1961).
[Germanicus], *Die Frankfurter Juden und die Aufsaugung des Volkswohlstandes* (Leipzig, 1890).
GERSTFELD, PHILIPP, *Städtefinanzen in Preussen. Statistik und Reformvorschläge* (Leipzig, 1882).
Geschichte der Frankfurter Zeitung 1856–1906 (Frankfurt, 1906).
Geschichte der Handelskammer zu Frankfurt am Main (1707–1908). Beiträge zur Frankfurter Handelsgeschichte (Frankfurt, 1908).
GIERKE, OTTO VON, 'Die soziale Aufgabe des Privatrechts', in Erik Wolf (ed.), *Quellenbuch zur Geschichte der Deutschen Rechtswissenschaft* (Frankfurt, 1949), 478–511.
GIZYKI, PAUL VON, 'Das Volksschulwesen', in Wilhelm Lexis (ed.), *Das Unterrichtswesen im Deutschen Reich. iii. Das Volksschulwesen und das Lehrerbildungswesen im Deutschen Reich* (Berlin, 1904), 1–232.
GNEIST, RUDOLF, *Die Selbstverwaltung der Volksschule. Vorschläge zur Lösung des Schulstreites durch die preußische Kreis-Ordnung* (Berlin, 1869).
—— *Die confessionelle Schule. Ihre Unzulässigkeit nach preußischen Landesgesetzen und die Nothwendigkeit eines Verwaltungsgerichtshofes* (Berlin, 1869).
GROH, KURT, *Ist der Versuch der Preußischen Unterrichtsverwaltung, den Frankfurter Lehrplan auf das Gymnasium zu übertragen, geglückt? Ein Wort zur Aufklärung* (Gütersloh, 1915).
'Grundsätze der Deutschkatholischen (freien religiösen) Gemeinde zu Frankfurt a.M.', in *Satzungen der im Jahre 1845 gegründeten Deutschkatholischen (freien religiösen) Gemeinde mit dem Sitze in Frankfurt a.M.* (Frankfurt, 1901), 21–2.
GÜNTHER, ADOLF, 'Die Belastung kleinerer und mittlerer Einkommen durch Verbrauchsabgaben seit Geltung des Zolltarifs vom 25. Dezember 1902', in Schriften des Vereins für Sozialpolitik, *Die Neuordnung der deutschen Finanzwirtschaft*, ii, ed. Heinrich Herkner, clvi (Munich/Leipzig, 1918), 189–268.
HALLGARTEN, CHARLES, *Neues über den Antisemitismus* (Frankfurt, 1897).
HARKORT, FRIEDRICH, *Die preußische Volksschule und ihre Vertretung im Abgeordnetenhause von 1848–1873* (Hagen, 1875).
HAUX, 'Die Taubstummen-Erziehungs-Anstalt zu Frankfurt a.M.', in *Deutsche Taubstummenanstalten, -Schulen und -Heime in Wort und Bild* (Halle, 1915).
HENNING, MAX (ed.), *Das freie Wort. Eine Auswahl von Beiträgen aus den beiden ersten Jahrgängen der Zeitschrift 'Das freie Wort'* (Frankfurt, 1903).
HERBER, Stadtschulinspektor, *Vom Volksschulwesen Frankfurts* (Berlin, 1914).

Jahresbericht und Rechnungs-Ablage des Haupt-Vereins der evangelischen Gustav-Adolf-Stiftung für das Jahr 1906 (Frankfurt, 1907).
Johannes von Miquels Reden, ed. Walther Schultze und Friedrich Thimme, ii–iv (Halle, 1911–14).
KANNGIEßER, OTTO, *Geschichte der Eroberung der Freien Stadt Frankfurt durch Preußen im Jahre 1866* (Frankfurt, 1877).
—— *Frankfurts Gegenwart und nächste Zukunft. Eine Denkschrift* (Frankfurt, 1892).
KAUFMANN, RICHARD VON, *Die Kommunalfinanzen. Großbritannien, Frankreich, Preußen*, 2 vols. (Leipzig, 1906).
KLOSE, WOLFGANG, 'Die Finanzpolitik der preußischen Großstädte', D.Phil. thesis (Halle, 1907).
KOCH, ADOLF, *Die neueren Schulgebäude der Stadt Frankfurt a.M.* (Frankfurt, 1904).
KÖRNER, OTTO, *Erinnerungen eines deutschen Arztes und Hochschullehrers 1858–1914* (Munich/Wiesbaden, 1920).
LANDSBERG, OTTO, 'Die Entwicklung des Gemeindeabgabenwesens in den preußischen Städten unter der Herrschaft des Kommunalabgabengesetzes mit besonderer Berücksichtigung der östlichen Provinzen', in Schriften des Vereins für Sozialpolitik, *Gemeindefinanzen*, ii/1. *Einzelfragen der Finanzpolitik der Gemeinden*, cxxvii (Leipzig, 1910), 1–42.
Leopold Sonnemann's siebzigste Geburtstagsfeier (Frankfurt, 1901).
LEXIS, WILHELM (ed.), *Die Deutschen Universitäten* (Berlin, 1893).
—— (ed.), *Die Reform des höheren Schulwesens in Preußen* (Halle, 1902).
—— (ed.), *Das Unterrichtswesen im Deutschen Reich*. iii. *Das Volksschulwesen und das Lehrerbildungswesen im Deutschen Reich* (Berlin, 1904).
LINDEMANN, HUGO (C. HUGO), *Städteverwaltung und Munizipal-Sozialismus in England* (Stuttgart, 1897).
—— 'Wohnungsstatistik', in Schriften des Vereins für Sozialpolitik, *Neue Untersuchungen über die Wohnungsfrage in Deutschland und im Ausland*, lxiv (Leipzig, 1901), 261–384.
—— *Arbeiterpolitik und Wirschaftspflege in der Deutschen Städteverwaltung*. ii. *Wirtschaftspflege* (Stuttgart, 1904).
—— *Steuern und Gebühren* (Berlin, 1906).
—— *Die städtische Regie* (Berlin, 1907).
LOENING, EDGAR, 'Die Unterhaltung der öffentlichen Volksschulen und die Schulverbände in Preussen', *Jahrbuch des öffentlichen Rechts*, iii (1909), 68–138.
LÜCKER, HEINRICH, *Gemeindefinanzen*, ii/3. *Die Entwicklung und die Probleme des Gemeindeabgabenwesens in den Städten und großen Landgemeinden der preußischen Industriebezirke*, Schriften des Vereins für Sozialpolitik, cxxvii (Leipzig, 1910).
LUPPE, HERMANN, *Mein Leben* (Nürnberg, 1977).
MANN, THOMAS, *Betrachtungen eines Unpolitischen* (Frankfurt, 1956).

MICHEL, FERDINAND, 'Jahrhundertfeier der Emanzipation der jüdischen Bewohner Frankfurts', in *Philanthropin. Realschule und Lyzeum der israelitischen Gemeinde zu Frankfurt a.M. Programm Ostern 1912* (Frankfurt, 1912), 35–49.

MILL, JOHN STUART, *Utilitarianism, On Liberty, Considerations on Representative Government*, ed. Harry B. Acton (reprint, London, 1991).

MIQUEL, JOHANNES, 'Verfassung und Verwaltung der Provinzen und Gemeinden des Königreichs der Niederlande', *Preußische Jahrbücher*, xxiv (1869), 312–40.

—— 'Einleitung', in Schriften des Vereins für Sozialpolitik, *Die Wohnungsnoth der armen Klassen in deutschen Großstädten und Vorschläge zu deren Abhilfe*, xxx (Leipzig, 1886), pp. ix–xxi.

MOMBERT, PAUL, 'Die Gemeindebetriebe in Deutschland', in Schriften des Vereins für Sozialpolitik, *Gemeindebetriebe*, i. *Neuere Versuche und Erfahrungen über die Ausdehnung der kommunalen Tätigkeit in Deutschland und im Ausland*, cxxviii (Leipzig, 1908), 1–77.

Monographien Deutscher Städte, vii. *Frankfurt am Main*, ed. Erwin Stein and Georg Voigt (Oldenburg i. Gr., 1914).

MOST, OTTO, *Gemeindefinanzen*, ii/2. *Die Gemeindefinanzstatistik in Deutschland. Ziele, Wege, Ergebnisse*, Schriften des Vereins für Sozialpolitik, cxxvii (Leipzig, 1910).

—— *Die deutsche Stadt und ihre Verwaltung. Eine Einführung in die Kommunalpolitik der Gegenwart*, 3 vols. (Berlin/Leipzig, 1913).

—— 'Die Gemeindefinanzen nach dem Kriege', in Schriften des Vereins für Sozialpolitik, *Die Neuordnung der deutschen Finanzwirtschaft*, ii, ed. Heinrich Herkner, clvi (Munich/Leipzig, 1918), 291–355.

MÜLLER, EDUARD JOSEF (ed.), *Aufklärungen über den Schulkampf im Jahre 1904 und 1905 in Frankfurt am Main* (Frankfurt, 1905).

MÜNZENBERGER, ERNST F. A., *Die Entwicklung des Frankfurter Schulwesens im letzten Jahrzehnt* (2nd edn., Frankfurt, 1880).

—— *Der stille Culturkampf auf dem Gebiet des Frankfurter Schulwesens* (Frankfurt, 1880).

NAUMANN, FRIEDRICH, *Die Wohnungsnot in unserer Zeit. Vortrag auf dem 6. Verbandstage Deutscher Mietervereine in Cassel* (Leipzig, n.d.).

NEUMANN, FRIEDRICH JULIUS, *Die Progressive Einkommensteuer in Staats- und Gemeindehaushalt. Gutachten über Personalbesteuerung auf Veranlassung des Vereins für Sozialpolitik* (Leipzig, 1874, reprint 1904).

OSTROGORSKI, MICHAEL, *Democracy and the Organisation of Political Parties*, i (London, 1902).

PALDAMUS, F. C., 'Zur Lage des Frankfurter Schulwesens', in *Einladungsschrift zu den am 29., 30., 31. März und 1. April 1871 stattfindenden öffentlichen Prüfungen an der höheren Bürgerschule* (Frankfurt, 1871), 3–23.

PAULSEN, FRIEDRICH, 'Der Sieg der Einheitsschule oder das Ende des klassischen Gymnasiums. Item: das Ende des Realgymnasiums', *Preußische Jahrbücher*, lxviii (1891), 866–75.

PERINI, C., *J. Vatter und die Taubstummen-Anstalt zu Frankfurt a.M.* (Friedberg, 1910).

PFLEIDERER, OTTO, 'Der Religionsunterricht in der Volksschule', *Preußische Jahrbücher*, lxix (1892), 402–16.

PIETZSCH, GEORG WILHELM, 'Erinnerungen eines Lehrers', ed. Wolfgang Klötzer, *Archiv für Frankfurts Geschichte und Kunst*, xlix (1965), 5–78.

POPPE, FRANZ, *Meine Erfahrungen an einer Simultanschule in Frankfurt am Main. Ein kritischer Beitrag zur Lösung der Simultanschulfrage* (4th edn., Frankfurt, 1880).

PREUß, HUGO, *Reichs- und Landesfinanzen* (Berlin, 1894).

—— 'Die staatliche Bestätigung der Mitglieder städtischer Schuldeputationen nach preussischem Recht', *Archiv für öffentliches Recht*, xv (1900), 202–25.

—— *Das städtische Amtsrecht in Preußen* (Berlin, 1902).

—— *Das Recht der städtischen Schulverwaltung in Preußen* (Berlin, 1905).

—— *Die Entwicklung des Deutschen Städtewesens. i. Entwicklungsgeschichte der Deutschen Städteverfassung* (Leipzig, 1906).

—— *Staat, Recht und Freiheit. Aus 40 Jahren Deutscher Politik und Geschichte* (Tübingen, 1926).

—— *Gemeinde, Staat, Reich als Gebietskörperschaften. Versuch einer deutschen Staatskonstruktion auf Grundlage der Genossenschaftstheorie* (reprint, Aalen, 1964).

Programm des Goethe-Gymnasiums in Frankfurt a.M. (Frankfurt, 1897).

Programm des Lessing-Gymnasiums zu Frankfurt a.M. (Frankfurt, 1903).

QUARCK, MAX, *Zur Naturgeschichte der Frankfurter Zeitung und der bürgerlichen Demokratie* (Frankfurt, 1896).

—— *Kommunale Schulpolitik. Ein Führer durch die Gemeindetätigkeit auf dem Gebiete der Volksschule* (Berlin, 1906).

REDLICH, JOSEF, and HIRST, FRANCIS W., *Local Government in England*, 2 vols. (London, 1903).

REINHARDT, KARL, *Die Frankfurter Lehrpläne* (Frankfurt, 1892).

—— 'Die Reformanstalten', in Wilhelm Lexis (ed.), *Die Reform des höheren Schulwesens in Preußen* (Halle, 1902), 328–42.

RÖßLER, HEINRICH, 'Die Sozialpolitik in unserem Gemeinwesen. Vortrag, gehalten im Demokratischen Verein', in *Gemeinnützige Blätter für Hessen und Nassau. Zeitschrift für soziale Heimatkunde*, iv (1902), 49–56.

—— 'Die Aufgaben von Reich und Staat in der Wohnungsfrage', in Adolf Damaschke and Heinrich Rößler, *Der Kampf gegen die Wohnungsnot* (Frankfurt, 1903), 7–23.

'Rückblicke auf die sozialistische Bewegung in Deutschland, kritische Aphorismen von ***', *Jahrbuch für Sozialwissenschaft und Sozialpolitik*, i (1879), 75–96.

SÄNGER, CARL, *Fest-Predigt gehalten bei der Einweihung des neuen Andachts-Saales der Deutschkatholischen (freien religiösen) Gemeinde zu Frankfurt a.M.* (Frankfurt, 1892).

SÄNGER, CARL, *1845–1895. Geschichte der freireligiösen Bewegung und der deutschkathol. (freien religiösen) Gemeinde zu Frankfurt a.M. Festschrift zur Feier des fünfzigjährigen Bestehens der Gemeinde* (Frankfurt, 1895).

—— 'Regierung und Bürgertum', in Max Henning (ed.), *Das freie Wort. Eine Auswahl von Beiträgen aus den beiden ersten Jahrgängen der Zeitschrift 'Das freie Wort'* (Frankfurt, 1903), 37–40.

Satzungen der im Jahre 1845 gegründeten Deutschkatholischen (freien religiösen) Gemeinde mit dem Sitze in Frankfurt a.M. (Frankfurt, 1901).

SCHLOTTER, PAUL, 'Fünfundzwanzig Jahre städtisches Arbeitsamt', *Frankfurter Wohlfahrtsblätter*, xxiii (1920), 11–16.

SCHOLZ, ERNST, 'Das heutige Gemeindebesteuerungssystem in Preußen. Unter besonderer Berücksichtigung des Westens der Monarchie', in Schriften des Vereins für Sozialpolitik, *Gemeindefinanzen, i. System der Gemeindebesteuerung in Hessen, Württemberg, Baden, Elsaß-Lothringen, Bayern, Sachsen, Preußen*, cxxvi (Leipzig, 1908), 279–318.

Schriften des Vereins für Sozialpolitik, *Verfassung und Verwaltungsorganisation der Städte*, ii. *Preußen*, cxviii (Leipzig, 1906).

—— *Verfassung und Verwaltungsorganisation der Städte*, i. *Preußen*, cxvii (Leipzig, 1906).

—— *Gemeindebetriebe*, i. *Neuere Versuche und Erfahrungen über die Ausdehnung der kommunalen Tätigkeit in Deutschland und im Ausland*, cxxviii (Leipzig, 1908).

SILBERGLEIT, HEINRICH, *Preussens Städte. Denkschrift zum 100 jährigen Jubiläum der Städteordnung vom 19. November 1908* (Berlin, 1908).

SONNENBERG, GEORG, *Deutschlands sozialpolitische Einrichtungen im Budget des Reiches, dreier Einzelstaaten, Preußen, Bayern, Baden, und dreier Großer Städte, Berlin, Breslau, Köln* (Berlin, 1912).

SOUCHAY, EDUARD FRANZ, *Was soll Frankfurt dem Staate entrichten und abgeben? Nach der Mittheilung der ständigen Bürgerrepräsentation beurtheilt* (Frankfurt, 1867).

—— *Was mag Frankfurt übrig bleiben? Nach den Mittheilungen der ständigen Bürgerrepräsentation vom 18. März 1867 beurtheilt* (Frankfurt, 1867).

Sozialdemokratie und Stadtverwaltung in Frankfurt a.M. Zugleich Rechenschaftsbericht der sozialdemokratischen Stadtverordneten-Fraktion zu den Stadtverordnetenwahlen 1906, ed. Sozialdemokratischer Verein (Frankfurt, 1906).

Sozialdemokratie und Stadtverwaltung in Frankfurt am Main. Zugleich Rechenschaftsbericht der sozialdemokratischen Stadtverordneten-Fraktion für 1907/08 zu den Stadtverordnetenwahlen 1908, ed. Sozialdemokratischer Verein (Frankfurt, 1908).

Sozialdemokratie und Stadtverwaltung Frankfurt am Main. Ein Rückblick auf zehnjährige Tätigkeit. Zugleich Rechenschaftsbericht der sozialdemokratischen Stadtverordnetenfraktion für die Jahre 1909/10 zu den Stadtverordnetenwahlen 1910, ed. Sozialdemokratischer Verein (Frankfurt, 1910).

SPECHT, FRITZ, and SCHWABE, PAUL, *Die Reichstagswahlen von 1867–1907* (Berlin, 1908).

SPIER, SELMAR, *Vor 1914. Erinnerungen an Frankfurt geschrieben in Israel* (2nd edn., Frankfurt, 1968).
STEIN, PHILIPP, 'Das Verhältnis der freiwilligen und zwangsgemeinschaftlichen Körperschaften in der Wohlfahrtspflege', in Schriften des Vereins für Sozialpolitik, *Gemeindebetriebe*, i. *Neue Versuche und Erfahrungen über die Ausdehnung der kommunalen Tätigkeit in Deutschland und im Ausland*, cxxviii (Leipzig, 1908), 427–40.
TROMMERSHAUSEN, ERNST, 'Beitrag zur Geschichte des landesherrlichen Kirchenregiments in den evangelischen Gemeinden zu Frankfurt a.M.', in *Programm des Lessing-Gymnasiums zu Frankfurt a.M.* (Frankfurt, 1897), 3–66.
—— *Über protestantische Erziehung* (Saarbrücken, 1904).
Verhandlungen des Ersten allgemeinen Preußischen Städtetages am 19. und 30. Januar zu Berlin (Berlin, 1901).
Verhandlungen des Zweiten allgemeinen Preußischen Städtetages am 23. und 24. Januar 1899 zu Berlin (Berlin, 1899).
Verhandlungen des Dritten allgemeinen Preußischen Städtetages am 29. and 30. Januar 1901 zu Berlin (Berlin, 1901).
Verhandlungen des Vierten allgemeinen Preußischen Städtetages am 6. und 7. Dezember 1904 zu Berlin (Berlin, 1905).
Verhandlungen des Fünften allgemeinen Preußischen Städtetages am 15. Januar 1906 zu Berlin (Berlin, 1906).
Verhandlungen des Sechsten Preußischen Städtetages am 5. und 6. Oktober 1908 zu Königsberg (Königsberg, 1908).
Verhandlungen des Siebten Preußischen Städtetages am 8. und 9. Oktober 1912 zu Düsseldorf (Düsseldorf, 1912).
Verhandlungen des Ersten Deutschen Städtetages am 27. November 1905 zu Berlin (Berlin, n.d.).
Verhandlungen des Zweiten Deutschen Städtetages am 6. und 7. Juli 1908 zu München (Berlin, 1908).
Verhandlungen des Dritten Deutschen Städtetages am 11. und 12. September 1911 zu Posen (Berlin, 1911).
Verhandlungen des Vierten Deutschen Städtetages am 15. und 16. Juni 1914 zu Cöln (Berlin, 1914).
Vorstand des Lehrer-Vereins zu Frankfurt a.M. (ed.), *Herr Direktor Dr. Georg Veith und die vierklassigen Volksschulen zu Frankfurt a.M. Eine pädagogische Abfertigung* (2nd edn., Frankfurt, 1887).
WAGNER, ADOLF, *Die Communalsteuerfrage. Ausarbeitung eines Referats im Verein für Sozialpolitik* (Leipzig/Heidelberg, 1878).
—— *Finanzwissenschaft*, iv. *Specielle Steuerlehre (Praxis der Besteuerung). Die deutsche Besteuerung des 19. Jahrhunderts* (Leipzig, 1899).
—— and PREUß, HUGO, *Kommunale Steuerfragen* (Jena, 1904).
WEBER, MAX, *Gesammelte Politische Schriften*, ed. Johannes Winckelmann (3rd edn., Tübingen, 1971).

WEBER, MAX, 'Science as a Vocation', in Hans H. Gerth and Charles Wright Mills (eds.), *From Max Weber: Essays in Sociology* (reprint, London, 1993), 129–56.
WEIGT, R., 'Die Stellung der Kirche zur Feuerbestattung', in Max Henning (ed.), *Das freie Wort. Eine Auswahl von Beiträgen aus den beiden ersten Jahrgängen der Zeitschrift 'Das freie Wort'* (Frankfurt, 1903), 58–62.
WERNER, JULIUS, *Deutschtum und Christentum. Gedenkreden* (Heidelberg, 1906).
—— *Der deutsche Protestantismus und das öffentliche Leben* (Hagen i.W., n.d.).
WOLFF, G., 'Leichenverbrennung und Körperbestattung in Geschichte und Vorgeschichte unserer Gegend', in *Alt-Frankfurt*, ii (1910), 101–8.
ZIEHEN, JULIUS, *Der Frankfurter Lehrplan und seine Stellung innerhalb der Schulreformbewegung* (Leipzig/Frankfurt, 1900).
—— *Über die Verbindung der sprachlichen und sachlichen Belehrung* (Frankfurt, 1902).
—— 'Schulpolitik und Pädagogik', *Zeitschrift für lateinlose höhere Schulen*, xvii (1906), 33–48.
—— *Aus der Werkstatt der Schule. Studien über den inneren Organismus des höheren Schulwesens* (Leipzig, 1907).
—— *Schulpolitische Aufsätze* (Frankfurt, 1919).
ZIELOWSKI, OTTO, *Die Millionärswirtschaft auf dem Frankfurter Rathause. Ein Rückblick für die Stadtverordnetenwahlen auf die städtische Verwaltung in den Jahren 1900 bis 1904* (Frankfurt, 1904).
Zu den öffentlichen Prüfungen in der katholischen höheren Töchterschule, genannt Englische Fräulein-Schule (Frankfurt, 1869).
Zur Verständigung über die Frankfurter Kirchenfrage. Für und gegen die Schrift: 'Die protestantischen Gemeinden der Stadt Frankfurt in Preußen' (Frankfurt, 1868).

D. SECONDARY WORKS

ACHINGER, HANS, *Wilhelm Merton in seiner Zeit* (Frankfurt, 1965).
ADICKES, ERICH (ed.), *Franz Adickes. Sein Leben und sein Werk* (Frankfurt, 1929).
ALBISETTI, JAMES C., *Secondary School Reform in Imperial Germany* (Princeton, 1983).
—— 'The Debate on Secondary School Reform in France and Germany', in Detlev Müller, Fritz Ringer, and Brian Simon (eds.), *The Rise of the Modern Educational System: Structural Change and Social Reproduction 1870–1920* (Cambridge, 1987), 181–96.
—— 'Systematisation: A Critique', in Detlev Müller, Fritz Ringer, and Brian Simon (eds.), *The Rise of the Modern Educational System: Structural Change and Social Reproduction 1870–1920* (Cambridge, 1987), 210–16.
—— and LUNDGREEN, PETER, 'Höhere Knabenschulen', in Christa Berg (ed.), *Handbuch der deutschen Bildungsgeschichte*. iv. *1870–1918* (Munich, 1991), 228–78.
ALDENHOFF, RITA, 'Das Selbsthilfemodell als liberale Antwort auf die soziale Frage im 19. Jahrhundert. Schulze-Delitzsch und die Genossenschaften', in Karl Holl,

Günter Trautmann, Hans Vorländer (eds.), *Sozialer Liberalismus* (Göttingen, 1986), 57–69.

ALEXANDRE, PHILIPPE, ' "Die Frankfurter Latern". Une Publication satirique editée par Friedrich Stoltze', Ph.D. thesis (Metz, 1980).

ANDERHUB, ANDREAS, *Verwaltung im Regierungsbezirk Wiesbaden 1866–1885* (Wiesbaden, 1977).

ANDERSON, BENEDICT, *Imagined Communities* (London, 1983).

ANDERSON, EUGENE N., 'The Prussian *Volksschule* in the Nineteenth Century', in Gerhard A. Ritter (ed.), *Entstehung und Wandel in der modernen Gesellschaft. Festschrift für Hans Rosenberg zum 65. Geburtstag* (Berlin, 1970), 261–79.

ANDERSON, MARGARET L., 'The Kulturkampf and the Course of German History', *Central European History*, xix (1986), 82–115.

—— *Windthorst. Zentrumspolitiker und Gegenspieler Bismarcks* (Düsseldorf, 1988).

—— and BARKIN, KENNETH D., 'The Myth of the Puttkamer Purge and the Reality of the *Kulturkampf*: Some Reflections on the Historiography of Imperial Germany', *Journal of Modern History*, liv (1982), 647–86.

ANDRICH, SUPHAN, and VEVERKA, JINDRICH, 'The Growth of Government Expenditure in Germany since the Unification', *Finanzarchiv*, Neue Folge xxiii (1963/4), 169–278.

ANGERMAIR, ELISABETH, 'München als süddeutsche Metropole—Die Organisation des Großstadtausbaus 1870–1914', in Richard Bauer (ed.), *Geschichte der Stadt München* (Munich, 1992), 307–35.

APPLEGATE, CELIA, *A Nation of Provincials. The German Idea of Heimat* (Berkeley, 1990).

—— 'Localism and the German Bourgeoisie: The 'Heimat' Movement in the Rhenish Palatinate before 1914', in David Blackbourn and Robert J. Evans (eds.), *The German Bourgeoisie. Essays on the Social History of the German Middle Class from the Late Eighteenth to the Early Twentieth Century* (London, 1991), 224–54.

—— 'Democracy or Reaction? The Political Implications of Localist Ideas in Wilhelmine and Weimar Germany', in Larry E. Jones and James Retallack (eds.), *Elections, Mass Politics and Social Change in Modern Germany* (Cambridge, 1993), 247–66.

ARNSBERG, PAUL, *Die Geschichte der Frankfurter Juden seit der Französischen Revolution*, 3 vols. (Darmstadt, 1983).

ASCHHEIM, STEVEN E., *Brothers and Strangers. The East European Jew in German and German Jewish Consciousness, 1800–1923* (Madison, 1982).

ASCHOFF, HANS-GEORG, *Welfische Bewegung und politischer Katholizismus 1866–1918. Die Deutschhannoversche Partei und das Zentrum in der Provinz Hannover während des Kaiserreiches* (Düsseldorf, 1987).

BANGERT, WOLFGANG, 'Baupolitik und Stadtgestaltung in Frankfurt a.M. Ein Beitrag zur Entwicklungsgeschichte des deutschen Städtebaus in den letzten 100 Jahren', Ph.D. thesis (Technische Hochschule Berlin, 1936).

BARKIN, KENNETH D., 'The Second Founding of the Reich: A Perspective', *German Studies Review*, x (1987), 219–35.
BARTELSHEIM, URSULA, 'Die Politisierung und Demokratisierung der kommunalen Selbstverwaltung. Kommunalpolitik in Frankfurt am Main 1850–1900', D.Phil. thesis (Frankfurt, 1995).
BAZILLION, RICHARD J., 'Liberalism, Modernisation, and the Social Question in the Kingdom of Saxony, 1830–90', in Konrad H. Jarausch and Larry E. Jones (eds.), *In Search of a Liberal Germany. Studies in the History of German Liberalism from 1789 to the Present* (Oxford, 1990), 87–110.
BECKSTEIN, HERMANN, *Städtische Interessenpolitik. Organisation und Politik der Städtetage in Bayern, Preußen und im Deutschen Reich 1896–1923* (Düsseldorf, 1991).
BEETHAM, DAVID, *Max Weber and the Theory of Modern Politics* (2nd edn., Cambridge, 1985).
BEHR, HANS-JOACHIM, 'Zwischen Vormärz und Reichsgründung', in Franz-Josef Jakobi (ed.), *Geschichte der Stadt Münster*, ii. *Das 19. und 20. Jahrhundert* (Münster, 1993), 79–130.
BELLAMY, RICHARD, *Liberalism and Modern Society. An Historical Argument* (Cambridge, 1992).
BENAD, MATTHIAS (ed.), *Gott in Frankfurt? Theologische Spuren in einer Metropole* (Frankfurt, 1987).
BERG, CHRISTA (ed.), *Handbuch zur Deutschen Bildungsgeschichte*. iv. *1870–1918* (Munich, 1991).
BERGER, STEFAN, *The British Labour Party and the German Social Democrats, 1900–1931* (Oxford, 1994).
BERGHAHN, VOLKER, *Imperial Germany, 1891–1914. Economy, Society, Culture and Politics* (Providence/Oxford, 1994).
BIAGINI, EUGENIO F., *Liberty, Retrenchment and Reform. Popular Liberalism in the Age of Gladstone, 1860–1880* (Cambridge, 1992).
BLACKBOURN, DAVID, 'The *Mittelstand* in German Society and Politics, 1871–1914', *Social History*, iv (1977), 409–33.
—— *Class, Religion and Local Politics in Wilhelmine Germany. The Centre Party in Württemberg before 1914* (New Haven, 1980).
—— 'Roman Catholics, the Centre Party and Anti-Semitism in Imperial Germany', in Paul Kennedy and Anthony Nicholls (eds.), *Nationalist and Racialist Movements in Britain and Germany before 1914* (Basingstoke, 1981), 106–29.
—— 'Die Zentrumspartei und die deutschen Katholiken während des Kulturkampfes und danach', in Otto Pflanze (ed.), *Innenpolitische Probleme des Bismarck-Reiches* (Munich/Vienna, 1983), 73–94.
—— 'Between Resignation and Volatility: The German Petty Bourgeoisie in the Nineteenth Century', in David Blackbourn, *Populists and Patricians. Essays in Modern German History* (London, 1987), 84–113.

—— 'Progress and Piety: Liberals, Catholics and the State in Bismarck's Germany', in David Blackbourn, *Populists and Patricians. Essays in Modern German History* (London, 1987), 143–67.

—— 'Catholics, the Centre Party and Anti-Semitism', in David Blackbourn, *Populists and Patricians. Essays in Modern German History* (London, 1987), 168–87.

—— *The Fontana History of Germany 1780–1918. The Long Nineteenth Century* (London, 1997).

—— and ELEY, GEOFF, *The Peculiarities of German History. Bourgeois Society and Politics in Nineteenth-Century Germany* (Oxford, 1984).

—— and EVANS, RICHARD J. (eds.), *The German Bourgeoisie. Essays on the Social History of the German Middle Class from the Late Eighteenth to the Early Twentieth Century* (London, 1991).

BLANKENBERG, HEINZ, *Politischer Katholizismus in Frankfurt am Main, 1918–1933* (Mainz, 1981).

BLESSING, WERNER K., *Staat und Kirche in der Gesellschaft. Institutionelle Autoriät und mentaler Wandel in Bayern während des 19. Jahrhunderts* (Göttingen, 1982).

—— 'Kirchengeschichte in historischer Sicht. Bemerkungen zu einem Feld zwischen den Disziplinen', in Anselm Doering-Manteuffel and Kurt Nowak (eds.), *Kirchliche Zeitgeschichte. Urteilsbildung und Methoden* (Stuttgart/Berlin/Cologne, 1996), 14–59.

BLOD, GABRIELE, et al., 'Unruhe im "Pfaffenstädtchen". Reaktion, "Neue Ära" und Kulturkampf (1850–1870)' in Heiko Haumann and Hans Schadek (eds.), *Geschichte der Stadt Freiburg im Breisgau*. iii. *Von der badischen Herrschaft bis zur Gegenwart* (Stuttgart, 1992), 130–64.

BLOTEVOGEL, HANS HEINRICH (ed.), *Kommunale Leistungsverwaltung und Stadtentwicklung vom Vormärz bis zur Weimarer Republik* (Köln/Wien, 1990).

BÖHM, HANS, 'Bodenpolitik deutscher Städte in der Zeit vor dem Ersten Weltkrieg', in Jürgen Reulecke (ed.), *Die Stadt als Dienstleistungszentrum. Beiträge zur Geschichte der 'Sozialstadt' in Deutschland im 19. und frühen 20. Jahrhundert* (St Katharinen, 1995), 19–55.

BÖHME, GÜNTHER, 'Schulpolitik, Volkserziehungswissenschaft und Universitätspädagogik—Aus Anlaß des 60. Todestages von Julius Ziehen (1864–1925)', in Günther Böhme (ed.), *Geistesgeschichte im Spiegel einer Stadt. Frankfurt am Main und seine grossen Persönlichkeiten* (Frankfurt, 1986), 122–39.

BÖHME, HELMUT, *Frankfurt und Hamburg. Des deutschen Reiches Silber- und Goldloch und Allerenglischste Stadt des Kontinents* (Frankfurt, 1968).

BOLENZ, JÜRGEN, 'Wachstum und Strukturwandlungen der kommunalen Ausgaben in Deutschland 1849–1913', D.jur. thesis (Freiburg, 1965).

BRANDT, HARTWIG, 'Zu einigen Liberalismusdeutungen der siebziger und achtziger Jahre', *Geschichte und Gesellschaft*, xvii (1991), 512–30.

BREUILLY, JOHN, *Labour and Liberalism in Nineteenth-Century Europe. Essays in Comparative History* (Manchester, 1992).

BREUILLY, JOHN, 'The National Idea in Modern German History', in John Breuilly (ed.), *The State of Germany. The National Idea in the Making, Unmaking and Remaking of a Modern Nation-State* (London, 1992), 1–28.
—— *Nationalism and the State* (2nd edn., Manchester, 1993).
BRIGGS, ASA, *History of Birmingham*, ii (Oxford, 1952).
—— *Victorian Cities* (reprint, Harmondsworth, 1990).
BROSIUS, DIETER, 'Die Industriestadt. Vom Beginn des 19. Jahrhunderts bis zum Ende des 1. Weltkriegs', in Klaus Mlynek and Waldemar R. Röhrbein (eds.), *Geschichte der Stadt Hannover.* ii. *Vom Beginn des 19. Jahrhunderts bis in die Gegenwart* (Hanover, 1994), 273–404.
BRUCH, RÜDIGER VOM (ed.), *Weder Kommunismus noch Kapitalismus. Bürgerliche Sozialreform in Deutschland vom Vormärz bis zur Ära Adenauer* (Munich, 1985).
—— 'Gesellschaftliche Funktionen und politische Rollen des Bildungsbürgertums im Wilhelminischen Reich—Zum Wandel von Milieu und politischer Kultur', in Jürgen Kocka (ed.), *Bildungsbürgertum im 19. Jahrhundert. Politischer Einfluß und gesellschaftliche Formation* (Stuttgart, 1989), iv. 146–79.
BRUNNER, OTTO, CONZE, WERNER, and KOSELLECK, REINHART (eds.), *Geschichtliche Grundbegriffe. Historisches Lexikon zur politisch-sozialen Sprache in Deutschland*, iv (Stuttgart, 1978).
BULLOCK, NICHOLAS, and READ, JAMES, *The Movement for Housing Reform in Germany and France, 1840–1914* (Cambridge, 1985).
BUNCE, JOHN THACKRAY, *History of the Corporation of Birmingham*, ii (Birmingham, 1885).
BUNCKHORST, HANS-DIETER, *Kommunalisierung im 19. Jahrhundert dargestellt am Beispiel der Gaswirtschaft in Deutschland* (Munich, 1978).
BÜTTEL, MINA, *Die Armenpflege zu Frankfurt a.M. mit besonderer Berücksichtigung der Kinderpflege im 18. und 19. Jahrhundert bis zum Eintritt der neuen Armenordnung im Jahre 1883* (Frankfurt, 1913).
CANNADINE, DAVID, and REEDER, DAVID (eds.), *Exploring the Urban Past. Essays in Urban History by H. J. Dyos* (Cambridge, 1982).
CASTELL RÜDENHAUSEN, ADELHEID GRÄFIN ZU, 'Die Überwindung der Armenschule. Schülerhygiene an den Hamburger öffentlichen Volksschulen im Zweiten Kaiserreich', *Archiv für Sozialgeschichte*, xxii (1982), 201–26.
CHROBAK, WERNER, 'Politische Parteien, Verbände und Vereine in Regensburg 1869–1914. Teil II', *Verhandlungen des Historischen Vereins für Oberpfalz und Regensburg*, cxx (1980), 211–384.
COETZEE, MARILYN S., *The German Army League. Popular Nationalism in Wilhelmine Germany* (New York/Oxford, 1990).
CONZE, WERNER, and KOCKA, JÜRGEN (eds.), *Bildungsbürgertum im 19. Jahrhundert.* Teil 1. *Bildungssystem und Professionalisierung im internationalen Vergleich* (Stuttgart, 1985).
CRAIG, GORDON A., *The Politics of the Unpolitical. German Writers and the Problem of Power 1770–1871* (New York/Oxford, 1995).

CREW, DAVID F., *A Town in the Ruhr. A Social History of Bochum, 1860–1914* (New York, 1979).
CROON, HELMUTH, 'Die Stadtvertretungen in Krefeld und Bochum im 19. Jahrhundert. Ein Beitrag zur Geschichte der Selbstverwaltung der rheinischen und westfälischen Städte', in R. Dietrich and G. Oestreich (eds.), *Forschungen zu Staat und Verfassung. Festgabe für Fritz Hartung* (Berlin, 1958), 289–306.
—— 'Das Vordringen der politischen Parteien im Bereich der kommunalen Selbstverwaltung', in Helmuth Croon, Wolfgang Hofmann, and Georg-Christoph von Unruh (eds.), *Kommunale Selbstverwaltung im Zeitalter der Industrialisierung* (Stuttgart, 1971), 15–58.
—— 'Aufgaben deutscher Städte im ersten Drittel des 20. Jahrhunderts', in W. Rausch (ed.), *Die Städte Mitteleuropas im 20. Jahrhundert* (Linz, 1984), 41–9.
CROSSICK, GEOFFREY, 'The Petite Bourgeoisie in Nineteenth-Century Europe: Problems and Research', in Klaus Tenfelde (ed.), *Arbeiter und Arbeiterbewegung im Vergleich. Berichte zur internationalen Historischen Forschung* (Munich, 1986), 227–77.
—— and HAUPT, HEINZ-GERHARD (eds.), *Shopkeepers and Master Artisans in Nineteenth-Century Europe* (London, 1984).
—— —— *The Petite Bourgeoisie in Europe 1780–1914* (London, 1995).
DAHRENDORF, RALF, *Society and Democracy in Germany* (2nd edn., New York, 1979).
DAWSON, WILLIAM HARBUTT, *Municipal Life and Government in Germany* (London, 1914).
DECHENT, HERMANN, *Kirchengeschichte von Frankfurt am Main seit der Reformation*, ii (Leipzig/Frankfurt, 1921).
DESAI, ASHOK V., *Real Wages in Germany, 1871–1913* (Oxford, 1968).
DILCHER, GERHARD, 'Genossenschaftstheorie und Sozialrecht: Ein "Juristensozialismus" Otto v. Gierkes?', *Quaderni Fiorentini per la storia del pensiero giuridico moderno*, iii/iv (1974/5), 319–65.
DOMINICUS, ALEXANDER, *Straßburgs deutsche Bürgermeister Back und Schwander 1873–1918* (Frankfurt, 1939).
DURCHHARDT, HEINZ, 'Frankfurt am Main im 18. Jahrhundert', in *Frankfurt am Main. Die Geschichte der Stadt in nevn Beiträgen*, ed. Frankfurter Historische Kommission (Sigmaringen, 1991), 261–302.
DUVERGER, MAURICE, 'Der Einfluß der Wahlsysteme auf das politische Leben', in Otto Büsch and Peter Steinbach (eds.), *Vergleichende Europäische Wahlgeschichte. Eine Anthologie. Beiträge zur historischen Wahlforschung vornehmlich West- und Nordeuropas* (Berlin, 1983), 30–84.
EICHLER, VOLKER, *Sozialistische Arbeiterbewegung in Frankfurt am Main, 1878–1895* (Frankfurt, 1983).
EIGENBRODT, AUGUST, *Berliner Tageblatt und Frankfurter Zeitung in ihrem Verhalten zu den nationalen Fragen 1887–1914. Ein geschichtlicher Rückblick* (Berlin-Schöneberg, 1917).

'*Eine neue Zeit . . .!*' *Die Internationale Elektrotechnische Ausstellung 1891*, ed. Historisches Museum Frankfurt am Main (Frankfurt, 1991).

EISENBERG, CHRISTIANE, 'The Comparative View in Labour History. Old and New Interpretations of the English and German Labour Movements before 1914', *International Review of Social History*, xxxiv (1989), 403–32.

ELEY, GEOFF, 'Notable Politics, the Crisis of German Liberalism, and the Electoral Transition of the 1890s', in Konrad H. Jarausch and Larry E. Jones (eds.), *In Search of a Liberal Germany. Studies in the History of German Liberalism from 1789 to the Present* (Oxford, 1990), 187–216.

—— *Reshaping the German Right. Radical Nationalism and Political Change after Bismarck* (2nd edn., Ann Arbour, 1991).

—— 'Army, State and Civil Society: Revisiting the Problem of German Militarism', in Geoff Eley, *From Unification to Nazism. Reinterpreting the German Past* (2nd edn., London, 1992), 85–109.

—— 'Society and Politics in Bismarckian Germany', *German History*, xv (1997), 101–32.

ERBE, MICHAEL, 'Berlin im Kaiserreich (1871–1918)', in Wolfgang Ribbe, *Geschichte Berlins*. ii. *Von der Märzrevolution bis zur Gegenwart* (Munich, 1988), 691–793.

EVANS, ELLEN LOVELL, *The German Center Party 1870–1933. A Study in Political Catholicism* (Carbondale/Edwardsville, Ill., 1981).

EVANS, RICHARD J., *Death in Hamburg: Society and Politics in the Cholera Years, 1830–1910* (Harmondsworth, 1987).

—— ' "Red Wednesday" in Hamburg: Social Democrats, Police and *Lumpenproletariat* in the Suffrage Disturbances of 17 January 1906', in Richard J. Evans, *Rethinking German History. Nineteenth-Century Germany and the Origins of the Third Reich* (London, 1987), 248–90.

—— *Rereading German History 1800–1996. From Unification to Reunification* (London, 1997).

FAIRBAIRN, BRETT, 'The German Elections of 1898 and 1903', D.Phil. thesis (Oxford, 1987).

—— 'Political Mobilization', in Roger Chickering (ed.), *Imperial Germany. A Historiographical Companion* (Westport, Conn., 1996), 303–42.

FAULENBACH, BERND, *Ideologie des deutschen Weges. Die deutsche Geschichte in der Historiographie zwischen Kaiserreich und Nationalsozialismus* (Munich, 1980).

FEHRENBACH, ELISABETH, *Verfassungsstaat und Nationsbildung 1815–1871* (Munich, 1992).

FERGUSON, NIALL C., 'Germany and the Origins of the First World War: New Perspectives', *Historical Journal*, xxxv (1992), 725–52.

—— 'Public Finance and National Security: The Domestic Origins of the First World War Revisited', *Past and Present*, no. 142 (1994), 141–68.

—— *Paper and Iron. Hamburg Business and German Politics in the Era of Inflation, 1897–1927* (Cambridge, 1995).

Bibliography

FISCH, STEFAN, *Stadtplanung im 19. Jahrhundert. Das Beispiel München bis zur Ära Theodor Fischer* (Munich, 1988).

—— 'Die zweifache Intervention der Städte. Stadtplanerische Zukunftsgesteltung und Kontrolle der Wohnverhältnisse um 1900', in Jürgen Reulecke and Adelheid Gräfin zu Castell Rüdenhausen (eds.), *Staat und Gesundheit. Zum Wandel von 'Volksgesundheit' und kommunaler Gesundheitspolitik im 19. und frühen 20. Jahrhundert* (Stuttgart, 1991), 91–104.

FISCHER, ANDREA, *Kommunale Leistungsverwaltung im 19. Jahrhundert. Frankfurt am Main unter Mumm von Schwarzenstein 1868–1880* (Berlin, 1995).

FISCHER, ILSE, *Industrialisierung, sozialer Konflikt und politische Willensbildung in der Stadtgemeinde. Ein Beitrag zur Sozialgeschichte Augsburgs* (Augsburg, 1977).

FLESCH-THEBESIUS, MAX, 'Der Frankfurter Sozialpolitiker Dr. Karl Flesch', *Archiv für Frankfurts Geschichte und Kunst*, xlvii (1960), 77–88.

FORSTMANN, WILFRIED, 'Frankfurt am Main in Wilhelminischer Zeit', in *Frankfurt am Main. Die Geschichte der Stadt in neun Beiträgen*, ed. Frankfurter Historische Kommission (Sigmaringen, 1991), 349–422.

FRASER, DEREK (ed.), *Municipal Reform and the Industrial City* (Leicester, 1982).

FREVERT, UTE, *Krankheit als Politisches Problem 1770–1880. Soziale Unterschichten in Preußen zwischen medizinischer Polizei und staatlicher Sozialversicherung* (Göttingen, 1984).

FRIEDEBURG, LUDWIG VON, *Bildungsreform in Deutschland* (Frankfurt, 1989).

FÜHR, CHRISTOPH, 'Die preußischen Schulkonferenzen von 1890 und 1900. Ihre bildungspolitische Rolle und bildungsgeschichtliche Bewertung', in Peter Baumgart (ed.), *Bildungspolitik in Preußen zur Zeit des Kaiserreichs* (Stuttgart, 1980), 189–223.

FÜHRBAUM, HELMUT, 'Die Entwicklung der Gemeindesteuern in Deutschland (Preußen) bis zum Beginn des 1. Weltkriegs', Ph.D. thesis (Münster, 1971).

GAGEL, WALTER, *Die Wahlrechtsfrage in der Geschichte der deutschen liberalen Parteien, 1848–1918* (Düsseldorf, 1958).

GALL, LOTHAR, *Der Liberalismus als regierende Partei. Das Grossherzogtum Baden zwischen Restauration und Reichsgründung* (Wiesbaden, 1968).

—— 'Die partei- und sozialgeschichtliche Problematik des badischen Kulturkampfes', reprinted in Alfons Schäfer (ed.), *Neue Forschungen zu Grundproblemen der badischen Geschichte im 19. und 20. Jahrhundert* (Karlsruhe, 1973), 93–132.

—— 'Liberalismus und "Bürgerliche Gesellschaft". Zu Charakter und Entwicklung der Liberalen Bewegung in Deutschland', *Historische Zeitschrift*, ccxx (1975), 324–56.

—— (ed.), *Liberalismus* (Königstein, 1980).

—— ' ". . . Ich wünschte ein Bürger zu sein". Zum Selbstverständnis des Deutschen Bürgertums im 19. Jahrhundert', *Historische Zeitschrift*, ccxlv (1987), 601–23.

—— *Bürgertum in Deutschland* (Berlin, 1989).

GALL, LOTHAR, *Europa auf dem Weg in die Moderne 1850–1890* (Munich, 1989).
—— (ed.), *Stadt und Bürgertum im 19. Jahrhundert* (Munich, 1990).
—— 'Das liberale Milieu. Die Bedeutung der Gemeinde für den deutschen Liberalismus', in *Liberalismus und Gemeinde. 3. Rastatter Tagung zur Geschichte des Liberalismus am 10./11. November 1990* (Sankt Augustin, 1991), 11–34.
—— (ed.), *Vom alten zum neuen Bürgertum. Die mitteleuropäische Stadt im Umbruch, 1780–1820* (Munich, 1991).
—— (ed.), *Stadt und Bürgertum im Übergang von der traditionalen zur modernen Gesellschaft* (Munich, 1993).
—— *Bürgertum, liberale Bewegung und Nation. Ausgewählte Aufsätze* (Munich, 1996).
—— (ed.), *Bürgertum und bürgerlich-liberale Bewegung in Mitteleuropa seit dem 18. Jahrhundert* (Munich, 1997).
—— and KOCH, RAINER (eds.), *Der europäische Liberalismus im 19. Jahrhundert. Texte zu seiner Entwicklung*, 4 vols. (Frankfurt, 1981).
—— and LANGEWIESCHE, DIETER (eds.), *Liberalismus und Region. Zur Geschichte des deutschen Liberalismus im 19. Jahrhundert* (Munich, 1995).
GALLINER, ARTHUR, 'The Philanthropin in Frankfurt. Its Educational and Cultural Significance for German Jewry', *Year Book of the Leo Baeck Institute*, iii (1958), 169–86.
GAUSE, FRITZ, *Die Geschichte der Stadt Königsberg in Preussen*. ii. *Von der Königskrönung bis zum Ausbruch des Ersten Weltkrieges* (Cologne/Graz, 1968).
GELLATELY, ROBERT, *The Politics of Economic Despair, 1890–1914* (London, 1974).
GERLOFF, WILHELM, *Die Finanz- und Zollpolitik des Deutschen Reiches nebst ihren Beziehungen zu Landes- und Gemeindefinanzen vor der Gründung des Norddeutschen Bundes bis zur Gegenwart* (Jena, 1913).
GERTEIS, KLAUS, *Leopold Sonnemann. Ein Beitrag zur Geschichte des demokratischen Nationalstaatsgedankens in Deutschland* (Frankfurt, 1970).
GNIFFKE, KAI, 'Max Quarck (1860–1930): Eine sozialdemokratische Karriere im Deutschen Kaiserreich. Zum Aufstieg eines bürgerlichen Akademikers in der Arbeiterbewegung im Spannungsfeld von revolutionärer Theorie und reformistischer Praxis', D.Phil. thesis (Frankfurt, 1992).
GOLLWITZER, HEINZ, *Vorüberlegungen zu einer Geschichte des Protestantismus nach dem konfessionellen Zeitalter* (Opladen, 1981).
GOLTZ, JOACHIM FREIHERR VON DER, 'Die Entwicklung der Selbstverwaltung innerhalb der staatlichen Verwaltung der öffentlichen Volksschule in Preußen', D.jur. thesis (Greifswald, 1914).
GOTTLIEB, GUNTHER, et al. (eds.), *Geschichte der Stadt Augsburg von der Römerzeit bis zur Gegenwart* (Stuttgart, 1984).
GRAF, FRIEDRICH WILHELM, *Die Politisierung des religiösen Bewußtseins. Die bürgerlichen Religionsparteien im deutschen Vormärz: Das Beispiel des Deutschkatholizismus* (Stuttgart, 1978).

Bibliography 365

GRASSMANN, SIEGFRID, *Hugo Preuß und die deutsche Selbstverwaltung* (Lübeck/Hamburg, 1965).

GREEF, KLAUS (ed.), *Das Katholische Frankfurt—Einst und Jetzt* (Frankfurt, 1989).

GROHS, WINFRIED, *Die Liberale Reichspartei 1871–1874. Liberale Katholiken und föderalistische Protestanten im ersten Deutschen Reichstag* (Frankfurt/Bern/New York/Paris, 1990).

GRÜNDER, HORST, '"Krieg bis auf's Messer"—Kirche, Kirchenvolk und Kulturkampf (1872–1887)', in Franz-Josef Jakobi (ed.), *Geschichte der Stadt Münster*. ii. *Das 19. und 20. Jahrhundert* (Münster, 1993), 131–67.

HAHN, HANS-WERNER, *Altständisches Bürgertum zwischen Beharrung und Wandel. Wetzlar 1689–1870* (Munich, 1991).

HALDER, WINFRID, *Katholische Vereine in Baden und Württemberg 1848–1914. Ein Beitrag zur Organisationsgeschichte des südwestdeutschen Katholizismus im Rahmen der Entstehung der modernen Industriegesellschaft* (Paderborn/Munich/Vienna, Zurich,1995).

HALLGARTEN, ROBERT, *Charles L. Hallgarten* (Frankfurt, 1915).

HAMER, DAVID A., *Liberal Politics in the Age of Gladstone and Roseberry* (Oxford, 1972).

HAMMERSTEIN, NOTKER, *Antisemitismus und deutsche Universitäten. 1871–1933* (Frankfurt/New York, 1995).

HANHAM, HENRY J., *Elections and Party Management* (London, 1959).

HARDTWIG, WOLFGANG, 'Großstadt und Bürgerlichkeit in der politischen Ordnung des Kaiserreichs', in Lothar Gall (ed.), *Stadt und Bürgertum im 19. Jahrhundert* (Munich, 1990), 19–64.

—— and BRAND, HARM-HINRICH (eds.), *Deutschlands Weg in die Moderne. Politik, Gesellschaft und Kultur im 19. Jahrhundert* (Munich, 1993).

HARRIS, JOSE, 'The Transition to High Politics in English Social Policy, 1880–1914', in Michael Bentley and John Stevenson (eds.), *High and Low Politics in Modern Britain* (Oxford, 1983), 58–79.

HAUMANN, HEIKO et al., 'Industriestadt oder "Pensionopolis"? Im Kaiserreich (1871–1914)', in Heiko Haumann and Hans Schadek (eds.), *Geschichte der Stadt Freiburg im Breisgau*. iii. *Von der badischen Herrschaft bis zur Gegenwart* (Stuttgart, 1992), 165–254.

HAUPT, HEINZ-GERHARD, 'Kleine und große Bürger in Deutschland und Frankreich am Ende des 19. Jahrhunderts', in Jürgen Kocka (ed.), *Bürgertum im 19. Jahrhundert. Deutschland im europäischen Vergleich* (Munich, 1988), ii. 252–75.

—— and LENGER, FRIEDRICH, 'Liberalismus und Handwerk in Frankreich und Deutschland um die Mitte des 19. Jahrhunderts', in Dieter Langewiesche (ed.), *Liberalismus im 19. Jahrhundert. Deutschland im europäischen Vergleich* (Göttingen, 1988), 305–31.

HAUSCHILD-THIESSEN, RENATE, *Bürgerstolz und Kaisertreue. Hamburg und das Deutsche Reich von 1871* (Hamburg, 1979).

HECKART, BEVERLY, *From Bassermann to Bebel. The Grand Bloc's Quest for Reform in the Kaiserreich, 1900–1914* (New Haven, 1974).

HEENEMANN, HORST, 'Die Auflagenöhen der deutschen Zeitungen. Ihre Entwicklung und ihre Probleme', D.Phil. thesis (Berlin, 1929).

HEFFTER, HEINRICH, *Die deutsche Selbstverwaltung im 19. Jahrhundert. Geschichte der Ideen und Institutionen* (Stuttgart, 1950).

HEIL, HEINRICH, *Zur Entwickelung der katholischen Presse in Frankfurt am Main. Ein Beitrag zur Geschichte der 'Frankfurter Volkszeitung' anläßlich ihres 50jährigen Jubliläums am 1. Oktober 1921* (Frankfurt, 1921).

HEILBRUNN, LUDWIG, *Die Gründung der Universität Frankfurt a.M.* (Frankfurt, 1915).

HEIN, DIETER, 'Badisches Bürgertum. Soziale Struktur und kommunalpolitische Ziele im 19. Jahrhundert', in Lothar Gall (ed.), *Stadt und Bürgertum im 19. Jahrhundert* (Munich, 1990), 65–96.

Heinrich Roessler, 1845–1924. Ein halbes Jahrhundert DEGUSSA-Geschichte, ed. DEGUSSA AG (Frankfurt, 1984).

Heinrich Rößler. Sonderabdruck des Physikalischen Vereins (Frankfurt, 1924).

HEITZER, HORSTWALTER, *Der Volksverein für das katholische Deutschland im Kaiserreich 1890–1918* (Mainz, 1979).

HENNEBO, DIETER, 'Öffentlicher Park und Grünplanung als kommunale Aufgabe in Deutschland', in Hans Heinrich Blotevogel (ed.), *Kommunale Leistungsverwaltung und Stadtentwicklung vom Vormärz bis zur Weimarer Republik* (Cologne/Vienna, 1990), 169–82.

HENNING, HANSJOACHIM, 'Arbeitslosenversicherung vor 1914: Das Genter System und seine Übernahme in Deutschland', in Hermann Kellenbenz (ed.), *Wirtschaftspolitik und Arbeitsmarkt* (Munich, 1974), 271–87.

HENTSCHEL, VOLKER, 'German Economic and Social Policy, 1815–1939', in Peter Mathias and Sidney Pollard (eds.), *The Cambridge Economic History of Europe*. viii. *The Industrial Economies: The Development of Economic and Social Policies* (Cambridge, 1989), 752–813.

HERRES, JÜRGEN, 'Das Preussische Koblenz', in *Geschichte der Stadt Koblenz*. ii. *Von der französischen Stadt bis zur Gegenwart* (Stuttgart, 1993), 49–102.

HERTERICH, HERMANN, 'Aus der Geschichte der Domschule', in *Handbuch*, ed. Vereinigung ehemaliger Domschüler Frankfurt a.M. (Frankfurt, 1929), 5–19.

HERZFELD, HANS, *Johannes von Miquel. Sein Anteil am Ausbau des Deutschen Reiches bis zur Jahrhundertwende*, 2 vols. (Detmold, 1938).

HETTLING, MANFRED, *Reform ohne Revolution. Bürgertum, Bürokratie und kommunale Selbstverwaltung in Württemberg von 1800 bis 1850* (Göttingen, 1990).

—— 'Von der Hochburg zur Wagenburg. Liberalismus in Breslau von den 1860er Jahren bis 1918', in Lothar Gall and Dieter Langewiesche (eds.), *Liberalismus und Region. Zur Geschichte des deutschen Liberalismus im 19. Jahrhundert* (Munich, 1995), 253–76.

HINDERLITER, ERIC LEE, 'Worker Protection in Imperial Germany: The Example of Frankfurt am Main 1869–1914', Ph.D. thesis (Providence, RI, 1977).

HOFMANN, WOLFGANG, 'Oberbürgermeister und Stadterweiterungen', in R. Dietrich and G. Oestreich (eds.), *Forschungen zu Staat und Verfassung. Festgabe für Fritz Hartung* (Berlin, 1958), 59–90.

—— *Die Bielefelder Stadtverordneten. Ein Beitrag zur bürgerlichen Selbstverwaltung und sozialem Wandel* (Berlin, 1964).

—— *Zwischen Rathaus und Reichskanzlei. Die Oberbürgermeister in der Kommunal- und Staatspolitik des Deutschen Reiches von 1890–1933* (Berlin/Stuttgart/Cologne/Mainz, 1974).

—— 'Oberbürgermeister als politische Elite im Wilhelminischen Reich und in der Weimarer Republik', in Klaus Schwabe (ed.), *Oberbürgermeister* (Boppard, 1981), 17–38.

—— 'Aufgaben und Struktur der kommunalen Selbstverwaltung in der Zeit der Hochindustrialisierung', in Kurt G. A. Jeserich, Hans Pohl, and Georg-Christoph von Unruh (eds.), *Deutsche Verwaltungsgeschichte* (Stuttgart, 1984), iii. 578–645.

HOLL, KARL, 'Überlegungen zum deutschen Sozialliberalismus', in Karl Holl, Günter Trautmann, Hans Vorländer (eds.), *Sozialer Liberalismus* (Göttingen, 1986), 227–32.

HOPE, NICHOLAS MARTIN, *The Alternative to German Unification. The Anti-Prussian Party Frankfurt, Nassau, and the two Hessen 1859–1867* (Wiesbaden, 1973).

HÜBINGER, GANGOLF, 'Hochindustrialisierung und die Kulturwerte des deutschen Liberalismus', in Dieter Langewiesche (ed.), *Liberalismus im 19. Jahrhundert. Deutschland im europäischen Vergleich* (Göttingen, 1988), 193–208.

—— *Kulturprotestantismus und Politik. Zum Verhältnis von Liberalismus und Protestantismus im wilhelminischen Deutschland* (Tübingen, 1994).

—— 'Confessionalism', in R. Chickering (ed.), *Imperial Germany. A Historiographical Companion* (Westport, Conn., 1996), 156–77.

HUNT, JAMES C., *The People's Party in Württemberg and Southern Germany, 1890–1914. The Possibilities of Democratic Politics* (Stuttgart, 1975).

HURD, MADELEINE, 'Tale of Two Cities. Socialists, Liberals and Democracy in Hamburg and Stockholm 1870–1914', in Bo Stråth (ed.), *Language and the Construction of Class Identities* (Gothenburg, 1990), 95–126.

HÜTTENBERGER, PETER, 'Die Entwicklung zur Großstadt bis zur Jahrhundertwende (1856–1900)', in *Düsseldorf. Geschichte von den Ursprüngen bis ins 20. Jahrhundert.* ii. *Von der Residenzstadt zur Beamtenstadt (1614–1900)* (Düsseldorf, 1988), 481–662.

—— 'Vom ausgehenden 19. Jahrhundert bis zum Ende des Ersten Weltkriegs', in *Düsseldorf. Geschichte von den Anfängen bis ins 20. Jahrhundert.* iii. *Die Industrie und Verwaltungsstadt (20. Jahrhundert)* (Düsseldorf, 1989), 7–262.

HYDE, SIMON, 'Roman Catholicism and the Prussian State in the Early 1850s', *Central European History*, xxiv (1991), 95–121.

JARAUSCH, KONRAD, *Students, Society and Politics in Imperial Germany. The Rise of Academic Illiberalism* (Princeton, 1982).

JEISMANN, KARL-ERNST, 'Volksbildung und Industrialisierung als Faktoren des sozialen Wandels im Vormärz. Dargestellt am Beispiel der Forderungen Friedrich Harkorts zur Bildungsreform', *Zeitschrift für Pädagogik*, xviii (1972), 315–37.

JERSCH-WENZEL, STEFI, 'Minderheiten in der bürgerlichen Gesellschaft. Juden in Amsterdam, Frankfurt und Posen', in Jürgen Kocka (ed.), *Bürgertum im 19. Jahrhundert. Deutschland im europäischen Vergleich* (Munich, 1988), iii. 392–420.

JOHN, MICHAEL, 'Liberalism and Society in Germany, 1850–1880. The Case of Hanover', *English Historical Review*, cii (1987), 579–98.

—— *Politics and the Law in Late Nineteenth-Century Germany. The Origins of the Civil Code* (Oxford, 1989).

—— 'Associational Life and the Development of Liberalism in Hanover, 1848–66', in Konrad Jarausch and Larry Eugene Jones (eds.), *In Search of a Liberal Germany. Studies in the History of German Liberalism from 1789 to the Present* (Oxford, 1990), 161–85.

—— 'Kultur, Klasse und regionaler Liberalismus in Hannover 1848–1914', in Lothar Gall and Dieter Langewiesche (eds.), *Liberalismus und Region. Zur Geschichte des deutschen Liberalismus im 19. Jahrhundert* (Munich, 1995), 161–93.

—— 'Constitution, Administration, and the Law', in R. Chickering (ed.), *Imperial Germany. A Historiographical Companion* (Westport, Conn., 1996), 185–214.

—— 'National and Regional Identities and the Dilemmas of Reform in Britain's "Other Province": Hanover, c.1800–c.1850', in Laurence Brockliss and David Eastwood (eds.), *A Union of Multiple Identities: The British Isles c.1750–c.1850* (Manchester, 1997), 179–92.

KAHN, ERNST, 'The Frankfurter Zeitung', *Year Book of the Leo Baeck Institute*, ii (1957), 228–35.

KAPLAN, MARION A., *The Making of the Jewish Middle Class. Women, Family, and Identity in Imperial Germany* (New York/Oxford, 1991).

KLAR, EMIL, 'Die Entwicklung des Wohnungswesens von 1870–1914', in *Das Wohnungswesen der Stadt Frankfurt a.M.* (Frankfurt, 1930).

KLAUSMANN, CHRISTINA, 'Politik und Bewegungskultur. Bürgerliche und proletarische Frauenbewegung in Frankfurt am Main 1876 bis 1914', D.Phil. thesis (Tübingen, 1995).

—— *Politik und Kultur der Frauenbewegung im Kaiserreich. Das Beispiel Frankfurt am Main* (Frankfurt, 1997).

KLÖTZER, WOLFGANG, 'Das Wilhelminische Frankfurt', *Archiv für Frankfurts Geschichte und Kunst*, liii (1973), 161–82.

—— 'Franz Adickes, Frankfurter Oberbürgermeister 1891–1912', in Klaus Schwabe (ed.), *Oberbürgermeister* (Boppard, 1981), 39–56.

—— 'Frankfurt am Main von der Französischen Revolution bis zur preußischen Okkupation 1789–1866', in *Frankfurt am Main. Die Geschichte der Stadt in neun Beiträgen*, ed. Frankfurter Historische Kommission (Sigmaringen, 1991), 303–48.

KLUKE, PAUL, *Die Stiftungsuniversität Frankfurt am Main 1914–1932* (Frankfurt, 1972).
KNUDSEN, JONATHAN, 'The Limits of Liberal Politics in Berlin 1815–48', in Konrad H. Jarausch and Larry E. Jones (eds.), *In Search of a Liberal Germany. Studies in the History of German Liberalism from 1789 to the Present* (Oxford, 1990), 111–31.
KOCH, RAINER, *Grundlagen bürgerlicher Herrschaft. Verfassungs- und sozialgeschichtliche Studien zur bürgerlichen Gesellschaft in Frankfurt am Main, 1612–1866* (Wiesbaden, 1983).
—— 'Staat oder Gemeinde? Zu einem politischen Zielkonflikt in der bürgerlichen Bewegung des 19. Jahrhunderts', *Historische Zeitschrift*, ccxxxvi (1983), 73–96.
—— 'Franz Adickes', in Günter Böhme (ed.), *Geistesgeschichte im Spiegel einer Stadt: Frankfurt am Main und seine grossen Persönlichkeiten* (Frankfurt, 1986), 101–21.
—— 'Liberalismus und soziale Frage im 19. Jahrhundert', in Karl Holl, Günter Trautmann, Hans Vorländer (eds.), *Sozialer Liberalismus* (Göttingen, 1986), 17–33.
KOCKA, JÜRGEN (ed.), *Bürgertum im 19. Jahrhundert. Deutschland im europäischen Vergleich*, 3 vols. (Munich, 1988).
—— 'German History before Hitler: The Debate about the German *Sonderweg*', *Journal of Contemporary History*, xxiii (1988), 3–16.
—— 'Bildungsbürgertum—Gesellschaftliche Formation oder Historikerkonstrukt?', in Jürgen Kocka (ed.), *Bildungsbürgertum im 19. Jahrhundert. Politischer Einfluß und gesellschaftliche Formation* (Stuttgart, 1989), iv. 9–20.
KÖHLER, JÖRG R., *Städtebau und Stadtpolitik im Wilhelminischen Frankfurt* (Frankfurt, 1995).
KÖLLMANN, WOLFGANG, *Sozialgeschichte der Stadt Barmen* (Tübingen, 1960).
KOSELLECK, REINHART, *Preußen zwischen Reform und Revolution* (Stuttgart, 1967).
KOSHAR, RUDY, *Social Life, Local Politics, and Nazism. Marburg, 1880–1935* (Chapel Hill, NC, 1986).
KÖSTER, Thomas, *Die Entwicklung kommunaler Finanzsysteme am Beispiel Großbritanniens, Frankreichs und Deutschlands 1790–1980* (Berlin, 1984).
KRABBE, WOLFGANG R., 'Munizipalsozialismus und Interventionsstaat. Die Ausbreitung der städtischen Leistungsverwaltung im Kaiserreich', *Geschichte in Wissenschaft und Unterrricht*, xxx (1979), 265–83.
—— 'Die Entfaltung der modernen Leistungsverwaltung in den deutschen Städten des späten 19. Jahrhunderts', in Hans Jürgen Teuteberg (ed.), *Urbanisierung im 19. und 20. Jahrhundert. Historische und Geographische Aspekte* (Cologne/Vienna, 1983), 373–92.
—— *Kommunalpolitik und Industrialisierung. Die Entfaltung der städtischen Leistungsverwaltung im 19. und frühen 20. Jahrhundert* (Stuttgart/Berlin/Cologne/Mainz, 1985).
—— *Die deutsche Stadt im 19. und 20. Jahrhundert* (Göttingen, 1989).

KRAMER, HANS-HELMUTH, 'Die Entwicklung der Preussischen Steuerverfassung im 19. Jahrhundert', D.jur. thesis (Kiel, 1970).

KRAMER, HENRIETTE, 'Die Anfänge des Sozialen Wohnungsbaus in Frankfurt am Main, 1860–1914', *Archiv für Frankfurts Geschichte und Kunst*, lvi (1978), 123–90.

KRAUL, MARGRET, 'Bildung und Bürgerlichkeit', in Jürgen Kocka (ed.), *Bürgertum im 19. Jahrhundert. Deutschland im europäischen Vergleich* (Munich, 1988), iii. 45–73.

—— *Das deutsche Gymnasium 1780–1980* (Frankfurt, 1984).

KROHN, HELGA, *Die Juden in Hamburg. Die Politische, Soziale und kulturelle Entwicklung einer jüdischen Großstadtgemeinde nach der Emanzipation* (Hamburg, 1974).

KROPAT, WOLF-ARNO, *Frankfurt zwischen Provinzialismus und Nationalismus. Die Eingliederung der 'Freien Stadt' in den preußischen Staat (1866–1871)* (Frankfurt, 1971).

KUHLEMANN, FRANK-MICHAEL, 'Niedere Schulen', in Christa Berg (ed.), *Handbuch der Deutschen Bildungsgeschichte*, iv. *1870–1918* (Munich, 1991), 179–228.

KÜHNE, THOMAS, *Dreiklassenwahlrecht und Wahlkultur in Preußen 1867–1914. Landtagswahlen zwischen korporativer Tradition und politischem Massenmarkt* (Düsseldorf, 1994).

—— *Handbuch der Wahlen zum Preußischen Abgeordnetenhaus 1867–1918. Wahlergebnisse, Wahlbündnisse und Wahlkandidaten* (Düsseldorf, 1994).

—— 'Die Liberalen bei den preußischen Landtagswahlen im Kaiserreich. Wahlmanipulation, Lokalismus und Wahlkompromisse', in Lothar Gall and Dieter Langewiesche (eds.), *Liberalismus und Region. Zur Geschichte des deutschen Liberalismus im 19. Jahrhundert* (Munich, 1995), 277–305.

KULLMANN, ADOLF, 'Die Stellungnahme der *Frankfurter Zeitung* zum Kulturkampf', D.Phil. thesis (Würzburg, 1922).

KUNZ, J. A., *Entstehung und Durchführung des Simultanschulsystems in Frankfurt a.M.* (Frankfurt, 1927).

LADD, BRIAN, *Urban Planning and Civic Order in Germany, 1860–1914* (Cambridge, Mass., 1990).

LAMBERTI, MARJORIE, 'State, Church and the Politics of School Reform during the Kulturkampf', *Central European History*, xix (1986), 63–81.

—— *State, Society, and the Elementary School in Imperial Germany* (New York/Oxford, 1989).

LANGEWIESCHE, DIETER, *Liberalismus und Demokratie in Württemberg zwischen Revolution und Reichsgründung* (Düsseldorf, 1974).

—— 'Die Anfänge der deutschen Parteien. Partei, Fraktion und Verein in der Revolution von 1848/49', *Geschichte und Gesellschaft*, iv (1978), 324–61.

—— *Liberalismus in Deutschland* (Frankfurt, 1988).

—— (ed.), *Liberalismus im 19. Jahrhundert. Deutschland im europäischen Vergleich* (Göttingen, 1988).

—— 'Liberalismus und Bürgertum in Europa', in Jürgen Kocka (ed.), *Bürgertum im 19. Jahrhundert. Deutschland im europäischen Vergleich* (Munich, 1988), iii. 360–94.

—— 'Deutscher Liberalismus im europäischen Vergleich: Konzeption und Ergebnisse', in Dieter Langewiesche (ed.), *Liberalismus im 19. Jahrhundert. Deutschland im europäischen Vergleich* (Göttingen, 1988), 11–19.

—— 'Bildungsbürgertum und Liberalismus im 19. Jahrhundert', in Jürgen Kocka (ed.), *Bildungsbürgertum im 19. Jahrhundert. Politischer Einfluß und gesellschaftliche Formation* (Stuttgart, 1989), iv. 95–121.

—— '"Staat" und "Kommune". Zum Wandel der Staatsaufgaben in Deutschland im 19. Jahrhundert', *Historische Zeitschrift*, ccxlviii (1989), 621–35.

—— 'German Liberalism in the Second Empire, 1871–1914', in Konrad H. Jarausch and Larry E. Jones (eds.), *In Search of a Liberal Germany. Studies in the History of German Liberalism from 1789 to the Present* (Oxford, 1990), 217–37.

—— 'The Nature of German Liberalism', in Gordon Martel (ed.), *Modern Germany Reconsidered, 1870–1945* (London, 1992), 96–116.

—— 'Reich, Nation und Staat in der jüngeren deutschen Geschichte', *Historische Zeitschrift*, ccliv (1992), 341–81.

—— 'Liberalismus und Region', in Lothar Gall and Dieter Langewiesche (eds.), *Liberalismus und Region. Zur Geschichte des deutschen Liberalismus im 19. Jahrhundert* (Munich, 1995), 1–18.

—— 'Kulturelle Nationsbildung im Deutschland des 19. Jahrhunderts', in Manfred Hettling and Paul Nolte (eds.), *Nation und Gesellschaft in Deutschland. Historische Essays* (Munich, 1996), 46–64.

—— 'Frühliberalismus und Bürgertum' in Lothar Gall (ed.), *Bürgertum und bürgerlich-liberale Bewegung in Mitteleuropa seit dem 18. Jahrhundert* (Munich, 1997), 63–129.

LÄSSIG, SIMONE, *Wahlrechtskampf und Wahlreform in Sachsen (1895–1909)* (Weimar/Cologne/Vienna, 1996).

—— and POHL, KARL HEINRICH (eds.), *Sachsen im Kaiserreich. Politik, Wirtschaft und Gesellschaft im Umbruch* (Weimar/Cologne/Vienna, 1997).

—— —— and RETALLACK, JAMES (eds.), *Modernisierung und Region im wilhelminischen Deutschland* (Bielefeld, 1995).

LEE, ALAN JOHN, *The Origins of the Popular Press in England 1855–1914* (London, 1976).

LEMBKE, RUDOLF, *Johannes Miquel und die Stadt Osnabrück unter besonderer Berücksichtigung der Jahre 1865–1869* (Osnabrück, 1962).

LENGER, FRIEDRICH, *Sozialgeschichte der deutschen Handwerker seit 1800* (Frankfurt, 1988).

LEPSIUS, M. RAINER, 'Parteiensystem und Sozialstruktur. Zum Problem der Demokratisierung der deutschen Gesellschaft', in Gerhard A. Ritter (ed.), *Die deutschen Parteien vor 1918* (Cologne, 1973), 56–80.

LERNER, FRANZ, *Bürgersinn und Bürgertat. Geschichte der Polytechnischen Gesellschaft 1816–1966* (Frankfurt, 1966).
LIBERLES, ROBERT, *Religious Conflict in Social Context. The Resurgence of Orthodox Judaism in Frankfurt am Main 1838–1877* (Westport/London, 1985).
LIEBERSOHN, HARRY, 'Religion and Industrial Society: The Protestant Social Congress in Wilhelmine Germany', *Transactions of the American Philosophical Society*, lxxvi, Part 6 (Philadelphia, 1986).
LIEBERT, BERND, *Politische Wahlen in Wiesbaden im Kaiserreich (1867–1918)* (Wiesbaden, 1988).
LÖNNE, KARL-EGON, *Politischer Katholizismus im 19. und 20. Jahrhundert* (Frankfurt, 1986).
LOTH, WILFRIED, 'Soziale Bewegungen im Katholizismus des Kaiserreichs', *Geschichte und Gesellschaft*, xvii (1991), 279–310.
LUEBBERT, GREGORY M., *Liberalism, Fascism or Social Democracy. Social Classes and the Political Origins of Regimes in Interwar Europe* (New York, 1991).
LUNDGREEN, PETER, KRAUL, MARGRET and DITT, Karl, *Bildungschancen und soziale Mobilität in der städtischen Gesellschaft des 19. Jahrhunderts* (Göttingen, 1988).
LUNTOWSKI, GUSTAV, 'Das Jahrhundert der Industrialisierung (1803 bis 1914)', in *Geschichte der Stadt Dortmund* (Dortmund, 1994), 215–355.
MÄCHLER, ANITA, 'Aspekte der Volksschulpolitik in Preußen im 19. Jahrhundert. Ein Überblick über wichtige gesetzliche Grundlagen im Hinblick auf ausgewählte Gesichtspunkte', in Peter Baumgart (ed.), *Bildungspolitik in Preußen zur Zeit des Kaiserreichs* (Stuttgart, 1980), 224–41.
MAI, GUNTHER, 'Konservative Stabilisierungsstrategien im Kaiserreich. Zur Praxis des Sozialistengesetzes in Frankfurt/M. 1878–1890', *Hessisches Jahrbuch für Landesgeschichte*, xxxiv (1984), 193–206.
MALY, KARL, *Die Macht der Honoratioren. Geschichte der Stadtverordnetenversammlung 1867–1914* (Frankfurt, 1992).
—— *Das Regiment der Parteien. Geschichte der Frankfurter Stadtverordnetenversammlung 1900–1933* (Frankfurt, 1995).
MARCUS, E., 'Dr. Georg Varrentrapp', in *Jahresbericht über die Verwaltung des Medizinalwesens der Stadt Frankfurt a.M.* (1886), 262–83.
MATTHEW, H. C. G., 'Disraeli, Gladstone, and the Politics of Mid-Victorian Budgets', *Historical Journal*, xxii (1979), 615–43.
—— 'Rhetoric and Politics in Great Britain, 1860–1914', in Philip J. Waller (ed.), *Politics and Social Change in Modern Britain* (Brighton, 1987), 34–58.
MATZERATH, HORST, *Urbanisierung in Preußen 1815–1914* (Stuttgart/Berlin/Cologne/Mainz, 1985).
—— ' "Kommunale Leistungsverwaltung". Zu Bedeutung und politischer Funktion des Begriffs im 19. und 20. Jahrhundert', in Hans Heinrich Blotevogel (ed.), *Kommunale Leistungsverwaltung und Stadtentwicklung vom Vormärz bis zur Weimarer Republik* (Cologne/Vienna, 1990), 3–24.

—— (ed.), *Stadt und Verkehr im Industriezeitalter* (Cologne/Weimar/Vienna, 1996).
MCLEOD, HUGH, *Religion and the People of Western Europe 1789–1970* (Oxford, 1981, reprinted 1990).
MEINECKE, FRIEDRICH, *Die deutsche Katastrophe* (Wiesbaden, 1965).
MENZE, CLEMENS, *Wilhelm von Humboldt* (Sankt Augustin, 1993).
MERGEL, THOMAS, *Zwischen Klasse und Konfession. Katholisches Bürgertum im Rheinland 1794–1914* (Göttingen, 1994).
MESSERSCHMIDT, MANFRED, 'Schulpolitik des Militärs', in Peter Baumgart (ed.), *Bildungspolitik in Preußen zur Zeit des Kaiserreichs* (Stuttgart, 1980), 242–55.
MEYER, FOLKERT, *Schule der Untertanen. Lehrer und Politik in Preußen 1848–1900* (Hamburg, 1976).
MIELKE, SIEGFRID, *Der Hansa-Bund für Gewerbe, Handel und Industrie 1909–1914. Der gescheiterte Versuch einer antifeudalen Sammlungspolitik* (Göttingen, 1976).
MITCHELL, BRIAN R., *European Historical Statistics, 1750–1975* (2nd edn., London, 1981).
MITTERAUER, MICHAEL, *A History of Youth* (Oxford, 1992).
MOELLER, ROBERT G., 'The Kaiserreich Recast? Continuity and Change in Modern German Historiography', *Journal of Social History*, xvii (1984), 655–83.
MOMMSEN, WOLFGANG J., 'Der deutsche Liberalismus zwischen "Klassenloser Bürgergesellschaft" und "Organisiertem Kapitalismus". Zu einer neuen Liberalismusinterpretation', *Geschichte und Gesellschaft*, iv (1978), 77–90.
MOSSE, WERNER E., *The German-Jewish Economic Elite 1820–1935. A Socio-Cultural Profile* (Oxford, 1989).
MÜLLER, DETLEV K., *Sozialstruktur und Schulsystem. Aspekte zum Strukturwandel des Schulwesens im 19. Jahrhundert* (Göttingen, 1977).
—— and ZYMEK, BERND, *Datenhandbuch zur deutschen Bildungsgeschichte. ii. Höhere und mittlere Schulen. Teil 1. Sozialgeschichte und Statistik des Schulsystems in den Staaten des Deutschen Reiches, 1800–1945* (Göttingen, 1987).
MÜLLER, PETRUS, *Liberalismus in Nürnberg 1860 bis 1871. Eine Fallstudie zur Ideen- und Sozialgeschichte des Liberalismus in Deutschland im 19. Jahrhundert* (Nuremberg, 1990).
NICHOLS, J. ALDEN, *Germany after Bismarck. The Caprivi Era 1890–1894* (Cambridge, Mass., 1958).
NIEHUSS, MERITH, 'Party Configurations in State and Municipal Elections in Southern Germany, 1871–1914', in Karl Rohe (ed.), *Elections, Parties and Political Traditions. Social Foundations of German Parties and Party Systems, 1867–1987* (Oxford, 1990), 83–105.
NIEWYK, DONALD L., *The Jews in Weimar Germany* (Baton Rouge, La., 1980).
NIPPERDEY, THOMAS, *Die Organisation der deutschen Parteien vor 1918* (Düsseldorf, 1961).
—— 'Grundprobleme der deutschen Parteigeschichte im 19. Jahrhundert', in Gerhard A. Ritter (ed.), *Die deutschen Parteien vor 1918* (Cologne, 1973), 32–55.

NIPPERDEY, THOMAS, 'Wehler's "Kaiserreich". Eine kritische Auseinandersetzung', *Geschichte und Gesellschaft*, i (1975), 539–60.
—— *Deutsche Geschichte 1800–1866. Bürgerwelt und starker Staat* (Munich, 1983).
—— 'Probleme der Modernisierung in Deutschland', in Thomas Nipperdey, *Nachdenken über die deutsche Geschichte* (2nd edn., Munich, 1990), 52–70.
—— *Nachdenken über die deutsche Geschichte* (2nd edn., Munich, 1990).
—— *Deutsche Geschichte 1866–1918*. i. *Arbeitswelt und Bürgergeist* (Munich, 1990).
—— *Deutsche Geschichte 1866–1918*. ii. *Machtstaat vor der Demokratie* (Munich, 1992).
NOLTE, PAUL, 'Gemeindeliberalismus. Zur Entstehung und sozialen Verankerung der liberalen Partei in Baden 1831–1855', *Historische Zeitschrift*, cclii (1991), 57–93.
—— 'Bürgerideal, Gemeinde und Republik. "Klassischer Republikanismus" im frühen deutschen Liberalismus', *Historische Zeitschrift*, ccliv (1992), 609–56.
—— *Gemeindebürgertum und Liberalismus in Baden 1800–1850* (Göttingen, 1994).
NONN, CHRISTOPH, 'Soziale Hintergründe des politischen Wandels im Königreich Sachsen vor 1914', in Simone Lässig and Karl Heinrich Pohl (eds.), *Sachsen im Kaiserreich. Politik, Wirtschaft und Gesellschaft im Umbruch* (Weimar/Cologne/Vienna, 1997), 371–92.
OFFER, AVNER, *Property and Politics 1870–1914. Landownership, Law, Ideology and Urban Development in England* (Cambridge, 1981).
OFFERMANN, TONI, *Arbeiterbewegung und liberales Bürgertum in Deutschland, 1850–1863* (Bonn, 1979).
OLLIGES-WIECZOREK, Ute, *Politisches Leben in Münster—Parteien und Vereine im Kaiserreich (1871–1914)* (Münster, 1995).
PADTBERG, BEATE-CAROLA, *Rheinischer Liberalismus in Köln während der politischen Reaktion in Preußen nach 1848/9* (Cologne, 1985).
PEUKERT, DETLEV J. K., *Grenzen der Sozialdisziplinierung. Aufstieg und Krise der deutschen Jugendfürsorge von 1878 bis 1932* (Cologne, 1986).
POGGE VON STRANDMANN, HARTMUT, 'The Liberal Monopolies of Power in the Cities of Imperial Germany', in Larry E. Jones and James N. Retallack (eds.), *Elections, Mass Politics and Social Change in Modern Germany. New Perspectives* (Cambridge, 1992), 93–117.
POHL, KARL HEINRICH, 'Die Nationalliberalen—eine unbekannte Partei?', *Jahrbuch zur Liberalismus-Forschung*, iii (1991), 82–112.
—— 'Sachsen, Stresemann und die Nationalliberale Partei. Anmerkungen zur politischen Entwicklung, zum Aufstieg des industriellen Bürgertums und zur frühen Tätigkeit Stresemanns im Königreich Sachsen vor 1914', *Jahrbuch zur Liberalismus-Forschung*, iv (1992), 197–216.
—— *Die Münchener Arbeiterbewegung. Sozialdemokratische Partei, Freie Gewerkschaften, Staat und Gesellschaft in München 1890–1914* (Munich/London/New York/Paris, 1992).
—— '"Einig", "kraftvoll", "machtbewußt". Überlegungen zu einer Geschichte

des deutschen Liberalismus aus regionaler Perspektive', *Historische Mitteilungen der Rancke Gesellschaft*, vii (1994), 61–80.

—— 'Die Nationalliberalen in Sachsen vor 1914. Eine Partei der konservativen Honoratioren auf dem Wege zur Partei der Industrie', in Lothar Gall and Dieter Langewiesche, *Liberalismus und Region. Zur Geschichte des deutschen Liberalismus im 19. Jahrhundert* (Munich, 1995), 195–216.

—— 'Liberalismus und Bürgertum 1880–1918', in Lothar Gall (ed.), *Bürgertum und bürgerlich-liberale Bewegung in Mitteleuropa seit dem 18. Jahrhundert* (Munich, 1997), 231–91.

—— 'Politischer Liberalismus und Wirtschaftsbügertum: Zum Aufschwung der sächsischen Liberalen vor 1914', in Simone Lässig and Karl Heinrich Pohl (eds.), *Sachsen im Kaiserreich. Politik, Wirtschaft und Gesellschaft im Umbruch* (Weimar/Cologne/Vienna, 1977), 101–31.

PREISSLER, DIETMAR, *Frühantisemitismus in der Freien Stadt Frankfurt und im Großherzogtum Hessen, 1810–1860* (Heidelberg, 1989).

PRINZ, MICHAEL, 'Wandel durch Beharrung. Sozialdemokratie und "neue Mittelschichten" in historischer Perspektive', *Archiv für Sozialgeschichte*, xxix (1989), 35–73.

PUHLE, HANS-JÜRGEN, 'Parlament, Parteien und Interessenverbände 1890–1914', in Michael Stürmer (ed.), *Das kaiserliche Deutschland. Politik und Gesellschaft 1870–1918* (Düsseldorf, 1970), 340–77.

PULZER, PETER, *The Rise of Political Anti-Semitism in Germany and Austria* (2nd edn., London, 1988).

—— *Jews and the German State. The Political History of a Minority, 1848–1933* (Oxford, 1992).

PYTA, WOLFGANG, *Landwirtschaftliche Interessenpolitik im deutschen Kaiserreich. Der Einfluß agrarischer Interessen auf die Neuordnung der Finanz- und Wirtschaftspolitik am Ende der 1870er Jahre am Beispiel von Rheinland und Westfalen* (Stuttgart, 1991).

REBENTISCH, DIETER, 'Politik und Rauplanung im Rhein-Main Gebiet. Kontinuität und Wandel seit 100 Jahren', *Archiv für Frankfurter Geschichte und Kunst*, lvi (1978), 191–210.

—— 'Industrialisierung, Bevölkerungswachstum und Eingemeindungen. Das Beispiel Frankfurt a.M. 1870–1914', in Jürgen Reulecke (ed.), *Die deutsche Stadt im Industriezeitalter* (Wuppertal, 1978), 90–113.

—— 'Die deutsche Sozialdemokratie und die kommunale Selbstverwaltung. Ein Überblick über Programmdiskussion und Organisationsproblematik, 1890–1975', *Archiv für Sozialgeschichte*, xxv (1985), 1–78.

RETALLACK, JAMES, *Notables of the Right. The Conservative Party and Political Mobilization in Germany, 1876–1918* (Boston, 1988).

—— 'Social History with a Vengeance? Some Reactions to H.-U. Wehler's "Das Deutsche Kaiserreich" ', *German Studies Review*, vii (1984), 423–50.

—— '"What is to be Done?" The Red Specter, Franchise Questions, and the

Crisis of Conservative Hegemony in Saxony, 1896–1909', *Central European History*, xxiii (1990), 271–312.

—— 'Antisocialism and Electoral Politics in Regional Perspective: The Kingdom of Saxony', in Larry Eugene Jones and James Retallack (eds.), *Elections, Mass Politics, and Social Change in Modern Germany* (Cambridge, 1992), 49–91.

—— 'Wilhelmine Germany', in Gordon Martel (ed.), *Modern Germany Reconsidered, 1870–1945* (London, 1992), 33–53.

—— 'Die "liberalen" Konservativen? Konservatismus und Antisemitismus im industrialisierten Sachsen', in Simone Lässig and Karl Heinrich Pohl (eds.), *Sachsen im Kaiserreich. Politik, Wirtschaft und Gesellschaft im Umbruch* (Weimar/Cologne/Vienna, 1997), 133–48.

—— ' "Why can't a Saxon be more like a Prussian?" Regional Identities and Political Culture in Germany, 1866–67', *Canadian Journal of History*, xxxii (1997), 28–55.

REULECKE, JÜRGEN, 'Bürgerliche Sozialreform und Arbeiterjugend im Kaiserreich', *Archiv für Sozialgeschichte*, xxii (1982), 299–329.

—— *Geschichte der Urbanisierung in Deutschland* (Frankfurt, 1985).

—— 'Bildungsbürgertum und Kommunalpolitik im 19. Jahrhundert', in Jürgen Kocka (ed.), *Bildungsbürgertum im 19. Jahrhundert. Politischer Einfluß und gesellschaftliche Formation* (Stuttgart, 1989), iv. 122–45.

—— 'Federal Republic of Germany', in Christian Engeli and Horst Matzerath (eds.), *Modern Urban History Research in Europe, USA and Japan. A Handbook* (Oxford, 1989), 53–71.

—— 'Stadtbürgertum und bürgerliche Sozialreform im 19. Jahrhundert in Preußen', in Lothar Gall (ed.), *Stadt und Bürgertum im 19. Jahrhundert* (Munich, 1990), 171–97.

—— 'Von der "Hygienisierung" der Unterschichten zur kommunalen Gesundheitspolitik', in Jürgen Reulecke and Adelheid Gräfin zu Castell Rüdenhausen (eds.), *Stadt und Gesundheit. Zum Wandel von 'Volksgesundheit' und kommunaler Gesundheitspolitik im 19. und frühen 20. Jahrhundert* (Stuttgart, 1991), 11–20.

RICHTER, GÜNTER, 'Zwischen Revolution und Reichsgründung (1848–1870)', in Wolfgang Ribbe (ed.), *Geschichte Berlins*. ii. *Von der Märzrevolution bis zur Gegenwart* (Munich, 1988), 605–87.

RINGER, FRITZ K., 'Bildung, Wirtschaft und Gesellschaft in Deutschland 1800–1960', *Geschichte und Gesellschaft*, vi (1980), 5–35.

—— *Education and Society in Modern Europe* (Bloomington, Ind., 1979).

RITTER, GERHARD A. (ed.), *Die deutschen Parteien vor 1918* (Cologne, 1973).

—— *Wahlgeschichtliches Arbeitsbuch. Materialien zur Statistik des Kaiserreichs 1871–1918* (Munich, 1980).

—— *Social Welfare in Germany and Britain* (Leamington Spa, 1986).

—— 'The Social Bases of the German Political Parties', in Karl Rohe (ed.), *Elections, Parties and Political Traditions. Social Foundations of German Parties and Party Systems, 1867–1987* (Oxford, 1990), 27–53.

—— 'Wahlen und Wahlpolitik im Königreich Sachsen 1867–1914', in Simone Lässig and Karl Heinrich Pohl (eds.), *Sachsen im Kaiserreich. Politik, Wirtschaft und Gesellschaft im Umbruch* (Weimar/Cologne/Vienna, 1997), 29–86.

ROBSON, STUART T., 'Left-wing Liberalism in Germany, 1900–1919', D.Phil. thesis (Oxford, 1966).

ROEDER, PETER MARTIN, 'Gemeindeschule in Staatshand. Zur Schulpolitik des Preußischen Abgeordnetenhauses', *Zeitschrift für Pädagogik*, xii (1966), 539–69.

ROHE, KARL, *Vom Revier zum Ruhrgebiet* (Essen, 1986).

—— 'Politische Kultur und ihre Analyse. Probleme und Perspektiven der politischen Kulturforschung', *Historische Zeitung*, ccl (1990), 321–46.

—— (ed.), *Elections, Parties and Political Traditions. Social Foundations of German Parties and Party Systems, 1867–1987* (Oxford, 1990).

—— *Wahlen und Wählertraditionen* (Frankfurt, 1992).

—— 'Politische Kultur—politische Milieus: Zur Anwendung neuerer theoretischer Konzepte in einer modernen Landesgeschichte', in Simone Lässig and Karl Heinrich Pohl (eds.), *Sachsen im Kaiserreich. Politik, Wirtschaft und Gesellschaft im Umbruch* (Weimar/Cologne/Vienna, 1997), 177–90.

ROHR, CORNELIA, 'Kommunaler Liberalismus und bürgerliche Herrschaft in den Städten Frankfurt am Main und Leipzig 1900–1924', *Jahrbuch für Liberalismus-Forschung*, vi (1994), 167–77.

ROHR, DONALD G., *The Origins of Social Liberalism in Germany* (Chicago, 1963).

ROLLING, JOHN D., 'Liberals, Socialists, and City Government in Imperial Germany: The Case of Frankfurt am Main, 1900–1918', Ph.D. thesis (Madison, 1979).

—— 'Das Problem der "Politisierung" der kommunalen Selbstverwaltung in Frankfurt am Main 1900–1918', *Archiv für Frankfurts Geschichte und Kunst*, lvii (1980), 167–85.

ROTH, RALF, *Gewerkschaftskartell und Sozialpolitik in Frankfurt am Main. Arbeiterbewegung vor dem Ersten Weltkrieg zwischen Restauration und liberaler Erneuerung* (Frankfurt, 1991).

—— ' " . . . der blühende Handel macht uns alle glücklich". Frankfurt am Main in der Umbuchszeit 1780–1825', in Lothar Gall (ed.), *Vom alten zum neuen Bürgertum. Die mitteleuropäische Stadt im Umbruch, 1780–1820* (Munich, 1991), 357–408.

—— 'Liberalismus in Frankfurt am Main, 1814–1914. Probleme seiner Strukturgeschichte', in Lothar Gall and Dieter Langewiesche (eds.), *Liberalismus und Region. Zur Geschichte des deutschen Liberalismus im 19. Jahrhundert* (Munich, 1995), 41–85.

—— *Stadt und Bürgertum in Frankfurt am Main. Ein besonderer Weg von der ständischen zur modernen Bürgergesellschaft 1760–1914* (Munich, 1996).

ROTHENBERGER, JULIUS, 'Von Miquel bis Adickes (1880–1912)', in *Jahrbuch der Frankfurter Bürgerschaft* (1926), 121–30.

ROXBOROUGH, IAN, 'Modernization Theory Revisited. A Review Article', *Comparative Studies in Society and History*, xxx (1988), 753–61.

SACHSE, CHRISTOPH, and TENNSTEDT, FLORIAN, *Geschichte der Armenfürsorge in Deutschland. Vom Spätmittelalter bis zum 1. Weltkrieg* (Stuttgart/Berlin/Cologne/Mainz, 1980).

SALDERN, ADELHEID VON, *Vom Einwohner zum Bürger. Zur Emanzipation der städtischen Unterschicht Göttingens, 1890–1920. Eine sozial- und kommunalhistorische Untersuchung* (Berlin, 1973).

—— *Auf dem Wege zum Arbeiter-Reformismus. Parteialltag in sozialdemokratischer Provinz Göttingen (1870–1920)* (Frankfurt, 1984).

SCHAEFER, HERMANN, ' "New Industries" and the Role of the State: The Development of Electrical Power in South Germany from c.1880 to the 1920s', in W. Robert Lee (ed.), *German Industry and German Industrialisation. Essays in German Economic and Business History in the Nineteenth and Twentieth Centuries* (London, 1991), 200–19.

SCHÄFER, KURT, *Schulen und Schulpolitik in Frankfurt am Main 1900–1945* (Frankfurt, 1994).

SCHAMBACH, KARIN, *Stadtbürgertum und industrieller Umbruch. Dortmund 1789–1870* (Munich, 1996).

SCHATZ, KLAUS, SJ, *Geschichte des Bistums Limburg* (Mainz, 1983).

SCHLOSSMACHER, NORBERT, *Düsseldorf im Bismarckreich. Politik und Wahlen, Parteien und Vereine* (Düsseldorf, 1985).

—— 'Der Antiultramontanismus im Wilhelminischen Deutschland. Ein Versuch', in Wilfried Loth (ed.), *Deutscher Katholizismus im Umbruch zur Moderne* (Stuttgart/Berlin/Cologne, 1991), 164–98.

SCHLOTZHAUER, INGE, 'Gleichstellung der Juden, 1816–1817', MA thesis (Frankfurt, 1982).

—— 'Die bürgerliche Gleichstellung der Frankfurter Juden im Urteil zeitgenössischer Schriften', *Jahrbuch für Hessische Landesgeschichte*, xxxiv (1984), 129–62.

—— *Ideologie und Organisation des politischen Antisemitismus in Frankfurt am Main 1880–1914* (Frankfurt, 1989).

—— *Das Philanthropin 1804–1942. Die Schule der Israelitischen Gemeinde in Frankfurt am Main* (Frankfurt, 1990).

SCHMIDT, GUSTAV, 'Die Nationalliberalen—eine regierungsfähige Partei? Zur Problematik der inneren Reichsgründung', in Gerhard A. Ritter (ed.), *Die deutschen Parteien vor 1918* (Cologne, 1973), 208–23.

—— 'Liberalismus und soziale Reform: Der deutsche und der britische Fall, 1890–1914', *Tel Aviver Jahrbuch für deutsche Geschichte*, xvi (1987), 212–38.

SCHMUHL, HANS-WALTHER, 'Bürgerliche Eliten in städtischen Repräsentativorganen. Nürnberg und Braunschweig im 19. Jahrhundert', in Hans-Jürgen Puhle (ed.), *Bürger in der Gesellschaft der Neuzeit* (Göttingen, 1991), 178–98.

SCHÖNEMANN, BERND, *Das braunschweigische Gymnasium in Staat und Gesellschaft. Ein Beitrag zur Schulgeschichte des 19. Jahrhunderts* (Cologne/Vienna, 1983).

SCHORSKE, CARL E., *German Social Democracy, 1905–1917. The Development of the Great Schism* (2nd edn., Cambridge, Mass., 1983).

—— *Fin-de-Siècle Vienna. Politics and Culture* (New York, 1985).
SCHREMMER, D. E., 'Taxation and Public Finance: Britain, France and Germany', in Peter Mathias and Sidney Pollard (eds.), *The Cambridge Economic History of Europe.* viii. *The Industrial Economies: The Development of Economic and Social Policies* (Cambridge, 1989), 315–494.
SCHWEMER, RICHARD, *Geschichte der Stadt Frankfurt am Main 1814–1866*, 3 vols. (Frankfurt, 1910–18).
SEDATIS, HELMUT, *Liberalismus und Handwerk in Südwestdeutschland. Wirtschafts- und Gesellschaftskonzeptionen des Liberalismus und die Krise des Handwerks im 19. Jahrhundert* (Stuttgart, 1979).
SEIER, HELLMUT, 'Liberalismus und Bürgertum in Mitteleuropa 1850–1880. Forschung und Literatur seit 1970', in Lothar Gall (ed.), *Bürgertum und bürgerlich-liberale Bewegung in Mitteleuropa seit dem 18. Jahrhundert* (Munich, 1997), 131–229.
SEITZ, WALTER, 'Kommunale Wohnungspolitik im Kaiserreich am Beispiel der Stadt Frankfurt am Main', in Hans Jürgen Teuteberg (ed.), *Urbanisierung im 19. und 20. Jahrhundert. Historische und Geographische Aspekte* (Cologne/Vienna, 1983), 393–428.
SHAPIRO, J. S., 'Was ist Liberalismus?', in Lothar Gall (ed.), *Liberalismus* (Königstein, 1980), 20–36.
SHEEHAN, JAMES J., 'Wie bürgerlich war der deutsche Liberalismus?', in Dieter Langewiesche (ed.), *Liberalismus im 19. Jahrhundert. Deutschland im europäischen Vergleich* (Göttingen, 1988), 28–44.
—— 'Liberalism and the City in Nineteenth-Century Germany', *Past and Present*, no. 51 (1971), 116–37.
—— *German Liberalism in the Nineteenth Century* (Chicago, 1978).
—— 'Deutscher Liberalismus im postliberalen Zeitalter, 1890–1914', *Geschichte und Gesellschaft*, iv (1978), 29–48.
—— 'Klasse und Partei im Kaiserreich: Einige Gedanken zur Sozialgeschichte der deutschen Politik', in Otto Pflanze (ed.), *Innenpolitische Probleme des Bismarck-Reiches* (Munich/Vienna, 1983), 1–24.
—— 'Nation und Staat. Deutschland als "imaginierte Gemeinschaft" ', in M. Hettling and P. Nolte (eds.), *Nation und Gesellschaft in Deutschland. Historische Essays* (Munich, 1996), 33–45.
SIMON, KLAUS, *Die württembergischen Demokraten. Ihre Stellung und Arbeit im Parteien- und Verfassungssystem in Württemberg und im Deutschen Reich 1890–1920* (Stuttgart, 1969).
—— 'Die soziale Struktur der württembergischen Volkspartei und ihre Auswirkung auf Programm und Politik der Partei (1882–1914)', in Gerhard A. Ritter (ed.), *Die deutschen Parteien vor 1918* (Cologne, 1973), 224–42.
SINZHEIMER, HUGO, *Der Sozialpolitiker Karl Flesch und seine literarisch-wissenschaftliche Tätigkeit* (Frankfurt, 1915).
SMITH, HELMUT WALSER, *German Nationalism and Religious Conflict. Culture, Ideology, Politics, 1870–1914* (Princeton, 1995).

SPECKER, HANS EUGEN (ed.), *Ulm im 19. Jahrhundert. Aspekte aus dem Leben der Stadt* (Stuttgart, 1990).
SPENCER, ELAINE G., 'State Power and Local Interests in Prussian Cities: Police in the Düsseldorf District, 1848–1914', *Central European History*, xix (1986), 293–313.
SPERBER, JONATHAN, *Popular Catholicism in 19th Century Germany* (Princeton, 1984).
—— 'Competing Counterrevolutions: Prussian State and Catholic Church in Westphalia during the 1850s', *Central European History*, xix (1986), 45–62.
—— *The Kaiser's Voters. Electors and Elections in Imperial Germany* (Cambridge, 1997).
SPIESS, ALEXANDER, 'Georg Varrentrapp. Gestorben am 15. März 1886', in *Deutsche Vierteljahresschrift für öffentliche Gesundheitspflege*, xviii (Brunswick, 1886), pp. iii–xxiv.
SPRINGHALL, JOHN, *Youth, Empire and Society. British Youth Movements 1883–1940* (London, 1977).
STACHURA, PETER D., *The German Youth Movement 1900–45. An Interpretative and Documentative History* (London, 1981).
STAGE, DETLEF, *Frankfurt am Main im Zollverein. Die Handelspolitik und die öffentliche Meinung der Freien Stadt Frankfurt am Main in den Jahren 1836–1866* (Frankfurt, 1971).
STEGMANN, DIRK, *Die Erben Bismarcks. Parteien und Verbände in der Spätphase des Wilhelminischen Deutschlands* (Cologne/Berlin, 1970).
STEINBACH, PETER, *Die Politisierung der Region. Reichs- und Landtagswahlen im Fürstentum Lippe 1866–1881* (Passau, 1989).
—— *Die Zähmung des politischen Massenmarktes. Wahlen und Wahlkämpfe im Bismarckreich im Spiegel der Hauptstadt- und Gesinnungspresse* (Passau, 1990).
—— 'Reichstag Elections in the Kaiserreich: The Prospects for Electoral Research in the Interdisciplinary Context', in Larry E. Jones and James Retallack (eds.), *Elections, Mass Politics and Social Change in Modern Germany. New Perspectives* (Cambridge, 1992), 119–46.
—— 'Politisierung und Nationalisierung der Region im 19. Jahrhundert. Regionalspezifische Politikrezeption im Spiegel historischer Wahlforschung', in Peter Steinbach (ed.), *Probleme politischer Partizipation im Modernisierungsprozeß* (Stuttgart, 1992), 321–49.
STEINMETZ, GEORGE, *Regulating the Social. The Welfare State and Local Politics in Imperial Germany* (Princeton, 1993).
STERN, FRITZ, 'Die politischen Folgen des unpolitischen Deutschen', in M. Stürmer (ed.), *Das Kaiserliche Deutschland. Politik und Gesellschaft 1870–1918* (Düsseldorf, 1970), 168–86.
STÜBLING, RAINER, *Die Sozialdemokratie in Frankfurt am Main von 1891 bis 1910* (Frankfurt, 1981).
STÜRMER, MICHAEL, *Regierung und Reichstag im Bismarckstaat 1871–1880* (Düsseldorf, 1974).

SUTCLIFFE, ANTHONY, *Towards the Planned City. Germany, Britain, the United States and France, 1788–1914* (Oxford, 1981).
—— (ed.), *The Rise of Modern Urban Planning 1800–1914* (London, 1984).
SUVAL, STANLEY, *Electoral Politics in Wilhelmine Germany* (Chapel Hill, NC, 1985).
TAL, URIEL, *Christians and Jews in Germany. Religion, Politics and Ideology in the Second Reich, 1870–1914* (Ithaca, NY, 1975).
TENFELDE, KLAUS, 'Historische Milieus—Erblichkeit und Konkurrenz', in Manfred Hettling and Paul Nolte (eds.), *Nation und Gesellschaft in Deutschland. Historische Essays* (Munich, 1996), 247–68.
TENNSTEDT, FLORIAN, *Sozialgeschichte der Sozialpolitik in Deutschland. Vom 18. Jahrhundert bis zum Ersten Weltkrieg* (Göttingen, 1981).
—— *Vom Proleten zum Industriearbeiter. Arbeiterbewegung und Sozialpolitik in Deutschland 1800–1914* (Cologne, 1983).
TEUTEBERG, HANS J., 'Historische Aspekte der Urbanisierung. Forschungsstand und Probleme', in Hans J. Teuteberg (ed.), *Urbanisierung im 19. und 20. Jahrhundert. Historische und Geographische Aspekte* (Cologne/Vienna, 1983), 5–22.
THEINER, PETER, *Sozialer Liberalismus und deutsche Weltpolitik. Friedrich Naumann im Wilhelminischen Deutschland, 1860–1919* (Baden-Baden, 1983).
THOMPSON, ALASTAIR PAUL, 'Left Liberals in German State and Society 1907–1918', Ph.D. thesis (London, 1989).
TILLY, RICHARD, 'Cyclical Trends and the Market Response: Long Swings in Urban Development in Germany, 1850–1914', in W. Robert Lee (ed.), *German Industry and German Industrialisation. Essays in German Economic and Business History in the Nineteenth and Twentieth Centuries* (London, 1991), 148–84.
—— 'Städtewachstum, Kommunalfinanzen und Munizipalsozialismus in der deutschen Industrialisierung: eine vergleichende Perspektive 1870–1913', in Jürgen Reulecke (ed.), *Die Stadt als Dienstleistungszentrum. Beiträge zur Geschichte der 'Sozialstadt' in Deutschland im 19. und frühen 20. Jahrhundert* (St Katharinen, 1995), 125–52.
TIPPS, DEAN C., 'Modernization Theory and the Comparative Study of Societies: A Critical Perspective', *Comparative Studies in Society and History*, xv (1973), 199–226.
TIPTON, FRANK B., Jr., *Regional Variations in the Economic Development of Germany during the Nineteenth Century* (Middletown, Conn., 1976).
TRAUTMANN, GÜNTER, 'Die industriegesellschaftliche Herausforderung des Liberalismus. Staatsintervention und Sozialreform in der Politikökonomie des 18./19. Jahrhunderts', in Karl Holl, Günter Trautmann, Hans Vorländer (eds.), *Sozialer Liberalismus* (Göttingen, 1986), 34–56.
TURK, ELEANOR L., 'German Liberals and the Genesis of the German Association Law of 1908', in Konrad H. Jarausch and Larry E. Jones (eds.), *In Search of a Liberal Germany. Studies in the History of German Liberalism from 1789 to the Present* (Oxford, 1990), 237–60.
ULLMANN, HANS-PETER, *Interessenverbände in Deutschland* (Frankfurt, 1988).

ULLMANN, HANS-PETER, 'Die Bürger als Steuerzahler im Deutschen Kaiserreich', in Manfred Hettling and Paul Nolte (eds.), *Nation und Gesellschaft in Deutschland. Historische Essays* (Munich, 1996), 231–46.

UNRUH, GEORG-CHRISTOPH VON, 'Die normative Verfassung der kommunalen Selbstverwaltung', in Kurt G. A. Jeserich, Hans Pohl, and Georg-Christoph von Unruh (eds.), *Deutsche Verwaltungsgeschichte* (Stuttgart, 1984), iii. 560–78.

—— 'Bürgermeister und Landräte als Gestalter kommunaler Leistungsverwaltung', in Hans Heinrich Blotevogel (ed.), *Kommunale Leistungsverwaltung und Stadtentwicklung vom Vormärz bis zur Weimarer Republik* (Cologne/Vienna, 1990), 43–55.

VALENTIN, VEIT, *Frankfurt am Main und die Revolution von 1848/49* (Stuttgart/Berlin, 1908).

Vereinigung ehemaliger Domschüler Frankfurt a.M. (ed.), *Handbuch* (Frankfurt, 1929).

VINCE, CHARLES A., *History of the Corporation of Birmingham*, iii (Birmingham, 1902).

VOLKOV, SHULAMIT, 'Soziale Ursachen des Erfolgs in der Wissenschaft. Juden im Kaiserreich', *Historische Zeitschrift*, ccxlv (1987), 315–42.

WACHSMUTH, RICHARD, *Die Gründung der Universität Frankfurt* (Frankfurt, 1929).

WAIBEL, RAIMUND, *Frühliberalismus und Gemeindewahlen in Württemberg (1817–1855). Das Beispiel Stuttgart* (Stuttgart, 1992).

WALKER, MACK, *German Home Towns: Community, State, General Estate 1648–1871* (Ithaca, NY, 1971).

WALLER, PHILIP J., *Town, City and Nation. England 1850–1914* (2nd edn., Oxford, 1991).

WEGNER, KONSTANZE, *Theodor Barth und die Freisinnige Vereinigung. Studien zur Geschichte des Linksliberalismus im wilhelminischen Deutschland (1893–1910)* (Tübingen, 1968).

WEHLER, HANS-ULRICH, *The German Empire 1871–1918* (Leamington Spa, 1985).

—— 'Deutsches Bildungsbürgertum in vergleichender Perspektive—Elemente eines "Sonderwegs"?', in Jürgen Kocka (ed.), *Bildungsbürgertum im 19. Jahrhundert. Politischer Einfluß und gesellschaftliche Formation* (Stuttgart, 1989), iv. 215–37.

—— 'Die Geburtsstunde des deutschen Kleinbürgertums', in Hans-Jürgen Puhle (ed.), *Bürger in der Gesellschaft der Neuzeit* (Göttingen, 1991), 199–209.

—— *Deutsche Gesellschaftsgeschichte 1849–1914*. iii. *Von der 'Deutschen Doppelrevolution' bis zum Beginn des Ersten Weltkrieges 1849–1914* (Munich, 1995).

—— 'A Guide to Future Research on the Kaiserreich?', *Central European History*, xxix (1996), 541–72.

WEITENSTEINER, HANS KILIAN, 'Karl Flesch—Kommunale Sozialpolitik in Frankfurt am Main', D.Phil. thesis (Frankfurt, 1976).

WENZEL, STEFI, *Jüdische Bürger und kommunale Selbstverwaltung in preussischen Städten, 1808–1848* (Berlin, 1967).
WERTHEIMER, JACK, *Unwelcome Strangers. East European Jews in Imperial Germany* (New York/Oxford, 1987).
WETTENGEL, MICHAEL, *Die Revolution von 1848/1849 im Rhein-Main Raum. Politische Vereine und Revolutionsalltag im Großherzogtum Hessen, Herzogtum Nassau und in der Freien Stadt Frankfurt* (Wiesbaden, 1989).
WHITE, DAN S., *The Splintered Party. National Liberalism in Hessen and the Reich, 1867–1918* (Cambridge, Mass., 1976).
—— 'Regionalism and Particularism', in R. Chickering (ed.), *Imperial Germany. A Historiographical Companion* (Westport, Conn., 1996), 131–55.
WIEGAND, FRANK-MICHAEL, *Die Notabeln. Untersuchungen zur Geschichte des Wahlrechts und der gewählten Bürgerschaft in Hamburg, 1859–1919* (Hamburg, 1987).
WILSON, JOHN A., *Seedbed of Protest. Social Structure and Radical Politics in Ettlingen, Grand Duchy of Baden, 1815–1850* (New York, 1992).
WINKLER, HEINRICH AUGUST, 'Vom linken zum rechten Nationalismus. Der deutsche Liberalismus in der Krise von 1878/1879', *Geschichte und Gesellschaft*, iv (1978), 5–28.
—— *Zwischen Marx und Monopolen. Der deutsche Mittelstand vom Kaiserreich zur Bundesrepublik Deutschland* (Frankfurt, 1991).
WITT, PETER-CHRISTIAN, *Die Finanzpolitik des Deutschen Reiches von 1903 bis 1913. Eine Studie zur Innenpolitik des Wilhelminischen Deutschland* (Lübeck/Hamburg, 1970).
—— 'The Prussian Landrat as Tax Official, 1891–1918. Some Observations on the Political and Social Function of the German Civil Service during the Wilhelmine Empire', in Georg Iggers (ed.), *The Social History of Politics. Critical Perspectives in West German Historical Writing since 1945* (Leamington Spa, 1985), 137–54.
—— 'Kommunalpolitik in Harburg zwischen Interessen lokaler Eliten und Entstehung einer modernen Leistungsverwaltung (1867–1914)', in Jürgen Ellermeyer et al. (eds.), *Harburg. Von der Burg zur Industriestadt* (Harburg, 1988), 219–49.
WOLF, SIEGBERT, *Liberalismus in Frankfurt am Main. Vom Ende der Freien Stadt bis zum Ersten Weltkrieg (1866–1914)* (Frankfurt, 1987).
WÖLK, MONIKA, *Der Preussische Volksschulabsolvent als Reichstagswähler 1871–1912. Ein Beitrag zur historischen Wahlforschung in Deutschland* (Berlin, 1980).
WYSOCKI, JOSEF, 'Kommunale Investitionen und ihre Finanzierung in Deutschland 1850 bis 1914', in Wilhelm Rausch (ed.), *Die Städte Mitteleuropas im 19. Jahrhundert* (Linz, 1983), 165–80.
ZANG, GERT (ed.), *Provinzialisierung einer Region. Regionale Unterentwicklung und liberale Politik in der Stadt und im Kreis Konstanz im 19. Jahrhundert* (Frankfurt, 1978).

ZERBACK, RALF, 'Unter der Kuratel des Staates—Die Stadt zwischen dem Gemeindeedikt von 1818 und der Gemeindeordnung von 1869', in Richard Bauer (ed.), *Geschichte der Stadt München* (Munich, 1992), 274–306.
—— *München und sein Stadtbürgertum. Eine Residenzstadt als Bürgergemeinde 1770–1870* (Munich, 1997).
ZIEBILL, OTTO, *Geschichte des Deutschen Städtetages. Fünfzig Jahre deutsche Kommunalpolitik* (Stuttgart, 1955).
ZIEGLER, DONALD J., *Prelude to Democracy. A Study of Proportional Representation and the Heritage of Weimar Germany, 1871–1920* (Lincoln, Nebr., 1958).
ZIMMERMANN, CLEMENS, 'Urbanisierung—Stadtgeschichte—Stadtentwicklung', *Neue Politische Literatur*, xxxviii (1993), 7–28.

Index

Adickes, Franz 27, 89–93, 116, 118, 127, 140–1, 247–53, 315
  secondary school reform 191–4
  social policy 226–38, 240, 242, 245, 290, 305, 318
  university 199–203
AG fur kleine Wohnungen 222, 225–6, 232, 234
Allgemeiner Deutscher Frauenverein 252
Alsace-Lorraine 73
Altdemokraten 66
Altonaer System 191
Anderson, Benedict 312
anti-Semitism 110, 126, 164, 165–7, 174, 183, 322
anti-socialist laws 69, 124, 224, 315
Applegate, Celia 196
artisans 42, 48, 103, 109, 110, 114–17, 121, 185, 215, 227, 244, 253, 302
Augsburg 16–17, 97 n. 233, 311

Baden 12–13, 20–1, 154, 311
Barmen 16, 48, 279
Bartelsheim, Ursula 25, 41, 89
Barth, Theodor 323–4, 326
Bauer, Heinrich 173
Berlin 19–20, 88, 167, 257, 266
Berliner Tageblatt 326
Bernstein, Eduard 240
Bezirksvereine 54, 102–3, 111–15, 142, 314
Bildung 147–9, 182, 199, 235
Birmingham 31, 326
Bismarck 6, 10, 33, 57, 71, 73, 98, 155, 205, 207, 212, 224, 240, 260, 261, 313
Blessing, Werner 165 n. 91
Blum, Robert 50, 60, 61, 72 n. 136, 169
Bochum 3 n. 7
Bockenheim 127, 133 n. 161, 137, 228–9
Bodelschwingh, Friedrich von 241

Bodenpolitik 116, 141, 229–32, 236, 251, 253, 317, 318, *see also* housing
Bornheim 156–7
Borscht, Mayor of Munich 297–8
bourgeoisie (*Bürgertum*) 1, 4–5, 7–9, 14–15, 38, 100, 141, 147–9, 170–1, 208, 309
  education 190–1, 199
  local government 41–2, 297, 321–2
  social policy 210, 239–40, 252
Breslau 19, 88, 181, 182, 319
Bülow Bloc 132 n. 156, 133
Bürgerschule 153, 156–7, 184
Bürgerrepräsentation 29
Bürgertum, *see* bourgeoisie
Bürgervereine 77, 102, 112–15

Calvinists 17, 35, 171–6, 177, 179, 316
camp 10–12, 98–9, 144, 313
Caprivi, Georg Leo Count von 261
Catholics, *see* German Catholics, Roman Catholics
caucus 94
Centre Association 105–8, 136 n. 179
Centre Party 2, 15, 16, 37, 40, 67, 69, 102, 104, 105–8, 119, 136, 137, 143, 145, 155, 160, 164, 204, 313
city council 3, 14, 16, 19, 20, 41, 42, 50–1, 74, 89, 93, 99, 102, 115, 153, 138–40, 311, 314–5, 318
  committees and offices 82–7
  education 156–8, 194
  municipal finance 285–6, 288, 290–1, 295, 300–1, 304, 308
  social policy 209–10, 225–6
city congress, *see* Städtetag
city ordinance, *see* Städteordnung
civic pride 64, 130–1, 145, 187, 195, 198, 199, 203 n. 266, 205, 311–12, 332, *see also* rhetoric
class tax, *see* Klassensteuer

Conservative Association 108–10
Conservatives 41, 43, 66, 88–9, 108–11, 130, 201, 264, 265
Cnyrim, Victor 113
Cologne 88, 205, 237, 250, 257, 274
council of elders 172–3, *see also* Calvinists
craftsmen 93, 115, 215, 222, 223, 227, 244
cremations 171, 316
Croon, Helmut 3
Curatorium für höhere Schulen, *see* school boards
Curti, Theodor 60

Das freie Wort 170–1
Democratic Association (*Demokratischer Verein*) 60, 63, 66, 225–6, 236, 249, 298
  organization 80–1, 95, 132–5
  programme 79–80, 82
Democratic Electoral Association (*Demokratischer Wahlverein*) 53–6, 62–3, 65–6, 79
Democrats 26, 32–3, 34, 58, 61–2, 95–6, 98–9, 223–5, 313, 314–16, 320, 323–5, 330–1
  before 1866 29, 41–9, 51–2
  city council 84–7, 102
  education 159–60, 179, 182, 184, 185–6, 204
  election of mayor 90–3
  elections 68–74, 83, 101, 112–15, 117–18, 119–22, 124–6, 132–6
  federalism 210–11
  left-liberal unity 323–6
  Magistrat 83, 87–90
  municipal finance 288–90, 298–303, 306
  politicization 75–9, 94–5
  programme 79–80, 143, 288–91
  Protestants 173, 174, 177, 179
  social policy 210–18, 222, 225–6, 231, 233–5, 236–8, 241–2, 245–9, 250, 252, 318, 324, 327
  teachers 287
  see also Bürgervereine, German Catholics, Jews, *Mittelstand*, rhetoric, Roman Catholics, SPD
denominational education 118–19, 149–50, 151, 152, 153–8, 159, 162, 164, 203–4
Deutscher Hof 166
Deutsche Volkspartei, *see* German People's Party
district associations, *see Bezirksvereine*
Doppelschule 157–8

Dortmund 14, 48, 97, 145
drainage 26, 34, 65, 116, 212, 263, 276, 281–2, 285, 288, 289, 292, 294
Düsseldorf 16, 17, 18, 145, 257
Dyos, H. J. 4

Ebeling, Mayor of Dessau 295–6
education, *see Bildung*, denominational education, primary schools, non-denominational education, secondary schools, *Vorschule*, workers' education
Education Act (1897) 275
education bill, Prussia 150, 175 n. 143, 181–2, 194, 329
Ehlers, Rudolf 172, 173, 177
Ehrlich, Paul 202
Eingemeindungen, *see* incorporations
Eisenach 210
Elberfeld 16, 219
elections 9–13, 15, 41, 66–7, 71–5, 97–9, 144, 328
  local 45–8, 50–1, 63, 78–80, 82, 83, 101–2, 109, 116–17, 118–19, 125, 126–8, 130, 133–8, 140, 142, 159–60, 175, 216
  national 67–9, 117–18, 124–5, 128, 132–3, 136, 225, 313–14, 342–4
  results 339–44
  state 69–74, 118, 340–1
  see also run-off elections
electricity 120, 217, 289–90
England 5, 87, 94, 209, 253, 255, 273 n. 57, 296, 305, 309, 310, 316, 326
Erbbaurecht 229, 231, 232–3
Erzberger, Matthias 267

Fay, Eduard 57, 61, 338
federalism 37, 67, 255, 312, 330–2
Fellner, Karl 72
Flesch, Karl 27, 90, 139, 141, 215, 236, 249, 252, 324, 326
  franchise 245, 246, 250
  and Miquel 220–3, 226
Flinsch, Heinrich 117
franchise 7, 8, 15, 29, 34, 37, 46, 54, 58, 76, 79–82, 123, 126–7, 130, 133, 140, 143, 197, 226, 239, 245–8, 250, 309, 314, 320–1, 323
Franco–Prussian War 63, 70
Frankfurt:
  annexation of 49–50, 58
  history of 28–30

liberalism, significance of 31–3, 36–7,
     322–32
  research on 23–6
  system 192–5, 201, 317, 330
Frankfurter Journal 47, 55–6
Frankfurter Latern 59–60, 75
Frankfurter Presse 75
Frankfurter Verein 48
Frankfurter Volksbote 45
Frankfurter Wahlverein, see National Liberals
Frankfurter Zeitung 32–3, 53, 54–6, 58–60,
     76, 79, 107, 134–5, 170, 178, 194, 322,
     left-liberal unity 324, 326, 327
freedom of trade 30, 46, 51, 59, 97 n. 233,
     223
Freiburg 16, 20–1, 144, 250
Freie evangelische Vereinigung 118–19, 162,
     174–5
Freisinnige Vereinigung 323–4
Freisinnige Volkspartei, see Progressive
     Liberals, Progressive People's Party
Fromm, Josef 165
Funck, Karl 32, 83, 118, 120, 170, 214, 231,
     323, 325, 326
Fuß, Mayor of Kiel 181–2

Gall, Lother 13, 14, 20, 21, 22, 38, 104, 198
Geiger, Berthold 92 n. 213, 94, 120, 124,
     139, 162, 213, 214, 291, 325
George, Henry 305
German Catholics 154 n. 34, 167–71, 316
German People's Party 26, 32, 61–2,
     68–70, 73, 117, 120, 134, 210–11, 232,
     236–7, 323–8
German question 29, 30, 45
Gesetzgebende Versammlung 51
gewerbliches Schiedsgericht, see industrial
     tribunal
Gierke, Otto 217, 230–1, 277, 321
Gneist, Rudolf 20, 153, 154, 180–1, 276,
     277, 321
Goethe 59, 72, 198
Göttingen 243 n. 202
Grimm, Otto 90, 194
großdeutsch 29, 30, 44, 58
Gründerzeit 211, 272
Guelphs 17, 18, 61–2, 67
guilds 115, 223
Gustav-Adolf-Foundation 177
Gymnasium 150, 189, 191–7

Hadermann, Nikolaus 45, 47, 56, 66, 78,
     213, 299

Hahn, Hans-Werner 14
Hallgarten, Charles 110, 167, 234, 324
Hammeran, J. A. 56
Hanover 13, 17, 18, 57, 61–2, 91, 96
Harburg 15
Hausbesitzer, see house owners, property
     owners
Haußmann, Konrad 327
Heidelberg Declaration 32, 74, 223, 225,
     261
Heimat 57 n. 94, 75, 196–7, 312
Heine, Heinrich 165–6
Hettling, Manfred 12, 19
Hirsch, Samson Rafael 161
Hirsch-Duncker trade unions 135
Hofmann, Wolfgang 3
Holthoff, Carl 60, 71, 75, 134 n. 167
homeless 214, 241 n. 192
Honoratioren, see notables
Hottentot elections 132
house owners 115–16, 209, 226, 267, 268
housing 26–7, 118, 211, 212, 217, 220–2,
     224, 225–6, 228–34, 276, 290, 305–6,
     317
Hübinger, Gangolf 179
Hugenberg, Alfred 227 n. 108
Hüttmann, Heinrich 139, 252

incorporations 127, 228–9, 233 n. 142, 276
industrial tribunal 222, 223, 226, 243,
     246–7, 287–8, 317, 318
Innungen, see guilds
Institut für Gemeinwohl 200, 251–2

Jews 29, 30, 35, 43, 44, 45, 46, 160–7,
     201–2, 316
John, Michael 13, 17
Junker 8, 264–5

Kanngießer, Otto 213
Kartell elections 32, 117, 124
Klassensteuer 301–2
Kleine Presse 134, 162
Koblenz 18
Kocka, Jürgen 7
Köllmann, Wolfgang 3
Kommunalabgabengesetz, see tax reforms
kommunale Daseinsfürsorge, see municipal
     socialism
Kommunalsteuernotgesetz 260
Königsberg 19, 88
Konstanz 20
Kreuzzeitung 121 n. 105, 201

Kühne, Thomas 13
Kulturkampf 15–18, 20–1, 39–40, 107, 108, 150, 153, 155–6, 164, 204, 205
Kulturprotestantismus 179

Laaß, Hermann 119, 165, 167, 175
labour exchange 27, 223, 236, 243, 244, 250, 288, 317
Lager, *see* camp
Langewiesche, Dieter 12, 38, 239, 245
law, *see* organic law
lectures 139, 234–5, 251, 317
left liberals 34, 50, 52–3, 58, 63, 64, 65, 66, 102, 167, 242, 327–8
    Bezirksvereine 104, 113
    education 159, 182, 194–7
    Jews 162–3
    local self-government 277, 321–2
    Magistrat 90
    mayor 91, 200
    Mittelstand 119–22
    municipal expenditure 288, 290–1, 297–8
    social policy 186, 223, 231–8, 243–4, 247–52
    SPD 122–45
    taxation 264–5, 299, 301, 302, 304–6, 309
    unity 33, 36–7, 323–7
    university 203–4
Lepsius, M. Rainer 9–10
Lessing, Gotthold 195, 198
Lex Adickes 228, 231
Liberal Party (Britain) 31, 206, 255
liberals, *see* Democrats, left liberals, National Liberals, National Socials, Progressive Liberals
Lloyd George, David 309
local government 2–4, 8, 14–22, 33, 42, 77, 97–9, 104, 114–15, 136, 150–1, 153, 165, 214, 245, 267, 294, 306, 310, 322
local identity 17–18, 312, *see also* civic pride, rhetoric
local patriotism, *see* civic pride
local self-government 20, 23, 83, 89–91, 131, 150–1, 153, 156, 165, 180–4, 194, 202–3, 204, 246, 256, 265–7, 275–8, 297, 299, 306, 309, 321–2
Luppe, Hermann 141, 143, 249
Lutherans 17, 176–80, 317

Magistrat 3, 14, 42, 83, 84, 87–90, 93, 127, 141, 153, 157, 200, 209–10, 220, 222, 229, 248, 286, 288–92, 304, 308, 314–15

Maly, Karl 25, 41
Mannheim 20
Mann, Thomas 1, 4, 8, 32
mass politics 12, 40, 42, 100–1, 136, 143, 313, 321
mayor 88, 89, 90–3, 193–4, 200, 315
meat and flour tax, *see* taxation
Meinecke, Friedrich 4, 8
Merton, Wilhelm 139, 200–1, 202 n. 258, 250–1
Metzler, Adolf 117
milieu 9–11, 13, 24, 38, 41, 98–9, 106, 144–5, 175, 178, 249
Mill, John Stuart 256
Ministry of Education 150, 158, 160, 202, 277
Miquel, Johannes 84, 89, 90–2, 314–15
    finance 31, 261, 304
    politics 37, 74, 117, 261, 330–1
    social policy 26, 218–26, 236
    see also tax reforms
Mittelschule 185
Mittelstand 34, 103, 115–26, 128, 131, 142, 143, 144, 314, 319–20
    education 162, 165, 167, 175, 185, 195, 198
    municipal finance 286–7, 302, 304, 309
    social policy 208, 223–4, 225, 227, 233, 235, 242, 244
    see also artisans, craftsmen, house owners, property owners
Mumm, Heinrich Daniel 26, 89–90, 91, 92
Munich 17, 27, 30 n. 132, 242 n. 197, 250, 297, 330
municipal:
    debt 36, 272–4, 282, 292–8, 306, 309, 335
    expenditure 36, 146, 213, 256–7, 259, 270–8, 279–92, 294–8, 306–7, 308, 333–4
    socialism 27, 35, 143, 226–45, 249–54, 307, 309, 318–19
    see also taxation
municipalization 27, 82, 93, 120, 129, 131, 211, 213–14, 241–2, 272, 275, 288–92, 295
Münster 15, 16, 18, 75 n. 147, 311

Nassau 49, 57, 154, 159
National Liberals 13, 15, 35, 59–60, 63, 66–75, 77, 78, 81–2, 96, 132, 139, 225, 287, 313, 314
    Bezirksvereine 113–14
    Calvinists 171–6
    city council 84–7

Index

Jews 162
left liberals, cooperation with 128, 130, 136–7, 143
Lutherans 178, 179
Magistrat 88, 90, 314–15
mayor 90–3, 226, 315
Mittelstand 116–19, 120, 121, 126, 142
primary education 186, 329
non-denominational schools 159, 160
social reform 212, 214–15, 227, 249, 252
National Socials 32, 110–11, 126, 324
Nationalverein 44, 45, 55
Naumann, Friedrich 32, 109, 110–11, 208, 316, 323, 324
New Course 148, 261
New Liberalism 35, 209, 331
newspapers 52–3, 54–6, 326, *see also* *Frankfurter Leitung, Frankfurter Journal, Frankfurter Latern, Kleine Presse*
Nipperdey, Thomas 8, 144–5
Nolte, Carl Wilhelm 153–5
Nolte, Paul 12–13, 21
non-denominational schools 79, 90, 118, 153–60, 163–4, 173–6, 183, 188, 315, 316, 317, 329
notables 3, 8, 12, 24, 29, 41, 66, 83, 92, 101, 114–15, 142, 150, 151, 165
Nuremberg 20

Oberrealschule 189, 191
Oeser, Rudolf 108, 121, 136, 323
Opificius, Ludwig 139
organic law 45, 49
Osnabrück 17, 91, 223, 224, 266, 311
Ostrogorski, Michael 94

party organization 14, 23, 31, 32, 33, 48, 53–5, 65–6, 73–5, 80–2, 94–5, 103–4, 106–7, 111–14, 132–5, 213, 313–14, 323–7
Passavant, Friedrich Ernst 51
Payer, Friedrich 323 n. 21, 325 n. 30, 327
People's Budget 331
petite bourgeoisie, *see Mittelstand*
Philanthropin 151, 152, 160–1
Pohl, Karl Heinrich 22
politicization 3, 14–21, 33, 38–42, 48–50, 65–6, 75–82, 83, 94–7, 104, 113–14, 138, 141–2, 311–15
poor relief 208–9, 211, 217, 219–20, 239, 267, 307

Posen 158
Preparatory school, *see Vorschule*
Preuß, Hugo 20, 208, 277, 321
primary schools 118–19, 149–50, 152–60, 183, 184–9, 197–8, 267, 316–17, 319, 329
Progressive Liberals 26, 66, 68–71, 74, 81, 82, 101–2, 123, 245, 247, 313, 314, 323–6
  Bezirksvereine 112–14
  Calvinists 173
  city council 84–7
  Mittelstand 120, 126
  municipal spending 289, 290, 291
  social reform 32, 143, 210, 213–15, 231
  see also Democrats, left liberals
Progressive People's Party 36–7, 323–8
property owners 118, 125, 263, 264, 266, 304, 305–6, 307
Protestantism *see* Calvinists, Lutherans
Protestantism, political, *see Freie evangelische Vereinigung*
Prussia 6, 13, 17–20, 29, 30, 45, 49–50, 56–66, 70, 72, 73, 75, 142
  education 150–1, 152, 158–9, 180–1, 189–91, 329
  finance 255, 257, 258–79, 292, 293, 295, 299, 304, 305
  see also West Prussia

Quarck, Max 108, 125, 128, 130, 137, 138–9, 252, 302
Quidde, Ludwig 122

Realgymnasium 189, 191–3
Realschule der Israelitischen Religionsgemeinschaft 151, 161
Reformed Church, *see* Calvinists
Reformverein 30, 44, 45
Regensburg 17
Reichsverein der liberalen Arbeiter und Angestellten 135, 326–7
Reinganum, Maximilian 63–4, 76, 80
Reinhardt, Karl 194, 196
Revolution (1848) 12, 19–20, 38–9, 41, 43–4, 104, 147, 168–9
Rezeß 62–3, 64, 70, 71, 79, 91
Rheinland 16
rhetoric 56–64, 71–5, 120–2, 128–30, 131–2, 142, 154–5, 311, 331–2
Richter, Eugen 32, 266, 323 n. 17, 325
Rive, Richard Robert 181–2

390 Index

Rohe, Karl 9–12, 15, 97–8, 144
Rolling, John 25, 41–2, 138, 140
Roman Catholics 16–17, 73, 105–8, 136–7, 138–9, 163, 204, 317, *see also* non-denominational schools
Rößler, Heinrich 86, 114, 134, 145, 216, 316, 323, 324–5, 326
 education 182, 186
 franchise 123, 130, 246–7
Roth, Ralf 24, 41, 65, 243
Rothschild, Carl Meyer von 50
Ruhrgebiet 11, 15, 16, 279
run-off elections 69–70, 108, 117, 120, 125, 130, 132, 136, 137, 167

Sabor, Adolf 117
Sänger, Carl 168, 169, 170–1, 316
Saxony 13, 66, 144, 244 n. 203, 248 n. 234
Schambach, Karin 14, 48 n. 51, 96 n. 229
Schlacht- und Mahlsteuer (meat and flour tax), *see* taxation
Schlossmacher, Norbert 15, 170–1 n. 125
Schmidt, Carl August 240
Schmidt, Wilhelm 139
Schöneberg 237
school boards 151, 152–3, 194
school reform, *see* secondary schools
Schuldeputation, *see* school boards
Schuldotationsgesetz, *see* education bill, Prussia
Secessionists 225
secondary schools 148, 150, 151–2, 185–6, 189–99, 317
Selbstverwaltung, *see* local self-government
Senate 43, 44, 45, 46, 47, 51, 58, 65, 89
Sheehan, James 2, 22, 227
Sonderweg 1–9
Sonnemann, Leopold 54, 55–6, 60, 62, 66, 73, 75, 77, 78, 86, 92 n. 213, 109, 122, 134, 312, 315, 325 n. 30
 and Adickes 92
 and *Magistrat* 89
 and Miquel 91–2
 German People's Party 32, 327
 Jews 162
 left-liberal unity 324, 325
 municipal finance 289–90, 298, 300–1, 302, 303–4
 social policy 210, 211, 212, 214–15, 217, 226, 234, 236–7, 250
speculation (housing) 4, 228–30, 233
SPD (Sozialdemokratische Partei Deutschlands) 3, 8, 11, 19, 68–9, 104, 120–1, 122–44, 159–60, 208, 309, 313–14, 318–20, 328
 education 185–7, 198, 204, 315
 municipal finance 291, 302, 305–6, 307, 319–20
 social reform 239–45, 247–8, 250–1
Sperber (Jonathan) 11–12, 40–1, 104, 133 n. 160, 320, 327 n. 36
Speyer, Georg and Franziska 202
Spiess, Alexander 220, 249
Städteordnung (city ordinance) 58, 79 n. 161, 83, 115, 181, 228, 269
Städtetag (city congress) 145, 181–2, 205, 237, 274, 277, 296–7, 330
Stadtrat, *see Magistrat*
Stadtverordnetenversammlung, *see* city council
Steinbach, Peter 9, 71 n. 135
Steinmetz, George 239–40
Steuerwehr 116
Stoltze, Friedrich 59, 60, 64, 72, 75
Strasbourg 237, 250, 289 n. 102
street clearances 112 n. 61, 146, 230, 232, 288
Stuttgart 21
Submissionswesen 103, 119, 120
Sunday closing 163

taxation 36, 151, 211, 214, 257–69, 270, 278, 298–306, 307–8, 329–30, 331
 church tax 177
 meat and flour tax 76, 79, 211, 258, 298–9
 Mittelstand 116, 227
 reforms 261–78, 303–4, 329
 SPD 131
 see also Währschaftssteuer, *Wertzuwachssteuer*
teachers 90 n. 205, 109, 135, 150, 151–2, 156–7, 184, 185, 275, 287, 291
technical schools 27, 211, 263, 322, 330
Thompson, Alastair 14
tolerance 35, 59, 128, 151, 164, 169, 171, 174, 175, 177, 178–9, 182–4, 196, 197–8, 199, 201, 202–3, 204–5, 314–17
town planning 4, 252, 253, 274–5
trade, *see* freedom of trade
trade unions, *see* Hirsch-Duncker trade unions
tramways 120, 135, 138, 140, 229, 241, 242, 244, 275, 276, 290, *see also* municipalization
Trommershausen, Ernst 174–5, 178, 179

Ulm 21
ultramontanism 164, 170 n. 125
Umlegung 228
unemployment insurance 27, 140, 236–7, 239–40
university 199–203, 204, 205, 315, 317
urbanization 28, 275, 276, 309, 332

Varrentrapp, Gustav 26, 59, 65, 74, 212
Verein der Fortschrittspartei, see Progressive Liberals
Verein für kommunale Wahlen 116 n. 80, 175
Verein für Sozialpolitik 26, 207, 220–1, 224, 257
Voigt, Georg 141, 143
Volks- Bau- und Spargesellschaft 234
Volksfreund für das Mittlere Deutschland 47, 56
Volksschule 184
Volksverein für das katholische Deutschland 106
Vorschule (preparatory school) 185–6, 204, 307
Vossische Zeitung 326

Wachensturm 43
Wagner, Adolph 257
Währschaftssteuer 305
Weber, Max 49, 95, 208
Wehler, Hans-Ulrich 7–8, 31
Weimar Cartel 316
Weiß, Guido 69 n. 132, 70
Wertzuwachssteuer 305–6
West Prussia 158–9
Wettengel, Michael 39
Wetzlar 14, 30
Wilhelm I 73
Wilhelm II 6, 122, 148, 192–3
Wilson, John A. 20
Wirth, Franz 217
Woell, Wilhelm 294–7
Wolf, Siegbert 24, 25, 110
Wolschendorff, Eduard 299
workers' education 234–5, 251 n. 235, 317
Württemberg 12–13, 20–1, 46, 49, 51–2, 120, 311, 323, 327

Ziehen, Julius 194, 201
Zielowski, Otto 252
Zollverein 29
zoning 141, 228